FLAUBERT POSTSECULAR

Cultural Memory
in
the
Present

Hent de Vries, Editor

FLAUBERT POSTSECULAR

Modernity Crossed Out

Barbara Vinken

*Translated by Aarnoud Rommens
with Susan L. Solomon*

STANFORD UNIVERSITY PRESS

STANFORD, CALIFORNIA

Stanford University Press
Stanford, California

Flaubert Postsecular was originally published in German in 2009 under the title *Flaubert: Durchkreuzte Moderne* © S. Fischer Verlag GmbH, Frankfurt am Main, 2009.

Printed in the United States of America on acid-free, archival-quality paper

Library of Congress Cataloging-in-Publication Data

Vinken, Barbara, author.
  [Flaubert. English]
  Flaubert postsecular : modernity crossed out / Barbara Vinken ; translated by Aarnoud Rommens with Susan L. Solomon.
      pages cm--(Cultural memory in the present)
  "Originally published in German in 2009 under the title Flaubert: durchkreuzte Moderne."
  Includes bibliographical references.
  ISBN 978-0-8047-8064-3 (cloth : alk. paper)--
  ISBN 978-0-8047-8065-0 (pbk. : alk. paper)
  1. Flaubert, Gustave, 1821-1880--Criticism and interpretation. 2. Religion in literature. 3. Modernism (Literature) I. Title. II. Series: Cultural memory in the present.
  PQ2250.V56 2015
  843'.8--dc23

                              2015011807

Typeset by Bruce Lundquist in 11/13.5 Adobe Garamond

To Moritz, to Anselm

Contents

Acknowledgments

First of all, I am happy to thank Susan Solomon and Aarnoud Rommens for their patience in translating my text. In the end, Susan and Katharina Simon were my guardian angels. Peter Dreyer went over the whole manuscript with great care and gave it its final polish.

A combined stipend from the Agence Nationale de la Recherche and the Deutsche Forschungsgemeinschaft has funded the translation of this long text, and the Center for Advanced Studies at Ludwig-Maximilians-Universität München has generously enabled me to take the time for revision and adaptation. I am grateful to Mieke Bal and Hent de Vries for welcoming this book in their series. I particularly thank Susanne Lüdemann, one of the readers for the Press, for her endorsement: she understood the project's point immediately. Pierre-Marc de Biasi, Anne Herschberg, Jacques Neefs, Agnès Bouvier, Philippe Dufour, and Françoise Gaillard from the Institut des Textes et Manuscrits (Paris) have offered spirited intellectual exchange despite many and heartfelt disagreements. I would like to thank Rüdiger Campe and Stephen Nichols at Johns Hopkins University, whose seminar offered stimulating discussion. In the Poetics and Theory Program at New York University, debate with John Hamilton and Martin Harries has sharpened the argument. Jürgen Paul Schwindt gave me the opportunity to explore Flaubert's "antiquity" further in the Heidelberg Colloquia. Michèle Lowrie has made long hours of swimming pass quickly by regaling me with stories of civil war's curse in ancient Rome. My son, Moritz, bore everything with his usual sparkling wit and, last but not least, my husband, Anselm Haverkamp, offered his habitually generous support when it was most needed.

FLAUBERT POSTSECULAR

Crossed Out

[W]hen the most masculine virtues and drives have been chopped off the god of
decadence, he will necessarily turn into a god of the physiologically retrograde, the
weak. They . . . call themselves "the good" . . .

Friedrich Nietzsche, The Anti-Christ: A Curse on Christianity

Habent sua fata libelli. Texts have their fate.[1] Flaubert is perhaps the
only nineteenth-century French prose writer who has not become historical, the way George Sand, Victor Hugo, and Honoré de Balzac have
been left behind in their century. In solidarity with Flaubert, the *nouveau
roman*, the French "new novel" of the 1950s, positioned itself, "contre
Balzac," whose realism does not so much concern the form as the narrative content. A position "contre Flaubert" is difficult to imagine. As one of
the founding fathers of modernism, Flaubert enjoys a glamorous international afterlife. Authors as diverse as Gertrude Stein, Franz Kafka, James
Joyce, William Faulkner, Nathalie Sarraute, and Claude Simon claim him
as their precursor. Gertrude Stein's *Three Lives* and James Joyce's short story
"Eveline" in *Dubliners* are reprises of Flaubert's *Three Tales*. Kafka speaks
of Flaubert as if he were immediate family and dreamed of reciting Flaubert's novel *A Sentimental Education* from beginning to end in a theater.
To a large extent, Claude Simon's oeuvre can be read as a meditation on
Flaubert's.[2] Critics like Foucault and Derrida never lost sight of Flaubert either. It is this sustained perpetuation that has made him one of the
canonical authors of world literature.

Through relentless work on his texts, Flaubert created a new, lapidary,
classical prose style with a dense lyrical texture resembling that of Tacitus.
This density is owing to the meticulous labor he devoted to his texts, in
which no word is superfluous. It is the result of an intricately woven intertextuality that transfers the great texts of antiquity into nineteenth-century

France. It is also owing to Flaubert's meticulous, decidedly philological research; few works of fiction are so embedded in topical research, in myth and biblical scholarship, or the emerging ethnology of their time. However, the explosiveness of Flaubert's oeuvre is above all derived from its being a testament against the Gospels and their patristic interpretation.

The paradoxical nature of Flaubert "the man," as well as the contradictory assessments of his oeuvre are not decisive for this afterlife, but rather symptomatic. If Flaubert is thought of as the realist author incarnate, his work is also treated as exemplifying art for art's sake, *l'art pour l'art*. Flaubert stylized himself as a secluded monk who had retreated to his Carthusian cloister in order to renounce all worldly pleasure and devote his life ascetically to his work alone; he signed texts with the name Saint Carpe, a stylite of late antiquity who had turned away from the world in disgust. At the same time he was the quintessential dandy; his mother was forced to sell a portion of land so that her son could pay off an exorbitant glove bill. He wrote charmingly flirting and teasing letters to Princess Mathilde, whose salon he frequented. After all, this was the heart of fashionable and intellectual Paris. A rentier in the provinces, where he lived with his mother and niece, Flaubert never became a proper adult in the eyes of his family: he was not married and did not have a career to speak of. In contrast to Balzac or Sand, who were able to live from their writing, Flaubert never earned a living for himself, nor did he see to his own affairs. He entrusted the management of his estate to the incompetent hands of his niece's husband, whose bankruptcy was only averted by the sale of almost all the lands and farms owned by the Flaubert family. His mother spent much of her life sick with worry over her son's so-called crisis. His niece never really appreciated the pains he took with her education, and reported on his attempts at teaching her ancient history as the efforts of the somewhat eccentric black sheep of the family.

In 1857, Baudelaire's *Fleurs du Mal* and Flaubert's novel *Madame Bovary* appeared and were charged with offending public morality in the first lawsuits against works of fiction in France. Flaubert's trial ended in an acquittal and *Madame Bovary* was again allowed to be printed and sold. The same society that had prosecuted him would later award him the *légion d'honneur*. This distinction was even bestowed by an emperor whose coup d'état Flaubert had compared in the pages of *A Sentimental Education* to the Roman civil wars, during which a crime worse than fratricide was committed: its legal authorization.

Flaubert stood out by swimming against the currents of his time. His flouting of contemporary orthodoxy endowed his work with a potential that is still far from exhausted. In the nineteenth century, the notions of "history" and "subject" were the two central ideological points of contention. Flaubert cannot be pinpointed as siding with one historically dominant position or the other within this ideological struggle between the French Republic, science, and the Church. Instead, he subverts all of them, thereby heralding a different modernity and opening a path that would later turn people as different as James Joyce, Thérèse de Lisieux, Edith Stein, and Luce Irigaray into his fellow travelers.

According to Hegel, the *Weltgeist* would unfold and come into its own with the end of history. In light of this happy ending, in some sort of narrative of worldly revelations, regressions and setbacks were redirected onto the path of salvation through the cunning of reason. Some speak of "secularization" in this context—this term is adequate if we understand it to mean the transference of Christian models onto worldly history.[3] Jules Michelet's interpretation of the French Revolution is presumably one of the best examples of such a Hegelian, so-called secularized version of a history fulfilling itself on earth. The new covenant forged through the revelation of the Revolution has come true in the here and now through a new Annunciation and Virgin Birth. At last, the Kingdom of Heaven has descended to earth. For Flaubert as well, all earthly history is articulated through the events of salvation history: through Pentecost and Babel, through the Crucifixion and Resurrection, the Eucharist and the fulfilling words of love of the living Spirit that transforms the text into the holy bread of redemption. The text that is the touchstone for Flaubert's literary writing is the Bible. The easiest formula that thematizes the relation of Flaubert's work to the Evangel, Scripture, is perhaps this: in the name of the Cross, the Gospel—the "good tidings"—is crossed out. His oeuvre is thus a kind of "non-Gospel" or *dys-angelion*—a body of "bad tidings"; it testifies against the New Testament. History proves the promise of salvation to be a lie; but history is nevertheless absolutely determined by the New Testament, since it is nothing but its per-version, its *per-versio*—its reversal. Only against the backdrop of this crossed-out promise of the unheard-of love of the New Testament, which is affirmed completely, does history make sense and reveal its horrible truth.

Throughout the nineteenth century, the issue of subjectivity—of the subject as either autonomous or subjected—was debated between Church and science and revolved around the phenomena of mysticism, visions, and ecstasies. From the outset, this discourse was gendered. Women were entranced, not by God, but, as psychiatry argues, by their sexuality. Science would quite sweepingly baptize this complex with the name "hysteria" and argue that frustrated sexuality was the cause of the symptoms. In the interest of bourgeois, misogynist gender ideology, the ideal of the virgin Bride of Christ had to be superimposed on that of the bourgeois wife and mother.

The self-authorization of the male as subject of knowledge is possible only at the expense of the woman who becomes the object of this knowledge. As she appears already in broad outlines in the eighteenth century, woman, according to this new science, is utterly subjugated to her gender and can therefore not conform to the norms of modern subjectivity. She is incapable of becoming an autonomous, self-determined subject. In this case as well, Flaubert, the self-confessed hysteric, does not commit to the ideal proffered by the Catholic Church—woman as the Virgin Bride of Christ—nor does he subscribe to the ideal erected by the French Republic—woman as fulfilled wife and mother. The aftermath of this discussion is still palpable today, beyond psychoanalysis and feminism, in the conflict between ego-centered philosophies, which present a theory of the subject where the ego is still master in its own house, and theologians, psychoanalysts, and philosophers who see the subject as essentially subjected.

Scriptural Kenosis

Flaubert: founder of modern literature? The centrality of Flaubert for the modern age was a thorn in Sartre's flesh. His conception of modernity had nothing in common with what he read in Flaubert. What Flaubert most sorely lacked, both in his life and his work, was what Sartre calls self-transcendence: a continuous work on the self in order to become the projected self, which Sartre envisages as essential to the modern individual and which for him typified the fulfillment, the implementation of the modern age. By contrast, Flaubert was completely lacking in active impulse. As a passive character he suffered, but not once did he voice his suffering. Sartre spent ten years trying to rid modernity of Flaubert by diagnosing him as an emblem of the detestable bourgeois neurosis pervading the modern age. In this perspective, Flaubert's texts are nothing but symptoms of failure: they are by no means merely the artworks of an individual, but rather the products of a collective neurosis that afflicted large parts of the bourgeoisie. This guaranteed Flaubert's success, but sealed the necessary end of his class, which, according to Sartre's criteria, was not fit for modern life.[4] Flaubert had to be analyzed exhaustively so that he could be done away with to finally enable the advent of man in Sartre's own image, the ultimate modern subject conceived in terms of self-transcendence.

In contrast to this passive view of Flaubert with all his suffering and pathos of character, I will paint a different picture of modernity in which Flaubert indeed plays an even more vital role.[5] Flaubert's fatal drive—Freud's *Triebschicksal*, which James Strachey translated as "instinctual vicissitude"—gains in dramatic effect since his work inscribes this fate in an anti-Christian Christian movement, namely, the tradition of pure love whose primal scene is Christ's act of renunciation on the cross. This is clearly not about self-affirmation or self-transcendence; what is at stake is forsaking the self and the suffering this entails. Flaubert articulated his *Triebschicksal* through a Christian matrix from late antiquity and the early Middle Ages.

As we can put it today, invoking Freud, Flaubert's work takes place on another scene, the scene of the other, the scene of the unconscious. This scene is always determined by the same dynamic, namely, that of the Oedipal and castration complexes. The complex bears the name of the Oedipus of Greek tragedy, since he transgressed the two taboos that founded culture: he murdered his father and had children with his mother. He is the bearer of the secret desire that must be suppressed by culture.

In this tragic genealogy, parricide, fratricide, and incest are decisive at the very outset of Flaubert's work and remain so until the end. In his early text "Quidquid volueris," an ape-man kills his "brother" and violates the wife of his foster father, his "mother." In his last work, *Three Tales*, the same constellation reappears in the figure of Saint Julian the Hospitaller, who stabs his parents to death; the stabbing of the mother is an obvious travesty of penetration. Both at the beginning and the end of his career, Flaubert's work evinces Freud's account of the violence the small boy experiences in witnessing the primal scene of copulation, which he sees as an act of mutilation against the mother, as an act of destructive homicide: the mother is castrated and pierced by the father.

Through castration anxiety, the boy reaches a way out of the Oedipus complex and its associated wish of killing the father so as to enjoy the mother in incest. The Oedipus complex propels the infantile theory of gender differentiation in castrated/phallic terms and translates it into the boy's fear of losing his organ of pleasure. In any case, the boy does not leave this phase unscathed, since the recognition of sexual difference seals the loss of the state of oneness with the mother. The fate of the mother, the boy fears, may also catch up with him if he persists in his aggressive stance toward the father, a result of the wish to take his place and to enjoy his mother. Therefore, the mother must be relinquished as an object of desire so as to enable the boy to substitute other love objects for her later in life. The relation with the father is desexualized, idealized, and ultimately internalized into the superego. This then opens up the path to identification and sublimation.

Flaubert mobilizes a battery of theological and historical sources in order to retell the drama of the Oedipus complex, with its focus on incest and parricide, over and over again. This explains his fascination with Tacitus's Nero, who supposedly had intercourse with his mother. In French history, this notorious scenario finds its most gripping variation in the story of one of the mistresses of François I, Diane de Poitiers, whom his heir Henri II would snatch from his father. For the rest of his life, Henri would remain under her spell, although, as we can read in Madame de Lafayette's *Princesse de Clèves*, she was no longer beautiful nor young: "For though she was no longer in possession of either youth or beauty, she ruled over him with an empire so absolute, that she was the sovereign of his person and the State."[6] Not in spite of the fact, but because she was no longer young, and because, as his father's mistress, she could have been his mother, Henri II remains devoted to her—she who dismisses his sovereignty and is unfaithful to him all her life. In Flaubert's work we encounter Diane de Poitiers in the castle of Fontainebleau under the mythical disguise of "infernal Diane"; Frédéric desires her, so to speak, posthumously. Her prototype ancestor is Hérodias, who, like Diana, is a huntress, and with whom we come face to face in *Three Tales*.

The desire of Oedipus is narrated and immediately sanctioned. Flaubert oscillates between desire and sanction. He lingers in the limbo of the dynamic between the Oedipus complex and the castration complex. Flaubert's interpretation of Saint Augustine's *civitas terrena*, onto which he inscribes the concept of incest—which is not prominent in Augustine—reads as a variation of the Oedipus complex. For Flaubert, the castration complex—namely, the incest taboo and the establishment of successive generations without any murder of the father, son, or brother—does not lead to the resolution of the Oedipus complex. This translates into a view of history governed by incest and fratricide.

Punishment follows swiftly, not only in the guise of the threat of death or castration, but also as self-sacrifice. For Flaubert, to desire means to be castrated and/or to die. Anyone entertaining the notion of not having to pay this price and who flaunts phallically is exposed by Flaubert as absurd. The oscillation between desire and castration takes on a sadomasochistic tone: death after incest in "Quidquid volueris," metaphoric castration in "Hérodias," and self-sacrifice after a disguised incest in "Saint Julian the Hospitalier." The sadomasochistic tone, however differently modulated, is also evident in the sympathy of the author with Emma Bovary in her death agonies, which, in a strange *imitatio Emmae*, makes him vomit with her, as well as in the aggression directed against her, which corresponds to Flaubert's view that, after all is said and done, all desire, and a fortiori all female desire, is death-bound. The mixture of sadism and masochism is unsurpassed in the passion of Mâtho in *Salammbô*, which the reader—in marked contrast with de Sade who displays no compassion for those who suffer—must suffer compassionately to an almost intolerable degree. The extremes of the Flaubertian corpus—be it the extreme pathos of empathic pity or incredible sadism—are thus caught within the primal scene: compassion with the mother as castrated, identification with the father as the castrator, the guilt ensuing from this identification, and self-punishment for the desire for the mother. The crude juvenile puns that abound in Flaubert's correspondence act as defenses against these unbearable dilemmas. However, things do not end there: there is still much to be learned from psychoanalysis for an understanding of Flaubert's art, for the unlocking of an oeuvre that developed at about the same time as the science of the unconscious.

The insistence of the castration complex is not overcome by adult knowledge of sexual difference. Freud still entertained the notion that the primacy of the phallus within his infantile sexual theory, centered as it is on the opposition castrated/phallic, could be overcome by knowledge of the biological difference between the sexes based on possession of either a penis or a vagina. However, for Jacques Lacan, as a reader of Freud, the relation between genders originating in the primacy of the phallus as construed by the child has a significant afterlife and further determines sexuality. For Lacan, the phallus/castration paradigm remains firmly in place, and Flaubert's writing is an excellent place to demonstrate this.

Freud offers fetishism as the prime example indicating that adult sexuality bears the indelible mark of infantile theories of sexuality. For the fetishist, the fetish, the substitute for the phallus of the mother, is essential for sexual arousal. These fetishist substitutes are typically what the boy has seen before he realizes the horrifying lack: shoes, lingerie, and, as a metonymy for pubic hair, fur. Out of fear and as a means to self-preservation, he denies the mother's castration, thus negating the possibility that he too could be castrated. To avoid the separation from the mother, he persists in his belief of her being perfectly phallic, although he has seen otherwise. Since he thus remains in a split position, he is able simultaneously to affirm and deny gender differentiation, thereby obfuscating the possibility of his own castration. Octave Mannoni rendered this in the inimitable formula "I know very well [that women have no penis], but all the same [I cannot believe it]."[7] As Freud puts it, fetishism "saves" (*bewahrt*) the boy from homosexuality. The homosexual cannot desire the "castrated" body of the woman, which, to him, conveys not only anxiety and a threat to his integrity, not to mention his "pride and joy," but also the separation from the mother. The fetishist creates an object which both recalls and blocks the threat of castration. Only supplemented women, made whole through a substitute for their lack, can become objects of desire. The fetish is the embodiment of the denial and the recognition of castration: at the same time it obstructs and marks gender difference. Above all, it allows for a position where the boy is not forced to give up his mother altogether as the unconscious object of his desire. This is crucial to Flaubert.

Symptomatic of the drama of the castration complex is the early, homosexually charged friendship of Flaubert with Alfred Le Poittevin. The most famous symptom is Flaubert's foot and shoe fetishism. As attested to by his letters to Louise Colet, Flaubert's shoe fetish was accompanied by a masturbatory fixation, and to assess the pertinence of this fixation, one need think only of Madame Bovary's little boots; of Madame Arnoux's open shoes, with their golden leather straps; or of Salammbô's sandals, adorned with hummingbird feathers. Shoes and feet never escape Flaubert's attention. In excerpts from the Song of Songs taken from Samuel Cahen's translation of the Hebrew Bible into French, Flaubert lovingly copied all things concerning shoes: "The rich ladies had slaves who carried their shoes in boxes. Plautus called them *sandaligerulae* [shoe porters]. Benoît Baudoin, who was a cobbler, dedicated himself to the study [of the subject] and came up with as many as twenty-seven different kinds."[8] In an unpublished manuscript of Flaubert's titled "Voltaire—Mélanges, critique littéraire et historique" held at the Morgan Library & Museum in New York, he goes into detail about foot fetishism in Spain: "A successor to the throne of a great monarchy loved only feet. In Spain, this is said to have been a rather common preference. By taking care to hide them, women attracted the attention of many a man to their feet."[9]

In Flaubert's correspondence with Colet, the profound split between tender and sexual feelings comes to light, resulting in his inability to experience "love"—at least as popularly understood. Flaubert usually associates love with death. His letters, as testimony to this incapacity to love, articulate quite poignantly the intimate connection between this impotence and fantasies of mutilation, which immediately surface when a woman threatens to become more than just a casual sex partner. There is no place for another woman in his life; his heart belongs to his mother. Flaubert's ineptitude regarding sexuality shows itself in letters to his male friends, with puns never going beyond dirty schoolboy jokes.

His hardboiled cold-heartedness in matters of love—the famous *trous nus* (naked holes) of the East, his visits to whorehouses masquerading as psycho-hygienic therapy—have soothed a great number of Flaubert admirers: here at least was a man who did not make himself dependent on the eternal Feminine, a manly man not in the clutches of all-consuming passions, a true man who, without prejudice or false modesty, enjoyed both the female and male prostitutes of the East, a man who, without complexes, paid visits to whores, and who appreciated sexual variation. This was a man who, thank God, never lost sight of the essential, who did not exhaust all his energy and was not to be sidetracked by love, but devoted his life—*génie oblige*—completely to his work.

Other readers might not have been reassured by such a display of masculinity. Adapting Freud, who claims that Leonardo da Vinci did research instead of making love, one could say of Flaubert that he wrote instead of loving. Flaubert imagines love as a deadly ripping apart of the heart, and, as Marthe Robert maintains, he erected his oeuvre to protect himself from this threat.[10] Thus, the true Flaubertian fetishes are not so much feet and shoes, but his work, whose artistic artificiality—"fetish" derives from "making," "producing"—Flaubert emphasized like no one else. Flaubert leaves no doubt that his texts are not the outpourings of the heart through the pen, nor are they the natural outbursts of genius. As Flaubert never grew tired of repeating, they were the result of the most toilsome, back-breaking labor, involving skill and artistry. As is well known, in the *gueuloir*—the "shouting room"—Flaubert shouted to himself until he was hoarse, to check the rhythm and sound of his prose.

His texts are veritable fruits of the library, as Foucault suggested.[11] This thesis has been amply confirmed by recent research. His works are the result of the most extensive readings and scientific studies, applications of the most advanced methods of modern philology. A well-wrought textual body is, to employ Flaubert's metaphorics, all male. Without exaggerating, one could say that the textual body is envisaged as an erect member from which all things feminine, the womanly, the unstrained, the supple, and the free-flowing, must be banished.[12] When describing his poetic praxis, Flaubert affirms his masculinity through a reduction of and a defense against all things female.

Yet I feel that at specific moments his poetic practice seems to run counter—*malgré lui* perhaps—to this ostentatious phallologocentrism. In his texts one can read what his letters often seem to refute, namely, that one can only preserve the phallus at the price of its surrender. Although Flaubert indeed writes in order not to love, the texts themselves do not assert the self-affirmative masculinity that his letters delineate in such a crude fashion. His texts do not establish phallic authority. Thus, in the transfer into the symbolic order of Flaubert's texts, the whole Oedipus complex comes to light through a seldom seen aggression directed at the authority of the symbolic fathers, above all, Hugo and Balzac. Flaubert destroys their authority; he overwrites and ridicules it. In stunning intertextual operations, he tears their textual fabrics asunder. The intertextual conflict, the anxiety of and resistance to their influence, is negotiated through the lexicon of phallic authorization and castration.[13]

What is made laughable in these precursors, is, as Derrida puns, their "good will to power," their will to assert themselves as authors and to raise themselves to the position of authority.[14] Flaubert does everything to avoid this mistake. He does so—and this constitutes the stylistic dimension of the dynamic of castration—by developing a style that is specific to him precisely by virtue of being divested of anything that could be called his own. Flaubert can only become himself by giving himself over to otherness. As with few other writers, entire libraries are incorporated into Flaubert's texts. However, in contrast to classical poetics and the poetics of the Renaissance, Flaubert's praxis does—to borrow a common image from classical rhetoric—not collect pollen with the aim of producing a particular honey of its own specific style. Instead, Flaubert strives for the highest form of self-denial and asceticism, proverbial impersonality.

In this regard one could speak of a surrender of the text to otherness, where the self can only be traced through the other. The *humilitas* of quotations, of commonplaces, which are inscribed in an authorless genre like the lives of saints, as well as the radical absence of an auctorial instance and what Roland Barthes has called the "degree zero of writing," in addition to the appropriation of textual fragments and their reorientation into new constellations—all this is a part of a labor that neither posits nor claims anything as its own. The refusal directly to state value judgments, coupled with the renunciation of orienting cues to the reader and the uncertainty of a point of view submerged in irony, also partakes of this labor. That is to say, one will not be able to treat Flaubert as he treated others. No one will be able to annihilate his authority—since he was neither so naive nor so insolent as to claim and assert it for himself. This ascetic overwriting of the self-assertive makes him the founder of modern literature.

Flaubert's contention with authority, and thus also his definition of what literature should be, does not so much concern authors or the scientific authorities of his time—although these are not to be underestimated—but the corpus of writing Flaubert assimilated, namely, the Old and New Testaments. It is in this context that one should reexamine Flaubert's obsession with literal accuracy, which went as far as having train timetables verified. Until now, this has been attributed to an understanding of realism's faithfulness to phenomenal reality, down to the pettiest detail.

However, it seems to me that this obsession with historical, factual truth pertains not so much to realism as to competition with the Bible. Flaubert insists that his texts not only contain the *sensus allegoricus* that typifies the poet's allegorical praxis, but indeed also harbor the *sensus historicus* that distinguishes the Gospels: "It happened; this is how it came to pass."

The principal intellectual concern of the nineteenth century, as the works of Chateaubriand, Hugo, and Nietzsche attest, revolved around the reconfiguration of the relation between the Old and New Testaments, Judaism, Christianity, and antiquity. In this respect, the nineteenth century is closer to the sixteenth century of the Reformation than to the seventeenth or eighteenth centuries. Issues of love and gender played a central role in this reconfiguration. Rarely had Catholicism been so consciously figured as a religion of blissful love and sensuality of the soul, as opposed to the killing spirit of the letter associated with the Old Testament. It was in the nineteenth century that Michelet transferred the love of the Bride of Christ to bourgeois marriage, and Charcot relocated the matrix of holiness to the psychological category of the hysteric. Flaubert has transferred this matrix in a very singular way; this is what makes him such an important figure for modernity. One might reformulate this transference as the "outdoing" of the castration that Christianity orchestrates. Flaubert thus stands in sharp contrast to his contemporaries, who, opposed to the castration anxiety and hysterical desire attributed to Christianity and specifically to Catholicism, mobilized antique virtues and "male instincts"—the latter incidentally a formula of Nietzsche's, but one that might just as well have been used by Zola or Michelet.

It is remarkable that Flaubert reformulates the dynamic of the Cross, which Saint Paul had traced in paradigmatic fashion in his Epistle to the Philippians in terms of Ascension and Fall, as a complicated dialectic between phallic omnipotence and castration. The argument in Philippians basically states that Jesus renounced and degraded himself beyond measure to an ignoble slave death upon the cross so as to be raised beyond measure through his victory over death. As a countermove, Flaubert detects a phallic chimera in the promise of resurrection, whose deconstruction he performs through his texts. While Flaubert's oeuvre hinges on the question of questions, the question concerning the Cross, his answer is not, as is often said, the same as Voltaire's. Although both authors are united in their visceral anticlericalism, religious satire never has the last word in Flaubert. Flaubert defines his work against and with the Book of Books and thus as both an anti-Christian as well as a Christian rewriting of the Scriptures. This grounding gesture of modern literature has remained invisible and illegible in scholarship on the subject, which has instead remained firmly grounded in the ideology of the secular French Republic. If there is a contemporary who at specific moments does share Flaubert's perspective, then it is none other than the Nietzsche of the *Antichrist*. Nietzsche too approaches his discussion of Christianity through the figure of castration.

Certainly, nothing would have been more foreign to Flaubert than the well-known and embarrassing remarks of Nietzsche about "the stronger races of northern Europe" and the cultivation of the *Übermensch*, whose future would become only too familiar.[15] His Social Darwinist talk on the will to power, which was so popular at that time, would have been immediately "chopped off" by Flaubert, so to speak. In addition, the no less calamitous palaver on Christianity's cardinal vice, the "active pity for all failures and weakness,"[16] which was to bear catastrophic consequences, was also alien to Flaubert. In this respect, the later Zola of *The Four Gospels* was much closer to Nietzsche. Nothing would have been further from Flaubert's sensibilities than the language of apodictic assertions. As with Pascal, Nietzsche despised Flaubert for his "unselfish" style. Flaubert was a decisive figure for modernism, since he was one of the few who resisted the flights of megalomania and self-aggrandizing. Inimical to the vitalistic, Social Darwinist will to power, he did not shy away from tackling the conflict of authority at its roots. Through *kenosis*—a relinquishing, or, if you will, a consensual castration—Flaubert endured, withstood, and was able to hold his ground.[17] If only they had known how to read his work, the aging Flaubert observed, then the civil war of 1870–71 would never have taken place. Extending a famous dictum by Shaw on Social Darwinism, one could say that it would never have come to a world war if people only had learned how to read Flaubert.

Read together, Nietzsche and Flaubert illuminate one another: Nietzsche's interpretation of the life and death of Christ becomes all the clearer through Flaubert's alternative. At certain points, Nietzsche seems to theorize Flaubert's praxis, although Nietzsche can hardly be suspected of having attained these epiphanies from reading Flaubert. Nietzsche thus sketches an astonishingly insightful account of kenosis, which he is quick to reject. Nietzsche juxtaposes the figure of Jesus and the practices of his dominant Christian followers, which approximate Flaubert's to a great extent, even while stressing different aspects. According to Nietzsche, the Christianity that has actually triumphed, owing to Paul's grotesque misinterpretations, turns the Gospel upside down. The Church—which for Nietzsche is nothing but the continuation and victory of Judaism, and thus the greatest of all historical disasters, as well as history's most poignant irony—

thus, under the guidance of Paul, restores "what the Evangel did away with." What would have been dismissed, however, with the Gospel "was the Judaism of the concepts of 'sin', 'forgiveness of sin', 'faith', 'redemption through faith'—the whole Jewish church doctrine was rejected in the 'glad tidings.'"[18] Against the official Church's dogmatic interpretation of the life and death of Christ, which, according to Nietzsche, is certainly not Christian but essentially Jewish, although not recognized as such, Nietzsche offers his interpretation of the Evangel: "What are the 'glad tidings'? That the true life, the eternal life has been found—it is not just a promise, it exists, it is in each of you: as a life of love, as a love without exceptions or rejections, without distance."[19] Flaubert sees things the same way. The Pauline-Jewish conception of sacrifice and reward stands as a model for the unchristian: the sacrifice on the cross is recompensed by the overcoming of death. This view of things is contrary to the Christian praxis that is not about some compensation in the future, but about every single individual in the here and now, "a feeling of the total transfiguration of all things."[20]

Nietzsche's trajectory starts with a provocative psychological portrayal of Christ as the personification of pathological-childish-idiotic decadence, only to end with an interesting biblical-hermeneutic and considerably softened reading. The life and death of Christ is reduced to a symbol for a state of the heart, imbuing everything in the here and now with a mystical *sensus anagogicus*. Nietzsche thus gets rid of what he finds so intolerable in the figure of Christ. As much as Nietzsche would have welcomed the overcoming of the Christian, that is, Jewish Church by Christian praxis, he becomes uneasy, even uncannily anxious when faced with his inquiry into the means of this overcoming. As opposed to Renan, who sees Christ as a "hero" and "genius" in his psychological account, Nietzsche detects an "idiot" in the original sense of the word; only someone like the author of *The Idiot*, Dostoevsky, he argues, could have a feel for the "distinctive charm that this sort of mixture of sublimity, sickness, and childishness has to offer."[21]

The substance of a Christian praxis with an Evangel without guilt, without punishment and redemption in an afterlife, is the complete relinquishing of self-assertion: "Christians act, they are characterized by a different way of acting. By the fact that they do not offer any resistance, in their words or in their heart, to people who are evil to them."[22] Christ does not redeem; his life and his death are symbolic of a state of bliss:

"[O]nly the practice of Christianity is really Christian, living like the man who died on the cross. A life like this is still possible today, for certain people it is even necessary: true, original Christianity will always be possible. . . . Not a believing but a doing, above all a not-doing-much, a different being."[23] Through his death, Christ shows how to live: "He does not offer any resistance, he does not defend his rights, he does not make a single move to avert the worst, what is more, he invites it. . . . And he begs, he suffers, he loves with those, in those people who did him evil. . . . Not to defend yourself, not to get angry, not to lay blame. But not to resist evil either,—to love it."[24] Nietzsche is disgusted by this praxis of kenosis, which he describes so brilliantly; he would prefer not to dwell in this "strange, sick world,"[25] with its mixture of the degenerate, the childish, the sickly, and the idiotic. But the longer he describes the truly and only Christian way of life, the more abstract everything becomes: "The 'kingdom of God' is not something that you wait for; it does not have a yesterday or a day after tomorrow, it will not arrive in a 'thousand years'— it is an experience of the heart,"[26] Nietzsche concludes, and we might add, turning to Flaubert, that this experience occurs "in a simple heart," the heart of an idiot. Nonetheless, Flaubert has more nerve than Nietzsche: instead of fleeing to ancient male virtues, Flaubert decides to dwell among those who are idiots at heart.

The Cross of History

Again and again, and always as if by chance, the centrality of crosses in Flaubert's work catches the eye on quite a superficial and literal level. The final string of words in *Madame Bovary* is "Croix de la Légion d'Honneur."[27] At the close of the chronicle that *A Sentimental Education* sets forth, just before its last *blanc*, which is then followed by a coda, Dussardier dies "les bras en croix." Crucified, Carthaginians and mercenaries hang from their crosses facing one another at the conclusion of *Salammbô*. The novel ends with its hero's passing through veritable stations of the cross. The *Three Tales* spatially render the figure of the Cross through the vertical dynamic of the final scenes, which are crossed horizontally by the carrying of the severed head of John the Baptist out of the vertical castle walls onto the plain of Galilee; as such, the tales delineate the mystical cross represented by the Greek letter τ (tau).

Flaubert's treatment of religion is not geared toward the contemporary conjuncture of a historicizing critique of the Bible and its resultant demythologization as practiced by Renan, whom Flaubert respected. Saving the Cross from its dogmatic Christian interpretation, which is what Flaubert's work is about, is not undertaken with a view to some kind of humanization, but rather to a more truthful imitation of Christ on the Cross, something utterly incomprehensible to the dominant humanist ideology. Flaubert inscribes the Cross into the praxis of pre-Christian human sacrifice, as the practice of scapegoating. This foundational structure for societal formation has neither been overcome nor redeemed by the victim on the Cross, Flaubert maintains: Christ is just one more scapegoat. The full pathos of the scapegoat, though, can only be seen in the light of the Cross. Only from the unprecedented love that enters the world with Christ's death on the Cross does the full horror of the human condition reveal itself.

The Catholic Church and, worse still, its secularized forms, deny and obfuscate the logic of the scapegoat, which, according to Flaubert, still informs nineteenth-century French society. They thus reinforce the general blindness. The self-serving illusion of bringing about an ultimately redeemed society through republicanism, socialism, scientific belief in progress, and the truth of realist literature is not salvational, but simply catastrophic. It results in the sacrifice of more scapegoats. Literature is at its worst when such a new, secularized evangelical authority assumes it is a legitimate harbinger of redemption. The Church and, to an even more disastrous effect, its secular transformations in the forms of socialism and republicanism are as obsessed with salvation as they are oblivious to suffering. As a whole, the bourgeois middle-class credo that prizes self-interest above all other things is the absolute antipode of a genuine imitation of Christ. Flaubert locates the seeds of this middle-class small-mindedness in, as Nietzsche would say, a Christianity turned upside down.

Flaubert thus sets out to subvert the ruling discourses of his time. First and foremost, it is the Hegelian conception of history as the unfolding of *Geist* into a worldly history and the subsumption of theological patterns within human history that provoke Flaubert's ire.[28] He employs the destruction of the secularized—and with it the destruction of the theologico-political—as a means for the deconstruction of the Christian sacrifice through love, thereby founding it anew. As such, Flaubert stands directly opposed to all the political, scientific, and religious currents that characterize his epoch; in the nineteenth century he is alone in his vitriolic skepticism, whose reverse is a unique pathos of suffering.

What all these currents deny despite their differences, what they all wish to abolish, what they all claim to overcome or promise to absolve arises *ex negativo* in Flaubert's writing: suffering. They share a denial of the Cross, which he inscribes into his writing as the sign and trace of what is real. The denial of the Cross is shared by socialism and the Catholic Church alike. The designation of "socialists" in the following excerpt can be substituted by any other discourse promising salvation:

This is the very thing that the socialists of the world, with their incessant materialistic preaching, refuse to see. They have denied suffering; they have blasphemed three-quarters of modern poetry, the blood of Christ that stirs within us. Nothing will extirpate it, nothing will eliminate it. Our purpose is not to dry it up, but to create outlets for it. If the sense of man's imperfection, of the meaninglessness of life, were to perish—as would follow from their premise—we would be more stupid than birds, who at least perch on trees.[29]

What are birds doing here, who, wiser than those who promise salvation, "perch on trees"? They follow Christ, who had been slain and "hanged on a tree."[30] Modern writing is a vessel for the blood spilt by the sacrificial victim and thus constitutes a counterdiscourse to all promises of redemption. Poetry alone—and not the Church—does something in memory of His suffering. Christ's suffering is synonymous with the inadequacy of all things human and the vanity of life—a fact that is easily forgotten, but that must be held in memory at all times. The Creation can be conceived after the medieval model of *allegoria entis*. The Creator, however, is only revealed as the crucified. Equally, history as creation testifies to the ceaseless staging of the event of the Cross. For Flaubert, there is no other *sensus anagogicus*. The Cross stands for the impossibility of fulfillment, for death in life, for the human lack.

The work of Flaubert thus becomes a chiasmus, a crossing out of the Cross. Crossed out is the promise of salvation in all its religious and secular variations. Like Nietzsche, Flaubert deploys antiquity against the Cross, but an antiquity that has nothing to do with *virtus*, with the assertion of masculinity. Against the Cross, Flaubert marshals an antiquity that is decidedly oriental in flavor. It is based on scholarly discoveries in the Bible and myth, as well as the early ethnology of Flaubert's time. It thematizes the return of

Babel as the mother of Rome, a Parousia in the guise of nineteenth-century Paris, the true Rome, and therefore also the new Babylon of its time. In the light of the East, modernity reveals its truth. Every one of Flaubert's texts spells out this Babylonian topos derived from Augustine's notion of the City of Man (*civitas terrena*). For Flaubert, Babylon is the byword for earthly-human history. However, it is only through the Christian promise of redemption and its secularized mutations that promise the dawn of the Kingdom of God on earth that the devastation of antiquity can attain its ultimate fulfillment. The Cross, which should have broken the vicious cycle of the eternal return of sacrifice once and for all, is exactly what will forever repeat itself throughout history. That which Christianity had pledged to overcome, namely, the logic of scapegoating, is resumed even more radically in the guise of the promise of redemption. Travestied as Roman Catholicism and its secular offspring, Babylon triumphs.

We are dealing here with complicated translations of antiquity to Christianity, which take, in the oriental Renaissance of the nineteenth century, an unprecedented turn in Flaubert. The schema of *interpretatio christiana*, which regulates the relation between antiquity and Christianity according to *umbra* and *figura*, between pagan prophecies and those of the Old Testament, is abysmally distorted. The implicit standard against which Flaubert gauges—and condemns—the world is that of a selfless love unto death that, perfectly gratuitous, did not redeem anything. The unheard-of pessimism of Flaubert's oeuvre is nourished by this unheard of love. Throughout his work, Flaubert thus implicitly establishes the same opposition that informs Augustine's *Civitas Dei*. It is after all a difference in love that characterizes the two cities. Like Augustine, Flaubert opposes love of self to love of God, self-invested love to selfless love.

From a rhetorical perspective, the crossing out of the Cross gives rise to a new chiasmus. Flaubert reverses the shorthand of Pauline hermeneutics: "littera enim occidit, spiritus autem vivificat"—"the letter killeth, but the spirit giveth life" (2 Cor. 3:6), or, to paraphrase: The letter of the law kills, while the spirit of love bestows life. Flaubert animates what is condemned to death, while literalizing the living Spirit, which hardens into catachresis, a dead metaphor.[31] The heart of Rodolphe, the seducer, is compared to a playground trampled flat by children, and on whose dead surface nothing can grow any longer: it is a vivid picture of a heart incapable of understanding and love. Flaubert thus puts the ossified catachresis of

the proverbial "heart of stone" vividly before our eyes. What is dead is illustrated in a lively manner—it becomes animated. By contrast, all sublimated things, all things vivified by the Spirit are turned into dead letters:
there is nothing more trite and clichéd than the ascension of Saint Julian.

The imagination of the writer who has the power to paint a vivid
picture before the eyes—"faire clair et vif," in Flaubert's words—is thematized in the topos *ut pictura poesis*: as is painting so is poetry. Only a handful of other works emphasize the role of art to such an extent as Flaubert's
texts; the amount of "illustrated" paintings is equal to that of quoted text.
Flaubert's texts are written with and against painting. The propensity for
vivid verbal portrayal occurs through this topos, and is put under erasure.
Flaubert is an iconoclast; he composes an "arid fictionality [that] tends to
denounce images, figures, idols, rhetoric."[32] Against the idolatrous fascination with the image, his texts counterpoise the esotericism of writing. Flaubert resisted the illustration of his works tooth and nail: "Every illustration
is antiliterary. Illustration is antiliterary. Would you want some idiot to
draw what I've almost killed myself trying not to show?"[33] In Flaubert's
presentation, the image falls on the side of Babel. Against its exotericism he
pits the esotericism of writing. In this respect too his texts are a testament
against the exoteric Gospels. If for the rest Flaubert has almost nothing in
common with Zola, he nonetheless shares with him a disgust for the first
pop art, that is, the religious mass kitsch of the nineteenth century, meant
to put the mysteries of faith vividly before the eyes of the believers. The asceticism of Flaubert's style culminates in the renunciation of the power to
inspire, to revive. To paint as vividly as possible is to surrender to the state
of Babylonian fallenness, where language cannot be but deception, delusion. Furthermore, the modern, Babylonian status of language can only
be articulated in a Babylonian fashion—there is no alternative. This entails exposing the sterility of language, its lethal banality. Against the living
Spirit, Flaubert juxtaposes the letter that subsists; puns sound the final re-
verberations of a heavenly echo.

Madame Bovary, the story of the ruination of a family in the province
of Normandy, is the history of a sacrificial victim upon which community
is founded. The victim is the adulteress, who is infamously driven to death
so as to be cannibalized. Flaubert writes the novel, which commemorates
her suffering, as a monument to the perverted Passion of the heroine. In
a world where every unselfish act comes across as lunacy, the Passion of

Emma Bovary is the only thing testifying, in its very perversions, to a self-less love—which is simply unheard of. Similarly, *A Sentimental Education* unveils history and the world as an equally gruesome and unsuspecting, fateful *perversio* of the Eucharist and Parousia. As a hidden matrix, these elements are inscribed into the novel; they are *ex negativo* present in the contemporaneous Babylonian condition. To paraphrase Adorno and Hork-heimer,[34] the text shows that the hope for redemption is not only outdated, but is fated never to be fulfilled. Inversely, *A Sentimental Education* reveals that maintaining the hope of a redeemed Kingdom of the World propa-gated by political theology is the very cause of catastrophic ruin. Ironically, the novel demonstrates how the promise of salvation justifies brutality and leads to nothing but an eternalization of the Cross, which informs the un-derlying logic of the scapegoat—as Flaubert's texts testify. The task of lit-erature is to make the irredeemable figure of the Cross legible throughout history and to convert it into text so as to keep its memory alive. The fail-ure of the promise makes the Passion of those who suffer, through its sheer pointlessness, perversity, and insanity, all the purer. The asceticism of writ-ing is the last means available for attaining this purity. Literature erects a Cross lacking salvation and is therefore an all the more intolerable *me-mento crucis*—the only consolation lies in its ability to testify to suffering. Refusing all subsumption into a salvational history, those who suffer in these stories are not destined for happy endings—they simply cannot func-tion within a teleology revolving around the moral category of the good. Instead, they withdraw into Flaubert's writing, and with it vanishes any good they could do or attain.

More than anything, one should stress what *Salammbô* is definitely not, despite the meticulous historical research that went into its composi-tion: it is not a historical novel. The premise of Hegelian historiography, which ruled historical thinking of the nineteenth century and which fixes history as a trajectory of self-becoming where the subject will finally attain full self-consciousness, is destroyed. In complete contrast to what could be called secularization, Flaubert provides no independent space for the *saeculum*. Even prior to Christ's Cross, the cross itself is the matrix of all earthly history. History is nothing more and will never amount to anything other than the crucifixion of ever-new figures. In *Salammbô*, sacrificial love is driven to the extreme and turns into a vertiginous escalation through a barbarous carnality: a kenosis that alienates kenosis from itself.

By virtue of their compressed intertextuality and their immaculate composition, the *Three Tales* have been compared to prose poems. They unquestionably offer the most cryptic crossing out of the Cross and have remained a thorn in the side of Flaubert scholarship precisely because of the hermeticism lurking beneath the text's smooth surface. Flaubert's work of deconstruction reaches completion with the *Three Tales*: a project that, from the perspectives of religion and of the history of ideas, should be grasped as a culmination as well as an abyssal form of self-renouncing kenosis that consummates Flaubert's writing. A great deal of what had hitherto only been implicit or just seemed a foible in his earlier texts becomes explicit in these three bizarre hagiographies. They are set in the sphere of theology. Their apparent theme is an unselfish devotion that goes to the point of self-denial. World and history recede, from here to eternity, even more lapidary than in the novels, into a grotesque perversion of the Banquet of Love and Pentecostal Parousia combined.

In *Three Tales*, the ascension to heaven, which transports both Saint Julian and Félicité, is sexualized. The topos of antique rapture by a phallic ancient god, with all of its deadly connotations, is superimposed onto the mystic ecstasy of the fulfillment of love through the Heavenly Bridegroom at the moment of death. The ascension, rapture, ecstatic elevation of the two saints turns out to be, in another chiastic movement, their deepest fall, thereby uncovering the idolatrous and phallic essence of Christianity. In the truest sense of the word, this "inflated" Christian promise outdoes paganism; death is after all still inscribed within ancient apotheosis. The passage from the Gospel of John cited in "Hérodias," "pour qu'il croisse, il faut que je diminue" (for him to increase, I must decrease),[35] shorthand for the essence of Christian love, will, by the end of the narrative, turn out to be the castration formula of the pagan Cybele cult. The selfless love of Félicité's "Simple Heart" borders on the idiotic. The topos of the spiritual night, in which the believer is metaphorically immersed in darkness, is literalized as Félicité loses her eyesight. Her way out of this dark night, which follows from the light of the *visio beatifica*, turns out not to be a revelation of truth, but a blinding illusion. Julian's love, modeled on psychiatric analyses, comes close to insanity and fulfills itself through an ascension that, at every step of the way, seems to be a homosexual love scene. But then again, in order to attain a true *imitatio Christi*, these strange saints abandon themselves to a total love, a perfectly gratuitous love marked by baseness and the earthly. The worst is yet to come: they are now burdened with the crossing out of the Cross, the cross of the Cross, and it is this second cross that purifies their Passion even further and realizes their true *imitatio* through the cancellation of its promise. Nothing remains but their pure, abject love.

"Quidquid volueris"

The Monstrosity of Civilization

The short story "Quidquid volueris" (the title references the motto of Rabelais's utopian Abbey of Thélème, "Fais ce que voudras"—"Do as you please"), which Flaubert wrote at the age of sixteen, stages a drama of sexuality and barbarism, conception and creation. In this ape-man story, Flaubert stages a poetics focused on the key term of (bad) mimesis, that is, imitation or *aping*.[1] Precisely this—aping—is what Djalioh, the ape-man, does not do. Djalioh—the freak of nature, the idiot who cannot read or write—is a figure of the author, Flaubert. A scene in which love is classified as incestuous and consequently conflated with death, which is repeated in one variation or another throughout Flaubert's work, makes its first appearance here. Short-circuiting sexual destiny [*Triebschicksal*] with poetics, Flaubert's story depicts the deadliness of sexual love bearing fruit, not in a child, but in self-sacrifice. The—bestial—poet becomes inimitable by strangely aping his predecessors. In his brutal expenditure, he stands diametrically opposed to the well-understood self-interest of society.

In his brutal overindulgence, the most bestial figure of the story is not the ape-man at its center, but the drama's sole survivor, who is simultaneously its initiator: the inhuman Paul de Monville. He is a model example of how to succeed in society. "Honor, power, riches, fame and the love of women"[2]—as Sigmund Freud's masculine ego notoriously pines for in his daydreams—fall into the lap of this Paul, who is more bestial than any beast could ever be. Paul is the only character to emerge without a hair on his head harmed. He profits from the whole drama, emerging from it, not only completely uninjured, but more respected, attractive to women, and richer. He is ruled entirely by his own self-interest. He does not marry for love, but because doing so doubles his fortune. This man, who conceitedly believes that all women are in love with him, perhaps not without some justification, in fact does not know what love is. "I see him as an eminently level-headed sort who hates poetry, who has a solid constitution and a dry heart, qualities needed to make your fortune and to live to be a hundred years old," Flaubert says of him. He "uses a woman's love like an occasional article of clothing and then tosses it aside among other old clothes, like discardable feelings that are no longer in style."[3]

"Quidquid volueris" begins with the concealment of a story that is not meant for the ears of women, let alone for those of brides. "Tell us of your trip to Brazil," Paul's aunt, Madame de Lansac, says to him on the eve of his wedding. "Adèle will enjoy it." Paul evidently doubts that the story of his Brazilian adventures would amuse Adèle—his bride to be—and begs off with empty phrases: "But Auntie, I assure you I had an excellent trip" (77). Later, among men at the wedding reception, he opens up, however.

If Paul is the epitome of the realistic bourgeois, then the ape-man Djalioh, whom Paul raises in place of a son, is its opposite: a passionate romantic. His becoming one with nature could have been drawn from the pages of Chateaubriand's *Atala*. Djalioh illustrates the grotesque; that is, the key concept of romantic poetics presented in Hugo's "Preface to Cromwell." While the coolly calculating Paul is ruled by base egoistic interests, Djalioh's love is limitless. His heart, in accord with the topography of the sublime, is "as vast as the sea and as immense and empty as the desert!" (82). The beauty of his soul shines through the ugliness of his body. Djalioh's heart is not dried up; he surely has received the gift of tears.[4] He is all poetry, passion, soul, and solitude: "Logic had given way to poetry, and passion had taken the place of knowledge" (82). And Flaubert summarizes: "That's the kind of natural monster who was befriended by Paul, who was himself a marvelous monster of civilization outfitted with all of its symbols, great intelligence, and shriveled soul" (83).

But who is Djalioh, who, as the text states, is half orangutan, half *nègre*? It is quickly clarified that unlike Paul, he does not belong in society *among* those who live off of their wealth as rentiers: he has no wife, does not go hunting, and doesn't smoke cigars. Nor is he an intellectual (the alternative to being a rentier). As Paul explains to his friends, Djalioh can neither read nor write.[5] On the eve of his wedding, Paul joins the circle of his male friends to tell about his Brazilian adventures and thus to reveal the mystery of Djalioh's identity. It is a story of bestial barbarism, committed in the name of science. Paul amused himself in Brazil, as he puts it, in a peculiar way. One of the slaves he bought was insufficiently compliant and, his vanity injured, he decided to revenge himself on her by using her as a guinea pig for breeding purposes. His experiment aspired to answer a question that perplexed the Académie des sciences: whether interbreeding between apes and humans is possible. Paul's scientific curiosity (which already pseudo-objectively conceals its own barbaric obscenity) serves as a cover for his drive for revenge. Because he believes that his slave has refused his advances because she finds him (the irresistible Paul!) as ugly as a wild animal, he purchases on one listless day the most beautiful orangutan he had ever seen and names him, suitably enough, Bell. His goal (to use the words of Shakespeare, from whom the story title, meaning "as you like it," appears to be borrowed) is an especially monstrous version of the *Taming of the Shrew*. When he leaves to hunt, Paul locks the purchased ape and the slave in his bedroom. On his return, he finds her crying and bloody from the animal's claws; the orangutan has escaped.

Cynical Paul, who shows no trace of sympathy for the raped woman, brings to light the cynicism of the academy. The slave becomes pregnant according to plan. On top of everything, his bet won him Mirsa, the slave of a colleague, as his bed slave. After seven torturous months, Paul's slave delivers her child on a dunghill and dies shortly after. Paul summarizes the results of his miserable experiment with the bravado of a Balzacian hero: "In short, I won Mirsa, was decorated at twenty, and on top of that I produced a child in a unique procedure" (90). The men standing around Paul react enthusiastically. This crossbreed between ape and human, the product of a bestial rape and of an even more bestial experiment, is Djalioh.

At the age of sixteen, Djalioh accompanies Paul back to Europe. He falls desperately in love with the blonde Adèle, Paul's betrothed and then wife. Djalioh loves her with his entire being. Adèle in contrast (like all women in Flaubert, blinded by beautiful appearances) loves Paul. She cannot discern the beautiful soul behind Djalioh's grotesque, ugly appearance. The only possibilities for Djalioh to express his passion consist in his playing the violin in a distorted manner at the wedding reception and in his out-of-sync rowing, when he takes the fulfilled couple on a lake cruise after their wedding night. The ape-man remains completely speechless.

The marriage between Paul and Adèle goes on to happily fulfill all of the clichés—at least until the moment when civilization's bestiality (of which Djalioh is a product) bestially breaks into civilization. The cause of this bestiality has certainly nothing bestial about it. Rather, it is that quintessentially occidental cultural refinement, an utterly romantic passion, something Paul, with his cold heart and calculating mind, is incapable of. Flaubert pulls out all the stops of romantic discourse: "Djalioh suffered the agonies of the damned. Imagine having all the passion necessary for love and having your soul consumed by flame, by the volcano where you are imprisoned! There you are, tied to a dry rock with your mouth athirst. Like Prometheus . . ." (92). The comparison with Prometheus charges the sensuous longing with heroism.

When the setting shifts from the provincial France to Paris, this deepest passion takes an utterly monstrous form. Djalioh reenacts the barbaric scene of his conception, making it even more terrible. Colonial bestiality migrates to the Faubourg Saint-Germain in the heart of Paris, where it no longer involves a black slave, but a blonde lady, the epitome of French civilization. It is perpetrated by an ape-man, who, more romantic than the most romantic hero, has a pure soul, a sensitive heart, passionate desire, and the gift of tears. He regresses into the role of his father, the orangutan—but only to conclude with the most romantic of all themes, a suicidal *Liebestod*.

Before we get to this catastrophic role reversal, there is a strange mirror scene between apes and men. The narrator begins the story as though he intended to avenge Djalioh's inexpressible passion, which is depicted with so much sympathy, on the conceited women who spurn such love. The scene begins as a meditation on aging women who take monkeys—supposedly the only beings who do not rebuff them—as lovers. Even Adèle, as the text suggests, will end up like Madame de Lansac, who enjoys the love of a monkey instead of a lover. The specific irony of the story may lie in the fact that Adèle does not reach this state of monkey love, because this pretty young woman will perish literally of a monkey love of an entirely different type. There follows a typical *vanitas* scene, which tells of the decline of all earthly, and a fortiori all feminine, beauty:

It's so sad but true. After losing their fresh complexion over the course of a dozen years and shriveling up like old parchment, they eat their dinner by the fireplace with a novel in hand. Accompanied by her cat and her maid, this angel of beauty will die and become a cadaver, a stinking corpse before turning into nothing except the fetid air trapped in a tomb. I constantly see skeletal people whose yellowish skin seems to take on the coloration of the earth that will contain them. (96)

Likewise Adèle and Djalioh will each end up as a skeleton and a stinking corpse.

In the end it comes to a commonplace comparison of apes' and humans' common traits. Apes hold up a mirror to humans: "I don't take to monkeys very much, and yet they do seem to imitate human behavior perfectly. When I see one of those animals (I'm not talking about men here), I seem to see myself in a magnifying mirror: the same feelings, same brutal appetites, a little less arrogance—and that's all" (96). If the apes play the lover to old women, they symbolize their spouses to the young. All human love seems to be a matter of aping, which is in fact human, all too human. Djalioh's tragic, bestial love cannot, however, be said to be mere "monkey business," an apish affair. The mirror relationship between apes and men is not at stake. Rather, cynical monstrosity, which by far exceeds all beastliness, engenders the most noble human love, which turns into unspeakable bestiality.

In spite of the expressed aversion to apes, the text blatantly apes contemporary great writers. Djalioh is a distorted imitation of the name of Esmeralda's goat Djali in Victor Hugo's *Notre-Dame de Paris*. The family resemblance between him and the hunchback Quasimodo is impossible to miss; each hides a beautiful, romantic, loving soul beneath a grotesque exterior. The fusion of soul and nature conjures up the work of Chateaubriand. Paul de Monville and Madame de Lansac echo the names of Paul de Manerville and the château of Lanstrac in Balzac's *A Marriage Settlement*. The settings of the château and of the house of Faubourg Saint-Germain are indebted to Balzac's interiors, as is Paul's cynical bravado to that of Balzac's hero. The entire novella reverberates with the contemporary literature between romanticism and realism that it mimics (including swans as the indispensable prop for romantic depictions of nature). That Adèle gets up early in order to read a novel by Balzac puts the poetological dimension of the narrative in a nutshell. This is also a story about *imitatio*: the relationship of an author to his predecessors, his fathers, is being negotiated. The scene with the apes is in *mise en abyme* with the story's own poetics: it apes. At the same time, Flaubert's ape story outdoes the literature he is aping. With his apes, he tells another story of the relation to the father. His *imitatio* is not about aping—or changes radically whatever we might have understood by this term. He tears the fabric of this literature apart with Djalioh's *griffe* (claw) in order to leave his own *griffe* (signature) upon it. As later in the cases of *Madame Bovary* or *Salammbô*, the classical metaphor of the textual fabric as a textile is crucial.

Djalioh's sensuously agonizing jealousy is not distanced by any ironic imitative gesture. His mystically flowing passion, whose tears have carved a deep channel in his soul, is as authentic as his bestial monstrousness and desire. He is speechless, however, and thus incapable of amorous sweet talk. Instead of falling back on clichés, all he can do is cry, sob, gesture, and shriek. In his inarticulate love, Flaubert nevertheless finds a language of his own. In order to kill Paul's son and wife, Djalioh must work his way through layers of precious textiles: "One morning (that's the day I'm speaking about) he got up and went out into the garden, where a one-year-old child slept, swaddled in muslin, netting, embroideries, and colored shawls, there in his boat-shaped cradle with its bowsprit graced by the sun's golden rays" (98). With each layer of precious fabric enveloping the child, Djalioh removes the veils of civilization and lays its monstrosity bare. He surpasses the barbarity of his own experimental conception when he reenacts that same savagery in the heart of culture. The soulful embodiment of romanticism becomes violence incarnate: "He picked him up, flipped him upside down, and threw him with all his might onto the grass with a thud. The child uttered a cry and his brain spurted ten feet away near a gillyflower" (98). At this point every trace of contemporary literature disappears; along with the textiles that had enveloped the child, Flaubert leaves the web of his predecessors behind. The tone of this murder belongs to Flaubert alone; we encounter it again many years later in *A Sentimental Education*, when Father Roque murders the blond young revolutionary and in the murder of Julian.

Strip, tear apart, rupture, unveil, lay bare: these are the actions that correlate the child's murder with the rape of Adèle. Stripped, torn apart, laid bare is also the basic formula of art and a fortiori of realism, which is supposed to imitate nature in a lifelike manner. With brutal force, the jungle breaks into an idyllic interior, as paradisiacally Parisian as it gets. Fragrant, melodious, radiantly beautiful nature, fused with all things feminine, is represented as pure civilization. Even the novel the woman is reading is naturalized; one hears the intoxicating rustling of leaves in the leafing of the pages. One cannot think of a nicer figure for the classical *silvae*, the woods to which the texts of tradition allude. Nature is beautiful only when imitated: the filtered sun penetrates the closed shutters; the twittering of birds comes out of the aviary; the flowers are preciously grown in a *jardinière*. The interior culminates in the woman reading Balzac, who "lay sprawled on a red velvet sofa. . . . Her dressing gown of flowing white muslin was open in front" (98–99). Her accessories, steeped in the scent of the room, are scattered everywhere: "Her white gloves were thrown onto the chair along with her belt, handkerchief, and small shawl, all of which exuded such an especially fine scent." Femininity and the interior permeate one another airily as if in an impressionist painting.

The fragrant flowers of rhetoric are plucked and the veil of civilization torn to shreds. The flowers are stripped of their petals, "Then he collected the flowers and strewed them all over the floor" (100).[6] The sofa, the locus of the art of love in a long European tradition cited by Flaubert, becomes a jungle vine, which Djalioh seizes, swinging like Tarzan: "he leapt on the couch, threw aside the pillows, leaned over the back and balanced himself for a long time in a seesaw motion, thanks to his flexible spine" (100). Adèle's precious fabric is brutally torn to pieces by Djalioh: "Djalioh held her by the back of her gown, which his nails gripped. . . . He began ripping her clothes with both hands, and tore away the sheer fabric that veiled her . . . dug his claws into her flesh and stripped her" (99–100). Even the "warm satin" of her skin is torn up by his claws. The naked truth of sex—no longer veiled by rosy curtains and shutters, but exposed by the harsh light of the sun—breaks into the classical *locus amoenus* as a ravaging, bestial, and ultimately deadly violence. Yet at the same time, in his ferocious brutality, Djalioh also shows what society as a whole is missing: tears and sobs. It is the non-language of the loving heart, which according to *the* received opinion belongs to humans only. Animals do not have it. In its paradoxical excess it becomes here the most sublime of all acts of charity: Djalioh has "nothing to offer her except the tears of an animal and the sighs of a monster" (99). Speechless and unspeakable, he remains in the passion that spells Adèle's death—and his own: "He uttered frequent ferocious cries, and stupefied and motionless, held out his arms. Then he gurgled with voluptuousness [*comme un homme qui se meurt*]" (100). The French metaphor for orgasm, *la petite mort*, is sinisterly literalized: Adèle's convulsions are not those of passion, but of death. The text states that this has to do with the Fall of Man—"like the first man to look upon a woman"—and perhaps alludes to the ape, who is depicted here as Adam, as assessor of man's fall. The bodies remain behind mauled, mangled, shattered; they lie bloody on top of one another, as in a macabre *Liebestod*. A sensitive heart and extreme bestiality do not stand opposed to one another as usual; instead the feeling heart in its speechless bestiality stands opposed to the monstrous, heartless society, cooled by its cynicism, but with language, law, and science on its side.

Djalioh the ape-man, created by Paul "in a unique procedure" and raised by him in the place of a son, takes the role of his biological father (the raping orangutan) during the rape scene, but also the role of his symbolic father Paul, Adèle's husband. In the end, Adèle looks exactly like Djalioh's mother, the black slave who is left bloody and mangled by the claws of the orangutan, with "deep scratch marks on her body" (101). After Djalioh kills his symbolic half-brother, Adèle and Paul's child, he rapes his father's wife. The vision of this rape, which is set up in the text as a primal scene, corresponds with the childhood sadomasochistic interpretation of the father making love to the mother. From the son's perspective, the father does violence to the mother. In this case, there is no *jouissance*, since sex means death here, even for the raping son. The transgression against the incest taboo leads to the death of the son; Djalioh is from the beginning doomed to the grave; he bears the stamp of death—as Flaubert thought he did himself. It was by no means a mere coincidence that he chose to give his antihero his own age.

For the monster Djalioh, lovemaking means killing, because Adèle, in league with this monstrous civilization, and even veiling its monstrosity, does not surrender herself to the monster as she does to Paul. The representation of the mother's unveiling rape, which is as brutal as it is soulfully empathetic, and leads to her and the rapist's deaths, is simultaneously the birth of the author, who in order to mark the world with his own *griffe* tears the textual fabric of his fathers—Chateaubriand, Hugo, Balzac— apart. Flaubert thus bares the monstrosity of civilization that these authors conceal. Brought forward then is the interplay between the heart and bestiality, an interrelation that had been expelled from human society. By giving a voice to this, or rather by putting it into writing, Flaubert comes into his own. Mimesis has to be something other than the *aping* of the fathers.

Or rather, Flaubert proposes a very different account of what aping might be. That is what Flaubert gives us to read in his ape story.

Flaubert's story, as Freud would say, is symptomatic of an Oedipal complex that has not been resolved by the castration complex. The son does not give up his mother as an erotic object. He adheres to her and thereby on one level accepts his castration; it has already happened, and he bears the stamp of death. He identifies with her suffering and remains with the childhood interpretation of lovemaking as a wounding to death. Mortally wounded, he too always already bears the stamp of death in life. In his life Flaubert will forsake love. In his work he will tell of incestuous as well as fatal cases of love, in which killing or mortal self-sacrifice and lovemaking are consistently the same—at least for those who don't have hearts of stone and who, unlike Paul or later Rodolphe in *Madame Bovary*, can love. Flaubert transfers his Oedipal aggression against the father to his symbolic fathers. He gives birth to himself as author through an aggressive tearing apart of his "fathers," against whom he sets up another "aping." By rupturing their textual web the castaway son brings to light a truth they had concealed, disguised, and veiled: the truly heartless monstrosity of this civilization.

The last chapter of the novella returns to the narrator and with him to societal clichés; again the style is openly ironic. The narrator describes how society, with its horrified and indignant "oohs" and "aahs," obviously enjoys the thrill of the sex and crime spectacle, which keeps all of Paris in suspense for weeks. The praise of the virtuous heroine found in every melodrama, who defends her innocence with a knife, is sung. That Djalioh kills himself is passed over in silence. In order to be exposed by Flaubert's language as clichéd, ossified convention, the tragic and bestial scene in which the perpetrator is simultaneously victim is literally covered up, shrouded, and veiled during the funeral: "draped in crepe trappings, candles, chanting priests . . . and men dressed in black with white gloves" (101).

The hypocrisy, the stark disconnection between what one says and what one does, is elaborately staged, as is the ridiculousness of those blind and deaf judges of Djalioh's outrageous passion who are so far from actually understanding it. They are themselves subject to the very egoistic and bestial desires that they denounce and ascribe to the criminal. They condemn his libidinal lack of self-control, but feast greedily on mutton and *haricots* (from *harigoter*: to tear up, shred, slice up). Flaubert seems a bit heavy-handed in spelling out the socially approved "moral of the story":

"'People must really lack discipline,' said the young grocer, while asking for the third time to have someone pass him the beans" (101). His later works shun such overkill.

The narrator puts forward another moral in the story: Adèle and Djalioh have gone the way of all flesh in a particularly terrible form. When she is exhumed for reburial two years later, she stinks to high heaven; one of the gravediggers throws up. For his part, Djalioh is dispossessed of all human traits and reduced to the animal drives that had been attributed to him. He falls victim to the same scientific spirit that created him and ends up as a superbly conserved skeleton in a zoological museum, a curiosity in a cabinet of curiosities. Only Paul is happy, wandering from one place of amusement to the other in the company of women, immune to life's challenges: "And Paul? What do you know: I almost forgot about him! He remarried. I saw him a while ago in the Bois de Boulogne, and this evening you'll see him at the theater" (102).

Quidquid volueris, as you like it: as moral as it is judicious, the folk saying self-righteously and self-affirmingly isolates libidinal, animalistic monstrosities from civilization so that the cynical bestiality of civilization can perpetuate itself undisturbed. Only a literature that "apes" in an entirely different way can unmask this truth—and not through reproduction, but at the cost of the self-sacrifice of its creator, a depraved freak.

Madame Bovary

Mœurs de province—Provincial Manners

Eating, Loving, Reading

I am the Lord, who heals you.

Exodus 15:26

Madame Bovary is a tale of adultery in provincial France. Emma, the wife of Doctor Charles Bovary, betrays him, first with a landowner, Rodolphe, then with a law clerk, Léon. The lifestyle that Emma holds to be necessary for love leads to her complete financial ruin, and in despair at being abandoned to her utter ruin by her lover, she kills herself with arsenic, obtained from the pharmacist Homais. Her only daughter, still a child, becomes a cotton spinner—one of the lowest forms of employment at the time, because of the often deadly damage to workers' health caused by the fine dust created in the process. Flaubert's novel is generally read as an example of the extreme aestheticization of lifestyle in modernity. Art—literature and music—becomes the model for life, with devastating consequences. Spiritual and sensory values get confused in the most corrupting way.[1] For Léon, the lace of his beloved's camisole is at least as appealing as the elevation of her soul, expressed through her purchase of a prie-dieu kneeler upholstered in tea-colored velvet. Emma's erotic charm in a riding habit, the so-called *amazone*,[2] leads to her first act of adultery; the "Parisian" custom of traveling in a fiacre triggers the second.

I read Flaubert's novel as a text on the aesthetic. From this perspective the novel's thesis can be summed up as follows: aesthetics offers no compensation for breaking away from the promise of salvation, and it is therefore not to be understood as a phenomenon of secularization. It is rather the outcome of an insatiable desire for God, misdirected toward the world, finding expression in the fetish and in drugs. In the end, this longing for transcendent salvation is not compensated for by aesthetics, but rather destructively deceived. *Only a literature that is no longer beautiful* can disabuse us of the beauty of the arts.

Research on *Madame Bovary* circles around three motif-complexes—food, love, reading—whose common nexus I would like to indicate with the help of a number of examples. The poetological topos of spiritual nourishment is the hidden structuring matrix of the narrative. The representational dimension of the novel rests on this topos, even though it does not appear as the primary focus of the plot and is therefore not visible on the level of the narrated events. The story of Madame Bovary is dominated by the symptoms brought about by the perversion of this very topos of spiritual nourishment. Flaubert's *Madame Bovary*, usually interpreted as the realistic novel par excellence, will here be read, by contrast, as the allegorical narration of the end of allegory. In this sense, it is a novel about reading—about aesthetic experience—or, to put it more exactly, about the now perverted readability of the world. As the epitome of all allegories of reading, which have tended in the modern period to become allegories of the no longer correctly readable world that can only be narrated in the no longer so beautiful belles lettres, Flaubert's *Madame Bovary* is fiction's Song of Songs. It is quite rightly celebrated as the novel of novels. My thesis is therefore that the aesthetic effect in Flaubert's avant-garde poetics is to be seen as an aftereffect of an older spiritual constellation that has been inscribed into Flaubert's modern aesthetics. The novel is therefore only apparently an exoteric text, easily understood by everybody; being densely encrypted, it is, indeed, esoteric beneath its smooth surface and is merely waiting to be understood by a handful of new readers each century.

As defined by Pierre Proudhon in 1866, nine years after the publication of *Madame Bovary*, adultery is "a crime that contains all other crimes."[3] A more matter-of-fact definition, with which Proudhon broadly concurs, is to be found under the heading "La femme adultère" in a volume in the series titled *Les Français peints par eux-mêmes*: "Adultery derives from a Latin verb that means 'to alter,' and nothing alters feelings and things more."[4] The writer goes on to explain that adultery is due to the natural and biblically attested lubricity of the woman and leads to all kinds of ruin, right up to prostitution and suicide. *Madame Bovary* is nothing but the working out of sexist clichés of its time, which are collected with unusual thoroughness in this article, Michael Riffaterre contends: like the adulteress in the article, Madame Bovary becomes addicted to novels and neglects her only daughter, who is confided to the care of a loveless nurse. But the novel, argues Riffaterre, goes beyond the reproduction of the contemporary clichés and produces an aesthetic surplus by its literalization of metaphors for adultery: "'Aller se promener au bois' [the context of Emma's first adulterous connection, with Rodolphe] and 'prendre le fiacre' [the context of the second, with Léon] are for a [French] woman cliché metaphors for having an affair."[5] The realism of the novel, according to Riffaterre, lies in its frank depiction of lust, unmasking the adulterous heroine as a fallen woman. Emma comes to recognize herself in the end, with her last, terrible laugh, as the whore in the blind beggar's song.

Intertextuality seems to me to work in a somewhat more subtle and, indeed, more sublimated manner here. The lust of adultery is not as banal as it "realistically" appears to be. It has an allegorical dimension: adultery is the figure of reading that has erred disastrously from the right path. The key sentence of the novel, if there is one, is not a typical contemporary commonplace. It is rather a psalm verse quoted in Augustine's *Confessions*. The *Confessions* is not in the least a book about aesthetic experience, and we find Augustine here transfixed by a text that was also a favorite of Flaubert's: the fourth book of the *Aeneid*. Augustine describes his identificatory participation in reading as an adultery: "non te amabam et fornicabar abs te"—"I had no love for you and committed fornication against you."[6] Caught up in "fictions," in the passionate reading of passions, Augustine is separated from God and so dies to himself. Wholly absorbed in the love and ruin of Dido, he commits adultery against God, his "spouse": "What is more pitiable than a wretch without pity for himself who weeps over the death of Dido dying for love of Aeneas, but not weeping over himself dying for his lack of love for you, my God light of my heart, bread of the inner mouth of my soul, the power which begets life in my mind and in the innermost recesses of my thinking. I had no love for you and 'committed fornication against you' (Ps. 72:27). . . . 'For the friendship of this world is fornication against you' (Jas. 4:4)."[7] This passage brings together addictive, fatal love with eating in the figure of adultery, which, as a worldly love, is the antithesis to love of God. Instead of God's wholesome nourishment, another, poisonous nourishment is taken.

One can formulate the error in reading *Madame Bovary* in the Augustinian terms of *uti* and *frui*: Emma wants to directly enjoy things, instead of using them as a reference to God. She rejects everything that does not serve the "immediate satisfaction of her heart's desires" (354); she is held by her fascination with sensory exteriority.[8] To this she is addicted, filled with insatiable desire, which by definition can never be fulfilled, but leaves her in unsatisfiable longing.[9] The contemporary clichés of the adulteress come into a new perspective through the lens of Augustinian epistemology. The corruption of the heroine's heart, described by Flaubert according to Augustinian topoi, brings to light the stony heartlessness of society. Heartlessly they take advantage of her corrupted heart, which, after all, is still a heart of flesh. If the novel were merely remobilizing misogynistic commonplaces, joining with the whole society in casting stones at the adulteress, then why would this society have put it on trial?

Using the example of the Dido episode, Augustine opposes the letters of literature to the letters of Holy Scripture. The passionate devouring of fictitious love stories leads to the loss of God and of the self. This loss of the self in passionate love is depicted in images of suicide, fornication, and adultery; the image of nourishment suggests its opposite in poisoning. The letter of belles lettres, which is greedily swallowed and is addictive like a drug, in short the letter that poisons, is in fact a persistent and central topos in the French discussion around the notion of fiction in the nineteenth century.[10] Flaubert's novel cites this commonplace in a general way. Literature is opposed to religion by Mother Bovary. Bookselling is declared to be a "poisonous trade" (103). Bournisien, the priest, argues in the same vein and takes his arguments from the Fathers of the Church via Rousseau's "Letter to D'Alembert."

"I know very well," objected the cure, "that there are good works, good authors. Still, the very fact of crowding people of different sexes into the same room, made to look enticing by displays of worldly pomp, these pagan disguises, the makeup, the lights, the effeminate voices, all this must, in the long-run, engender a certain mental libertinage, give rise to immodest thoughts and impure temptations. Such, at any rate, is the opinion of all the church fathers." (174–75)

Flaubert demonstrates that, contrary to what is claimed by the theologically educated enemies of literature from Augustine to Pierre Nicole, belles lettres are not necessarily the epitome of seductive, deadly reading. Novels—at least Flaubert's novels—do not mystify, but rather demystify. In the allegory of love, they tell of false reading, including the false reading of literature; as such, they are novels against novels, antinovels. Therefore, love stories are always also stories of reading. It is Sade who, instead of seeing so-called fiction as illusion, defines the novel as the very medium in which the blinded reading is staged as such. Only the novel, as the science of the deluded heart, brings to light the truth about human blindness, and as such, it is as edifying as it is true. In this precise sense, *Madame Bovary* is also a story about the dangers of false reading, about a false relation to the world. This false relation is illustrated by the fatal reading of novels. The theme of the book is corrupted reading and corrupted love, as illustrated in the figure of adultery. Augustine opposes to this destructive and god-forsaken mode of being the redeeming love of the Savior.

In the nineteenth century, the paradigm of the salvific, healing love of God faced competition from medicine, the new science of truth and salvation.[11] Flaubert illustrates this competition between the institutions of medicine and of the Church by having the commode at the sickbed of Madame Bovary transformed from a pharmacy into an altar: "they were clearing the night-table of its medicine bottles and turning it into an altar" (170–71). The medicine bottles give way to another promise of salvific introjection: Holy Communion. Later, the doctor appears "like a god" at the heroine's deathbed; people no longer expect salvation from religion but from the doctor, and the village crowds around him as if he were a saint. Flaubert's coup lies in presenting the competing discourses of religion and medicine as equally literal knowledge, without any touch of spirituality, and hence not as knowledge of life but as knowledge of sheer, unredeemed death. Their competition is revealed as a mere surface phenomenon, covering over the deeper affinity in their shared heartless, obtuse literality. The pharmacist Homais and the priest Bournisien both remain equally blind in their committed literality. The final solidarity between priest and pharmacist comes to light during the funeral meal, over the corpse of the heroine in her room sprayed with holy water and chlorine. The new belief turns out to be far more disastrous than the old one. Where the priest is merely obtuse in a well-meaning way, the self-interested Homais, in his liberal republican belief in progress, pursues everybody without mercy. The helpless blind man, who involuntarily proves the impotence of his science, is his most obvious victim. Having long lost faith in her own power, the Church turns those who turn to her over to the institution of medicine. The truth of the powerlessness of the institution of medicine, which believes itself to be all-powerful, is in an interesting chiasmus soberly announced by a doctor, a priest without god: "There is nothing more to be done" (254). Larivière acknowledges his own impotence upon seeing Emma on her deathbed. He is the only one who does not have a heart of stone and sheds tears in sympathy with the suffering dying Emma.

Literature, religion, and medicine converge in the trope of the antidote/poison. The pharmacy, which transforms poison into medicine through the art of the correct dosage, is so prominent in the novel because literature, in the topos of the sugared pill, is itself a *pharmakon*. Homais, the pharmacist, refers to this affinity of literature and medicine: "'Of course,' pursued Homais, 'there is bad literature as there is bad pharmacy . . .'" (174). But just as drug laws do not succeed, and the drugstore, like the Church, deals out death rather than salvation, literature functions, not as the sugared pill, but, in a dizzying, irresistible spiral, as an addictive poison. All three are as drugs the reverse of the saving spiritual meal that stills hunger: it nourishes instead of poisoning. They are to be decoded by reference to this implicit backdrop. In Flaubert, the novel becomes the site at which the truth of the deadening letter is produced by deconstructing the *allegoresis* of the Fathers.[12]

Realism does not reveal crude carnal lust to be the final truth about women. Realism results from a desire for God gone astray. The symptoms of this going astray appear in the flesh. The sober desire for God is converted into a numbing, drunken debauchery, into hysterical symptoms such as convulsions and paralysis, and finally into self-destruction through poison. In terms of rhetoric as well as of poetics, realism does not present the topos of the naked truth—carnal lust—but is the result of the collapse of allegoresis: in search of spiritual nourishment, Emma becomes a drug addict.

The heroine's carnal devotion to the world, her fatal poisoning, her deviant love of a perverted heart[13] are nothing but expressions of how this longing for spiritual nourishment, for the sweetness of the letter, for fulfilling love have gone astray. In the name of morality and law, this society lovelessly and heartlessly profits from the heroine's misdirected love. She is exploited without mercy.

Let us begin with the sublime aspect of Madame Bovary's love, with its mystical/erotic/religious complex. As one can already perceive in the titles of his other novels and novella, Flaubert, contrary to the tradition of his family, was more fascinated by the reversal of religion than by the hegemonic discourse of medicine: "A Simple Heart," "Saint Julian the Hospitalier," and *The Temptation of Saint Anthony* are all inverted histories of saints, stories of religion gone wrong. Such misdirected devotion (*religio*) is a key element in the case brought against *Madame Bovary* by the state prosecutor in 1857. What is taken to be offensive is the strange mixture of religion and love: one of the two charges is that it is an "insult to religious morality" (*offense à la morale religieuse*). The novel, according to the *avocat impérial*, mixes sexual immorality and religion; it brings the language of adultery into the shrine of divinity. "One day voluptuous, the next day religious" (326), Madame Bovary would whisper the same endearments to God as to her lovers. The novel thus appeared as a celebration of adultery.[14] The long-untreated question of Madame Bovary's worldly love and her love of God has been thematized by Micheline Hermine, who compares Thérèse de Lisieux and Madame Bovary.[15] The comparison between a virginal saint and a character in a novel seems at first absurd, but it reveals a convergence in the coding of love: both the love of the adulteress and the love of the nun follow the model of the *sponsa Christi*, the virginal consecrated spouse of Christ, developed in Christian mysticism. In *Madame Bovary*, Flaubert draws the portrait of an inverted *sponsa*.

The model of the *sponsa Christi* was very much present to Flaubert during the writing of this novel, when, as he wrote to Louis Bouilhet, he was absorbed in the works of the most famous of all the brides of Christ, Teresa of Ávila (1515–82). A hundred years later, she is cited by Lacan as the principal reference in the question of female desire for God. In letters to his mistress, Louise Colet, which make up a kind of workbook to *Madame Bovary*, Flaubert speaks of his ecstatic and passionate heroine as "a girl, who dies a virgin mystic" (*une fille, qui meurt vierge et mystique*). In a letter to his longtime correspondent Marie-Sophie Leroyer de Chantepie on May 30, 1857, he writes that he had originally imagined his heroine as a "virgin, living in a provincial milieu, growing old miserably, and thus attaining the highest stages of mysticism and dreamed-of passion."[16] Emma does not turn out to be this mystical virgin, whom we find in distorted form in "A Simple Heart," but rather an earthly erotic, loving woman (the *avocat impérial* called her a "lascivious" woman). The sensual fulfillment at the beginning of her love affairs does not silence her desire for absolute love. After the deceptions and disappointments of marriage and adultery, Emma regularly turns to religion for what she cannot find in earthly love.

Linking human and divine love and attempting to bring the two into a new configuration by recasting the model of the *sponsa Christi* is characteristic of the second half of the nineteenth century. A great deal of realist literature of that era propagates the new idea of the wife and the mother by translating, rather than dismissing, the mystical model of the *sponsa Christi*. The shrine of the new, laicistic religion of the nineteenth century would no longer be the Church, but the family; the wife, excluded from the world, became simultaneously the priestess of and the sacrifice on the altar of the home. Jules Michelet's treatises *L'amour* (1858) and *La femme* (1859) bring this ideology into focus. The woman, hitherto the enemy of men, of the French Republic, and of progress, has to be torn from the claws of the priests, from the bosom of the Church. The ideal of the chaste nun, of the Bride of Christ, is stigmatized as mere frigidity or hysteria and replaced by the new norm of the wife and mother. Émile Zola's *Lourdes* illustrates this new ideal in polemical opposition to the ideal of the virginal saint. Drawing on the work of the neurologist Jean-Martin Charcot, Zola depicts the *sponsa* as a hysteric. In contrast, thanks to her husband and children, the new woman, wife, and mother is both useful and happy. She no longer has to sacrifice herself to God, but to her family, which becomes the religion proper to the woman.

The linkage between the *sponsa Christi* and the wife and mother, so determining in Michelet's writings, fails in Flaubert's. And the new, bourgeois ideal of the loving wife and mother, so important throughout the nineteenth century, and presented by Zola in opposition to the *sponsa*, especially in his later work, fails in a more gruesome manner. In Flaubert, the *sponsa* and the wife mutually destroy each other. Motherly love and marital love are certainly not for Madame Bovary what they are for Michelet or for Zola's positive heroines: the fulfillment of female nature and female desire with religious overtones of redemption. Flaubert minutely measures out the stations of a fulfilled female life in order to show Madame Bovary's unfulfilled nature all the more starkly. The wedding night, which transforms the girl into a woman, passes over her without leaving a trace. The commonplace contemporary view was that regular marital sex prevented hysteria in women. Here, marriage causes Emma's hysterical symptoms. Marriage is hysteria-inducing. The birth of her child, the highlight of a woman's life, causes Madame Bovary to fall into a swoon of disappointment. Instead of living to love her baby only, a state hymnically represented in contemporary literature, Madame Bovary immediately hands her child over to a wet nurse. It is on the way to the wet nurse, a few weeks after the birth, that her first affair begins. What was seen at the time as the fulfillment of every true woman is, for Madame Bovary, nothing more than a role, which she acts with virtuous brio in accordance with literary models. "She claimed to love children; they were her consolation, her joy, her passion; and she accompanied her caresses with lyrical outbursts that would have reminded any one but the inhabitants of Yonville [where the Bovarys live] of the penitent nun Sachette in *Notre Dame de Paris*" (88–89). Emma cannot be satisfied by husband and child: she is consumed by another desire. This other desire is satisfied by adultery only for a little while. It continues to draw her further, to suck her in, even when she is satiated by it to the point of revulsion.

This leads me into the second complex: eating. In contrast to that of religion, this one has been widely treated in the novel's critical literature, from Erich Auerbach to Jean-Pierre Richard and Victor Brombert. Eating has been declared to be the real theme of the novel.[17] In general, because of its sheer fullness of detail and truth to life, the treatment of food and eating in *Madame Bovary* is taken as an indicator of realism. The turn in the interpretation of the novel away from "realism" and "representation" crystallizes around this complex. Richard phenomenologically determined Flaubert's relation to the world by way of the metaphor of eating: not only the author, but also his characters are guided by these metaphors. Brombert began to work out the "symbolic-allegorical" moments in the theme of food. Jonathan Culler, in his "The Uses of Madame Bovary," indicates that representation or "realism" enters into crisis precisely when it is a matter of food; it is then that the signifier and not the signified begins to direct the movement of the text. It is not only that so much veal is eaten in the novel. Calves and cattle populate it through a proliferation of signifiers for *veau* and *bovine*: the mayor of Yonville is named Tuvache ("Thou Cow"), Léon marries a Mlle Lebœuf ("Miss Steer"), and the architect of Emma's tomb is called Vaufrylard ("Veal-Fry-Fat"). Culler makes a Flaubertian pun of this, joking that *Madame Bovary* is not "a novel of realism, but of vealism."[18]

In every place that we might think we encounter realistic details, what we find is in fact a play on words. The theme of food, or better of incorporation, has been further developed in an intricate psychoanalytical reading by Avital Ronell.[19] Incorporation is the corporeal model of introjection, which lies at the basis of the metaphorics of the spiritual nourishment, as well as of the psychoanalytic function of identity formation. My own discussion can be understood as presenting the patristic-topological backside to Ronell's psychoanalytic foreground.

The allusive complex of food, love, and reading, the nexus of the novel, hidden in the depth of realistic details, brings together the topos of love of God/love of man with those of eating/addiction and food/drug. The *avocat impérial* prosecuted the novel as adultery's Song of Songs (*le Cantique de l'adultère*).[20] With this phrase, he hit the nail on the head, though not in the way he intended. For the Song of Songs has been for almost two thousand years the central text upon which every *interpretatio christiana* learned to distinguish the spiritual and the literal sense of allegorical reading and to unfold the connection of spiritual and earthly love. Henceforth, reading and loving have belonged inseparably together.

Translated back into the oldest hermeneutic formation, the theme of *Madame Bovary* is contained in an often-cited verse of Paul in 2 Corinthians 3:6: "the letter killeth, but the spirit giveth life." Flaubert unfolds this antithesis within the same set of metaphors, which ever since the Fathers of the Church have served to represent the concealed spiritual sense of the word. This is precisely why eating is so prominent in the novel. Other, complementary metaphors, like that of the cloth and the veil, stemming from the same tradition, and which have entered into the novel in the same way, have been similarly overlooked in their function.

With the metaphorics of eating, the novel is determined by a structuring paradigm concealed in the surface text and not unfolded in the narrative—namely, the Eucharist. In the sacrament of the Eucharist, one incorporates the body and the blood of Christ in the form of bread and wine. As meta-allegory, as the figure of figuration, the Eucharist provides the model according to which the world is to be deciphered. It guarantees feeding on the Scripture, and not merely on the bitter letter that kills, but also the sweetness of the life-giving spirit. Christ's sacrificial death transforms the bitter into the sweet. Sweetness and bitterness are the semantic isotopes organizing *Madame Bovary*. Their metaphorical significance had to remain unrecognized as long as the basic underlying paradigm was not seen. Flaubert reverses the Eucharistic model of sweet readability into bitter blind literality: his novel perverts the figure of *conversio*, effected by Christ's sacrificial death. Flaubert's novel thereby reverses the New Testament, which was, in a Paulinian hermeneutics, read as converting the letter that kills into the spirit that gives life.

Developing on Henri de Lubac's monumental standard work, Klaus Lange and Hans-Jörg Spitz have collected the metaphorics of the spiritual meaning of Scripture with impressive erudition. Lange was also one of the first to point out that the metaphors coined by the Fathers of the Church, which had laid the foundation for all medieval allegorical scriptural interpretation, were still very much alive in the nineteenth century. To support his case for the ongoing relevance of metaphors to designate the *sensus spiritualis*, he cites the example—and it could not be more suitable for the present context—of a letter of Flaubert's to Louise Colet, in which he writes: "For two days already, I have been trying to figure out what young girls dream about and I am thus navigating in the milky oceans of writings about castles and troubadours in white-plumed velvet caps."[21] Flaubert's "milky oceans," according to Klaus Lange, cites "an allegory on the basis of the secularized milk metaphor with the meaning *simplex doctrina*, as coined by the New Testament."[22] Let us give another example of the unbroken career of exegetic metaphors in the same correspondence. Flaubert, writing again to Colet, faults the style of her novel *La servante* as follows: "At the stage you are at, linen shouldn't smell of milk . . . go back, tighten up, compress the breasts of your heart."[23] The "breasts of your heart" should have sufficed to alert readers to an allegorical dimension and made it clear that it is not, as Janet Beizer suggests, a matter of an *écriture féminine* or of drastic interventions in the feminine body.[24] The milk that flows too easily from the breasts—and that then becomes rancid and smelly in the laundry—contrasts with solid food. So that what is being said is that Colet should produce less easily digestible and more solid food, suitable, not for children of the spirit, but for adults: writing that does not remain stuck at the level of the *simplex doctrina*, but leads into the mysteries—in other words, write a less didactic and naive, more complex and deeper text. Flaubert unfolds the metaphor of milk and butter alluded to here in another passage. Isidore of Seville uses the metaphor in his commentary on Genesis to distinguish literal and spiritual meanings. The Gospel, the spirit, crystallizes out of the law the way butter hardens out of milk. Gregory the Great says more precisely that the butter of the spiritual meaning first originates through "beating" (*pressio*), which signifies an applied contemplation of the written text, of the milk of the literal meaning. When Flaubert therefore says of an unfinished text that the style is still "soft, slack, it's cream that hasn't been beaten enough,"[25] so that what is now necessary is hard work in order to beat already whipped cream into butter, he is once again referring to the same topos.

In the following analysis of *Madame Bovary*, the focus has to fall rather upon topoi than on concrete intertexts; this also corresponds to the form of the transmission. The exegetic tradition was systematically collected in allegorical lexica, gleanings called *spicilegia*. These topoi were even familiar to authors who had grown up in atheistic families, like Flaubert and Michelet. They evidently belonged to the mnemotechnical knowledge of the Latin West, whose function was first recognized by Ernst Robert Curtius. The legal system contemporary to Flaubert showed greater sensitivity to these nuances than do modern interpreters.

Flaubert's biting irony lies in his entirely literal use of metaphors signifying nonliteral spiritual reading in order to illuminate the false world-relation of his protagonists. To name only two examples: the absent spiritual sweetness is replaced by actual sugar, the modern substitute for honey, which, since antiquity, has incarnated the *dulcedo* of the Scriptures. In Madame Bovary's house, too much sugar is used (sugar still being very expensive at the time). This is because Félicité (whose name signifies "happy"), Madame Bovary's maid, cannot draw sufficient sweetness from her evening prayer and has to console herself with the real stuff: "Félicité every evening took a small supply of sugar that she ate alone in her bed after she had said her prayers" (51).

Charles Bovary chews bovinely: "his heart full of the joys of the past night, his mind at rest, his flesh at ease, he went on, re-chewing his happiness [*il s'en allait ruminant son bonheur*], like those who after dinner taste again the truffles which they are digesting" (29). The discovery of the spiritual sense is metaphorically conveyed here by the French verb *ruminer* (meaning both "chew" and "chew the cud, ruminate"). The search for the *sapor* of the text, the search for spiritual sweetness, corresponds, in solid food, to the process of chewing (*ruminatio*); it is a matter of repeated reading and applied reflection. Charles always remains attached to knowing the letter by heart—"learning all the old questions by heart" (13)—but he only knows it outwardly and, never touched by its spirit, never understands anything. What he ruminates is the earthly flesh, which entirely satisfies him. His horizon does not extend beyond his wife's silk skirts. Nor can he draw spiritual sweetness from the medical journal to which he subscribes, suggestively titled *La ruche médicale* (The medical hive) (52); tired out by the work of digestion, he falls asleep over it.

Madame Bovary does not find such enjoyments in food or in love; in contrast to her husband, she gets no satisfaction and is always only briefly satiated. Hence she repeatedly turns to the Heavenly Bridegroom in order to still her consuming hunger and thirst. Listening to the bells of the Angelus, she finds herself transported back to her convent education: in the line of white veils, drawn over the prie-dieu, she sees "the gentle face of the Virgin amid the blue smoke of the rising incense" (92). It compels her to sink into pious reverie, and without knowing how it happens, she finds herself on the way to the church where the priest is teaching the catechism to the children to prepare them for their First Communion. The priest meets her under the sign of food: "He had just eaten his dinner" (93), unmistakably. Madame Bovary's visions of immaculate purity are destroyed by his soutane with its many food stains: his skin too has "yellow spots" (*macules jaunes*). The conversation between Madame Bovary and the priest also stands under the sign of food, both literal and allegorical. It circles implicitly around Matthew 4:4: "Man shall not live by bread alone, but by every word that proceedeth out of the mouth of God." With this sentence, Jesus, after forty days of fasting, resists the temptation of the devil to change stones into bread. As the subsequent conversation shows, the Gospels have become completely unintelligible to the priest, who reads everything literally. Every sense of the spiritual nourishment and its sweetness has passed from him, so that readers concerned about the state of the souls of the children confided to his care might justly wonder precisely what kind of satisfaction from the Communion Abbé Bournisien actually promises the children.

Bournisien interprets Madame Bovary's suffering in a physical sense and explains it with the most banal material cause possible, namely, the weather. En passant, he names Saint Paul, who coined the formula of the letter that kills and the spirit that gives life, the determining figure of all allegoresis. The topoi about spiritual nourishment, to whose allegorical sense this priest is totally blind, are grotesquely literalized. The privilege of prescribing remedies has been ceded by the priest Bournisien to the medical doctor. Emma is referred back to the very cause of her suffering, marriage. The "doctor of the soul" refers her to the "doctor of the body," her husband. Madame Bovary insists that "it is no earthly remedy I need" (93) and pleads for respite: "you solace all sorrows" (93). As an example of his general capacity to alleviate suffering, the priest at once cites the dropsical cow, and, via the root "bovine," brings the husband, Bovary, back into the discussion. The pastor cannot imagine that those "who have bread and have no . . ." might be lacking anything; the very notion of a hunger for spiritual sweetness is to him unheard of. His sympathy goes to those who are without bread: the "housewives there, virtuous women, . . . real saints" (94). He refers Madame Bovary's dizziness back to her digestion and recommends that she return home and drink a glass of sugar water. The conversation is a travesty of a pastoral conversation, and the pastor himself is a grotesque figure. Priests of his stamp were cruelly mocked by Baudelaire, who also draws the relevant parallel between Church and pharmacy. Madame Bovary, he writes, "calls on the Church for assistance. We expect the Church to be like the divine mother, ready at all times to extend a helping hand, like a pharmacist who always has to be available."[26] Disappointed by the Church, Madame Bovary will in fact eventually seek her salvation in the drugstore.

Such a Mother Church cannot satisfy Madame Bovary's hunger for spiritual sweetness. Following the great Teresa of Ávila, the little Theresa, Emma's compatriot Thérèse of Lisieux (1873–97), subsequently elevated to the status of the latest Church teacher, was able to satisfy her consuming hunger for the Eucharist by swallowing the body of the Lord daily. In her search for spiritual nourishment, however, Madame Bovary meets Rodolphe Boulanger de La Huchette: "Rudolph Baker of the Little Bread Bin [or perhaps Dough Bowl]," whose name twice bespeaks bread. In the famous seduction scene at the country fair—once again cows are present—Rodolphe utters romantic platitudes as a kind of commentary on his expressive name. The second voice to this discourse comes from offstage, from a gentleman with the no less striking name of Lieuvain—the empty or idle place—who apparently confines himself to the most neutral commonplaces. But this empty phrase-maker takes up one metaphor for the production of the spiritual meaning out of the letter after the other.

In conclusion, he even describes the love feast of Holy Communion, which brings this transformation to its literal point. In question is the transformation of "the wheat, which, being ground, is made into powder by means of ingenious machinery, issues from there under the name of flour, and is then transported to our cities, soon delivered to the baker, who makes it into food for poor and rich alike" (117). In the topos of the spiritual meaning emptily taken up by Lieuvain, the milling of the corn into meal is the repeated metaphor for the words of Scripture, which are to be freed from the rough husk of the letter and purified into fine meal, in which the spiritual sense of the Word can come to light. Thus, Saint Paul is shown transforming the corn brought to him by the Prophets into meal in one of the windows in the Basilica of Saint-Denis, described by Émile Mâle, which one could still admire in Flaubert's day—he had a weakness for stained glass (*vitrail*). At first it appears as if love for Rodolphe, the baker, might satisfy Emma's hunger by her partaking of the exegetic promises of his name.

Through her love for Rodolphe, Madame Bovary is "transfigured" (131). Her love radically changes everything. It can move more than mountains: "nothing around them seemed changed; and yet for her something had happened more stupendous than if the mountains had moved in their places" (130). Flaubert's echo of Paul in 1 Corinthians lets an overtone of what is missing, namely, love, be heard in the moving mountains. Madame Bovary is seduced by Rodolphe into what Flaubert calls "pure crap" (*simple fouterie*) in his letters to Louise Colet, invoking the Song of Songs—"Be my friend, my sister"—and the pure rapture of the Virgin Mary: "In my soul you are as a Madonna on a pedestal, in a place lofty, secure, immaculate" (129). In the course of her love, the initial transfiguration is converted into its opposite, into corruption and ruin. Thrown back onto the "defilements" (*souillures*) of marriage by her adultery, Emma is addicted, but not satisfied. Her passion is drunkenness (*ivresse*), a carnal "beatitude which left her numb." The dizzying drunkenness—"and her soul sunk deep into this intoxication [*ivresse*] and drowned in it, all shrivelled up, like the duke of Clarence in his butt of malmsey" (154)—stands in contrast to the topos of the sober intoxication with which the sweet wine of the Gospels makes drunk and inflames love.

The reference to the duke of Clarence in Shakespeare's *Richard III* illustrates the historical precision and the abyssal nature of the intertexts woven through Flaubert's apparently so very simple, readable text. Already in Shakespeare, the Clarence episode is a gruesome parody of the Communion. Clarence's stabbed but not yet entirely dead *corpus* is dipped in the wine, like the host in the Communion (as the commentary to the Arden Shakespeare has it), in which he drowns. In drawing the parallel between Emma and the duke of Clarence, Flaubert compares Emma's *concupiscentia carnis* with a drowning in sensuality, which shows itself in the inverted wine; this wine does not inflame the spirit, but numbs it, like the blow that strikes the unfortunate Clarence before he is drowned, as a perversion of the Eucharist.

The relationship to Léon unfolds the transformation of a redeeming, spiritual meal into an intoxicating and addictive poison in an intensifying reprise. Léon is addicted to Emma like a drunkard: "then, when he heard the creaking of her boots, he felt his courage desert him, like drunkards at the sight of strong liquor" (223). Emma turns to her preferred drug, to letters, in order to give the flesh its necessary spice (223). Thus the structure of the novel as a perverted conversion is confirmed. The conversion of absolute longing for transcendent eternal love, through which one is transformed, reverses itself into adultery, or, to put it another way, into an unredeemed, very carnal attachment to the world—"et fornicabar abs te," to cite Augustine once again, who chooses adultery as a metaphor for this wrong attachment to the world. As far as I can see, this is the first suggestion of the modern structure of fetishization, in which "the exaltation of her soul" and "the lace on her petticoat" (209) become equally valid objects of admiration. It is this inversion of the desire for God into all things worldly that stamps the latter with the mark of the fetish or the drug—both, fetish and drugs, being forms of confused, inverted reading. The failed transcendence in the *conversio* leads to the death of the soul: Emma is "drunk with sadness" (*ivre de tristesse*), a "phantom" and an "automaton" before she is actually dead. The remedy turns out to be poison, redemption turns into ruin: and the locus of this reversal is the pharmacy.

The Passion of Madame Bovary

This brings me to Emma's death scene. Emma is ruined, ruined by her lovers, who did not give her life or still her hunger, but rather left her numb and addicted, dependent on the honey-sweet discourse of the extortionist Lheureux, the only one whose words are modified by the adjective "honeyed" (*mielleux*), a term (Latin *mellifluus*) also used by Saint Bernard of Clairvaux in his commentary on the Song of Songs. Far from elevating Emma's soul to God, Lheureux's honeyed discourse traps her ever more profoundly in the materiality of the world. Lheureux does not work at the salvation of her soul out of a love for God: "Did you think, my dear lady, that I was going to go on to the end of time providing you with merchandise and cash, just for the love of God?" (233)—but rather through treachery and deception at her destruction, by which he profits. The letter of the law is always on his side. It is no accident that Lheureux shouts instructions through a peephole (in French, *judas*); the word identifies the extortionist.

Arsenic, "white powder" (249), is systematically associated with sugar in the text. Emma takes the poison in the laboratory of the pharmacy, what Homais refers to as his "sanctuary." She learns where it is stored, because the apprentice, on another occasion, is accused of having inadvertently almost mixed some arsenic into the sugar used to sweeten the jams. Madame Bovary, says Homais, to cover up the fact of suicide and his responsibility in it, had inadvertently taken arsenic instead of sugar to sweeten a vanilla cream (*crème à la vanille*). Sugar comes up again when Emma is dying of arsenic poisoning; in offering some to Doctor Larivière for his coffee, the vain, affected chemist Homais refers to it by its Latin name, *saccharum*.

Arsenic is not life-giving like the spirit, but deadly, like the word that kills. Emma dies by the word, by the imbibing of the word from which she cannot draw spiritual nourishment, but only earthly and sensual addiction, only intoxication and finally poisoning. She dies from false reading and false loving, which draw her ever deeper into the carnal enjoyment of this world, in adulteries that are more against God than against her husband. The dramatic highpoint of the novel is thus a reversed peripeteia. Flaubert stages it in a pointed reversal of the topos that effects the conversion of the bitter word into spiritual sweetness, through the "wood of life," Moses's piece of wood, prefiguring Christ's cross. Klaus Lange and Hans-Jörg Spitz record that this conversion from bitter to sweet is uniformly present in Origen, Saint Jerome, Isidore of Seville, Pseudo-Beda, and Rabanus Maurus. In Exodus 15:23–25, Moses transforms the bitter water of Marah into sweet potable water with a piece of wood. This was read as a *figura* for the *conversio* brought about by Christ. Origen's homilies on Exodus speak of the wood of the "wisdom of Christ" and of the "mystery of the cross," transforming the law in its literal sense into the sweetness of its spiritual meaning.

But this is exactly what does not happen in Flaubert's novel. The bitterness does not turn into sweetness. It becomes on the contrary more and more unbearably bitter: with her dying strength Emma presses "the fullest kiss of love that she had ever given" onto the "body of the Man-God" (375), onto Christ on the cross. It does seem that the Communion she then receives has healed her, as if she were reborn to life, or at least as if she could pass away peacefully, having atoned for her sins. But Communion does not lead to a gentle death. Flaubert confronts us instead with a very bitter death: a *mort amère*—indeed, with one of the most drastic, atrocious death scenes ever written. The convulsive distortions of Emma Bovary's body wracked by unbearable pain obscenely mimic the motions of the lustful body.[27] In dying she spends all of her passion in the Dantean mode of a *contrapasso*. In a grotesque, mechanical pseudo-resurrection, she becomes a galvanized cadaver. A posthumous expulsion of black bile follows. It smells like ink and stains her immaculate white silk wedding dress, which becomes her shroud.[28]

Emma's head was turned towards her right shoulder, the corner of her mouth, which was open, seemed like a black hole at the lower part of her face; her two thumbs were bent into the palms of her hands; a kind of white dust besprinkled her lashes, and her eyes were beginning to disappear in a viscous pallor, as if covered by a spiderweb. The sheet sunk in from her breast to her knees, and then rose at the tips of her toes, and it seemed to Charles that infinite masses, an enormous load, were weighing upon her. (260)

Flaubert's portrayal of the dead Emma Bovary does not owe its verisimilitude to the morgue or to an anatomical handbook, but to a statue in the Sansevero Chapel Museum in Naples, Giuseppe Sanmartino's *The Veiled Christ* (1753). Flaubert gives no hint of this source, but those who have seen this sculpture are bound to recall it vividly when reading the book. Conversely, readers of *Madame Bovary* who happen to see Sanmartino's statue in Naples will inevitably call to mind Flaubert's description of Emma's corpse. Death's hopeless finality has seldom been presented more vividly than by these two works of art.

The shroud of Sanmartino's *Veiled Christ* reverses a classical effect of sculptural representation, in which a thin veil serves to reveal a provocative nakedness. Though Christ's head is veiled by the thinnest of fabrics, he could scarcely be any deader. Seen in a certain light, he seems, like Emma, to have a black hole instead of a mouth in the lower half of his dead face. Like Sanmartino's shroud, too, the sheet covering Emma's body sinks from her breast to her knees, then rises at the tips of her toes. Something like a cobweb veils her decaying eyes, not unlike the thin veil covering Christ's face.

The last thing Emma hears, the blind beggar's song about the gleaner Nanette speaks for itself. With it, Flaubert identifies his novel as a gleaning (*spicilegium*),[29] which expunges every trace of *conversio*, of true readability, by rehearsing the topoi that organize the conversion of literal into spiritual meaning. As a result, in its realism, the novel remains a true canticle to the cross of its heroine. But this is not all: Flaubert takes his heroine's passion upon himself: *imitatio Emmae*. With her he feels the inky taste of the poison in his mouth; with her he vomits. The impersonality of the style only makes a more pathetic memorial to the heroine forsaken by God and the world. In setting up a memorial to the Passion and the cross of Madame Bovary, Flaubert judges and condemns a society that can award Homais the Cross of the Legion of Honor—the novel's last words are *la croix d'honneur*.

What remains in this modern *spicilegium* is not the spiritual meaning, the love of God and the resurrection of the flesh, but literal consignment to death of a flesh that is specifically configured as feminine. This is what the blind man sings of: Nanette, while gleaning the corn, bends over the furrows and dreams of love. Her skirt is blown up by the hot summer wind. In this erotic posture—Freud would say *a tergo*—the genitals are exposed. Sexual love turns out to be fatal. In the gathering of the corn—which has to die to bear fruit (John 12:24)—the beggar's song makes yet another allusion to bread and to the Eucharist, to death and resurrection. But here this is reversed: no resurrection is to be hoped for, no redemption has taken place. Even after Christ, we are still in a postlapsarian world: sex equals death. Both, sex and death, are consequences of the Fall. The equality of death and pleasure is underlined by Madame Bovary's last gasp, which occurs at the same moment as the exposure of the female genitals in the song. In death, through the topos of the hysteric, Emma incarnates the antique mask of the Medusa.[30] The radically disillusioning Medusa reveals the truth of the attractions of the flesh. In her passion gone wrong, Madame Bovary turns out to be the Arachne she always was. In an acerbically medical but nonetheless baroque register, like a seventeenth-century Dutch still-life *vanitas*, Flaubert shows us Emma's dead, already decaying body, with a black hole in the place of the mouth and eyes beginning to disappear "in a viscous pallor, as if covered by a spiderweb" (260).[31]

. . .

Blind literality remains, which the author jokily personifies as an artist called Vaufrylard ("Veal-Fry-Fat"), "a friend of Bridoux's, who never ceased to make puns" (272). Emma's mausoleum, designed for her by Vaufrylard, also involves a play on words. Homais comes up with the inscription "Sta viator, amabilem conjugem calcas," which is generally understood to mean "Halt, traveler, you stand at the grave of a dear spouse,"[32] but can also be translated as "Halt, traveler, you are trampling a dear spouse underfoot."[33] This is precisely what has happened to Flaubert's hapless heroine.

The Scapegoat and Homo Sacer

> He that is without sin among you, let him first cast a stone at her.
>
> John 8:7

As we have seen, Jonathan Culler hits the bull's-eye in observing that *Madame Bovary* is not a novel "of realism, but of vealism"—a witticism reminiscent of a Flaubertian pun.[34] In Flaubert's later novel *Salammbô*, cattle also play a significant role. The sacrificing Carthaginian priests damningly vociferate: "These are not men but oxen!"[35] The crude disavowal expresses the intolerable truth: the Carthaginians feed, not oxen, but their own children to the all-consuming, burning Moloch. The cows, oxen, calves, which, in all their possible varieties, are so pervasive in Flaubert's novel of a family's ruin in a Normandy village, concern neither the rampant proliferation of signifiers indifferent to all sense, as Culler has in mind, nor are they due to a commitment to realistically portraying meat and dairy farming in Normandy. The ox, bull or *bovis*, is the primordial sacrificial animal organizing all signification in this novel of *Bovary*.

As Michel Butor first noted, *Madame Bovary* is the history of an expiatory sacrifice: "Victim of an expiatory sacrifice, Mme Bovary takes on the endemic evil in Yonville like the scapegoat of the Hebrews. At the same time, she is the sacrificing priestess."[36] Because she is a scapegoat, the novel is populated by oxen, cows, and calves. Without a doubt, Emma Bovary is a woman who fully lives out her desire.[37] However, probably never before has literature written so unrelentingly and mercilessly about the fatalness of such desire. Living out their desire is also what Dido and Phaedra do—to the point of suicide. Loving is a form of dying: poisoned by passion, Phaedra poisons herself; pierced and burned by love, Dido chooses the sword and fire. Like Emma Bovary, both fall prey to their passion: "Venus in all her might is on her prey."[38] They succumb to the torture and torments of desire, its pitiless pursuit; the flames of Eros consume them, its sword pierces them, its poison seeps into their marrow. It is the ancestral line of Phaedra and Dido that shows Emma Bovary in the light of myth.

Madame Bovary is generally celebrated as the birth of Flaubert the author as well as the birth of the modern novel. The scalpel has been proposed as a metaphor for this new style, because it ruthlessly penetrates the deepest layers of the heart. However, to my mind, Flaubert's writing is better elucidated by a different framing metaphor: *ex oriente lux*—light comes from the East. The light of the Orient brings the truth of his society into full view. Not only medicine, but ethnology as well, served as a model for his writing. At that time, ethnology had made great strides thanks to Max Mueller, whom Flaubert had read, and would be further developed by Malinowski and Freud. Through foreign eyes Flaubert observes his own, familiar world. This alien perspective on what is familiar informs—at least if we are to believe Maxime Du Camp, Flaubert's friend and companion on his journey across the Middle East—an oriental coloring of Normandy:

Moreover, his future novel preoccupied him; "I'm obsessed by it," he told me. Gazing on African landscapes, he dreamed of the Norman countryside. On the borders of lower Nubia . . . , as we were watching the Nile beating on outcroppings of black granite, he let out a cry: "I've got it! I've got it! Eureka! Eureka! I'll call her Emma Bovary"; and he repeated it several times, savoring the name Bovary, which he pronounced with a very short *o*.[39]

Madame Bovary's name thus came to light in the East. The short pronunciation of the *o* clearly brings out the root *bovis* and its reference to the sacrificial animal. The problematic of fertility and sacrifice was central to early ethnology. Flaubert, who closely followed contemporary biblical research, was well aware that the Jews of ancient Palestine had striven unremittingly, albeit ineffectually, to control the Eastern sacrificial cults and abolish human sacrifice. The fruitlessness of their condemnation of human sacrifice prompted Flaubert's formula "Jehovah = Moloch."[40] If one reads the sources and considers the clear evidence of the Old Testament, one must conclude that Judaism remained an Eastern religion, still thriving on idolatry, the cult of the sun, and human sacrifice, despite all its efforts at containment. This was at least the conclusion Flaubert came to. As a consequence, Christ's sacrifice on the cross undergoes a radical reinterpretation. In essence, Flaubert's work is a new reading of the cross, illuminated by the light of the Orient.

As in *A Sentimental Education* later in his career, Flaubert already shows in *Madame Bovary* that contemporary society, in defiance of its own Christian or enlightened secular self-understanding, is still ruled by the logic of the scapegoat. The sacrifice on the cross has not overcome this logic—society is still governed by it. Flaubert's shorthand for societies under the sway of this logic is Babel.[41] Like the Paris of *A Sentimental Education*, Rouen and Normandy are bathed in the light of the Orient: "the ancient Norman city was like a gigantic metropolis, like a Babylon into which she was about to enter."[42] In Yonville one feels oneself "transported into the midst of a dream from the 'Thousand and One Nights'" (124); its two small hanging gardens constitute the town's own Babylonian Wonder of the World. "The clerk, too, had his small hanging garden" (84). From beginning to end, the pharmacist Homais appears illuminated by signal flares called Bengal lights: Emma sees him for the first time as "beyond them, as in a Bengal light, the silhouette of the pharmacist can be seen leaning over his desk" (62). From beginning to end, he mixes eastern ingredients for his concoctions: "Arabian racahout" (ibid.), a powder of acorns, cacao, and sugar, among other things, used for a beverage, at the beginning and *revalenta arabica*, an invalid food made of lentil and barley flour, at the end (271–72). For the sake of a prestigious cross of his own, the *croix d'honneur*, he prostitutes himself in the most abysmal of all Flaubertian ironies: "Homais hankered after the Croix de la Légion d'Honneur. . . . He sold, in a word, prostituted himself" (273). Invoked by the signifier of prostitution, the Great Whore of Babylon appears. Lheureux comes on stage as the epitome of Babel, replete with its universal style (the people of Babel were scattered all over the world after the confusion of languages), in which the exotic Eastern element predominates in the form of three Algerian scarves (87). Emma's Judas, this profiteers' profiteer, will deliver her to

her execution in exchange for his foul lucre. Further highlighting the oriental motif, Lheureux refers his greed to the shopworn antisemitic stereotype:
"'We are no Jews!'" he exclaims (ibid.).

The charge of nihilism that Nietzsche levels at Flaubert, with which
many have concurred, is thus revealed to be utterly mistaken. If it is true
that the romantic faith in a redeeming love and the future collapsed into
a desire for nothingness between 1830 and 1850, then this is exactly what
does not happen in *Madame Bovary*.[43] Christendom, romantic literature, science, and politics, which Flaubert reads as forms of secularization, mask the social reality. They are part and parcel of an overarching
illusion, which is taken full advantage of by those who stand to gain a
profit from it. Literature, science, and politics, in their guise as the self-
appointed agents of redemption, have carried over the old sacrificial logic
under false appearances. They deliver up the scapegoats, the sacrificial victims, who, as though drugged, are intoxicated by the idea of romantic love,
and thus led to the altar like lambs to the slaughter. More uncompromisingly than anyone else, Flaubert puts his own time and its morality on
trial. Society, which prosecuted Flaubert's novel, is what Flaubert himself
prosecutes, shames to the core, and condemns as guilty. There is no question of nihilism.

Almost everyone in Yonville scrambles for a share in the spoils and
profits from Madame Bovary's death: "Then everyone began to collect
what they could" (269). The usurer and cloth-dealer Lheureux and the
pharmacist Homais are the ones who gain most from it. Both are connected to literature: Homais, the pharmacist, through the metaphor of literature as *pharmakon*, as a sugarcoated pill; Lheureux, the cloth merchant,
through the metaphor of the text as fabric. The "substance" Lheureux deals
in is Emma's undoing. He has so profitably ruined the Bovarys through
chicanery based on capitalist credit that he is now able to open a large
coach business, "Les Favorites du commerce." Soon he will have a monopoly on travel to Rouen and the intermediate stops; in the end, Madame
Lefrançois, the owner of the Lion d'or hostelry, is as good as ruined too.
Bit by bit, Lheureux succeeds in becoming the master of the Babylonian
relay, whose heart is Paris. For his part, Homais has managed to ruin
Bovary's medical authority; one after the other, the physicians are successfully driven out of Yonville, thus enabling Homais, the pharmacist,
to permanently take up the position of physician without legal sanction.

Homais is an unscrupulous usurper. "Since Bovary's death three doctors have succeeded one another in Yonville without any success, so effectively did Homais hasten to eradicate them. He has more customers than there are sinners in hell; the authorities treat him kindly and he has the public on his side" (275).

Set off by his Bengal lights, Homais serves a weird clientele.

. . .

In the Augustinian lexicon, adultery is the formula for an error of reading, which comes down to defective love: "although adultery is not a death of the body, it is worse—it is the death of the soul."[44] The misreading is premised on a *carnal* practice of reading; that is to say, a practice of reading that puts the onus on a lethal literalness to the detriment of a spiritual interpretation. The relationship to the world, which is in this sense utterly fleshly, is propelled by concupiscence (*concupiscentia*), a desire intent on producing self-profit. Flaubert's novel, which takes up this Augustinian theme, foregrounds the deadliness of carnal understanding by bringing together two complexes, an operation that quite literally illustrates the movement from the spiritual to the material: the complexes of eating and love and of love and fabrics are interlaced in a quid pro quo.

Sex and Slaughter

Madame Bovary is marked by the systematic coupling of food and sex.[45] Love stories are already being dished out to Emma and her father on the way to the convent where Emma Rouault is to be raised. They eat their supper from painted plates depicting the romance of King Louis XIV and Louise de La Vallière: "The explanatory legends, chipped here and there by the scratching of knives, all glorified religion, the tenderness of the heart, and the pomps of the court" (30). After having been replaced by Madame de Montespan as the king's favorite, Louise de La Vallière became a Carmelite nun under the name of Louise de La Miséricorde. In the novel, the sublimity of this adulterous love, in which the mistress becomes a suffering Mary Magdalen, is lacerated by the cuts of the knife that accompany the violence of eating.

At the ball in Vaubyessard, so crucial for Emma's fate, adulterous love is again coupled with food. She watches the old duc de Laverdière, who "had . . . slept in the bed of queens," "eating, letting drops of gravy drip from his mouth." Absorbed by the meal, he wants to sample everything: "A servant behind his chair shouted in his ear, in reply to his mutterings, the names of the dishes that he pointed to" (42). This sampling is an echo of his youthful amorous exploits. As if trapped together in a sandwich with two other lovers, the duke had reportedly been "the lover of Queen Marie Antoinette, between Monsieur de Coigny and Monsieur de Lauzun" (42). He had "devoured" his family's assets and eloped with many women (ibid.). His hanging lips, stained by the drops of sauce falling from his mouth, do not disturb Madame Bovary's fascination, much like the scratches did nothing in her eyes to distort the charm of the depictions on the plates. The affinity between the two episodes is underlined by the similarity between the two names: *de La Vallière* and *Laverdière*. The men at the ball, who are descended from the duke's family, assume the brutal domination of women and animals, as if they were mere things, to be their God-given birthright: "Their indifferent eyes had the appeased expression of daily-satiated passions, and through all their gentleness of manner pierced that peculiar brutality that stems from a steady command over half-tame things, for the exercise of one's strength and the amusement of one's vanity—the handling of thoroughbred horses and the society of loose women" (45). From there, it is only a small step to their consumption.

Like blood, love gushes forth from Emma; through love, she is bled out like cattle at slaughter: "love, the more she repressed it, flowed freely, in joyful effervescence" (145).[46] She will die, since she bleeds to death out of love. "She suffered only in her love, and felt her soul escaping from her in this memory, as wounded men, dying, feel their life ebb through their bleeding wounds" (248). The first encounter between Rodolphe and Emma happens under the sign of gushing blood: Charles performs a bloodletting on Rodolphe's servant. Homais, who attends the procedure, has no problem with seeing other people's blood, but under no circumstance can he stand the sight of his own—an issue that will be examined later. Since Rodolphe is introduced to the reader as a man with "much experience of women and . . . something of a connoisseur" (106), it is ominous that he thinks of Emma from the outset as a kind of thing, in serial, dehumanized, and objectified terms that strip her of all individuality: "*it* would adore you [*cela vous adorerait*]."[47] Rodolphe imagines Emma as a carp on the kitchen table, ready to be cut up and consumed: "She is gasping after love like a carp gasping on a kitchen table after water" (106). Later, he describes her as a show horse, sold on the cattle market: "Fine teeth, black eyes, a dainty foot, a figure like a Parisienne!" (ibid.). He strips her naked in his mind's eye. This Rodolphe, serial seducer, fallen Don Juan, cheap Valmont, is only nominally—as de La Huchette—affiliated with aristocracy, which in the novel has dominion over women and horses as if they were things. He decides, in spite of all of the unpleasantness that adultery brings with it, to replace his previous lover, an actress from Rouen, with Emma. Before this love has begun, it is already over. From the very start, Rodolphe is mentally done with Emma and wonders how to dispose of her afterwards—or should we say "it": "but how to get rid of it afterwards?" (106).[48] The eating habits of the actress enter into his decision; Rodolphe regards her predilection for pink shrimp with distaste. "His love letters" (161), and other love trophies, piles of locks of hair, "hair . . . lots of hair! Some dark, some fair" (162)—following the romantic motif of "trophies of my lovers gone"—are kept by Rodolphe in "an old Rheims cookie-box" (161). Love is like a sweet tooth—the letter of love is intended for immediate consumption. *These* billets-doux have lost their sweet touch, however; they have become flavorless, meaningless dead letters. The reference to the "old Rheims cookie-box" alludes to the city where French monarchs received their anointment—*le sacre de Reims*—with the right to rule "by the grace of God," of which men like Rodolphe de La Huchette enjoy but a paltry imitation. Rodolphe, the hunter, writes his farewell letter to Emma "under the stag's head that hung as a trophy on the wall" (161), an allusion to both cuckolded Charles—the one who is made to wear the horns—and Emma, whom Rodolphe hunted down like prey. He hides his lethal weapon, the letter, underneath vine leaves and fragrant apricots and lets a servant take it over to Emma's house in order to avoid the long-planned elopement he never meant to happen. Since the apricot—*l'abricot*—is a euphemism for a woman's vulva in French (rather as in former times an attractive female could be called a peach in English), by sending his letter to Emma under such fruit, Rodolphe signals that he no longer wishes to consume it. He thereby exposes the deadliness of Eros concealed under the sweet-smelling illusion of love. The apricots divulge the essence of the quid pro quo of food and sex. The flesh of the fruit becomes a metaphor for the fatal word.[49] The vine leaves invoke the drunken addiction in which *agape*, the love banquet, a stupefying and intoxicating fattening prior to slaughter, becomes legible as a reversal of the Eucharist. The reading of the letter sends the blood rushing into Emma's veins, her heart "beating irregularly in her breast like the blows of a battering ram" (165).[50] The *terminus technicus*, "ram," conjures up the classical sacrificial animal, the scapegoat.

Frustrated in spite of the regular marital intercourse, Emma eventually blossoms thanks to Rodolphe's caresses. The flowering of her beauty has met with a chorus of praise, but praise, I am afraid, that is rather misplaced, since Flaubert takes great pains to strip this beauty of all ideality. Emma's beauty is not the mirror of a beautiful soul; it does not shine forth through her eyes. Flaubert drives his message home through a masterful reversal of the ocular trope. Emma's eyes are, so to speak, sealed off by several layers of shining enamel. They are wholly impermeable and do not allow the least bit of a soul to shine through. The viewer, like Narcissus, sees only his own reflection. Emma's fully blossomed, sensuous beauty is owing solely to the corrupting satiation of her flesh, which is destined to lead to a weariness that is as inevitable as it is repetitive. Rodolphe, hunter and lady-killer, personally manages his farms. He also cultivates Madame Bovary through fertilization. When he runs into Emma's husband after her death, he talks of nothing else, only seeming to talk about something completely different: "The other [Rodolphe] went on talking of agriculture, cattle and fertilizers" (274). In Flaubert's story "Hérodias," Aulus Vitellius, the lover of the emperor Tiberius, famous for his orgies on the island of Capri, is called a swamp flower (*fleur de fange*). Similarly, Emma is compared to a dung blossom; her beauty is like that of "a flower feeding on manure" (157). Perversion is framed through the same comparison in each case, and both comparisons reduce the other to a flesh that is consumable for the sake of desire, regardless of sexual preference: "He made her into something at once malleable and corrupt" (154). For Flaubert, Eros is not a counterforce to Thanatos: they are identical.[51]

The right of man to dehumanize, to objectify, and to consume leaves its marks on his sacrificial victims; it subjects them by making them all equal. Emma Bovary becomes like those who profit from her. This is the real meaning of her becoming more and more like a man, which scholarship has never tired of noting ever since Baudelaire's analysis.[52] One can read *Madame Bovary* as a grotesque bildungsroman in which a woman is totally masculinized, becoming a total whore in the process. From the outset she wears male outfits, and she grows into them as the novel progresses:

"Like a man, she wore a tortoise-shell eyeglass thrust between two buttons of her blouse" (17). She usurps the power of the head of the family, as established by the Napoleonic Code, to handle the income and possessions of the household as he sees fit. Coaxed by Lheureux, the assistant of notary Guillaumin, she will strip her husband of all his power through a thousand tricks. And, *par procuration*, she counters the interventions of her mother-in-law in order to become the ruinous empress of the family estate. Much like Lheureux, she entangles her husband in a web of lies. She not only metamorphoses into Lheureux—"She had profited by Lheureux's lessons" (202)—in order to cheat and steal from her husband, the same way Lheureux deceives and betrays her, but also eventually—in keeping with the metaphor of an infamous death—to pull the wool over his eyes in cold blood. Fruitlessly, she incites her lover Léon to commit larceny, which would have ruined him, exactly the way she was cheated to the point of ruination: "A diabolic determination showed in her burning eyes which were half closed in a lascivious and encouraging manner" (236). She thereby also transforms into Rodolphe. Madame Bovary does not forgive, nor does she repent. She acts according to the logic of an eye for an eye, a tooth for a tooth, and her violence is mimetic: what has been done unto her, she will do unto others who are weaker than her, just as she has been treated as weaker by those who are stronger. Léon becomes *her* mistress, just as Rodolphe took her as his. With the same words Rodolphe used to ask himself how he would get rid of her at the very moment when he started the affair, Emma now asks herself how "it"—that is to say, Léon—will be disposed of, since he will become tedious after the conquest. She is seized with the same desire that guides the men who profit from her and ruin her, the same arrogance, the same vanity, the same brutality, the same hate, and the same drive to destroy the other:

[I]t seemed to her that Providence pursued her implacably, and, strengthening herself in her pride, she had never felt so much esteem for herself nor so much contempt for others. A spirit of warfare transformed her. She would have liked to strike all men, to spit in their faces, to crush them; she kept walking straight on . . . almost rejoicing in the hatred that was choking her. (241)

Emma's death scene carefully omits the slaughter of the sacrificial animal, substituting an ignominious suicide in which no drop of blood is shed. Instead, the scene is accompanied by a meal that knows no end, entangling sexuality and food through the figure of the slaughtered sacrificial victim, put to death and consumed for the benefit of the community. The sacrifice on the cross and the Last Supper are made into a travesty. We are in the middle of Lent in Rouen, which, as the new Babylon, turns into an ancient amphitheater through Flaubert's descriptions. As the locus of Rome's bloodiest spectacles and massacres of martyrs, the amphitheater later also figures in "Saint Julian the Hospitalier."[53]

Mid-Lent, also called the Feast of the Washerwomen (*fête des blanchisseuses*), fuses with another great Lent carnival, namely, the *promenade du bœuf gras*—still known today as Mardi Gras. As such, the carnival already fuses fabrics and sacrificial victims, washerwomen and beef. On the day of the celebration, Emma dances at a masked ball. As in the ancient cults of Cybele, wild music is played to accompany the sacrifice—her sacrifice—and she dances in a frenzy. Her transvestism—she is disguised as an aristocratic man—is also an allusion to the cult of Cybele, where men dressed as women: "She danced all night long to the wild sounds of the trombones; people gathered around her, and in the morning she found herself on the steps of the theatre together with five or six other masked dancers, dressed as stevedores or sailors" (231). There follows another reference to "the rhythmical pulsation of thousands of dancing feet" (232).

Suddenly, we are no longer in contemporary Rouen, but in a ritual celebration of the Cybele of Middle Eastern antiquity, with its furious, stomping, rhythmic sacrificial dances. This, though, is by no means the honeymoon *à l'orientale* about which Emma had fantasized. In glaring contrast to romantic orientalist kitsch of the time, it is in a brutal oriental style, and it will be Emma's first and last trip. From now on, she is ostracized from the community of the living. Her fainting after the dance prefigures her death. The community of the living is figured in the community of devourers: "The others began to eat; she ate nothing" (231). The only thing left for her is poison. The sky heralds the sacrifice: "Day was breaking, and a large purple stain was spreading across the pale sky in the direction of the St. Catherine hills" (232). Her stations of the cross begin at the Croix rouge (Red Cross), the hotel that is the stopping place of the Hirondelle (Swallow), the weekly coach that takes her to her adulterous rendezvous.

It is there, in the Croix rouge, that Emma, before she runs into Homais, notices a picture of the Tour de Nesle (Nesle's Tower) in her room, which discloses the true face of "God's Glory," depicted on the scratched plates telling of Louise de La Vallière's affair with Louis XIV. It is not golden, glorious light, but the blood-red horror of the Passion: the *Croix rouge*. The "tender-nesses of the heart and the pomps of Court" (30) reveal their bloody truths in the Tour de Nesle. The fourteenth-century tale revolves around the alleged adultery committed in Nesle's Tower, in Paris's old city wall, by the wives of the heirs to the French throne. King Philippe IV's eldest daughter, Isabella, the wife of Edward II of England, reported this to the king, perhaps with a view to furthering the claim to the French throne of her own son (the future Edward III of England). The so-called Tour de Nesle Affair arguably contrib-uted to a change of dynasties, in which the Capetians were replaced by the Valois, and to the Hundred Years' War (1337–1453).

The betrayal and discovery of the love affairs is followed by the cruel executions of the lovers, a pair of brothers, who are flayed alive in the mar-ketplace, castrated, and then hanged on the gallows—and the imprison-ment of the two women, one of whom is strangled with her own hair by her husband when she is on the point of becoming queen of France. Flaubert interlaced this monstrous story into his novel based on Alexan-dre Dumas's 1832 play *La tour de Nesle*, hence perhaps the brevity of his allusion to the picture in Emma's room in the Croix rouge hotel. What becomes even more outspoken when placed alongside the life of Emma Bovary, whose future is debased by this image and reduced to a trivial, hackneyed aristocratic level, is the legal status of adultery: since it cannot be adduced as grounds for divorce, it cannot but end up necessitating mur-der—the newly crowned French king does not think twice and remarries four days after killing his wife. As for the second adulteress, the pope re-garded her more favorably and, instead of risking the slaughter of another woman, he granted permission for a divorce; she was buried alive in a nun-nery. In the end, the double adultery in the French reigning house leads to a change of dynasty, enabling the English King Edward III to claim the French throne.

On a much smaller scale in Yonville, the Homais dynasty will replace the dynasty of doctors. Flaubert underscores this parallel by making the phar-macist often speak in English: like the English king, who asserted his illegit-imate claim for the French throne, Homais makes an illegitimate claim to the doctor's position. Emma hardly has time to take in the depictions of the Tour de Nesle. Four lines later, she is promptly confronted with the words proclaiming her death sentence, glaring out in capital letters: "By power of the king, the law, and the courts, Mme. Bovary is hereby ordered . . ."

(232). The order of the auction of her property is to be executed, which, as Lheureux observes cynically, has never actually killed anyone. However, as always with Flaubert, the signifiers know better, and the words "legally binding" (*exécutoire*) will be true to the letter. Before the public auction, however, the extortionist Lheureux blackjacks her more brutally than he would club an animal: he has sent Vincart, whom he tellingly characterizes as "fiercer than an Arab" (225), to track her down, and she is "more overcome than if felled by the blow of a club" (233). The Babylonian tone is pursued to the end.

.   .   .

Now utterly stunned and soullessly, "mechanically obeying the force of old habits" (236), Emma returns to Yonville, escorted by Homais. From Lheureux, who administered the deadening sacrificial blow to Bovary, she is delivered into the hands of Maître Hareng, who has come from Buchy, which evokes *bucher*—the funeral pyre—and his assistant, who carve up the carcass as if it were a sacrificial animal. She encounters Homais at the Croix rouge. Emma has traveled the way of the cross in reverse, from the Lion d'or, the hostelry where she spent her first evening in Yonville, whose name obliquely refers to Jesus, the Lion of Judah, as the golden, resurrected Christ, to the Croix rouge. When he runs into Emma, Homais is on his way to the rue Massacre to buy his wife's favorite food: turban-shaped bread rolls called *cheminots* (railwaymen), which conjure up the image of the "heads of Saracens":

Madame Homais was very fond of these small, heavy rolls, shaped like turbans which are eaten during Lent with salt butter: a last relic of Gothic fare, going back, perhaps, to the Crusades, and with which the hardy Normans would stuff themselves in times gone by, thinking that they saw, illuminated in the golden light of the torches, between the tankards of Hippocras and the gigantic slabs of meat, the heads of Saracens to be devoured. The druggist's wife crunched them up as they had done, heroically, in spite of her wretched teeth. (237)

On his way in the rue Massacre, Homais shows Emma the way to her massacre. Homais can chatter all he wants about the progress and humanity of Western civilization: it is the distorted image of an Orient whose high point is the sacrificial meal of cannibalism, at which enemies are devoured.[54]

Emma's ruin is carried out by Guillaumin, the notary, who intends to profit from it twice, in collaboration with Lheureux. It is in the dining room that Monsieur Guillaumin wants to consume her. That the Bovary who shows up before him has now fallen out of grace with the order of civilization becomes all the more apparent as the notary abandons all manners: with complete ease of mind he sets out to dine while she is present, without offering her anything. He appears *à l'orientale*; palm trees adorn his dressing gown (239). The occidental register is also alluded to through the "tiger," which, as Guillaumin knows very well, refers to Lheureux, but with whom he does not want to be seen consorting (240ff.). Like a sacrificial animal, Madame Bovary, already clubbed, is roasted in preparation for her consumption: "[W]ithout interrupting his lunch, he turned completely round towards her, so that his knee kept brushed against her boot; the sole was beginning to curl in the heat of the stove" (240). Guillaumin proceeds directly from his cutlets to gorging himself on Emma's hand, which he kisses "greedily" (240). Faced with the prospect that he will be unable to consume her after all—"You shamelessly take advantage of my distress, sir! I am to be pitied—not to be sold!" (241), Emma protests—he pulls himself together and calms down, admiring his oriental footwear, his "fine embroidered slippers. They were a love gift" (ibid.).

Emma's agony is attended by a lavish banquet offered by the pharmacist, in which almost the whole village participates. It includes all and everyone; this is wittily captured by Flaubert in the image of the tear that falls on the jabot of Doctor Larivière, evidently the only character with some humanity, symbolically linking even Jesus, who wept when faced with suffering, in the community of those who nourish themselves with human sacrifice. Overcome, Larivière leaves the banqueting room, but the pharmacist promptly calls him back: "À table, docteur!" Between servings of pigeon and pork chops, Homais flaunts his erudition in truly Babylonian fashion, not really knowing what he is talking about, but touching upon nothing less than the foundation of the ritual of sacrifice. Confusedly citing cantharides, manchineel (a poisonous Caribbean tree), the upas (an Indonesian tree whose latex was used for arrow poison), and the viper, he invokes both the unredeemed Fallenness of Man and the logic of the scapegoat. The prominence of the apple tree, which grows at almost every corner of the novel, much like the prominence of cows and wolves, cannot be accounted for by alluding to local flora and fauna. They give the novel its local flavor, but much more important, they indicate that it should be read not in a realist mode, but allegorically. Perhaps anticipating Bovary's being struck down from beyond the grave by his wife's toxicity, Homais rambles on about oversmoked *boudins*: "I have even read that various persons have been poisoned, and struck down, so to speak, by blood sausage that had been too strongly smoked" (255; modified).

Doctor Canivet, the physician from Neufchâtel who amputated the leg of the Lion d'or's stable boy, Hippolyte, and whom we encounter at Emma's deathbed, brings out, *ex negativo*, the bloodiness of this sacrifice without bloodshed. During the amputation of Hippolyte's leg, he had boasted that without batting an eye, he would cut up any God-fearing Christian just as he would a chicken—"it doesn't matter to me whether I carve up a Christian or the first fowl that comes my way" (148), he asserts—but he does not wish to see "the spectacle of Emma dying" (254). Similarly, Larivière's bon mot also points to the bloodiness of this bloodless sacrifice, with Emma's death throes taking place simultaneously with the meal. Larivière's reply to Madame Homais's worried inquiry into the thickness of her husband's blood plays on the homophony of the French words *sang* (blood) and *sens* (sense): "Oh! ce n' est pas le sens qui le gêne" (French ed., 468).[55] Homais has no problem watching the blood flow from others. Aided by Canivet's grotesque incompetence, he drives Emma to her death. In playing on the homophony of *sens* and *sang*, sense and blood, Larivière inadvertently exposes the central Babylonian characteristic: an inability to establish meaning, to make sense—and shedding blood instead.

The community-founding meal, at which the parish priest and the pharmacist make their peace over the corpse, is a meal dedicated, not to life, but to death; not to the death of the body, but to the death of the soul. With their "stomachs thrust forward," the pharmacist and priest already resemble the dead: "they moved no more than the corpse by their side, that also seemed to be sleeping" (263). Then they eat; the Mass could not satisfy the hunger of the priest, who says: "'I must say that I wouldn't mind taking some sustenance.' . . . they ate and drank, chuckling a little without knowing why . . . 'We'll end up good friends, you and I!'" (264). The sacrifice of the scapegoat, Madame Bovary, concludes in gluttonous love at the funeral banquet—a love offering that perverts the Eucharist and the communal bond, founded in Communion.

The tone for this kind of consumption at the heart of social relations, which feed on the dead that in the end turn out to be sacrifices, is set by Lestiboudois at the beginning and the end of the novel. In Yonville, whose abbey gave the village its name before it disappeared from the face of the earth without leaving a trace—not even ruins remain—all roads lead to the cemetery, which is at the same time used as a potato field: "Beyond this there is nothing to see at Yonville . . . one soon reaches the graveyard" (62). Lestiboudois, "who is at once gravedigger and church sexton (thus making a double profit out of the parish corpses), has taken advantage of the unused plot of ground to plant potatoes. . . . 'You feed on the dead, Lestiboudois!'" (62–63).

Lestiboudois, whose name alludes to the blood sausage (*boudin*) made after the annual "slaughter festival," feeds on the dead. This holds in a double sense, as the text shows. At the end, after Emma's funeral, everyone is fast asleep, including Rodolphe and Léon. Only those who truly loved her, Charles Bovary and Justin, are awake. The orphan boy sobs heart and soul on her grave. In this mythological novel, Justin functions as Cupid. Like Cupid, as an innocent young boy, almost still a child, he has introduced Madame Bovary to love as well as death, men, and poison, whose effects coincide in that they all result in corruption and decomposition. Lestiboudois finds Justin in tears on her grave and cannot imagine anyone weeping out of love for the dead rather than exploiting them for profit. He concludes that Justin is stealing potatoes, which thrive there, fertilized by the dead (268).

As a vile whore, Emma is excluded from the community. In the most literal sense of the word, her death is "infamous" (*infâme*)—the word "suicide" appears only once in the entire novel. Her death is doubly infamous because—as a suicide—she could not have been given a Christian burial in hallowed ground. Homais, who supplied the poison for her suicide via Justin, who did not know what he was doing, self-interestedly attributes her death to a tragic mistake—Emma had confused arsenic with sugar. Yet, even before her infamous death Bovary was already infamously treated like a whore, and even before she turned into one: "So she set out towards La Huchette, unaware that she was hastening to offer what had so angered her a while ago, not in the least conscious of her prostitution" (244).

The Roman Spectre of Proscription

Emma's desperate attempt to scrape together enough money to stave off the public auction ordered by the court is marked from the outset and throughout the narrative by prohibition and ostracism: all of a sudden, she is no longer treated by the whole world as a respectable citizen, a wife and mother, but as a whore. The motif of the whore rings through from the very start. Her wolfish giving of herself to Rodolphe like a courtesan or sultana sets the tone. The motif is finally articulated, first by Lheureux, who says to Emma: "There, that'll do! Any one'd think you wanted to seduce me!" (233); then by Léon, who subsumes her under the category of "women": "And he admitted that his landlord didn't like his having 'women' there" (235). Finally, the auctorial voice characterizes her doings as "prostitution" (244).

The stocktaking of all her possessions preceding the public auction prompting her suicide is no longer carried out on a living body but on a cadaver: "and her whole existence, to its most intimate details, was stretched out like a cadaver in an autopsy before the eyes of these three men" (234). *Madame Bovary* ends, like *A Sentimental Education*, with the dissolution of a household.[56] As is the case with Madame Arnoux in the latter novel, the inventorying of her belongings reads like a rape and at the same time like the cutting up of a body. Maître Hareng's and his two colleagues' penetration into the most intimate aspects of her life—her linen and letters—is described as a collective violation: "This made her furious to see this coarse hand, with red moist fingers like slugs, touching these pages against which her heart had beaten" (235).

The next morning Emma wakes up to find the entire village out and about in the marketplace, all reading the poster with the public announcement of the auction. Justin wants to avert her public disgrace and tear down the announcement, but he is called to order. Later, after her death, the scapegoat is carved up and cannibalized. "Chacun se mit à *profiter*"— Flaubert drives the message home by putting the last word in italics—and all of them start to swindle and steal from Charles. That the public auction not only affects the married couple but also ruins their young child is illustrated by the tattered socks and rags that hang like scraps from poor Berthe's body—she, whose mother had ruined herself for the sake of the precious fabrics of her clothing and her interiors: "He suffered, poor man, at seeing her so badly dressed, with lace-less boots, and the arm-holes of her pinafore torn down to the hips" (270). No sharper contrast is imaginable with the sobering and inevitable fate in store for Berthe than the pretty picture her father paints for himself while she is still a child: "[H]e wanted Berthe to be well-educated, to be accomplished, to learn to play the piano . . . they would find her some good young fellow with a steady business; he would make her happy; this would last for ever" (157).

Berthe's raggedness excludes her from the community of children—"the pharmacist's children saw less and less of the child. In view of the difference in their social positions, Monsieur Homais had chosen to discontinue the former intimacy" (270)—and isolates her in their house with her father, whom no one ever visits: "No one came to see them" (270). Flaubert estimates the ruin of the daughter to the last penny: "there remained twelve francs and seventy-five centimes, just enough to send Mademoiselle Bovary off to her grandmother" (275). The journey of the twelve-year-old is a journey into death. Berthe already suffers from consumption: "she coughed sometimes, and had red patches on her cheeks" (273). The dramatic present tense at the end of the novel highlights the death sentence that society has pronounced over the innocent in the here and now: "She *is* poor, and sends her to a cotton-mill to earn a living" (275; emphasis added). The vertiginous social fall to the status of a female worker in a cotton mill is all the more poignant considering the "yarn-mill" (85) the Bovary family once visited on a Sunday outing when Berthe was still a baby. For Berthe, exposure to the fine dust of the cotton mill—lethal in the long run even for healthy people—will be a death sentence; provincial manners.

It becomes evident here that in addition to the motif of oriental human sacrifice in the interest of communal ties, the Flaubertian text harbors a further, classical subtext. As *A Sentimental Education* will also do later, *Madame Bovary* presents four elements that, taken together, point to a very specific historical event. Emma's vile immolation, the confiscation of the Bovarys' goods, the multigenerational ruining of their family, and the isolation that subsequently stifles Charles and Berthe all constitute a pattern that is reminiscent of the proscriptions to redress political power relations both during the second Roman civil war under Sulla (82–81 BCE) and later under the second Triumvirate of 43 BCE, following Caesar's death. These ancient purges, whose radical excesses remain a mystery to this day, are an essential constituent of Flaubert's Roman world. The proscriptions—law that repealed all law—marked the high point of tyrannical violence, and *proscriptio* became a word imbued with terror during the Roman civil wars. Touching upon the heart of the matter without even realizing it, after she read the notice announcing the forced auction of her mistress, Emma's maid Félicité calls it "an outrage" (239).

In short, proscription notoriously combines the arbitrary execution of citizens according to public lists of names, with the confiscation of property: "The death penalty was imposed on the proscribed, enforceable by anyone and linked to the confiscation of assets. Anyone could murder them with impunity and was rewarded for it."[57] Those who had helped the outlawed were killed in their turn. The children of the proscribed were not excluded from the burdens, but from the full honor of public office, and thus ended up ruined. Flaubert's *Sentimental Education* distributes the two elements of proscription, at the climax of the Roman civil war, which is about to tip over into tyranny, namely, execution and public auction, between two characters, Dussardier and Madame Arnoux. In *Madame Bovary*, both elements are crystallized in the figure of Emma Bovary, the ruined, plundered, and infamously cannibalized sacrificial victim. Her household is torn up at the roots. Juridically, the procedure of confiscation and public auction attendant on bankruptcy—one need only think of Balzac for images of the ruin and dishonor of bourgeois life—is based on the Roman foreclosure law; even its wording, with the distinction between *proscriptio bonorum* and *publicatio bonorum*, is derived from its Roman predecessor: "Emma read with a glance that her furniture was for sale" (239). Moreover, in both cases Flaubert incorporates all the moments involved in the execution of the process according to the Roman model: the public shaming, the rape, the slaughter, the body-stripping, and the exile or ruination of the children.[58]

If both proscriptions share in financial motivation, then the proscription of the later triumvirate is marked by its painfully exact pseudo-legal justification. The triumvirate did not retroactively dress up acts of personal vengeance into legal forms as Sulla had, but "proceeded with cold calculation and with a plan in which almost all particulars had been determined; above all they made pains to adhere to the formal legality of the steps taken."[59] This is distinctive of Lheureux's procedure against Emma. His "slaughter" is perfectly legal; the king, the law, the state vouch for it. It serves to protect the interests of Lheureux and his intermediaries. Lheureux stresses the legality of the procedure: "Too bad! The court has recognised it! There's a judgement. You have been notified" (233).

By weaving a refined net of double meanings, Flaubert draws a parallel not only between Emma's death and ruin and that of human sacrifice, but also with the *homo sacer* condemned to death through proscription.

He compares the France of his time, not only with the idolatrous cults of the East, which relied on human sacrifice, but also with one of the most infamous episodes in Rome's history. In Flaubert's interpretation, the French nation has inherited, not Roman glory, but Roman infamy. The political abyss of Flaubert's era is embodied in the abysmal tragedy of *Madame Bovary*.

Arachne, Deadly Eros

A picture of the goddess Minerva hangs on the wall in Emma Rouault's girlhood room. However, Emma is no Minerva; she is an Arachne, the goddess's human antagonist. Arachne's undoing was precipitated by her provocation: she, as a human, dared to challenge Minerva to a contest to determine who could weave the most lifelike representation. Arachne is thus an example of hubris. As a precursor to the poet Ovid, she weaves the metamorphoses of the gods into human form, driven as they are by their lust for human women. The first story she weaves is the abduction of the king's daughter Europa by Zeus transformed into a bull: "Arachne shows Europa tricked by Jove in [the] semblance of a bull upon the sea, and done so naturally you would have thought the bull and the waves he breasted were both real," as Ovid sums up her achievement (*Metamorphoses* 6.140–50).[60] Arachne's theme, Eros, is—quite literally— enlivening, while that of Minerva on the other hand, with its focus on metamorphoses of punishment that immediately follow, evokes death. Arachne therefore wins the contest ipso facto, but only herself to embody what Minerva has depicted on her fabric. Arachne's perfect, lifelike representations, her immaculate stories of desire, with which not even the most discerning eye could have found fault, are ripped up by Minerva as an offense against heaven, *celestia crimina* (6.131). Made to realize her impiety by the goddess, Arachne hangs herself; but Minerva transforms her into a spider, condemning her and her offspring to weave in perpetuity. Arachne wants to hang herself, and would thereby illustrate the impotence of her merely fictive power of creation. Through poison, Minerva transforms her into a spider. Ovid's *Metamorphoses* is an allegory of art, moving most artfully between life and art.

Flaubert denounces Arachne's weaving, with its metaphors of lust illustrating the power of desire to give a deadly illusion of life, *enargeia*, through Eros. Adopting the perspective of Ovid's latter-day antagonist Saint Augustine—who sees adultery as a fundamentally false relation to the world, which, instead of spiritualizing and thereby giving life to everything it encounters, objectifies and makes everything carnal, leading to the death of the soul—he registers the truth about desire: its deadliness. Emma's deadly desire, rendered in such vivid strokes before our eyes, is "living" proof of this.

The fate of Arachne put forth in Ovid's *Metamorphoses* will fulfill itself literally in the case of Emma Bovary and her daughter. Mutatis mutandis, the fate of Emma Bovary and her daughter is that of Arachne in Ovid's *Metamorphoses*. It is her metamorphosis, woven through the whole text of the novel, that informs the story of Emma and accumulates so many details that seem insignificant at first glance. Charles's first wife, the jealous Héloise, immediately recognizes Emma as "some one who knows how to . . . embroider" (18), who had "learnt tapestry work" (ibid.) in the convent. Héloise accordingly attributes immense powers of seduction to Emma.[61] Emma's initiation to love is indeed a result of her convent education, which brought together letters, desire, and fabrics. An old noblewoman ruined by the Revolution, who helps mend the nuns' linen, slips romance novels into the laundry. Letters and linen again supplement one another. Right at the beginning and once again later in the story, Emma retraces Arachne's first metamorphosis of desire: she transforms Charles Bovary—who carries the ox in his name—into a bull. She restores his manhood by finding his mislaid bull's pizzle (*nerf de bœuf*) riding crop for him, evoking the tension of the erect male member as captured in the connotation of the French verb *bander* (get hard).[62] But this restoration will not last, and Emma has to look elsewhere. In the manuscript version of the novel, Rodolphe comes to Emma as the bull that Charles, in his impotence, has failed to be for her and promises to ravage her the way Zeus raped Europa. The original description of Rodolphe as bull made the first interlaced metamorphosis erupt into the picture, but Flaubert omitted it from the published text, presumably because it was all too obvious: "His open shirt revealed his fat neck. His tight red flannel stirrup pants exhibited the muscles of his thighs, and Emma's grudge against Rodolphe vanished, enchanted as she was by his strength and virility."[63] The mythological subtext is apparent in the thigh muscles bulging from Rodolphe's oxhide-colored pants.

At the beginning of the novel Emma pricks her finger while sewing and licks away the blood. This gesture, linking her back to Arachne's web, embodies the deadliness of eroticism. Texts like textiles prove fatal: they induce Emma's downfall. She gets caught in them, as when her wedding dress gets caught in thorns, or when her dress gets entangled on her way to an adulterous encounter. She remains caught in the materiality of this world; she goes to her grave shrouded in her wedding dress and covered with green velvet. The path of her passions is her Via Dolorosa. Her raptures, into which she is inveigled by her bulls, like Europa, will not lead to the naming of a continent. Turning Arachne's poetics upside down, Flaubert's novel flawlessly—one is tempted to say, like Arachne—illustrates the ruin of Europa/Europe.

On the way back from the ball at château Vaubyessard, Charles finds a cigar case lined with green silk. His wife believes it to be the vicomte's. It becomes the pre-text of her Passion, the text(ile) of passion:

Perhaps it was a present from his mistress. It had been embroidered on some rosewood frame, a pretty piece of furniture, hidden from all eyes, that had occupied many hours, and over which had fallen the soft curls of the pensive worker. A breath of love had passed over the stitches on the canvas; each prick of the needle had fixed there a hope or a memory, and all those interwoven threads of silk were but the continued extension of the same silent passion. (49)

Emma remains bound to the vicomte—who crops up at the crucial moments of each station of her Passion—through cloth. The green fabric of the silk case reappears at the very end of her earthly voyage in the green velvet that Charles spreads over her coffin. At the beginning of her affair with Léon, she finds a scarlet silk ribbon, which again she attributes to the vicomte.

Whenever Emma dreams about romantic travels, in which she desires to be abducted and transported to another country, much as Europa was carried off by Zeus in the guise of a bull, weaving and fabrics invariably turn up: not spider webs, but fishing nets that look uncannily like spider webs. This occurs, for instance, in the land of her dreams to which Rodolphe is to take her: "And then, one night they came to a fishing village, where brown nets were drying in the wind along the cliff and in front of the huts. It was there that they would stay; they would live in a low, flat-roofed house" (158). In the Robinson Crusoe fantasy à deux of her "honeymoon" with Léon, the nets not only pop up in Emma's imagination but are real: "They sat down in the low-ceilinged room of a tavern with black fishing-nets hanging across the door" (202). It is in these nets—the promise of life-giving lust—that Emma will get entangled and die. As fishing nets they refer back to the mud at the bottom of the river that Emma glimpses at the end of her affair with Rodolphe—"their great love, in which she had lived immersed, seemed to run out beneath her like the water of a river absorbed by its own bed; and she could see the bottom" (139). This brings us back to the simile of the gasping carp to which Rodolphe compares her on seeing her for the first time. Her entire life will transform into a web of lies, which veil her love: "From that moment on, her existence was one long tissue of lies, in which she wrapped her love as under a veil in order to hide it" (213).

Emma Rouault sews her wedding trousseau herself. But she does not lift a finger for the child she is expecting: "she gave up looking for the layette altogether and had it all made by a village seamstress, without choosing or discussing anything. Thus she did not amuse herself with those preparations that stimulate the tenderness of mothers, and so her affection was perhaps impaired from the start" (74). Flaubert opposes erotic love to motherly love through the medium of needlework. Emma only works on fabrics in the name of Eros. The lack of maternal tenderness, which makes her the anti-mother par excellence, is made manifest through the role of the *soulier*, the French equivalent to Christmas stocking, which marks the extreme void between Emma and her daughter in the death scene. Psychoanalytically speaking, "Emma is not more man than woman; she is above all a *non-mother*."[64]

Through the birth of her daughter Esmeralda, Sachette, the heroine of Victor Hugo's *Notre-Dame de Paris*, eventually turns from a whore into a mother, and nothing less than a martyr for maternal love. A comparison with Hugo is always instructive. Hugo elucidates the dramatic reversal from a loose woman to a loving mother through a change of name, thus establishing a parallel with the change of name a nun takes when she dies to the world to enter the convent: Paquette la Chantefleurie changes into Sachette. In *Madame Bovary*, in contrast, Hugo's conversion occurs as a change in the opposite direction. It is the becoming-mother of Bovary that makes her go astray: "Madame Tuvache, the mayor's wife, declared in the presence of her maid that Madame Bovary was jeopardizing her good name" (77). At a time when mothers were still considered taboo before they had been ritually purified after having given birth, Emma is already publicly on the path to adultery, led on by Léon.[65] Whereas Hugo's Sachette is the proverbial incarnation of the Passion of motherly love, Emma involuntarily parodies the vocation of motherhood: "She claimed to love children; they were her consolation, her joy, her passion, and she accompanied her caresses with lyrical outbursts that would have reminded any one but the Yonvillians of Sachette in *Notre-Dame de Paris*" (89). Sachette expresses the exclusive love for her daughter through embroidery: one of the charming baby shoes she embroidered for her Esmeralda remains her only keepsake of the child stolen by gypsies. She preserves it like a relic, while an old gypsy woman hangs the other shoe around Esmeralda's neck. In the context of Emma's death, however, Berthe's *soulier*, the equivalent of the lavishly hand-embroidered shoe that is the redemptive mark of mutual recognition between mother and daughter in Hugo's novel, signifies alienation and failed deliverance.

Carried to her dying mother in the middle of the night, little Berthe mistakes the occasion for New Year's Day or the mid-Lent Festival (*mi-carême*), festive days when she is woken up very early in the morning "to fetch her presents" (252). Accordingly, the little girl looks for her *soulier*: "But I can't see my little stocking" (ibid.). Without knowing what she is looking for, Berthe is searching for the sign of recognition that stands for the conversion of sexual love into maternal love in Hugo. Perhaps the wet nurse has taken it away? she thinks, revealing a deeper knowledge that will remain forever hidden from her. The wet nurse had opened the path of desire for her mother and had been a constant companion in Emma's Passion. Flaubert inverts Hugo's scene of recognition into a scene of misrecognition. Berthe does not recognize her own mother: "Oh, how big your eyes are, mamma! How pale you are! How you sweat! . . . I'm frightened!" (252). This mother has entangled herself so deeply in the materiality of the world and is so totally wrapped up in its trappings that she is no longer able to free herself from its chains. Instead of a mother she has become the whore.

In another instance, Flaubert illustrates the inversion of Hugo's *conversio*, not just with a *soulier*, but, worse, with an oriental slipper. Appropriately, Emma finds the gondola-shaped cradle that she has denied her own daughter—a bed in the form of a gondola—at the Hôtel de Boulogne, site of her adultery with Léon. The pink silk curtains and the bonnet that she wanted to embroider for Berthe's cradle (157) reappear in Flaubert's erotic fetish par excellence, namely, the pink satin slippers, embroidered and adorned with swan feathers. Coquettishly, Emma balances her "whim" on the tip of her feet, "held on only by the toes of her bare foot" (209), having now actually become "a living part of her own fantasies, . . . fulfilling 'the love-dream of her youth'" (131). Although she renounces all her desires when buying things for Berthe, she realizes all her fantasies at the expense of the child. Berthe scarcely recognizes her mother on her deathbed, and like Little Red Ridinghood (Charles Perrault's "Le Petit Chaperon Rouge," published in 1697) who finds a wolf in bed instead of her grandmother, she unwittingly exposes Emma's true, wolfish nature by saying: "Oh, how big your eyes are, mamma!" Emma's wolfishness has already announced itself in the discussion of wolves when Charles paid his first visit to her father's farmstead: "First they spoke of the patient, then of the weather, of the great cold, of the wolves that infested the fields at night" (16). The French word for wolf, *loup* is related to the Latin word *lupanar*, "brothel." Emma does not love her child passionately as Sachette does, but sacrifices Berthe to her passions without batting an eyelash. She has not only destroyed Berthe's future but lies to Léon that nothing has happened between her and Rodolphe, "swearing on the head of her child" (212). Leaving Rodolphe's château in despair—he has just refused her a loan of 3,000 francs to settle her debts—she smashes her nails like a trapped wolf on the lock of a gate in a ha-ha (or sunken wall—*saut-de-loup*, or "wolf jump," in the French, 456). In short, references in the novel to wolves have little to do with the actual presence of wolves in Normandy. Rather, they reflect Emma's wolfish nature. Emma oscillates between whore and Virgin Mary, whose Marian blue accompanies her like a trademark.[66]

Having become Madame Bovary and a mother, Emma, née Rouault, employs a wet nurse, Mère Rolet. Both women weave, sew, embroider, and knit uninterruptedly from beginning to end. Both carry the spinning wheel, *rouet*, in their names. The materials out of which Emma knits and weaves are dreams of love; only seemingly enlivening, they turn out to be deadly delusions. In quite a literal sense it is the wet nurse who serves as a go-between. On her way to see Rolet, Emma starts her affair with Léon; the wet nurse becomes the intermediary of their love correspondence. Emma spends the last weeks before her death neither with man and child nor with her lovers, but with the wet nurse and Lheureux, the agents of her ruin, who both supply her with deadly drugs of choice: fabrics and books. She has a limitless need for both, since she merely sets them aside after superficial consumption: "But her reading fared like her pieces of embroidery, all of which, only just begun, filled her cupboard; she took it up, left it, passed on to other books" (102f.). Her death is accompanied by the weaving wet nurse: "Nurse Rollet . . . took her wheel and began spinning flax" (243). Emma spots a "large spider that was crawling along the crack in the beam above her head" (ibid.), and after her death her eyes are covered with what looks like spider webs: "and her eyes were beginning to disappear in a viscous pallor, as if covered by a spiderweb" (260).

Entangled in fatal dreams, this modern Arachne rushes to meet her fate: "in sua fata ruit," Ovid says of the Arachne of the *Metamorphoses* (6.51); her child will do likewise after her. When Emma's maid, Félicité, asks for a bit of her hair, Homais makes "two or three great cuts at random that left white patches" (263), marking her corpse as Minerva marks Arachne. Emma's daughter Berthe will weave like a spider; as Ovid has the goddess say to Arachne: "you must indeed live on, you wicked child: so that your future will be no less fearful than your present is, may the same punishment remain in place for you and yours forever!" (6.194). Berthe will be a spinner in a cotton mill. However, Flaubert does more in *Madame Bovary* than merely illustrate the Ovidian intertext and question religion by deploying art's enlivening power as classical *enargeia*. He does more than dialecticize the relationship between life and fiction, and Thanatos and Eros, by parodying and destroying Hugo's undialectical ideology. Flaubert perspectivizes Ovid through the Augustinian metaphor of adultery as the death of the soul, showing the deadliness of desire spinning its webs. The text's overarching interchangeability of weaving and text, of threads and words, demonstrates the fatality of such voluptuous interlacing. The metaphor of the death of the soul, which Emma undergoes in this weaving, in this texture, becomes literal to the letter in her death by poison, and the deadliness of weaving becomes literally true in the death of Berthe, the spinner.

Phaedra: Foot by Foot

At the center of the novel, according to the poetics of tragedy that inform it, we come to the peripeteia. The failed surgery on the clubfoot of the unfortunate Hippolyte, the stable boy employed at the Lion d'or hostelry in Yonville, is this moment of reversal. Charles, who as a mere health official, is not authorized to perform such operations, is nonetheless talked into it by his wife and Homais. In truth, he only performs the operation to satisfy Emma's pride: if he succeeds, Charles, her husband, would become an authority in the field and thus be worthy of her. Unceremoniously, their marital knot is tied faster by the severing of poor Hippolyte's Achilles tendon; the affair between Rodolphe and Emma is cut like a string.[67] But the restoration of the marriage after the end of the affair will not last long. After Charles's pathetic failure, the ghastly miscarriage of the operation, which ends with an amputation, "the ridicule of his name would henceforth sully hers as well as his" (149). Charles becomes dead to Emma, and her adulterous love for Rodolphe revives: "She repented of her past virtue as of a crime, and what still remained of it crumbled away beneath the furious blows of her pride. She revelled in all the evil ironies of triumphant adultery" (150).

The triumph of adultery precipitates Emma's plunge to death; it is the peripeteia that will lead up to the catastrophe of her suicide. At this turning point, Flaubert alludes to and surpasses an intertext whose influence runs structurally deeper in the novel than the contemporary reference to Hugo. Racine's *Phèdre*, the *nec plus ultra* of French classicism, is as important for the novel as are Ovid's *Metamorphoses*. Emma outdoes Phaedra's perfidy word for word; she is the new Phaedra, in the same way that Racine's Phaedra went beyond Ovid's Hippolytus (15.497ff.) by invoking Seneca's version.

I know my baseness, and do not belong
To those bold wretches who with brazen front
Can revel in their crimes unblushingly.[68]

Obviously a "bold wretch" in contrast to Phaedra, Emma enjoys her adulterous love for Rodolphe from the outset, and can "revel in their crimes unblushingly" to use Phaedra's words.[69] Through her adultery Emma strikes back at her fate, which, as she believes, has withheld happiness, passion, and love. Now, after the failed operation, all values are perverted: Emma declares her virtue to be a crime. From now on, she does not enjoy her adultery out of love for Rodolphe, but gives herself perfidiously to him only for the sake of being unfaithful to her husband. If she blushes, it is not out of shame like Phaedra but, like Arachne, out of anger:[70] when, after the failed operation, Charles turns to her for comfort, she pushes him away "flushed with anger" (150). Emma will commit the incest that Racine's Phaedra so madly desires with Léon, the son she wished for but never had: "Do you love me, child?" (209), she asks him. The wet nurse leads the way, as in Phaedra's case: "Heaven in my heart lit an ill-omened fire. / Detestable Oenone did the rest."[71] Emma, who poisons herself like Phaedra, nevertheless exceeds Phaedra in perfidy, as Flaubert's tragic novel exceeds Racine's tragedy.

Although the embodiment of vileness, Emma is also associated with Phaedra's victim Hippolytus, who has been defamed by his stepmother on the advice of the nurse and will thereby find his death. Like that of Racine's Hippolytus, that of the stable boy, Hippolyte, bears on horses. The parallel between Emma's suffering and the martyrdom of Hippolytus, which plays no role in Ovid but is emphatically present in Racine, is conspicuous. The surgery on Hippolyte's clubfoot and Emma's poisoning exhibit a parallel structure. Both are spectacles in this small town; both events are on everyone's lips. Each time, Doctor Canivet travels from Neufchâtel and the priest Bournisien is called to the sickbed. The Christian context of martyrdom is inscribed within the logic of pagan sacrifice in both Hippolyte's and Emma's suffering. Emma's *Liebestod* recalls the Passion of Christ, while Hippolyte's operation evokes the martyrdom of Saint Hippolytus of Rome, who, like his mythological namesake, was said to have been dragged to death by his feet.

The association of Emma's fate with the Passion is just as obvious as the allusion to the legend of the holy Hippolytus: Lheureux, the Judas, betrays Emma for the sake of profit. She is ridiculed and jeered at: "Some of them laughed in her face; all refused" (235). She is forsaken by all: "Everything within her and without, was abandoning her" (237). Later the word "whipped" (243) appears. Like Christ stumbling under the weight of the cross, Emma drops to the ground. Christ's hour of death on the cross is explicitly cited by the wet nurse: "Nearly three" (244). The motif of the gambling for Christ's clothes under the cross by the Roman soldiers is echoed in the fight for Emma's clothes between her husband and her mother-in-law and their theft by the servant.

But it is not only on this basis that the stable boy Hippolyte precedes Emma in martyrdom, an offering topped by her way of the cross. In both Passions, the antique, pre-Christian motif of sacrifice is inscribed. Emma is driven to suicide; Hippolyte is forced into the operation. He is sacrificed on the altar of Science and Progress, while Emma perishes on the altar of Capitalism. What Hippolyte is promised by Homais in the journal *Fanal de Rouen*: "and who knows if . . . we shall not see our good Hippolyte appear in the midst of a bacchic dance, surrounded by a group of gay companions" (145), Emma will realize in his stead at the carnival in Rouen. She will be the one to dance like a bacchant, while Hippolyte hobbles on one leg. Like Emma, Hippolyte is likened to an animal for slaughter: Canivet, the bombastic physician from Neufchâtel who amputates his leg, says that it makes little difference to him whether he is cutting up a Christian or a chicken (148). The analogy culminates in Hippolyte's howls of pain during the amputation, he having received no anesthetic: "the last cries of the sufferer, following each other in long-drawn modulations, broken by sharp spasms like the far-off howling of some beast being slaughtered" (150). Hippolyte thus literalizes the etymology of the Greek word *tragedy*, which originally meant "goat song." Here, too, Emma surpasses Hippolyte; the ox, embodied in her married name, is the most magnificent sacrificial animal.

As a stable boy, Hippolyte takes care of the horses at the Lion d'or. In Racine's *Phaedra*, taking fright at a sea monster, Hippolytus's horses—which he has fed with his own hands—drag their master to his death, leaving a trail of blood: "The traces of his blood showed us the way."

I have beheld, my lord, your ill-starred son
Dragged by the horses that his hand had fed.
His voice that called them merely frightened them.
Onward they flew—his body one whole wound.[72]

Such horrible incidents, which, through teichoscopy, are scattered throughout *Madame Bovary*, reference horses. When Charles arrives for the very first time at the Rouault farm, his horse shies away, like those of Hippolytus (15). Before setting to work on the amputation, the first thing Canivet does is feed his horse with his own hands, just as Hippolytus used to do: "for on arriving at a patient's he first of all looked after his mare and his gig" (148).

In Racine's tragedy, the death of Hippolytus, where enormous amounts of blood are spilled—"de son sang généreux"—is already contrasted with the icy poison that cools Phaedra's burning heart, where no drop of blood is shed:

I have instilled into my burning veins
A poison that Medea brought to Greece.
Already it has reached my heart and spread
A strange chill through my body.[73]

Phaedra's chilly suicide by poison stands in contrast to Hippolytus's bloody death, and blood is notably lacking in Emma's suicide too. On her deathbed, she writhes, like the stable boy Hippolyte, "seized with convulsions" (252), but her corpse does not bleed; instead, "a stream of black liquid, like vomit, flowed from her mouth" (262). *Ex negativo* it becomes clear that her death of the flesh is merely a manifestation of a soul long since dead. When she finally expires, she had already been dead inside for a long time. This is why no drop of live, generous blood is made to flow. The vividly evoked smells of Hippolyte's gangrenous leg and Emma's corpse contrast with the bloody, open, live wound that is Racine's Hippolytus. The rotting of the stable boy Hippolyte's living flesh anticipates Emma's arsenical corruption. She in fact embodies corruption in her life, on her way to death, and in death. She is already dead and poisoned while alive. Decomposing through the effects of poison, which had already permeated her like a dung blossom, she corrupts everything she touches. "Why was her life so unsatisfactory, why did everything she lean on instantly rot and give away?" (223). She is nauseated by everyone, including herself: "She was as sick of him as he was weary of her. Emma found again in adultery all the platitudes of marriage" (231). Her actual death is therefore the literal confirmation of the death of her soul, with adultery as its metaphor, which she suffers from as much as she enjoys it during her lifetime. Beyond the grave she corrupts her husband, who, in an Ovidian metamorphosis, changes into her. In the dream he dreams every night, "[h]e approached her, but when he was about to embrace her she fell into decay in his arms" (272). The death of the soul, for which adultery is a metaphor in Augustine, is the driving force consummated in Emma's adultery. Its figure is the bloodlessness of the sacrifice of both Hippolyte and Emma, replacing blood with black liquid. Beneath the intertextual staffage of Ovid's and Racine's models, Augustine emerges as a conceptual force.

Gender Equality Before God

in adulteras adulteri saeviunt

Augustine, *De adulterinis coniugiis*

In the end, Emma Bovary kills herself out of pride, just like Arachne. She cannot bear the thought that Charles is superior to her: "This thought of Bovary's magnanimity exasperated her. He was bound to find out the catastrophe, whether she confessed or not, now, soon, or tomorrow; so there was no escape from the horrible scene and she would have to bear the weight of his generosity" (242). Flaubert alternates between the pagan register of hubris and the Christian register of guilt, which, through the echoes of "And forgive us our debts, as we forgive our debtors" (Matt. 6:12), fuses the notions of guilt and debt (*debita, debitoribus*). Quoting blindly, Emma grasps Charles's ability to grant her forgiveness through the words of the Lord's Prayer. Grumbling under her breath like some wild animal, she acknowledges that her husband would forgive her even if he were to be ruined by her: "Yes, . . . *he* will forgive me, the man I could never forgive for having known me, even if he had a million to spare! . . . Never! never!" (242). On the other hand, in her scandalous inability to forgive, Emma is not prepared to pardon her husband under any circumstance. It is unforgivable to her that he has known her, that is to say, because of the carnal knowledge he has of her. Flaubert exhibits a strange pre-Freudian insight into the taboo of virginity, where the woman cannot forgive the man for robbing her of her virginity. This makes Freud advocate reverting to the old custom of not marrying virgins.[74] Madame Bovary, whose debt society does not forgive, cannot forgive her debtor, who is her husband.

The central question of adultery and forgiveness, which Flaubert explores in his novel of manners in the provinces, is treated by Augustine in his pastoral treatise *De adulterinis coniugiis*.[75] (He also discusses adultery and its connection to marriage, virginity, widowhood, and abstinence in *De bono coniugali*, *De sancta virginitate*, *De bono viduitatis*, and *De continentia*.) Since not only adultery, but rather the forms of coexistence of the sexes in general are negotiated in *Madame Bovary*, the novel begins and ends with Charles Bovary, who marries a widow, only to die a widower after his second adulterous marriage. Right from the start of the book, as a schoolboy, Charles is faced with the din of charivari, and such derisive "rough music"—notably heard in France in an earlier time when a widower or widow remarried too soon[76]—punctuates the entire novel.

Madame Bovary is an outspoken counterdiscourse to Augustine's doctrine. The novel pointedly contradicts the interpretation of adultery Augustine proffers in *De adulterinis*. Flaubert insists that the world is not redeemed. The conclusions Augustine draws therefore do not apply. The blood of Christ has not washed away anything. Yet the unredeemed nature of this world becomes legible only in the light of the blood He shed. Flaubert does not think the ancient texts—the tragic metamorphosis of Arachne and its history of reception, the tragedy of Phaedra, Dido's tragic death, the tragic myth of Cupid and Psyche—have been overcome and left behind by Christianity. On the contrary, finding them reconfirmed in the Christian West, he employs these ancient tales, in even more tragic form, against the Gospel, which was intended to overcome and supersede them.

Augustine's redeeming message is cancelled out through Flaubert's invocation of the ancient pre-texts, which Augustine meant to overcome. The opposite occurs of what had taken place in an exemplary fashion in the exchange of letters between Abélard and Héloise: modeled on the representation of passion in antique literature, their passionate love as expressed in their correspondence is redeemed through the love of Christ. This way, the ancient sources were overcome and at the same time preserved—sublated—in this new Christian love. *Madame Bovary* performs the opposite process: the ancient passion, surpassed in Emma's perverted Passion, belies the Gospel. In this novel, everything, even the love of God, is read *à l'ancienne*: not according to the living spirit, but in the name of the flesh. This carnal fashion of reading always stumbles solely upon the deadening letter. This reversal of the hermeneutics of Abélard and Héloise's epistolary love in Flaubert's novel might shed light on why Charles's first wife is called Héloise.

Flaubert's first novel of love and family is set in France, known both as the eldest daughter of the Church and the Fatherland of Human Rights. But in this France, no trace of the redeeming love propagated by Augustine is left. Especially the men lovelessly testify to this cruel lack. Like Père Goriot, Lheureux covets money and gets off by ruining women. The onanist Binet lives in proud isolation. Homais cannot owe his proclaimed expertise in all things female to his own wife, whose motherhood has erased all femininity. He thus has to practice adultery. In his untrammeled pursuit of lust, the bachelor Rodolphe, a seedy Don Juan, cannot bear to take care of a child. The married notary Guillaumin has mistresses and tries to profit doubly from the ruin of women by coaxing them into intercourse without ever getting his hands dirty. Emma's father remains a widower only to pursue his pleasures. He sacrifices his only daughter to these pleasures, since he sees Charles as a profitable opportunity for giving her away without a dowry. Charles's father, the eternal womanizer, has the hots for his daughter-in-law. Charles marries a mendacious widow because of her supposed riches, only to get married a second time to a virgin who will corrupt him beyond the grave. All these family stories illustrate a love gone wrong, a love that only seeks profit. It is precisely against this love that Augustine develops his doctrine of selfless Christian love.

The exactitude and detail with which *Madame Bovary* counters Augustine is in itself worth a book-length study. For our purposes it will suffice to reflect on the central point of contention, namely, the stain of original sin, as materialized in the stain of adultery. *Madame Bovary* is all about maculation. Emma oscillates between *immaculata* and *maculata*. Sick of herself, before she unconsciously sets out on the path to sacrifice, Emma dreams of "realms of immaculate purity" (232). That Emma is maculated to the tips of her hair is a detail that only appears in the manuscript version: after a rendezvous with Léon, she has to go to the hairdresser to get the semen stains out. A black liquid emitted from her corpse stains her virginal wedding dress. Emma, corrupted and corrupting, is the epitome of maculation.

Augustine's remarks revolve around these stains of adultery. His treatise focuses on the practical, ecclesiastical question of whether a woman or a man, whose partner has committed adultery, can divorce to remarry. This question is answered in the negative: marriage binds man and woman until death. As long as both partners are still alive, each new marriage constitutes adultery. Augustine does not deem adultery to be a real, that is to say, Christian problem. With Christ, adultery has lost its terrifying aspect, since His blood also washes these stains away; as a physician He heals the infection spread by adultery. Adultery is therefore no longer an ontological category. It is a sin, which, like all other sins, is forgivable, and has therefore no deeper existential implications. This is the revolutionary, and one is tempted to say, feminist message of Augustine's treatise.

Against the grain of late antiquity's horizon of expectation, Augustine argues that faith makes reconciliation possible. "It appears harsh to you that, after adultery, spouse should be reconciled with spouse. If faith is present, it will not be harsh," he admonishes one Pollentius, who argues in favor of recognizing adultery as grounds for divorce. The hypocrisy of those who "themselves adulterers, rage at the adulteress" is clear.[77] This is a radical interpretation of Christ's words demanding that he who is without sin should cast the first stone. Augustine interprets the sin referred to by Christ, not just as original sin, but as the specific sin of adultery—which he assumes has been committed by all the men who have gathered to stone the adulteress. But is "adultery" understood here in its everyday meaning? Augustine's treatise plays on the ambiguity between the literal and the figurative.

Why do we still reckon as adulterers those who we believe have either been cleansed by baptism or have been healed by penance? Under the Old Law of God, no sacrifices wiped away these crimes, which, without a doubt, are cleansed by the Blood of the New Covenant. Therefore, in former times, it was forbidden in every way to take unto oneself a woman sullied by another man. . . . But now, afterwards, Christ says to the adulteress: "Neither will I condemn thee. Go thy way, and from now on sin no more" (John 8:11). Who fails to understand that it is the duty of the husband to forgive what he knows the Lord of both has forgiven, and that he should not now call her an adulteress whose sin he believes to have been eradicated by the mercy of God as a result of her penance? (Augustine, "Adulterous Marriage," 108)

Again calling for rhetorical affirmation, the question posed by Augustine presupposes an interlocutor still ignorant of the fact that it is the divine compassion (*divina misericordia*) of the Lord of both (*dominus amborum*) that extinguishes the debt. As the treatment of adultery separates the Old from the New Testament, so it separates the City of Man (*civitas terrena*) from the City of God (*civitas Dei*). Their outlook on adultery separates Christians from both Jews and pagans. Since they have been redeemed by the blood of Christ, which has vindicated and washed away the stains of original sin, married couples can forgive one another without losing face after doing penance. Augustine is well aware that the legislation of his time does not follow Christian precepts; for him, as for Flaubert, however, the condemnation of the adulteress is a mark of the unredeemed depravity of the City of Man: "after her participation with Christ, she may not be called an adulteress."[78]

The commandment to forgive, which at the same time is a proscription of vengeful bloodshed, is, as Augustine emphasizes, a *skandalon*, a stumbling block lodged at the heart of the issue of gender. Christ's abhorrence of the assembled lynch mob he denounced to their faces was so radical in late antiquity that, according to Augustine, there were those who sought to rewrite the Gospel. Not making a woman who had inflicted the stain of adultery on the heads of similar men pay with her blood was intolerable to the male avengers admonished by Jesus, although many of them were adulterers themselves. In their view, only the lethal shedding of her own blood could cleanse an adulteress of these stains. What separates the Augustinian understanding of adultery from its Jewish and pagan counterparts is the radical novelty of the absolute equality of the sexes. The sexual act is no longer perceived as the staining of the woman by the man. Rather, the figure of sinning against God is encapsulated for both genders in the metaphor of the adulterous sexual act: adultery is the formula in the *Confessions* for a turning away from God that leads to the death of the soul.[79]

Flaubert's attack on the deep-rooted hypocrisy of branding female adultery a social scandal notwithstanding that it is so common among men has its unrivaled model in Augustine. In saying, "He that is without sin among you, let him first cast a stone at her" (John 8:7), Jesus pronounces a judgment that *Madame Bovary* and Augustine reiterate: "themselves adulterers, they rage at the adulteress." Augustine expresses the hope that "the chaste man" who is "without *that particular* sin" (emphasis added), but who is nonetheless not so vain as to think he is without sin *in general,* will "not be savagely harsh. In the knowledge that they are not without sin, they forgive." In sketching the sphere of social depravity in all its complexity, however, Flaubert does not share that hope.[80]

This is an admirable example of rhetoric in which literal adultery is a metaphor for a deeper break that represents *fornicatio* against God as a fundamentally distorted relationship to the world. It is the merciless condemnation of adultery that prompts men to stone adulteresses in order to guarantee the fidelity of their own wives and to safeguard their own adultery with whores, which becomes the mark of true adultery: the death of the soul. They are not so much adulterers because they fornicate as because they are without love and compassion: "while adultery may be death, it is not the death of the body; what is worse, it is the death of the soul."[81] Since Augustine's reading of the Gospel of John, the Church has held that the rights of men do not override human rights: men may no longer spill blood to wash away the stains of their wives.

The male choir of protest against gender equality in conjugal morality and sexual fidelity is ironized by Augustine. He wittily mimics their presumptuous tone, which is infused with an arrogance relying on the self-evident superiority of masculinity, seen as a legal guarantee for male preferential treatment: "We are men; will the dignity of our sex sustain this affront?" ("Adulterous Marriage," 109). Augustine retorts with a caustic question openly poking fun at their arrogance: does the honor (ancient Roman *dignitas*) of our sex (*sexus nostri dignitas*) have to bear injustice (*iniuria*) like women do when we give ourselves to women who are not our wives? (cf. ibid., 108). Wounded in their male pride, their privileges curtailed, men find it outrageous to have to endure the same punishment as women for the same offense. Augustine caricatures their grotesque grandiosity in their cry for blood, which he puts into the mouths of these self-righteous men: if adultery is no reason for divorce, then the adulteresses should at least be killed so that the men can take a new wife (ibid., 125ff.). For Augustine, a bloodthirsty avenging mob law is not an option; forgiveness is the only solution, since the act of forgiveness carries within itself the hope for the forgiveness of one's own sins and for God's help in maintaining one's own chastity.

Based on Flaubert's scrutiny of it, French society under King Louis Philippe continually contradicts the standards upheld by Augustine. Christianity has turned against itself. This turning against itself is apparent in Emma Bovary, the adulteress, who cannot forgive her husband, although he would forgive her. According to Flaubert, the perversion of Christianity takes the form of a kind of political theology, in which by divine authority, aristocratic men have rights over women similar to those they have over their horses: Louis XIV thus unceremoniously replaces Louise de La Vallière with his new mistress. This is why the motif of aristocracy is so important in Flaubert's novel; it is not a question of social mobility, but of the order of the sexes. Women, according to Flaubert, idolize this type of aristocratic man who exercises this divine right—Charles's mother does, and so does Emma. Therefore, in Flaubert's view at least, women are the pillars of phallocracy, to which they—or their femininity—fall victim. If women had lovers—as was the rule for French kings—then they were killed or buried alive in convents. Woven into the text of *Madame Bovary*, French history and its kings by Divine Right exhibit what Augustine would have regarded as the epitome of horror: if the pope did not dissolve the marriage, an adulteress was strangled to remove the obstacle to the king's remarriage. This is the story told by the painting of the Tour de Nesle scene in the Croix rouge hotel.[82]

The bourgeois male inherits the male royal rights against, or better yet, *in the name of* France's widely proclaimed human rights.[83] No one shows any concern over Rodolphe and his endless affairs, over the married notary Guillaumin and his mistresses, or the affairs attributed to Léon. A pronounced sex life serves as proof of masculinity. On the other hand, everyone in the entire little town gossips about Emma Bovary's affairs. Wallowing in their own depravity, the bourgeois of Yonville are only too willing to cast the first as well as the last stone at her. In a concerted effort, they all work together to bring about her ruin and all make a killing from it. Lheureux blackmails her with his knowledge of her adultery and bankrupts her all the more effectively by doing so. In the society depicted by Flaubert, the adulteress is not redeemed by the blood of Christ. For men, adultery is routine; for women, as in ancient Jewish or pagan societies, it means a death sentence.

Yet more decisive than Flaubert's affirmation of a brutal pre-Christian, pagan reality in a society that claims to be Christian—or better still, enlightened—is his insight that this society consists of metaphorical adulterers. This is a community of adulterers, who, in a permanent state of Augustinian *fornicatio*, rage against adulteresses. In this adulterous society of a universal death of the soul, women are reduced to things, to fetishistic props and mere pieces of décor. In his marriage to Emma, Charles lives in spiritual adultery against God, since he knows nothing beyond his sensual fulfillment. However, this is only the least harmful form of adultery Flaubert portrays: through Charles's capacity for forgiveness he will be forgiven. In contrast, nothing absolves the more deadly versions: Lheureux's mad desire for money, Homais's merciless ambition for honor, Rodolphe's heartless self-interest in pleasure, and Guillaumin's greed for profit. From this perspective, the structure of such a society grasped in its totality—and *A Sentimental Education* will introduce another variant of this constant—can be encapsulated in the motif of prostitution. Emma is the figure whose individual fate makes the general structure of adultery, which brings to light the death of the soul, readable as the societal human condition. Through her, adultery against God is referred back to literal adultery, the Augustinian primal scene of moral decay leading away from God. Even

Emma's kiss of love pressed on the crucified Christ at the moment of her death remains an inevitably tragic adultery against God. The tragedy lies in the fact that no alternative is at hand: there is no other love. The Gospel has remained unheard. In its immaculate prose, the novel makes legible the stain of original sin, which no amount of blood has washed away—not even that of the Son of God—through its most ancient and most modern example: adultery.

Salammbô

The Fruit of Passion: Carthage Lives

Ah! How I'd like to be a scholar! To write a fine book titled "On the Interpretation of Antiquity"! I'm sure I'd be in the tradition, and what I'd bring to it would be modern sentiment.

Flaubert to Louise Colet, March 27, 1853

I wasn't trying to write the *Iliad* or the *Pharsalia*.

Flaubert's response to Sainte-Beuve, 1862

Flaubert's novel *Salammbô*, which appeared in 1862, was a "grand, grand succès," as Baudelaire wrote.[1] Contemporary criticism could not change that fact, though it considered the novel a failure. As Michel Butor observes, it is a cruel, glittering oriental fantasy that has something in common with the Rome of Hollywood cinema,[2] ironized so inimitably by Gore Vidal's screenplay for the 1980 film *Caligula*.[3] In tune with a spirit of the times in thrall with the East, *Salammbô* launched a veritable fashion: Empress Eugénie considered—and ultimately rejected—the idea, inspired by the heroine of the novel, of making her entrance to the court's masked ball wrapped in nothing but a veil. Surrounded by scandal, the emperor's mistress, the divinely beautiful countess Castiglione, was not tormented by such scruples of respectability and provocatively presented herself as an oriental princess.[4] Sarah Bernhardt derived inspiration for her interior decoration and fashion from Flaubert's heroine. Today, the novel shines like a dead star. If it were not for *Madame Bovary* and *A Sentimental Education*,

Salammbô would likely have fallen into oblivion. It accords with today's taste as little as the vast, wall-filling historical paintings of the nineteenth-century Academy.[5]

Flaubert's *Salammbô* narrates the consolidation of a national body politic through sacrifice rather than the history of a war.[6] The transitivity between acts of war and cult sacrifice is shaped through the fluent transition between enemy and victim: "The body of the enemy is sacred"[7]—here Flaubert evidently cites Joseph de Maistre.[8] Throughout the war, which is nothing but a sacrificial cult, the national body politic thereby constituted is the perversion of the body of the Church as founded on Holy Communion and Christ's loving sacrifice. This is a bond founded not on love but on revenge: "the Elders thought it was clever thus to have combined the whole people in a single revenge" (154).[9] Contrary to the Passion of Christ, the sacrifices do not engender a spiritual community of love grounded in the Eucharist or found a living bond between loving hearts through the ingestion of the transubstantiated flesh and blood of the Lord. Instead, "mystic pleasure" (241) and "mystic lasciviousness" (277) are instituted, which are communions and celebrations of love of an altogether different kind and orgiastically unite the city in a delirium of sex and violence. "Carthage was as if convulsed in a spasm of *titanic* joy and *boundless* hope" (282; emphasis added). In Flaubert's Babylonian-Roman matrix, *titanic* references the Titans, who were defeated in a cosmic battle, and whose seven graves became the hills Rome was founded on, while *boundless* alludes to both the immoderate pride of the builders of the Tower of Babel and the *imperium sine fine*, the endless empire, predicted for the Romans by Vergil. (Flaubert's technique of allusion is discussed further below in regard to *A Sentimental Education*.)

The key question of the novel concerns the nature of sacrifice. I propose that the Carthaginian sacrifices in *Salammbô* are to be read as perversions of Christ's sacrifice out of love, of Holy Communion, and of their figurations in the Old Testament: the sacrifice of slave children and the burnt offering of children, which are fed to Moloch, distort Abraham's intended sacrifice of Isaac, as well as the sacrifice of Christ on the cross. In the case of the mercenaries, at stake is a kenotic intensification of the motifs of the Cross and the Eucharist. The slaughter of the Balearics by the Carthaginians; the cannibalism committed by the mercenaries, who eat the flesh of their brothers-in-arms in order to survive; the homosexual love of the mercenaries forced by the Carthaginians to duel against one another, battles that end in erotic embraces in which each must take the other's life, death as a sacrifice out of love for the other; Mâtho's way of the cross; and Salammbô's death for the sake of love are all examples of kenotic intensification. In terms of rhetoric, this kenotic crescendo occurs through a de-sublimating literalization of the flesh: as the Credo has it, "And made flesh was of Spirit Holy" (*et incarnatus est de Spiritu Sancto*). Flaubert presents this incarnation of the Word in a reversal of the usage of manuscripts in the *Iliad*, to give one example, where the names of the warriors are inscribed in columns to immortalize them, as was still common practice on triumphal arches up to the nineteenth century.[10] The mercenaries, however, bear the traces of their heroic fights for Carthage in their flesh; their bodies serve as monuments: "With this appeared the marks of the great blows they had received for Carthage's sake; they looked like inscriptions on columns" (259). A transfiguration of the flesh is nowhere in sight.

What Flaubert writes with *Salammbô* is—to put it succinctly—a text that reconfigures and reinterprets the central events of the New Testament, namely, the sacrifice on the cross and the Last Supper. Flaubert's relation to religion has been largely overlooked. When it conspicuously comes to the fore, as it does in *Three Tales*, it is considered playfully ironic. But this is a crude underestimation. Flaubert's oeuvre erects a monument to a message of love that remains the touchstone for human behavior by exceeding what is humanly possible. Aesthetics is therefore not a compensation and secularization of a promise of salvation transferred onto the indifferent beauty of art. Rather, aesthetics is the hollow mold—the negative—of a promise of love and redemption that was never realized in the here and now. This crossed-out promise is encoded in history. It has to be deciphered and remembered. Flaubert's work is a *monumentum crucis*. It crosses out the promise of salvation. Art takes the place of religion without thereby becoming a religion of art, which would be just another cult. Literature becomes the only space where the salvational promise is disenchanted. History and politics are nothing but the blind, perpetual erasure of the promise of redemption. In Flaubert's work, history becomes legible, giving us an insight into its blind truth. Flaubert deciphers history against the backdrop of the sacrifice on the cross, which is latently inscribed in all history: history is nothing but the unfolding of this sacrifice. In the worst-case scenario, it is its perversion; in the best of cases, it is its abysmal kenosis.

But what does this have to do with Carthage and the Orient, an Orient to which, as Sainte-Beuve never tired of emphasizing, the Bible could be no valid guide?[11] How is this relevant to a historical novel set after the First Punic War, exactly 241 years before Christ? In the following section, I approach *Salammbô* as the systematic erasure of the salvational promise tied to the Crucifixion. The Passion and the Eucharist are the persistent subtexts against which the suffering in *Salammbô* can be deciphered. The Passion of Christ is the matrix of the oriental novel. Criticism has so far only focused, again and again, on specific moments of this fundamental structure, without recognizing its systematic meaning. Sainte-Beuve already saw the great Carthaginian general Hamilcar as a counterpart to Abraham. Generally, the parallel between the suffering of Mâtho and Christ's way of the cross is acknowledged. However, the meaning of this parallel remains under contention.[12]

This matrix of the sacrifice on the cross and the Last Supper determines all of Flaubert's works and shatters the genre distinction between the contemporary and the historical novel. He treats the East and Normandy, Carthage, Rome, and Paris merely as different guises of this configuration, thus seamlessly integrating *Salammbô* into an underlying stratum binding together all of his writings.[13] "Carthage is not only the reverse side of Rome, it is the reverse side of Paris, of Yonville. We encounter the same characters in all of those cities, in extraordinary disguises," Butor says.[14] Rome's hidden side and the reality of contemporary France are both revealed in Carthage: "Everything in this city is dual: here and there, antiquity and us, today and back then."[15]

From offstage, Flaubert tells the truth about all history. "Carthage must be destroyed [*Ceterum censeo Carthaginem esse delendam*]," Cato the Elder notoriously proclaimed. The totalitarian body politic consolidated in Carthage through the sacrifice of Mâtho will before long disappear without a trace from history as a result of the Second Punic War, waged by Hannibal.[16] This is a dead civilization that disappeared from the face of the earth. As Flaubert and criticism never failed to point out, we know nothing about it. And yet, razed to the ground, Carthage lives.[17] For Flaubert, the war of the Carthaginians against the mercenaries becomes the key to understanding what remains ever the same story across space and time—*sine fine*. What Flaubert shows with the example of *Salammbô*—and, for that matter, with all his other works in their meticulous, even obsessional attention to historical detail—is not a well-defined historical epoch, but the all-embracing truth of history, whose sign is the cross. It is a structure that holds true for all times: the cross becomes the paradigm for what humans do to each other time and time again, degrading others, turning them into animals or machines, reducing them to bare life. In this story of a ruined city, Flaubert unveils the truth of all history: it is the perversion, unfolding, and cryptic hyperbole of the sacrifice on the cross.

To define *Salammbô* as a historical novel is to misjudge Flaubert's aim and interest.[18] Ultimately, his text does not compete with historical discourse but with Revelation, which shows itself in the course of history if the latter is read carefully.[19] It may come as a surprise that Flaubert, the father of the modern novel, wrote only starkly anti-secular texts. For him, there is simply no history independent of Revelation. As such, he crossed paths with the writers of his generation, who spell out an earthly history in the mold of salvation history. Flaubert directs his work against this theological foundation of earthly politics; he inverts this process. Flaubert, who conducted unbelievable research following a truly philological method—for *Salammbô* alone he painstakingly studied and excerpted from ninety-eight books and seemingly suffered from a strange craze for the letter—puts his faith in the letter, in the Word.[20] He thereby invokes a schema that Erich Auerbach calls the *figura verborum*.[21] Something must exist in writing for it to have a place in his novel,[22] much in the same way the New Testament exists by virtue of the words of the Old Testament, which through it acquire their full, true meaning for the first time. The relation between *Salammbô* and its sources corresponds to the relation between the Old and New Testaments: the *figura verborum,* into which turn all the gathered texts, finds fulfillment in Flaubert's work. The truth becomes dimly visible in their interplay, making Flaubert's text legible. The *implementum* often lies in an ironic twist, in a reversal of direction overturning the historical order. Thus, set against its Christian interpretation, the cross in *Salammbô* takes on a new meaning. Like "Saint Julian the Hospitalier," *Salammbô* comprehensively fuses texts from all around the world, from the most diverse areas and epochs. In this sense, these texts are timeless, sub specie aeternitatis, because although they are set within a certain time, with an appropriate *sensus historicus*, as in the Bible, they contain an additional, allegorical dimension. Carthage is also Babel, Jerusalem, Rome, Paris, and Washington, antiquity before the birth of Christ, the

France of the Terror, of Napoleon, and of the 1848 Revolution, the America of slavery and the Civil War.

In this respect, Flaubert's wild syncretism—which, echoing the archeologist Wilhelm (*dit* Guillaume) Froehner, one could only qualify as an absurd montage of sources if one were to take historical veracity as one's criterion—is nothing but the expression of this deeper universal truth happening always and everywhere.[23] How else could one narrate the war of the mercenaries against the Carthaginians short-circuited with Hannibal's Second and Third Punic Wars against the Romans; or base the siege of Carthage by the mercenaries on Ezekiel and the Book of Kings, with the siege of Jerusalem by Nebuchadnezzar as model? How else could the Book of Kings be the source for Carthaginian sacrificial practices, the debates in the Carthaginian senate borrow elements from the proceedings of the U.S. Congress, Salammbô's dressing up and perfuming draw on the Book of Esther, Mâtho's description of her sleeping evoke Apuleius's story of Cupid and Psyche, and the love scene between Salammbô and Mâtho cite the Book of Judith, while referring to Vergil's love scene between Dido and Aeneas? How else could the love between Mâtho and Salammbô exhibit traces of the mid-nineteenth-century psychiatric discourse on hysteria?[24] How else could the Moloch of the Carthaginians, based as he is on the Old Testament, and above all on the Book of Kings, be at the same time modeled on the cannibal god of the Druids, a reference Flaubert owes to de Maistre, who cites Caesar's *De bello Gallico*? How else could Schahibarim's last sacrificial gesture be modeled on Aztec sacrificial rituals as related in de Maistre, while at the same time tied to the iconography of the nineteenth-century French cult of the Sacred Heart? How else could Flaubert's description of leprosy, incarnated in *Salammbô* in Hanno's flesh, refer to Polybius, where it is a metaphor for the corruption in Carthage, and at the same time draw on the description of elephantiasis as described in the Old Testament,[25] and on the sickness of the Roman tyrant Galerius in Chateaubriand's novel *The Martyrs*?[26] Flaubert always emphasized this all-embracing, ahistorical, universal character of his work. Thus it cannot come as a surprise that his Carthage, in following the biblical opposition between Babel and Jerusalem, turns into yet another Babel, while Jerusalem itself, however, as in "Hérodias" later on, appears in the guise of Babel, and it is only natural that for Flaubert, Rome is nothing but another Babel. These are all empires of the earthly realm; in following the path laid out by Augustine, Flaubert molds all of them in the form of the City of Man.

Contrary to literary lore, *Salammbô* does not stand out as an erratic block in Flaubert's oeuvre, nor is it simply a roman à clef set in a distant Carthage. In fact it refers to Paris after the Revolution, from the time of Napoleon I to the Second Empire.[27] History is the same always and everywhere: the unfolding of incarnation and crucifixion. Flaubert sees this Christian *mysterium* as the recasting of an older solar religion. On the one hand, Christian religion is the blind staging of a mythical, archetypal pattern, which, in the final analysis, constitutes a natural myth.[28] On the other hand, however, Flaubert stresses Christianity's fundamental break, in the form of a rejected love offering, with these mythical cults. Its promise did not come true, but the memory of this sublime love is kept alive in history. It is the standard against which all things earthly must be measured. As a testament against the Gospel, Flaubert's work stages the Passion anew and outdoes its kenotic moment in a kenosis of kenosis. The literary method of this outdoing is literalization—the desublimated, nonsublime incarnation of the *passio*.

Psychoanalytically, one might speak of an unfolding of the Oedipus and castration complexes. It is an Oedipus complex not resolved by the castration complex, which Flaubert endows with both mythical and cosmic dimensions. The final tableau of *Salammbô* frames the primal scene, just like the final tableau of Flaubert's early work "Quidquid volueris." It is a scene depicting a love that is as incestuous as it is deadly; only corpses remain. On the mythical, cosmic level, we have *the sun/the son*, here Moloch, diving into the sea/the mother (*la mer/la mère*), here Tanit. This cosmic scene is doubled by the Passion of Mâtho and Salammbô. Their "lovemaking" is at the same time the death of both; after the lacerated son, Mâtho, topples over backwards and succumbs, the woman, Salammbô, grown stiff and pallid, expires in her turn, her head falling backwards on her throne. Deadly desire penetrates the scene and finds its only expression in the pathetic formula of the loosening of the hair. The figure of the sinking sun—Moloch—is split into father and son. The sacrifice of the son is made to appease the father, who is the only one to emerge unscathed from the story: in the pulsating heart of the son offered to him, he completes the sacrifice offered by the son to the mother in carrying out the castration/death of the son. Perhaps this explains why the sacrifice on the cross—all theological complications aside—in which a father offers up his son, is so crucial to Flaubert.

After *Madame Bovary*, but before *A Sentimental Education*, alternating between the East and France, Flaubert chose to set the novel in distant Carthage.[29] But *Salammbô* is no mere exotic escape from an odious reality to the Orient, although this orientalist misreading—readers' perceptions of what they took to be a colorful, luxuriant world of uninhibited sex and power—was undoubtedly responsible for its succès de scandale. Like *Madame Bovary*, *Salammbô* succeeded with the public for all the wrong reasons. The truth of history that emerges in Flaubert's Carthage is of a different order than that propagated by Hegelianism and the historical novel. *Salammbô* is also—though not only—the destruction of Hegelian versions of history; the novel tells history in a way that shows the absurdity of the modern concept of politics. As heir to a specific Christian tradition, Flaubert is the forefather of Benjamin, Bataille, and Agamben. Against the emancipatory history of the modern age, determined by subjects able to liberate themselves from their subjugation, and who self-confidently and self-determinedly become the masters of their own historical fates, Flaubert posits a history of violence incarnated in those subjected to it. Civilization is grounded in barbarity; in its pursuit of power, money, and lust, humankind has never stopped inflicting inhuman suffering upon its own kind. By rejecting all things human, humans become abject and abjected. For Flaubert, the primal scene of this self-negation, of this subjection, is the becoming-human of God, who dies the most abject of deaths and renounces all divine attributes through the becoming-flesh of the Word: "The Jews demand miracles and the gentiles seek wisdom, but as to us, we preach JC crucified, who is a scandal to the Jews and madness to the gentiles."[30] This *skandalon* is repeated and outdone by Flaubert in *Salammbô*. Here, all humanity is denied to human beings: they are used as machines of birthing and desiring, as beasts of burden, as sacrificial animals. They are turned into nothing but flesh—indeed, flesh for slaughter. Compassion for and identification with the downtrodden, with those reduced to an inhuman state—this is the almost impossible demand Flaubert makes on the reader. He uses all his skills to further this compassion.

It is the crux of compassion that makes Flaubert's texts so very difficult. The reader is led up the garden path, initially identifying—as the good bourgeois and self-determining subject he holds himself to be—with those who consistently follow their transparent self-interest. After all, the behavior of a Rodolphe or a Homais in *Madame Bovary* is presented as perfectly understandable. Evildoers are not seen in terms of their stigmas, and judgment is never explicitly passed on them as, for example, in Balzac. Hanno's leprosy, which virtually turns his body into a heap of rotting flesh, illustrates his malice, which reaches all the way to the marrow, a malice eating away at the Carthaginian body politic at large. In unimaginable cruelty, Hanno vents his anger on the poorest of the poor: he tortures cripples and children, allows his soldiers to rape women before they are killed, and lays waste to ruins. His obviously allegorical sickness is probably the most explicit condemnation to be found in Flaubert.

The trash and scum of humanity, the poorest of the poor, the "idiots," so to speak, who have joined the army of the barbarians—"there could be seen, behind all the others, men with the features of animals and giggling with idiot laughs; wretches ravaged by hideous diseases, deformed pygmies" (208)—have been subsumed by readers on a par with Hanno under the signifier of "monstrosity." Nothing shows better the incredible extent to which Flaubert has been misunderstood.[31] It is a lot to ask of readers—and seemingly too much—that they identify with the rejected and the abject and suffer with them. Reading Flaubert is thus a very difficult education of the heart, a lesson in overcoming great resistance. This education is as Aristotelian as it is Christian. The heart should be formed through "gaping horror" (*horreur béante*), on the one hand, and learn the gift of tears, on the other. While the gift of tears is granted to the mercenaries and slaves,[32] the eyes of the Carthaginians remain dry. Yet at least they are not sanctimonious and do not deceive with crocodile tears like Rodolphe, Flaubert's quintessential modern man, whose heart is hardened like a playground trampled by children.

Flaubert rarely creates characters who have pity on those who suffer. The reading is not steered by the voice of an evaluating narrator who explicitly judges and takes sides, nor is there a stand-in (*Rückenfigur*) for the reader. Those who inflict pain and suffering are not openly condemned, and no direct voice is lent to compassion. Unlike one of his most evident sources, Michelet, Flaubert does not show his disgust at the cowardice of the Carthaginians torturing Mâtho. Nor does he legitimate these actions like another important source, Polybius. Critics have thus spoken of Flaubert's "affectless tone" (*ton sans affect*), of a "lack of human presence" (*déficit de présence humaine*), "atony" (*atonie*), and "the degree zero of conscience" (*degré zéro de conscience*).[33] Although this description is apt, the conclusions drawn from it seem to me all the more erroneous: namely, that violence, simply characterized as being portrayed according to a "stylistics of indifference,"[34] becomes something picturesque, just part of the décor. Mâtho's torture, for example, is thus regarded as an *écorché de beaux arts* exhibiting Flaubert's "tranquil anatomical knowledge."[35] Since in Flaubert, much as in Titian's *Punishment of Marsyas*, nothing stands between the gaze of the viewer and the work, it constitutes a "tranquil meditation on the quick of death."[36]

Nothing strikes me as more inadequate than this description, pertaining to both Flaubert and Titian, of the impression of the torture scene made upon the reader. Rarely has the concept of Flaubertian "impassiveness" (*impassibilité*) been so misjudged. The reading of this torture scene is simply unbearable. This is not due to the tranquil display of anatomical knowledge; nor is it owed to our musing about what people are capable of doing to each other. The reading of this scene is unbearable because one almost dies of compassion. What is left blank in terms of moral judgment or a passionate taking of sides is filled in with the art of description. Flaubert relies completely on the artistic skill of his illustration of suffering, his ability "to represent vividly" (*faire vif*)[37] in order to move the reader to compassion. The cool objectivity and display of inhumanity without commentary is carried out with an eye to maximizing horror and compassion. The exposure of man as an abject being whose depravity consists in rejecting all things human reproves the humanistic faith in man and shows it to be a lie. The reader undergoes the full force of this exposure of the human as inhuman and is deprived of all hope. As Flaubert does not justify civilization but shows its bottomless cruelty, and indeed shows cruelty as the very foundation of civilization, compassion is not turned off, but is intensified to the height of pathos. *Salammbô* is an intolerable mirror,[38] but its unbearableness lies less in a narcissistic injury inflicted by the representation of what people are capable of than in its focus on the horror of man as perpetrator who sacrifices all compassion. A reader who does not feel horror at Hamilcar's pitilessness or has no compassion for the workers and slaves caught in lifelong torture is a mystery to me.[39] This intensification to the highest degree of pathos through a style renouncing all formulas of pathos is summarized by Michel Butor: "As we suffer with Mme Bovary we shall suffer with

Mâtho, even though he is in part his own sacrificer."[40] And thus we suffer, one could add, with the slaves and a fortiori with the father whose child is sacrificed instead of Hamilcar's son, Hannibal. Whoever can read this text without their heart standing still, not blinded with tears, is beyond hope.

Perhaps nowhere else in Flaubert's oeuvre is the rhetorical device of vivid representation (*faire vif*) deployed with such allegorical force as in *Salammbô*. Mâtho's martyrdom evokes the Passion of Christ, Hector's mutilation in the *Iliad*, and the flaying alive of Marsyas.[41] Flaubert makes of the writing just such a martyrdom, such alive self-sacrifice. Like the bodies of the mercenaries, the text is threatened with mutilation. He has to "rip out a lot of pages" (*disloquer quantité de pages*), Flaubert writes to his friend Louis Bouilhet.[42] "Literature, for me, is torture," he says.[43]

Salammbô also performs a destruction of the historical novel, as outlined by Sainte-Beuve: the historical novel is all the more relevant and interesting, affecting us in the truest sense of the word, if it tells of epochs in the not too distant past, whose traces are still palpable in the present. The history Flaubert narrates amounts to a negation of the basic pattern of romantic historiography, as practiced by both Sainte-Beuve and Michelet. Following the example of Montesquieu, these two writers portray the struggle between Rome and Carthage as a "decisive battle": Michelet presents it as a battle between races, in which the Semites (Carthaginians) fight against the Indo-Germanics (Romans), while Sainte-Beuve sees it as a fight in which "our" Roman past asserts itself against the "foreign" Orient. Our entire tradition is at stake in this moment, the culminating point of a law of historical, inner necessity. For "us," descendants of the Romans, this fight is of the highest importance—it concerns us directly. This historiography is not only teleological but serves first and foremost as a means of self-legitimization. The war of the mercenaries with Carthage, a forgotten, utterly vanished city, is insignificant from the perspective of a teleological historiography. Through this insignificance, this eccentricity, Flaubert's novel destroys the teleological, meaningful schema of historiography, as well as the historical novel à la Walter Scott. *Salammbô* is therefore not a historical novel, but a novel about history written against historiography. *Salammbô* distorts the image of history in which rationality, through the cunning of reason, would have the last say. The story told leaves no room for a history oriented toward the good; there is no way leading up to the advent of a humanity peopled with self-conscious, self-determining subjects.

The mercenaries do not suffer in the name of good: nothing can legitimate their sufferings. It cannot be made to bear fruit and demands only this: to be remembered. History, as it is disclosed in Carthage, can no longer be interpreted according to the criteria of goal-directedness, unity, and truth. This means that all contemporary representations of history—history as the expression of the rationality of the future, running a predictable course, informed by messianism, or teleologically structured with a specific terminus in mind—are rendered null and void.[44] Gathered from all four corners of the earth, the barbarians wander around aimlessly and haphazardly in this North African space, so far away from their homeland. Blind chance has thrown them into this alien land; they can only dimly recall where they came from, and they know even less of what is in store for them: this is an allegory of humanity's being in history. A strategically ingenious action, based on the mastery of space and the optimal use of its features, leads the Carthaginians to victory. However, this is merely a Pyrrhic victory, and before long the victorious civilization will have vanished from the face of the earth. However, what is put to rest above all else is the notion that the history of mankind, through becoming-subject and through emancipation, will inherently work out for the best. It is impossible to justify the cruelty of this war by taking recourse to a moral, noble aim: "It is not that history is missing its purpose, but that a purpose is missing in history."[45] Insofar as cruelty without ideological justification is brought to light in all its nakedness in *Salammbô*, antiquity is "more human" than modernity with its ideological motivation of cruelty and the moral hypocrisy of invoking the common good, or any other imvoking of "historical necessity" with beautiful words to legitimate brutality. The heap of corpses produced by the mercenary war does not quite make one's blood freeze as much as the "[s]omething white . . . on the edge of the grating,"[46] left there after Père Roque's murder of the young rebel during the June Days of the 1848 Revolution, in *A Sentimental Education*.

The models invoked by the novel to endow this war with meaning and purpose, and thereby subordinate the monstrosity of violence to a reasonable goal and significance, are marshaled only to be disavowed. At first, the war is briefly presented as a slave revolt or uprising of the poor against their exploiters. The mercenaries are initially supported by the debtors of rich Carthaginians and Libyan farmers ruined by Carthaginian taxes. However, Spendius, who champions this ostensibly just war in the hopes of never being enslaved again, is the first to buy himself a slave.

Secondly, at the beginning, the Carthaginian mob of "Unclean-Eaters" (162) seems to show solidarity with the mercenaries; they disappear from the city and later actually fight side by side with the mercenaries. As such, the war would seem to be a class conflict of rich against poor, tinged with racial aspects. Yet in the end, the rich and the poor and all races alike unite in the torture of Mâtho. Thirdly, for a moment it looks as if the story revolves around a colonial war against the foreign rule of the Phoenicians. However, out of self-interest, the Numidian Narr-Havas will ally himself later with Carthage. Fourth, Rome refuses to accept the mercenaries' offer to change sides. Does Rome thereby embody lawfulness? The rationale for this Roman decision is not the observance of the treaty of 241 BCE, reached after the First Punic War with Carthage. Contrary to Polybius's account (Flaubert follows Sallust's), the Romans deliver food to the mercenaries and profit quite brazenly from the latter's uprising by seizing control of Sardinia.[47] The Romans only recall their treaty with Carthage when a mercenary victory threatens to unleash anarchy, which would jeopardize the legitimacy of every form of government.[48]

The question is whether it follows from *Salammbô*'s resolute refutation of a rational, teleological history of progress that Flaubert offers a decadent or nihilistic worldview. Or, to put it differently, whether the nullity of all ideological values leads to an aestheticization of nothingness "[s]ince writing, or art, to put it like Flaubert, have that advantage over popular opinion that they turn the ideological nothingness of values into the aesthetic value of nothingness," as Françoise Gaillard observes.[49] What is at stake is also whether or not the distinction between the violent barbarians and the supposedly civilized Carthaginians is shattered in a general orgy of violence. Or is it rather that a different opposition is worked out between mercenaries and Carthaginians than that of "barbarity" and "civilization," an opposition the novel effectively breaks down anyhow? Is the clash between the two camps really one that ends, again and again, in the heaping up of ever more torn bodies? Are Mâtho and Hamilcar truly equal in their "fratricidal fury that precedes them by far"? Is it really the case that "the recognition of their brotherhood, laid open by the identity of their courage and their virility, pits them against each other even more savagely"?[50] Is *Salammbô* a fratricidal tragedy?

Does purely strategic thinking not triumph in Hamilcar, and does he not, with his calculating mind, clearly subordinate everything to the primacy of utility, of profitability? Hamilcar's astounding aptitude for split-second, cold calculation is revealed when he acknowledges that his daughter has been rendered worthless in the patriarchal system by her defloration. It only takes him the blink of an eye to sell her off to the first man who comes along: deception for betrayal. The barbarians, thanks to Spendius, make the occasional cunning decision, but for the most part wander around aimlessly, straying off into the scenery, afflicted by *ennui* and melancholy. In contrast, Hamilcar is a master of shrewd and ingenious strategic thinking. He simply makes no mistakes. Consider for instance how he uses his deadly efficient knowledge of the terrain against the barbarians. The barbarians give in to their passions with no regard for their losses; Hamilcar only lets his passions—revenge and rage—take over when he can afford to: only when he can cruelly destroy the helpless and subjugated with impunity. Does Mâtho, on the other hand, not live beyond all calculation, embracing his passionate love to the full? This love, incidentally, is not so manly but is punctured by hysterical moments—one need only think of the masturbatory gesture of polishing his sword. His passionate love comes literally true in the end in his martyred body.

In this view, Hamilcar and Mâtho would not represent the same principle—heroic masculinity in all its perfect beauty, its Nietzschean fascination making the female readership swoon without the slightest resistance—but two opposite principles. The Carthaginians are somewhat cowardly and underhand; they finish off their enemies from behind, they cheat and do not keep their promises. Is the tearing of the body an emblem for the absence of a historical purpose, and is it therefore, in historical terms, a symptom of decadence? Does Flaubert really disallow either side any insight into the historical situation—are both camps devoid of a political or moral vision?[51] Without a doubt, there is at least one figure who has such a political vision, namely, Hamilcar: his son Hannibal must perpetuate his name and secure the destiny of the city by exacting vengeance on Rome and immortalizing Carthage as an empire. He is to perpetuate a hatred that can never be appeased: "The future Hannibal does not so much inherit a historical mission as an indelible hatred, which he is to prolong into the future. And the shape his destiny takes in his father's dreams is one of perpetuation not of fulfillment."[52] Fulfillment may be *our* political interest in history. To destroy Rome and found an everlasting Carthaginian empire, to avenge Dido, queen of Carthage, whom Aeneas abandoned, in

Vergil's account, in order to settle in Italy, leading eventually to the founding of Rome—this is without any doubt a political project.

Salammbô—and this is often overlooked—does not end on a battlefield littered with slain corpses. On the contrary, the end of the novel is very edifying indeed, and this is precisely its inexpressible horror. What it relates is a story of becoming-whole, the consolidation of a totalitarian, unified national body politic, the way Hamilcar envisioned it. This unification of the Carthaginian body politic is carried out through universal mob law. Its crowning moment is the temple prostitution. Just as in René Girard's account of it, the sacrifice of the scapegoat, which Mâtho becomes, enables this ecstatic unification of a body politic torn apart by self-interest. Every civilization, to paraphrase Walter Benjamin, is founded on barbarity.

The Fulfillment and Inversion of Christ:
Mercenaries and Carthaginians

One can reimagine the provocation Flaubert's text stirred up in the France of his time by taking another look at the arguments of Sainte-Beuve, probably the most influential of contemporary critics. Almost indignantly, Sainte-Beuve rejects the mirror Flaubert holds up to French society through the reflection of distant Carthage. This is hardly surprising, since with the hidden face of that other Rome he makes visible in Carthage, Flaubert touches on the core of our self-understanding. As Butor writes: "Rome, for us, has two fundamental aspects, which are the two pillars of our cultural history, the two testaments upon which the whole of our civilization is built: on the one hand, there is Imperial Rome, and following from that classical antiquity, that of the humanists and of Greek and Latin studies; on the other hand, there is the Christian Rome, the Holy See of Saint Peter."[53] Carthage is "the hidden face of its two fundamental aspects: antiquity and Christianity."[54] And it is exactly both these legacies, both these foundations, that Flaubert gives us to read anew, against the grain of the ruling ideological stances of his day. *Salammbô* is without question as anti-humanistic as it is anti-Christian in a very specific sense.

Sainte-Beuve not so much questions historical veracity as the relevance of Flaubert's novel to the France of his time, its interest to the contemporary reader. The tenor of his critique is that the Orient, as described by Flaubert in *Salammbô*, has absolutely nothing to do with us and our present. It simply does not speak to us, as Sainte-Beuve harshly puts it. *Salammbô* is a text so absurd and outlandish that it would require a dictionary to understand it. The novel, set in the margins of history, in a "country of monsters and ruins, Africa,"[55] lacks all humanity. Not even once does the Greek Spendius raise the voice of reason against all this barbarity; the voice of the West, in short, of humanity, is muted. Flaubert took to the margins just to allow his sadistic imagination free rein.[56] Apart from the fact that the reported atrocities, like the sacrifice of children to Moloch, are purely and simply unbelievable, nothing in the novel concerns us at all: "How does the duel between Tunis and Carthage concern me?" Sainte-Beuve asks. "Tell me about the duel between Carthage and Rome, fine! I'll listen to that, I'll be moved by that. In the grim dispute between Rome and Carthage, the whole future of civilization is already at stake, your very own [society] depends on it."[57] So much cruel barbarism, so much unspeakable brutality can only remain unintelligible, unrepresentable to a civilized, humanistic world, in short, to our world. To the rightful heirs of antiquity and Christianity, Carthage should have remained forgotten and buried and not resurrected by this novel. Sainte-Beuve finds it an ungrateful story. He turns away disgusted and leaves Flaubert behind in his lamentable, wholly individual instinctual vicissitude and propensity to sadism.

So much resistance suggests denial. Flaubert reacted to this criticism by stressing the burning actuality of his novel. The gruesome spectacles in *Salammbô* had their parallels in eighteenth- and nineteenth-century French history and in the events of the Civil War in the United States, even then taking place, which became a struggle for the abolition of slavery. The mutilation of the corpses committed by the Carthaginians after the murder of the Balearic mercenaries is dismissed by Sainte-Beuve as contrary to human nature, and is thus a fabrication in his view. Flaubert justifies himself by reminding him of the most recent history of France and America: "And you are astonished that the vanquished, despaired, enraged barbarians should at least once pay back tit for tat, and this time only? Do I have to remind you of Mme de Lamballe, of the [Gardes] Mobiles in '48, and of what is happening right now in the United States? I have on the contrary been very restrained and temperate."[58]

During the massacres in revolutionary Paris in September 1792, the princesse de Lamballe, who had allegedly had a lesbian relationship with

Marie Antoinette, was decapitated, the labia were cut off from her corpse and pasted onto her face like a moustache, and her head was stuck on a pike and displayed to the imprisoned queen by a spiteful populace. In *A Sentimental Education*, the Garde nationale militia, the Mobiles, are represented as having massacred insurgents during the June Days of the 1848 Revolution.

Where Sainte-Beuve postulates a radical break between monstrosity and humanity, a reasonable antiquity and intolerable barbarity, human sacrifice and the humanity of Christianity—in short, between the West and the East—Flaubert sees continuities. Flaubert does not emphasize the singularity of Carthage but its everlasting humanity, or, to be more precise, its everlasting inhumanity, the universality of the Carthaginian situation, which reaches all the way through history to the present: the Terror of the 1790s, the Revolution of 1848, the Second Empire, American slavery and the Civil War in the United States. Cruelty is not alien to the West, but lives among us. Ignoring barbarity is hypocrisy. Carthage is here and now: "You wonder where I got 'an idea such as that of the Carthaginian Council'? But of course from nowhere other than from all the analogous environments in times of revolution, from the [French National] Convention to the American Congress."[59]

History is not subject to development; it is the eternal return of the same immemorial cruelty in different guises. Consequently, the novel subverts the very idea of progress from the start and undermines the dichotomies championed by Sainte-Beuve between the marauding, murdering horde of mercenaries and the ancient world, supposedly heeding a slow but steady civilizing project mirrored in its institutions, which Carthage already possesses in exemplary fashion.

All in all, Flaubert claims to have gone further in his indictment of humanity in his realistic, contemporary novel of adultery, *Madame Bovary*: "I even think I was less hard on humanity in *Salammbô* than in *Madame Bovary*."[60] Although this might not seem obvious in view of the atrocities committed in *Salammbô*, one cannot help but agree with Flaubert's self-assessment. Flaubert judges humanity in this oriental novel less harshly than the society in which his story of adultery takes place. Indeed, what else to make of a society driven by self-interest alone, a ruinous, deceitful, blackmailing usurer, a heartless, careerist pharmacist, a mindless, apathetic priest, a lover with a heart of stone, and a cowardly, ambitious notary employee who, out of unmistakable self-interest, does not even let the death of the heroine stand in his way but keeps hiding behind noble and morally superior principles to justify his self-righteousness? Aren't they more despicable than a commander who lets a herd of elephants trample over prisoners tied hand and foot, begging on their knees for mercy? Compared to the hypocrisy that hides civilization's "healthy" egoism under the mantle of the common good, progress, and the struggle for humanity, the cruelty of the Carthaginians comes across as sincere. At least they frankly express and follow their self-interest.

So far, the opposition between Carthaginians and barbarians has been framed most aptly through the confrontation between "humanity" (the barbarians) and "civilization" (the Carthaginians).[61] I shall attempt to grasp this opposition in economic terms and thereby specify it. Flaubert pits economy against its privative opposite. What is central is the issue of sacrifice and its use. It is their sacrificial practice that separates the barbarians most clearly from the Carthaginians. A well-calculated, instrumental sacrifice of others stands in counterpoint to a sacrifice out of love, which, in the mode of loving self-sacrifice, renounces all calculations of profitability. *Salammbô* portrays the progress of the barbarians toward such sacrifice. Suffering to the point of death, the ultimate privation of economy, constitutes withdrawal from the world-governing economy of reification. Suffering to death, which is a process through which one comes to understand oneself as part of suffering Creation, amounts to the way out of Babel.

The war begins with Babel-like incomprehension. The mercenaries are unable to understand one another, and the Carthaginians cannot understand them either. The Greek Spendius poisons the translator so as to take his place and causes an eruption of violence by his deceitful translation (as the Italian proverb has it, *traduttore, traditore*: "translator" = "traitor"). The hopelessness of seeking mutual understanding is staged quite radically through the identity of word and murder: *frappe*. Every single utterance of this word is instantly successful: it produces a victim. The departure from Babel does not lead to a new land abounding in milk and honey, but, like in "Hérodias," is nothing but the stations of the cross. The novel shows this development toward the loving sacrifice whose paradigm is Christ's suffering. "Development" is perhaps the wrong word here, since it recalls the bildungsroman, which centers on a subject who reaches self-understanding through increasing self-knowledge. It would be more accurate to say that a slow suffering through violence leads to a love offering, a process of pure passivity, an actual Passion in which the ego is renounced so as to become one with the suffering creature: "They were our brothers" (265), the Gaul, remembering the crucified lions, says to Spendius just as he dies on the cross. Christ's sacrifice is the quintessential sacrifice perpetuated in the present.[62]

This is only possible because its dogmatic meaning has been inverted. Christ, the novel tells us, has not ended the praxis of human sacrifice. The sacrifice and consumption of a scapegoat remains in all societies—and above all in Christian societies—the foundational structure. They are thus daughters of Babel. Christ amounts to nothing more than the most prominent of all scapegoats. However, since his love was so great that it led to self-sacrifice, an alternative to the logic of the scapegoat becomes visible. It is only in the light of this love that the horror of the logic of the scapegoat can be recognized and condemned.

The Passions shine through all the descriptions of sacrifices in *Salammbô*. Each sacrifice—both that of the barbarians and that of Christ—casts a new light on the other. As martyrs, the tortured mercenaries start to resemble Saint Sebastian; at the same time they are offerings to the dead, like the enemies that were killed on graves in antiquity. The Christian cult of martyrdom and the sacrificial cults of antiquity are superimposed:

The two thousand Barbarians were tied up against the steles of the tombs in the Mappalia; and merchants, kitchen porters, embroiderers, even women, widows of the dead with their children, anyone who wanted to, came along to kill them with arrows. They took slow aim, to prolong the torment. . . . Then these crucified corpses were kept standing, looking like so many red statues on the tombs. (154)

The novel is a displacement and condensation of the Passion and Eucharist. The difference between barbarians and Carthaginians is certainly not leveled out. It becomes clearer and clearer. Hamilcar and Hanno mark the negative of the sacrifice on the cross; they are Christ's antitypes. Hamilcar's refusal to sacrifice his son Hannibal, modeled on the intended sacrifice of Isaac, and his ruse to replace him with a slave child instead, the "least of his brothers" (Flaubert of course does not use this word; he illustrates it, as usual), marks Hamilcar/Hannibal as an antitype to Christ: "Inasmuch as ye have done it unto one of the least of these my brethren, ye have done it unto me" (Matt. 25:40). Hannibal sacrifices Christ once more. Hanno, on the other hand, is altogether incapable of sacrifice. Faced with death, he betrays his homeland and brothers-in-arms without much ado in inconceivable cowardice—he would sacrifice everything in a heartbeat to save his miserable life. Hanno's body, embodying the corruption of Carthage, falls decomposed in scraps from the cross.

In the figure of the barbarians, however, Flaubert performs the impossible: the outdoing of the epitome of kenosis, the sacrifice of Christ. Flaubert outdoes the cross. The renunciation, the nullification of the cross in the figure of the barbarians, is systematically effected through literalization and thereby introduces dimensions of depravity. The latter is what Chateaubriand wanted to erase under all circumstances through an ennoblement, or, rather, a sublimation of sacrifice. Sainte-Beuve, and perhaps we readers too, would prefer to sweep this abyssal depravity under the rug, to pretend we know nothing about it. What is unbearable is this degradation of the human, this reduction to bare life, man's debasement to a machine or mere object of desire, to a beast of burden, or his animalization into cattle for slaughter. The "sadistic" and "aesthetic" reading variants are, in their cold distantiation, defenses against this *skandalon*, which provokes horror and unspeakable compassion.[63] The outdoing of the cross does not so much consist in the inflationary devaluation of this sign as in its total degradation for the sake of its elevation.[64]

With the question of sacrifice and atonement Flaubert embarks on the final assessment of the Greek historian Polybius, who tries to justify the cruelty of the Carthaginians, in his view owed to the excesses of the mercenaries. But the atrocities of this war that defy the imagination prompt Polybius to speak of an "irredeemable war."[65] That is why the decisive reshaping by Flaubert of his most important source for the sequence of events—Polybius and his recapitulation in Michelet's *Histoire romaine*—is not the leveling, as has been pointed out repeatedly, of the hierarchy emphasized by Polybius between barbarians and Carthaginians: Carthaginians and barbarians are equally savage.[66] Nor is what matters a simple about-turn of the contrast between the barbarous and the civilized as sketched by Michelet: the Carthaginians are the true barbarians. For Flaubert, this inversion is but the first step. Central to Flaubert's narration of the war between Carthage and its mercenaries after the end of the First Punic War is the opposition between egoistic, calculated, profitable, and productive sacrifice (Carthaginians) and selfless, senseless sacrifice (barbarians). Polybius justifies the cruelty of the Carthaginians by the barbarians' excessive demands and their excessive violence: the Carthaginians thus had no other choice than to fight and exterminate them completely, as if they were wild animals. The reversal of the assessment of Carthaginians and barbarians appears in outline in Michelet's *Histoire romaine*. In the face of Mâtho's torture, Michelet speaks of the cowardly barbarity of the Carthaginians.[67] Michelet too highlights the signifier "expiation." In his case, however, it does not revolve around excessive violence that no war can atone for, but around the cruelty of Carthage as a commercial metropolis, which wages war as if it were a commercial enterprise geared to profit. Carthage's structural cruelty is expiated by the war of the mercenaries against the city. What the Carthaginians let loose on the world comes back to haunt them: "These bands, without country, without law, without God, this impious and sanguinary Babel, whom she had set upon other nations, now fell upon her."[68]

Michelet consistently emphasizes the structural power of the commercial metropolis of Carthage, which, although the pinnacle of civilization at the time, he describes as barbarian: "the barbarous monopoly of the Carthaginians."[69] In idolatrous rapture, the Carthaginians revere money as god and king,"[70] ruthlessly subjugating everything; their fatherland is neither heaven nor earth, but profit. For the Carthaginians everything, even all the bloodshed, is a matter of maximizing profits. In their choice of mercenaries they prove to be good managers and savvy businessmen using their commercial expertise as with any other product on the market. The crucial point of Michelet's presentation is that Carthage turned war into a business in which people become consumer goods and their deaths a question of investment and return. The businessmen of Carthage were too valuable to die during the war, and it proved more worthwhile to replace them with cheaper blood:

This tariff of blood being thoroughly known, [Numidians were likely more expensive than Greeks] Carthage commenced a war as she would a mercantile speculation. . . . She could expend fifty thousand mercenaries in this enterprise better than in that. If the returns were good, they did not regret the capital; they again bought men, and all went on well.[71]

As a source on Carthage's cruel tyranny and absurd despotism, for which no price is too high for maintaining its commercial monopoly, Michelet cites Montesquieu's *De l'esprit des lois*: "all strangers, who traded to Sardinia and towards Hercules' pillars this haughty republic sentenced to be drowned. Her civil polity was equally extraordinary; she forbade the Sardinians to cultivate their lands, upon pain of death. She increased her power by her riches, and afterwards her riches by her power."[72] Since no one knows any-thing about Carthage any longer, Michelet draws historical parallels with other colonial powers: with Venice, and more topically, with the Spanish colonization of Peru, with the English and Dutch colonial powers plun-dering the world and senselessly hoarding all that money in the coffers of a handful of oligarchic families. In Carthage, these plundering oligarchies were called "the Hundred." For their sake, millions of people perished. This kind of commercial monopoly is more destructive than any war.[73] Using the example of Carthage, Michelet criticizes contemporary colonialism. Flaubert continues down this path by looking at colonialism and slavery in America. Like Michelet before him, the decisive factor for Flaubert is the universal, all-embracing economic exploitation that in heartless reification destroys all humanity.

Flaubert illustrates Michelet's insight that everything in Carthage is determined by profitability.[74] Carthaginians differ from the mercenaries in that the former know how to count, whereas the latter do not. "[C]onstantly repeating the same sum, [the mercenaries] drew figures on the sand with their fingers" (43). Their relation to money is entirely chimeric. Not greed but their sense of justice is outraged when Carthage withholds their pay. The mercenaries do not even notice when the Carthaginians swindle them out of their money. Gisco, however, whom "the Hundred" cold-bloodedly sacrifice to their stinginess, is, as a Carthaginian, able to count, and sees his death sen-tence written in black and white in the fraudulent figures calculating what is owed to the mercenaries. Flaubert fleshes out the question of profitabil-ity through the question of sacrifice, which becomes his focus and pivotal point. The illustration of this principle takes on grotesque traits in its over-emphasis: the Carthaginians need hair for their war machine to function. Cutting off the hair of the two thousand women held captive in Carthage intended for prostitution abroad—whose hair would be most suitable since it has been become resilient through constant oiling—would cause too great a loss of revenue: with their hair cut, their commercial value would plum-met. Thus they resort to their own wives. The women of the Carthaginian oligarchy sacrifice their hair without the slightest resistance; it is presumably worthwhile, considering the properties they possess in Carthage. Perhaps the money of prostitution also flows indirectly into their coffers. The women of the populace refuse. In his reading, Butor points out that this makes citizens of nineteenth-century Paris Carthaginians.[75]

This merciless principle of measuring in terms of cost and benefit knows no compassion. Through restless inventorization, it negates the figure of the human together with the structure of sympathy. Hamilcar does not know what compassion is. Even his *clementia* heeds the iron logic of cost-benefit calculation. Hamilcar does not see his fellow human being as his neighbor, let alone as a brother: to him, other people are just a means to an end. He perceives others not as human, but purely from the perspective of their usefulness to his needs, in their exploitability. The fact that he disfigures his serfs to inhuman degrees and makes them suffer torture, during which they beg for their death and not their lives in an appeal to his compassion, is of no interest to him. To grant mercy would be unprofitable:

They went through other corridors and other rooms, finally arriving at a door where, for greater security, a man was attached by the belly to a long chain sealed into the wall, a Roman custom recently introduced into Carthage. His beard and nails were abnormally overgrown, and he swayed to right and left with the continuous rhythm of a captive beast. As soon as he recognized Hamilcar he rushed towards him, crying: "Mercy, Eye of Baal! Have pity! Kill me! It is ten years since I saw the sun! In your father's name have mercy!" Hamilcar did not answer. (128)

The principle of profitability reduces the human to an artistic technique—taught at the slave school in Syracuse—of manipulating and disciplining bare life. Modernity has become even more cynical than antiquity in this process of exploitation; less brutal on the surface, it puts to use, in increasing refinement, the "humane," the "heart"—the capacity for love. Catherine Leroux in *Madame Bovary* and Félicité with her simple heart exemplify this.

Hamilcar is for Flaubert the embodiment of the principle of the reduction to bare life for the sake of profit maximization. His brutality stems from always having a calculating, rational eye on his advantage and profit. Human labor power, sexuality, and even death—the only way out of exploitation—are used in a rational way to increase gains. Hamilcar's slave master lacks the talent for the art of optimal exploitation. He buys the wrong slaves, locks them up, keeping men and women apart, so that they are unable to produce offspring and increase their owner's revenue. He wears them out, so that they are too exhausted to work, and pointlessly mutilates them. Hamilcar's inspection of his possessions is a crash course in the management of human resources: "He was amazed at the small number of children. 'Each year, Giddenem, the household must have children born! You will leave their huts open every night so that they can mix freely'" (133). Rendered worthless, the slaves are curtly and cheaply disposed of. A Samnite with a broken leg—a punishment inflicted by Giddenem, the slave master—"tottering like a wounded heron" (133), is strangled without further ado in the dung heap. The right to death is disclaimed for those who are serfs to another; they are condemned to live out their lives as mere things. Exceptions to this rule do not occur out of a recognition of suffering or heroism—after all, the death wish is the only human expression remaining to these slaves, since it resists their absolute exploitation, a salvaging of their humanity—but are simply the result of a slightly more complicated cost-benefit analysis: "'Ah! you want to die?' said the Suffete scornfully. And the slave boldly answered: 'Yes!' Then, heedless of the example or the financial loss, Hamilcar said to the servants: 'Take him away!'" (133). Flaubert consistently highlights how this subjugation robs them of all dignity and degrades them to a mere animal-like existence. Half-starved, his slaves forget all decorum. Their denudation comes to the fore against the background of the ceremonialism of refined clothes and the dominators' exquisite gestures:

Men were pushing with chest and arms, while others pulled, in harness. The bridle rubbing round their armpits had formed purulent scabs such as one sees on a donkey's withers, and the loose black rag that hardly covered their loins hung down at the end, beating against their calves like a long tail. Their eyes were bloodshot, their ankle fetters clattered, their chests all drew breath in unison. Round their mouths, fixed by two bronze chains, they wore a muzzle, to make it impossible for them to eat the flour, and their hands were encased in fingerless gloves to prevent them taking any.

At the master's entrance the wooden bars creaked still louder. The grain crunched as it was ground. Several men fell to their knees; the others, continuing, walked over them. . . . Hamilcar signed to him to undo the muzzles. Then all of them, with cries like ravenous beasts rushed upon the flour, and devoured it, burying their faces in the heaps. "You are wearing them out!" said the Suffete. . . . "It was hardly worth sending you to the slave school at Syracuse." (132–33)

Salammbô centers on what human beings are capable of doing to each other. The erasure of the human is the theme of the novel, giving short shrift to any kind of humanism. The violence they are subjected to subjects them. It merges with their flesh and blood; it becomes their very nature: nothing human remains of them. There is nothing noble about these victims; they are truly abject, worse than animals. Their sight borders on the intolerable. This is perhaps the crucial difference separating Flaubert from the romantics. In Sand or Hugo, the victims exude something sublime, moving, and often heroic. Flaubert's victims are utterly debased. They incarnate nothing but this denudation. Hamilcar stigmatizes his servants and slaves—like cattle—with the abusive sign of the coward, which he has burned into their foreheads. The corpses of the mercenaries not only display their wounds, making their bodies testaments to their history; their serfdom is equally tattooed onto their bodies:

The Mercenaries could be recognized by the tattoos on their hands: Antiochus's old soldiers carried a hawk; those who had served in Egypt, a baboon's head; service with the princes of Asia was shown by an axe, a pomegranate, a hammer; with the Greek city-states by the profile of a citadel or the name of an archon; and there were some to be seen whose arms were entirely covered with these multiple symbols, which mingled with their scars and fresh wounds. (196)

The bodies of the mercenaries, strewn with scars from defending Carthage, are compared to columns. Columns, like the column in the Place Vendôme in Paris or Hadrian's Column in Rome, are, however, memorials to battles. Since the mercenaries are nothing but flesh to him and not monuments immortalizing the sacrifice for his fatherland, Hamilcar will destroy them mercilessly.

The mercenaries only have their destructible and mortal bodies; by contrast, Hamilcar has possessions, which, as extensions of his body, allow him to live on in eternity. They are invested with divine attributes: "It [his wealth] was inaccessible, inexhaustible, infinite" (129). The secret threshold to self-transcendence is etched into his flesh: complicated marks on his arm encrypt the access to his possessions. Hamilcar is the finest example imaginable of an owner who projects his existence onto his possessions, attaching greater importance to them than to his life because possession stretches beyond the narrow limits of his temporal existence, outlasting his physical dissolution, thus functioning as the earthly and tangible embodiment of the immortal soul. In Hamilcar, Flaubert condenses the triumph of a capitalist patriarchy where man immortalizes himself through his possessions and passes on his name to his son. Because he believes he will attain divinity, Hamilcar makes fun of the god Baal; *his* empire, *his* name—and not that of some god—will become everlasting and limitless, passing from his sons to his sons' sons. The other is manipulated for the purposes of this male mission of self-realization; there is no room for an *other* in the sense of an irreducible counterpart. The price for one's own deification is the effacement of the figure of the human in the other, and, more radical still, the effacement of what embodies otherness in its purest form, that is, sexual difference. Lacking both faces and voice, Salammbô's and Hannibal's mothers, as well as Hamilcar's wife, remain disgracefully anonymous. Slaves, cattle with human faces; slaveholders, who profit from their slaves; and female bodies like Salammbô's, used to secure powerful alliances, are constantly reified. Because Hamilcar wants to marry her off to his advantage, he excludes Salammbô from services to the lower Tanit, that is, temple prostitution. The climax of the Carthaginian cost-benefit analysis—"Such a sacrifice should not be [in] vain [*inutile*]" (243)—is the holocaust of their own children to Moloch. The Carthaginians sacrifice their own children out of self-preservation. It is a successful, worthwhile sacrifice: the fertilizing, saving rain starts to drop with the charred corpses of the children still smoking.

Flaubert writes, not mainly against the historical novel, but against what one might call a Christian epic, against the productive inflection of the idea of sacrifice as summed up in Chateaubriand's *The Martyrs*, which serves as a countermodel to *Salammbô*. Christianity, or rather, a specific interpretation of Christianity, has, according to Flaubert, usurped and perverted Christ's loving sacrifice by inscribing it within a teleological narrative, where victory and redemption are transferred onto a triumphant history materializing in the here and now, misusing the story of the sacrifice to ground politics through theology. Christianity has battened onto the sacrifice on the cross, whose adoption has destroyed its dynamics of radical dispossession. With *Salammbô*, Flaubert inscribes himself into a history of ideas ranging from de Maistre's *Éclaircissement sur les sacrifices* to Chateaubriand's *The Martyrs*. The debate over sacrifice and redemption was arguably the nineteenth century's most significant, and it extended into the twentieth in the work of Bataille, Girard, and Agamben. *Salammbô* is a treatise against de Maistre's *Éclaircissement* and a reversal of the final scene of Chateaubriand's *The Martyrs*.[76]

De Maistre was crucial for Flaubert's project. The two central scenes of sacrifice in Carthage—the burning of the children sacrificed to Moloch and the tearing-out of Mâtho's heart—have elements going back to de Maistre. For Mâtho, Flaubert follows de Maistre's description of Incan sacrifice: "The sacrificing priest opened the chest of the victim and quickly tore out the still beating heart."[77] In Flaubert, this becomes: "With one blow he split Mâtho's chest, then tore out his heart, put it on the spoon, and Schahabarim, raising his arm, offered it to the sun" (282). The burning of the children takes up motifs of de Maistre's portrayal, which he in turn quoted from Caesar's *De bello Gallico*. "Some of them filled certain colossal statues of their gods with living men; they covered them with pliant branches and set them on fire; and thus the men perished in the flames."[78] In his letter to Sainte-Beuve, Flaubert characterized *Salammbô* as a counterproject to Chateaubriand's *Martyrs*.[79]

The Martyrs is a cosmic drama in which the pantheon of idolatrous gods spearheaded by Astarte, in tandem with the devil, battle against the archangels and heavenly hosts of the God of the Christians. It illustrates the struggle of idolatrous polytheism against the one, true God. The repulsiveness of idolatrous religions, and more specifically the Druidism ruling Gaul, is depicted through the practice of human sacrifice. Chateaubriand thereby gives political weight to the *translatio* school of thought, opposing a return to proper origins. Polytheism goes hand in hand with a specific type of government, namely, tyranny. The mission of *The Martyrs* consists in abolishing human sacrifice through the renewal of the Passion of Christ, which is to lead to the rehabilitation of the Roman Empire and the triumph of the one, true God over polytheism. Through his triumph, the true God avenges himself—resembling the jealous, vengeful God of the Old Testament to an astonishing degree—against those who have inflicted suffering on innocent martyrs. This God also interprets martyrdom as a true human sacrifice: "The victim [*l'hostie*] was accepted: the last drop of the blood of the just was about to cause that religion to triumph, which was to change the face of the earth."[80] The word *hostie*, the host, not only refers to the transubstantiated body of Christ, but also to the stranger, the prisoner, the guest who, as derived from de Maistre, is the chosen victim, the sacrifice.[81] Thus, not only the sacrifice of Christ, but also the sacrifice of *The Martyrs* as human victims fulfills the figure of the Old Testament in which the Jews did not offer human sacrifices but only animal sacrifices, as opposed to the idolatrous peoples surrounding them.

The "blood wedding" through martyrdom of Eudore and his bride, Chateaubriand observes, "recalled to mind one of the peace-offerings of ancient days, when the sons of Aaron sacrificed to the God of Israel a dove and a young bullock."[82] No sooner do both martyrs receive the blessing of martyrdom than a light in the form of a cross appears in the sky, thunder starts rolling over the eternal city, and "a voice, like that which was formerly heard in Jerusalem, exclaimed: 'The gods are departing!'"[83] With respect to this final victory, Chateaubriand inserts a truly Eusebian moment, announcing the need, in the present tense, of an empire for the sake of salvation:

God thunders from the height of heaven; the standard of the cross is borne aloft; Constantine strikes; Maxentius [the new tyrant who wants to arrogate all powers to himself] is thrown into the Tiber. The conqueror enters the queen city of the world. . . . The warlike eagle of Romulus is decorated with the pacific cross. On the tomb of the young martyrs, Constantine receives the crown of Augustus, and on this same tomb he proclaims the Christian religion the religion of the empire.[84]

This *gloria passionis* is without doubt the story of a useful and successful—and one is tempted to add, profitable—sacrifice, which seals the victory of the one God over the idolatrous powers of darkness, heralding the worldwide triumph of the Cross. Everything—even the emperor of Rome and most powerful man on earth—bends to the will of Christ in the end. "Mission accomplished" could be written underneath the last lines of *The Martyrs*. But what mission, exactly? It would seem that it concerns the sealing of a difference. Yet the difference between the two is lost: namely, the difference between the pagan gods who require human sacrifice and who recompense those who do the sacrificing, and this God who accepts human sacrifice as the precondition for the triumph of Christianity. Pagan gods and Christian God fatally resemble one another. Secretly, Chateaubriand has mutated the God of the Christians into a pagan god who demands human sacrifice. Suffering leads to triumph and, on that account, it is as justified as it is meaningful.

De Maistre captures the close connection between Christianity and paganism in a different—and undoubtedly more fascinating—manner. According to him, the practice of human sacrifice was no absurd, childish outgrowth of superstition whose eradication required only a tiny bit of logic, as Voltaire claimed. Instead, it should be seen as an anthropological constant. People, de Maistre claims, have always made expiatory sacrifices to gods whom they believed to have angered. The model of sacrifice thereby follows the logic of *contrapasso*: having become guilty through the flesh, through the blood, through the entrails—which becomes shorthand for sexuality in de Maistre—one can only be washed of one's sins by blood, through a kind of baptism in blood. The logic of sacrifice heeds the logic of substitution: instead of the perpetrator, an innocent, an animal, is sacrificed, having taken on all the sins of the transgressor to become the proverbial scapegoat. According to de Maistre, the perversion of this sacrificial thought arose out of the substitution of human sacrifice for animal sacrifice and its universal implementation. Christianity put an end to this praxis through a sacrifice that annulled sacrificial logic by fulfilling it. Christ redeemed us from Satan with his blood. Since the flesh led to our fall from grace, God had to become flesh himself:

The flesh having separated man from heaven, God took on flesh to unite himself to man by what had separated him from it; but this was still too little for an immense goodness attacking an immense degradation. This flesh divinised and perpetually sacrificed is presented to man under the exterior form of his privileged nourishment.[85]

By the Word becoming flesh, and by its incorporation during Communion in the form of bread instead of sacrificial victims, mankind—according to de Maistre's curiously literal logic—is purified of its stained insides, the locus of lust. Thus, this last sacrifice, which brought the practice of human sacrifice to an end, shows what humanity has always believed: "its radical degradation, the substitution of the merits of the innocent paying for the guilty and SALVATION BY BLOOD."[86] De Maistre's sacrificial logic obeys the primacy of the economic to an almost absurd degree. Against this theory of an economic, meaningful sacrifice, Flaubert posits a senseless, indeed absurd, sacrifice. In this sign, in the sign of the cross, nothing will ever be conquered, but everything is always catastrophically lost. That's why it is the only thing worth erecting a monument to. Nevertheless, Flaubert does not memorialize Christ's sacrifice in *Salammbô*. He affirms it by a radical desublimation. Through the art of his words, Christ's sufferings are incarnated anew in the most terrible way. It is precisely this that makes reading the novel so unbearable.

The Perversion of Kenosis:
The Carthaginians and Their Sacrifices

Let us begin with the *figura* of Christ's sacrificial death, Isaac. Sainte-Beuve sees in the figure of Hamilcar, the father of Hannibal, an inverted Abraham. In contrast to Abraham, Hamilcar is a father rebelling against the imposed sacrifice of his son.[87] Who is Abraham? The father who is willing to kill his only son as a burnt offering upon the pile of wood he had the boy collect himself for the designated sacrifice, who is willing to slaughter him by his own hand for the sake of his God. Why Abraham, in defiance of the divine prophecy—"in Isaac shall thy seed be called" (Gen. 21:12)—was willing to go through with it was something Saint Paul also asked himself. Abraham staunchly believed, at least following Augustine's explanation interpreting Paul, in the resurrection: "'God was able to raise him up, even from the dead.' The apostle [Paul] then adds, 'From whence also he received him in a figure.' But a figure of whom, if not of Him of Whom the apostle says, 'He spared not His own Son, but delivered him up for us all'?"[88] The burnt offering of Isaac, for whom, thank God, a ram trapped in thorns is substituted, is thus a prefiguration of the sacrifice fulfilled by Christ, the Lamb of God, wearing a crown of thorns, in the New Testament. Decisive for the sacrificial dynamics is the substitution of a human sacrifice with an animal sacrifice; both human and animal sacrifice are fulfilled and simultaneously sublated by the self-sacrifice of the human son of God.

The semantic intersection of the Isaac and Hannibal episodes stands out. A sacrificing father, an only son, a burnt offering, the replacement of one sacrifice through fire by another: these elements are evident in both stories. Both episodes, the one in the Bible as well as Flaubert's text, are determined by a dynamics of substitution of what is to be sacrificed; the first time the son is replaced by an animal, a *figura Christi*, while the second time a slave child, the least among Christ's brothers, takes the place of the son, the victim to be. As with Isaac, the hope of the father for an empire and for the immortality of his name lies in the child, in this case, Hamilcar's son, Hannibal. In contrast to Hannibal's empire, which is unambiguously an empire of this world, Isaac does not announce an earthly kingdom. Thus, the biblical dynamics is reversed: Hamilcar and Hannibal are antitypes of Abraham and Isaac, and ultimately also of Christ. Flaubert works out the contrapuntal parallel between Christ and Hannibal via these moments: both boys are represented as single-parent children. A motherless child, Hannibal is entirely the child of his father, who also acts like his mother: "Like a mother finding her lost firstborn, he flung himself on his son; he clasped him to his breast, he laughed and wept at once, called him by the sweetest names, covered him with kisses" (235). However, Christ is the son of a most prominent mother—iconographically, he is *the* mother's son par excellence. Both Hannibal and Jesus are the only children to escape massacres: only Christ eludes the murder of children in Bethlehem, while only Hannibal escapes the sacrificing of the city's aristocratic children. Both child massacres serve as a means of preserving ruling powers. In the offspring of the House of David, Herod fears rivalry to his rule; Carthage feels threatened with ruin and believes it can only stave this off by sacrificing the children of the ruling class. Both Christ and Hannibal are chosen, as a countermove to this escape, to become expiatory sacrifices on a world-historical scale. Christ expiates the sins of the world; through his war, Hannibal gives the Romans the chance—at least from a Vergilian vantage point—to expiate Aeneas's amorous betrayal of Carthage's founder, Dido, by shedding their blood in this cruel war. In Christ, the promise of a worldly empire finds no fulfillment; in Hannibal, the destruction of an earthly empire is realized. In fulfilling the supplication of the city's founder Dido, spilling the Romans' blood to expiate Aeneas's betrayal of love, Hannibal destroys not only his own life but also his own empire, Carthage. Hannibal's war with Rome was already predicted to him as a child: he catches an eagle, the symbol of victorious Rome, which is imposed with every Roman standard upon the world. He crushes it against his chest and, lacerated by the scratching of the beast's beak, his blood mixes with that of the eagle. Hamilcar is willing to do everything to spare his son, destined for this decisive battle. So as not to be offered to Moloch, the boy is hidden from his priests inside his father's house. He enters his father's home for the first time "covered in a goat-hair cloak" (221), calling to mind the animal that took Isaac's place. Hamilcar sees in his son, like Abraham in Isaac, the guarantee of the everlastingness of his name. But whereas Abraham would become the founder of a kingdom not of this world (John 18:36) that would find fulfillment through Christ, Hamilcar sees his name as the perpetuation, through his son's guidance, of a worldly empire.

Whereas Christ fulfills a promise of love, Hannibal will avenge Dido, whose love was cheated and betrayed by Aeneas. Through him, Dido's entreaty will be answered: he will engulf the Romans in blood. Hannibal takes revenge for Aeneas's betrayal of love, and makes the Romans pay. Hamilcar dreams of the immortalization of the Barca name, who were originally enemies of Carthage and Dido: "Aren't you concerned about peoples who share these lands you have settled? / We are surrounded: . . . /

South lies a region of desert and thirst and of savage Barcaean / Nomads,"
Dido's sister, Anna, says in the *Aeneid*.[89] It is a Barca, though, his son, who
will make the curse of the city's founder against the Romans come true.
Jupiter's promise of a boundless, everlasting empire for Aeneas and his
progeny cannot be changed by Dido; she can only hurt him by going after
his army (4.614–15). As far as Aeneas is concerned, Dido's curse already
comes true in the *Aeneid*; he himself will never see the empire he founds.
It will equally come true with respect to the future of both cities, Rome
and Carthage. However, the price for this fulfillment is the destruction of
Carthage, which ruins itself quite literally through the fulfillment of the
ruinous wish by the ruined Dido:

This is my prayer; these final words I express with my life-blood:
Tyrians, drive with relentless hate against his stock and every
Future brood, and dispatch them as ritual gifts to my ashes.
No love must ever exist between our two peoples, no treaties.
Rise from my bones, my avenger—and there *will be* an
avenger!—
So you can hound these Dardan settlers with hot fire and cold steel,
Now, or some day in the future, whenever that strength coalesces.
Menace of coast against coast and of waters hurled against waters,
Arms against arms, I invoke. Let them fight, they themselves and
their grandsons!

(4.621–29)

From a Roman perspective, Carthage fulfills its historical destiny with the
fulfillment of Dido's mission: it will come to ruin. This ruinous historical
mission befalling Hannibal—as one must suppose—is read by the sacrificing
high priest in his prophesying stones, allowing the deceit to take place tacitly:

When the fourteenth child was brought up everyone could see him [Hamilcar]
make a great gesture of horror. . . . On the other side of the statue the High Priest
remained as immobile as he. Bowing his head with its Assyrian mitre, he looked
at the gold plate on his breast covered with fateful stones, to which the reflection
of the flames imparted irridescent gleams. He paled in dismay. Hamilcar bent his
head. (*Salammbô*, 240)

What is protected by Hannibal's survival is not—as his father had hoped—
eternity, but the final destruction of an empire; his name will become the
everlasting testament to and remembrance of this destruction.[90]

When the priests are standing in front of the door to take the child to the burnt offering, Hamilcar ties up and gags his son, not in order to sacrifice him, but to hide him: "With one hand he seized Hannibal, tore off with the other the edging of a garment lying about, bound his feet, his hands, stuffed the end into his mouth as a gag and hid him under the oxhide bed, under a wide drapery hanging down to the floor" (232). The oxhide hiding Hannibal prefigures the later sacrifice of the children in the holocaust, about whom it is said that they are not people but oxen (241).

In spite of his perceptive comparison between Abraham and Hamilcar, Sainte-Beuve overlooks the most abyssal aspect of the scene. Not an animal, but the least of his brothers is substituted for the destined fire victim, Hannibal, the only son: "Inasmuch as ye did it not to one of the least of these, ye did it not to me" (Matt. 25:45). In the slave child, Christ is sacrificed once more. Hamilcar does not recognize the slaves and this child as his brothers: "He had never thought—so vast was the gulf separating the two of them—that they might have anything in common" (233). In *Salammbô*, through the animalization of man, Flaubert persistently illustrates the figure of the "least of my brothers": "He was a poor child, both thin and puffy; his skin looked as grey as the filthy rag hanging round his waist; his head was sunk on to his shoulders, and with the back of his hand he rubbed his fly-infested eyes" (232).

The son to be sacrificed is the abject child of an equally abject wretch living in the house: "an abject-looking man, one of the wretches who lived as best he could in the household" (233). The flies in the eyes of the child immediately make one think of an animal. They are also associated with the crucified lions, with the mercenaries scaring away the flies from their eyes with stones. The misery of the slave child does not move Hamilcar to compassion. He overcomes his outrage and disgust for the sake of his son and travesties the slave child, hurriedly adorning him with the insignia of rule and wealth. The child has no clue what is happening to him. He smiles happily, almost becoming a normal child: "The child smiled, dazzled by such splendour, and growing bolder he was even beginning to clap his hands and jump about when Hamilcar led him off" (233). The miserable father, who, at the risk of his own life, revolts out of love for his son, is symbolically slaughtered like an animal by Hamilcar: "He answered with a look colder and heavier than an executioner's axe; the slave, fainting, fell to the dust at his feet" (233). Hamilcar robs the slave father of his be-all and end-all: his son. If he spares the father, it is not from a sense of justice or even compassion, but out of selfishness: superstitious as he is, Hamilcar fears that killing the slave father might turn fate against his own son. The emaciated man is fobbed off with a "sacrificial meal," the anticipated remains of the holocaust, the holocaust of his child: a piece of billy goat, of scapegoat, is put in front of him. His hunger pangs are so sharp that he forgets everything and stays behind *repu*, satiated, like an animal. The thing that makes him human are the tears he sheds for his consumed "child," the sacrificial animal for whose death he obtains food: "his tears fell into the dishes" (234). These tears of desolation counter the triumphal tears of joy shed by Hamilcar for the salvation of his son.

Augustine makes Abraham the founder of the City of God and opposes him explicitly to Rome—the earthly counterpart to the Heavenly City. Hannibal is also contrasted with Rome, but in the name of an empire of this world. As the founder of Babylon, one of the empires of this world, Augustine writes, Hannibal is a "hunter against the Lord" (*De civitate Dei* 16.4.703), standing in for the hunter Nimrod. Rome is the successor of Babylon, the model of the City of Man (ibid., 2.280). The iconography of the blessing child marks Hannibal once again as the antitype of Christ: "He talked as he dreamed, back resting against a scarlet cushion; his head fell back a little, and his small arm, thrust out from his body, remained quite straight in an imperious attitude" (*Salammbô*, 234–35). Hannibal, wearing in the scarlet the color of dominion, blesses an empire of this world; the infant Jesus blesses with this very same imperial gesture, but an empire that is not of this world. In Flaubert, Rome and Carthage fuse into one city: the new Babel. The divisiveness of the City of Man appears in the absolute, mutual hatred mutually connecting its inhabitants. They are united in strife.

At the close of the novel Hamilcar once again brings together empire and sacrifice in inverted Christological terms; while the empire of Christ, not of this world, is founded by his death on the cross, the Suffete sees cross and empire as opposites. Hamilcar has either to submit to a shameful death on the cross, fit only for slaves, or to rule an empire without limit and without end, to borrow a phrase from Vergil. He will rule in the name of his dynasty, the Barca: "He had, though, never felt such anxiety; if he succumbed it meant the destruction of the Republic and he would perish on a cross; if, on the other hand, he won, by way of the

Pyrenees, Gaul, and the Alps he would reach Italy and the Barca's empire would be eternal" (268–69).

The irony of history of course lies in the fact that his son will indeed set out "by way of the Pyrenees, Gaul and the Alps." However, while Hannibal does, in the sense of arriving, "gain Italy" (*gagner l'Italie*; French ed., 362), he will not found an everlasting empire but definitively lose an empire, Carthage, which will disappear from the face of the earth. Of the name of the Barca nothing will remain. Nothing at all will come of it—except Flaubert's novel, which illustrates the Christian promise *ex negativo* through Hamilcar and Hannibal, trapped in the vanity of all things earthly.

The reversal analyzed by Sainte-Beuve does not primarily concern the reversal of the figure of Abraham in Hamilcar; more crucial is the reversal of the logic of substitution itself. As a result, the relation between *figura* and *implementum*, between promise and fulfillment, is turned upside down. On a purely formal level, the substituted, the sacrificed slave child, becomes the equivalent of the ram as *figura Christi*. In him, as in the sacrificial ram, the sublation of the logic of human sacrifice should thus be announced. However, the slave child is a figure of Christ only in a completely negative sense. He is just another victim in an endless chain of sacrifices. Christ's suffering does not redeem the sins of the world. Flaubert declares the salvational promise even before it is uttered as null and void. The sacrificed child illustrates that Christ's Passion is nothing but just one more suffering, pure and simple, to the same bitter end, to death. In this being unto death, Christ is our brother. Using identical word material and plot parallels, Flaubert inscribes his "reversed Abraham" into that scene of the Old Testament that foreshadows the promise of the New—death and resurrection through the sacrificing of the only son. He thereby not only inverts Abraham through the figure of Hamilcar, but more crucially reverses the promise of salvation.

In parallel, the children offered to Baal as food are a perversion of the Eucharist. The children take the place of sacrificial animals: the priests throwing them into Moloch's glowing furnace insist that they are not people, but oxen. Flaubert thus turns the sublimated structure of the Christian sacrificial logic on its head. In the story of Isaac and Abraham, it is an animal, a ram, that takes the place of the child. Christ as the Lamb of God, as a sacrificial lamb, is not sacrificed to God; rather, through him God sacrifices himself for our sake. God—according to the Christian logic—sublates the human and animal sacrifice once offered to the gods, while He sacrifices himself through his son, his divinity in a sacrificial human form. Human nature is not denied in this sacrifice, but instead comes to the fore all the more: *ecce homo*. The children sacrificed to Moloch by their parents are reduced to meat, to the meat of sacrificial animals. Only through such a denial of humanity can this sacrifice go on. The barbarians, no strangers to violence, are left "aghast with horror" (242) at the sight of this spectacle. As Flaubert's novel seldom registers sympathetic reactions, they become especially significant. There are two such reactions to suffering in *Salammbô*, and both times they come from the mercenaries who for a short moment become stand-ins for the reader. The voice of humanity in *Salammbô* belongs to the barbarians. It ties together the scene of the crucified lions, which leaves the mercenaries speechless at such cruelty, with the scene of the burning of the children. Both scenes revolve around the central sacrificial chiasmus between man and animal. The body politic of Carthage is strictly hierarchical and utterly split against itself. This is a society where it is every man for himself and God against all. The social fabric is torn apart by merciless exploitation of the weaker for the sake of the iron logic of self-interest. The result is the animalization of humanity, expressed in a disavowal, but fully realized in the children who are thrown to Moloch: "These are not men, but oxen!" (241). It is at this very moment that the body politic of Carthage is united in a delirium of sex and murder. The scene thereby highlights *ex negativo* the loving Eucharist and sober headiness of the united body of the Church. "If the author wanted to show at work one of those infamous, infernal, devastating religions that do not care in the least about human lives, and of which Christ has rid the world, he has succeeded," Sainte-Beuve writes.[91] But contrary to what Sainte-Beuve believed, Flaubert does not show a religion overcome by Christianity. He depicts instead the terror of this Carthaginian religion, sub specie aeternitatis, as it were, through Christian figures and their recasting. By erasing the Christian figure, the unholy, eternal truth of the practice of sacrifice is revealed. But it is only in the light of Christ's Passion that the passion of the victims gains its full pathos. Their sacrifice is illuminated by the sacrifice on the cross. Only in the light of the promise of a kingdom not of this world is the irredeemable depravity of this world's empires decipherable.

A Kenosis of Kenosis:
The Mercenaries' Eucharist and Sacrifice of Love

The crosses in *Salammbô* are impossible to ignore. Irrespective of any historical accuracy—these crucifixions occur around 250 BCE—they have been read as a comment on Christianity. Karl Heinz Bohrer has read the vast number of crucifixions as an inflation, as a devaluation and empty-ing of the Christian symbol. Indeed, crucifixions are omnipresent: lions die on the cross, the leaders of the mercenaries as well as the Carthaginian councilmen end up on the cross, each facing the other—one could almost say—in harmonious unison in neat rows of ten on the hills surrounding the town, making the scene a true Calvary. In the place of devotion, *reli-gio*, empathy, identification, and sincere compassion, an aestheticization of suffering comes to the fore—this is the argument: instead of grief, pain, and pathos, distance and a detached, fascinating superficiality manifest themselves.[92] It seems to me that the aesthetic aloofness that is attributed to Flaubert again and again is nothing but a trope giving expression to a defense against too much empathy through *passio*. Surreptitiously, the pa-thos of *passio* is mobilized through *impassibilité*. This means that empathy is all the more sorrowful, since it concerns a *passio* beyond the purvey of salvation.

The parallel between the mercenary uprising and the Crucifixion of Jesus is already established through the first murder of the mercenaries at the hand of the Carthaginians. The replay of the Passion begins with the ordeal of the mercenaries. The Last Supper is literalized in the cannibal scene. It continues with the crucifixion—modeled after that of Christ—of the ten diplomats at the site of skulls surrounding the city, a true Golgotha, to be followed by the stations of Mâtho's way of the cross throughout Car-thage, only to end in a scene invoking the Sacred Heart. This whole pro-cess restages Christ's suffering: the crucifixion of the ten ambassadors on the mount of skulls, the hillside surrounding the city, and the novel's end-ing with Mâtho's death is a displacement and condensation of the Passion.

Throughout, the figure of kenosis can be observed in the literaliza-tion of the Passion, which is attained through incarnation, a fundamen-tal becoming-flesh—or, worse, becoming meat. The moment of abjection is decisive in this regard; it appears, for example, in the violation by the Carthaginians of the corpses of the Balearic mercenaries, which are cut up like cattle and "hung up in bits in butchers' shops" (49). The Balearic troops, who did not get out of Carthage in time, are driven against an iron gate in the city wall and crushed to death by the Carthaginians. The latter act out of revenge for the destruction wrought during the banquet: The only survivor, Zarxas, who escaped the massacre half mad, reports: "'Yes killed, all of them, all! Crushed like grapes! The fine young men! The slingers! My companions and yours!' They made him drink some wine, and he wept" (48). Crushed grapes, blood, and wine form the signifiers of his story. The symbol of Christ is the vine, often twining around the wood of the cross. Christ spills his blood, which, like pressed grapes, turns into wine; his blood is drunk in the form of wine. Flaubert's obsession with the signifying material of the Eucharist appears in the subsequent, vampiric act of Zarxas, who literalizes and subverts the figures of the Eucharist in a gruesome way:

Zarxas ran up, knocked him down and plunged a dagger into his throat; pulling it out, he flung himself upon the wound—and with his mouth glued to it, with grunts of joy and spasms which shook him from head to foot, he pumped out the blood with all his might; then he quietly sat down on the corpse, lifted up his face and threw back his head to breathe more freely, like a deer which has just drunk from a stream . . . ; he called on his dead brothers and invited them to a feast; then he dropped his hands in his lap, slowly lowered his head and wept. (161–62)

Instead of blood transformed into wine, Zarxas drinks the blood of a victim who did not sacrifice himself, but whom Zarxas killed singlehandedly; he does it for the memory of his dead, butchered brothers. However, this does not make them come alive, not in the least. Like the deer thirsting after the spring, so does he thirst for the blood of more victims. This very same thirst will take possession of Saint Julian in the *Three Tales*. This thirst for blood replaces the soul's thirst for the enlivening Word of God. The events of the war are narrated through the degrading figures of Crucifixion and the Eucharist. Quite literally, the lives of the mercenaries are marked by the Cross from the very outset. According to Spendius, their lives are stamped by the "the constant threat of the cross" (31). The mercenaries embark on their Carthaginian enterprise under the sign of the Cross when passing by the crucified lions. The relation between the barbarians and the lions also illustrates this development. After all, Christ is, as Revelation tells us—referring back to the Old Testament—the Lion of Judah: "And one of the elders saith unto me, Weep not: behold, the Lion of the tribe of Juda, the Root of David, hath prevailed to open the book, and to loose the seven seals thereof" (Rev. 5:5).[93] The lion is thus a metaphor for Christ. Furthermore, the lion is the king of beasts, and Christ on the cross is ridiculed as the king of the Jews. The unbelievable cruelty of the Carthaginians, which is a closed book to the barbarians, becomes manifest for the first time when they are crucifying the lions. Flaubert, in his description, relies in detail upon the iconography of the Crucifixion. The anatomically exact description of the lion's body conjures up the image of the crucified body of Christ before the eye of the reader:

It was a lion, its limbs fastened to a cross like a criminal. Its huge muzzle drooped on to its chest, and its two forepaws, half concealed under its luxuriant mane, were widely separated like the wings of a bird. Its ribs stuck out, one by one, beneath the taut skin; its hind legs, nailed one on top of the other, rose a little; and black blood, flowing through the hair. . . . The soldiers stood round amusing themselves; they called it consul and Roman citizen and threw stones at its eyes to drive away the flies. (38)

As the Jews mocked Jesus, nailing him to the cross as INRI, king of the Jews, so the mercenaries now mock the lion as consul and Roman citizen—of course, had Christ been either consul or citizen, he would never have been crucified. Cross and power, empire and death are intertwined. The skillfully elaborated difference between the barbarian and the civilized is inverted from the beginning and turned against the Carthaginians. Through the infinite refinement of their cruelty they appear as the true barbarians. The barbarians themselves are horrified at the viciousness of the Carthaginians: "'What sort of people are these,' they thought, 'who amuse themselves by crucifying lions!'" (ibid.). Mâtho, the leader of the mercenaries, is associated with lions and death early on: "Mâtho, naked as a corpse, was lying prone on a lion skin, his face in his hands" (41).

Let us now skip to the end without working out further the subtext of sacrifice and Eucharist in every single scene. Before Mâtho is caught like a wild animal, "his arms and legs in a cross" (273), tied to an elephant, two mounts of Golgotha rise over Carthage. On the one mount hang the leaders of the mercenaries, on the other the elders of the council of Carthage. "But Hamilcar wanted first to show the Mercenaries that he would punish them like slaves. He had the ten ambassadors crucified, side by side, on a hillock facing the town" (263). On the other side "the thirty corpses of the elders appeared right on top, in the sky" (265). If the mercenaries, in a pointed inversion of the Christian cult of love, see themselves as "the pontiffs of universal vengeance" (268),[94] by the end of the story they will become figures of Christ. In the last conversation between Spendius and the Gaul Autharitus, echoing the words exchanged between Christ and the two criminals crucified by his side, Autharitus acknowledges the crucified lions as their brothers: "'They were our brothers!' replied the Gaul as he died" (265). The crucified lions thus become the *figura* of the crucified mercenaries, and consequently also *figura Christi*. But the message they preach is different from the promise on the cross. Their reward will not be "today shalt thou be with me in paradise" (Luke 23:43) as Christ proclaims but will be nothing but the recognition of brotherhood in suffering. The cross does not overcome death nor does it lead to eternal life but instead leads to an everlasting deliverance from slavery through death: "certain as he [Spendius] was of an almost immediate and eternal liberation" (265).

The crucifixion scenes and Mâtho's way of the cross form a diptych. Taken together, the scenes reiterate all the events of the Passion. The tearing apart of Mâtho's body, his complete diremption, in which all Carthaginians take part, establishes Carthage as a united body politic. Mâtho's suffering ends under the sign of the Sacred Heart. Already from the beginning, his sacrificial body experienced the religious reverence that befell the body of Christ only after his sacrifice on the cross: "This victim's body was something special for them, endowed with an almost religious splendor" (279). He is close to Christ in that he undergoes his martyrdom for the sake of all the mercenaries. Mâtho ceremonially goes through the stations of the cross of the Lord in full. Like Christ, he breaks down several times and always takes up his path again, only to be subjected to new torments: "he slowly collapsed on the pavement. . . . Six paces further and he fell a third, a fourth time again; and fresh torture brought him up each time" (280–81). Finally, just as Jesus reveals his own heart in contemporary Sacred Heart iconography, Mâtho's heart is exposed:

A man rushed to the corpse. . . . With one blow he split Mâtho's chest, then tore out his heart, put it on the spoon, and Schahabarim, raising his arm, offered it to the sun. The sun was going down behind the waves; its rays like long arrows struck the crimson heart. The great star went down into the sea as the beating lessened; at the last palpitation it disappeared. (282)

Like the heart of Jesus, Mâtho's heart testifies to his love unto death.[95] Just as Mâtho's way of the cross evokes the suffering of Christ, this description evokes the Sacred Heart. The priest who holds Mâtho's heart up to the sun is garbed like a Catholic priest on Good Friday. Flaubert condenses the two discourses surrounding the discussion of the cult of the Sacred Heart in nineteenth-century France: anatomical descriptions of the heart intersect with religious-mystic evocations of a love cult. The anatomy of Mâtho's flayed body calls to mind the "flayed man" of medical illustrations. In the broaching of a live body, we encounter the horrifying wish of all anatomy: to be able to dissect a living body, to unearth the origin of life—the beating of the heart—not in the dead, but in the still living flesh. Zola boasted that, unlike the anatomist, the novelist can dissect living people; he can "cut to the quick" (*trancher sur le vif*). At the same time, cutting open a corpse to find a beating heart is every anatomist's worst nightmare. Iconographically, the Sacred Heart appears in the popular religious art of Flaubert's era in the exact same way Mâtho's heart appears; that is, surrounded by a golden nimbus: "its rays like long arrows struck the crimson heart" (282). Indeed, what occurs in this scene is exactly what the critics of the cult of the Sacred Heart always emphasized: it is a carnalization of a spiritual bond. According to the *Dictionnaire de théologie catholique*, which appeared a little after *Salammbô*, Jesus openheartedly points to his own heart as a sign of his love; he has bled to death to give life.[96] Mâtho's Passion does not lead to life but death. This is stressed with the setting sun. When Salammbô, the embodiment of the Carthaginian republic, dies, the republic goes down in an orgiastic ecstasy. Like the crosses of the mercenaries, the Sacred Heart is also the sign of the irredeemable. In the ruins of Carthage, the future of all empires of this world is revealed. It is a future that Flaubert might also have predicted for the French Second Empire: after all, Paris would seek to expiate the crimes of the Commune by erecting the Sacré-Cœur Basilica in Montmartre (begun in 1875, consecrated 1919). In Carthage, we have ruins upon ruins lined with crosses of vengeance. The corpses are devoured by vultures and left to rot. The hope for a kingdom not of this world, promised by Christ, never materializes.

Flaubert's extensive portrayal of the wounded and mutilated, but above all of putrefying bodies, is perhaps so intolerable because Flaubert paints these scenes so vividly, inscribing this graphic, glaring disarticulation of the body with such horrific irony against the promise of the resurrection of the flesh. The pity one feels for these indiscriminately and mercilessly butchered and butchering creatures in this total war, whose fraternal link with wild animals comes to the fore in that they are hunted like wild animals, while also hunting like wild animals, is only intelligible against the backdrop of the Christian Passion. And it is all the more heartrending since the hope of salvation appears, only to be extinguished in the very same moment. Only the mercenaries, and maybe the slaves and the poor, possess the innocence of wild animals. By contrast, the ruling Carthaginians in their shrewd cruelty are beyond all innocence. The body of Hanno, the allegorical figure of the Carthaginian state, is so putrefied that it simply cannot be crucified. It falls apart.

Nevertheless, Flaubert was right when pointing out to Sainte-Beuve that he had handled humanity more gently in *Salammbô* than in *Madame Bovary*. While the East preserved a great deal of innocence in its brutality, virtually all of this innocence has been lost in the hypocritical West. In the East—the land of the rising sun—everything had already come to an end even before the beginning of the West—the land of the setting sun. The truth of all history is the selfishness that always leads to fratricide: it is the ruinous foundation of every empire of this world. The novel erases the only hope for a different history: the cross. Sainte-Beuve, who believed in humanity, in reason, in culture, civilization, and constant progress, was deeply antipathetic to all of this. History, however, bore out not Sainte-Beuve, but Flaubert; the twentieth century turned out more horrifying than Flaubert could ever have imagined.

Venus and Mars

Vita femina. . . . But perhaps that is the strongest magic of life: it is covered by a veil of beautiful possibilities, woven with threads of gold—promising, resisting, bashful, mocking, compassionate and seductive. Yes, life is a woman!

Friedrich Nietzsche, *The Gay Science*

In Flaubert's novel there is a story unsubstantiated by any source detailing the mercenary revolt: the love story between Mâtho, the leader of the mercenaries, and Salammbô, the daughter of Hamilcar.[97] This love story is pure and simply Flaubert's own invention. Flaubert weaves a host of intertexts into the novel's essential quid pro quo between love and war. In this composition, the political dimension of the connection between love and destruction, rescue or founding of an empire is central. It is dominant in all intertexts relevant to *Salammbô*: the abduction of Helen leads to the destruction of Troy; through her seductive beauty, Judith succeeds in reaching the tent of Holofernes, decapitates him, and thereby saves her kingdom from destruction by his hand; Iphigenia is willing to sacrifice herself to Diana in order to save her fatherland; the bloody wedding of the lovers Cymodocée and Eudore in Chateaubriand's *The Martyrs* becomes the basis for the Catholicism of the Roman Empire. This political dimension of love is most poignantly—and most disastrously—illustrated in Vergil's *Aeneid*. Its main protagonist is Dido, the *genius loci* of Carthage.

Through the diacritics of the typeface, foremost in Flaubert's mind, Salammbô and Mâtho are interconnected. The *o* and *a*, each marked by a circumflex, refer to the end and beginning of the Greek alphabet, the all-embracing order of letters, and with it the condition of possibility of representation. Christ is the *alpha* and *omega*. The Marian antiphon, in which the all-embracing perfection of the heavenly is contained in the first and last letter of the alphabet, resonates in the names of both, where *â* and *ô* are the decisive vowels. The novel begins with the promise of a wedding between Salammbô and Mâtho, and ends in their blood wedding. At the beginning, Mâtho falls in love with Salammbô, and she pours him wine, an act that the mercenaries gathered around them interpret as foreshadowing a wedding. This love is triangulated: Narr'Havas, Salammbô's designated bridegroom, first betrays the Carthaginians to become an ally of the mercenaries. In a renewed betrayal, he later turns against them with Hamilcar. As a reward he acquires Salammbô, already deflowered by Mâtho, as his bride: deception for betrayal. Narr'Havas already tried to kill Mâtho, his destined rival, during the disastrous banquet at the beginning of the novel. At the end it is Narr'Havas from whom Salammbô demands the death of Mâtho in pledge of her betrothal. This seems to be the only thing Salammbô desires of Narr'Havas, who otherwise, in his stunning beauty—modeled after Hasdrubal who perished in the Second Punic War—seems more like an older sister to her than a man she desires. Mâtho is caught in a net by Narr'Havas. It is a literalization of his love for Salammbô: "Oh, if only you knew, how in the midst of war I think of you! Sometimes the memory of a gesture, a fold of your robe suddenly grips me and traps me like a net!" (185). He is tortured to death during the wedding celebrations of Salammbô and Narr'Havas. But instead of marrying, Salammbô dies as well, entangled in the meshes of her dress and bound in her pomp as if in a trap, right at the moment when she should toast to Carthage with

Narr'Havas and seal their love bond with wine. Witnessing the enormity of Mâtho's suffering, which she knows "was her work" (282), Salammbô realizes that she loves him, her true bridegroom, and dies literally of that love rather than uniting orgasmically—*la petite mort*, "the little death," is a metaphor for orgasm in French—with Narr'Havas. As Flaubert sums it up in his outline for the chapter: "His torture—along the streets—on the day Pyrrha's wedding is to be celebrated, the young girl gazes on Mâtho's torn body—she loves him—it is he who is her spouse—they are wedded by death—she grows pale and collapses into Mâtho's blood."[98] In the last scene, Salammbô has become the "the very genius of Carthage, her soul incarnate" (278), *genius loci* in the most literal sense. What Anna says to her sister Dido in the *Aeneid* holds true of Salammbô's death as well: "You've killed me and yourself, the Sidonian people and senate, sister, your city as well" (*Aeneid* 4.683–84). Salammbô's death marks the ruin of Carthage just as much.

Before engaging with the intricate interweaving of love and war with the *genius loci* of Carthage, let us start with the most evident intertext, namely, Chateaubriand's *The Martyrs*, already discussed above. In *Salammbô*, Flaubert fuses two types of classically opposed women: the woman who brings about death, the femme fatale, and the woman who brings about salvation. Chateaubriand's Cymodocée, Eudore's bride, and his beloved Velléda, the fatal druid priestess whose love kills body and soul, were both models for Salammbô. Eudore and Cymodocée's martyrdom, their blood wedding, becomes the truly productive, fertile *fundamentum* of a new empire. Before the two lovers are thrown to wild animals, Eudore slips a wedding ring dipped in his blood on Cymodocée's finger, betrothing them at the place of their martyrdom, the circus:

"Let us increase; let us multiply for eternity; let us fill heaven with our virtues." At the same instant the heavens opened and celebrated these sublime nuptials: the angels chanted the canticle of the spouse; the mother of Eudorus presented to God her united children, who were soon to appear before the throne of his Eternity; the virgin-martyrs wove the nuptial crown for Cymodoce; Jesus Christ blessed the happy pair, and the Holy Ghost bestowed on them the gift of an everlasting love.[99]

Empire and salvation unite on the tomb of the martyrs.

By contrast, the blood wedding between Mâtho and Salammbô prefigures not the foundation, but the devastation and destruction of an empire illustrated in the splendor of its sacrificial victim. Salammbô is connected to Velléda through the opening scene in which, at night, a virgin priestess relates the destiny of her people before a group of soldiers, highlighting the prominent position of women. She is connected to Velléda through the poison of love, intoxicating both Mâtho and Eudore: "we breathe in their atmosphere a poison that intoxicates us."[100] Finally, the comparison of Velléda with Dido and her destructive love that leads to death links Velléda to Salammbô.[101]

In *Salammbô*, Flaubert transfers the close connection between love and war onto a sacrificial love. The deadliness of love has no alternative for Flaubert. Unlike in the cases of Cymodocée and Velléda, the Virgin Mary and Venus, or, to put it in terms of the title of Jean Eustache's film *La maman et la putain* (1973; released in America as *The Mother and the Whore*), femininity is thus not split into two opposed aspects as usual but instead those are bound up in one figure. This is expressed succinctly in the formula "sweeter than wine and more terrible than death" (42). The beloved of the Song of Songs is sweeter than wine, thereby becoming the *figura* of the salvational effect of the New Testament, while woman is more bitter than death in Ecclesiastes.[102] In Salammbô, as the culmination of her ambivalence, salvation and ruin are combined. She is both the corrupting Eve responsible for the Fall that brings about death and ruin, and is illuminated by Pentecost. She addresses the mercenaries in every language, speaking to those having come from all four corners of the earth: "She was using simultaneously all the Barbarians' idioms" (27). Peculiarly, the representation of Salammbô swings back and forth among Eve, Venus, and Mary. The syncretism, established in the Catholic figure of Mary, uniting elements of Cybele, Venus, and Diana, is projected back onto the figure of Salammbô. Like Mary, she is an immaculate Virgin, not born of men: "not like any daughter of men" (42). Flaubert does not stigmatize this love—as Chateaubriand does in the case of Velléda. He does not outlaw it or reject it in favor of a love that is purer, happier, and more fruitful, in short, redeeming. Equally, he does not juxtapose it to sexual satisfaction. For Flaubert there is no better love than a love that leads to death. Emma Bovary's seducer Rodolphe Boulanger de La Huchette is unquestionably erotically successful and sexually fulfilled, but his heart is dead, and no one would ever dare elevate him as the Flaubertian ideal of love. Similarly, for Emma, the "solution" cannot be for her to read less and act more "realistically" within her environment. If she did, she would just be like the wife of the pharmacist Homais.

Flaubert affirms the mystically hysterical love through the splendor of the sacrifice that founds nothing, since nothing turns fertile except the praxis of this love, fatal to all. The fact that Flaubert considered de Sade the paragon of the Catholic author is enough to give one pause. It is a love, which, in its terrifying beauty and its reckless abandon to death, contrasts sharply with the bourgeois ideal of a fertile, profitable, satisfying love. It is also opposed to the fruitful sacrificial victim in the name of the fatherland: not in the Bible, but rather in its reception, Judith surrenders her body to get the head of Holofernes so as to save her native land. Iphigenia bleeds willingly in order to win over Artemis for the sake of her fatherland: "freely I offer my body for my country and all Hellas" (*Iphigenia in Aulis* 1553).[103] Salammbô's love, in its groundlessness, also contrasts with a founding love; it stands against a fertile sacrifice of love, which becomes the *fundamentum* of a new empire, as in *The Martyrs*.

The opposition Flaubert sets up within love is between the hysteric and mystical, that is to say, figurative love and a strictly carnally fulfilling bourgeois love. Teresa of Ávila, de Sade, Mâtho, and Salammbô are paradigms of mystic-figurative love.[104] Rodolphe in *Madame Bovary*, Paul de Monville and his wife Adèle in "Quidquid volueris," and briefly also Salammbô, after her amorous encounter with Mâtho, are examples of bourgeois love. "Salammbo had turned bourgeoise. No more exaltation, she saw at things as they were," Flaubert notes in his outline for the first chapter,[105] thereby affirming the mystic-hysterical complex, found in men and women alike, that only fulfills itself in the death agony. Contrary to prevailing modern sexological science and to the beliefs of Zola or Charcot, Flaubert does not believe hysterical-mystic love can be cured by a healthy sex life.[106] In *Madame Bovary*, he quite ironically inverts the figure of therapeutic sex: marriage is supposed to cure hysteria, but Emma only starts to show signs of it after she gets married.

This Flaubertian love doctrine is articulated most clearly in *Salammbô*. War and love are generally interchangeable. Love is a continuation of war; war is a form of love. The motive for war is love, which is a kind of war. The name "Salammbô"—"bringer of peace"—is therefore ironic.[107] This is evident in battles described as though they were erotic embraces: "When there were no weapons left to hold they wrestled bodily with each other;

chests cracked against breastplates and corpses hung with head thrown back between stiffening arms" (147). Male desire and force of arms do not only stand for one another metaphorically, as in the classical metaphor of the sword or dagger as penis piercing or spearing the woman during the sexual act. War and love are interchangeable and have become one and the same: when he eagerly eyes the singing Salammbô, Narr'Havas's "belt bristled with so many darts" that it "made a bulge in his full cloak" (27). Salammbô is excited by "naked swords," which for her indicate "the excitement of all these men" (28). Love is a battlefield, and the metaphor of the *petite mort* is literalized: "I will kill her," says Mâtho, and Salammbô, on her part, desires his death. The lover feels undone and/or would like to destroy the other. Flaubert does not stop there, however: on top of pitting the meaningful, founding sacrifice against the groundless, senseless sacrifice, he turns the sadistic moment into a masochistic one, so to speak. The dynamic of violence is sublated through the sacrifice of love into a formula that might run something like this: love means torture; to love is to sacrifice. It is not by chance that Salammbô and Mâtho make love on a lion's skin for the first and only time. Since the lion is a symbol of Christ, as we have seen, both their sacrificial deaths are alluded to. Both are *figurae Christi*. Mâtho's bloody stations of the cross are already decided with "the red door with the black cross" (29, 82) behind which Salammbô disappears twice. His Calvary is prefigured in his bloodstained face and the gaping arrow wound Narr'Havas inflicts in a conspicuous literalization of Cupid's arrows. The sexual act, which, as a murderous tearing, is equated with martyrdom, is prefigured in Mâtho's "military tunic," whose "bronze plates tore into the purple covering of the couch" (27). The story of the veil, the "zaïmph," is also a story of torn fabrics, body coverings, and textiles. Although the recovery of the veil was successful, Salammbô must pay for it with her defloration, a torn veil, the tearing of her hymen, which is symbolized through the breaking of her small foot chain.[108] But Mâtho, the one who does the tearing, does not leave unscathed. The torn hymen returns in the torn tarpaulin of Mâtho's tent, presaging the tearing of his skin at the end of the novel, his flaying, the unveiling of his anatomy by the population of Carthage. "I am the wound and I the knife!" Mâtho might say with Baudelaire.[109]

Sacrifice and wedding, love and power cross paths in Salammbô's visit to Mâtho's tent. The Carthaginians claim a sacrifice, which sounds like a warrant on Iphigenia: "To appease the Baalim there must no doubt be offered something of inestimable value, some being who was young, beautiful, virgin, of ancient lineage, descended from the Gods, a human star" (165). However, instead of sacrificing Salammbô immediately, her self-sacrifice to Mâtho is demanded in order to return the veil. Schahabarim, the high priest of Tanit, considers her surrender to death and acceptance of the loss of her virginity as a reparation for her crime: she is found guilty of the loss of the veil and the subsequent misfortune of Carthage. Like the sacrifice exacted on Iphigenia by Artemis/Diana, hers is demanded by the Rabbet, by Tanit/Venus/Diana. Like the sacrifice of Iphigenia in Aulis, the offering of this virgin must expiate the fatherland. Salammbô understands her mission as sacrificial victim all too well: right before her journey, precisely like Iphigenia, she feels "like a victim at the foot of the altar awaiting the stunning blow" (170). Love and sacrifice are introduced through the motif of the blood wedding. After dressing her in the costume prescribed for Tanit, her nurse thinks that Salammbô could not look more beautiful, not even on her wedding day. When Salammbô leaves, the nurse sees it as an omen of her mistress's death: "from a distance, in the moonlight, she made out, in the cypress avenue, a gigantic shadow walking diagonally on Salammbo's left, which was an omen of death" (176). Death and love meet in the cypress, which is simultaneously the tree of Venus and the tree of death, growing to this day in the cemeteries of Italy. The symbolic value of this tree—love, death—is evoked once more in the small table made out of cypress wood where the dagger lies with which Salammbô—almost like Judith—would like to have killed the sleeping Mâtho. Her nurse mourns for Salammbô as she leaves, as if she were already dead: scratching her cheeks, tearing out her hair, beginning the lament for the dead.

This sexualization, which is not foregrounded in the Iphigenia episode, is underlined through the additional reference to the biblical Judith scene. This happens first in the scene where Salammbô is dressed, while in the second instance it is more explicit: Salammbô is overcome by a burning bloodthirstiness and contemplates killing Mâtho with the dagger. Flaubert evokes not only texts, but also paintings: his portrayal of sleeping Mâtho just before his decapitation is unmistakably modeled on Horace Vernet's *Judith and Holofernes* (1831): "Mâtho, like a drunken man, slept lying on his side, with one arm projecting over the edge of the couch. . . .

A smile parted his teeth, gleaming amid his black beard, and in his half-closed lids there was a silent and almost outrageous gaiety" (188).

The word "drunken" alludes to the drunken Holofernes; in view of the unavoidable, persistently posed question of whether or not the sexual act did or did not take place in the tent, or whether Mâtho is impotent, it is not insignificant to note that Flaubert describes his sleep in terms of drunkenness. Drunkenness incapacitates Holofernes in the biblical story, as is widely known. We might want to keep this in mind, considering that other interpreters can only see the "postcoital" moment, as if it were self-evident and right there for all to see.[110]

Before setting off to Holofernes's camp, Judith dresses up to seduce the men with her charm (Judith 10:3–4). If the biblical Judith leaves unspoilt from the tent of Holofernes—"my countenance hath deceived him to his destruction, and yet hath he not committed sin with me, to defile and shame me" (Jth. 13:16)—it is her ultimate weapon, namely, erotic fascination, that she deploys for the salvation of her people. The bat of an eye lies between the enthralled Holofernes and his severed neck. Or, as Judith's triumphal song—or should one say, triumphal howl?—formulates it: "Her sandals ravished his eyes, her beauty took his mind prisoner, and the fauchion passed through his neck" (Jth. 16:9). Judith's scene is invoked as a counterimage: *Salammbô* is not concerned with saving a national community with the help of Eros, and neither is it about a murdering/castrating woman. The sacrificial love of man and woman in the blood wedding amounts to its countermodel. Mâtho flings the anguish of the entire world at Salammbô's feet and they unite in a grand death scene. However, this death does not mark a fruitful beginning but the final destruction of a great empire.

Infelix Dido

Contrary to what the moderns have decided, primitive opinion held that Noga and Cochab [the Hebrew names of Venus and Mars] were above the sun.

Flaubert to Sainte-Beuve, December 23–24, 1862

The association between love and war is a densely populated allegorical field; it is most obvious in the story of Venus and Mars.[111] The motto of the flower power generation, "make love, not war," may count as its last echo for the time being. In the most favorable of cases, Mars can be satisfied by Venus; the war is brought to an end through love, or—to speak metaphorically—shifted onto a different terrain. After all, the "little death" is not an actual death, and the woman enjoys being "speared" or "pierced." Love pacifies war; it generates life and not death. "The Carthaginian Venus, who dominated the region" (39), seems, despite being referred to as "the All-Fertile" (79), unable to hold out the prospect of such a happy, pacifying, and indeed fertile ending. Dido remains infertile, left behind in a house where, to her desolation, no little Aeneas is playing; the same fate awaits Salammbô.

It is precisely this—the interchangeability of love and war, love as war, and war as love—that accounts for the tradition of Carthage, as narrated by Vergil, *ab urbe condita*, from the founding of the city onwards. The self-destructive love of Dido, founder and queen of Carthage, for Aeneas, founder of Rome, prefigures the city's destruction by the Romans. Dido having slain herself with the sword of Aeneas, her body will burn on the funeral pyre destined for a sacrificial victim. Aeneas's mother, Venus, callously mobilizes love as a weapon of war, as a means of destruction and annihilation, while Juno, the goddess of marriage and protector of Carthage, fails to defend Dido but foolishly plays into Venus's hands. The horrifying irony of the story is that it is Juno who destroys Dido/Carthage. In this case, and contrary to Juno's hopes and best intentions, marital union does not found an everlasting peace between two cities (*Aeneid* 4.99) but results in a perpetual war ending with the downfall of Carthage (4.167–70).

Flaubert's novel is guided by the dynamic marking Dido's disastrous love. The violence Dido wants to direct against others ends up turning against herself, in all its self-destructive force. She threatens to have Aeneas's fleet go up in flames (4.604); instead, Dido will go up in the flames of the funeral pyre. This irony in Vergil's Roman text becomes especially cruel with respect to the vanquished antagonist, Carthage, whose destruction Vergil prefigures in Dido's suicide. From the Carthaginian, or rather from the barbarian perspective, which coincides with Flaubert's perspective, this irony vanishes into thin air. It is sacralized into the dynamics of sacrifice. So, for Flaubert there can be no victor, no "Aeneas, the pious" who, blessed by the gods and obeying their will, accomplishes his mission and founds an empire. Both Mâtho and Salammbô undergo Dido's ordeal. In the love scene between Mâtho and Salammbô in the tent, the ill-fated union between Venus and Juno leading to Dido's ruin is echoed in the thunderclap. As Flaubert clarifies writing to Sainte-Beuve, the rolling thunder is the sign of a wedding in the heavens.[112] As intimation of a heavenly marriage, it is a quotation from the *Aeneid*, where earth and sky join in thunder and lightning, signifying the union of Dido and Aeneas. The thunderstorm is summoned by Juno to break up Dido and Aeneas's hunting trip. They flee to a cave looking for shelter and wind up alone together, ending in the act of love that will prove fatal for Dido. Just like the sexual act in the *Aeneid*, *Salammbô's* union partakes of the double coding as sacred heavenly marriage, through which earth and sky are reconciled, and as a violent profanation, exposing marriage as but the veil for human beings living together as wild animals, as Dido observes shortly before her suicide (*Aeneid* 4.556).

Equally driven by the disastrous intervention of the gods, the love of Mâtho for Salammbô, like the love of the founder of Carthage, is a love unto death, presaging the ruin of the city. Under the sign of Mars and Venus, Mâtho and Salammbô meet; as in Vergil's tale, they do not meet as mere individuals, but as incarnations of the gods. In her first appearance, Salammbô enters under the sign of Venus-Derceto, Tanit-Astarte, whose symbols are the cypress, the pomegranate, and the fish; Mâtho stands under the sign of Moloch.[113] Both suffer and embody the gods. The love scene in the tent allows them to fuse, during the *hieros gamos*, the cosmic marriage of the gods, with both divinities. "Moloch, you are burning me" (*Salammbô*, 187), Salammbô exclaims. For her, Mâtho incarnates Moloch, just as Salammbô becomes Venus for Mâtho: "Are you not omnipotent, immaculate, radiant, and beautiful like Tanit?" (184), he asks. On the other hand, Mâtho feels cursed by Moloch, just as Tanit exacts her revenge on Salammbô through erotic obsessions, since Salammbô does not know the goddess in her popular guise, namely, in the figure of temple prostitution—"She knew nothing of obscene effigies" (55). Profanation and sacralization also inform the scene in the tent. Unlike Vergil's gods, whose intentions do not seem entirely evil, Flaubert's gods are patently ruinous.

War devours love. The destructive principle wins out over the principle of fertility. On their way to Sicily, the doves, symbols of Venus, drop into the burning throat of Moloch / the sun: "the whole horizon was coloured red as blood. The doves seemed to be coming down towards the sea, gradually; then they disappeared as though swallowed up and falling of their own accord into the sun's maw" (173). But the price to be paid for fertility is not merely the destruction of what is generated. Something different is at stake: What is subverted is the opposition between a love unto death and a love that leads to life.

The story of Dido sets up the quid pro quo of war and love right from the start. During Aeneas's recounting of the ruination of Troy, Dido fatefully falls in love. In his prologue, Aeneas tells of the horrors of the Trojan War, revealing exactly what will become of Dido, whose love is here already paralleled with the devastation of Troy: it comes down to the revival of an inexpressible love, an inexpressible pain, and conveys, in the case of Troy, as well as in the suicide out of love by the queen, extreme suffering and misery, portraying heartrending scenes, which provoke tears in all who hear the story (*Aeneid* 2.3–13). Already in the story of Dido, the rhetorical figure of literalization takes center stage: through her death Dido literalizes the metaphor of a love that wounds and inflames to death. To inflame Dido with love is the order Cupid receives from his mother, Venus: "My plan is then: Strike first; take the queen by a ruse, with encircling fences of fire so she won't change course through divine interference" (1.673). Fatally struck by the secret wound she received in her heart of hearts, Dido is consumed to the marrow by the flames of love (4.65). In the end, she really does die, pierced by the sword of Aeneas, on the pyre whose flames engulf her body. Another metaphor for the lethalness of love is poisoning—Cupid is to bewilder the queen through poison (4.65). Dido drinks the love poison in Vergil's narrative: "Infelix Dido lonqumque bibebat amorem"[114]—"Dido, unfulfilled, drank deeply of love's heady vintage" (1.749). Flaubert plays upon the poisonous drink of love. Like Vergil, he literalizes the metaphor of the flame and the wound.

For *Salammbô*, Vergil's metaphor of the hunt for love is vital. This hunt is undertaken, not only with weapons, but with nets as well. Cupid should ensnare the queen as a cunning hunter would lure his prey into his nets ("capere ante dolis et cingere flamma" [4.65]). As usual, Cupid is successful in this undertaking, and Dido is thus entangled in her passion ("turpique cupidine captos": "Cupid's slaves in a shameless love" [4.194]). The motif of *capta* (4.330), of being restrained and ensnared, runs throughout Vergil's text. The meshes and nets that hold one captive are mentioned as hunting tools in the disastrous love scene: "fine nets, snares" (4.131) and Dido appears, "draped in Sidonian fabric with needlework fringes" (4.137). It is here that Flaubert jumps in. More important than the comparison of the queen with a shot and mortally wounded hind who, punctured by a deadly arrow, wanders around like a lost soul, are the metaphors of nets, meshes, snares, and being tied up—all images taken from the iconology of the hunt. Mâtho dies à la Dido, caught in the net of Narr'Havas, to be chained up and set on fire at the very end: "two flames came from his eye sockets which seemed to go up to his hair" (*Salammbô*, 281). Salammbô too dies à la Dido, "sheathed in a net of narrow mesh imitating a fish's scales, . . . a wide cloak, white as snow, fell back behind her, and with her elbows in, her knees tightly together, with diamond bracelets at the top of her arms" (277).

In Flaubert, both Mâtho and Salammbô are modeled on Dido; there are however more areas of overlap between Dido and Mâtho. The fact that Aeneas encounters Dido as if he were Apollo shortly before the fateful love scene (*Aeneid* 4.144) does not make the devastation of this love any more reassuring for Mâtho. The figure of radical self-abandon characterizes Dido's love, and through the example of Mâtho, Flaubert illustrates it most forcefully. If Dido imbibes love in drawn-out gulps, then Mâtho literally ingests love word for word in the drink poured for him by Salammbô; like Dido, Mâtho is completely beside himself from love, even to the extent that he takes after Salammbô and incarnates her.

The lovesickness consuming Dido also allows Mâtho no rest, and like the queen he cannot find sleep. Nothing can cure him of his sickness— neither women, wine, nor play can distract him. Mâtho fears to be what Dido had become: a burnt offering doomed by the gods: "I suppose I am the victim of some holocaust she has promised the Gods?" (*Salammbô*, 41). Like Dido, Mâtho's love delirium keeps him in chains: "She holds me fast by some invisible chain. If I move she comes forward; when I stop, she rests!" (ibid.). Actually surrounded by flames (*cingere flamma*), Mâtho awakens in his tent after his lovemaking: "a fearful glare blazed behind the canvas. Mâtho lifted it up; they saw huge flames engulfing the Libyans' camp" (188). Like Dido, who erects a funeral pyre on which she piles everything Aeneas left behind, all the things that remind her of him—his weapons, his clothes, but, above all else, the bed that heralded her downfall (*Aeneid* 4.497–99, 508)—Mâtho burns the whole tent in which he made love to Salammbô: "Then Mâtho stood up. He took a still smoking ember and threw it contemptuously on to the debris of his tent. Then with the toe of his boot he pushed into the flames any objects that spilled over, so that nothing should remain" (199). The devastations of this love suddenly surface: "Twelve hours later all that remained of the Mercenaries was a heap of wounded, dead and dying" (195). Mâtho must suffer Dido's curses to the bitter end, up to his woeful torture, and, indeed, the "barbarian" is punished: "you'll drink retribution in deep draughts, often invoking Dido's name. When I'm absent, I'll chase you with dark fire! . . . My destination is yours. There'll be no impunity. You'll pay" (*Aeneid* 4.383ff.).

Gisco believes, against all odds, in victory and the survival of the city, and Dido and Salammbô come together in his speech. However, the shameless surrender of Salammbô to the enemy signals the final ruin of Carthage from his perspective. Gisco translates into plain language what the *Aeneid* only metaphorically stages: the association between Dido's surrender and the sacking of the city by the Romans. The ambivalent wavering between sacred bond and violent profanation, between *hieros gamos* and crude carnal lust, is performed by Gisco's oration, which reveals what is not put into words during the love scene proper: the visual description of the sexual act remains blanked out with an ellipsis. Furthermore, Gisco did not see, but only heard. The love rage of Dido, which the *Aeneid* does not illustrate but only names and thereby bashfully veils, is crudely expressed. Gisco introduces the comparison with Dido, who, consumed by a blazing desire, callously ignores all laws of decency (*Aeneid* 4.27) and in her sensual madness abandons her renown and reputation (4.91). In addition, the comparison with wild animals through which Dido condemns herself is cited only to be outdone. Worse than a wild animal, Salammbô shamelessly abandons herself to her desire right under the very eyes of her father:

But now all is over! All is lost! The Gods execrate her! Curses on you who hastened her ruin by your ignominy! . . . I heard you moaning with love like a prostitute; then he told you of his desire and you let him kiss your hands! But if you were driven on by your shameless frenzy you could at least have behaved like wild animals who do their coupling in secret, and not display your shame right under your father's eyes! (*Salammbô*, 190)

Before Hamilcar, Gisco goes on about Hamilcar's daughter's disgrace: "To please him she has put on the Goddess's robe; and as she yields her body, she delivers up the glory of your name, the majesty of the Gods, the country's vengeance, the very salvation of Carthage!" (ibid.). Gisco curses Salammbô.

Regarding Representability:
The quid pro quo of Fabric and Skin

What really happened in the tent, and whether or not the sexual act did take place, is a question that has led to heated debates. What is clear however is that Flaubert did not achieve what he set out to do, namely, write a steamy love scene such as his thoroughly male-dominated age had never read about before: "I'm onto something big right now in this book," he tells Ernest Feydeau. "It has to be simultaneously dirty and pure, mystic and realistic! Slobbering the likes of which nobody has ever seen before made visible."[115] The reader does not see a thing: the act is never shown. The dynamic of the erotic scene—that of a progressive undressing, the baring of the woman—is reversed: Salammbô is naked before she goes to Mâtho, so as to disappear under more and more veils. Above all, and Flaubert cannot insist on this enough, Salammbô is veiled. The love scene is a story of fabrics, a story about cloth, and a story narrated through the metaphor of fabrics. It is a veiled story. Salammbô cannot get enough of veils and envelops herself in layer after layer of cloth: "over a first tunic, thin and wine-coloured, she drew on a second . . . over all these clothes she put on a black cloak . . . a long yellow veil over her hair . . . a scarf round her neck" (175–76), "despite all her veils" (178). Under the veil, Salammbô dreams. Veiled to the point of unrecognizability, she arrives as a moon goddess at Mâtho's tent, under the sign of Mary, Venus, Diana, and Tanit. "But she had over her face a yellow veil with black flowers and so many draperies round her body that it was impossible to guess anything about her. From the top of the terrace [Mâtho] considered this vague form rising like a ghost from the shadows of the night" (181). Veiled—in this case by the moon—Salammbô appears in Mâtho's reveries: "It looked like a veil hiding your face" (187). Salammbô looks like the women photographed by the fascinated psychiatrist Gaëtan Gatian de Clérambault (1872–1934) a little while later. They are completely veiled, and there is literally nothing to be seen but fabrics, fabrics, fabrics. This fascination with the veil is a correlate of the occidental desire to see what nobody is allowed to see: the naked oriental woman, or, to echo Flaubert's own vulgar expression, "les cons nus."

There is unquestionably a problem with the love scene, but some critics resort here to language reminiscent of *Animal Planet* rather than Flaubert. One writes: "But [Mâtho] was not simply an aroused male about to possess the woman for whom he longed. He was also a hysteric and dreaded such a fulfillment, another extraordinary intuition of Flaubert's."[116] Flaubert does everything in his power to cast the shadow of impotence over his thoroughly male hero. In the manuscript version, Mâtho suffers from a "physical, abnormal weakness." As a result, Salammbô feels humiliated: "Elle se sent humiliée." All that remains of this in the published text, in which the lovers' discourse oscillates between the alternatives of destroying or being destroyed by the other, is the moment of anguished tension and collapse: "Pale, fists clenched, he quivered like a harp whose strings are about to snap. Suddenly he was choked by sobs, and collapsing to his knees" (186). Tears take the place of semen.

The instrument with strings taut to the point of snapping is the same image Flaubert uses to describe his impotence to Louise Colet. Impotence is interpreted here as the sign of an extraordinary love. He highlights the abnormality of this phenomenon for an otherwise healthy and ever potent man—the way he portrays himself as well as Mâtho. In the novel, both the astonishment about this fiasco of impotence and the humiliation of the woman spelled out in the letters are banished to the notes.

What a terrible lover I am!—Do you know that what has happened to me with you has never happened to me before? (I've been so exhausted for three days and as tense as the string of a cello). If I were somebody who took himself seriously I would have been bitterly vexed indeed. I felt sorry for you. I was afraid you might have supposed terrible things, others might have concluded that I offended them, they would have thought me cold, disgusted, used. I was very thankful for your spontaneous intelligence, which nothing could surprise, whereas I was surprised as though of an unheard of monstrosity. I thus must love you, and very much, since I felt the very opposite of what I had with all the others, those are of no matter.[117]

Like in the correspondence, the novel couples impotence with the uniqueness of love. With no one else, Flaubert explains to Colet, has it ever come to such a fiasco. Love renders one impotent; impotence is the proof of love. Only for Salammbô does Mâtho have this "infinite adoration" (184). As Flaubert also asserts of himself, Mâtho usually avails himself as indifferently and as sovereignly of women for the purpose of his lust as if they were a mere, indifferent function of his desire. "Am I a child? . . . Do you think their faces and their songs still touch me? We had women to sweep out our stables in Drepanum. I have had them in the middle of attacks, under ceilings that were crumbling and while the catapult was still vibrating! But that one, Spendius, that one!" (42).

The scene in the tent is under an absolute visual ban: to view the body of the naked woman is strictly prohibited. What is visible of Salammbô's body is associated with the scene of temptation in paradise, where the snake tempts Eve with the forbidden fruit. The "unknown fruit" (183) is the body of Salammbô, and like Eve, Mâtho is driven by an uncontrollable curiosity (ibid.) to touch her. Just as with Hérodias later on, the snake writhes between Salammbô's breasts: "and in his imagination he was lost in the narrow cleft between them, down which hung a thread holding an emerald plaque, which could be seen lower down under the violet gauze" (ibid.). Sexuality, equated with curiosity or *libido sciendi*, is here synonymous with original sin. According to the Church Fathers, the consequences of original sin are sexuality and death. As is usual with Flaubert, love and death fatally collapse into one. This is made particularly clear in Flaubert's sketches: Salammbô is wrapped in her veil like in a shroud, and only when she is quite literally invested with death will Mâtho make love to her. "He covers her with the coat—as if it were a shroud, he holds her close, and finally he fucks her."[118] However, wherever there is danger, there is also the possibility of salvation, to quote Hölderlin. Original sin—and its corollary, death—is phallically overwritten through the soaring snakes on the tarpaulin. Moments before the female sex becomes naked in a certain sense—in the tearing of another veil, that of the hymen—the symbol of defloration, the breaking of the small golden chain, that links her feet, turns into a phallus: "Mâtho seized her heels, the golden chain snapped, and as the two ends flew off they struck the canvas like two vipers recoiling" (187).

To obtain the veil of Tanit, Salammbô tears the veil from her face with her hand: "and with her other hand [she] tore the veils from her head" (183). This violent gesture of ripping frightens Mâtho, who seems to be afraid of one thing only: to see. "He fell back, drawing in his arms, gaping, almost in terror" (ibid.). She is hardly unveiled, as an additional veil now covers her: "The zaïmph fell down, covered her" (187). Her presumably naked legs are immediately covered by Mâtho: "he even spread the zaïmph over her legs like an ordinary rug" (ibid.). The secret of Mâtho's attraction to Salammbô is that her body is a body wrapped in fabrics: "for him her clothes were fused with her body" (183). Nature and art, body and fabric seamlessly merge to be nothing but a splendid glow. Her flesh is transmuted into shimmering fabrics and precious stones.[119] "The shimmer of the material, like the splendour of her skin, was something special and peculiar to her. Her eyes and her diamonds flashed; her polished nails were a continuation of the fine jewels on her fingers" (183). Her shoulder becomes moist and shiny. It is the same shimmer that drew Charles Bovary so irresistibly to Emma. Salammbô is nothing but glamour.

Two typically fetishistic moments are constitutive for the fascination Salammbô exudes. Firstly, a phallic symbol comes into play—the snakes that leap up at the moment the female sex comes into focus. They are phallically connoted, since at the beginning of the novel, Salammbô makes love with a snake. Secondly, the natural body is turned into an artifact. It is a body made of fabrics and precious stones. It is this artificiality that makes the shining body desirable and an object of worship. It has been rightly pointed out that the "gloss" (*Glanz*) of Freud's famous "a glance [*Glanz*] on the nose" is not merely an error of translation but also refers to the gloss of the glans of an erect penis: it stands for desire.[120] In this respect Salammbô's whole body is a phallus—and thus also a fetish—erected in counterpoint to woman's lack of a penis and the associated castration anxiety. The unrepresentable sexual act—it must not be seen because there is nothing to see—is shown in deferral. In the sexual act with the snake, the love scene is metaphorically anticipated in the sequence of undressing, arousal, fulfillment: "it tightened round her its black coils striped with golden patches. Salammbo gasped beneath this weight, too heavy for her, her back bent, she felt she was dying; and with the tip of its tail it gently flicked her thigh" (174–75). The sexual act is consummated in the final death scene with its "great death."[121] Flaubert also deploys this technique, which one is tempted to call cinematographic, in *A Sentimental Education*: in the forest of Fontainebleau, what is happening in Paris at that same moment becomes legible. What happens in the tent is foreshadowed by the episode with the serpent, a scene whose true meaning is revealed during Mathô's torment.

That it does come to the act of love in the tent is not only made manifest through the tearing of Salammbô's small foot chain. The love scene disintegrates into a before/after: the unrepresentable sexual act, overwritten as original sin and Fall, leads to a radical fall in the rhetorical register. Sublimity is lost. After that has happened, everything becomes strangely disenchanted, robbed of luster. An infinitely worshipped glamorous, immaculate goddess, whose iconography mixes those of Venus, Tanit, Diana, and Mary, is derided as a whore moaning with lust; a divinity making everything vibrate in harmony becomes fodder for a crude sex scene. Above all, however, this mythical veil, magical sealer of fates, whose recovery motivated this entire scene, turns into nothing but a mere piece of cloth. It suffers a rhetorical, vertiginous debasement. Mâtho throws the zaïmph over Salammbô's legs as a simple rug. Later she hurriedly wraps it around her waist before getting together her various coverings: "She threw the zaïmph round her waist, swiftly collected her veils, her cloak, her scarf. 'I go there in haste!' she cried" (190). If the veil was previously the talisman of Carthage, on which the entire fate of the city depended, now it is nothing but a piece of fabric: "and when she had looked at it thoroughly she was surprised not to feel the happiness she had once imagined. She stayed wrapped in melancholy before the fulfilment of her dreams" (189). The veil loses the power ascribed to it of being able to turn the sad fate of the city around: "recovery of the zaïmph had not sufficed" (219). After this turn of events, Salammbô is no longer a venerable being not entirely of this world, but a practical, almost sporty woman who, no longer hindered by her small foot chain, takes giant strides: "With her teeth she held up the hem of her robe which hampered her, and in three leaps she found herself on the platform" (191). In the patriarchal society she lives in, she had always been but a means to her father's political ends: "He was reserving her for some match that might serve him politically" (54). As an exchange object, the veil is devaluated by her defloration and must immediately be brought back to the men. After the consummation of love, Salammbô loses her exchange value and, much more shockingly, her sacred aura.

This becoming lackluster is overturned by the love-death. The violence of the sacrifice restores the splendor. Mâtho's torture scene spells out what lovemaking means for Flaubert. The ellipsis of love is filled. The desire to know somebody in the flesh is horrifyingly literalized. Both scenes are anchored in the myth of original sin, which Flaubert reads as a desire to come to know somebody in the flesh (make love). The thirst for knowledge, curiosity, and lovemaking stem from the same desire; the untamable thirst for knowledge, which prompts Mâtho to touch Salammbô's naked flesh, has as its counterpart "an infamous curiosity, a desire to know him completely" (279), driving the women of Carthage in their urge to come face to face with the murderer of their children and men. Skin and fabric are to be understood as quid pro quo. The skin, which is torn in shreds from Mâtho's body, making him utterly naked, is prefigured in the tearing of the tents: "he ripped away a strip of canvas to let in some daylight; the zaïmph had disappeared" (191); "they were beaten in advance through the loss of the zaïmph . . . the tents, with the canvas torn to shreds" (195). Finally, it is announced with Mâtho's tent, whose material is ripped: "The torn canvas flapped in the wind; sometimes its long strips passed in front of his face" (199). What stands out above all else is a contrast between clothed and naked bodies. Against the veiled body of Salammbô, whose torn virginal membrane is covered up with all those layers of clothing she is able to heap on before leaving the tent, stand the bodies of the soldiers. The description of their bodies focuses almost obscenely on their nakedness in death. The text showcases even their state of decay according to racial type. In Mathô's torture scene, love itself finally appears naked, in all its carnality. It is only representable as a body destined to death: a flayed body, whose skin is torn away. The desiring, loving body is representable only as a sacrificed, immolated body.[122]

The scene of Mâtho's torture is a tightly woven text, whose most evident intertexts are the skinning of Marsyas in Ovid's *Metamorphoses*, the desecration of Hector's corpse by Achilles in Homer's *Iliad*, and the Passion of Christ. Like Mâtho, Hector is sacrificed by the will of the gods. The opposition determining representation in the *Iliad* is between naked, injured, flayed, and disfigured male bodies versus fabrics and coverings from the outset associated with women. Already in the very beginning, when Achilles chases Hector around the city, they twice come across a spring where women are hanging out the wash. The future, disgracing nakedness of Hector's wounded body is foregrounded through the veiled women. The interchangeability of skin and cloth is underlined through the metaphor of shreds: upon hearing what happened to her son, Hector's mother throws away her wonderful veil, while Andromache, who is "weaving at her loom . . . working flowered braiding into a dark red folding robe" (*Iliad* 22.517–18),[123] halts her work. Andromache sobs, saying that Hector's corpse will remain wholly naked, while his palace abounds in "stores of clothing laid up in the halls, fine things, a joy to the eye, the work of women's hands" (599–600). She wants to burn these instead of the body, since they can no longer serve as his shroud (600ff.).

Hector is killed by Achilles as a sacrifice and his corpse is violated by the Greeks: "not a man came forward who did not stab his body" (22.372).

This scene is recalled in the gesture of the Carthaginians who all show their nails after having grown them longer with the sole purpose of making them more suitable as instruments of torture. Every Carthaginian, man and woman alike, wants to have a share in this torture, just as every Greek thrusts his sword into the body of their worst enemy.[124] And as if this were not enough, Hector's disfigured corpse, lacerated by thousands of cuts, is dragged around the city by Achilles. It is striking that in Achilles' hate speech to his enemy, the word "scrap" is obsessively repeated, thus short-circuiting fabric and skin or flesh. The corpse of Hector must, Achilles decrees, be torn to shreds by dogs. What Achilles would like most is to devour the scraps of raw meat himself. However, Achilles does not succeed in satiating his beastly desire to disgracefully destroy and devour Hector's corpse. The gods restore Hector's human form—they make it whole. One more time, the tearing of the body is called forth in the negative. Every day at sunrise the cruel, revengeful Achilles drags the corpse three times through the dust of the grave site. Apollo cannot stand this desecration. He piously protects Hector's body with a golden film, so that no scratch can touch the skin (24.1–27). While Phoebus Apollo preserves the intactness of the skin, Aphrodite envelops him with the scent of roses so that the dogs will not eat him. Thus, Hector's corpse remains miraculously unharmed in spite of all the defacement: "his body has not decayed, not in the least, nor have the worms begun to gnaw his corpse . . . how he lies there fresh as dew, the blood washed away, and no sign of corruption. All his wounds sealed shut, wherever they struck and many drove their bronze blades through his body" (24.488–96). Eventually, the gods see to it that the corpse is clothed in precious fabrics and burnt on the pyre, in accordance with the Trojan cult of the dead. Homer averts his gaze from the mutilated body: the nonrepresentation of the violated corpse corresponds with the restorative gesture of healing. It is left to the imagination of the reader, but it is never actually shown.

Such an Apollonian—in the truest sense of the word—gesture has no place in Flaubert's work. The horrific disgrace visited upon Hector's corpse is outdone by Flaubert via Ovid. In unmatched graphic cruelty, the absolute, mangled nakedness of a living body is represented *à vif*. The Western ideal, namely, to put vividly before the eye, is literalized to an insufferable degree. Death comes alive. Flaubert achieves this rhetorical set piece via Ovid's description of the flaying of Marsyas. In its very briefness,

Ovid's narrative has always been seen as a masterpiece of unmatched vividness. Against the calm, composed Apollonian conception of art, Ovid puts a more "vivid" art before one's eyes. At the moment of death, life reveals itself, in all its vivacity, through the figure of the torn body. What becomes visible is that which is concealed. The skin is stripped off as if it were a mantle, a piece of fabric to bare flesh and blood. Mâtho/Marsyas is nothing but a wound, "He's all entirely one wound."[125] Flaubert follows Ovid's anatomical representation almost word for word:

He's all entirely one wound:
blood runs out everywhere, and his uncovered
sinews lie utterly exposed to view;
his pulsing veins were flickering, and you
could number all his writhing viscera
and the gleaming organs underneath his sternum.

(*Metamorphoses* 6.555–60)[126]

"[H]e was just a long shape, completely red" (*Salammbô*, 281) illustrates "He's all entirely one wound"; "his broken bonds hung along his thighs, but could not be distinguished" (ibid.) reverses "you could number"; "the tendons of his wrists which had been completely stripped of flesh" (ibid.) takes up "uncovered" and "utterly exposed." The motif of the "wrists . . . completely stripped of flesh" (ibid.) conjures up the attribute of Saint Bartholomew: the hands of the flayed martyr always hang as empty skins.

However, the most evident intertext of Mâtho's torture is the Passion of Christ. The Passion is first evoked in the reversal of Mâtho's victory march through the city, just after he had stolen the zaïmph: "However he remembered once before having experienced something similar. It was the same crowd on the terraces, the same looks, the same anger; but then he was walking free, everyone drew aside, a God covered him" (280).

This reversal restages the opposition between Palm Sunday—the triumphant entry of Christ into Jerusalem who is celebrated as a new king—and Good Friday—the way of the cross, where Christ's reign as king of the Jews ends. In Hebrew, *zaïmph* signifies phallus,[127] a meaning that could not have escaped Flaubert. The Mâtho then endowed with the phallic attribute stands in contrast to the now castrated Mâtho. His "castration" is represented as a displacement of the wounds of Christ. The evocation of the stations of the cross becomes loud and clear in the stations Mâtho passes, the four times he stumbles and falls, and in the fact that, like Christ, each time a new torture forces him to resume his march: "Six paces further and he fell a third, a fourth time again; and fresh torture brought him up each time" (281). Like Christ on the cross, sponges are held up to him on sticks. And exactly as Christ's thirst is not alleviated by the sponge soaked with acid vinegar, Mâtho's pain is not alleviated, since these sponges do not serve to wipe away sweat and blood, but merely stain: "others with sticks on which were stuck sponges soaked in filth dabbed at his face" (280). Like Christ, Mâtho is laughed at and mocked. Both wounds inflicted upon Mâtho are displacements of Christ's side wound. One could say that the wound in his side has doubled, slipping to the neck and hip: "On the right side of his throat spurted a stream of blood . . . his blood streamed out from a wound in his hip" (ibid.).[128] The wound in the neck recalls the beheading of Holofernes and thus refers back to the Judith story; the "spurting" of his blood is characteristic of the iconography of the decapitated Holofernes and is illustrated in an especially impressive manner in Caravaggio's *Judith*. Decapitation as a displacement of castration is not only a traditional device,[129] but is worked out explicitly by Flaubert in the close relation between the Tetrarch and John the Baptist in "Hérodias": his decapitation is anticipated by the "collapse" of the rigid Tetrarch. Through metonymical proximity, the wound in the hip points to the genitals. The sexualization of torture, in its association with castration, seems clear. Finally, the side wound inflicted upon Christ is called forth in the still pulsating heart torn from Mâtho's body to be held up to the sun with an instrument used in animal sacrifice. The Catholic cult of the Sacred Heart is thereby brought close to animality—"sacred meats" (282)—and in this "meatification" radically desublimated.

The opposition between veiled women and naked, injured men—as in the *Iliad* and in the tent scene of Flaubert's novel—structures the most iconic and most powerful image of European art: the image of a wholly shrouded Mary, whose clothes merge with her body, as opposed to the naked, wounded body of Jesus. This opposition marks the representations of the Mother of God with the infant Jesus, with the mother completely covered while the child is always nude. Invariably, the lethal wounds of this baby child destined to be sacrificed are symbolically alluded to. Bellini goes so far as to superimpose the iconography of the Pietà onto the Mother-with-child scene: his naked infant Jesus is lying deathly still in his mother's lap. The naked corpse of Christ in the lap of his veiled mother shines through.

This opposition of naked versus clothed comes to the fore most forcefully in the enfolded *mater dolorosa* underneath the cross and in the Pietà. Completely veiled, she holds the naked, dead, pierced body of her son in her lap. Her heart is figuratively pierced by seven pangs of love. It is precisely such a metaphoric anguish of love, which proves fatal to both Salammbô and Kleist's Penthesilea, while the male bodies stay behind, torn to shreds. The actual body of the Virgin and Mother of God remains in every regard *intacta*, whole. The only thing given to view is also what in the case of Salammbô signals an increasing nakedness in both of her appearances: her breasts. In contrast to the breast-feeding bosom unveiled by a *maria lactans*, Salammbô exposes the tempting breasts of Eve: at one point, a chain, like a snake, coils itself between her breasts; on another occasion, her bosom is naked and the nipples only are covered by caps. The other moment when the iconography of the Mother of God and that of Salammbô overlap and are played out against one another occurs in the motif of the hair coming loose as a sign of most intense pain. Mary's hair comes loose when she is undone by suffering under the cross. At the moment of her death, Salammbô's hair is completely unbound, contrasting with her wholly bound, covered body. The body of Mâtho is by contrast the most naked, the most wounded, the most open of all bodies imaginable. In the figure of the violated Marsyas, this body has become the wound of wounds. It is *nothing but* a wound. On the one hand, the Mary/Jesus opposition is reinforced by the heightened dressed/naked opposition; on the other hand, it is sexualized. In Salammbô's case this occurs through the breasts—decidedly not the breasts of a nursing mother, which, in line with Marian *allegoresis*, provide spiritual nourishment. In Mâtho's case, castration is inscribed onto the tortured body.

For Flaubert, this is what making love amounts to: the son affirms his castration which he suffers for the mother;[130] his tattered body is his love offering. The taking upon himself of the wound by the son, the incarnation of the son as a wound, is the price to be paid so that the mother can be kept as an object of love. The mother is seen as *intacta*, her castration is only articulable through displacement and is immediately veiled. But the castrated son, nothing but a wound, also remains strangely whole—wholly destroyed, that is. The beloved women are, as in all love scenes in Flaubert, always *intacta*, if only because they lack desire. They truly lack for nothing. Making love in the flesh is a degradation, an absolute disempowerment. It robs everything of its aura and magic; it is utterly disenchanting. Poetically speaking, the most beautiful moment of *A Sentimental Education* is therefore without doubt the final *acte manqué*: sex simply does not happen. This fall—with its glaring reference to the scene of original sin that appears in Flaubert's manuscripts under the name of the "tentation du Serpent"—can only be restored through the love sacrifice, which allows love to fully shine in all its intact glory.[131]

Let us end with the veil. The story of *Salammbô* is one of transgression and atonement, narrated after the model of *contrapasso*. Everything begins with an unveiling in Hamilcar's garden that leads to devastation and sacrilege. A paradisiacal opening scene turns into a Babel in which no one understands anyone else. Everyone is blinded by self-interest. The sacrilege committed in Hamilcar's garden finds fulfillment in the sacrilege of sacrileges, the penetration of the holy of holies in the temple of the goddess, the murder of a priest in the sanctified sphere of the temple, and the seeing, touching, and theft of the veil. The veil is not the goddess, but her *virtus*, her potency. Like the phallus that, as Lacan reminds us, is only seen veiled, the veil/phallus is a simulacrum. In itself, it is nothing, and it can therefore only be described metaphorically: as such, the veil is the universe, it is creation itself, and tells the story of Creation. Following the logic of *contrapasso*, the mercenaries must do penance for their sacrilege through their Passion. This is most visible in the Passion of Mâtho, whose body is "unveiled" into the most extreme nakedness. Veils and defloration are introduced from the very outset. Already in the second encounter between Mâtho and Salammbô, events revolve around the lethal exchange of veil for veil. Like lovemaking, the veil is also bound up with the will to knowledge, the Fall that drove humanity out of paradise, short-circuiting original sin and sexuality. Heeding the topos of Babel, Flaubert ties the moment of sexuality to language. Spendius, the deceitful sophist whose words precipitate the disastrous uprising of the rebels, is the son of a Greek rhetorician and a Campanian prostitute. Prior to his enslavement, he made his money as a pimp and a trader in women. After Salammbô experiences her Fall, after having known Mâtho and let herself be known in the flesh and tearing her veil, that same veil loses its transfiguring, enchanting power; everything is brought down to a dull state of fallenness. Salammbô is reduced to her exchange value and sees things how they are: she sees the world as fallen—the true state of affairs. But this is the real sin, the reification, to put it in Marx's terms, to which the bourgeoisie submits everything in a disenchanted world. To it corresponds a matter-of-fact sexuality geared to satisfaction as well as the rhetoric of the nonrhetorical: a nonfigurative authenticity. Like the nineteenth-century bourgeoisie, the Carthaginians know of nothing else. This language proper does not correspond to naturalness or some originary, unspoilt state, but is always already a figure of fallenness.[132] Like all of Flaubert's texts, *Salammbô* presents a biblical story in the guise of a secular story, narrating through the revolt of the mercenaries the temptation by the serpent, the Fall, the fratricide, the story of Babel, the Diaspora, all the way up to the Passion on the cross.

Like his contemporaries, Flaubert sees the *saeculum* as determined by the Bible. The cross has always been the matrix of history. In his work on Michelet, Claude Lefort has shown that secularization meant exactly that: the translation of Christian figures in order to interpret earthly history.[133] Michelet as well allows for no historical realm undetermined by the structure of "salvational events." In contrast to Flaubert, Michelet writes earthly history as a salvation history. By replaying and refiguring the Virgin Birth, the Passion, and the Resurrection, the French Revolution institutes a New Covenant here on earth. Flaubert counters this view by deciphering history as the erasure of the promise of salvation. This is achieved by perverting Christ's sacrificial love-death and the Banquet of Love, the Holy Communion. In the refiguration of the Passion, the kenosis of the sacrificial victim is followed through, in vertiginous hyperbole, to the extreme. The terrible truth of catastrophic history becomes legible only against the backdrop of the evangelic, salvational promise. The task of literature is to passionately stick to the cross and thus make history legible as the erasure of the salvational promise.

Let's take a last look at the veil and Flaubert's notes on it, held in the Morgan Library & Museum in New York. The veil, a cosmic device, binds man and universe; it is the starry sky above and simultaneously the human body, into which the secrets of what is to come are inscribed as the future is inscribed into the constellation of the stars. "The form of man [*La forme de l'homme*]," as Flaubert summarizes Adolphe Franck's interpretation of the Kabbala, "is a covering veil [*est un voile qui le couvre*]." Flaubert then proceeds to excerpt the following section, "the veil," from Franck's *La Kabbale, ou la Philosophie religieuse des Hébreux*:

On the veil, which is the firmament that envelops the whole universe, we see constellations, formed by the stars and the planets, to reveal hidden things and deep secrets. On the skin that envelops our body, there are drawings and marks, which are our body's planets or stars. All those drawings have a hidden meaning and the wise men who can read the faces of men, concentrate on those.[134]

In short, the veil is what endows the world with meaning—it is what makes the world intelligible and legible. No wonder, then, that it is considered to be an inscribed piece of fabric, a textile, a text. In 1859, Flaubert's friend Frédéric Baudry sent him excerpts from an article by Renan discussing the "peplos d'Astarté," with the comment: "Think about this new transformation of the peplos, which this time is not a pallium any longer, a coat, but a fabric covered with writing."[135]

Salammbô is the story of a veil—not a dance of veils, but a war of veils. One veil, Flaubert's novel, disavows the other veil, the veil of Tanit. Tanit's veil depicts the origin of the city, and perhaps also the origin of the universe. Since it is an attribute of Tanit—indeed, her *virtus*—and embodies her power, it stands for Tanit's fertility, that is, her ability to generate life, to create. That it is a male genital organ—the "zaïmph"—acting as the attribute of the goddess further strengthens the bond between Creation and the veil, as the goddess is conceived as phallic. Against this power testifying to sexuality, against this ability to create life stands a different veil: Flaubert's novel, which he also referred to as the "crimson web [*toile de pourpre*]." Making alive (*faire vif*)the vivid portrayal in words, of putting things before one's eyes, is Flaubert's aesthetic ideal. For Flaubert, the metaphor for this ability to make things come alive is not sexual procreation, but a wound, a skinning, an "unveiling," the wound of all wounds, the purple flesh, the purple paper soaked in blood.

Flaubert's novel does not see itself as a representation of what has already been created, but as *creatio ex nihilo*. Carthage is a vanished civilization, with only alien texts testifying to its existence. Not only the object of representation, but language itself must be invented anew; it must be translated out of nothing: "Nothing more absurd has been tried since literature came into being. To give a language to people in which they never thought," Flaubert writes to Ernest Feydeau.[136] "At every line, at every word, language fails me,"[137] and he underscores the need for never-ending translation.[138] Salammbô is not Flaubert's creation from the flesh, but from the letter. Like the Christian Word, like the Jewish Word[139]—but unlike the carnal fertility of Tanit—Flaubert creates a world through his texts. The veil has no hermeneutic function; there is no truth hiding behind the veil, no deeper meaning shimmering through. The novel is nothing but the best possible illustration of the poetics of *faire vif*, and as such it is an allegory of his writing. The price for this art à la Marsyas, of this enlivening of a dead culture, is the self-sacrifice in which the flesh becomes Word—the Word that resists every transfiguration of the flesh and thereby hopes to become more vivid than ever before.

A Sentimental Education
The Story of a Young Man

Paris/Rome: Flaubert's *Pharsalia*

A tree is an edifice, a forest is a city, and . . . the forest of Fontainebleau is a monument.

Victor Hugo

A little more than a year has passed since the Franco-Prussian War of 1870–71 and the French civil war called the Commune, which tore Paris apart. Like ancient Rome, nineteenth-century Paris has succumbed not to barbarian invaders but to internecine strife. "I am appalled by the state of society. . . . I'm filled with the sadness that afflicted the Roman patricians of the fourth century: I feel irredeemable barbarism rising from the bowels of the earth," Flaubert writes to Ivan Turgenev three years after the publication of his novel *A Sentimental Education*. "Since 1870 I've become a patriot. Watching my country die, I feel that I loved her. Prussia may lay down her arms: we can destroy ourselves perfectly well without her help."[1] "Rome herself is being ruined by her own power," Horace wrote at the end of Caesar's civil war (49–45 BCE), which left the Republic in ruins.[2] Civil war would remain a perpetual threat in the postrepublican era—a sword of Damocles suspended over imperial Rome.[3] Flaubert's diagnosis of his own time is modeled on this Roman precedent.

Rooted as it is in Rome's prehistoric era, Vergil's *Aeneid* is overshadowed for Flaubert by its successor, Lucan's blood-drenched epic *Pharsalia: De Bello Civili* (*Pharsalia: On the Civil War*), in which Rome is portrayed as having been founded from its inception in civil war, only to have the latter seal its eventual fate as well. "Rome is overwhelmed by her own might," Lucan says. In *A Sentimental Education*, Flaubert depicts the Revolution of 1848 as a civil war analogous to Lucan's ancient Roman one between the adherents of Julius Caesar and of Pompey and the Roman Senate. He famously claims in a letter that the Paris Commune could have been prevented had people only known how to read his novel. Many of his contemporaries likewise invoked ancient Rome to interpret current events, of course, but Flaubert's analysis of the political differences that had inflicted new waves of violence on France ever since the great Revolution of 1789 differs radically from theirs.

In order to gauge this return of Rome in the interpretation of contemporary French history, we have to go back to late antiquity, to the fourth century, which Flaubert compares to contemporary Paris in his letter. Broadly speaking, two distinct reactions to the fall of Rome would guide the interpretation of European history for centuries to come: Augustine's letter *De excidio urbis Romae*, written in 410, immediately after the sack of Rome by the Visigoths,[4] and that of Saint Jerome, who was following the earth-shattering events from distant Bethlehem and believed himself to be witnessing the end of mankind, which for him would coincide with the completion of the Vulgate.[5] In contrast to Jerome, Augustine remains astonishingly cool. He does not see the fall of the city as a unique, let alone apocalyptic, event. Instead, he ranks it among the long lineage of destroyed and punished cities of the Old Testament: Rome is thus a variation of Sodom and Gomorrah. Vergil had prophesied Rome's endless rule,[6] but for Augustine the city symbolizes *vanitas*; it is merely another illustration of instability and transitoriness, of the deceit of the earthly. Later, in his *The City of God Against the Pagans* (*De civitate Dei contra paganos*), Rome becomes the archetypical City of Man (*civitas terrena*): no longer just one example among many others, but the city of cities, a body politic torn apart by carnal desire (*concupiscentia),* the fate of all things earthly.[7]

For those concerned with the kingdoms of this world, Rome had an altogether different significance. This seminal role of Rome became amenable to modern thought already through Eusebius, whose theology offers a political alternative to Augustine's dark diagnosis as regards the City of Man.[8] For Eusebius, the Roman Empire was foundational to the global spread of Christianity. This was not only a matter of the political legitimacy of the new Christian world order. Eusebius rewrites Roman history into a narrative replete with prophetic salvational dimensions. Thus, the expansion of the Roman Empire and its descendants was already a cultural advance toward Christian fulfillment. European history appeared to be determined of old by a continuity that reached from Roman times through the Middle Ages. French history is marked by the equation of Paris with Rome in such terms as *translatio imperii et studii*. Up to the French Revolution, the emperor Augustus remained the orienting central figure: Henri II was Augustus, Louis XIV was Augustus, and finally Napoleon was yet another Augustus, putting an end to the civil war represented by the Revolution.[9] The philosophers of the Enlightenment and the politicians of the Revolution played off the virtuous republic against the decadent empire: Cato was Rousseau's model; Robespierre cast himself in the role of Brutus. History is performed twice over: first as tragedy and then as farce, as Marx wrote referring to the Revolution of 1789, the tragic return, and the Revolution of 1848, a second-rate, bloody slapstick comedy. Both revolutions come in the garb of antiquity and their heroes are dolled up as Romans.[10] This was, however, only the tip of the iceberg. Europe is the return of innumerable variations of Rome.

The poets write the scripts for the various rebirths of Rome. Seeking to be to Henri II what Vergil was to Augustus, Pierre de Ronsard writes the *Franciade*, a new *Aeneid*, in which Paris figures as the new Troy instead of Rome. This is why, as Racine explains in the preface to his *Andromaque*, Ronsard had Astyanax—the son of Hector and Andromache and Trojan heir apparent—survive the sack of Troy, whereas in all the ancient texts, he is killed by the Greeks. Ronsard made Astyanax the founder of Paris and as a result also the forebear of the French royal family; Paris thus becomes the direct successor of Troy and thereby the true Rome.[11] Despite or maybe because of all those glamorous predictions, Ronsard's *Franciade*, born under an unlucky star, was never finished. Like his predecessor Corneille, Racine—who lived at a time when the heights of literature and art attained by Paris rivaled those of its ancient model—instructs the absolute monarch, Louis XIV, in the Roman virtues of self-restraint and clemency (*clementia*). Paris had become the new Rome.

Configurations of this equation remained decisive in the postrevolutionary nineteenth century. Again as a reincarnation of Vergil, Hugo asserts that in the person of Napoleon, Paris had become an improved version of the Rome of the empire. With Napoleon, prefigured by Alexander, Caesar, and Charlemagne, not only French, but European history at large reached its apotheosis in Paris. The emperor completes the salvational dimension of European history, which becomes legible in Hugo's work as history finally fulfilled. According to Hugo, Napoleon turned Paris into what the poet Joachim du Bellay could only dream of for Henri II: he built a more magnificent Rome, replete with triumphal arches, victory columns, and obelisks.[12] The auspicious prediction—du Bellay's *bienheureux présage*—that Rome and Paris stood on an equal footing were superseded by the reality of imperial Napoleonic Paris. In contrast to the Roman ruins, whose foundation walls are stained with the blood of fratricide, the ruins of Paris exhibit immaculate holiness, Hugo the prophet announces. In Hugo's eyes, whatever takes place after Napoleon, after the fulfillment of history and the overcoming of Rome by Paris, can no longer aspire to the name of history. It amounts to no more than the meaningless bustle and hustle of forgettable trivialities, trifling events, leaving no trace.

However, for Émile Zola, history was also to be fulfilled in a French empire to come, envisaged as the precise antithesis of the Second Empire.[13] Zola imagined Paris becoming a third, finally true Rome, as the title of his *Three Cities Trilogy: Lourdes, Rome, Paris*, bears witness. This third Rome perpetuates the heritage of neither the Rome of the caesars nor that of the popes, both of which Zola deemed to be possessed by the Roman demon of an excessive will to power.[14] Instead, he envisaged the Paris to come as an anti-Rome that would convert Rome's sterile perversions into a fertile humanity spreading imperially around the globe: these are Zola's glad tidings announcing a French empire bringing salvation. He promises to this empire what Jupiter promises in vain to the Roman Empire in Vergil's *Aeneid*: it would be endless, unlimited in space and time.

Against these variations on fourth-century Eusebian self-interpretation, post-Renaissance France also experienced a different equation with Rome, which even if it subscribed, like Zola, to the "against Rome" tradition, was not tied to the paradigm of Rome's theologico-political merging of salvation and empire. Although this alternative tradition, this negative *translatio Romae* was extremely influential in the French interpretation of history, it has hardly ever been taken into account by scholarship. It concerns a deeply skeptical concept of history that fundamentally contradicts Petrarch's optimistic idea of Renaissance and its implications for the historiography of the modern. What else, as Petrarch's rhetorical question asks, is history but a hymn of praise to Rome?[15] If so, a skeptic might reply, history reproduces Rome's disastrous beginnings, the fratricide that stamped itself on Roman literature ever since Romulus murdered Remus. Transferal (*translatio*), the perpetual reenactment of the Roman curse, condemns all history to the blind repetition of the Roman fate of fratricide and civil war. Looking back on the lost Roman Republic, Lucan's *Pharsalia* sees Caesar's civil war as an absurd enlargement (*amplificatio*) of Roman history conceived of as founded on fratricide. Lucan pits this "fulfillment" of Roman history against Vergilian fulfillment, which takes the form of a timeless and boundless empire sanctioned by the gods. The *Pharsalia* refutes and seeks to erase the *Aeneid*.[16] The image of the torn body is its leading metaphor; it represents the split body politic that results in civil war. In the *Pharsalia*, it is fortune and not providence that reigns over history. The latter does not follow a salvational logic but figures instead as a history of damnation, of violence and bloodshed without end. Its primal scene is the act of violence committed out of lust for power: "A brother's blood wetted our city's earliest walls" (*Pharsalia* 1.9).[17] History is the bloody unfolding of this original sin/sacrilege, which hovers over Rome like a curse and realizes itself anew in the horrors on the Thessalian battlefield at Pharsalus, where the outcome of Caesar's civil war was decided.

Augustine's break, in his *City of God*, with Eusebian theologico-political theorizing was motivated by Lucan's *Pharsalia*, an account of Caesar's civil war written under Nero, in 60 CE, over a century after that war. According to Eusebian imperial theory, an *interpretatio christiana* of Vergil, the earthly Roman Empire is the precondition for the spread of the Christian faith (*praeparatio evangelica*), while simultaneously prefiguring the heavenly empire in the *pax romana*. The bold Vergilian prophecies promise an everlasting empire of divine predestination spanning the globe. The theologico-political *interpretatio christiana* makes this empire the prerequisite for the all-embracing Catholicism of the Roman Church. Augustine distinguishes the City of Man from the City of God, worldly history from the history of salvation. From the outset, the City of God undoes the theologico-political interpretation of the Roman Empire. Empire and redemption do not mix well in this world; the prospects of a *civitas permixta* are so questionable, much like Augustinian political theory itself, that the discussion lingered on well into Flaubert's time.[18] What can be said with some degree of confidence given the uncertainty of the source material is that Flaubert's reading of Augustine goes against the grain—be it out of disagreement or sheer ignorance—and resists the ideologically colored reception of political Augustinianism that was so prevalent at the time. It would therefore be careless, or even downright misleading, to bring this political Augustinianism to bear on the reading of Flaubert's texts. Luckily, there are some leads we can follow for Flaubert's reception of Augustine. As with all sources Flaubert consulted, his intensive reading of Augustine shaped his published work, and he also left us with a faint paper trail in the form of excerpts and notes, although unfortunately only a few of these have been preserved.[19] However, Augustine belonged so much to the traditional French higher educational regime that for Flaubert knowledge of his writings would have been second nature. What does seem remarkable, though, is the explicitness with which Flaubert swam against the tide of Augustine's political reception. In so doing, he obtained insights into aspects of *The City of God* that would not be fully appreciated by *The City of God* studies until the late twentieth century. Augustine exerted a decisive influence on Flaubert; it is all the more astonishing that Flaubert research has overlooked the Augustinian influence.

The meticulous confrontation with political theology is decisive for the historical working through of the literary and philosophical material Flaubert mobilized in his novels and enlisted in *A Sentimental Education* for a veritable historical critique of the contemporary ideological climate of the Second Empire. Flaubert the exegete was opposed to the widespread confusion of ideas attending distorting political interpretations of the *civitas* concept. He recognizes aspects of it masked by ideological overpainting that would only be discovered much later by theologico-philological studies of Augustine. "The notion *Civitas Dei* is a concept arising out of the Christian exegesis of the Old Testament," Joseph Ratzinger, later Pope Benedict XVI, writes.[20] The crucial insight, which in retrospect confirms Flaubert's reading, is as follows: the idea of the City of God was originally a hermeneutical construct on the part of the Fathers of the Church, but became a veritable metaphorological syndrome, in which theologico-political misreading of Augustine proliferated. The spread of this misconception, which borders on sheer ignorance, is exposed as lucidly as possible by Flaubert, precisely through his own writing.

As Flaubert sees it, already Augustine—writing during what he perceives as the last throes of a Roman City of Man whose earthly term has run its allotted course—connected that city with the catastrophic notion of history that was incarnated for him in the Roman concept of an all-encompassing world empire, originating with the Babel of the Old Testament. He identified these elements, ran them together, and revised them. Arguably, in *A Sentimental Education*, Flaubert now extends the idea of the City of Man to Paris, radicalizing the critique of the state derived from political Augustinianism à la Pascal. In any case, what he finds in this radically anti-politicized Augustinianism is precisely the bone of contention fought over by the Christian denominations in twentieth-century Augustine research, the theological stumbling block that Augustine "saw each and every state, including the Christian state, as a *civitas terrena* or *diaboli.*"[21] Understanding the consequences entailed for this controversy, he traced out a reading that early on definitely deduced from Augustine "the susceptibility of all *regna* to the counterorder that takes the form of *latrocinium* [meaning robbery, brigandage, piracy; *De civitate Dei* 4.4]."[22] The emphasis Flaubert puts on this state of things was already common knowledge in the Middle Ages. It is the contextual elaboration, however, that warrants closer attention; the issue is to gauge to what extent Flaubert went back to the original textual milieu of the fourth century before turning to and interweaving its subsequent French reception since Jansenism. "In fact, conversion meant the discovery of a new history from the time of Adam and Eve up until contemporary events," is how Arnaldo Momigliano characterizes the decisive moment of the fourth century, which becomes central in Flaubert.[23] Augustine's interpretation restored the Babylonian schema of the Prophets and virtually laid the groundwork for the subsequent critique of ideology. Flaubert's contribution, hostile as he is to conversion—in this hostility he is no longer following Pascal—pertains to another consequence: the literary anchorage of the critical moment. Only in and as literature—starting with the reading of *The City of God* as literature—can this ideological critique avoid turning into a new ideology, as is made obvious by the ubiquitous French revolutionary slogan "Liberty, Equality, Fraternity," which Flaubert reads as a historical echo.

Let us therefore turn to the main features of the history that Flaubert discerns in *The City of God*. The universality and eternality of salvation history does not entail that every political community can be questioned as to its achievement in *praeparatio evangelica*. Inversely, the existing earthly societies do not reach their aim of earthly peace any more easily *in temporibus christianis*. For Augustine, there cannot be an *imperium christianum*; the more visible the City of God becomes, the more pronounced its categorical difference from earthly things. Augustine identifies a pagan analogue to the story of Cain in Lucan's primal scene from the history of Rome, which locates fratricide at its heart. He quotes Lucan verbatim: "The first walls of Rome were wet with a brother's blood [*Fraterno primi maduerunt sanguine muri* (De civitate Dei 15.6)]."[24] Augustine comments: "The first founder of the earthly city, then, was a fratricide; for, overcome by envy, he slew his brother, who was a citizen of the Eternal City and a pilgrim on this earth."[25] The difference between both primordial fratricides is that both Romulus and Remus were citizens of an earthly *civitas*. Abel however, in contrast to Cain, did not found a state but, "by grace he was a pilgrim below, and by grace he was a citizen above," a *civis* of the City of God.[26] The City of God, whose figure is the Church, is never wholly of this world; it remains on earth in exile, *ecclesia peregrinans*, on a pilgrimage to the heavenly homeland. For Augustine, fratricide becomes the archetype of earthly history; it is the figure of a body politic that is fundamentally torn, divided. Inner conflict and division are figured in civil war. With Cain, the founder of the city—this being the exegetic hook connecting the concept of *civitas* with Rome—the City of Man runs its earthly course, reaching a first, horrific culmination in Babel with Nimrod, heir to Cain. The most powerful paradigm of the City of Man, though, is Rome, since its beginning—as Augustine explains quoting Lucan's epic— blindly follows the pattern of Cain's fratricide. In retrospect, humanity can be divided into two species, the Cains and the Abels (paradigmatically contrasted in Baudelaire's poem "Révolte" in *Fleurs du Mal*, roughly contemporary with *A Sentimental Education*).

Decisive for Flaubert's reading of the City of Man is its internal division: since everybody is only interested in his or her own advantage, everybody is at war with everybody else. Like every earthly community built upon the glorification of worldly goods, the foundation and progress of Rome can be ascribed to lust for power and thirst for fame. Justice reigns nowhere; consequently, no earthly realm has the right to speak of itself as a *res publica*. The driving force of the earthly state is the desire to dominate, *libido dominandi*. It drives states to expand and compels them to universal domination; it determines the internal structure of every *civitas* as a community of lordship and bondage. The domination of the masters over the slaves within is as violent as the expansion of power in the domination of other peoples. Both relations of violence generate antagonisms and discord. And since the discord in the City of Man is constant, the only way this vicious circle becomes ever more vicious is by ever more violence. Augustine's profane history is a *series calamitatum*. Determined by violence, betrayal, and prostitution, it leads to nothing—to use Flaubert's rendering of Augustine's *series calamitatum*—but a ruinous "eternal destitution of everything [*éternelle misère de tout*]."[27] This is the common denominator to which Flaubert reduces French history in the Palace of Fontainebleau. For world history and especially for Paris, the latter-day Rome, the fratricide exemplified by Rome, is an irreducible burden. All earthly history remains bound to the conflict that Augustine found prefigured in Lucan.

"Lucan versus Vergil" sums up the conflict of interpretations in French literary history from the Renaissance to the twentieth century. Most recently, perhaps, this dichotomy informed the work of Claude Simon (1913–2005), one of Flaubert's most prominent literary heirs (Simon's *La bataille de Pharsale* and *Les Géorgiques* being obvious examples). The Roman paradigm—but of which Rome?—manifests itself as a dominant model of self-interpretation of French history in *A Sentimental Education*. Flaubert's contemporaries preferred variations of the Eusebian imperial model, based on Vergil. The institution of the French Third Republic through the civil war represented by the Paris Commune—the flip side of Roman glory— was too hard for them to stomach.

Joachim du Bellay was the first modern writer to become aware of the Lucanist construction underlying the Augustinian interpretation. With Lucan and against Ronsard—the new Vergil—du Bellay writes about the disastrous subtext of the transferal to France of the Roman model, a curse that inevitably split the political and social body to the core.[28] This constellation of ideas informs Flaubert's novel, in whose Paris no one recognized the intertextual model of Lucan's Rome.

Set in France between 1840 and 1867 and revolving around the events of the 1848 Revolution and "Prince-President" Louis-Napoléon Bonaparte's 1851 coup d'état, *A Sentimental Education* is Flaubert's interpretation of the politics of the time. The question of Flaubert's political engagement has been raised over and over again in terms of the hackneyed binaries of reactionary versus progressive, Left versus Right, bourgeois versus proletarian. Many frustratedly contend that Flaubert missed his rendezvous with history—*Histoire* with a capital *H*. One feels one would have known better and judged more clearly; one would have expressed oneself more uncompromisingly, and would have unequivocally chosen sides. For Flaubert, however, the question posed itself quite differently. Like Hugo and Zola, he interpreted French history according to the Roman prototype, but he framed its transferal to Paris quite differently. The Palace of Fontainebleau is one of the most prominent locations in Flaubert's *A Sentimental Education*. There is perhaps no other place so manifestly connected to the idea of the Roman prototype. It was here that François I asserted, by means of an astonishingly elaborate program of architecture and painting, that France was heir to the Roman Empire. It was here that Napoleon I abdicated in 1814 in favor of his infant son, whom he had titled the king of Rome. The dream of a worldwide French empire with Napoleon in the role of Caesar Augustus thus came to an end, but oscillating between the 1789 Revolution and the collapse of the Second Empire in 1870, attempts to transfer the Roman paradigm to Paris persisted; for Flaubert it is a *basso continuo*.

At first sight Rome plays no significant role in *A Sentimental Education*. However, Dussardier does draw the tried-and-tested historical comparison between the demise of the Roman and French Republics: "Now they're killing our Republic, just as they killed the Roman Republic" (429). The name of the eternal city comes up as the last home of Madame Arnoux, who lives there with her son, who, incidentally, as *lieutenant de chasseurs*, exercises a scarcely concealed Babylonian profession. Nimrod, the founder of Babel, offspring of Cain, was a hunter in defiance of the Lord according to both Augustine and Hugo. This lapidary formulation is a good example of the mode of cryptic inscription we will have to deal with: "She must be in Rome now with her son, a cavalry lieutenant [*lieutenant de chasseurs*]" (457). In Paris all roads lead to Madame Arnoux, "every street led towards her house" (76). By mentioning her last residence, Flaubert slips a key into our hands. Since all roads lead via Madame Arnoux to Rome, he has them end at the source of the catastrophe of civilization that culminates at this very moment in Paris, the new Rome.

The calamities of fratricide, civil war, and barbarian self-destruction, diagnosed by Lucan in Rome and turned by Augustine into the model for the transhistorical *civitas terrena*, are the fates doomed to be repeated by Flaubert's protagonists, who are deaf to the lessons of history. Flaubert interprets the events of the 1848 Revolution through Lucan's *Pharsalia* and its reception in Augustine's *De civitate Dei*. The fact that *A Sentimental Education* perpetuates the reasoning of the *Pharsalia* has gone unnoticed. It is cryptically inscribed by means of a refined intertextuality. In the novel, Augustine's far-reaching historical and philosophical exposition finds an abyssal, anti-Augustinian response. Flaubert agrees with Augustine that society, which manifests itself in the form of the state, cannot be seen as the initial stage or fulfillment of the Kingdom of God. Rather, society is simply the eternal return of the selfsame, deathly discord of the City of Man. More disillusioned than Augustine, Flaubert leaves no room in *A Sentimental Education* for a *civitas Dei peregrinans* that would inaugurate on earth the pilgrimage toward the heavenly homeland. Enthralled by utter self-love, contemporary France, like the Roman Empire, is solely of this world. *A Sentimental Education* seeks to erase every possible political realization of a salvific kingdom of this world as promoted by revolutionaries of all political stripes. Flaubert tells his story of the 1848 Revolution and the following coup of 1851 according to the structure Augustine had analyzed for the City of Man.

Rightly, the Fontainebleau episode is *A Sentimental Education*'s most famous passage. It owes its beauty, indeed its very sublimity to its underpinning in Lucan's pathos-laden *Pharsalia*. "Fratricide is my song," Hölderlin translated the opening of the epic with a sense for its perversion in mingling the beautiful with the horrible.[29] Readers sympathetic to the June Days Uprising have overlooked in the heat of the Paris battles how Flaubert's description of the forest of Fontainebleau echoes Lucan's preamble, which portrays a Rome destroyed from the ground up. Rosanette and Frédéric's escapade to Fontainebleau occurs during the second phase of the 1848 Revolution, the "June Days," when the working classes turned against the bourgeois government established in February after the fall of King Louis Philippe. In June 1848, General Louis-Eugène Cavaignac, invested by the National Assembly with dictatorial powers, ordered the army and Garde nationale to suppress the insurgents, their brothers-in-arms in the February Revolution. "Some travellers who had just arrived told them [Rosanette and Frédéric] that a terrible and bloody battle was raging in Paris" (350). The opposition between a Paris torn apart by executions and slaughter and the rural idyll of Fontainebleau, which structures the plot, collapses through the intertext of the *Pharsalia*. Flaubert inscribes onto his description of the forest of Fontainebleau, in objective, dramatic irony, unfolding behind the back of clueless Frédéric and Rosanette, the fratricidal furor that takes at this very moment hold of Paris. He thus unveils the Roman fate that in this instance is once more fulfilled in the contemporaneous destruction of Paris through civil war. The description of the forest of Fontainebleau as a Rome-in-ruins anticipates the outcome of a wrecked Paris and holds a mirror up to the revolutionary prophesy of redemption.

At the Palace of Fontainebleau, Frédéric and Rosanette come face to face with the ideal of Renaissance France, "when mankind sought to transform the world into a dream of the Hesperides" (347). In the forest of Fontainebleau, the Hesperidian dream returns as a nightmare.[30] The novel opposes a barren realm strewn with brambles—the outcome of the civil war—to the paintings in the palace with delightful blue-golden love scenes. "Desolate Hesperia," as Lucan writes, "bristles with thorn-brakes" (1.5). Flaubert's description of the forest of Fontainebleau is not modeled after just any dead and ruined city. It shows us one particular city: Rome, at a precise moment in history, devastated at the end of the civil wars, and seen by one specific poet, Lucan. Paris, the new Rome, is like its ancestor, "wetted with a brother's blood" (1.9). In Flaubert's transferral, the Roman curse fulfills itself in this very moment and its result, utter ruin, unfolds before our eyes in the forest of Fontainebleau.

While portraying the forest, Flaubert gives en passant a pastiche of romantic clichés, from Hugo's poem "À l'Arc de triomphe" to the "Promenade dans Rome au claire de lune" in Chateaubriand's *Voyage en Italie*. History ends here on a melancholy note in aesthetically enjoyable ruins, thus transcending the transitoriness of all things earthly in a pacifying light that turned Paris into an improved version of Rome, but Flaubert's forest of Fontainebleau is filled with irredeemable signs of a tragic, bloodstained, and fatally recurring history. Following the oppressive lead of antique topoi, history fades into the ancient image of limitless pride and inevitable ruin. Of the trees of the forest, Flaubert says: "Some were astonishingly tall and bore themselves like patriarchs or emperors; some linked branches and with their long trunks they looked like triumphal arches; some grew obliquely from the ground like pillars about to fall" (351).

The immodest loftiness of patriarchs or emperors, the tall shafts of triumphal arches, the awe-inspiring pillars in danger of collapsing—nothing could more vividly convey Lucan's comment: "It was the fall which no eminence can escape; it was the grievous collapse of excessive weight, and Rome unable to support her own greatness" (*Pharsalia* 1.9).

Huge gnarled oaks rose convulsively out of the ground, embraced one another, and, solidly established on their torso-like trunks, threw out their bare arms in desperate appeals and furious threats, like a group of Titans struck motionless in their anger. An oppressive atmosphere, a feverish languor hung over the pools, whose still waters were hemmed in by thorn bushes; the moss on their banks, where the wolves came to drink, was sulphur-coloured, as if it had been burnt by witches' footsteps. (*Sentimental Education*, 351–52)

With the oak tree and the wolf conjuring up the symbols of Rome, the forest is identified as Roman. The oak trees of the forest, which stretch up from the ground as if cramped in distorted pain, resemble a group of Titans frozen with rage, hurling vicious threats while crushing each other to death in a violent embrace. With the figure of the Titan Flaubert cites the prehistoric foundational myth of the city of Rome. In insurgent fury and wild revolt the giants confronted the gods, who slammed them to the ground. The Seven Hills of Rome are the graves of the Titans. Lucan correlates the struggle of the Titans with the civil war—both are unlawful, monstrous wars bringing only chaos.[31] Flaubert exploits the ambiguity inherent in *étreindre*, which oscillates between "embrace" and "crush," in order to bring out the motif of fratricide. The victory of the gods over the giants, which, from Vergil to Horace, guarantees the order of the universe, was a model of the *pax romana*. In Lucan's text, however, Rome is not faced with chaos. Rather, Rome is the soil where chaos cannot but recur and renew itself ad infinitum: "Pharsalia nostra vivet"—"Our Pharsalia will live, no generation will banish us to the shadows!"[32] During the golden age of Latinity with its panegyric Roman poetry celebrating Augustus's world domination as a victory against the forces of chaos, the Rome of *Pharsalia* is presented as the living empire of chaos, which Flaubert transposes onto contemporary Paris.

From the start, Lucan introduces the outcome of the tragedy set to unfold in the *Pharsalia*. What remains is a wasteland; Rome is ruined. This is exactly how the forest of Fontainebleau is portrayed:

The sound of iron, a succession of hard blows, rang through the air; it was some quarrymen striking the rocks on a hillside. These rocks became more and more numerous, finally filling the whole landscape; cube-shaped like houses, or flat like paving-stones, they propped each other up, overhung one another, and merged together like the monstrous, unrecognizable ruins of some vanished city. (352)

The stone quarry stretches out into a landscape of ruins, where isolated people wander and wild animals live. Flaubert describes the forest of Fontainebleau, a new Hesperia, in Lucanian terms. As a consequence of its civil wars, Rome was transformed into an almost depopulated region overgrown by thornbushes, with half-destroyed houses and gigantic ruins at the feet of crumbling fortress walls. With "fury" and "chaos," Flaubert's text finally names both keywords of the *Pharsalia*. It was *furor* that, in pitting father-in-law against son-in-law, hurled everything into chaos. Flaubert takes up Lucan's analogy between the chaos of Roman history and the originary chaos of nature. For Lucan, the ruined Rome plunged into blind rage and wild fury is the mirror image of the discord of primal chaos: "Once the world's framework loosens and its final hour, drawing all time to a close, seeks out ancient chaos once more, fiery stars will hurtle seaward . . . ; the whole discordant cosmic machine will fly apart, its laws confounded."[33] Flaubert compares the stone quarry that expands into a landscape of ruins with natural catastrophes and, like Lucan, short-circuits both imperial history and natural history in its cosmic expansion: "But the frenzied chaos in which they lay conjured up rather thoughts of volcanoes, floods, great unknown cataclysms" (352). It is the history of the eternal renewal of catastrophe. Chaos, as formulated by Flaubert via Lucan, is the image of disunity and self-division thematized in and through history and stands for a fratricidal, destructive discord. As bloody as it is tragic, it constitutes for both Flaubert and Lucan the beginning and end of history. Rosanette, who turns away from this spectacle because "it would drive her mad" (ibid.), is right, even without realizing what she is saying.

The deafening stone quarry has been read as an allegory of Paris during the 1848 Revolution and as a symbol of Paris in the 1860s when Flaubert was writing his novel: as a truly corrosive commentary on the Paris newly renovated by Haussmann.[34] More crucial however than the Paris of the Revolution and of the Second Empire is Lucan's Rome, showing through the woods and stone quarry at Fontainebleau. Haussmann's Paris turns out to be the ignorant heiress of Rome, the latest embodiment of the City of Man. The comparison between political history and natural history, between revolution or civil war and natural catastrophe is a constant in the text; the seizure of power by the people at the Tuileries Palace is represented in the metaphor of the Flood. Through the "flood" and the "swarming mass . . . like a spring-tide pushing back a river" (313), it is stylized as a natural disaster. The simile, through which the *Pharsalia* draws parallels between the downfall of the empire and the destruction of the universe, reiterates the Vergilian analogy between universe and empire, only to turn it into an ironically negative typology. Rome is the image of the cosmos and here that means the locus of primal discord or chaos. Against Vergil's teleological perfection, Lucan pits a cycle of disintegration and ruin, which Augustine then reads within the allegorical frame of the *interpretatio christiana*. In Flaubert, the return of Rome does not mean Roman glory bestowed upon Paris, but the return of the Roman curse.

Shortly before Frédéric and Rosanette's escapade, stand-ins for the two chief characters of the *Pharsalia*, Caesar and Pompey, father-in-law and son-in-law (Pompey having married Caesar's daughter Julia), make their appearance, representing the driving force of Lucan's Roman civil war, ferocious rage (*ira ferox*).[35] Monsieur Dambreuse and Monsieur Martinon both back law and order and are against the workers' uprising. Though both prospective father-in-law and son-in-law do not lash out at each other in civil war *fureur* as they do in Lucan, they are united in rage. Dambreuse, speculator, banker, and filthy rich capitalist, is by all appearances a cultured upper-class gentleman. Now he has lost all measure and manners. He is so furious that he goes about with a blackjack: "He had become so fanatical on this subject that he carried a cosh in his pocket" (344), and not to be outdone, his future son-in-law, Martinon, decides to carry one as well. They do not practice fratricidal violence personally, but delegate it. Dambreuse's steward (*régisseur*),[36] Père Roque, is charged with realizing the interests of his master at the price of deception, extortion, and murder (368). At the time of Frédéric and Rosanette's escapade to Fontainebleau, Père Roque, wearing the antiquated uniform of the Garde nationale, murders a defeated insurgent in Paris. Regardless of political inclination, almost everyone in *A Sentimental Education* participates with fratricidal fervor in civil war. It is not the working class that behaves most repulsively; it is the bourgeois victors who make no bones about brutally slaughtering the defeated.[37] Thus perhaps not the law, but certainly all sympathy in *A Sentimental Education* is on the side of the vanquished, with the insurgents of the June Days, the republicans. *A Sentimental Education* represents the Second Empire, established after the 1851 coup d'état, as a regime that has legitimized fratricide—one is hard-pressed to find a stronger condemnation in Marx or Hugo. With Lucan, *A Sentimental Education* sings a song of fratricidal warfare, or, in Lucan's words, "war worse than civil. . . . Justice given over to crime" (1.2).

The story that unfolds in *A Sentimental Education* is one of revolution. Yet it is not a revolution that revolutionizes, but one that repeats unconditionally, and what it repeats is the curse of fratricide. The specter of fratricide seeks out the 1848 Revolution from the start. Variations on the revolutionary paradigm of Liberty, Equality, Fraternity and its progressive erasure drive its story forward. Dussardier is loyal to the Republic because he sees it as a regime built on brotherly love and not on fratricide. He hates the authorities:

One day, at the age of fifteen, outside a grocer's shop in the rue Transnonain, he had seen some soldiers with their bayonets red with blood, and hair sticking to their rifle butts; and from that time on, he had loathed the Government as being the very incarnation of Injustice. He tended to confuse murderers with policemen; in his eyes a police informer was as bad as a patricide. (251)

People love poking fun at Dussardier, that insignificant office worker who is barely literate and has only read two books in his lifetime: he confuses everything and is really not a man of the world. Nevertheless, and this is the terrible irony of the entire narrative, Dussardier is the one who will be right in the end: the soldiers will indeed emerge with bloodied bayonets and hair caught in the shafts from the slaughter of the June Days, after killing those who had been their brothers-in-arms just a few weeks before. The Garde nationale and gendarmes will become *parricides*. Sénécal, who turns into a police informer for the dictatorship, becomes a fratricide in killing Dussardier, his comrade-in-arms of many years. In the service of authority, he kills the one who tried to save him from the authorities. The tyrant arising from the coup d'état will declare these crimes lawful.

Dussardier's mission is to prevent fratricide—only to fall victim to it in the end. In the scene where he is introduced, Dussardier, the blond Hercules, protects a boy, still just a child, against police brutality without any consideration for his own safety. The second time, at the barricades of the June Revolution, he is fighting with the Garde nationale against the rebels and risks his life to save one of the insurgents from being shot to death; he barely escapes with his life and is heavily wounded. The scene takes place at the end of the June Revolution when the rebel workers are already all but quashed by Cavaignac. This scene is so important in the economy of *A Sentimental Education* because it is here, in the context of the Revolution of 1848, that fratricide makes its first appearance. It is all the more central since Flaubert superimposes Delacroix's famous painting of the 1789 Revolution—*Le 28 Juillet: La liberté guidant le peuple* (1830)—onto this scene in June 1848. The role of Marianne/Liberté wrapped in the Tricolor, as Delacroix had paid homage to her in what at the time had become a national icon, is played here by a boy:

The previous Saturday a boy wrapped in a tricolour flag had shouted to the National Guards from the top of a barricade: "Are you going to fire on your brothers?" As they moved forward, Dussardier had dropped his musket, pushed the others away, leapt up on to the barricade, felled the young rebel with a well-directed kick, and snatched the flag from him. He had been found under the debris, his thigh pierced by a copper slug. (362)[38]

The ambivalence of the sentence is arresting, since "felled" (*abattre*) can also mean "killed." Finally, too, who exactly is lying injured under the rubble—the rebel boy or Dussardier, the national guardsman? The ambiguity of personal pronouns emphasizes their interchangeability, equality, and fraternity. The scene in which Dussardier, the almost illiterate, painfully dim-witted sales clerk (*commis*), marches with the Garde nationale against the revolutionaries and saves his "brother" in disregard of his own life repeats itself the other way around, in a specular fashion, when he is stabbed to death by his "brother" Sénécal.

The curse of fratricide comes to fruition in a now-foreseeable manner—and will carry the force of law—before the eyes of a shocked Frédéric at the moment of the coup d'état in 1851 by Louis-Napoléon Bonaparte. The protagonists Sénécal and Dussardier belong to Frédéric and Deslauriers's circle of friends; side by side, and changing sides all the while, they struggle throughout these days. Sénécal, whose hero is the revolutionary socialist Auguste Blanqui, sides with the defeated insurgents, while Dussardier fights alongside the Garde nationale and is injured. When Sénécal lands in prison because of his involvement in an attempted bomb attack, Dussardier does everything in his power to save him. Subsequently, however, Sénécal becomes a police agent and defender of the coup d'état that would seal the fate of the Revolution and inaugurate the end of the Republic. He stabs

Dussardier, who, after the reversal of their political positions, dies for the republican cause:

But on the steps of Tortoni's a man stood firm, as motionless as a caryatid, and conspicuous from afar on account of his tall stature. It was Dussardier. One of the policemen, who was marching in front of his squad, with his three-cornered hat pulled down over his eyes, threatened him with his sword. Then Dussardier took a step forward and started shouting: "Long live the Republic!" He fell on his back, with his arms spread wide. A cry of horror rose from the crowd. The policeman looked all around him, and Frédéric, open-mouthed, recognized Sénécal. (450)[39]

With its protagonists Dussardier "motionless as a caryatid" and Sénécal blinded by "his three-cornered hat pulled down over his eyes," the fratricide is performed in the trappings of classical antiquity, à l'antique. In this scene, what the novel has been building up to step by step finally comes about; the crowd witnesses the murder, Frédéric recognizes the fratricide. Dussardier collapses "with his arms spread wide" (les bras en croix) in the sign of the cross (we'll come back to the cross later).

This is given emphasis by what Proust calls Flaubert's "blanc": sixteen years pass virtually unrecorded after Frédéric recognizes Sénécal.[40] "He [Frédéric] travelled the world," is how Flaubert transitions into the following chapter: "He tasted the melancholy of packet ships, the chill of waking under canvas, the boredom of landscapes and monuments, the bitterness of broken friendship" (451). Synchronous with the legibility of history in the forest of Fontainebleau—in a technique that reminds one of cross cutting—the novel tells of a place in the Tuileries where the vanquished are crowded together and brutally murdered by the Garde nationale and the army—all of whom were once brothers-in-arms during the February Revolution.[41] Mad with hunger, shaking with fever, lying amongst their own excrement and rotting corpses, they are pierced with bayonets the minute they try and move closer to the bars for a breath of air. Although the Revolution was crushed, it proved victorious across the board: its ideal, equality for all, has finally been attained. But égalité and fraternité are by now invested with a meaning, radically different from the one propagated in the formula. Equality has been reached: all are reduced to "brute beasts," more bloodthirsty than wild animals. Shocked and broken at the core, reason has regressed into barbarous brutality. Cold-bloodedly, Père Roque shoots a young man, still no more than a child, crying out for bread. Accompanied by the crowd's howl of shock, a howl we hear again only when Sénécal murders Dussardier, this scene presages this fratricide as well as the coup d'état. In a comment without a trace of irony that could not have been more auctorial, Flaubert models his conclusion on the events of 1848 on the *Pharsalia*.[42] Like Lucan, he contrasts *furor* with *ratio* and *pietas*, comparing men to wild animals in their bloodthirstiness, and the civil war to a cosmic catastrophe (cf. *Pharsalia* 1.73–82, 4.240):

By and large the National Guards were merciless. . . . Despite their victory, equality . . . asserted itself triumphantly: an equality of brute beasts, a common level of bloody atrocities. . . . The public's reason was deranged as if by some great natural upheaval. Intelligent men lost their sanity for the rest of their lives. (363–64)

The most monstrous scene of *A Sentimental Education* is bloodcurdlingly brutal. In bestial cruelty, the sword is turned against its bearer, against yesterday's comrades who are now a weak, helpless, and defeated people crying for bread in pure desperation:

One of them, a youth with long fair hair, pressed his face to the bars and asked for bread. Monsieur Roque ordered him to be silent. But the young man went on repeating in a pitiful voice: "Bread!" . . . To frighten them he aimed his musket at them; and the young man, carried up to the ceiling by the crowd pushing behind him, threw his head back and cried once again: "Bread!" "Right! Here you are!" said old Roque, firing his musket. There was a tremendous howl, then nothing. Something white remained on the edge of the grating. (364)

Death, rather than the Bread of Life, is thus dished out by Père Roque, "Father Rock" (*roque* being regional Middle French for *roche*), the respectable citizen and steward upon whom Monsieur Dambreuse relies and builds (cf. Matt. 16:18: "upon this rock I will build my church"). After the murder, Roque, as craven as he is vengeful, returns to his daughter and property to slurp his soup in the coziness of his home. The soup gets stuck in his throat.

The revolutionaries hope the revolution will bring about the opposite of fratricide—that is, an era of equality and brotherliness, a union of justice and brotherly love here on earth that knows no class or gender hierarchy.[43] This new state of an all-embracing, brotherly love is tied to a new form of government, the socialist republic: "All the Christianity I find in Socialism appalls me!" writes Flaubert to George Sand in 1868.[44] In *A Sentimental Education*, the Revolution of 1848 explicitly stands for hope of the advent of this new empire of love. On this all revolutionaries can agree, regardless of what specific political faction they belong to. "The others . . . listened to [Sénécal] talking about universal suffrage, which would result in the victory of Democracy and the application of the principles of the Gospel" (282). And Dussardier, the man of two books, the only one who will actually sacrifice himself for the ideal of unselfish brotherliness, exclaims after forty-eight hours of battle, after having witnessed the occupation of the Tuileries and the proclamation of the Republic in the February days: "I've just come from there. All is well! The people have won! Workers and bourgeois are embracing! Oh, if only you'd seen what I've seen! What wonderful people! How splendid everything is!" (316). In the French Revolution, the manly virtues of the Roman Republic were staged according to the model of ancient rhetoric, with Robespierre playing Cato the Elder, while Saint-Just does Brutus. During the February and June Revolutions, the Roman Republic returns, dressed up doubly, in the garments of the 1789 Revolution, which was the first to appropriate Rome:

[A]nd as it was customary for every person in the public eye to model himself on some famous figure, one copying Saint-Just, another Danton, and yet another Marat, he himself [Sénécal] tried to resemble Blanqui, who in his turn imitated Robespierre. His black gloves and his close-cropped hair gave him a severe look, which was extremely becoming. (327)

A pathetic déjà vu, were it not for a minor, decisive difference that is already announced in Michelet and developed by Proudhon; *A Sentimental Education* relies on the Proudhonian version. The promise of a return of the Roman Republic—its Second Coming, so to speak—goes now hand in hand with the Christian notion of redemption.

The "Club de l'Intelligence" is an assembly of Charismatics who, with a kind of Pentecostal hope, await the coming of the all-embracing love that will bring about the new covenant. As one of the speakers, representing the position of Proudhon and the Saint-Simonists, formulates it: "The time had come to inaugurate the reign of God. The Gospel led straight to 1789. After the abolition of slavery would come the abolition of the proletariat. The age of hatred was past; the age of love was about to begin" (329). But instead of an age of love, the reader witnesses a fight of all against all. Instead of a Pentecostal moment of universal understanding, a grotesque Babel of voices ensues, in which no one can understand anyone else—literally so when someone speaks in Spanish. Their watchword may be charity, but the deafest, dumbest, blindest kind of self-love is the rule. The "club of intelligence" reveals itself to be the club of universal insanity (329ff.). It proclaims brotherly love but wages internecine warfare; Sénécal deliberately nips Frédéric's candidature in the bud. *A Sentimental Education* rises to a crescendo: the shouting gets louder and louder, while mutual understanding grows weaker and weaker, until the initial chaos boils over and explodes precisely in—of all places—the "Club de l'Intelligence," where the frenzied cacophony reaches its climax in a Babel of voices. How skillfully and laboriously Flaubert worked on this cacophony becomes clear when one considers that to evoke Babel, he translates an actual speech made there in French by a Spanish patriot back into Spanish word for word: everybody talks in their own language and no one understands a single word, because what people understand is only *their own* opinion, which is in turn nothing but the expression of the will to power and must therefore inevitably clash with the claims to power of others: *every man for himself and God against them all.*

The new covenant of love is, following the New Testament, a unique event through which history fulfills itself and an unrepeatable turning point is experienced. In Flaubert's text, the emergence of this unique event is framed as a tasteless quotation and a return of the same—it follows a pattern, whereas it should have eliminated all patterns. It comes to the fore in the light of a second-rate slapstick comedy. *A Sentimental Education* does not fail to expose the hyperinflation of proclamations that, through the sheer fact of repetition, undermine their own claims to salvation. It therefore comes as no surprise that the oustanding protagonist of this new empire of love is an actor, the handsome Delmar, who has "a mission"—he is becoming the Messiah (189).[45] Two central Christian notions—the mission and the *imitatio Christi*—are reduced here to bad theater: missionary work is confined to proclaiming one's own fame, while the *imitatio* only concerns hairstyle: "He had long black hair arranged in the style adopted by Christ" (80). Against the advent of the new bond of love and fraternity in a reborn republic, another recurrence of Roman history is operative in *A Sentimental Education*. This Roman history has always been conceived of as cyclical and it subjects the history of mankind to a fatal eternal return. In *A Sentimental Education*, the sacrifice of love that should overturn the fratricidal state is travestied. Instead of a salvational conversion through the Incarnation and Crucifixion, inner conflict reappears in the form of tragic farce—"cataclysms" and "upheavals" tricked out as redemption. In Flaubert there is no space for salvation beyond disaster. The opposition between the two collapses, since the scope of disaster expands in the guise of salvation. To put it in Augustinian terms, the promise of the City of God serves as a cover-up for the expansion of the City of Man. In the alleged furtherance of the empire of love, the empire of hatred unfolds, culminating in fratricide. In this novel where everyone cheats, lies, and betrays their fellow human beings, here where resentment, jealousy, and hatred are sovereign and where Frédéric's "education" consists of a hardening of the heart, everything is sugar coated with the hypocritical, sweetish rhetoric of the good heart, the compassionate heart, the golden heart, the genius of the heart. When it manifests itself in the narrative, fratricide is the figure—and herein lies the labor of *A Sentimental Education*—of a heart only driven by self-interest, a heart obeying only the laws of the desire to dominate, *libido dominandi*. It is a heart—in the Pauline sense of the phrase—of stone, not governed by charity but by pride, by rage and fury, lust for power, self-gratification, greed, lies, and deception, by boredom and envy, jealousy and hatred.

Flaubert erases the opposition between salvation and catastrophe by overlaying his writing with a Balzacian intertext. In Balzac's *Lost Illusions* (*Illusions perdues*) a set of artists and scientists calling itself the Cénacle des Treize (Coterie of the Thirteen) stands in contrast to a corrupt Paris, pitting love of one's neighbor against self-love. This literary coterie is supposed to give birth to a better, wholesome future and to create bonds of fraternity and solidarity that will in the end overcome the corrupt self-love that has Paris under its sway. If the reader still held any illusions after reading Balzac, *A Sentimental Education* will exorcise these once and for all. Like that sketched by Balzac for his Cénacle des Treize in *Illusions perdues*, Flaubert's "circle of friends" in *A Sentimental Education* (which Flaubert refers to as "le cénacle" in his notes)[46] is staged as based on ideal friendship (*amitié pure*) (235); Frédéric and Deslauriers are its core, but Dussardier, Sénécal, Pellerin, Martinon, Regimbart, and Cisy also belong. Deslauriers testifies that the Cénacle was a youthful ideal, betrayed by Frédéric: "At school we vow[ed] . . . to form a phalanx in later life, like Balzac's *Thirteen*" (167). The word "cenacle" refers especially to "the upper room in which the Last Supper was held, and in which the apostles met after the Ascension" (*Oxford English Dictionary*). Balzac underscores the Christian connotations by calling the main protagonist of his "circle of friends" Michel Chrestien. However fascinatingly Balzac might present Paris as a worldly counterspace—and therein lie the aesthetic stakes of *Illusions perdues*— there remains a corruption-free space of work and self-sacrificing charity, of monastic restriction and renunciation. It shines forth all the more brightly when contrasted with the space of ambition, self-gratification and avarice, extortion, bribery, betrayal and cheating, and all other vices that Balzac's novel subsumes under the metaphor of prostitution. Illusions may well go to seed, but this space of self-sacrificial love survives in Balzac. No flaw blemishes his Thirteen. It is precisely this immaculate pureness that sparkles against Balzac's evocation of a Paris luxuriating in the artificial flowers of evil. In stark contrast to Balzac's Thirteen, the "circle of friends" in *A Sentimental Education* is ruled only by self-interest; they all betray and drag one another down along the path of depravity, which will end in fratricide.

Let us return once more to that long-haired blond boy who asks for bread and gets death in return, and to Dussardier who lies dead on the ground, with his arms forming a cross at the end. Fratricide ends with the signs of bread and the cross. The terrible irony of history, which is at the same time its tragic pathos, manifests itself in the continued production of figures of Christ—the blond boy, the unlucky Dussardier—which return, like stigmata, as blind marks of the fratricidal course of history, without any conscious participation of those subjected to it. The pathos of Christ's cross lives on in the crossing out that is performed in *A Sentimental Education* on the pathetic figures of the cross and Christ; the force of their pathos is reduced to the mark of the cross. Regardless of the intention of the actors involved, the crosses are scattered throughout the text. Thus, even the actor Delmar, the most contemptible of all protagonists of *A Sentimental Education*, perversely stars as Christ. And when, before his duel with Frédéric, the aristocrat Cisy faints in fear, he falls to the ground in a crosswise position: "His head tilted backwards, his arms spread out, and he fell on his back in a faint" (247). Finally, prior to his death under the sign of the cross, Dussardier twice pathetically forms it, imagining that with this sign he is victorious and able to announce glad tidings: "The whole world free! The whole world! And sweeping the horizon with a single glance, he stretched out his arms in a triumphant gesture" (316). In a similar vein he pleads to all who are of good intentions. Yet, sobered by the political events, Dussardier can no longer put his hopes on the angels' singing to announce Christ's birth. Instead, "He put both hands to his forehead; and then, stretching out his arms as if he were in terrible pain," he again unconsciously performs the cross, saying: "Yet if only people tried! With a little good faith, they could reach an understanding. But it's no use. You see, the workers are no better than the middle classes" (429). Flaubert's intimations almost seem to follow the demonstration by the Lollard martyr Sir John Oldcastle, the original of Falstaff in Shakespeare's *Henry IV*, Part One, of being the cross that proved his destination: he "spread his arms abroad [and said] 'this is the very cross, yeah, and so much better than your cross of wood, in that it was created of God.'" Flaubert alludes to this famous inquisition scene against the grain of Shakespeare's romantic reception: the cross as sign of salvation recedes in his text from a triumphant emblem into a cryptic mark, which signals absolute hopelessness and pure suffering for a martyr, Dussardier, who incarnates what he endures without the consolation of a martyr's confessed testimony. Spread out on the steps, the martyr Dussardier's body merely coincidentally forms a cross, whose catastrophic signature is inscribed with "invisible ink" (as in Walter Benjamin's favorite simile) into history by the art of Flaubert. The cross inscribed fails to free history from fratricide; it never did. In Flaubert, however, it does more: it reveals fratricide to be history's final and eternal truth. In this cross, the tragic pathos of history comes to life: it rises from the dead. In it, the cross becomes the sign of pure pathos in the full ancient sense, pure through the crossing out of its message of salvation. Salvation and redemption are crossed out. But Flaubert sticks to the figure of the cross; he does so in memory of the victims of history, but also in His memory. Ultimately, Flaubert's text is the monument of a covenant of love that was never to come about, but survives, crossed out, in his writing. Outside of his text no trace is left of it.

What, then, does Flaubert do by presenting Paris, during the events of 1848 that ended in a coup d'état, through an ingenious intertextual montage with Lucan's Rome, torn by civil war? What does he achieve by staging the Revolution and its suppression by the coup d'état as the blind repetition of the primal scene of an unredeemable earthly history, the primal scene of the City of Man, the curse of Roman fratricide? He gives a new interpretation to this Revolution. He reveals the truth of history, in which the players, driven by concupiscence, are blindly entangled. He shows the quashing of the Revolution and a fortiori the Second Empire to be illegal. The Second Empire makes the worst of crimes, fratricide, lawful. Strange as it may seem, however, this does not entail that Flaubert takes the side of the revolutionaries. He sees them as ideologists who promise throughout the political upheaval the salvation of fraternity, thereby knotting together republicanism and redemption. Contrary to their own rhetoric, they do not act out of brotherly love but, like everybody else, out of sheer self-love, thus reactivating blindly the old schema of catastrophe. They too succumb to this ruin. By siding with the sacrificial victims, Flaubert discards all forms of political ideology, including the ideology of the Republic, which will replace the Catholic Church to take on the status of a secular religion in France. In it, he recognizes the absolute hypocrisy of self-interest.

By no means did Flaubert miss his rendezvous with History.[47] But like Saint Augustine, who taught him how to interpret history, he does not think that earthly history can be salvific. To him it is nothing more than the "eternal destitution of everything," which, in the Palace of Fontainebleau, shows itself as the Augustinian synopsis of earthly history as a series of calamities. Flaubert erects his oeuvre as a monument to the cross of history.

Flaubert inscribes himself in the conflict of interpretations that is continuously renewed in Rome and the transferal of Rome to Paris. In this conflict the same question is posed time and time again: are earthly and salvation histories to be considered as one or should they be sharply distinguished? How does literature relate to politics? The romantic and republican view of history takes precedence in the 1848 Revolution. People like Michelet and Hugo stand for that hope of a republic to come that will in the here and now save history from the curse of fratricide and self-love. They theologically legitimate forms of government by transferring theological patterns onto history. For Flaubert, this type of political theology is the original sin. Sénécal and Hussonnet incarnate its most depraved variation when they justify the Saint Bartholomew's Day massacre, "that old story about the massacre of St Bartholomew's Day" (153), in the name of one faith and one kingdom. In their grotesque wording, the Catholic League of the sixteenth-century French wars of religion was the herald of "the dawn of democracy, a great egalitarian movement against the individualism of the Protestants" (ibid.). Flaubert agrees with Augustine, but without the latter's belief in a City of God to come. Thus in Flaubert, the relationship between literature and politics can never be a glorifying one, as is the case in Hugo or Michelet who endorsed the 1789 Revolution as a revelation. Literature can only illustrate the theologico-political delusion and decipher it as a catastrophic blinding. Neither glorification nor disenchantment—this is the only point everybody in nineteenth-century France agrees upon—have ever occurred more strikingly than in ancient Rome, whose literature and stones do not reveal glory, as Petrarch claimed, but the terrible, infamous truth of history.

Paris/Babel: Love and Politics

"A young man from the college of Sens and who lacked it."

Following Genesis, Augustine recounts the history of the building of the Tower of Babel (*De civitate Dei* 16.5–6). Nimrod, descendant of Cain, hunter in defiance of the Lord, whom we encounter again in "Saint Julian the Hospitalier," sanctions the building of Babel. Through this ancestry— Cain is synonymous with possession (15.17)—Babylon becomes emblematic of the rule of property and the proud desire to become godlike. Its name already presages the destiny which will overtake the city: as Augustine already notes, Babel means confusion, division.

And the whole earth was of one language, and of one speech. And it came to pass, as they journeyed from the east, that they found a plain in the land of Shinar; and they dwelt there. And they said one to another, Go to, let us make brick, and burn them thoroughly. And they had brick for stone, and slime had they for mortar. And they said, Go to, let us build us a city and a tower, whose top may reach unto heaven; and let us make us a name, lest we be scattered abroad upon the face of the whole earth. And the Lord came down to see the city and the tower, which the children of men builded. And the Lord said, Behold, the people is one, and they have all one language; and this they begin to do: and now nothing will be restrained from them, which they have imagined to do. Go to, let us go down, and there confound their language, that they may not understand one another's speech. So the Lord scattered them abroad from thence upon the face of all the earth: and they left off to build the city. Therefore is the name of it called Babel; because the Lord did there confound the language of all the earth: and from thence did the Lord scatter them abroad upon the face of all the earth. (Gen. 11:1–9)[48]

In Augustine's reading, the building of the Tower of Babel resumes and completes the Fall. The origin of man is marked by pride. Man desires to become God's equal, to make himself God. This desire drives Eve to eat the apple. In the story of the construction of the tower, pride literally leads to a self-aggrandizing storming of the heavens. To elevate oneself, to follow one's own will and make oneself the principle and ground for self-creation and self-idolization, amounts to a fall from grace. "Thou castedst them down while they were being exalted" (Ps. 73:118). "[T]hey were cast down even while they were being exalted: their very exaltation was itself a kind of abasement," Augustine explains.[49] The split results from the self-aggrandizing self-building. The revolt within the self against the self, of brother against brother, leads to the division of the social body, the revolt of all against all. The tower, which was supposed to be a monument of unity, leads to dispersion. The worldly dispersion, diaspora, corresponds to the expulsion from paradise.

The story of the building of the tower is represented in *A Sentimental Education* through a doubling, distorting, disfiguring repetition that leaves its mark throughout the work. The story of the construction of the tower furnishes the poetics of Flaubert's novel. In general, no original materials but only substitutes are used in the biblical story: instead of stones we have brick and instead of mortar we have mud ("slime"). Historically speaking, the bricks and the mud, as substitutes for stone and mortar, do not constitute signs of degradation, but signal settlement and the cultural techniques that follow from it. But the substitutive repetition, which matters so much to Flaubert, does not amount to a fulfillment but rather to a degradation perpetuated in the confusion of tongues. New languages appear as caricatures of a lost language. If language once served communication, now it only functions as a vehicle of unintelligibility or misunderstanding. The multiplicity of languages is an allegory of division, an allegory for the conflict dormant in oneself and the other. Everyone merely says the same thing in a variety of different ways, only always expressing their self-interest; no one will ever understand the other. After the fall of the tower, language becomes the expression of a distorted, false relation to the self and the other. The words for this deranged, topsy-turvy self-relation, used by Augustine and the intellectuals of Port-Royal, Pascal, and then by Flaubert, are *passion, concupiscence*, and *convoitise* (covetousness). It is the will to absolute sovereignty—to be like God—which leads to enslavement (cf. *De civitate Dei* 14.28). All worldly relations are controlled by people who are unable to control themselves and are ruled by greed for money and pleasure, and lust for power and domination: that lust for mastery which belongs in its purest form to the whole Roman people (1.30). In the end, avarice, in its destruction and exploitation of the one by the other, leads to ruin. It is because man, who imagines himself the foundation of himself alone, is helpless: "Man is like to vanity" (14.15; Ps. 144:4; trans. Dyson 612). *A Sentimental Education* is a book about the passions of pride, rage, vengeance, miserliness, deception, pedantry, lasciviousness, self-righteousness, lust for and worship of power. The furious lust for vengeance is vented against dead objects: glass and porcelain are smashed, mirrors are broken. Frédéric's friends begin on a small scale in other people's houses what the people will continue, on a grand scale, with the looting of the Tuileries in the first phase of the 1848 Revolution, prefigured in the City of Man:

Even anger itself was defined in ancient times as being no more than the lust for revenge; although a man is often angry even with inanimate objects which cannot feel his vengeance, as when, in a rage, he smashes his stylus or breaks his pen when it writes ill. . . . Thus, there is the lust for vengeance, called anger. Again, there is the lust for money, called avarice; the lust for victory at any price, called obstinacy; the lust for glory, called vanity. . . . [T]he lust for mastery, . . . the evidence of civil wars shows how great a sway it has over the minds of tyrants. (*De civitate Dei* 14.15; trans. Dyson 613–14)

And as dominating as the lust for power itself, which leads to fratricide and civil war, is the lust for sex. Augustine names incest amongst the latter's prime examples:

The act itself which is performed under the influence of such lust [for sexual intercourse] shuns the public gaze. This is true not only of those debaucheries which need places of concealment, but also of the practice of fornication, which the Earthly City has made into a lawful form of wickedness: a kind of lust which is permitted and not punishable by any law of that City. . . . A natural sense of shame ensures that even brothels make provisions for secrecy; and it was easier for unchastity to dispense with the fetters of prohibition. (*De civitate Dei* 14.18; trans. Dyson 617)

As Henry James so strikingly puts it, *A Sentimental Education* leads its abject hero Frédéric Moreau nowhere—just as the inhabitants of the City of Man in Augustine get nowhere. The life of the young graduate of the college of Sens makes and has no sense, just as the story qua History with a capital *H* lacks sense. The novel proves the name of its protagonist's alma mater to be a lie: this life makes no sense. Frédéric comes, with his *grande passion* and a series of as many senseless as indifferent homosexual and heterosexual affairs, to nothing: "Et ce fut tout" (621)—"and that was all" (455), "he had affairs with other women" (451). His ridiculous dreams of becoming a great author or, alternatively, a great painter, come to nought. *A Sentimental Education* culminates aimlessly in recollections of a whorehouse, a nonplace where—as the two friends later recognize, having senselessly wasted them—the most beautiful thing in their lives has taken place: nothing.

The whorehouse in which *A Sentimental Education* effectively concludes testifies to the powerful Babylonian topos; for Augustine, the Great Whore of Babylon is synonymous with the City of Man. The Paris that appears in *A Sentimental Education* is torn into pieces and bloodstained by struggles, death-ridden and ruined from the outset, indulging in idolatry and consumed by self-interest—it is a Paris refracted through the lens of the topos of the City of Man. The rewriting of the Lucanian paradigm of civil war through the Revolution of 1848 is molded by this Babylonian topos. Unlike for the generation of romantics that included Hugo, Lamartine, and Michelet, the coup d'état and the ensuing tyranny are not, for Flaubert, the antithesis to the 1848 Revolution: revolution and coup d'état heed the exact same Babylonian logic. The Revolution ends in fratricide and incest; the Republic leads to tyranny; and great love reveals itself in the midst of mindless phrasemongering as the desire for a delusion that merely serves self-aggrandizement. A political model—that of Lucan—becomes a negative typological model in the reception of Augustine. Since Babel is the prototype of the City of Man, the daughter of this mother, the second Babel, is Rome: "the city of Rome was founded and as a kind of second Babylon; the daughter, as it were, of the former Babylon" (*De civitate Dei* 18.22; trans. Dyson 848).

Frédéric imagines Roman succession quite differently. He sees Paris as Rome's successor in the role of city of love—following the palindrome "Roma summus amor"—and as the "mother of the sciences and arts." He applies this Roman cliché to Paris right from the start, when he still sees himself as poor and condemned to the provinces: "Paris!—for in his mind Art, Knowledge and Love, those three faces of God, as Pellerin would have put it, were the exclusive purview of the capital" (101). Later he longs for Paris's "heady atmosphere of love and intellectual stimulus" (113). In his half-educated ignorance he cites the Renaissance motif that marked

Henri II's translation of the Roman paradigm to Paris and owes its popularity to the historicist revival of the Renaissance in the nineteenth century. But instead of the loving bride and fertile mother, only the great whore remains in the end: the brothel of the Turkish woman. Against the commonplace of the time, the Roman paradigm turns out to be the offspring of Babel, whose granddaughter Paris now is.

On March 29, 1862, the Goncourt brothers mention a new book project by Flaubert in their journal: he wants to write either about the "modern Orient" or produce "an immense novel, a great tableau of life, connected through an action where everybody destroys everybody else."[50] Either the Goncourt brothers misunderstood or the two projects eventually fused into one, mutually illuminating one another during the praxis of writing: *A Sentimental Education* shows France, through its oriental lighting, as a modern Babel, dividing everyone from within and without, and leading to mutual destruction. In this Paris everybody talks at cross-purposes, and everyone self-destructs, since all are equal when it comes to misunderstanding, to their blind egoism in politics, economy, and love. Thematically, the Babylonian topos is developed through prostitution, idolatry, and tyranny. What is more, *A Sentimental Education* razes to the ground the entire great tradition of the French novel since Hugo and Balzac, which untiringly constructed the image of the Roman Paris—as the true Rome, the new Jerusalem, but also as an equivocal city in which a fascinating Babel stands side by side with an eventually victorious Jerusalem. What is also destroyed is the alternative, which searches for the salvation and the averting of the city's corruption by turning to a rural idyll. But the dichotomy between orientalism and the modern also breaks down. The oriental topos no longer signifies the absolute other; Babel rules sovereign in the heart of Europe, in the capital of modernity. Nothing but spectral ruins remain of the contemporary topoi informing realism and romanticism.

A Sentimental Education is thus a realist novel only insofar as it is the locus classicus of an "allegory of reading," as Paul de Man sketched it and distilled it from two readers of Augustine, namely, Pascal and Rousseau. Hermeneutics—or more exactly its perfect failure—is the theme of this novel. According to an old pattern, love is an allegory of one's relation to the world.[51] As such, the Babylonian paradigm has a poetological component: parallel to the protagonists' inability to understand anything but their self-interest, Flaubert worked diligently on his text to make it less readable. This riddling, which asks for deciphering, has a typological side: the hermeneutic schema of *figura* and fulfillment gives way to degrading repetition. The adoption of the Babylonian paradigm has a consequence with regard to the philosophy of history: the city, here Paris as Rome, and Babel before that, becomes the negative type of history. It has a religious implication: blinding idolatry takes the place of knowledge. It has a moral and political correlative: a social body driven by self-interest leads to tyranny.

This Babylonian topos, which as an allegory of reading allows us to make sense of the apparently disjointed coexistence of politics and love in *A Sentimental Education*, has racked the brains of many interpreters. Love and politics, informed by the same Babylonian paradigm, illuminate each other: corrupted and divided against and in itself by concupiscence, the heart conjures up the counterimage of the straightforwardness and simplicity of the loving knowledge of charity. In this respect, this text, like all of Flaubert's texts, inverts the figure that defines the connection between the Old and New Testaments in Saint Paul. Paul poses the living spirit of a writing that is understood by hearts of flesh against the dead letter of the law, which is read by hearts of stone. The action of *A Sentimental Education* can be described as a hermeneutic development centered on a reversal of the Pauline dynamic: in Flaubert, the spiritual is systematically reified. Once this process of reification of all things spiritual is complete, the novel has reached its end.

While the protagonists of the novel blindly succumb to this reification, the reader's task is to learn to decipher their terrible reading error. By learning to decipher the error in reading to which all the protagonists succumb, the reader of the novel is made literate. *A Sentimental Education* is then foremost an education in reading. It is a reading lesson, which Flaubert undertakes painstakingly, with patience and care. In no other novel is the difference between the perspective of the reader and that of the protagonists highlighted as starkly as in *A Sentimental Education*. We can only find a similarly stark contrast in Dante's hell. Following *A Sentimental Education*, realism is the spelling out to a reader of a world that makes no sense. The reader is to grasp the Babylonian matrix in all its facets as the human condition, to the truth of whose unchanging history our eyes need to be opened. The Babylonian condition is catholic in the most literal sense. It is comprehensive and all-embracing. Thus it determines the course of history always and everywhere. Modernity—in this respect Flaubert also writes a history of decay and decadence—is Babylon under intensified, doubly twisted, completely blinded conditions. With the advent of Christianity, the Babylonian condition is sped up all the more disastrously in the guise of a radical break with Babel. To become conscious of this blinding is the anti–sentimental education the novel holds out. It did not fall on fertile soil with its contemporaries: what is possibly Flaubert's greatest novel was initially seen as a catastrophic failure. The book's contemporaries refused to recognize themselves in the less than flattering mirror with which *A Sentimental Education* confronted them. This is hardly surprising, since the novel uncompromisingly crushed the ideals of the day and shattered the self-image of the epoch. The aggressiveness that characterized the book's rejection attests to the striking truth of Flaubert's presentation.

In Augustine, the building of the Tower of Babel is a case of false mimesis, which is also the subject of *A Sentimental Education*. As an artist's novel, it is about imitation in music, theater, art, and literature. Imitation comes always as stereotyped reification. It is a déjà vu all over again: see Frédéric's planned novel about *Sylvio, the Fisherman's Son*. Flaubert illustrates the idolatrous reification by reconstructing the world in his novel as if it were an image, a painting. Particularly the women are not painted after reality, but after paintings. They are staged as paintings; they reduplicate icons. Erotic desire is dependent on the representation of femininity as an idol to which the protagonists themselves willingly succumb, but which is thwarted and crossed out in the writing. For Flaubert, literature is thus the medium where the truth of a reified world becomes legible. As a unique praxis, this writing is able to make the Babylonian truth readable. It is precisely this mode of reading, which the nineteenth century, in its fascination with Saint Paul, had chosen in the name of the heart and against which the exteriority of the letter is foregrounded, that Flaubert treats with unrelenting irony, revealing it as the paragon of an ossified stereotype.[52] The ironic distancing is set against the grain of contemporary, self-blinding intensification of Babylonian conditions, which were literally fulfilled in the Second Empire, which, in Flaubert's eyes, is but a name for tyranny. Tyranny was made possible in the name of the values the New Testament once mobilized against Babel: in the name of a kingdom of generous love renouncing the self, and in the name of a new bond, a new Pentecost promised by the Revolution, which would abolish the Babylonian condition. With the "Club de l'Intelligence" frequented by the hero, *A Sentimental Education* presents a perverted Pentecost, the dinner with the calf heads "serves" up a perverted Eucharist, and the circle of friends around Frédéric and Deslauriers amounts to a perversion of Christ's circle of disciples at the Last Supper. Taken together with the embodiment of Christ by the actor Delmar, Flaubert unmasks the Revolution of 1848 as a grotesque travesty of the Christian promise of love and redemption that it prides itself on.

In contrast to Victor Hugo's Paris, which pursues a world-historical salvational telos, Flaubert's Paris is the capital of recurrent calamities. Flaubert addresses first of all the fatal political optimism of his time, which is nothing but a republican version of political theology. The City of Man, whose first full-blown manifestation was Babel and whose actual manifestation is according to Flaubert modern Paris, is not only the counterimage to the City of God. The City of Man is for Flaubert as for Augustine also the opposite of a true republic.[53] Flaubert develops his reading of Augustine against the republican conception of the political and specifies his point down to the last political detail. The pertinence of his point gains even more perspective against the background of the contemporary reception of Saint Paul.[54] The romantic generation had hoped that the Revolution would bring about a republic structured according to the Pauline model of the new covenant, as a union in love. Republican secularity would thus depend on a structural transfer from the religious to the secular sphere. Augustine's *De civitate Dei,* on the contrary, was written against such a theological justification of the political. In Augustine's view, the Roman political ideal of the republic, from Livy to Cicero and all the way down to Lucan, is simply unrealistic in the context of the City of Man. For him, only the City of God was a true *res publica.* Flaubert not only had no interest in the City of God, however, but also believed a true republic in the here and now to be an impossibility. *A Sentimental Education* shows the disastrous effects of the hope of a new covenant within the political sphere:

Thus, justice is found where the one supreme God rules an obedient City according to His grace, so that it sacrifices to none but Him; and where, in consequence, the soul rules the body in all men who belong to that City and obey God, and the reason faithfully rules the vices in lawful order. In that City, both the individual just man and the community and people of the just live by faith, which works by love: by that love with which a man loves God as God ought to be loved, and his neighbor as himself. But where there is not this justice, there is certainly no association of men united by a common agreement as to what is right and by a community of interest. And so there is no commonwealth (*res publica*); for where there is no "people," there is no "property of the people" (*res publica*). (*De civitate Dei* 19.23; trans. Dyson 959–60)

As the embodiment of the City of Man, Paris figures in *A Sentimental Education* as the opposite, not only of the City of God, but also of what Augustine calls the "res publica." The Paris of the Revolution, the Republic, and the coup d'état is a republic fatally struck by self-love and self-interest. In a strict reversal of Augustine's definition of the *res publica*, the soul is ruled by the body and reason by the passions. No sacrifices are made in the name of the true God; sacrifices are made in honor of the idols of Power and Property. Dominated by prostitution, and indeed even incest, Paris is divided by the hatred vented through the Revolution and which finds its completion, as fratricide, in the coup d'état. Utterly divided, this city is the exact opposite of the unified social body of the commonwealth (*res publica*) as Augustine understands it in *De civitate Dei*. His accentuation of unity couldn't be stronger: *one* jurisdiction overseen by God; *one* power, exercised by *one* God; the people love the *one* God as the *one single* judge; here, one loves one's neighbor as oneself. Only here, in *one single* body *united* by the bonds of love, can there be a *res publica* in the *civitas*. Flaubert underpins the political self-description of those days, which articulates conflicts within the body politic as a struggle between the Left and the Right, between socialists and reactionaries, as a fight of the republic against monarchy, or of the republic against tyranny, with another, more fundamental schema. It turns the political oppositions between Right and Left and between the workers and the bourgeoisie into mere surface phenomena. This opposition is grounded in a single, deeper structure of civil war universalized in Augustine's reading: the division of the self, which leads to a division with the other and a split body politic.

Loveless: Equality, Fraternity

A Sentimental Education evinces a kind of historical development in the application of its negative typological schema, which lies in the heightening of terror. It is always the same, but it always gets worse. This

political development finds its allegorical shape in the three women in Frédéric's life: Madame Arnoux, the bourgeois muse of bohemia, embodies
for a short moment the possibility of a real republic; Rosanette, the demimondaine, shows the face of the actual republic, which carries the coup
d'état within itself; Madame Dambreuse, representative of the upper class,
foreshadows tyranny. Her Advent is the Second Empire. To this political degeneration corresponds an increasing hard-heartedness in the three
women. Completely in keeping with the tradition of the Christian doctrine of tears, Flaubert articulates this through their weeping.[55] Madame
Arnoux suffers the Passion with her son and sacrifices her desire for his
sake. Rosanette cries desperately for her dead child. Yet the eyes of the
selfish and, incidentally, infertile "bookkeeper" Madame Dambreuse only
weep for herself. While weeping over the loss of her money, her eyes remain dry at the sight of misery: "the rags and tatters of the poor left her
dry-eyed. An innate selfishness revealed itself in her habitual expressions"
(420). She mourns her lost property like a mother mourns her dead child:
"A bereaved mother beside an empty cradle could not have been more pitiable than Madame Dambreuse before the gaping strongboxes" (414).

Since the three women are allegories of political forms, love and politics are articulated through each other. Structuralist analyses have shown
the strict parallel between the amorous encounters and political events.
The argument that the novel is a failure, since it does not manage to unite
politics and love but instead leaves them side by side in a disjointed state, is
thus untenable.[56] However, what matters is to recognize exactly what kind
of parallel between love and politics is proffered by the novel. Its contours
only become visible when one grasps that the novel is to be read according to the Babylonian matrix: love and politics, sex and violence are func-
tionally equivalent. Both are the effects of the Fall—they generate death
in their wake. Flaubert's great Parisian novel unites love and politics to
show that both are determined by the same structure, namely, equality and
brotherliness. The generally accepted meaning of these central values of the
Revolution is turned upside down in the course of the novel. They are no
longer ideals, but descriptions of a state of affairs: the Fall. The most important political categories of the Revolution, equality and brotherliness,
are decomposed through the parallelism of love and politics.

Love is the great leveler. Whores and the bourgeoisie are all the same:
for sale. The nexus between love and money unites the demimondaine

Rosanette, the middle-class Madame Arnoux, and the upper-class Madame Dambreuse in the register of prostitution. Since everyone strives after their own profit, love does not unite but instead divides. Madame Dambreuse and her husband hate each other to such an extent that they are compelled to escape the moment of togetherness of a warm summer evening and flee to the theater. The Arnoux family is riddled by marital strife. So as not to have to endure any tête-à-tête, they constantly drag in Frédéric as a mediating third. Love and money are so closely interwoven that the context of prostitution is omnipresent. There is no such thing as "free love." Deslauriers sums it up succinctly: "Those who don't cost you anything take up your time; that's another form of money, and I'm not a rich man" (195). Madame Dambreuse married her husband for his riches; she is worth her price because she has increased his symbolic capital tenfold. In the end she is swindled out of her profit by her husband's illegitimate daughter. Monsieur Arnoux marries his wife without a dowry out of love; as a bourgeois muse she is a veritable goldmine for him at first. An *homme à femme*, he has no scruples about cheating on his wife. He ruins his family because of his weakness for women and is despised by his wife, whom he drags along with him to his ruin without bothering to inform her of their impending doom.[57] When Frédéric hears that Madame Dambreuse, whom he is about to marry, has lost her property, he turns pale; he has unwittingly contributed to this. Even the love story between Madame Arnoux and Frédéric turns out to be a tale of money. And yet this is not all.

Even if Frédéric does not manage to sleep with Arnoux's wife, he nonetheless sleeps with the same woman Arnoux does, since they share the courtesan Rosanette. The opposition, so central to nineteenth-century morality, between the respectable woman and the tart dissolves in an incessant quid pro quo. Between the Arnoux household and that of Rosanette, men, candlesticks, porcelain, and cashmere scarfs wander in and out, making the two women so similar that the one could be mistaken for the other. Madame Arnoux sees herself treated as a prostitute by her husband. She recognizes Frédéric's love by a kiss between glove and sleeve, which Rosanette also receives from him. Rosanette, who prostitutes herself, is not an easy lay for Frédéric, but on the contrary, a distinctly difficult one. Conversely, Madame Dambreuse surrenders without the least resistance and reveals herself to be so available that Frédéric hardly notices it: "Madame Dambreuse closed her eyes and he was astonished at the ease of his victory" (395). The interchangeability of Madame Arnoux and the famous eighteenth-century singer Sophie Arnould, the cause of the duel between Cisy and Frédéric, casts a shadow over Madame Arnoux's immaculate respectability; singing functions as a metaphor for sensuous surrender in *A Sentimental Education*. Inversely, the *bourgeoise déclassée* Rosanette really wants only one thing: to marry and become a respectable woman. In the end, with the arrival of the Second Empire, she will succeed. The subtext of prostitution manifests itself in the continual, systematic approximation of Madame Arnoux and Rosanette, which is staged through the same stylistic means: Flaubert conceals the references of the personal pronouns. In the husband's comparison of the courtesan with his wife, it is not immediately clear who exactly has the more beautiful thighs: "he extolled Rosanette's qualities, even contrasting her with his wife. There was really no comparison. It was impossible to imagine lovelier thighs" (343). Frédéric sleeps with Rosanette as a substitute for the missed love encounter with Madame Arnoux. Later he will become the lover of the upper-class Madame Dambreuse. On the very same day she has been left by her lover, she beckons Frédéric in her boudoir as a substitute. After cheating on Madame Arnoux with Rosanette, Frédéric henceforth cheats on Madame Dambreuse with Rosanette, and on Rosanette with Dambreuse. He repeats the same oaths of love to both word for word; he sends both the same bouquets with the same love notes, simultaneously. He justifies this infidelity by citing his unrequited love for Madame Arnoux. Hardly has Frédéric begotten a child with Rosanette when he prepares to marry Madame Dambreuse, whose husband has happened to die at the right moment. When Rosanette announces that she is pregnant, the stunned Frédéric imagines how nice it would have been to have had a child with Madame Arnoux instead. Frédéric has promised to marry his country sweetheart, Louise Roque, too, but when his mother—proud of her socially ascendant son's prospective Balzacian dream match with the filthy-rich Dambreuse and one of the largest fortunes in Paris—tells the supposedly love-struck Louise that her marriage to Frédéric is off, she immediately replaces him with his best friend, Deslauriers. Frédéric tells each of the four women in quick succession that she is his one and only.

Not only the women are interchangeable, quid pro quo, in the equation of sex and money. Frédéric has substitutions on the male side as well. Arnoux's lust is his, too, just as his is that of Deslauriers, who has sex with the first woman who comes along to settle a bet with him. That night,

Frédéric cannot sleep in his own bed because his roommate Deslauriers is lying in it with someone else. Later, Deslauriers faithfully does what Frédéric suggests and cheats systematically on his friend. He vainly tries to seduce Madame Arnoux, believing her to be Frédéric's lover, but scores with Rosanette, who has just been abandoned by Frédéric, and finally manages—the height of his triumph—to marry Frédéric's former sweetheart Louise. So much desire and jealousy make the libertine novel look like a school play. But while the quid pro quos of the libertine novel tend to lead to desire fulfilled and love found,[58] the imbroglios of *A Sentimental Education* are endlessly frustrating. Everybody ends up with the wrong person in the wrong bed at the wrong time. No one is happy.

This heterosexual interchangeability puts the characters all on the same footing: there is a substitute for everyone. However, the homosexual register has been almost overlooked here.[59] From start to finish, Deslauriers and Frédéric are the only stable couple in the novel. Starting with a romantically exaggerated boyish enthusiasm for each other, by the end of the novel, wallowing in memories of their youth, they are united before the hearth—*douceur du foyer*—like Philemon and Baucis "by that irresistible element in their nature" (456).[60] The final scene of the shared visit to the brothel in which no sexual act takes place, referenced at the beginning of the novel, is elevated into the best thing that ever happened to them. They conclude, in unison, on the same note: "that was the best time we ever had," Frédéric exclaims, and Deslauriers echoes: "Yes, perhaps you're right. That was the best time we ever had" (459).

Frédéric and Deslauriers are presented as a couple since their schooldays, when their togetherness sets them apart from the other students. Their intimacy at college is tinged with eroticism: "From that day on, their friendship was complete" (17).[61] Nonetheless, "After fits of verbose exaltation they would relapse into profound silences" (18); "a feeling of suffocation came over them and they lay down on their backs, dazed and elated . . . and they felt as sad as if they [had] been deep in debauchery" (ibid.). Increasingly, they get mutually excited: "The headmaster claimed that they were bad for each other" (ibid.).[62] "A close watch was kept on their friendship. This merely strengthened the affection between them" (ibid.).[63] During the first evening of their impatiently longed-for reunion upon Frédéric's return from Paris, they walk, embracing like lovers, wrapped in the same coat: "Frédéric put part of his cloak over his friend's shoulders. They both wrapped themselves in it and walked along, side by side, holding each other round the waist" (20). They embrace for a long time before they part ways (22). Deslauriers calms Frédéric's mother by saying, somewhat suggestively, that her son will "sleep at home tonight" (21).[64] After a long separation, they can no longer embrace as affectionately in public as they would like to. Deslauriers succumbs to Frédéric's feminine charm, and Frédéric feels like an unfaithful wife when, having received an invitation to Madame Arnoux's birthday party that same evening—as usual, at the wrong moment—he spends his friend's long-expected first evening in Paris, not with him, but with the Arnouxs: "Seeing Deslauriers, Frédéric began to tremble like an adulterous wife beneath her husband's gaze" (50). As his friend watches, he dresses up for the occasion like a bridegroom: "Anybody would think you were getting married," Deslauriers says (50). "A man like Deslauriers was worth all the women in the world," Frédéric thinks (49). Nevertheless, he goes out with the intention of paying court to Madame Arnoux (52). Deslauriers feels cheated by Frédéric's love for her, while Frédéric feels cheated by Deslauriers's love for Sénécal, who, later on, Frédéric believes to have taken his place in the communal lodgings after our hero has been forced to give up his Paris existence for lack of money.

As in heterosexual love, love triangles proliferate in homosexual love. Frédéric's passion for Madame Arnoux never gives rise to the deadly despair that overcomes him when he hears that Sénécal and Deslauriers are living together. Then: "He wanted to die" (102). Deslauriers behaves like a husband when he hears of Frédéric's inheritance, assuming that they have inherited jointly: "we're going to have it easy now!" (122). He feels duped when he finds out that Frédéric has spent the money he was promised on the other, on Madame Arnoux, and not on him. Through the ambiguity of personal pronouns it becomes clear that both Madame Arnoux and Deslauriers stand in a love relationship with Frédéric in which each can take the place of the other: when Frédéric comes home from the Arnouxs' party, rapturous about "the one," he hears Deslauriers snoring: "it was the other [c'était l'autre]" (108).[65]

That said, Frédéric's romance with Madame Arnoux is modeled on Flaubert's youthful infatuation with Elisa Schlesinger and is not a screen for the inexpressible but genuine homosexual love between Flaubert, Alfred Le Poittevin, and Maxime Du Camp. Flaubert, who had already been put on trial for a harmless novel of adultery, would have shrunk from publishing even more inflammatory writing. In short, *A Sentimental Education* is not a bildungsroman.

If the structural correspondence between the two forms of love is puzzling, the key is that sameness divides in each case. Being together is being apart, a conflicted being with the other that leads in short order to separation. The ambivalence of pronominal relations highlights the quid pro quo between characters. "Fraternity" is homosexually connoted so as to bring out in greater relief the similarity, indeed, the sameness of jealousy and betrayal, the split, the separation of the self within the self: Deslauriers identifies with Frédéric and becomes Frédéric in trying to seduce Madame Arnoux.

The close "cohabitation" of murder and sex is as valid for heterosexual as it is for homosexual relations. Frédéric shares lovers with Jacques Arnoux and both hope thereby to get their money's worth through the financial deception of the other. But Frédéric also shares Arnoux's bed. In order to spend an undisturbed night with Rosanette, Arnoux asks Frédéric under false pretenses to take his place in the Garde nationale (338). However, it is not Arnoux and Rosanette who finally lie together undisturbed, but Arnoux and Frédéric who spend the night in the same bed. Arnoux overestimates himself; exhausted he has to leave Rosanette after just a few hours. Drowsy with sleep, he whispers sweet caresses in Frédéric's ears, caresses he has already whispered in hers: "My darling! My little angel!" (341). Caught up in the fantasy of enjoying Madame Arnoux undisturbed, Frédéric considers killing Arnoux with the loaded gun the latter takes to bed with him, the muzzle of which winds up tucked into his armpit in his sleep. All Frédéric need do is press the trigger with his big toe and it would fire: "le coup partirait" (469). Ejaculation and death thus are woven together in the double entendre *tirer un coup*, "fire a shot," but also "screw."

In another scene, Arnoux saves Dambreuse from the fury of the people by embracing him, only to be delivered by him to his ruin. What binds these figures together is also what separates them: in their "bond," embrace, and bed, they pursue nothing but their own interests, which are so deadly because they are identical to the interests of the other.

A closer reading, all of a sudden, reveals the abysses in the love relations between Madame Arnoux and Frédéric, Frédéric and Rosanette, Madame Dambreuse and Frédéric. Love turns into hatred. This inversion of love into hatred propelled by pride is systematic. Hatred always marks the end of the idyll, whether with Rosanette in Fontainebleau—"His love suddenly weighed upon his conscience like a crime. They sulked at one another for an hour" (358)—or with Madame Arnoux in Auteuil—"for he was beginning to hate her, and it was only right that she should share his sufferings" (295). When Madame Arnoux, agonizing over her dying child, does not show up for a rendezvous, Frédéric is "filled with angry pride . . . and, like a leaf carried away by a hurricane, his love disappeared" (304). This is all the more inexcusable since Frédéric has seen with his own eyes how sick Madame Arnoux's son is and has been "astonished at the child's feverish appearance" (295). Frédéric's love, which encloses him like a dungeon, is the counterimage of the love that "beareth all things, believeth all things, hopeth all things, endureth all things" (1 Cor. 13:7). With Madame Dambreuse, Frédéric's "sentimental atrophy" gives rise to an idyll that lasts only one dinner long. And this only because the lovers keep their mouths completely shut out of mutual distrust.

In homosexual liaisons as well, love turns to hatred. Love always has a bestial flavor. Without exception, Frédéric experiences "brutal lust [*convoitise brutale*]" (578) for every woman who arouses him; for Rosanette, "while her personality irritated him more and more, a sensual urge, bestial and violent, would still impel him towards her, producing a momentary illusion which always turned to hatred" (422); for Mademoiselle Vatnaz, "suddenly, in the presence of this ugly woman with the lithe body of a panther, Frédéric felt an overwhelming lust, a bestial longing for pleasure" (275); for Madame Arnoux, "once again he was filled with desire, a frenzied, rabid lust such as he had never known before" (455). The "animality" of love is underscored by the favorite position of all of Flaubert's male heroes: they approach love *a tergo*, from behind. Charles and Emma Bovary are in this position in their first erotic encounter: Charles approaches Emma from behind, who is stooping down over sacks of flour, looking for his horsewhip. When Rodolphe spots Emma from behind stooped over a bowl, his desire is ignited. Frédéric is aroused as he approaches Madame Arnoux from behind: "One day he came up behind her when she was crouching on the lawn, looking for violets" (291). Frédéric moves closer to Rosanette from the back, causing her to blush. Sodomy, which once referred to sex between a man and a female animal and by extension also signified homosexual love, finds its common denominator through this position. This sexual position unites, through sodomy, heterosexual with homosexual love, making the one the quid pro quo of the other. Homosexuality is a continuous stratum of *A Sentimental Education*, calling to mind—through the favored position—the name of sodomy, and it activates the topical, nineteenth-century association between the cities of Babel, Sodom, and Gomorrah, which would not be fully unfolded until Proust.[66] In Hugo's *Orientales*, "Le feu du ciel" gives an account of the destruction of Sodom and Gomorrah, the sister cities of Babel: "Babel, accomplice of their guilt, was seen / O'er the far hills to gaze with vision keen!"[67] Animal and by association homosexual love is ascribed proverbially, in a homophobic and xenophobic fashion, to Oriental, possibly "Turkish dogs."[68] In *A Sentimental Education*, homosexual love is not foreign, ostracized, or out of place. In Paris, the new Babel, it is an utterly domestic kind of love.

In this Babylonian condition, we witness a breakdown of three fundamental oppositions that make man and woman, heterosexual and homosexual love, and love and hatred interchangeable and indistinct. With this breakdown, the very possibility of meaningfulness, of making sense, is shattered. All love ends the same, and in love all are equal, which merely means: arbitrarily interchangeable, indifferently replaceable. Love is thus fundamentally brought down to a measurable scale in which anything can be exchanged for anything else: the standard of money. Love unites the classes and sexes in "fraternal" hatred, in bestial avarice, in jealousy and murder. United, they are torn apart by self-interest, obeying the same hostile divisiveness. As far as love is concerned, the pledge of this revolution has become quite literally true: it really equalizes everybody, men as well as women, heterosexual as well as homosexual love, whores and respectable women. This comprehensive triumph of the Revolution also amounts to its abyssal breakdown: this equality entails absolute division and is therefore an absurd caricature of the ideals aspired to.

The love stories of *A Sentimental Education* illustrate not only a radically different *égalité* from that of revolutionary thought, but also a radically other *fraternité*. Everyone is indeed so similar that no one stands in solidarity with the other: instead, everyone turns against everyone, since each desires that which the other also desires.[69] The equality of the people does not lead to community, but to betrayal and deception, only to come to fulfillment in fratricide and incest. The people are united in division: competition, envy, jealousy, hatred. The ruin of Madame Arnoux, the most prominent example in the novel, is owed to the jealous, envious, and hateful collaboration of the "courting couple," Sénécal and Deslauriers, with Madame Dambreuse, who takes revenge as the cheated third against Madame Arnoux, whom she believes to be Frédéric's mistress. United they stand, only to ruin everything and everybody.

In principle, brotherhood leads to ruin and fratricide. Incidentally, the same holds for sisterhood: in their desire to inflict mortal pain on the other and thereby ruin him/her, the genders are in all actuality equal. Driven by jealousy, Mademoiselle Vatnaz is out to ruin Rosanette; out of jealousy Madame Dambreuse ruins Madame Arnoux. Ruination also resounds in the word "fate"—*fatalité* (620)—in the apparently idyllic final scene by the fireside between Deslauriers and Frédéric. Brotherliness is marked by equality through hatred: Deslauriers wants the women Frédéric has, Frédéric wants the woman Arnoux has, and sooner or later each of these "brothers" will entertain the thought of killing the other, or at least of striking a fatal blow to cause the other's ruin. Flaubert's *A Sentimental Education*, a paragon of modern realist literature, folds open to reveal none other than the Babylonian structure of the City of Man analyzed by Augustine. The oriental topos, which illuminates Paris in a Babylonian light and which, following the Augustinian interpretation of the City of Man, constitutes the poetics and theme of *A Sentimental Education*, reveals itself in perpetually new facets. Flaubert's Paris lights up as the true Rome, in which the Babylonian structure, which Augustine already certified with regard to the first Rome, comes about once again, only more terribly.

Negative Typology: Histories of Calamity

In a laconic, or, if you prefer, realistic fashion, *A Sentimental Education* tells of the aftermath of Cain's fratricide in the founding of the first city, with Babel as its fulfillment and culminating point. In Augustine's view, Babel is the direct result of the Fall of Man, and it is as an effect of the Fall that Paris appears in *A Sentimental Education*. After the Fall comes the Flood, whose destructive potential is echoed in the metaphor of the Revolution as a natural force, as a deluge rushing through Paris and wrecking everything in its wake. Paris, much like Babel, is demolished, ruined, and crushed as a consequence of the Fall. In the forest of Fontainebleau, Paris appears as the ruined Rome destroyed by civil war. In short, it is the Babylonian matrix, which organizes the representation of contemporary reality, right down to the last of the details that were researched with such unbelievable meticulousness.[70]

A Sentimental Education presents all events and descriptions—everything that appears in the text—as pertinent to this matrix. Everything is filtered through this matrix in order to profile the Babylonian leitmotif that orchestrates the novel's registration and ordering of reality.

Raw data from the social context or history are sometimes subjected to distortions in order to serve their selection. All of *A Sentimental Education* can be read in negative allegorical terms. Rosanette's pregnancy is a striking example: it lasts an incredible twenty-five months, thus coinciding with the duration of the Second French Republic.[71] The embodiment of this republic, Rosanette becomes pregnant with a child sentenced to death. This child is born only in order to die immediately. The pregnant Rosanette and her dying child betray the allegory of a republic that is pregnant with a tyranny bent to its allegorically preset ending.[72]

What comes to the fore in the novel is what makes the implicit Babylonian topos decipherable. Yet, everything is represented in a Babylonian fashion. It is never expressly formulated or put in plain speech. There is no Babylonian plain text. *A Sentimental Education* resists hermeneutics. Its plot must be read and deciphered through its *discours*,[73] namely, in the isotopy of networks of signification, in the parallelizing of scenes, and in the overlapping of different temporal layers. The technique of presentation is reminiscent of the technique of the cross cutting, through which actions are placed in parallel, so that one segment of action illuminates what happens in a different one, which can thereby become a metaphor for the other.[74] The most tried and tested stylistic means of making the Babylonian logic legible is metonymy. It is generally the figure that disjointedly cuts through syntagms, while arbitrarily ordering elements—as if by a throw of the dice—in a chaotic fashion, putting things side by side, and making them commensurable by the mere act of juxtaposition, which results in an endless series where each term is joined together by nothing more than "and." It only appears that the events in the Paris of *A Sentimental Education* are strung together in arbitrary senselessness to build a historical magma of anecdotal coincidences. Metonymically unmotivated, the seeming randomness of the array of events informs the subjacent metaphoric operations of the anonymous, of the infamous—its name kept a secret—paradigm, which Augustine called Babel. Metonymy is metaphorically guided by the paradigm of Babel.[75]

· · ·

Rosanette's pregnancy, the death of her child, the ruin of the Arnouxs set in motion by Madame Dambreuse's jealousy, the forced auctioning of Madame Arnoux's household goods orchestrated by the hate-filled and vengeful Sénécal and Deslauriers, Deslauriers's betrayal of Frédéric's friendship by marrying Louise Roque—all these are events not only parallel with revolution, civil war, fratricide, and coup d'état: they are equivalent. The shared Babylonian matrix reciprocally illuminates each event. The rhythmicization of the story through the triple resumption of social gatherings—in the housewarming party of the socialists with Frédéric, the punch party with Dussardier, the meeting of the "Club de l'Intélligence"—corresponds to the three diners of the reactionaries at the Dambreuse house. In this case as well, political contrasts only hide the same logic that unifies rather than distinguishes the events.

What is shown is that beyond political divisions the same disastrous dynamic determines both circles. In crescendo, the catastrophe unfolds quite literally; word for word the voices become louder, ending by shouting, so that one cannot make out one's own words. The Babylonian topos is increasingly profiled, while remaining hidden from its actors through objective irony. They have no clue of the historical play they are actors in and remain blind as to their reality. In the camp of the socialists, the Babel-like confusion of tongues becomes manifest; in the salon of the Dambreuses, idolatry of power reigns supreme, together with a readiness for violence and the brazen dance around the Golden Calf of Property. Flaubert, who makes the disaster legible, is thus, contrary to the general view, an absolutely committed author. Maxime Du Camp recalled: "In June 1871, as we were standing together on the terrace beside the Seine, looking at the blackened carcass of the Tuileries, [Flaubert] said to me: 'If people had understood *A Sentimental Education*, none of this would have happened.'"[76] This is entirely plausible. However, Flaubert cannot be interpreted as expressing a specific political position. His book has to be read as a manifesto against the "political."

The Topos of Babel

The conventional meaning of the topos of Babel plays no role in *A Sentimental Education*: Flaubert's Paris is spelled out according to the Augustinian subtext. Flaubert does not pit the fascinating corruption of the metropolis against the purity of country life in the opposition Rousseau made the springboard of his critique of civilization. The opposition, so central for the realist novel, between Paris and the provinces is already inverted from the outset only to collapse: Frédéric does not travel from the provinces to Paris, but from Paris to the provinces. In *A Sentimental Education*, the countryside is subjected to the same rules as Paris. Iron self-interest rules without limitation. Here as over there, the big capitalist Dambreuse causes ruin through his steward (*régisseur*), Père Roque, in order illegally to profit from it later.[77] Frédéric's mother, described by Flaubert as a perverted Saint Monica, lives in the provinces; she can be called perverted because, unlike Saint Monica, the mother of Augustine, she is not concerned with her son's spiritual welfare but only with his worldly success, which she tries to enhance as best she can: "Provincial family crookednesses matching those of the Parisian world," is how Flaubert sums up this parallel.[78]

The opposition between countryside and city is cited in *A Sentimental Education* so as to subvert both its Rousseauian and Balzacian molds. For Balzac's novels, the opposition of the provinces and Paris is decisive;[79] the road to success led to Paris. Balzac's hero Rastignac epitomizes the struggle to make it in Paris, characteristic of so many novels, and Deslauriers holds him up as a model for Frédéric. En passant, Flaubert discredits Balzac's novels, reckoned the last word in realism, and holds them up to ridicule as artificial fever dreams. As opposed to the childish faith in the omnipotence of the human will and its ability to manipulate chance that informs Deslauriers's Balzacian perspective on the world, Flaubert represents the truth of his leaden times, in which the actors, enraptured by their delusions of self-love, blindly bring about the fulfillment of a blind destiny:

Never having seen society except through the fever of his ambition, Deslauriers pictured it as an artificial creation, functioning in accordance with mathematical laws. A dinner in town, a meeting with an important official, the smile of a pretty woman, could, through a series of actions following logically one upon the other, produce amazing results. Certain Paris drawing-rooms were like those machines which take material in its raw state and give it out with its value increased a hundredfold. He believed in courtesans advising diplomats, rich marriages obtained by intrigue, the genius of criminals, the submissiveness of fortune to a strong will. (87)

In *A Sentimental Education*, things happen exactly the same way over here as over there, in the provinces as in Paris. Both are equally corrupt; Babel is everywhere. After his ideals are wrecked, Frédéric falls from one cliché into the next, resolving to flee the corruption of the city to embrace the idyll of country life. This occurs shortly before the coup d'état:

He forgot about the Marshal, and did not even worry about Madame Arnoux, thinking only of himself and nobody else, lost among the ruins of his hopes, sick with grief and discouragement; and, in his hatred of the artificial world in which he had suffered so much, he longed for the freshness of the grass, the peace of the country, a sleepy life among simple-hearted folk, in the shadow of the house where he was born [à l'ombre du toit natal]. (448)

As a sentimental topos, "the shadow of the house where he was born" and purity of the heart are conjured up as the counterimage to Paris only to be smashed immediately. Deslauriers's ultimate betrayal of Frédéric's friendship takes place in the countryside, to which Frédéric travels in order to find again the woman whom he believes to have been the only one who truly loved him. Frédéric vowed to Louise Roque that she was the one and only, but he meanwhile betrayed and lied to her, as he did with every other woman. At the very moment Frédéric steps off the train, his "intended," Louise, and his best friend, Deslauriers, leave the church as bride and groom. The provinces and Paris are placed in parallel through the resumption, like a trumpet resounding through the text, of the dramatic leitmotif of the triplicate "ruined, robbed, done for!" (100; ruiné, dépouillé, perdu [164]). This is how Frédéric reacted the first time in 1840 upon hearing the news of his mother's renewed poverty, which made his life in Paris impossible. In the provinces, where there is, at least as he sees it, neither love nor intellect, his existence strikes him as hopeless. He returns only to witness the betrayal of friendship and love: "Shamefaced, beaten, crushed" (449)—honteux, vaincu, écrasé—upon seeing Louise and Deslauriers marry ten years later, he immediately goes back to the station and returns to Paris, where all his dreams have been shattered. Paris and the provinces are simply different playgrounds in the same unchanging Babylonian condition. With a universalized Babel, a distinctive structural feature of the great Parisian novels of the nineteenth century is fundamentally overturned.

In Flaubert's work, the counterpart to Babel is neither the countryside nor the heavenly City of God, but literature. Self-interest is the very essence of Babel. It divides the self against the self as well as the other. The cause of this split is not difference, but sameness: everybody desires the same because it is what the other desires. Literature, on the contrary, is founded upon the renunciation of the self to the other; it is the very locus of selflessness. "Only an honest person [*un honnête homme*] can have the gift of observation, for to see the things in themselves, you must be without any personal interest," Flaubert notes.[80] Literature is all about this disinterested participation, which involves the sacrifice of the self to the other and not self-affirmation: "The artist has to act in such a way as to make posterity believe that he never existed."[81] Literature shows society as divided through its own self-love. Flaubert's novel intends to educate its readers to recognize the Babylonian topos.

The structure of degrading repetitions is comprehensive: nothing in *A Sentimental Education* arises as original. Everything appears as déjà vu, as a hackneyed quotation, a trite stereotype. Everything is a distorting, disfiguring imitation. The historicism of Flaubert's time, the romantic rediscovery of the Renaissance and the Middle Ages, becomes the epitome of this clichéd reification for him. Thematically, this moment comes to the fore in the career of Arnoux, which can be read as an example of Walter Benjamin's work of art in the age of its mechanical reproduction. Flaubert systematically reduces the spiritual to the material; all spirituality is debased in the name of a profitable deal. With "industrial art [*art industriel*]," which Arnoux manages according to the motto "the sublime at a reasonable price" (45; *le sublime à bon marché* [95])—*horribile dictu* to Flaubert's ears—Arnoux's ruinous descent assumes increasingly stronger forms of mechanical production, starting with arts and crafts and ending with the industrial production of devotional objects. The ruin is not only financial, but above all rhetorical-hermeneutic; the produced object becomes increasingly base, culminating in the sordid idolatry of cheap and sickly-sweet devotional objects, the first real pop art. The crucial artist and critic of *A Sentimental Education* is called Pellerin, alluding to Jean-Charles Pellerin, founder of the Imagerie d'Épinal, which mass-produced cheap cut-out paper dolls representing edifying subjects such as "The Family of Emperor Napoleon I" and religious kitsch. In the figure of Félicité in his story "A Simple Heart," Flaubert shows how everything spiritual is reduced to a blinding, gaudy gleam in these fetishistic images. Ironically, in *A Sentimental Education*, Christian hermeneutics is reversed in religious pictures. Arnoux's career, summed up by such images, petrified into clichés, shows Christian iconography to be a form of idolatry. From divine understanding we have descended to the bright superficiality of kitsch. Although utterly incomparable, salvation and money are equated: Arnoux "had become a dealer in ecclesiastical objects, hoping in this way to secure both his salvation and a fortune" (425). In both his first and his last appearance in the novel, Arnoux literally emerges in the light of this idolatry, under the sign of sex, gold, and the cross. On the ship where Frédéric sees him for the first time, he is toying with the decorative golden cross adorning the décolletage of a maidservant. The last time we see him, the female sex has literally gone to his head. A wreath of rosebuds adorns his temples: a metaphor for the female sex that is, however, also a literal description of syphilitic lesions encircling the forehead, a condition bearing the poetic name *corona veneris*. Arnoux's crown of Venus, which incarnates Mary's love in a truly inverted manner through the symbol of the rose, shines in the reflection of the golden cross lit up by the sun.

Every repetition is a grimacing distortion. Frédéric's ambition is to become France's Walter Scott, an author Lucien de Rubempré, the hero of Balzac's novel *Lost Illusions*, likewise desires to emulate a quarter of a century earlier—and he presumably wasn't alone in this. Deslauriers imagines a future devoid of originality for Frédéric, seeing him as a Balzacian hero of a novel, a sort of Rastignac of the *Comédie humaine*, who succeeds through skillful marriage politics. It strikes him too that by doing so he says nothing really new: "this is just the way the world goes. Remember Rastignac in the *Comédie humaine*. You can do it, I'm sure you can!" (21).[82] Frédéric himself writes the caricature of a romantic novel. His "autobiographical" novel, *Sylvio, the Fisherman's Son*, inspired by his "great passion," takes place—how could it be otherwise?—in the romantic city par excellence, Venice, and revolves around love and power. The table of contents, a trite, absurd hodgepodge, already makes one yawn. Pellerin dithers over artists he ought to imitate, making stereotypes of them: Rosanette à la Titian? "In his memory he went through all the great portraits that he knew, and finally decided on a Titian, which would be set off with touches in the style of Veronese" (163). For the portrait of the dead child, the possible models are legion. Madame Arnoux, a collage of female stereotypes of her time, also appears as a "ready-made" figure. Rather than looking forward to the future as any revolution should, the Revolution of 1848 is fixated on the past, nostalgically looking back on the Revolution of 1789 and thereby never going beyond the level of seedy comical theater. The indisputable star of this second-rate comedy is the actor Delmar, who finally returns as Christ himself: "his biography, which was on sale in the intervals, depicted him as caring for his aged mother, reading the Bible, and helping the poor, in fact as a combination of St Vincent de Paul, Brutus, and Mirabeau. People spoke of 'our Delmar.' He had a mission; he was turning into a Messiah" (189). Claiming to be crucified for art's sake, he presents himself as its incarnation *tout court*. "In a poster addressed 'to the People,' in which he spoke to them in familiar terms, the actor boasted that he really understood them, and that for their sake he had allowed himself to be 'crucified by Art,' with the result that he had become their incarnation, their ideal" (325). His overpowering attraction, and herein the text leaves no doubt, Delmar owes exclusively to his sensuous fascination, to which all women succumb. As with Martinon, whose counterpart is Delmar in the bohemian milieu, this fascination derives, as in this case with the women in the novel, from being perceived as a painting, a statue, or a porcelain figurine in three-quarter profile. Martinon has solidified in a Babylonian material, Sèvres porcelain: "Martinon was standing near them, his hat under his arm and his face in half-profile, so elegant that he looked like a piece of Sèvres porcelain" (254).

The hermeneutic schema of *figura* and *implementum*, which regulates the relation between the Old and New Testaments, is turned upside down in *A Sentimental Education*. A degrading, distorting, grimacing, and disfiguring doubling is the general pattern. Misunderstanding, which sows discord, is a constant theme, and the repeated occurrence of signifiers intensifies the vapid, dead literalness, emptying the text of all fulfilling spirituality. Some examples will suffice to record the pointed unfathomability of every single case of misunderstanding: the duel between Frédéric and Cisy presumably ensues on account of a mix-up between Madame *Arnoux* and a famous eighteenth-century singer, Sophie *Arnould* (or Arnauld), who was not exactly known for her immaculate virtue. More fundamentally, the confusion of Madame Arnoux with the easygoing singer gives singing an erotic charge and binds it to prostitution. Frédéric's great passion, his "pure" love, is thereby infected by the topos of the Whore of Babylon. The motivation for the duel is hence so opaque that nobody agrees on who fights for whom. Rosanette, Madame Arnoux, and Arnoux all think that Frédéric duels for their sakes. Interchangeability, confusion, and indifference, binding everyone to everyone, are apparent.

Meetings between friends degenerate into the hollowest of phrases, in defamation, jealous criticism, fraud, lies, drunkenness, the furious smashing of porcelain and glass, and, finally, in swordplay in the duel, all

culminating in fratricide. Rosanette's and Frédéric's tears, even if shed together, refer to radically different causes. They cry about different things.
Their tears are not signs of love, but of its betrayal. Rosanette, Frédéric,
and Madame Dambreuse all cry at the same time: Rosanette weeps at the
death of their child, and Frédéric for the definite loss of Madame Arnoux,
while Madame Dambreuse sheds tears of fury because she believes that
Frédéric retains Madame Arnoux and her money:

Was he not her real husband? And as it was borne in on him that he would never
see her again, that it was all over, that she was irrevocably lost, he felt his whole
being torn apart; his tears, which had been gathering all day, overflowed. Rosanette noticed. "Ah! So you're crying like me? You're unhappy?" "Yes! Yes! Terribly
unhappy!" He clasped her to him, and the two of them sobbed in each other's
arms. Madame Dambreuse was crying too, lying face down on her bed, with her
head in her hands. (439)

Not once do the characters understand that no one understands the other.
There is no concord in their discord. Locked in self-interest, which degrades the other to a means to an end, there is no possible union. The
lie driven to absurdity, which isolates all from all, turning everyone into
victim and culprit, no longer obeys any pragmatic need in the case of
Rosanette and Frédéric. The world of lies of *A Sentimental Education* is so
all-embracing that they do not expose each other but, one is tempted to
say, ironically complement each other harmoniously.

The impossibility of understanding is not only shown thematically.
It also determines the grammar throughout the novel. The becoming-illegible of the text, the confusion of the reader, is the principle of its presentation. Flaubert's work on the text consists of a systematic dis-illumination.[83]
Part of this obfuscation is the quid pro quo of all differences and oppositions: between hatred and love, between man and woman, between animal
and man, between friend and enemy, between high and low, between the
material and the spiritual. The disintegration of contrasts through quid pro
quo is achieved with syntactic juxtaposition, which effects the coordination
and leveling of what is semantically strictly hierarchized—a fact stressed in
most of the literature on Flaubert. If we were to pick out only one arbitrary
example for this general structure, the syntactic equation of the cathedral
with the sausages of Chartres would count as paradigmatic: "He praised
its cathedral and its pies" (265). Perhaps the most telling example is the description of a painting by Pellerin: "It showed the Republic, or Progress, or

Civilization, in the form of Christ driving a locomotive through a virgin forest" (323–24). The figure of the zeugma, the syntactic yoking together of semantic differences, is not an isolated figure of speech, but is "ratified and internalized" as a general structure of experience. The outcome is a world "where every categorization, organization or even hierarchy starts to slip out of control," a world of a "universalized zeugma" in which everything is leveled and becomes undifferentiated.[84] It is a contingent world of incoherent randomness, of chaotic unconnectedness.

The structure of what has been described in terms of rhetoric as a zeugmatic experience can be analyzed more precisely: it is the carnalization of the spiritual. This phallic Christ who as engine driver deflowers an untouched forest with his locomotive, and who, in addition, alternatively represents progress, the republic, or civilization is such a sexualizing carnalization of spirituality. In this respect Flaubert illustrates, through the syntactic equation of semantic dissimilarities, a world where not only does nothing make sense any longer, but everything is of equal value and thus indifferent. It stages, in the chiasmus of spirituality and carnality, the idolatrous structure that determines this world. What is presented as an internalized and ratified experience of contemporaries is not to be shared by the reader; to read (through) them—and this means not to reenact them blindly in one's mind, but to analyze this structure of experience—is the reader's task. Flaubert makes this universal blindness readable. To decipher universal discord is the reader's burden.

The systematic dis-illumination and confusion persists in the grammatical structure. It is quite obvious that Flaubert worked hard to consistently obfuscate the reference of personal pronouns. An example would be the above-mentioned episode in which Dussardier, who is fighting at the side of the Garde nationale in the June Days of the Revolution, saves the boy fighting on the side of the insurgent workers from being shot by his own troops. Still, even the most seasoned reader must read this passage several times to understand what really happens: Who saves whom, and who lies injured under the rubble of the barricades? Let us have another look:

The previous Saturday a boy wrapped in a tricolour flag had shouted to the National Guards from the top of a barricade: "Are you going to fire on your brothers?" As they moved forward, Dussardier had dropped his musket, pushed the others away, leapt up on to the barricade, felled the young rebel with a well-directed kick, and snatched the flag from him. He had been found under the debris, his thigh pierced by a copper slug. (362)[85]

The grammatical game of dis-illumination has a definite Babylonian subtext in that the interchangeability of Dussardier and the boy, of the Garde nationale and the rebels, comes to the fore through a resemblance leading to a mistaken identity. The Babylonian signifier "fratricide" crystallizes in the murder of what is closest and most similar. Furthermore, love, through the quid pro quo with prostitution, points to the impossibility of meaning since both found an arbitrary indistinctness leveling all difference into a meaningless equality.

Reading Illegibility

The dis-illumination of the text, its systematic becoming-illegible, the progressive obfuscation Flaubert worked on, has yet another aspect that can hardly be overstated. It concerns not only the fact that the motif of incoherence and randomness, in which everything is of equal and thus of no worth—in short, chaos—is remarkably unchaotic. It is indeed orchestrated in the most systematic and well-planned manner.[86] The myriad historical details in the conversations of *A Sentimental Education* pertaining to economics, to politics, to the gossip papers are never explained. Few readers of the novel were likely to remember the Lafarge and Choiseul-Praslin cases in the 1840s, long before its publication.[87] Flaubert knows this. The strategy of making illegible is not an end in itself, but serves a becoming-legible of something different, that is, the decipherability of the Babylonian condition of this society.

The Babylonian topos is referenced both by the technical terminology of Arnoux's ceramics workshop and by the Choiseul-Praslin and Lafarge affairs; and Flaubert surely also had in mind the rioting at Buzançais in central France in 1847 as a result of famine (suppressed by Louis-Philippe's government with excessive force—three villagers were guillotined). Critics treat the details of ceramics production and the completely opaque speculations about kaolin mines as no more than "realistic" touches illustrating Roland Barthes's "effect of reality" (*effet de réel*). Nevertheless, without the slightest intention of signaling a detailed, "realistic" arbitrariness, a Babylonian brickworks is made to surface in the burning of clay to produce stoneware or porcelain in ceramics production, and the close Babylonian association prepares the ground for the opening of a ceramics factory by Arnoux and his speculation in kaolin, the raw material for porcelain production. The imitative moment of the building of the Tower of Babel, which substitutes brick and mud for stone and mortar, thus becomes manifest not merely through kaolin and ceramics, but also in the secondary imitative, foundational copying of Arnoux's factory itself: Arnoux builds his factory directly beside an old one with the intent to profit from the proximity. He wants to profit from the symbolic capital of the earlier establishment by metonymy.

The Lafarge and Choiseul-Praslin affairs—murder cases involving married couples—profile the ruling functional equivalence of sex and murder in the City of Man; both are consequences of original sin. The first question Frédéric is asked in his mother's salon after his return from Paris concerns the fate of Madame Lafarge, accused of killing her husband. On September 2, 1840, she was sentenced to life with hard labor for the murder of her husband—a murder she denied until the very end. The Choiseul-Praslin affair is mentioned en passant par Sénécal during his celebratory punch party upon his release, touching upon the discovery of the corpse of the duchess of Choiseul-Praslin. The duc de Choiseul-Praslin, who was considered guilty of the murder of his wife, committed suicide in prison. Flaubert inscribes the continuous overturning of sexual desire into murder, of sex into violence, characteristic of these two affairs, in a Babylonian way, into the plot of the novel. The motif runs through *A Sentimental Education* like a red thread: the murder at Fontainebleau in 1657 on the orders of Queen Christina of Sweden of her presumed lover Monaldeschi becomes a cryptic allusion to the way of the world, revealing the sinister underside, the Babylonian matrix, of all politics.

The disastrous pattern of the course of history becomes manifest most clearly in what "sentimental" means in *A Sentimental Education*: the mode that idolizes the heart in order to pursue one's own interests heartlessly with all the less disturbance. Ironically, it is precisely the heart—which hermeneutically speaking counters all reification—that has become the fetish par excellence in this society: it must pay off. Those who have it perpetually on their lips show no heart—their actions disprove their words. La Vatnaz, who unites women with men only to profit later from aborting the product of their couplings, and who systematically skims off the fruits of her female staff's labor by pocketing the stolen goods herself, is—in the most flagrant contradiction between her actions and words—a fervent admirer of the wisdom of the heart (*génie du cœur*), as well as an ideological champion of a kingdom of love in which men and women are equal. Inspired by—of all things—the writings of the romantic Flaubert despised most, Alfred de Musset (1810–57), Frédéric inscribes what he regards as his great love unto death for Madame Arnoux into the sublime tradition of literary figures like Dido, Phèdre, Werther, and the chevalier Des Grieux in *Manon Lescaut*, "forgetting" that he is lying and cheating even as he speaks these words: not only are he and Rosanette living together as husband and wife, but he is simultaneously betraying both Madame Arnoux and Rosanette through his affair with and planned marriage to Madame Dambreuse. Madame Arnoux, who cannot stand all this talk about the heart and counters such phony sublimity with a bourgeois belief in the preservation of virtue out of self-interest, has the best heart of them all, as Frédéric rightly sees. The truth of the novel remains concealed from the protagonists, in whom the fallen human condition blindly enacts itself. This is why these heroes— at the ball in the Alhambra or later during the ball at Rosanette's—have something mechanical, almost puppet-like, about them. They are remote-controlled agents of a ruinous destiny; they do not speak, but are spoken. Completely ensnared in blindness, they are in no case and in no regard stand-ins for the reader.[88] They are molded into willing executors; they are not educated, but pulled in. Frédéric's "sentimental education" amounts to his becoming hard-hearted, and the peak of this hard-heartedness resides in the fact that he carries out this hard-heartedness in the name of the heart he capitalized on and cashed out long ago. Corrupted and ruined, they all mutually corrupt and ruin one another—without ever truly knowing what they are doing. They are blinded by self-interest; they see the world distorted through their passions. Against the bourgeois concept of educational formation, in which one learns to understand oneself and the society in which one lives, thus enabling free will, Flaubert poses tragic repetition, destined for blind misrecognition, and hopeless entanglement. One is not master in one's own house, but subject to Babylonian logic. Ironical objectivization is a key element of the novel.

The irony with which Flaubert objectivizes his characters does not, however, prevent him from empathizing with them. *A Sentimental Education* has obvious autobiographical resonances: Flaubert's homosexual friendships with Alfred Le Poittevin and Maxime Du Camp inform the relationship of Frédéric and Deslauriers, and his youthful infatuation with

Elisa Schlesinger informs the love story of Frédéric and Madame Arnoux, just to name the most obvious examples. Flaubert does not exempt himself from objectivizing irony. He as well, insofar it concerns his non-writing persona, is but an actor within the Babylonian logic that governs everyone. From that point of view, *A Sentimental Education* is self-therapeutic. Above all, however, it is a text in which the author does not exclude himself from the conditions represented, thus avoiding self-righteousness.

A Sentimental Education can be summarized in two words, which are progressively revealed: fratricide and incest. Both are perversions of family ties and the result of original sin. The Babylonian logic of all of worldly history becomes readable again in Flaubert's Paris. Concupiscence takes the place of charity; self-love usurps the place of love for the other. The word "incest" appears when Frédéric does not sleep with Madame Arnoux. Sénécal's murder of his "brother" Dussardier actually does take place, but without the actual word being necessary. In the Babylonian topos, tyranny is indissociable from fratricide and incest. Revolution and republicanism are the breeding ground for tyranny. The idols of the Right are Power and Property, while the Left fetishizes Society. Despite their rhetoric of liberty, equality, and fraternity, Flaubert reproaches the socialists for wanting to organize society based on the Babylonian trinity of the barracks, the brothel, and commerce, condemning "[t]he whole cartload of Socialist writers—those who wanted to reduce mankind to the level of the barrack room, send it to the brothel for its amusement, and tie it to the counter" (149). Their enthusiasm for the model of Sparta, echoing Rousseau, is not an expression of their love for the Republic but the epitome of Babylonian tyranny: "And out of this mixture he had evolved an ideal of a virtuous democracy . . . , a sort of American Sparta in which the individual would exist only to serve the State, which would be more omnipotent, more absolute, more infallible, and more divine than any Grand Lamas or Nebuchadnezzar" (ibid.).

In the absolute omnipotence of Nebuchadnezzar, the Babylonian topos becomes as clear as day: in the guise of a republic that would in fact be a tyranny more absolute than ever before, Babel is the socialists' program. Concord rules in this society only in the truly Babylonian cry for tyranny, which becomes audible across all ideological camps. From the Left, Sénécal quotes Robespierre to justify tyranny: "A dictatorship is sometimes indispensable. Long live tyranny, provided the tyrant does good!" (404).

The reactionary camp sounds exactly the same. Soon everyone is shouting in unison for a leader and the iron fist of power: "It was necessary to 'restore the principle of authority.' It did not matter in whose name it was wielded, or where it came from, provided it was strong and powerful. The Conservatives now talked like Sénécal" (421). Frédéric, who had long since changed to the reactionary camp, is utterly confused by this unheard-of unanimous Babylonian roar for a tyrant from the two enemy camps. The great, unspoken—and therefore also most conspicuous—absence is Napoleon III, who is never once mentioned in the novel, as though he were already no more than an infamous memory.

Rome is mentioned at least three times at significant moments in *A Sentimental Education*, but the name of Babel remains as unspeakable as that of the emperor. However, it is alluded to in Frédéric's fantasies. Having become a wealthy heir through the fortunate death of an uncle, he returns heady with excitement from the provinces to Paris, dreaming of the life to come: "Like an architect designing a palace, he planned the life he was going to lead. He filled it with luxuries and splendors; it rose into the sky" (113). Later on the same journey to Paris—rise and fall—the counterpart of this Babylonian hubris already appears in the form of a ruined city, as if ravaged by divine wrath: "This part of Paris had changed beyond recognition. It looked like a town in ruins" (114).

Bengal Lighting

In the nineteenth century, the East was neither geographically nor religiously strictly defined; it stood for all that was foreign or other and was shorthand for exoticism. Islam was not the smallest common denominator of all things oriental, but only one part of the concept of the Orient. In the East lay the origin, the cradle of our culture; therefore, the Phoenicians, the Babylonians, the Egyptians—the peoples of the Old Testament—counted as oriental. But Africans and of course North Africans were also considered oriental. Even chinoiseries passed as oriental. "Asiatic" and "oriental" were used almost synonymously. The Hebrews were oriental—and by extension also the Jews—but also, in the middle of Europe, the Spaniards, who loved more boldly and fervently.[89] Perhaps inspired by Goya, Manet's Spanish motifs, in his depiction of women in lace mantillas and of bullfighters, were expressions of orientalism. Andalusia was considered especially oriental. The East was simply the other, every-thing not part of Western modernity.

In *A Sentimental Education*, the fashionable orientalism that Flau-bert considered the signature of his time has deeper implications. The op-position between East and West, the foreign and the familiar, the self and the other, Babel and Paris, and the exotic and the domestic, upon which this fashion rests, breaks down in the novel. Orientalism here is more than a reigning style, more than a stylish allusion evocative of an exotic alter-native world. In *A Sentimental Education*, the oriental is in fact not in es-sence the other, the East, or Andalusia, but Western Europe itself. Modern Paris, the "capital of the nineteenth century," in Walter Benjamin's words, turns out to be the true Babel.

Let us take our cue from what catches the eye. The Paris of the sec-ond half of the nineteenth century appears in Flaubert's text as déjà vu in the arts, interior decoration, fashion, architecture, and even cemetery ar-chitecture: an endless mimicry, a random juxtaposition that universally gathers the styles of all epochs and all areas. Thus, even in its oriental cita-tions, the Babylonian structure reverberates, that is, in a universality that is truly scattered over the entire earth through a degrading repetition. This motley collection quotes randomly. Disjointed citations and fragments are put in abrupt juxtaposition: snippets of China and Japan are placed next to ancient Greece and Rome, the Italian Renaissance, oriental Venice, all the way to Meissen china, while covering epochs of French history rang-ing from Louis XIII, François I, Henri II, to Louis XVI. They are united in their disunity.

In this universal Babylonian style the erotic register stands out. In the form of the Andalusian, the oriental finds its dominant variant: it is the one that is "most romantic." On account of its Moorish history, Andalusia is a byword in both Hugo and Balzac for a more poetic kind of love, a love not yet tainted by the stigmas of modernity.[90] Owing to her dark skin, Frédéric takes Madame Arnoux to be an Andalusian or even a Creole woman. Her exoticism is underlined by the figure of the black nanny, freshly imported from the islands, Martinique or Guadeloupe. The music accompanying this *amour à l'orientale* is consequently a *romance orientale*, featuring dag-gers, flowers, and stars. It sounds like a pastiche of Victor Hugo's cycle of poems *Les Orientales*. Small wonder that Frédéric later finds that Madame Arnoux "looked like the women you read about in romantic novels" (13).

She is the embodiment of the romantic-oriental déjà vu. Oriental motifs are thereby fundamentally drawn into the Babylonian perspective: orientalism namely always appears as a cliché, a degrading repetition.

The romanticization of the East in terms of a promise of a more poetic love is called upon only to be dismantled. Hugo positions the morally edifying love of the Christian West against the enticement of orientalisms. Flaubert dismantles the promise of more poetic, orientalist love through the Babylonian model itself: through a reiterating distortion. The absurd lining up of daggers, flowers, and stars in the scene of the first meeting of lovers already foreshadows nothing good. Madame Arnoux does not hold what Frédéric projects onto her. She turns out to come from the trite provinces and a petty bourgeois background. Chartres is not exactly a city that inspires exotic fantasies. At Frédéric's housewarming party the poetic aspect of the opening scene, bathing as it does in the shine of Hugo's verse, tips over into a clip-clop, mechanical nursery rhyme presented by Hussonet: "assez d'Andalouses sur la pelouse" (117)—"We've had enough of Andalusian women" (65). Much more poignant is that the "Andalusian" Madame Arnoux is travestied in a way that contaminates high love with prostitution. The Alhambra, a pleasure dome in the middle of Paris filled with Moorish galleries, is the counterpart to Madame Arnoux's house and its indiscriminate piling up of historical citations. Like the Arnoux household, the Alhambra is on the road to ruin. In the Alhambra, too, there is an Andalusian, who is not an object of adoration, but who is a marquise working as a prostitute. Hired to organize an "oriental rout [raoût oriental]" for Hussonet's friends, she fears moreover that she may not cover her expenses. When Delmar wails a sentimental song titled "The Albanian Girl's Brother," it reminds Frédéric of the one sung by the beggar on the river steamer after he had seen Madame Arnoux for the first time: "The words reminded Frédéric of the song the man in rags had sung on the boat, between the paddle-wheels" (81).

The histrionic gestures of this prototype, who was no actor, are horribly exaggerated by the ham actor Delmar. The uniqueness of a love at first sight, with its overtones of courtly love, is in this repetition scene disfigured through distorting duplication. Andalusian-oriental is revealed as a style promoting the sale of sex. The oriental, for the romantics still the standard of an exotic poeticization of love, becomes in the course of Flaubert's novel, for men and women alike, the register of prostitution. Almost without exception, this includes both sexes. That "rare flower" (254) (*une fleur de haute culture* [358]) Madame Dambreuse, an upper-class lady with aristocratic pretensions, signals orientalist prostitution most clearly.

Frédéric's first self-furnished dwelling has a drawing room "hung with yellow damask and furnished in the Louis Seize style, like the Marshal's" (154); doubtless this alludes to the conqueror of Algeria, Marshal Thomas Bugeaud (d. 1849), and, needless to say, "The three Algerian curtains were carefully drawn" (63). Frédéric is in fact accommodated like a whore.[91] His plan for the renovation of the Dambreuse house after his planned marriage, the coronation of his successful prostitution, is to fulfill his earlier dream of a Moorish palace, "reclining on cashmere divans, beside a murmuring fountain, attended by Negro pages" (61). Naturally, "Turkish baths" (408) are a must. All the women appear at least once in an oriental light. They are thus integrated into the circle of prostitution. But the men are no exception: Arnoux is cast from the beginning—with curled hair, pulled together extravagantly—as the embodiment of the Jew and thus as the paradigmatic oriental, while Deslauriers ends up as "director of colonization in Algeria," and "secretary to a pasha" (456).

At the birthday party in Saint-Cloud, Madame Arnoux is wearing a black velvet dress, "and, in her hair, a long Algerian headdress of red silk net which was caught in her comb and hung over her left shoulder" (52). She has sprung out of a painting of Manet and looks like one of his Spanish ladies, who, together with Manet's entire Spanish cycle, are evidently orientalist. In Frédéric's imagination, Madame Arnoux appears à la Delacroix or à la Ingres as a harem girl on yellow cushions. Rosanette and Madame Arnoux own a cashmere shawl bought from a Persian that will confirm Arnoux's adultery for his wife. Rosanette wears an "Oriental burnous" (163) at the horseraces and has Turkish divans and Turkish tobacco in her apartment; she enjoys adopting the "the provocative expression of a slave-girl" (279), as if she were an oriental fantasy springing from Delacroix's imagination, complete with tyrants. La Vatnaz wears an Algerian headscarf and "an Oriental sash round her waist" (389), as in François Gérard's painting *Madame de Staël as Corinne*. A jealous Rosanette compares the dryness of Mademoiselle Vatnaz's hands to castanets. When Tunisian emissaries are received in Madame Dambreuse's salon, the flimsily dressed upper-class beauties present remind Frédéric of a harem, even a brothel: "and this gathering of half-naked women suggested a scene in a harem; whereupon a cruder comparison came into the young man's mind" (173–74). The ruined philanderer Arnoux leaves Paris, "lui et toute sa smala" (595), the term *smala,* deriving from the Arabic for "tribe," signifying family and household in the French of Hugo and Daudet. In oriental disguise, the demimonde go about their murky business just like the respectable upper classes. Bathed in oriental light, Paris reveals its true nature as the Great Whore of Babylon.

As with Saint Augustine, the family stories in *A Sentimental Education* illustrate the results of the Fall, pithily summarized by Rosanette: "What luck for her if she hasn't got a mother!" (354). The quid pro quo, the equivalence of sex and murder, shapes the paradigm that unfolds in these ruinous tales. These are especially salient examples of how the Babylonian matrix informs the metonymies of the surface, where everything seems arbitrary and yet nothing is accidental. The prehistory of Frédéric's parents introduces the metonymic juxtaposition, the causally unmotivated, chance encounter of the Babylonian trinity of money, sex, and violence, in the form of a dowry, a pregnancy, and a stroke of the sword. The history of his mother, Madame Moreau, is sketched in laconic fashion: "She came of an old gentry family, now extinct. Her parents had married her to a man of plebeian origin, who had died of a sword wound while she was pregnant, leaving her an encumbered estate" (14). In the same way, the Babylonian trinity is found in the stories of sex and the pregnancy of Rosanette, in which murder, that is to say, abortion, and incest, as the intensification of sex and violence, are juxtaposed without any connection, by mere chance, seemingly unmotivated—Babylonian indeed. La Vatnaz, who catches Rosanette in bed with her lover, Delmar, dishes up Rosanette's story to Frédéric, precisely as the cheated third party, hoping her jealousy will stir him up into denouncing Rosanette's amours with Arnoux. She hopes this will rob Rosanette of her livelihood and ruin her. Among other things, Frédéric is told that Rosanette sleeps with two brothers: "But it doesn't matter. And when she was in a mess, I settled everything," Vatnaz says (178). Here, abortion and incest are linked by accident. Only much later, during Rosanette's pregnancy, will the paradigm of original sin show through and the Babylonian matrix start to reveal itself, subterraneously propelling seemingly chance events, in its interchangeability of violence and sex.

Madame Moreau marries for money to please her parents; Deslauriers's father marries his wife for her dowry; Madame Arnoux marries Arnoux without a dowry, only to be ruined; Madame Dambreuse marries for the money, only to be disinherited. Marriages are a kind of prostitution, in which sex is traded for money: one buys and sells. The relation between children and parents is characterized by incest or violence, and the relation of married couples is determined by sexual or financial rapacity. The orphaned Dussardier, a bastard child, is therefore, one is tempted to say, lucky to have no family. Parents and children sue one another over inheritances, as Deslauriers does his father for his mother's legacy. Fathers like Arnoux ruin their wives and children by womanizing. Through lechery, fortunes are passed on to children born out of wedlock, and the lust for symbolic or real capital is bequeathed with it, as in the case of the daughter of Dambreuse and Louise Roque. The relationship between Arnoux and his daughter has a whiff of incest about it—he spoils her rotten and lets her get away with the most sexually suggestive little moods; he "lift[s] her up to kiss her" (51). Following the iron logic of *A Sentimental Education*, and rounding off the contamination of the family, it is thus no coincidence that, eroticized at such a young age, she ends up—after marrying and moving to Bordeaux—in a brothel, reached by way of a cloister. The signifiers *bordelais* and *bordelaise*, meaning inhabitants of Bordeaux, are first associated, apparently only by chance, with the Arnouxs; after dark, when the irrepressible creases in Madame Arnoux's dress have disappeared, Arnoux visits a Bordeaux bar (*estaminet bordelais*); and his last lover is a *bordelaise*: "Arnoux was in fact letting the Bordeaux woman exploit him, with all the indulgence of an infatuated old man" (382). Following the logic of the hunter Nimrod, builder of the Tower of Babel, the Arnouxs' son becomes a *chasseur*—read a hunter in defiance of God—in Rome, the first daughter of Babylon, whose second daughter is Paris, the successor to Rome.

Like Deslauriers, children are brutally beaten by their fathers and forced into crippling labor, or prostituted like Rosanette, whose mother's alcoholism ruins her family. Doubt is shed on their legitimacy when their mothers fall for other men. Frédéric's duel in defense of Madame Arnoux's honor illuminates the mysterious sword blow that killed his father, who perhaps fought a duel on a similar account. Madame Arnoux imagines her son wounded in her lap after being obliged to fight a duel for the sake of her lost honor if she has an affair with Frédéric and is thus compromised. Not only the fortune inherited by Madame Moreau is compromised— which is to say, riddled by debts—but so too is her honor, and with it

Frédéric's legitimacy. According to Père Roque, Frédéric should in any case renounce his father's name in favor of the noble name of his mother, which Roque intends to regain for Frédéric should the latter marry his daughter as planned. Cécile, Dambreuse's natural daughter, inherits everything since the childless wife of her father has a well-publicized affair with Frédéric and is thus cheated of the gains of her matrimonial prostitution. Martinon, Cécile's future husband, lover of her "aunt" Madame Dambreuse, has manipulated this affair with an eye to the inheritance. Thanks to the early death of her mother, the unmarried virgin Louise Roque becomes, in spite of her illegitimacy, an acceptable, and even a good match owing to the illegitimate dealings of her father. Because families are not ruled by love but by money, sex, and power, which are passed on from generation to generation like original sin—since adultery and therefore the illegitimacy of succession and bequest are the order of the day—the questions pertaining to inheritances in the political discussions between the law students Deslauriers and Frédéric, and in the examinations they sit for, are not as insignificant as they may appear in isolation. They all illuminate the Babylonian topos.

The identity of sex and murder is established in Frédéric's first sexual act in the novel with Rosanette—whose nickname "la Maréchale" stands for war—which parallels the outbreak of the February Revolution. In a dream, the horny Rosanette sits astride him, "tearing him open with her golden spurs" (140). What the text betrays remains, as usual, completely hidden from the protagonists. Caught in the Babylonian inability to understand, they are unable to recognize the Babylonian condition. They know not what they do. The parallel between the fratricide at the end and sexual gratification at the outbreak of the Revolution is highlighted by Italian names, underscoring the Roman subtext. "Opposite Frascati's" (304), Moreau glimpses the windows of "la Maréchale," Rosanette, and goes over to make love to her; Dussardier is stabbed to death in the name of the Republic "on the steps of Tortoni's" (411). In the name of the Revolution—naively dubbed a "reformation" in the beginning—Rosanette and Frédéric spend their first night together. Rosanette, who initially seemed to Frédéric to be a "difficult woman," turns easy the moment the Revolution takes hold. She even goes as far as to encourage Frédéric to do what he had not done thus far: to demand sex in return for the favors he has shown her. Frédéric pledges change: "I'm following the fashion. I've reformed" (305). Hearing this, Rosanette is won over. Meanwhile, in a sexually suggestive scene, "The officers of the National Guard, on the other hand, flushed with enthusiasm, kept brandishing their swords and shouting: 'Reform for ever!' Every repetition of the word 'reform' set the two lovers laughing" (305).

The deadliness of sex and civil war, the fatal interchangeability of the one for the other, finds its metaphor in the erotic appeal of silk. Frédéric associates the sound of the execution of civilians with the sound of silk being torn: "when, all of a sudden, there was a crackling noise behind them like the sound of a huge piece of silk being ripped in two. It was the fusillade on the Boulevard des Capucines. 'Ah! They're killing off a few bourgeois,' said Frédéric calmly" (306). Reformed sex is the opposite of empathy. Wrapped in utter self-absorption, Frédéric passes the crowd with cold-blooded indifference: "There are situations in which the kindest of men is so detached from his fellows that he would watch the whole human race perish without batting an eyelid" (306). That very same day, Frédéric makes love for a second time—this time out of hatred. "Then, as a refinement of hatred, in order to degrade Madame Arnoux more completely in his mind, he took Rosanette to the house in the rue Tronchet, and into the room prepared for the other woman" (306). Rosanette is promptly roused a few moments later by the clamor of fighting: "she was awoken by distant rumblings" (ibid.). The text, which has seemingly become engrossed in the playfully frivolous tone describing the lovers' sensuous happiness to the extent that it appears to have become oblivious to politics, cites the hellish poetics of tragedy, by quoting Dante's shipwreck of Odysseus: "noi ci allegrammo, e tosto tornò in pianto"—"we rejoiced, but soon our joy was turned to grief" (*Inferno* 26.136, Singleton I, 279). Laughter—"[e]very repetition of the word 'reform' set the two lovers laughing" (305)—turns to tears: "and she saw him sobbing with his head buried in his pillow" (306). When Frédéric wakes the next morning, when "the sound of gunfire roused him suddenly from his sleep" (309), he has not missed the Revolution or his encounter with History—with a capital *H*—because he chose to devote all of his attention to carnal knowledge. Rather, he has transposed it to another scene: without being aware of it, he has literally and faithfully lived the Babylonian topos in which sex and revolution are born of the same hatred and have the same fatal consequences. Therefore, intercourse can take the place of revolution, the disdain in love can take on the guise of murder in fratricide. The same happens in both.

The Revolution, which should herald a new age of love based on liberty, equality, and fraternity, appears instead like the family, under the sign of murder and fratricide, prostitution and rape. "Ex-convicts thrust their arms into the princesses' bed, and rolled about on it as a consolation for not being able to rape them" (314). The statue of Liberty is embodied by a prostitute: "In the entrance-hall, standing on a pile of clothes, a prostitute was posing as a statue of Liberty, motionless and terrifying, with her eyes wide open" (ibid.). Rosanette compares the Second Republic, which she embodies, to a whore Frédéric loves, and whom she should thus be jealous of. Politics and the military are joined in the courtesan; Rosanette's nickname "la Maréchale" suggests war, and her anteroom resembles that of a minister. Women like her will get really rich during the Second Empire, and, as the omniscient narrator à la Balzac knows, set against those fortunes, Rosanette's gorgeous display, though it blinds Frédéric now, will seem like mere destitution. In this superior knowledge of the author it is not the opposition, but the continuity between the Second Republic and the Second Empire that reveals itself under the sign of prostitution.

Sentimental Idolatry

Medusa and my error turned me to stone,
dripping with vain moisture

Petrarch, "Prayer to the Virgin"

Self-aggrandizement, which is the foundation for all idolatry and division,[92] is the most disastrous outcome of Babel, symbolized by the building of its Tower. According to Augustine it is not so much a matter of worshipping a false god; rather, the false god, the idol, is a symptom of a false relation to God, the other, and the self. There are two forms of idolatry in *A Sentimental Education*: the simple, crude form and its refined, sentimental variation. The brutal idolatry reigning over Paris with absolute dominion is the worship of power. For its sake almost everyone prostitutes themselves unscrupulously. Already from the very beginning of the Revolution, society is heading toward tyranny. Following Augustine, Flaubert considers the desire to dominate, *libido dominandi*, to be the strongest passion of the City of Man. Corrupt and hypocritical to the core, the ensemble gathered at the Dambreuse household venerate power through a limitless and all-embracing conformity and opportunism, without bothering with political principles. Unconditionally, indeed, with utter pleasure, one submits to it: "Most of the men there had served at least four governments; and they would have sold France or the whole human race to safeguard their fortunes, to spare themselves the least twinge of discomfort or embarrassment, or simply out of mere servility and an instinctive worship of power" (257–58). Only through death is Dambreuse released from his submission to his revered god: "How many people had he flattered with smiles and bows! He had acclaimed Napoleon, the Cossacks, Louis XVIII, 1830, the workers, truckling to every government, worshipping Authority so fervently that he would have paid for the privilege of selling himself" (408).

Idolatry, corruption, and prostitution are summed up in this brilliant, paradoxical formula that goes to the heart of the matter: "he would have paid for the privilege of selling himself [*il aurait payé pour se vendre*]." Apart from power, property is idolatrously worshipped: "Now property was raised to the level of Religion and became indistinguishable from God. Attacks on property were regarded as a form of sacrilege, almost as cannibalism" (320). Property takes the place of God: a more straightforward and coarse definition of idolatry is difficult to imagine. These idolaters, dancing frantically around the Golden Calf, try through the comparison between cannibalism and the attack on private property to distance themselves from the "savages." Flaubert's devastating irony unmasks them as just as "savage." Cannibalism finds an uncanny echo in the corpse robbery, and the strange, almost sacrificial meal attended by Parisian high society, at the forced auctioning off of Madame Arnoux's belongings. Both strands of idolatry—that of power and that of wealth—which are primarily found among the upper class, are shamelessly exhibited in the Dambreuses' salon and are diagnosed and condemned by the author without a hint of irony.

Sex is a means for the accumulation of wealth and power. Madame Dambreuse uses it, only to end up cheated out of its rewards. The men, more successful at jumping from one bedroom to another, are thus the real whores of the story. Less explicitly and therefore more elegantly than Maupassant later, Flaubert's *A Sentimental Education* already anticipates the theme of *Bel Ami*. Martinon and Delmar are men who get lucky with women.[93] Women, falling for their beauty, are ruined by their sensuality. As successful as they are unscrupulous, both beaux gain power and money in exchange for sex. Martinon is the *mondaine* counterpart to the *bohème* Delmar. Frédéric follows them, so to speak, into the beds of Rosanette and

Madame Dambreuse. Madame Dambreuse, Martinon's lover, hates her "niece" because of her marriage to him, just as Delmar's lover La Vatnaz hates Rosanette because of her affair with Delmar. For Martinon, women and money are equivalent; as the object of their desire, he takes care to maximize his sex appeal so as to enrich himself as much as possible. This is his talent. Initially, Martinon lives with a working-class woman, "and, with fifteen hundred francs a year and the love of this simple woman, he was perfectly happy" (27). After that, he abandons his modest origins and starts climbing the social ladder: "with him [Martinon] was a woman of about fifty, ugly, superbly dressed, and of doubtful social status" (82). Later he becomes Madame Dambreuse's lover and ultimately marries the excruciatingly plain "niece" of his mistress, Cécile, who is actually Dambreuse's illegitimate daughter. This confronts him with the delicate question of "how to rid himself of Cécile's aunt" (366) while simultaneously swindling her out of her fortune, which according to his plan, should drop into his lap through his marriage to the illegitimate daughter, Dambreuse's only child. As always, Martinon figures out an elegant solution by handing down Madame Dambreuse to Frédéric. Completely clueless and under the spell of his own narcissism, Frédéric is puzzled when he realizes the deadlock between Martinon's marriage to the "niece" and his seduction of Madame Dambreuse: "and he was no more successful in seducing her than was Martinon in getting married" (393). Frédéric replaces Martinon in a dazzling round of musical chairs: practically the very same day Martinon abandons her to go on his honeymoon with Cécile, Frédéric goes to bed with Madame Dambreuse, who is still in tears over the loss of his predecessor. By virtue of Martinon's skillful plotting of her new liaison with Frédéric, Madame Dambreuse compromises herself according to plan, which ensures that the tremendous fortune of her husband falls into Martinon's hands via Cécile. As expected, Martinon enters on a brilliant career: he becomes a senator in the Second Empire.

In Flaubert's modern scenes—as opposed to those in *Salammbô*, for instance—this idolatrous adherence to the iron law of self-interest, no matter whether it results in piles of corpses or not, is always cloaked in the mantle of sanctimony and respectability. The new idol worship effaces the older cult of the Church. The mourners at the Dambreuse funeral, devoted tooth and nail to the cult of private property and power, are simply no longer conversant with Catholic rites: "With a few exceptions, those present were so profoundly ignorant of things religious that the master of ceremonies motioned to them from time to time to stand up, kneel down, or sit" (410–11). *A Sentimental Education* skewers these people—the financial and political elite of the Second Empire—authoritatively and without mercy.

In Flaubert, the more refined kind of idolatry bears the name "sentimental." It is exactly this sentimentality that he analyzes as the driving force behind the Revolution of 1848 and that he denounces with vitriolic sharpness. "I want to write the moral history of the men of my generation—or more accurately, the history of their *feelings*," he declares.[94] *A Sentimental Education* overturns the positive valuation that romanticism ascribes to the sentimental, which it analyzes as a form of perverse self-reference. Flaubert frames the sentimental history of his generation by condemning all forms of self-interest, however enlightened or judicious.[95] Sentimentality is a historically determined form of self-love (*amour propre*) that mistakenly identifies itself as true love.

Love and politics are marked by the same structure of idolatrous self-glorification and its attendant pleasure. The cult of love, which Frédéric dedicates to Madame Arnoux, is analogous to the sentimental devotion of the revolutionaries to the Republic. In this cult, before all else, one principally loves oneself as a noble lover of all that is noble.[96] Since it serves only to enhance the self, devotion to an ideal—be it the Republic or a One and Only Love—comes down to the form of idolatry Flaubert calls sentimental.[97]

In *A Sentimental Education*, sentimentality appears as the epitome of perversion: love, which is supposed to surrender the self to the other, instead folds back upon the self with the aim of self-aggrandizement and the pleasure this entails. Augustine identified this structure of abusive and inverted transcendence, which recoils back upon the earthly, in terms of having the use and enjoyment (*uti* and *frui*) of something.[98] The object is no longer used in order to lead to God, who should be the sole aim of enjoyment. Instead, nothing is enjoyed but the self, which is capable of such, only seemingly selfless, adoration of the ideal. The perverted structure of this cult of the ideal, which is, in fact, an idol, is illustrated by Flaubert through a universal literalization, a carnalization of the spiritual, or, to use more contemporary vocabulary, through reification and fetishization. The sacralization of the worldly, the deification of the earthly, and conversely, the secularization of the sacred, are as characteristic of sentimentality as they are of crude idolatry. In contrast to base idolatry, which is single-minded and uninhibited in its egoistical aims, sentimentality does however pursue an ideal. It takes itself to be driven by a love that does not seek its own profit, thus deluding itself as being selfless. The sacralization of the worldly in the form of the promise of salvation through the coming of a reign of Liberty, Equality, and Fraternity, a reign of Love and the sacrosanctity of heterosexual love, is what Flaubert refers to as "sentimentality." Love and politics are worldly religions; their sentimentality is due to their desire to enjoy, in the here and now, that which is not of this world. Without transcendent relation, the sentimental subject is condemned to enjoy his/her own self tautologically.

Only Madame Arnoux and Dussardier, who cling selflessly to love and to the Republic, display genuine feeling in *A Sentimental Education*. They become martyrs to their love, and all hope—hope that was still alive with the advent of the Revolution of 1848 in spite of everything—is buried with them. They are the sacrificial victims of a society that from the beginning of the Revolution has paved the way for the coup d'état. Dussardier, who stands up for the Republic, is murdered by Sénécal in the name of the new order. Madame Arnoux, who senses that with the outbreak of the Revolution something sinister is brewing, turns out to be right: everyone is now conspiring against her. Ruined, she is forced into exile. Two distinct scenes are linked as in a diptych. On the one hand, there is Dussardier's corpse, with its limbs arranged in such a way that they form a cross—a corpse that vanishes from sight as if without a trace. On the other hand, there is the scene of the picking over of Madame Arnoux's possessions—although she is only symbolically dead, her hallucinatory presence resembles that of a corpse perversely desecrated and devoured. The parallel between Madame Arnoux and Dussardier is also highlighted through their actions. Both give money to Frédéric. Dussardier gives Frédéric all his savings, without asking anything at all in return, to prevent the seizure of Rosanette's property by Mademoiselle Vatnaz, now his lover, who is seeking in this way to take revenge for Rosanette's amorous escapade with her former lover Delmar. Frédéric, less as a token of his financial but rather of his complete moral bankruptcy, accepts the money. Madame Arnoux, who lives in impoverished exile, returns the money Frédéric lent her. Dussardier's commitment to the cause of the Republic, to freedom and brotherhood, does not serve his own ego, just as

Madame Arnoux is not intent on self-aggrandizement through love. This love is not something that she feels entitled to, as Frédéric does, or believes she owes to herself, as Madame Dambreuse does: rather, it is something that takes her by surprise.

In Frédéric, the novel offers a central character who seems destined to subvert, pervert, and betray this religion of sentimentality. In this respect, Frédéric undergoes some development of character, in contrast to Martinon, Madame Dambreuse, or Rosanette. However, his "formation" consists in his adoption of an egoistic notion of love to the detriment of a selfless love. It consists of his transformation from a lover who does not seek self-gratification—"he loved her without reservation, without hope, unconditionally" (92)—into a cynical, hardened seducer who betrays, lies to, and cheats everyone. His "devotion" is later restricted to the meticulous observance of a schedule dividing his time between two women: he "religiously" spends his afternoons with Madame Dambreuse, while his evenings are occupied with Rosanette. In the final scene, his trite words make him sound like Rodolphe in *Madame Bovary*. But the modern seducer is not only morally, but also aesthetically speaking in absolute decline compared to his great eighteenth-century forebears Lovelace, in Samuel Richardson's novel *Clarissa*, and Valmont, in Choderlos de Laclos's novel *Les Liaisons dangereuses*. Frédéric quotes Valmont quite literally, echoing the words the latter writes about Madame de Tourvel to Madame de Merteuil: he does not want to take Madame Arnoux; she must give herself to him. Lovelace is cited when Frédéric thinks of "absurd, monstrous things, perhaps a nocturnal assault using drugs and skeleton keys" (185), mirroring the counterfeit keys and drugs Lovelace uses in his rape of Clarissa, since he is unable to seduce her. Rodolphe, who has "a broad experience of women and was something of a connoisseur" (*Madame Bovary*, 116), is stylistically outclassed by Lovelace as well as Valmont: their sense of the aesthetic is peerless. After all, they do not limit themselves to phrase-mongering; their *esprit* is legendary. This is what Rodolphe utterly lacks; lacking much imagination, he seduces women by means of extravagant clichés. Neither Lovelace nor Valmont are so pettily obsessed with their own advantage, their own profit and sensory gratification as Rodolphe is. Like Rodolphe, all Frédéric wants in the end is for his love for women to pay off. Cheap like Rodolphe, who quite literally refuses under any circumstance to make a bad bargain, Frédéric at least never suffers gratis.

The economic discourse, which is diametrically opposed to the romantic discourse of love—where love is deemed beyond price—is introduced in the final scene between Madame Arnoux and Frédéric, a scene that is the inverted mirror image of the last encounter between Madame Bovary and Rodolphe. Madame Arnoux repays her debts to Frédéric; Madame Bovary needs money from Rodolphe to pay her debts. Madame Arnoux does not accept Frédéric's money, which could have saved her from ruin, because she is afraid that by accepting she will have surrendered to him and thus, like a whore, have exchanged sex for money. Conversely, Emma Bovary runs to Rodolphe without being conscious of the fact that she is prostituting herself by doing so.

Frédéric uses the same stale clichés as Rodolphe, who, debating with himself whether to seduce Madame Bovary, wonders how he will eventually get rid of her: "Oui, mais comment s'en débarrasser ensuite?"[99] This is echoed in Frédéric's reservation when pondering the question whether or not he should make love to Madame Arnoux: "D'ailleurs, quel embarras ce serait!" (620). After Rodolphe sleeps with Emma Bovary for the first time, and the "Madonna on a pedestal, sublime, secure, immaculate" has toppled from her pedestal, he immediately reverts to type, "a cigar stuck between his teeth" (*Madame Bovary*, 143). Similarly, Frédéric lets all sublimity go up in smoke through the prosaic gesture of rolling a cigarette: "to avoid degrading his ideal, he turned on his heel and started rolling a cigarette" (455). He is intoxicated by his own sentimental commonplaces. The uniqueness of love, for which there is no substitute, is brutally reduced to a stereotype and déjà vu; it turns into the cheapest ersatz, precisely through Frédéric's cashing in on its uniqueness. When he hears about Madame Arnoux's love, Frédéric concludes, in accordance with his cheap, sentimental logic, that he has broken even: "He regretted nothing. His former sufferings were redeemed" (453).[100]

Whereas time stands still in the first encounter between Madame Arnoux and Frédéric, their final meeting occurs under the sign of time passing. Madame Arnoux's dark locks have turned white. She appears under the agonizing tyranny of the clock, with its mechanical measuring of every minute: if Frédéric had once lost track of time in the eternity of the meeting of their eyes, now the minutes pass agonizingly slowly. The clock hand, upon which Madame Arnoux rivets her gaze, creeps forward all too slowly for the both of them, who are separated already before they have to separate. Each of these moments is too much; this is merely an empty time drained of all meaning. Their time, which was once a timeless dawn, in the end turns into a timetable. Never did a novel relate a more depressing, a more hopeless "consuming" of a passion or a more merciless interchange-ability of things, where everything ends in meaningless seriality—"he had affairs with other women" (451)—and where everything, equally insignifi-cant, turns to nothing—"And that was all" (455).

The text provides its autopoetics. Borrowing from romantic dis-course yet again, Frédéric thinks: "I can understand Werther not being put off by Charlotte's bread and butter" (453).[101] Now, given Werther's love for Charlotte, dislike of her bread and butter was never an issue: nothing would be more absurd than to voice concern about her buttering bread for her brothers and sisters so maternally, chastely, and housewifely. We may thus deduce that Frédéric's thought has nothing to do either with Madame Arnoux's lack of rhetorical finesse, to which it is notionally applied. It is precisely in this hackneyed discourse that the truth of her love may be de-tected. Flaubert believed human, Babylonian language to be ill-equipped for expressing love in both a true and effective manner. If it were effec-tive, it would not be true; it would merely be the tool for seduction. If it were true, it would be ineffective and remain unheard. Such is the Babylo-nian tragedy in which truth cancels out the effect, and the effect the truth, "since no one can ever tell the precise measure of his own needs, of his own ideas, of his own pain, and human language is like a cracked kettle on which we beat out tunes for bears to dance to, when what we long to do is make music that will move the stars to pity" (*Madame Bovary*, 170). The bread and butter stands in for Frédéric's strategically employed empty phrases of seduction. In the end, he becomes intoxicated by his own rheto-ric: "Frédéric, drunk with his own eloquence, began to believe what he was saying" (*Sentimental Education*, 454).

In his professed ideal love, Frédéric loves only himself. This truth is progressively uncovered by the novel. Frédéric's sin is pride, in the sense Saint Augustine gives to the term: "For 'pride is the beginning of sin.' And what is pride but an appetite for a perverse kind of elevation?" (*City of God* 14.13, 608). This vanity is what Frédéric chases after, all the while blinded by the idolization of his supposedly noble self. Flaubert frames Frédéric's decadence through what Augustine sees as the main criterion for distinguishing between the City of God and the City of Man, namely, the distinction between self-love and love of one's neighbor or love of God. Frédéric's love is merely a means to his self-glorification: "He thought that the happiness his noble soul deserved was slow in coming" (6). Love does not make him humble or grateful. Instead, he thinks "disdainfully of all the human beings lying asleep behind those walls, those who lived without seeing her, unaware of her existence!" (56). In his grotesque conceitedness, Frédéric believes he has found his calling through love, and soon sees himself as a great painter and author. "Love is the stuff of genius. Great emotions produce great works of art" (20). In the figure of his antihero, Flaubert en passant satirizes romantic aesthetics, according to which great works are produced thanks to great passions:

Then he was seized by one of those tremblings of the soul in which you feel yourself transported into a higher world. An extraordinary talent, object unknown, had been bestowed upon him. He asked himself in all seriousness whether he was to be a great painter or a great poet; and he decided in favor of painting, for the demands of this profession would bring him closer to Madame Arnoux. So he had found his vocation! The object of his existence was now clear, and there could be no doubt about the future. (56–57)

Perhaps the most devastating aspect of Flaubert's style are the exclamation marks. The scene ends with an invocation of Narcissus. Mesmerized by his own beauty, utterly self-absorbed, Frédéric gazes into the mirror: "His face appeared in the mirror. He thought himself rather handsome, and stood there for a minute gazing at himself" (57–58). The following day, upon starting his sublime calling as a great painter, he goes and does some shopping.

The motif of Frédéric's self-love—narcissistic, self-idolizing, and thus constantly frustrated—pervades the entire novel. The duel is not so much an attempt by Frédéric to defend the honor of someone else as a way to enhance his own image. In his own eyes, Frédéric's nobility and grandeur will grow exponentially: "The thought of fighting for a woman magnified him and elevated him in his own eyes" (244). He resembles Boccaccio's Fiametta, whose ambition is to be the most tragic lover ever.

A Sentimental Education is thus no education, but a tale of the perversion of the heart. The worst thing about Frédéric's sentimental education is neither the perfidy of his lies nor "the apathy that lived in his heart" (451). It is that he does not spare a single thought for the victims: the ruin and exile he causes Madame Arnoux, the supposed love of his life;

Rosanette, whom he ruthlessly abandons; ruined Madame Dambreuse, his promise of marriage to whom he breaks. He cares only about the destruction of his own dreams and his own ideals, "thinking only of himself and nobody else" (448). Frédéric's ultimate downfall is sealed by his moral bankruptcy. In the end, his ideal does not enable him to act selflessly, but rather serves to justify his cruel behavior[102]—first in order to excuse his betrayal of Rosanette and Madame Dambreuse in the name of the unattainability of his ideal and, finally, in order to excuse his unjust scolding and abandonment of Rosanette and, as the text informs us, his "execution" of Madame Dambreuse. All of this occurs in the name of the ideal, in the name of a devotion to love, whose religious origin is uncovered through a language that invokes the words of the Fathers of the Church to designate God's love—"Was she not the substance of his feelings, the very essence of his life?" (435), "Was he not her real husband?" (439)—only to distort that love absolutely. The catastrophe of *A Sentimental Education*, thus already turning the title into a grim irony, is—contrary to the host of interpretations thus far—not so much the fact that Frédéric wrongheadedly hangs onto an ideal: if only he had taken a dose of realism, he might have gained control over his life, his love for Rosanette or Madame Arnoux, and achieved happiness. This alternative, where through some magic touch of realism Frédéric would have turned into a second Martinon, surely misses the point. Flaubert had already dismissed such bourgeois desires for success.[103] On the contrary, hence showing that in the text the ideals are not so much destroyed as they are deconstructed, *A Sentimental Education* affirms the ideal of selfless love. Nevertheless, it cannot present this in a positive way—which would only produce a kitschy caricature and lead to idolatrous self-enjoyment—but only negatively.

At first, Frédéric's love for Madame Arnoux was not driven by any kind of self-interest, as Flaubert remarks in his notes.[104] With Madame Dambreuse, no trace of such a generous, selfless love is left; to Frédéric she is nothing more than a springboard for his career and wealth—just a means to an end. Madame Dambreuse for her part does not want to give herself away for nothing; he owes her a great passion. Frédéric fails miserably in his attempts to remain faithful to his ideal; in the rift between ideal and reality Frédéric's narcissism comes to the fore. The systematic and close interweaving of the Arnoux and Dambreuse homes also serves to bring out the caricatural duplicate of the love for Madame Arnoux. If Frédéric's great love and great art were misguided and blinding ideals from the start, then his falling in line with the values of this society, for which he scrupulously prostitutes himself, is a revolting descent instead of an uplifting story of personal growth. Frédéric is a sellout: he forsakes his love for Madame Arnoux while passionately declaring his love to Madame Dambreuse by telling her what he felt for Madame Arnoux. In the most literal sense of the word he coins his feelings. Because his heart remains numb, he tells Madame Dambreuse what he felt for Madame Arnoux; since his senses are not aroused, he falls back on the image of his lovemaking to Rosanette. His love thus never comes for free—it always pays off. The good life, becoming rich, enjoying political success: these are the ends so despised by Flaubert, and the ends that Frédéric, in the end, pursues as unsuccessfully as Martinon is successful.

Frédéric ends up with nothing because, when all is said and done, he is willing to renounce everything for his ideal. And this is indeed the worst-case scenario, since his ideal proves at that very moment to be an idol. His affirmation of the ideal is so disastrous because, as an idol, it is but a mere pretext for his uninhibited self-idolatry, enabling him to destroy anything that does not conform to it without a hint of *caritas*. Unable to see the beam in his own eye but always ready to point out the splinter in that of others, Frédéric leaves Rosanette whom he wrongly holds accountable for the ruin of Madame Arnoux, while he "executes" Madame Dambreuse—after having unintentionally contributed, through their liaison, to the loss of her considerable property—because she refuses to accept his ideal love for Madame Arnoux. In his "loyalty" to Madame Arnoux—a passion, one is tempted to say, he cashes out and uses to his own profit— he elevates and adulates nothing but his own noble self.

Madonnas and Whores

The decomposition of the ideal, its exposure as an idol through which Frédéric blindly worships his own self, is effected by the text on different levels. The most ingenious mode of this disintegration takes place through a Flaubertian self-commentary. In the course of *A Sentimental Education*, it is not only Frédéric who mutates into Rodolphe. Even more disconcerting are the parallels between Madame Bovary and Madame Arnoux. Madame Arnoux is the virtuous wife and mother, always with needlework in her lap, always embroidering, knitting, and sewing for her little ones, faithfully following her ruined and ruinous husband into exile. She is the counterpart to Madame Bovary, the voluptuous adulteress and ruin of her family. According to Michael Riffaterre, the contrast between the two women—the virtuous woman and the whore—is underscored in the difference between Madame Arnoux's skirt that cannot be lifted (309) and Nanette's little skirt blown up by the wind in the blind beggar's song, a song greeted with horrific laughter by Madame Bovary on her deathbed, "a ghastly, frenzied, despairing laugh" (*Madame Bovary*, 290), as she recognizes herself as the whore. But Flaubert's text reinforces the bourgeois opposition between the virtuous wife/mother and the whorish adulteress, which, ultimately, does nothing more than confirm the clichés of a middle-class worldview and guarantee its neatly ordered hypocrisy, only on the surface. He establishes this opposition only to decompose it. The unmistakable parallels between Madame Bovary and Madame Arnoux are disconcerting. On a purely superficial level this parallel is already announced by the fact that both women are incessantly doing needlework.

These unsettling parallels bring the distinction between whore and virtuous wife/mother to the point of collapse. With every fiber of his being, and as hypocritically as possible, Frédéric must hold onto this distinction for the sole purpose of his self-aggrandizement; he hates Rosanette, who as a "whore" visited a "saint," Madame Arnoux, and thereby as it were desecrated the latter's sanctorum. That the text does not consolidate but rather subverts this distinction already becomes apparent in that it is not only the conceited Frédéric who holds it so dear, but that there are even bigger idiots who find it so essential: Regimbart, for instance, idolizes virtuous women. Madame Arnoux does indeed represent the two protagonists of the Annunciation, the virgin mother and the angel, and thus absolute pureness, in her names: Marie and Angèle. But on closer inspection, she is not so much the opposite of Madame Bovary, the soiled adulteress, as her uncanny double. Madame Arnoux embroiders a garnet-colored velvet case for Frédéric, just as Madame Bovary embroiders a garnet-colored cigar case for Rodolphe. On two occasions, Madame Arnoux lets out the same hopeless laughter of recognition that shakes Emma on her deathbed. As a sign of utter despair, her laugh betrays the same recognition as Emma's: she is but a cog in an economic machine governed by prostitution. The first time Madame Arnoux breaks out in laughter is when Deslauriers comes to her and declares his love, in hope of replacing Frédéric in his presumed role as her lover: "She gave vent to a burst of laughter: shrill, heart-rending, terrible laughter" (266). She has just realized that because of her husband's financial straits and her love for Frédéric, she is being treated like a prostitute by this man.

Next, to collect on Jacques Arnoux's debt to her, Rosanette formally seeks to penetrate their home, where she has already secretly been before to make love to him. The highly significant "apparition" of the Annunciation is transferred to Rosanette and thus, upon a second reading of this first scene, profaned. Frédéric's perspective on Rosanette's visit to Madame Arnoux as the profanation of a "holy" space by an impure woman is thus undone by the text: "A common whore like you, and the saintliest, sweetest, kindest woman in the world!" (442).[105] The scene is the mirror image of a previous scene in which Frédéric, looking for Madame Arnoux, interrupts Jacques making love to Rosanette. Instead of her lover, Jacques, Rosanette finds Frédéric, the father of her child, her "husband," who enjoys the delights of newlywed life at home with her, in a tête-à-tête with Madame Arnoux. She surprises Madame Arnoux and Frédéric embracing in their first and only kiss, virtually in flagrante. Rosanette, the courtesan, behaves like a wife, who, without wasting words, curtly drags her husband back home from a scene of adultery. The well-bred Madame Arnoux handles the contretemps as delicately as possible, but as soon as the door is shut, "a shrill, piercing laugh came down to them from the top of the staircase" (386); it is heard all the way to Rosanette's carriage.

Just as uncanny as the laughter Madame Arnoux and Madame Bovary both indulge in, which signals their recognition of themselves as whores, is another motif that connects the two women, namely the mutilating cutting of a lock of hair and the play of black and white it entails. At Charles Bovary's request, Homais cuts off some of Emma's beautiful black hair: "Homais hacked off two or three thick locks at random, leaving white gaps in that beautiful head of black hair" (297). The white lock of Madame Arnoux's hair cut "close to her head" to give to Frédéric as a memento of her love corresponds here: "With an abrupt gesture she cut off a long lock close to her head" (455).[106] In so doing, she says good-bye to her femininity, dying as a woman. Once as black as Emma Bovary's, her hair now parallels Emma's exposed white scalp.

Ave Maria: Carnalization of the Spiritual

In the figure of Madame Arnoux the dichotomy between Madonna and Whore is established only to be torn down;[107] the opposition of respectable wife and mother versus adulteress and whore does not find confirmation, but is undermined. That the madam of a brothel the young Flaubert and his friend Alfred Le Poittevin frequented was actually called Arnould,[108] although in itself irrelevant to the text, becomes pertinent taking into account the presumptive cause of the duel between Frédéric and Cisy: the confusion of names between Madame Arnoux and Sophie Arnould, one of the most famous singers of the eighteenth century, who had quite a reputation for being frivolous: "Sophie Arnoux . . . everyone knows about that," Cisy says.[109] What is revealing in terms of the connotations of incest is that Frédéric's mother, in the first drafts of the novel, is not called Madame Moreau, but Madame Arnout. Mother, lover, madam: all these roles are compressed into this one name and become interchangeable.[110] If Madame Arnoux and Rosanette, as saint and whore, constitute absolute opposites for Frédéric, they nevertheless make a melodious match; while the one enchants the heart, the other titillates the senses (248). Not only is the breakdown of the opposition between respectable wife/mother and courtesan framed within the general, Babylonian economy of prostitution. Idolatry, as the cult dominating Babel, is furthermore joined to it. Idolatry, obviously, revolves around the question of the image. The idol blinds and fascinates. After all, the idol is nothing but the mirror image of the self, a rising of the ego to a state of completion so that it can become its own object of enjoyment. Read between the lines, the text signals that Frédéric succumbs to idolatrous illusion when he meets Madame Arnoux for the first time. Self-blinding is already inscribed in the moment of this first appearance. Frédéric's love for Madame Arnoux—and this is evident from the very start—is, as a love cult, a religion where the sacred and the profane, the spiritual and the carnal, are at stake. It is as an idol, both a Renaissance Madonna and harem girl, that Madame Arnoux enters the picture.

At the outset of the novel, Madame Arnoux appears in a world that, in the most literal sense of the word, is Babylonian: conceived as death-ridden, senseless, and unintelligible chaos consisting of nothing but traces of decay. She is the antithesis to this world, the counterimage to the vulgarity, ugliness, the devastated ruin and decay of a wasted world: "People arrived, out of breath; barrels, ropes and baskets of washing lay in everybody's way; the sailors ignored the passengers; . . . and the general din merged into the hissing steam, escaping through some iron plates, wrapping the whole scene in a whitish mist, while the bell in the bows was clanging incessantly" (5). An incredible confusion, an absurd jumble, a disjointed juxtaposition that turns into an obstacle course, a painful chaos of sound and fury where one is unable to hear one's own words, a world where the eyes are always deceived; in short, the breakdown of all understanding, recognition, and meaning is what this initial tableau sketches out.

Nothing is whole in this world. Flaubert illustrates the moment of the non-whole, the defiled, the fragmentary—one is almost tempted to say—as wholly and comprehensively as possible through the figure of clothing fabrics. The textiles have faded, become threadbare, frayed at the edges, pierced. Tainted, soiled, and torn to shreds, they hang about in tatters. The only refuse is what remains after consumption: nutshells, cigarette butts, pear peels, sausage skins. Hermeneutically, this corresponds to the metaphor of the spiritual sense of the Scriptures in which what is shed once the spiritual core is recovered is left behind as chaff, as the meaningless shell. Madame Arnoux appears against the backdrop of this foul, meaningless world, arbitrarily held together by the incoherence of chance, a world in which nothing remains intact and everything is under the spell of decay, this world where no one is understood and recognized but where everyone rushes about in reckless abandon. She is "like an apparition . . . silhouetted clearly against the background of blue sky" (8), absorbed by the embroidery in her lap. Eternity stands opposed to *vanitas*.[111] Frédéric greets this apparition, like the angel greeting the Madonna, lifting her head. Though he does not bend his knees he does lower his shoulders. As soon as their eyes meet (9), this sublime fulfillment is shattered by her husband's question. Both are called back to the punctual temporality of timetables: Madame Arnoux is about to disembark. The contrapuntal aspect of her husband's interruption with the Marian Annunciation is only covertly decipherable through a second reading.

However, the world, against whose background Madame Arnoux appears, already profiles *ex negativo*, and almost to the point of obsession, the Marian attributes with exceptional completeness. Most pronounced is her intactness, wholeness, and undefiled nature, which is not torn apart and pierced, her immaculacy as well as her uniqueness, her overpowering glow, the light she emits, her beauty, her purity and perfection, all of which set her apart from the meaningless chaos of the world, its overwhelming ug-liness, all worn-out and ragged, its decay, filth, clamor, and refuse. Our Lady, Star of the Sea (*stella maris*) is evoked, since Madame Arnoux travels by ship and since her shawl is about to slip into the water. The scene of the apparition, though, subverts the opposition constitutive of the figure of Mary, who is not a vain idol, but "vera beatrice." Mary's Conception, through which the word becomes flesh, performs a hermeneutic rever-sal: the ability to discern true knowledge, as given through and by Mary, stands in contrast to the delusional and blinding idolatry that character-izes the worldly. In Flaubert's text, however, Madame Arnoux alias Maria appears between the lines as the antithesis of that to which she is tradition-ally opposed: as an idol.

Whether the shine that sends Frédéric into raptures is the ray of light from her eyes pouring into his soul, or whether he is blinded by his own eyes, is not clear in Flaubert's French, but Baldick's English translation re-solves the ambiguity: "he could not see anybody else in the dazzling light which her eyes cast upon him" (8).[112] That their eyes have yet to meet at this point is first suggested and then later emphatically underscored when they finally do connect: "Their eyes met [*se rencontrèrent*]."[113] Here Frédéric experiences, not transfiguration, but blinding.[114] The text erects the anti-thesis between world and apparition only to subvert it at the same time. Between the lines we can read that Frédéric is deceived by an illusion.

The apparition of Madame Arnoux is the epitome of clichéd femi-ninity. She appears to Frédéric in the guise of an image, as an icon, re-peated ad nauseam, of the contemporary ideal of beauty, namely, as a Raphaelesque Madonna.[115] The background of blue sky evokes a painting in which the oval of the face and the folds of the dress allude to the com-monplaces in descriptions of Marian apparitions. However, Flaubert fur-ther layers this icon with a reference to the contemporary classicist school of the Ingristes, bound to the explicitly Raphaelesque, ancient, classical, timeless ideal of beauty. "Her straight nose, her chin, her whole figure was silhouetted clearly against the background of the blue sky" (8).[116] The de-scription of Madame Arnoux corresponds to art historical descriptions of the classicist Ingristes, in which clear contours and the antique straight nose play a prominent role. This school extracted from Raphael's oeu-vre a calcified and stereotypical ideal of beauty, which, through its wide-spread reception, became somewhat of a standardized, easily reproducible gimmick. The straw hat that substitutes for the Virgin Mary's halo sums it up nicely: it is bathetic.

One stereotype follows the other, and in this case that of the oriental-exotic—as a wink to the reader, perhaps an allusion to Ingres's *Le bain turc* (1862), or *La grande odalisque* (1814)?—is projected onto the ancient ideal of beauty, the Madonna. The Madonna motif of sheer purity is from the outset framed within the oriental register of sexual availability. The fact that the phrase "it was like an apparition" is a quotation from the Egyptian diaries of Maxime Du Camp is of no consequence to the reader. To know that this is a quotation merely underlines what the text itself already provides in terms of its orientalism, namely, the fundamental erotic connotation of this register as applied to women. With this sentence, Du Camp captures the moment of the apparition of the courtesan Koutchouk-Hânem, whom Flaubert and Maxime Du Camp visited together during their oriental journey. Delineated by the blue of the sky, both Koutchouk-Hânem and Madame Arnoux, the whore and the Madonna, are reified and fetishized by the male gaze.[117] Madame Arnoux is reduced to a cookie-cutter image, a two-dimensional object, in Frédéric's eyes.[118] And it is this fetishization, this reification that turns both Madonna and odalisque alike into objects of desire.

This image is an idol, which functions as such for Frédéric but not for the reader. The does and undoes the idolization: it stages the apparition through an ossified, rigid, clichéd image framed as a quotation and déjà vu. Frédéric's perspective is thus shown to be an illusion. The image is exposed by the text as an idol. The description inscribes that which Frédéric cannot see, but we can read. The antithesis between *vanitas* and eternity is established only to be undermined. The Madonna turns out not to be in opposition to worldly death and chaos. The Babylonian world is the one true world, while the apparition of the Virgin Mary is but a delusion. Since Frédéric already knows what Madame Arnoux embodies, what he sees in her is not what is individual and unique but an idolized femininity turned into an image, rigidified into a cliché, and thus marketable. At the core of idolatry is a literalization of the spiritual, or, to borrow Saint Augustine's expression, a debasing of the spiritual through the carnal—the praxis of the City of Man—instead of a spiritualization of the carnal—the *proprium* of the City of God. The Annunciation is the primal scene of the overturning of the one into the other: through Mary, who before conceiving in the flesh conceives in her heart, a hermeneutic revolution is initiated. Flaubert folds this transfiguration back upon itself: a *perversio* of the *conversio*.

The fetishistic cathexis of the things surrounding Madame Arnoux is already heralded during their first encounter. The reification of their love, in which a small case takes the place of a person, will find its fulfillment at the auction of her household property. Already from the outset, Frédéric's interest in Madame Arnoux is fetishistic in the Freudian sense of the word; his curiosity is not piqued by the body of the loved one, but shifts and focuses on what the body has come into contact with (metonymy) and what takes its place (metaphor): "He longed to know about the furniture in her room, all the dresses she had ever worn, the people she mixed with; and even the desire for physical possession gave way to a deeper yearning, an aching curiosity which knew no bounds" (9). Frédéric's idolatry is ultimately less directed at Madame Arnoux than devoted to his self. Above all, Frédéric's love elevates his own pride through a complete reversal of the religious topos where love leads to humility. This is why, from the outset, the motif of curiosity is so prominent as the classical moment of reification and self-elevation. This "love" is therefore nothing but a form of self-deception and a tautological self-affirmation of Frédéric's potency.

The work of the text is to literalize the signifiers of the first encounter, dismantling the ideal as an idol. In this literalization, the idolatrous deception of the first moment becomes readable. The ideal will reveal itself to be an idol. Step by step, the ideal is pursued by a devouring doppelganger, tearing apart all transcendence. This de-idealization follows the path of reification, or, to invoke Augustine, the path of carnalization of the spiritual. Rhetorically, this is effected through literalization. *A Sentimental Education* does little more than elaborate the progressive literalization of the Annunciation. With the achievement of its literalization, reification, and carnalization, the *education* reaches its completion.

Let us first take a look at the scene where Deslauriers—almost Frédéric's alter ego—tries to seduce Madame Arnoux. In his eyes, as a "society woman" (264), Madame Arnoux is the very embodiment of the luxury object. "A poor man, he yearned for luxury in its most obvious form" (264). Deslauriers's call on Madame Arnoux is marked by a concern for money and contracts. Deslauriers wants to be paid in sex for his financial aid. Sex for money fits the Babylonian trope of prostitution; from the outset, Deslauriers sees Madame Arnoux as an adulterous woman. A lover, he presumes, is easier to replace than a husband. The defining moments of the scene of the initial encounter between Frédéric and Madame Arnoux thus become explicit in this scene in which Deslauriers overtly identifies himself with Frédéric, even to the point of becoming a second, debased Frédéric: Frédéric takes Madame Arnoux for an Andalusian; Deslauriers ascribes to her a southern, Mediterranean origin. He is immediately disillusioned upon finding out that Chartres is her place of birth. If Frédéric is blinded by the overwhelming radiance of her apparition in a metaphorical sense, in the case of Deslauriers this glare quite literally becomes a technical-mechanical radiance owing to his spectacles: "he looked her straight in the eyes, through his gleaming spectacles" (265).

The tenor of the first meeting between Madame Arnoux and Frédéric sets the tone for the way she is presented throughout the text. She is described against the backdrop of the iconography of the life of Mary, whose most salient stations are the Annunciation, Virgin and Child, Stabat Mater, and Pietà. Mary's attributes play a dominant role in the depiction of Madame Arnoux: she is the Star of the Sea (*stella maris*), a "rose without thorn," the cloaked virgin (*vierge au manteau*). The ideal of the virgin mother is what Frédéric worships in her. Both signifiers, "virgin" and "mother," are related through Frédéric's impotence: the virgin Louise Roque wants to surrender herself to him, but seized by fear, he is unable to take her. Madame Arnoux wants to surrender to him, but because of his fear of incest, which automatically produces the unspoken signifier "mother," he is unable to take her. The Annunciation is not just alluded to in her first meeting with Frédéric; through her names "Angèle" and "Marie," Madame Arnoux represents its two protagonists, the Angel and Mary. Frédéric projects a lack of eroticism onto her, which, in his eyes at least, marks her as blessed among women, able to conceive in all purity without the taint of sexual lust. Her immaculacy appears only negatively, however, through the contrast with the stains of original sin that mark all the other women in the novel and that in Babylonian fashion place sexual desire and murder under the rubric of the Fall. Louise Roque is stained, as is Rosanette. As a young girl, Louise Roque already envisages the sexual bliss of becoming Frédéric's wife. The next day she weeps over her sins and at night she is woken up by a nightmare; Frédéric had read her *Macbeth* "in Letourneur's straightforward translation," and in her nightmare she shrieks: "'A spot! A spot!' Her teeth were chattering, she was trembling, and, fixing her terrified eyes on her right hand, she kept rubbing it and saying: 'Here's yet a spot!'" (105). Given its context, Macbeth's regicide and the bloodstains it leaves behind are associated with Louise's precocious sexual desire.[119] The equivalence of sexual lust, reproduction, and murder is metonymically underscored by the close temporal proximity of her father's murdering of the captive rebel, and her nightly, passionate search for Frédéric, provoking jokes about her possible pregnancy with the men of the Garde nationale. Sex and murder: family affairs, affairs that are kept most literally within the family. As to Rosanette, she is equally stained through her pregnancy, which she reveals to Frédéric when he is about to strike her in a fit of rage: "Don't kill me! I'm pregnant!" (387). She bears the stains of original sin, both of murder and of sexual lust and its consequences: "Her skin was unusually puffy, and flecked with little yellow spots" (ibid.).

For Frédéric, Madame Arnoux is free of such taints; alone of all her sex, he has placed her beyond the human. Frédéric is not jealous of Jacques Arnoux, because he finds it inconceivable for Madame Arnoux to be naked and have sex: "he could not imagine her other than clothed, her modesty seemed so natural, hiding her sex in a mysterious darkness" (77). Her natural sense of shame is matched by his propriety: "An invincible sense of decency restrained him; and he could not find any example to follow, since she was different from other women. His dreams had raised her to a position outside the human condition" (185). The motif of the "Madonna with the sheltering cloak" reinforces the Marian iconography: "Besides, he was restrained by a sort of religious awe. That dress of hers, merging into the shadows, struck him as enormous, infinite, impossible to lift; and precisely because of that his desire increased" (215).

Frédéric parallels his cult of love with the Catholic service. "She called him Frédéric and he called her Marie, worshipping that name, which he said was made specially to be breathed in ecstasy, and which seemed to contain clouds of incense and trails of roses" (293). He sounds like one of Zola's heroines who, during the Marian devotions of May, already enjoy the sensuous bliss of adultery even before the moment of its consummation. The furnished room in which Frédéric hopes to make love to Madame Arnoux for the first time, which he unhesitatingly rents for an entire month, has its two exits—as the landlord does not fail to point out—arranged practically and prosaically for the purpose of adultery. In this room one can escape being caught in flagrante delicto by using the second exit. Frédéric makes of this sordid room a shrine in which Madame Arnoux's naked body is to take the place of the consecrated host: "more reverently than somebody decking out an altar of repose, he moved the furniture about, hung the curtains himself" (297). In Flaubert, the image of the altar recurs obsessively and is always accompanied by a fragrance ("he went to three shops to buy the rarest of scents" [ibid.]); flowers, the classic violet ("violets on the chest of drawers" [ibid.]); lace ("he bought a piece of imitation lace" [ibid.]); by the color blue—here in the gleam of the satin of his slippers—and by gold. Were it up to Frédéric, Madame Arnoux would appear in the golden gleam of a completely gilded room, just like the host in the gold of the monstrance: "he would have liked to pave the whole room with gold" (ibid.). These sacred moments appear as modes of idolatry, whose latest contemporary version is incarnated by the sordid shine of the reified world of consumer goods. The fragrances are perfumes bought and mixed together, the lace is fake, and the golden-tiled room breathes an air of vulgarity. With Flaubert, the Corpus Christi altar is the place par excellence of Catholic idolatry, an actual dance around the Golden Calf, where a deadly petrification takes the place of a life-giving transcendence. This distorting solidification of the luster of the world of commodities is also what characterizes this altar of love.

This deadliness recurs later in the laid-out body of Rosanette and Frédéric's dead child, a substitute for the body of Madame Arnoux on the Corpus Christi altar, who was replaced in this same room by Rosanette. The corpse of the dead child, disfigured beyond recognition, dead as could be, a "real still-life" (433) (*véritable nature morte*), in the thoughtless words of the artist Pellerin, takes the place of the living presence of the Body of Christ: "the two women had devoutly arranged him in this fashion. On the mantelpiece, which had been draped with a lace cloth, there stood some silver-gilt candlesticks, interspersed with bunches of holy box; aromatic pellets were burning in the vases at each end; all this, together with the cradle, formed a sort of altar of repose" (438). The Babylonian moment is also inscribed via the "aromatic pellets [*pastilles du serial* (600)]," which, just like the Corpus Christi altar and the idolatrous dance around the Golden Calf, come from the Orient.

May 24 is Madame Arnoux's saint's day, that of Saint Angela, which Flaubert expressly moves from January to the Marian month of May. And yet, Madame Arnoux does not reveal herself as Mary in the rose garden.

She is no rose without thorns and cannot love without the sting of the flesh. Her love, like that of the Virgin Mary, does not overcome death. For her saint's day her husband presents her with a bunch of roses as a gift, which he has thoughtlessly wrapped in a sheet of paper and pinned together with a needle, which pricks her. This becomes a thorn in Madame Arnoux's side, because through it she comes to realize that she is a cheated wife. The paper in which these literally and metaphorically thorny roses are wrapped is actually a letter from the procuress La Vatnaz, who has arranged a rendezvous between Rosanette and Arnoux on the evening of his wife's saint's day.

The Marian iconography the text evokes are the Annunciation, in the scene where Frédéric and Madame Arnoux first meet; the Virgin and Child, in the scene where, after an unsuccessful stay of three years in the provinces and ending up penniless, Frédéric meets Madame Arnoux again, seated in front of the fire with a boy about three years old on her lap (187); the Stabat Mater; and the Pietà, when Frédéric is waiting to make love to her, while she is sitting alone at the bedside of her son who is struggling with death. These scenes from the life of Mary are immediately profaned. We thus have a travesty of the stations of the life of Mary and of the attributes associated with her. Hardly have the eyes of the lover and the beloved met, in a scene modeled on the iconography of the Annunciation, when the prosaic husband shouts "Are you ready, my dear?" (9), a comic paraphrase of the Ave Maria, in which the angel inquires after Mary's preparedness to conceive, with Mary replying, "Be it to me according to your word." Obviously—the child on her lap is proof—roughly around the same time that Madame Arnoux answered her husband's question with a yes, she indeed conceived. Already from the start the travesty of the Annunciation is thus heralded. After the Annunciation comes the Virgin and Child. In these often idyllic settings, the hallowed death of the infant Jesus, his sacrifice by the Father, is iconographically inscribed, through vine grapes and certain birds like the siskin, which symbolize his sacrifice to come. Madame Arnoux comically voices exactly this fear as the father takes the child from her lap. "You're going to kill him! For heaven's sake, stop!" (120), she cries out as Arnoux playfully throws his son in the air. Madame Arnoux sitting through the agony of her child is associated with the motives both of the Stabat Mater—Mary under the cross—and of the Pietà—Mary holding the dead Christ in her lap. The iconography of Stabat Mater is emphasized through the parallel between the child's death throes and Christ on the Cross via the motif of the protruding rib cage. The image of the Pietà is evoked by a fantasy of Madame Arnoux at her dying son's bedside: she imagines him, at that time still a small child, as an adult involved in a duel to defend the honor of his mother, whose reputation has been stained through an affair with Frédéric. He is carried home injured.

It is the supposed purity of Madame Arnoux that both arouses and paralyzes Frédéric's desire and turns her into a sexual taboo for him. The core of this taboo is the incestuous desire for the mother. As Freud puts it: "When they love, they do not desire, and when they desire, they cannot love."[120] *A Sentimental Education* reads like an exposition on this avant la lettre. One can read Flaubert with Freud, or read him with Saint Augustine. In fact, he negotiated his own sexual difficulties in the figure of Frédéric: fear of sex; incapacity to love; psychic impotence; Casanova-like promiscuity (since no love object would ever be enough as long as his incestuous attachment to his mother and sister remained unresolved); homosexuality; foot fetishism. In his correspondence with Louise Colet, he elaborates.

The text captures Frédéric's inability to make love to Madame Arnoux in Augustinian terms. "For some men, the stronger their desire, the more difficult it is for them to act. They are hampered by mistrust of themselves, daunted by the fear of giving offence" (273). Flaubert's continuous insistence on Frédéric's "cowardice [*lâcheté*]" also points to his sexual inability vis-à-vis Madame Arnoux. Augustine sees male sexuality, which does not obey the will, as a lasting memento of the disobedience of humanity to divine will. Just as man failed to obey God, an erection fails to submit to the will of a man:

But not even those who love this kind of pleasure are moved either to marital intercourse or to impure vice only when they so wish. Sometimes the urge arises unwanted; sometimes, on the other hand, it forsakes the eager lover, and desire grows cold in the body while burning in the mind. Thus, strangely, then, does lust refuse to serve not only the desire to beget, but even the lust for lewd enjoyment. Although it is for the most part wholly opposed to the mind's control, it is not seldom divided against itself: it arouses the mind, but it does not follow through what it has begun and arouse the body also. (*De civitate Dei* 14.16, 614–15)

Lust splits man: when the mind is aroused, it may well be that the body does not share in its excitation. Frédéric's sentimental education contaminates Madame Arnoux with sexual desire. Her purity becomes legible as

Frédéric's fantasy. Madame Arnoux herself however does not deny this sexual desire. Up to the final scene she does not subscribe to her supposed virtuousness. Only at the very end, in the final scene, when her love has gone to seed and become a cliché, does she idolize this love as something unique. As with Frédéric, her love turns out to be in the end both idolatry of the self and contempt for others, like the two sides of a coin. In the end, she despises all the women with whom Frédéric has slept, is sleeping, or will sleep, and, just when Frédéric has ceased to love her, she believes that no woman could ever be loved as much as she is. Babel has finally caught up with Madame Arnoux; she eventually sings her own praises through a love she now also idolizes. Her whole family is called home to Babel. Her daughter marries and goes to live in Bordeaux. This name not so much designates an actual city as it evokes the whorishness the novel confers upon this signifier. Her son becomes a *chasseur* in Rome, a word that evokes Nimrod, the hunter in defiance of God and builder of Babel; and with Rome, where Madame Arnoux will settle down with her son in the end, we have finally reached a penultimate Babylon—until the Paris of Flaubert's novel.

Secondly, the text brings out the true nature of Frédéric's feelings for Madame Arnoux by literalizing the spiritual: little by little, the ideal reveals itself as an idol. This reification, which runs parallel to political developments, fulfills the Babylonian logic. On the one hand, this happens through a grimacing distortion. The Alhambra, as temple of pleasure, is as it were the double of Madame Arnoux's dwelling; she has her own double in the introductory figure of the Andalusian courtesan. The systematic contamination of Madame Arnoux with sexual desire is what makes this possible. She, who is elevated to the status of immaculate purity by Frédéric and set against her naturally licentious husband, is like all women receptive to Jacques Arnoux's salacious flattery. The proof is the little boy she conceived at the time of her first meeting with Frédéric. An erotic mating call escapes from the virginal Louise's throat just when she is on the point of surrendering herself to Frédéric—which, as the text emphasizes, is the very moment when Madame Arnoux admits her love for him: "A cry, as soft as the coo of a dove, came from her throat; her head fell back; she nearly fainted; he held her up. It was not even a matter of conscience. This pure young girl offering herself had given him quite a shock. . . . He spoke no more words of love" (272). We in fact already heard such love-struck cooing in the singing of Madame Arnoux, her ruling passion since she was a little girl. The erotic subtext of the latter's song is thus made explicit: "Her bosom swelled, her arms stretched out, her neck swelled slightly as she trilled, as if receiving ethereal kisses" (55).[121] When in the end Louise leaves her husband, Deslauriers, and elopes with a singer, the erotic aspect of singing is again underscored.

It is Frédéric's bitter task to finally reveal the betrayal of his ideal and its decline into idolatry—but the bitterest aspect of it is that he does not notice it and never will. In the scene where Frédéric's desire for Madame Dambreuse is portrayed, all elements are taken up to illustrate the Babylonian dynamic of the carnalization—that is to say, the literalization, the reification—of the spiritual, as analyzed by Augustine.

Dambreuse is not a virgin mother, but an infertile courtesan. For Frédéric, she does not stand out from the surrounding world as was the case with Madame Arnoux; rather, she is its very epitome, the incarnation of the commonplace, of respectability. Love has deteriorated into a routine, into the fulfillment—to the letter—of convention, which Madame Dambreuse incarnates and provokes in him: "He set to work to do whatever was necessary" (392). Frédéric becomes her lover not by breaking convention, but by strict adherence to it. In this love nothing is unpredictable and nothing is unique. She turns into an utter stereotype. Every sentence has been spoken at least once before. The climax of Frédéric's rhetoric of seduction is the rhetoric of the a-rhetorical: "To my mind all that high-flown stuff is a profanation of true love" (395). At this moment there is no trace of true love left for Frédéric—not even its illusion. Frédéric's love for Madame Dambreuse profanes his love for Madame Arnoux; the aim of this profanation is to accentuate Frédéric's moral decline. Nevertheless, this decline is more of a gradual nature and does not concern a specific event: already from the outset Frédéric was subject to this decay, and the text merely works to highlight its progression.

As early as his first encounter with Madame Arnoux, self-deception and self-idolatry were, as demonstrated above, inextricably entwined. After making love to Madame Dambreuse—so "facile" that Frédéric almost does not notice that she gives herself to him—the topos of the sublime is evoked: "the whole universe seemed to have come to a standstill" (395). This corresponds to the scene where he first meets Madame Arnoux; then, "His world had suddenly grown bigger" (13).[122] The idea of romantic love of course supposes that this is something that can only be experienced once, in a unique fashion. The religious topos of conversion is evoked only to be reversed: in this act of love, Frédéric does not shed his old self, but instead completely embodies it. He has not become humble but instead haughty in the grotesque overestimation of his own power, which is strangely reduced to serial measurability: "Going down the staircase, Frédéric felt that he had become a different man. . . . Nothing was impossible now! He felt he could travel five hundred miles on horseback, work for nights on end, without the slightest fatigue; his heart was brimming over with pride" (395–96). His desire does not target Madame Arnoux's body; his curiosity extends to everything she has ever come into contact with. Madame Arnoux ensouls everything. Through her touch, things become alive. She endows them with an aura, as if they were major works of art: "her comb, her gloves, her rings were things of real significance to him, as important as works of art, endowed with life almost human; they all possessed his heart and fed his passion" (63). This is a fetishism that goes to the heart of the animation of the inanimate. Conversely, Frédéric is interested in Madame Dambreuse as if she were a thing: the typically valuable, unusual object in a cabinet of curiosities. She is a rarity.[123] If Madame Arnoux animates the objects of her environment and breathes a soul into them, then conversely, Madame Dambreuse is turned into a lifeless object, reified into a particularly unusual and therefore very precious collector's item: "he desired her as an exotic, inaccessible object, because she was noble, because she was rich, because she was devout, telling himself that she had delicate feelings as exquisite as her lace, with holy medals next to her skin and modest blushes in the midst of debauchery" (393).[124]

The two characteristic moments that typify the curious glance that does not seek beauty but instead revels in the abnormal and the difficult come to the fore here. Madame Dambreuse's piety is devoid of spirituality and reduced to purely external signs, the amulets she wears against her skin, with the word "amulet" evocative of the naïve fetishism of "savages." The objectification of the spiritual is summed up in the comparison of the delicacy of feelings with the intricacy of lace. Devotion—and with this perversion it becomes total—enhances the arousal of carnal love. *A Sentimental Education* presents love as something decidedly no longer sublime. There are of course specific genres for the presentation of nonsublime love: while tragedy features a love sublime and exclusive, farce, comedy, bawdy poetry and ribaldry, or operas like Mozart's *Così fan tutte* feature the comic interchangeability of serial sexual partners. It is in these forms that love is affirmed as sexual desire, since the survival of the species depends upon it. They illustrate that love is a business that will benefit all, a transaction where everyone will get their money's worth.

This does not hold in Flaubert's case. The last thing he does is to ask for less sublimity and more realism in matters of love. The implication of his method is double; on the one hand, it makes the trend toward the carnalization of the spiritual and the concomitant self-aggrandizement of the idolater already legible right from the outset. On the other hand, however, the ideal of sublime love always emerges paradoxically as one already lost, at last sight, in its true and absolute beauty. The ideal of love, which finds its most succinct formulation in Mary's loving conception according to the heart, is deconstructed: it is unreservedly confirmed in its erasure. Only because of this absolute affirmation do author and reader show so much compassion for those characters who have never come to know this love, depraved though they may be.

Rosanette has no idea of the sweetness of love; she is ignorant of the Song of Songs and has never heard of the cedars of Lebanon, one of the many metaphors for the striking beauty of the beloved whom the singer pines for in lovesickness: "his countenance is as Lebanon, excellent as the cedars" (Song of Songs 5:15). She thinks that Lebanon is somewhere in China. Instead of Frédéric, she will marry her first patron under the Second Empire, the old and wealthy Oudry, and will be widowed soon afterward. She adopts a child to take the place of her dead son. Apparently, this does not bring her any closer to love. As a consolation for the lack of the sweetness of love, she eats an entire jar of jam as a girl, while fearfully awaiting the man to whom her mother has sold her virginity. Rosanette, whose waist was once so slender, becomes monstrously fat during the Empire: she must have devoured many a jar of jam during her marriage—blatant prostitution—to compensate for the lack of love's sweetness.

The carnalization of the spiritual finds its ultimate form in the chest that in the end becomes the pars pro toto for Madame Arnoux. It concludes the auction scene where the impounded goods of the ruined Arnoux household, who have meanwhile fled to the provinces, are sold. In the glittering chest, the reification of Frédéric's love, the dazzlement of their first meeting are signaled and condensed. In the course of the novel, Frédéric identifies the chest as a quid pro quo for Madame Arnoux.

The Renaissance style chest was a present from Arnoux to his wife. Later, amongst many other items of the Arnoux household, Frédéric rediscovers it at Rosanette's: "there was a chased silver casket. It was Madame Arnoux's! He felt deeply moved, and at the same time horrified, as if by sacrilege. He longed to touch it, to open it; but he was afraid of being seen, and he went away" (280). Instead of Madame Arnoux, instead of her body, Frédéric would like to touch the small chest and open it. The sanctity of the beloved is transferred onto the chest; its presence in the household of the courtesan is therefore scandalous. The fact that the chest has become a metaphor for the sex of Madame Arnoux is stressed at the time of the auction by the designation "A jewel [*bijou*] of the Renaissance" (446). As in the title of Diderot's novel *Les bijoux indiscrets*, *bijou* is a metaphor for the female genitals: "a little casket with silver medallions, corners, and clasps. It was the casket he had seen at the first dinner-party in the rue de Choiseul; afterwards it had passed to Rosanette before coming back to Madame Arnoux; his gaze had often fallen on it during their conversations" (446). In the place of the lovers' fused gazes in the greeting scene, "leurs yeux se rencontrèrent," Frédéric now recalls that his eyes often wandered over the chest during his conversations with Madame Arnoux. The chest thus takes the place of the melting of one soul into another. The mysteriously oriental Andalusian character Frédéric ascribed to Madame Arnoux upon first sight now returns in the form of silver polish, "blanc d'Espagne." The brilliance of her appearance has become the shine of polished silver: "With a little whiting [*blanc d'Espagne*] you'll get a lovely shine on it!" (446).[125] Madame Dambreuse makes a point of buying Madame Arnoux's silver chest with Frédéric as her witness. She pays an excessively high price—being wealthy, the price tag is no obstacle for her—for something Frédéric regards as invaluable, priceless. She thus turns Madame Arnoux, whom she suspects to be Frédéric's true love, into what she herself is in Frédéric's eyes, namely, a rarity in a cabinet of curiosities. Frédéric's vehement objection to this appropriation by his future wife—"but there's nothing remarkable about it" (446)—feigns lack of interest.[126] However, as the antithesis to the loving, enlivening gaze, the glance of mere curiosity is the epitome of the reifying, deadening gaze. With it, the carnalization of the spiritual, the reification of the ideal reaches its culminating point.

Here, the Babylonian topos surfaces in the signifiers and becomes explicit. During the auction, the Arnouxs' furniture and household articles are lined up according to outward, measurable criteria such as size, thus tearing them out of their living fabric: there they stand, utterly disjointed and meaningless. In this way they illustrate nothing but the *vanitas* that makes all worldly things meaningless, reduced as they are to the common denominator of money. This alludes to the scene of the Desecration of the Temple, since for Frédéric, Madame Arnoux's home was a sanctuary. The auction, described as an indifferent and pitiless picking-over-the-bones, as the dismemberment and devouring of a corpse, is to be read as a perverted burial and therefore as a counterpart to the murder of Dussardier, whose funeral is lacking.[127] The two scenes are thus also hermeneutically connected, inasmuch as the Babylonian substrate surfaces and becomes legible in both. The auction is chaired by a man called Berthelmot, who bears the stamp of Babel doubly in his name, as a stupid word no one can understand, a *bête mot*, and as Behemoth, an Old Testament monster, entangled in corruption. Created as a counterpart to the female sea monster Leviathan, the male Behemoth is revered by the animals of the earth. Both are of Babylonian origin. In the end, they establish an apocalyptic reign of terror, while fighting each other, locked in eternal battle.[128] As partners of the devil they tempt their victims into committing idolatry. After the apocalyptic final battle, which ends in mutual destruction, the Day of the Righteous dawns, during which they are consumed by the other animals, or, as other traditions have it, they are eaten by the righteous in an elaborate banquet.[129] They often have human bodies with animal heads.[130]

This Babylonian myth recurs in the auction of the estate of the Arnouxs. The missing body of Madame Arnoux is evoked by the auctioning of her underwear, fingered by all. A "gleam of white flashed through the air" (445), and her flesh seems present in this whiteness. As for Frédéric, "the distribution of these relics, which vaguely recalled the shape of her limbs, struck him as an atrocity, as if he were watching crows (*corbeaux*) tearing her corpse to pieces" (ibid.).[131] In Frédéric's vision, a desecrated body is devoured by ravens. However, in a twist of the myth, these ravens do not represent the righteous, but are carrion-devouring birds, which, following Augustine, are not undivided birds like the dove, but, like all carnal beings, are split at the core and are locked in constant internal struggle. In a complete reversal of the myth, it is not the body of the monsters or that of the depraved that is devoured, but the body of Madame Arnoux, who is one of the two righteous characters in *A Sentimental Education* and who has been sacrificed, much like Dussardier, the latter having fallen prey to a revolution turned into tyranny. Sénécal murders Dussardier, while Madame Arnoux, through the alliance of Sénécal and Deslauriers, is driven into exile and ruin by Madame Dambreuse.

The auction, described as the communal consuming of a body, is thus a sacrificial meal. It is a reversal of the Eucharist. This reversal already operates on the level of temporality: it takes place even before Dussardier has been killed. Through the sacrificial meal a community is founded and preserved; whoever partakes of the body of the sacrificial victim belongs to the community. One becomes part of the community as soon as one incorporates the sacrificial victim.[132] The sacrificial meal at the end of *A Sentimental Education* is not the messianic sacrifice by the righteous, which would prefigure a different temporality attendant upon redemption. Instead, it heralds the triumph of the infernal Babylonian monsters. The victory of Monsieur Berthelmot, who resolutely and mercilessly submits everything to the rap of his hammer, seals the final victory of the City of Man.

Republican Hope: Stabat Mater and Brothel

And yet, *A Sentimental Education* has two "republican moments," which could have steered history away from the bleak variation on the Babylonian topos. In the peripeteia of the novel, at the moment of the decisive missed encounter that seals both Madame Arnoux's and Frédéric's fates—we are in the middle of the outbreak of the February Revolution—a miracle happens. Eugène, Madame Arnoux's little son, just barely survives croup at the last minute. This completely unexpected, unbelievable reversal of fate, leading not to catastrophe but to healing and life, defies all truth and probability. Madame Arnoux does not believe her eyes and strains to convince herself of the truth: "He's out of danger! Can it be true?" (303). Just this once it is salvation that triumphs instead of ruin. The deliverance from prolonged agony almost amounts to a resurrection from the dead. Deserted by her equally indifferent and oblivious husband, who has other things on his mind, and surrounded by inept doctors, the desperate Madame Arnoux remains alone by the side of her child, who is struggling against death: "The hours went by, heavy, dreary, interminable, heartbreaking; and she counted the minutes only by the progress of this death-agony" (303). This time that passes is the naked time of dying. The mother has

already averted her eyes so as not to witness the death of her son. Chronologically speaking, the agony of mother and son coincides exactly with the
moment of adultery that should have taken place instead, at just this point
in time: the suffering at the bedside of her son takes the place of the lust in
the bed of the lovers. This parallel is underlined by the sweet nothings the
mother stammers to her son, who locks his arms around her neck in mortal
fear: "Yes, my love, my angel, my precious!" (ibid.). At that moment, she
might just as well have spoken these same words to Frédéric. This miraculous recovery—and here Flaubert does not leave us in any doubt whatso-
ever—owes nothing to the science of medicine.

The indifference and incompetence of the doctors is earth-shattering;
Flaubert refrained from including the originally planned scene where the
windpipe of the croup sufferer was to be cut open out of medical necessity. The description of the suffering is medically speaking absolutely
correct, up until the moment when the child regurgitates a piece of parchment—and is cured. "The spasms of his chest threw him forward as if they
were going to break him up; finally he vomited something peculiar which
looked like a tube of parchment. What could it be? She supposed that he
had thrown up a piece of his bowels" (ibid.). Never have there been any accounts even suggesting that the croup can simply disappear like this. The
regurgitating of parchment thus has, as incredible as it is untrue, not even
the faintest whiff of realism about it—even if we grant the medical precision of Flaubert's description (in this case of the symptoms of diphtheria).

The impossibility—in the form of the revelation of an unmistakable
miracle—of a realistic reading signals the inevitability of an allegorical interpretation of this moment of dramatic peripeteia. At the same time, a possible reversal of the Babylonian logic comes into sight. At the moment of
the peripeteia, the mode of reading is also inverted. The scene of the death
struggle and healing is but one moment in a general series of reversals. The
topos informing endless variations of nineteenth-century novels is itself inverted: the child of the adulteress dies and the mother interprets this death
as a punishment for her sin. Instead, in this case the child threatens to die
in place of adultery, *passio* for *passio*; his death struggle prevents the mother
from committing adultery. After the miraculous salvation, Madame Arnoux
sacrifices her first and only passion, before it is consummated, in the equivalent of an Old Testament burnt offering: "Jumping to her feet, she flung
herself on the little chair; and, sending up her soul with all her strength,

she offered God, as a sacrifice, her first love, her only weakness" (304).[133] In this scene of healing, agony is overturned into redemption, as in a deus ex machina. Its poetological counterpoint is the lovemaking of Frédéric and Rosanette that takes place instead of the consummation of his love for Madame Arnoux. Obeying the poetics of tragedy, happiness is turned around into the most wretched of catastrophes; laughter turns to tears. It is the day Frédéric begins his liaison with Rosanette, which will get her pregnant. The day a son is begotten, only to die as a baby, is also the day the son of Madame Arnoux spits out something resembling a piece of "parchment" (*parchemin*). "Pergamena, charta," as the *Petit Robert* explains, is a piece of parchment for writing down important documents or, as pars pro toto, *charta*, a "charter." The child throws up, from the depth of his bowels, the Constitution of 1848 that is choking him. The text remarks later—strangely devoid of irony and in an emotional tone that is quite uncharacteristic of Flaubert—that this constitution was the stipulation of the most humane legislations ever to have seen the light of day: "In spite of the most humanitarian legislation ever passed" (320).[134] It was not to last, and its nullification ended the hopes of 1848.[135]

The moment of hope is captured in the miracle of the grueling coughing up of the parchment, in the miraculous healing of the son who had almost fulfilled his suffering to the point of death. Instead of the equivalence of sex and power, instead of the horrific begetting of death and fratricide, a text is born out of the agony of a mother and son. As the Word born out of the Flesh, it inverts the Annunciation. Since the Word is not devoured—as it is by the prophets—but is instead choked up with difficulty, the logic of prophesy is overturned. This republican moment adheres to the iconography of the Stabat Mater; the parallel between the suffering of the child and the Passion of Christ is highlighted graphically through the forceful foregrounding of the ribs, which are visible in the majority of Crucifixion scenes. Beside the Stabat Mater, the Pietà is also accentuated: Madame Arnoux imagines a duel, which her son would have to fight so as to defend her reputation tarnished from her liaison with Frédéric; injured, he is carried home. For a crucial moment within the general structure of reversals, a republican hope flares up, before the world resumes its blind, Babylonian course.

The second republican moment is located in the brothel. The topos of the Great Whore of Babylon lets *A Sentimental Education* end with an oriental brothel scene. In the novel, all love is subsumed under the sign of prostitution, which receives its oriental name only at the very end, brought under the common denominator "La Turque" (459): *A Sentimental Education* closes with a recollection of Frédéric and Deslauriers's youthful visit to a brothel run by Zoraïde Turc, who is as Turkish as Madame Arnoux is Andalusian. Yet again, the oriental topos is inverted. It does not lead to the poeticization of love, but to the poeticization of prostitution. Against the *communis opinio*, which self-righteously draws a hypocritical dividing line between virtue and vice, this brothel does not figure as the place of depravity in *A Sentimental Education*. This society, head over heels in total and absolute prostitution, unambiguously condemned the brothel as a "den of iniquity" (459) while upholding itself as paragon of virtue through the sanctimonious exclusion of prostitution. Flaubert's pen transforms the brothel into the idyllic space par excellence. With the brothel, poetically transfigured through the splendor of the Orient, Flaubert not only overturns the way the romantics mobilized this topos. Of all places, it is the brothel that functions in *A Sentimental Education* as a heterotopia, as the one and only place that has nothing in common with the Babylonian.

This women's sanctuary is heterotopic in quite a literal sense: it lies beyond the novel's space and time. The brothel visit of Deslauriers and Frédéric, which is already alluded to in the opening scene, is recounted at the end, thus framing the novel as a whole. The visit took place in 1837, thus prior to the setting of the novel, which starts in 1840. The brothel is located in a nameless space in-between: "You know where I mean . . . that street . . . below the Bridges" (459). As a space of innocence, it is the infamous *u-topos* of the brothel that becomes the counter-topos of contemporary society, a counter-topos to prostitution, a counter-topos to a universalized Babel, and thus classically, almost all too classically, it serves as a counter-topos to the Catholic Church. This life-giving Marian Church is traditionally cast as the antitype to the Great Whore of Babylon. The Church is founded at Pentecost and is saved from all things Babylonian by an all-embracing, life-endowing understanding. Not in *concupiscentia*, but in *caritas* it leads to life, and shuns death. Church and brothel, Mary and the Great Whore, are confronted at the end of *A Sentimental Education*.

In the short description of the visit to the bordello—one of the scenes Flaubert polished the most—no word is superfluous.[136] One Sunday, while the community has assembled in church for vespers, Deslauriers and Frédéric make their way to the "Turque." Their walk brings to mind the Corpus Christi procession, which moves along bestowing blessings to the fields. Like the children in this procession, the "cherubs," Frédéric and Deslauriers have curled their hair. Like the angels of the procession, they carry flowers and blossoms. Like the Corpus Christi procession, they pass through fertile fields:

One Sunday, when everybody was at Vespers, Frédéric and Deslauriers, their hair freshly curled, picked some flowers from Madame Moreau's garden, and then set off through the gate leading to the fields. After a long detour through the vineyards, they came back along the river-bank and slipped into the Turkish House, still holding their bunches of flowers. (459)

And like the cherubs of the procession, these curly-headed, bouquet-bearing boys, intent on performing a rite to manhood, seem almost asexual in their innocence. Why does Flaubert evoke the Corpus Christi procession? To point out what is absent from this walk through the fields, that is, the *corpus Christi* in the golden monstrance as equivalent to the Golden Calf, the embodiment of idolatry. To the extent that the Corpus Christi is presented as the dance around the Golden Calf, Catholicism is, in Flaubert's view, an idolatrous, Babylonian religion.[137]

The radically anti-romantic, economic context of the brothel, where men pay for sexual intercourse and where women are turned into products for consumption, is inverted. The brothel becomes a place of gift and courtship, a place, so to speak, of priceless love. Like a lover to his bride, Frédéric offers his bouquet: "Frédéric presented his flowers, like a lover to his betrothed" (459). The analogy with the Song of Solomon displaces this topos of Marian devotion of the High Middle Ages. It is not Mary and the Church but the brothel that is imagined as *hortus conclusus*, as *locus amoenus* through the signs of water and the shady coolness sheltering from the summer heat. The bowl with the goldfish can be read as a metaphor for Mary, the sealed vessel; the symbol for Christ is the fish. With wine (*les vignes*) and fish (*la Pêcherie*), the two central symbols for Christ are brought up. The place that should evoke sex without love becomes the place where there is only love and no sex, an emotion so intense it makes Frédéric turn pale: since Sappho the sign of a love sublime.

The logic of the gaze is inverted since the subjects of the gaze are in this case the prostitutes. The spectacle does not so much fix upon the women, who are indeed displayed as commodities for inspection and possession.

Rather, the focus is upon the young men who are incapable of performing the transaction: Frédéric's bashfulness makes the whores laugh. In the entirety of *A Sentimental Education*, a communal, happy, joining laughter in which no one is ridiculed occurs only once, and it is precisely in this women's refuge. In the entire scene no word is spoken; the idiom of Fallenness is not to be heard. Quietly, the women sing in their husky voices.

As a counterimage to the Great Whore of Babylon, the brothel becomes an almost paradisiac space of innocence, a place prior to the Fall whose ultimate consequence would be Babylon. The result of the Fall is the emergence of sexual desire, procreation, and death, aspects that are all left out in this scene. What is also absent is the determination of gender through the sexual act: Frédéric and Deslauriers do not become men. They remain angelic, just like Adam and Eve before the recognition of gender. Instead of a manly bond securing their masculinity, we are met with cheerfully laughing women. With this the whole constellation of business, commerce, and commodity exchange also recedes—possession refers to Cain, who is the forefather of Babylon. With his money in his hands, Frédéric flees, and Deslauriers has no choice but to follow him. In the oriental bordello of the Turkish woman, all that the Great Whore of Babylon brought into the world is simply absent: reification, sexual desire, mutual ruination, deception, and lies. They have all changed places and define the community, which has hypocritically gathered in the church and has presumably just begun singing the Magnificat, the hymn of praise to Mary. In the transvaluation of all values—in which the Marian Church has become Babylonian, and the Great Whore has become Mary—*A Sentimental Education* thus ends with a recollection of the brothel, the *u-topia*, the "no-place" where all things Babylonian simply do not take place, have no place.

Three Tales

Common Speech: Realism and Christianity

Are you inspired by the Bible? For over three years I've read nothing else at night before going to sleep.

Gustave Flaubert to Louise Colet, October 4, 1846

Erich Auerbach's investigations of realism have the inestimable advantage of putting the representation of reality in a rhetorical frame right from the start. Following Hegel, Auerbach discusses realism as the unfolding of a paradoxical figure: the becoming flesh of the word, the incarnation of God.[1] Following Auerbach's theory of realism, developed from, among other works, Flaubert's *Madame Bovary*, it can be said that realism ditched the classical ideal of poetry valued until the eighteenth century. There, high class had been solidly combined with high style. Now, in the new realism, humble people and the humble things of everyday life are no longer scoffed at. They are no longer the objects of comedy, but are shown in their own seriousness—they may indeed be tragic. The portrayal of their lives awakens feelings that used to be the province of an elevated, sublime style.[2] The development of style as a category of representation does not begin in the nineteenth century. As Auerbach meticulously elaborates in his study of Latin late antiquity, it begins with Christianity upsetting the rhetorical hierarchy of ancient forms.

Saint Augustine is Auerbach's crown witness. In the *Doctrina christiana*, Augustine closely follows Cicero's *De oratore*, but vehemently distances himself from him. He follows him in the tripartite division of styles, which he also subdivides into high (*flectere*), middle (*vituperare sive laudare*), and low (*docere*). Nevertheless, in Cicero, the stylistic register is solely motivated by the nature of the interpreted text and the requirements of the situation. The close association in Cicero between his stylistic register and content is rejected by Augustine. The rise of Christianity includes a break with the classical rhetorical and literary tradition.[3]

This break is motivated by a crucial paradox of Christian Revelation: the Gospels tell the story of a God who becomes man.[4] This God does not come into the world in a palace, but in a miserable stable. He is born of parents who belong to the poor. He does not reveal himself to highborn families, to well-to-do, educated people, but to those of rather humble birth, the rejected, even the despised, the powerless, and the ridiculed. To fishermen and shepherds, tax collectors, whores, and wretches designated by the euphemisms "uneducated" and "rough," since often they can neither read nor write. The Creator of things decides to spend his existence on this earth among the condemned, beaten, mocked, laughed, and spat at and elects to suffer the most abject of deaths, death on the cross.[5] It took a considerable effort of interpretation to convert this rough picture into the idyll of Christmas and the sublime story of the Passion. The most sublime and the base collide; the elevated reveals itself drastically in the lowest, thus breaking down the ancient antithesis *humilis—sublimis*.

Auerbach brings together three moments: firstly, the lowness of style in the Bible—*sermo humilis*, common speech—which was written not by learned rhetoricians but by—so it must have appeared to an educated audience—half-educated sectarians using a strange and tasteless style full of absurd superstitions; secondly, the lowness of the object; and, thirdly, the lack of education of those whose ears, or rather whose hearts would be penetrated by the glad tidings. As an example of *humilitas*, Auerbach cites the incarnation in Saint Paul's Letter to the Philippians. The epistle mentions a God "born in the likeness of men. And being found in human form, he humbled himself by becoming obedient to the point of death." Indeed, even to the point of the most shameful and contemptible of deaths, "even death on a cross" (Phil. 2:7–9). This lowering into human form, kenosis, was translated by Luther as *Entäußerung*, renunciation.[6] The lowness of the subject matter, the degradation, corresponds with the style of the text that chronicles it—*humilis*—and with the status of the audience. Christianity sees itself, as the feast of Epiphany indicates and in contrast to Judaism, not as an esoteric religion oriented to an educated, chosen elite, but as an exoteric religion with glad tidings intended for all, but especially for those who are poor in spirit, like children. The break with ancient rhetoric manifests itself in a revaluation of the word *humilis*, which does not merely characterize a low style, but describes the life and death of Christ, his becoming flesh. The negative connotations—rejected, pitiful, helpless, shabby, subordinate, rough, and so on—make way for a more positive inflection, which can be summarized most succinctly under the heading of humility, which is now opposed to pride: "Christus humilis, vos superbi." Humility, and not learning, is vital for an understanding of the mysteries of religion. However, humility mixes with and becomes the vehicle of a new sublimity. Sublimity, because its subjects, the salvation of the soul and the mysteries of faith, are elevated; sublime, since the simplicity of style veils religious mysteries that remain hidden and kindle a desire for understanding in the faithful; but sublime also since the affects to be awakened belong to a higher register.

As an exemplary instance of the new rhetorical power of the *sermo humilis*—it is hard to explain why he did not consider "A Simple Heart"—Auerbach chooses a story from the third century: the Martyrdom of Saints Perpetua and Felicitas, which took place in Carthage during the reign of the emperor Septimius Severus and is traditionally celebrated on March 7. The first part of this Martyrdom was probably written by Perpetua herself. It is the most important subtext of Flaubert's "A Simple Heart." The sublimity of this extremely graphic and detailed portrayal of a martyrdom takes as its self-evident model the story of Christ's Passion. Auerbach points out how the holy sublimity of the event arises from the everyday, from the lowest and most ordinary. Following his insights, I want to show how Flaubert developed his style in *Three Tales*—a sublime realism, in fact—as a poetics of kenosis, of renunciation and debasement, in order to stage the *skandalon* of the Gospel anew. In *Three Tales*, Flaubert set this "realism" up as a testament against the Gospel, in an alienated and reified world forsaken by God.

Kenosis applies to different aspects: to the author and the impersonal style perfected in *Three Tales*, to the form of the legend, and, more specifically, to the sanctity brought to life in Félicité and Julian. Gerald Wildgruber has drawn attention to Flaubert's ideal of *impersonnalité* as reflecting a long and rich tradition in France of an *imitatio Christi* in terms of kenosis: "Flaubert's art form and the realistic ideal of objectivity appear as the concealed renewal of the thought of religious self-renunciation now invested in the medium of art."[7] The point of departure here is Nietzsche's question concerning the ideal of objectivity in the realm of literature:

Nowadays I avail myself of this primary distinction concerning artists of every type: is it hatred of life or superabundance of life that has become creative here? In Goethe, for instance, superabundance has become creative, in Flaubert it is hatred: Flaubert, a new edition of Pascal, but as an artist, based on the instinctive judgment: "Flaubert est toujours haïssable, l'homme n'est rien, l'œuvre est tout." [Flaubert is always detestable, the man is nothing, the work everything.] He tortured himself when he wrote, just as Pascal tortured himself when he thought— they both felt un-egoistic. Selflessness—that principle of decadence, the will to the end in art as in morality.[8]

Wildgruber attributes Nietzsche's comparison of Flaubert to Pascal to a religious affect grounding the principle of the negation of the subject. For Wildgruber, Nietzsche's criticism of Flaubert serves as a model situating this specific form of renunciation in the discourse of an *imitatio Christi* that could be attested to by an endless string of quotations in Flaubert's correspondence. While for Nietzsche, Goethe exemplifies the forceful man—*Gewaltmensch*—who, as a great personality, creates the world in his own image, modernity succumbed to the misconception of having to renounce the self and surrender, out of sheer self-loathing, to the work of art. The art of the moderns amounts to self-denial informed by the desire to become an object, and is then sold under the name of "objectivity"—Flaubert would be the case in point. As Wildgruber summarizes Nietzsche's critique:

This "misunderstanding" of the moderns, exemplary in Flaubert, is to have understood *impersonnalité*, not as the sovereign expression of an act of world appropriation, but rather as, in its origin still to be examined, the persisting of the mere negation of the subject. That is to say, modern "self-contempt" becomes the ideal of objectivity . . . and an excuse for the praxis of self-denial.

As Wildgruber observes, "the objectivity of modernity, its *ideal* of impersonality, which wants to adapt the art form of the novel to the methods of science, is for its part extremely *interested*, but in a destructive way: it realizes the 'desire for nothingness.'" Nietzsche thus treats "self-contempt" and "self-renunciation" as synonymous.[9]

This religious, or, more accurately, this specifically mystical piety, has a tradition in France, notably in the theory and practice of *pur amour* (pure love) formulated by Fénelon and Madame de Guyon. Fénelon's attempt to explain, systematize, and theorize the spiritual experiences of the mystics in his *Explication des maximes des saints sur la vie intérieure* (1697) already effected a change in genre: the account of a spiritual praxis is transferred into theory. After being condemned by Pope Innocent XII (*Cum alias*, 1699), the praxis of *pur amour* by no means came to an end; instead, it moved into a different medium, literature, where it always already had a place, and later to psychoanalysis. Apart from theological complications, the smallest common denominator seems to be self-forgetfulness, self-renunciation, self-denial. It consists in the surrender of all that can be called one's own. Self-mortification is carried out indifferently, without any concern for redemption. The incredible proverbial patience of the folkloric Griselda, made famous by Boccaccio, exemplifies this kind of devotion, accepting the most terrible and unjust suffering without the slightest protest.[10] Such self-understanding is diametrically opposed to the modern striving for self-assertion, self-affirmation, and self-reflection; in short, it is incompatible with the ideal of the autonomous subject.[11]

Kenosis as a technique of the self, or rather as paradoxical work on the self is the main gambit of the Christology of Paul's Epistle to the Philippians, quoted by Auerbach. It concerns the self-emptying of the divine in human nature through the Incarnation. The self-emptying of the divine goes to the most scandalous extreme of the human, to the death on the cross, which is as painful as it is infamous. In the Gospel of Matthew, Christ not only does die the most gruesome death possible; he feels abandoned, forsaken by the Father, whose will he has fulfilled in all its bitterness, attested to by the final cry: "My God, my God, Why hast thou forsaken me?" (Matt. 27:46). The self-relinquishing of God is a double implication of being incarnate: God emptied himself in Christ to humankind, but Christ also emptied himself as man in death, thus destroying his substance. This specifically human doubling of the imitation of Christ is taken up by mysticism. Here, the life of Christ is seen less as the guarantee of one's salvation. Rather, what matters is to emulate this sacrifice as self-emptying in a *via negativa*. The decisive scene of this self-surrender, which even leads to the acceptance of the nonexistence of God, has always been this cry of the dying Christ on the cross, "this unthinkable eclipse of divinity,"[12] "a Father, whose will allowed despair to invade the abandoned Son."[13] In its harshest consequence, this kenotic attitude follows the loving self-sacrifice of Christ indifferent to redemption, and reaches the paradoxical peak of a perfect *imitatio* in the form of an atheist Christianity.[14]

Hans Urs von Balthasar (1905–88) cites Pierre de Bérulle and Charles de Condren as authorities. De Bérulle says:

I thus honor this destitution in which the humanity of Jesus is bereft of his own subsistence. . . . I renounce all power, authority, and freedom, that I have to dispose of myself as I wish, from my being. . . . I go further; and I wish there to be no more ME in me; . . . and that I should be nothing but a naked capacity and an emptiness unto myself.[15]

But it is perhaps Charles de Condren's formulation of participation in the Sacrifice of the Mass as the sacrifice of the self that comes closest to Flaubert's view: "In this act we must annihilate ourselves and become nothing but Christ's limbs, offering and doing what he offers and does, as if we were not ourselves."[16] Flaubert's formulation is as impressive as that of any theologian. His understanding of Christ's sacrifice, his spiritual experience of the Cross, goes as far as total physical participation in which one's own body painfully becomes the body of another: it is not our blood that flows in our veins, but the blood of Christ shed on our behalf. The flowing of the sacrificial blood in us, this everlasting pain, is the only thing that will last eternally. However, besides one's own body transfigured into the suffering body of Christ, Flaubert adds another medium serving as the vessel for the blood of Christ: modern literature. In the name of the blood shed by the Man of Sorrows—and for Flaubert this means in the name of the vanity of life and the flaws of all things human—modern literature is seen as a counterdiscourse to the blasphemous salvational promises of the socialists:

This is the very thing that the socialists of the world, with their incessant materialistic preaching, refuse to see. They have denied suffering; they have blasphemed three-quarters of modern poetry, the blood of Christ that stirs within us. Nothing will extirpate suffering, nothing will eliminate it. Our purpose is not to dry it up, but to create outlets for it. If the sense of man's imperfection, of the meaninglessness of life, were to perish—as would follow from their premise—we would be more stupid than birds, who at least perch on trees.[17]

The birds, who "perch on trees," are wiser than socialists since they follow Christ, "perché sur l'arbre de la croix" (hanged on a tree) (Acts of the Apostles 10:39). Flaubert interprets the whole of Creation as a recollection and visualization of the sacrifice on the Cross. God does not appear to him in all his glory, but crucified. It is this implicit allusion, hidden in wordplay, which conveys how familiar this thought was to Flaubert.

Contrary to what Wildgruber maintains, in Flaubert the mystical practice of self-denial is not hidden; nor is it travestied in an impersonal style and cloaked in the modern form of scholarliness. Not only does it shift to "form, through which Flaubertian writing constitutes itself as discourse."[18] It is also explored thematically in terms of a relation to the self and the world. Flaubert claims that it is no longer the Church, no longer theology but—aside from our bodies—modern literature that is the space of this radical dispossession, a disinterested relinquishing of all that is one's own. The religious model of renunciation can also be found in the style of *Three Tales*—criticism has generally pointed out the fact that a point of view or the perspective of a narrator cannot be determined—and in the form of the legend that "Saint Julian the Hospitalier" and "A Simple Heart" follow, as well as in the form of holiness corresponding to this *forma vivendi*. Julian and, to an even greater extent, Félicité are perfect examples of a saintliness in which the self is surrendered as an act of absolute hospitality to make room for the other. The *Three Tales* thereby follow the tradition of *pur amour*.

They show three figures who love unto death, who sacrifice themselves to others. The question whether this love is stronger than death—this is the promise of the Cross—is at the center of the *Three Tales*. Through the death of their selves, John the Baptist, Saint Julian, and Félicité follow the example of the suffering Christ. Bearing witness, their testaments separate them radically from their surrounding worlds. Through them, a love becomes manifest that Flaubert had so far only employed in the negative, as an implicit standard of human behavior. In the relinquishment of the self, in utter self-abandon, the figure of man in these saints is lost to idiocy, in animalistic nature, in material decay, in empty mechanics. The process of renunciation has a hermeneutic dimension, in that the saints surrendering to self-renunciation take on the form of the fallen, godforsaken world. They abandon themselves to the forms of God's disappearance from this world: to bitterness and despair, fetishism and idolatry, the stultifying language of catachresis. But going to the extreme, this self-renunciation does not save them. It *is* unto death.

In becoming exemplary, the saint changes and transforms into something different. Having renounced his self, he becomes the sign of the activity of someone else, the work of God. Flaubert follows the pattern of the legend; he adds nothing of his own. Rather, he delivers himself to given forms, whose hospitality he accepts with a peculiar twist. Following André Jolles, Wildgruber concludes that the legend "organizes forms of condensed repetition that, as discursive gestures within a text, serve as intermediary devices for the praxis of self-renouncing *imitatio*."[19]

The form of the legend, heeding the demand of its self-renouncing character, thus generates texts whose linguistic composition presents itself as a narratively reorganized articulation of hardened discursive entities, which appear as if congealed through repetition. From these discursive gestures every trace of concrete individuality, of personal style, has been removed; therefore they can serve, as *loci communes* (and as such also as a no-man's-land), as aspirations to saintliness.[20]

Although impassively extinguishing all subjectivity in abandonment to the work, Flaubert inscribes his autobiography cryptically into his legends. Both Julian and Félicité bear autobiographical traces. Any originality or claim to something of his own is written in the mode of self-renunciation, processed through commonplace discursive gestures.

Thematically, kenosis consists of a paradoxical transformation of the self into a reified, godforsaken world, in which the promise of redemption appears solely in stereotypes and the empty husks of words. In the cases of Julian and Félicité, the paradox of transformation is intensified to the extreme. The saints' legends are revived from their catachrestic torpor only to satisfy self-renunciation. Stultified religious platitudes are broken open and filled with new life in order to poetically produce a new testament against the Gospel, a testimony against the false appearance of glad tidings. Flaubert's point is a chiasmus: what is destined to death comes to life; what is living spirit petrifies into catachresis.

At the heart of the rhetorical procedure is a reversal of the Pauline hermeneutics, turned by Corinthians into the handy rule of the letter that kills and the spirit that gives life. This formula is chiastically overturned. Also, the vertical dynamic of humiliation and ascension in Philippians is reversed. At first glance, Flaubert's legends seem to simply stage this dynamic: out of the deepest degradation, with Julian almost turning into mud and Félicité becoming deaf, blind, and idiotic in her body's decay, both protagonists are raised up to become God's lovers. Their approaching ascension to God's blue shining magnificence counters the dying Christ's desolate cry on the Cross. The ecstatic ascension, with God manifesting himself in the figures of the Son and the Holy Spirit in golden, fragrant azure in the first two of the *Three Tales*, involves a peculiar stylistic break with their otherwise restrained, lapidary, and even terse tone. The apotheosis of his saints has remained the crux for bewildered critics. Only readers like James Joyce and Gertrude Stein were at first able to appreciate this.

The death scenes furnish commonplaces of the lives of saints found in the illustrated broadsheets of the Imagerie d'Épinal, an edifying popular Alsatian product. Death—visualized as a moment when the Christian God appears in the splendor and deadly eroticism of the antique gods—turns out to be the culmination of kenosis. In the deaths of these saints, the pinnacle of delusion, the most intense moment of idolatry imaginable is reached. The Christian promise of salvation reveals itself to be the return of ancient idolatry. The reversal of deepest humiliation into elevation is the distinctive structural feature of the primordial kenotic scene. Vertical dynamism is decisive in more than one way:

Wherefore God also hath highly exalted him, and given him a name which is above every name: That at the name of Jesus every knee should bow, of things in heaven, and things in earth, and things under the earth; And that every tongue should confess that Jesus Christ is Lord, to the glory of God the Father. (Phil. 2:9–11)

Utter degradation leads to absolute exaltation. The vertical is doubled and thereby underscored: from completely above to completely below, from the heavens to hell, everything falls to its knees before this peak.

Flaubert inverts this structure in that he makes the ascending moment appear as the climax of a blinding illusion: ecstasy is entrancement, transfiguration turns out to be nothing but a pagan metamorphosis to death. The delusion of idolatry includes a turn to the clichés and commonplaces of the Christian world. Paradoxically, the humiliation, degradation, and self-renunciation are staged as a self-surrender to the false promise of Christian salvation. While they lose, these saints win in a cryptic manner.

In the hackneyed ascension, Christianity is considered an idolatrous religion in line with antiquity; indeed, it is seen as even surpassing the ancients in their idolatrous potential. Paradoxically, it is this atheist variant of *pur amour* that renders Christianity superior to antiquity. By imitating the godforsaken Christ, it brings forth the one thing that deserves to be monumentalized: a love that renounces the self in favor of the other, even the most abject other.[21] Flaubert's kenotic writing in *Three Tales* immortalizes his saints. However, what he immortalizes is their gratuitous love. The martyrs' ancient glory and fame no doubt live on in their *gloria passionis*, but with that *gloria*—which is to say, with the splendors of antiquity and its gods—Flaubert renounces art's potential for illusion. Since he figures their apotheosis as the highest form of kenosis, Flaubert also points to—and thus also disenchants—the illusionary potential of art, which he captured in the maxim, "The first quality and aim of Art is *illusion*."[22] He crosses out the art of illusion with stereotyped endings that reveal transfiguration to be a mode of illusion.

Flaubert's Cathedral: Notre-Dame de Rouen

The irony that Flaubert, that most sophisticated of realists, left *Three Tales*—hagiographies, after all, however unconventional—as his ultimate literary legacy has often been remarked on with surprise. Although they were written down quite late, these stories had occupied Flaubert his entire life. Through their extremely well-structured composition and thick intertextual fabric, they come close to prose poems one must know by heart to interpret. Not only do they offer an intertextual rejoinder to Flaubert's work, but they comment on prominent literary currents of the nineteenth century: "A Simple Heart" is a rejoinder to *Madame Bovary* and the realistic novel; "Saint Julian the Hospitalier" to *The Temptation of Saint Anthony* and the romantic view of the Middle Ages; and "Hérodias" to *Salammbô* and the state of Christology after Ernest Renan's *Vie de Jésus*. Above all, *Three Tales* stands out as Flaubert's *summa* because it demolishes the edifying substructure of his contemporaries', the secular poet-prophets', conception of literature.

Already by virtue of its title, *Three Tales* stands under the sign of three. With antiquity, the Middle Ages, and modernity the stories replicate the three-part division of European historiography. Against the historical order of things, the three stories begin in the contemporary modern world, in nineteenth-century Normandy, with Félicité, a rather slow-witted, illiterate, unmarried housemaid, who adores a parrot as the Holy Spirit. The middle ground of the Middle Ages is covered by the legend of Saint Julian: a butcher and parenticide, who does penance and ultimately ascends to Heaven with Christ. The trio closes with the primordial scene of Christian antiquity shortly before Christ's crucifixion, with Salome's dance and the decapitation of John the Baptist. These exemplary events testify to the catastrophic state of affairs in the tragic sense of a final turn to decline instead of the glad tidings announcing the Messiah. In a letter to his friend Louis Bouilhet in 1856, Flaubert already extolled the use of this historical pattern: "So in 1857, I could provide some modern, some Middle Ages, and some antiquity."[23] It would take another twenty years for the project to reach publication.

Beneath the threefold scheme of history, the *Three Tales* unfold another, even more prominent trinity: the Trinity of Father, Son, and Holy Spirit. More than history lessons, tales offer knowledge and tidings of God, "theo-logy." With the prophecies of John, which closely follow the prophecies of the Old Testament, "Hérodias" is written under the sign of God the Father, "Saint Julian the Hospitalier" under the sign of the Son, and "A Simple Heart" under the sign of the Holy Spirit.[24] The Holy Spirit appears especially marked, taking effect *ex negativo* in "Hérodias" with Salome. Like an inverted Holy Ghost, who descends in tongues of fire, scintillating and lisping, Salome unites men in a love bond of a very special kind. The dove, symbol of the Holy Spirit, hangs as a lamp above the little Julian's feather-down, soft-padded cot. But the Holy Ghost's most spectacular appearance happens in the metamorphosis in which the stuffed parrot hovers in the sky above the dying Félicité. The Trinitarian feature has been successfully quantified down to the formal level of the ternary sentence structures prevailing in "A Simple Heart."[25] And finally, "Saint Julian the Hospitalier" and "Hérodias" are each divided into three parts.

A theological motif stands out in *Three Tales*: the revelation of the divine. It is featured as prophetic speech and as vision. John, the lonely caller in the desert, is the harbinger of all that will happen after him. Prophecies also accompany the birth of Julian. Later, the deer, a figure of Christ, forewarns of doom. From the start, Félicité's parrot does not only play the role of prophetic bird; it even proves this ability: the parrot laughs at Bourais when he sneers at Félicité's stupidity. the bird, in fact, foresees Bourais's fate, to which everybody else remains blind. Pride comes before the fall. Beside prophecy there is vision: Félicité actually sees the Holy Ghost. Julian sees Christ in all his glory. In his rapture, Phanuel sees God face to face.

The theological moment of *Three Tales* is underscored by the paradox of a unity of place and time outside of space and time. Despite their spatial and historical distance, Flaubert's three stories evince a unity of time and place: a space and time not of this world. "A Simple Heart" is set in Pont-l'Évêque ("bishop's bridge") in Normandy, where Félicité sees a painting of the Annunciation. Salome and Saint Julian can be found nearby: the latter's legend is depicted by a stained-glass window in Notre-Dame de Rouen Cathedral, in the tympanum of whose north façade Salome dances. Flaubert translates these motifs into his text, which thus proves to be a strange cathedral itself.[26]

In his transposition, technically a *translatio*, from the space of the church into that of the book, from painting and sculpture into letters, the age-old debate over which medium is able to represent more truthfully takes a new turn. At first it may seem as if the *Three Tales* restage the old rivalry between the arts. This is perhaps most conspicuous in "Saint Julian the Hospitalier," which takes up the topos of *ut pictura poesis* explicitly, since its model is a stained-glass window "in my country" (70).[27] However, the question of which art can portray things most vividly turns out to be a trompe l'oeil; what is at stake is no capacity for illusion, but the capacity for truth. The text's stained-glass windows, Épinal prints, and Roman coins stamped with the image of Caesar Divus—divine Caesar—all evoke idolatry, fetishism, and fascination. In contrast, through his lapidary style, Flaubert renounces the illusory intention of art. He does not put things vividly before our eyes. Contrary to the legend's traditional thrust, his writing is not *de propaganda fide*. The true church of letters is erected against the idolatrous use of images from whose representational repertoire the letters of truth are to be extracted.

True unity of place and time is found, not in world history, but in the church, whose architecture already analogically—in *sensus anagogicus*—evokes redemption.[28] The protagonists of the *Three Tales* all belong to the same mystical register, and the end of each is marked by ecstasy: Félicité dies enraptured in bliss; Julian likewise ascends in rapture; and Phanuel is "in rapture" (105) when he comes to understand what John the Baptist is saying. The Baptist is the prototype of the martyr whose hagiographical pattern is followed by "Saint Julian the Hospitalier."[29] Conversely, the

life of Félicité is marked by the kenosis of the "small saints" who are far removed from such grandeur but magnificent in their humility.[30]

Given these apparently very happy endings, *Three Tales* constitutes
a novelty in Flaubert's career, sharply differing, it has been said, from the
pessimism of his earlier work. Michel Tournier finds them to be an unequivocal appeal to the divine,[31] and, more alarmingly perhaps, even Sartre
sees in them an onset of hope, inspired by God, in Flaubert's hitherto un-
relieved despair. It has been supposed that Flaubert might have written "A
Simple Heart" for George Sand, to prove that desolation was not his only
register ("What are we going to do? You'll surely spread desolation, while
I preach consolation," Sand wrote to him in December 1875).[32] Consequently, in contrast to many of his other works, the *Three Tales* were well
received during Flaubert's lifetime; the life and death of his saints had
something oddly comforting about them.[33] Against the grain of these feelings, I am afraid that in its pessimism, the heavenly blue of these saints'
ecstasies outdoes even the blackest aspects of *Madame Bovary*.

Let me explain and explore the metaphor of edification as Flaubert
uses it in the cathedral erected by his writings. As a writer of hagiographies, Flaubert once tongue-in-cheek portrayed himself as a pillar of the
Church: "If I continue like this, I shall find my place among the Lumi-
naries of the Church. I'll be one of the pillars of the temple. After Saint
Anthony, Saint Julian, and finally John the Baptist, I won't get rid of the
saints. At that, I'll have to try not to 'edify.'"[34] Hardly "edifying," in fact,
his saints' lives are based on, and confront, the Old and New Testaments
and their patristic interpretation. Faced with this flabbergasting state of affairs, the politically correct have developed the appropriate defense mechanism: it's nothing but irony, of course. Flaubert is making fun of religion.[35]
The assumption that Flaubert's relation to his saints is ironic seems to me
disproved from the very start, since "A Simple Heart" thematizes precisely
this reaction: Bourais laughs at Félicité (21) and Madame Aubain insults
her bottomless simple-mindedness (30). By making them laugh at her in
middle-class cold-heartedness, Flaubert leaves the bourgeoisie to its ruin.
Just as *Madame Bovary* is not just a story of adultery in the provinces, written with sociological distance, neither is "A Simple Heart" an anthropological study of religious hysteria. Flaubert would leave this task to Zola,
who, under the title of *Four Gospels*, intended a new faith over and against
the old. Flaubert is too close to his saints. They are too involved in and in-

extricably tangled up with his autobiography. He cannot depict them with distancing irony nor with the cold detachment needed in the treatment of case histories.

Why does Flaubert build a cathedral where stone and paintings are translated into letters? Why the theological discourse on the divine? Why this insistence on edification, which turns into an abysmal ruination in *Three Tales*? What is ruined and keeps ruining? And where does this unbelievable, deeply uncanny aggressiveness come from, which does not rest until everything is erased? The "anxiety of influence" is one notorious answer.[36] Indeed, but influence must in this case be understood in a wholly literal sense: "Your poetry became a part of me like my nurse's milk," Flaubert writes to Hugo.[37] He takes up the classical topos of the text as nourishment to be digested.[38] More than any other nourishment, a mother's milk is key for the survival of the child; one will never be as dependent on anything else in life. Hugo as a nurse, Flaubert as a baby: Hugo's writing has become flesh in Flaubert. In our reading of *Madame Bovary*, we have come to understand Flaubert's infatuation with "milk as nourishment." Milk contrasts with solid food. Considered as milk and by metaphorical implication as easily digestible, the text is aimed at the childish spirit that fails to appreciate the mysteries of faith. Milk is a metaphor for the didactic format of a text. However, Flaubert deems milky texts disastrous: "For two days already, I have tried to figure out what young girls dream about and I am thus navigating in the milky oceans of castle literature, troubadours with caps and white feathers."[39] A more ambivalent compliment to Hugo is hardly imaginable. What has been fed to Flaubert must be inverted in digestion, and the most radical form of a reversal of digestion is vomiting. Thus, one might say, the *Three Tales* perform a vomiting of the milk of devout minds. "The milk of human kindness"—Macbeth quoting Saint Paul—has turned sour.

To call Flaubert's relation to wet nurses ambivalent is a crass understatement. In his oeuvre, nurses do not nourish, they poison. Their milk is not life-giving but brings death. In *A Sentimental Education*, Rosanette and Frédéric's child, placed with a wet nurse in the countryside, grows dangerously thin; "his lips were covered with white spots; the inside of his mouth looked as if it were full of clots of milk."[40] Upon hearing her ill-fated daughter mention the wet nurse, Emma Bovary turns her head on her deathbed, "as if in disgust at the taste of a different, harsher poison in her mouth."[41] The nurse's milk had earlier led to stains on Madame Bovary's dress; the second time, these poisonous stains are not white but black, and taste bitter like ink. The milk Berthe gets to swallow contains a good deal of *eau de vie*; the nurse takes brandy in exchange for her milk. This does not agree with poor Berthe: she vomits on the dress of her mother. The stain of this milk prefigures the black liquid bursting out of the dead Emma, bitter and black like ink, staining her white wedding dress, which is now a shroud, black on white. The "water of life" turns out to be the water of death. The poisoning by the letter and the poisoning by the nurse's milk is encapsulated in this stain.

Instead of breast-feeding nurses, Flaubert—out of sheer anxiety of influence about what has been forced down his throat—clings to the classical she-wolf. He holds the writings of Lamartine and his school—again one is reminded of *Madame Bovary*—in very low esteem indeed: the poetry of Lamartine's school, he writes to Colet, is "a dribble of sugary water. But those, who have sucked the milk of the she-wolf (I mean the suckling of the ancients) have a different blood in their veins."[42] This type of literature is, worse than Hugo's, not even suitable to be fed to children. It is a cheap substitute for anything masquerading as spiritual: it is sugar water, like what Madame Bovary drinks, instead of the sweetness of the spiritual sense of the word; it is sugar, which her maid Félicité steals to swallow to make up for the sweetness she does not find in prayer. Flaubert cannot be fed by it; he has a better milk, the milk of the (Roman) she-wolf, the letters of the ancients. It is their kind of writing that is destructively turned by Flaubert against Lamartine and Hugo, the poets of the 1848 generation before him.

In his enormously successful novel *Notre-Dame de Paris*, Hugo had built a new temple directed against the cathedral of that name. His is erected not out of stone, but built of living spirit: "This will kill that." *Madame Bovary* echoes *Notre-Dame de Paris* and like all echoes disfigures and distorts meaning. Against the firm fortress of the whore turned into a chaste mother in Hugo stands the wife and mother who turns out to be an adulterous whore of corrupt ruination. Flaubert overturns the role in which Hugo and some writers of his generation cast themselves. They saw themselves as prophetic writers, as consecrated poets sent by God. Paul Bénichou has described this generation's literary aim and ambition, introducing a secular age of "laicist" power, with great empathy. For them, literature is conceived of as the third, secular testament of a new covenant celebrating the postrevolutionary state.[43] To convince oneself of the successful institutionalization of literature as the founding ground of the new republic, one need only look at the Panthéon, a temple of classical proportions superimposed on the medieval church grounds of Sainte-Geneviève, patron of Paris, now consecrated to the nation's great men. And as far as the living spirit of these men is concerned, one need only attend the literature seminars of French universities, where each of these authors has an exegete of his own, who preaches his pure doctrine to this day.

The most important exponents among this generation of newly sacred authors of a secular Gospel are the ones addressed by Flaubert: Hugo and Lamartine. They are the most prominent contemporary "influences" on Flaubert. Both conceive of themselves as godsends. Their literature is to "build" and to "enlighten"—*édifier et illuminer*—the grounding metaphors in Flaubert's *Three Tales*. Lamartine's ambition is to become Bernardin de Saint-Pierre's successor by writing a type of literature in the vein of a simple heart, which is supposed to be like the Gospel as well as a substitute for it. This ambition is shared, as it would turn out at the end of the century, with Zola's *Four Gospels*, by almost all authors of the epoch. In this rewriting of the Gospel, applied to the present time, they almost indiscriminately participate in the "political theology" initiated by de Maistre and called, albeit belatedly, by its apt name by Carl Schmitt. Across tremendous political divisions from the royalist restoration to the Commune, reaching from the various foundational scenes of the Republic to the blatant announcement of a worldwide French imperium by Zola, the vast majority of the French authors of the nineteenth century are preoccupied with finding a theological fundament and giving it to politics. One cannot overestimate this powerful current that puts the literature of the time in an unholy alliance with the national politics of the time. Flaubert's laconic opposition to such self-declared national or republican sacredness connects him to Baudelaire. In their polished prose, the *Three Tales* stand as a monument, a singular bulwark against the political theology of his day.

As a revised version of the Gospel—and for no other reason—Bernardin's *Paul et Virginie* and Lamartine's *Geneviève: Histoire d'une servante* figure as intertexts for "A Simple Heart." The new national literature needed a poet sent by God. Lamartine sums up: "God must raise up a popular genius, a working-class Homer, a plowman Milton, a soldier Tasso, an industrialist Dante, a thatched cottage Fénelon . . . , a beginning of literature, a poetry; a sensibility of the people!"[44] Thus, the new Gospel must be a Gospel of feeling: "The Gospel of sentiment is like the Gospel of sainthood: it shall be preached above all to the simple minded and in a language as simple as the heart of a child."[45] Exoteric like the Sermon on the Mount—"let the little children come to me," "blessed are the poor in spirit"—Lamartine's Gospel is directed at the simple hearts. It strangely merges class and hermeneutics; simple hearts are what distinguishes the people, the lower classes. This literature must not remain dead letter, but preach the living word in a spirit of love.[46] It is not to be sermonized on Sundays by the priest, but by the mother with her family gathered around her within the home, creating a living bond of love. Gospel-like, the people are to be nursed, and their natural thirst for love and recognition has to be satisfied.[47]

With Lamartine's transposition of the Gospel to literature, which had a variety of precursors in the Reformation, a special rhetoric with its representational effects stands out: the Pauline mode. It pits the living spirit against the letter that kills and the living body of the Church against the Old Testament's temple of stone. The strength of the Word—Saint John's overtones of the Word that was in the beginning—that is not written in hearts of stone, but is poured into hearts of flesh, is what founds this living temple.[48] The people—as a class in the political order—have become the addressee of the founding word, the edifying word, through which unification is achieved. This word, this literature, in fact, should give birth to a nation. Seeing themselves as successors of the apostolic disciples of Christ, the literary operators of this political theology were not afraid to invoke the Last Supper.[49] The new covenant of democratic humanism aims directly at a republic of the Heavenly Jerusalem, superseding Lamartine's earlier ideal of the divine right of kings, in which the monarch stood in for Christ. In *A Sentimental Education*, Flaubert destroyed this old version of a theological foundation of the political through literature. "A Simple Heart" completes the course of hermeneutical ruination running down the theology of foundations.

Victor Hugo was, of course, a prophet and visionary, the consecrated poet on a messianic mission at large. He is the embodiment of the institutionalized literary sphere in the nineteenth century.[50] He confirms his higher calling by sometimes casting himself in the role of Saint John the Divine (as in *Odes* 5.14),[51] and at other times posing as Saint John the Baptist: "Apparais dans la foule impie / Tel que Jean, qui vint du désert" (*Odes* 4.2).[52] As a suffering poet he is successor to the saving sacrifice of Christ. Bestowed with a heavenly inspired genius, he acts as mediator between God and man, becoming as it were God's translator. Hugo, marked out by God, produces a sublime poetical surplus: "Celui que le seigneur marqua, parmi ses frères, / De ce signe funeste et beau" (*Odes* 4.1).[53] While Lamartine confined himself to the pastoral, Hugo presents himself in his poetry as the one who carries the light and shows the way to those coming after him: he reveals the providential course of history. Two of Hugo's works, *La légende du beau Pécopin* and *Fin de Satan*, the central intertexts of "Saint Julian the Hospitalier," feature a cosmic final battle between good and evil, where out of the deepest misery the highest blessing appears and out of mortal danger salvation arises: Saul becomes Paul.

Hugo too preaches a Gospel. More dramatic and of greater amplitude than Lamartine's, his Gospel unfolds through the figure of Paul's conversion on the road to Damascus, which he models as a transfiguring fall, interpreted as the grounding metaphor of Western and French history, the figure through which history, in a series of illuminations, moves toward a truer light.

For Hugo, the course of French history is nothing but the unfolding of Paul's conversion—a miraculous example of secularization that can hardly be outdone:

The enlargement of a mind by the in-breaking of light, the beauty of the seizure of a soul by the truth, shine forth in his person. Herein, we insist, lies the virtue of the journey to Damascus. Whoever, henceforward, shall desire such growth as this, must follow the pointing finger of Saint Paul. . . . The light . . . shall increase in intensity; after having been revelation, it shall be rationalism: but it shall ever be the light. Paul, after his august fall, arose again, armed against ancient errors with the flashing blade of Christianity; and two thousand years after, France also, struck to earth by the light, arouses herself, holding in hand the flaming sword of Revolution.[54]

Historical progress follows the pattern of *conversio*. Before it can get any better, it cannot get bad enough; if things turn out well, it means that, at best, it went quite badly. Under such visionary guidance, at some point in time, a universalized French nation will reach the secular version of the

Heavenly Jerusalem. This realm is located in the here and now: it resides in the work begun by Hugo.

Of this edifice no stone is left standing after Flaubert's passage. From the perspective of a history of ideas, one could say that he turns Hugo's Christianity upside down. From a Nietzschean point of view, on the other hand, closer to Flaubert, Hugo's Paulinian religion had little if nothing in common with Christ's original message, since with Paul, according to Nietzsche, the basic ideas of Christ were perverted to the core. Against a holy empire of this world, against the march of world history toward the Jerusalem preached by Hugo, Flaubert pits an Augustinian perspective sharpened by the experience of high modernity. It is the hope for a possible realization of a City of God in this world that cruelly aggravates the City of Man discarded by Augustine and intensifies a hopeless condition through false slogans and fake promises of salvation. Hugo, every now and then assuming the role of a Vergil, is in Flaubert's eyes the explicit spokesman of this disastrous hope. The poisonous promise of literature, which has become the modern agent of salvation, rises during the Revolution of 1848 with the intention of inaugurating a republic of love and brotherhood. All it does instead in its progression is to further civil war.

Flaubert not only undoes the philosophy of history that marked his century. Above all, he sees the secularized, quasi-religious mission of literature as an absolute evil that must be fought. Thus, the ruinous fervor of the *Three Tales* is not so much directed against the Church itself, but— as in *Madame Bovary* and in *A Sentimental Education*—against its secular heir, the French Republic. For the anticlerical Flaubert, who finds in this political turn something like a literary mission, the Church is an unholy institution, entangled in blind worldliness. For a long time now, priests have been deaf to the message they preach. Their hearts are of stone, no less merciless than those of the representatives of political salvation through progress. Christ's sacrifice of love, which they commemorate day after day in the Sacrifice of the Mass, is a closed book to them. In Flaubert's eyes, the Church is an institution that has reduced itself to absurdity. But the secular agents of salvation are even worse, because more real in their delusion. *Madame Bovary* and *A Sentimental Education* tell a story about revolution and medicine, in which Flaubert diagnoses a radical secularization of the salvific promise in the sciences, in politics and literature. The subject matter of the *Three Tales* is the secular potential of literature as an institution of modern redemption that claims to pronounce a new Gospel of the living spirit in building works of literature, instead of cathedrals, as the groundwork of a *res publica*.

The cathedral, which Flaubert's *Three Tales* erects in a most refined "mimesis unto death"—the type of mimesis Horkheimer and Adorno might have had in mind, since a more fitting phrase is hardly imaginable to describe Flaubert's aim here—is a critical fiction.[55] Prophets and visionaries appear in the iconographic ground plan of this cathedral, with its windows and pillars, but they do so as set pieces of false legends like those written by Hugo and colored by Lamartine. They do not present authentic voices and forces, as intended and employed by Hugo and Lamartine. In Flaubert's profiling, the writers of 1848 mutate from pretentious authors to worn-out stereotypes. The gnostic battle between good and evil in Hugo is perturbed in Flaubert's rewriting through the quid pro quo of Christ and Satan, inverted word for word in the homosexual ascension of Julian. The crystal-clear juxtaposition of Mary and Eve misused by Lamartine is flatly rejected, crossed out. In the place of the life-giving spirit, the deadly letter takes over—spirituality, taken at its own word, is driven out. In Flaubert, the spirit works through the witty pun to be excavated from the materiality of the arbitrary sign. The vertical dynamic of Pauline *conversio*, the basic pattern of Hugo, is inverted. The upward dynamic of redemption is turned upside down: it proves to be anagogical nonsense. The luminous death of Félicité is a delusion par excellence, while the darkness of Emma's death reveals the truth.

At the very end, Flaubert's *Tales* draw yet another cross, like the one concluding *A Sentimental Education* and *Madame Bovary*. A true cross, it crosses out the vertical force of Paul's cross. At the close of the third story, the way of Christ's disciples leads horizontally out of Herod's fortress, with John descending to the dead to proclaim Christ. But only if one projects the vertical movement of the ascensions of both John and Christ onto this incomplete cross does the entire figure of a cross arise.[56] The upward-flying vertical lines that lead to eternal life with the transfiguration of Julian and Félicité are an abysmal reversal of the salvational promise, a reversal which, like a classical metamorphosis, ends in death. Redemption topples over in the opposite direction—not to everlasting life, but to death-bound delusion.

The sign of the Cross is crossed out: seen as a sign of redemption that brings the old sacrificial logic of the scapegoat to a happier ending, the

Cross—no small crux of this text—is transformed by Flaubert into a universal sign of history as repetition. Colossal in the larger-than-life format of both ascensions, it demands scapegoats to the end of time. Mankind is based on the ruinous gutting and consumption of scapegoats: Dussardier, Madame Arnoux, Madame Bovary, Félicité, Julian, and John already. The cross: an instrument of torture; Christ: no savior, but another pawn in the unending series of *homines sacri*. While Flaubert's literary testament elaborates and exposes the true meaning of the cross, he devastates the Pauline intention of the new evangelists of his time, Hugo and Lamartine.

If, finally, Christ's dying on the cross exposes the institution of the *homo sacer* in a nutshell, it does so because his death makes it possible to decipher the unbearable truth of history in the very light of the cross that is cast by the crossing out of the Cross. Only in the light of His scandalous love unto death, in the light of the new covenant founded on the Last Supper can Flaubert come to grips with the terror of history and conceive of it in his writing. Thus the Cross even in Flaubert does mark an epoch. To the Carthaginian Hamilcar in *Salammbô*, as even to John the Baptist in "Hérodias," there was nothing beyond the logic of sacrifice, nothing beyond the logic of the *homo sacer*. His sense of an ending seemed a given; nothing else could be imagined. It was merely a matter of not becoming a *homo sacer* oneself. Only in the crossing out of the Cross, the paragon of all formulas of pathos, is the pathos of Flaubert's work released. Only literature is able to preserve the hidden figure of this scandalous love unto death. Only latently, as *figura cryptica*, can the Cross be deciphered in the perverted patterns of History. Unheard-of, this love can be read in Flaubert.

"A SIMPLE HEART"

[A]rid fictionality tends to denounce images, figures, idols, rhetoric. An iconoclastic fiction must be thought.

Jacques Derrida, *On the Name*

A Legend of Modernity

It is 1876. Flaubert is sitting at his desk in Croisset, his hermitage in Normandy, writing to his niece Caroline. Before him is a stuffed parrot and surrounding him is a small reference library of religious and specialized medical literature: the breviary of a choirmaster he uses to study the Corpus Christi procession, a medical treatise about pneumonia, Caroline's prayer book, the missal of Lisieux, which belonged to her great-grandmother, Flaubert's grandmother. Flaubert gathers the tradition of his family—religion, the female sphere, and medicine, the business of men—and inscribes himself in it. Like in *Madame Bovary*, in the story of "A Simple Heart" the two salvational promises cross: the old, fading religion and a new medical knowledge. If the failing promise of medicine was the focus of *Madame Bovary*, "A Simple Heart" foregrounds the failure of religion.

To prevent the bankruptcy of the daughter of his most beloved sister—also named Caroline—Flaubert has just, as he phrases it, "ruined" himself by selling his inheritance from his mother. Destitute, he commences his final work to be published, *Three Tales*. In these three legends of saints, the autobiographic slant is impossible to ignore. Flaubert inscribes his life into these legends. Close to Pont-l'Évêque, the setting of "A Simple Heart" and his mother's hometown, Flaubert had just sold the Toucques farm, which his character Madame Aubain in "A Simple Heart" is able to rescue from her financial debacle. Like Madame Aubain's children Paul and Virginie, Flaubert often spent his holidays there as a child. In many respects, Félicité is an autobiographical projection of the author. Like her, he could not read for a long time; like her, he was "the idiot of the family."[1] Just like her, he collapses and loses consciousness on the icy road from Pont-l'Évêque to Honfleur only to wake up and continue on nonetheless, stained in blood. A carriage at full gallop passes by, just as it does with Félicité.[2] And like her he loves Loulou: this is what he called his prematurely deceased sister Caroline, as well as her daughter. "A Simple Heart" constitutes an anti-Gospel that rejects the Pauline interpretation of Christianity. Just as the Gospels contain a *sensus allegoricus* and *sensus historicus*, this negative Gospel displays its *sensus historicus* in these autobiographical moments. Its *sensus allegoricus* will turn that of the Gospels upside down. When Flaubert thus writes in a letter to his lifelong friend Edma Roger des Genettes that with all these stories of saints, he was turning into a pillar of the Church, the irony goes deeper than one might think.[3] In his *Three Tales*, which, true to the actual lives of the saints, are without a trace of sentimentality, if somewhat shocking, Flaubert demolishes the edifying genre in which Lamartine excelled.

In "A Simple Heart," overlooked by a stuffed parrot called Loulou, Flaubert writes the laconic life story of a tormented, illiterate spinster of depressing simplicity, which ends with her idolizing the worm-eaten remains of a stuffed parrot as if it were the Holy Spirit. The absurd contradiction between the life of a saint and parrot mania has kept readers on tenterhooks. Enlightened spirits have read "A Simple Heart" as a satire on religion or as a study of pathological female religiosity in provincial France. In this view, the tale shows that holiness is nothing but a life-negating neurosis, nonetheless bringing irony and some tenderness to the lot of some of its unfortunate victims.[4] Others speak of the triumphant spiritual journey of the good Félicité, whose life and deeds reveal the work of the Holy Spirit.[5] Beyond this controversy around enlightenment and religion, "A Simple Heart" has also been read as Flaubert's statement on his poetics.[6]

The satirical surface of the tale is not without theological depth. But something more is at stake than an enlightened critique of religion. Even if he meant it in a quite different sense, Nietzsche was right: "The stories of the saints are the most ambiguous pieces of literature in existence."[7] In "A Simple Heart" Flaubert engages with the theological substrate to develop his poetics. He also revises the outrageous *skandalon* of the Gospel in the face of a Church that he sees as entangled in an unholy alliance with bourgeois society. In literal dullness, this blind and deaf Church covers up the founding *skandalon*. What Flaubert transfers onto modern times through the figure of Félicité is the *skandalon* of a God who out of love took on the basest human form and died the most contemptible of all deaths. But this inconceivable love was gratuitous, and no salvation resulted, Flaubert asserts.

The doctrine of pure love has the death of God as its ultimate horizon. Such a radical take on kenosis confirms the Christian value par excellence: devotion extending to self-renunciation through the love of one's neighbor. It is indifferent to the Gospel's promise of resurrection, which sees the Son triumph over death by virtue of his renunciation through his loving sacrifice on the cross. Radical kenosis thinks what Jacques Derrida called "the worst violence": crucifixion and the death of God without resurrection.[8] In "A Simple Heart," Flaubert pictures this extreme horizon anew: both the love that does not seek any profit and is completely gratuitous and the death of God. In spite of her most perfect love, Félicité cannot give life, but always gives birth to death. Her own ecstatic death, her godforsaken apotheosis, is a cryptic reversal of the vertical dynamic as formulated in 3 Corinthians: since Jesus has emptied himself of his godly nature and taken upon himself the human form—the form of a slave or servant, *forma servi*—and utterly degraded himself, he is raised above everyone. The enraptured death of Félicité does not transport her to eternal life in the heavens, but ends in irredeemable death. The salvational promise is inverted into the ruinous sign of death. "A Simple Heart" bespeaks a poetics of kenosis—it is the *écriture* of kenotic emptying out into the outwardness of the dead letter, into the fetishized image—that brings Flaubert's work to completion. The ambivalent reactions to his blissful heroine Félicité and her stuffed parrot testify to the effectiveness of the provocation of the Christian *skandalon* of kenosis. The format of *imitatio*, which defines the form of the legend, successfully discloses its kenotic intensification. The literary result is as ruinous for religion as it is for Enlightenment and most of all for the philosophy of history. Its fatal success is achieved only as a monument to its heroine, the maidservant with the simple heart. Theological kenosis finds its most astonishing literary expression in "A Simple Heart."

"A Simple Heart" tells the story of a woman who has nothing endearing about her—she lacks all charm. Early on she becomes an orphan and is sent to work as a maidservant on a farm. As a small child, she lives in abject poverty and isolation, trembling in her rags, drinking water from puddles face down with the cows. She is falsely accused of having stolen a few pennies and is chased away in ignominy. Everyone she loves abandons her or dies. As Flaubert laconically narrates it, she falls in love with a man who ends up marrying a rich widow; her mistress's daughter—whom she follows around like a pet animal with "dog-like devotion" (27)[9]—dies of

tuberculosis as a little girl; her nephew Victor bleeds to death in the colonies, under the eyes of heedless, incompetent doctors; an old man she cares
for dies of cancer. Finally, in the isolation caused by her increasing deafness and blindness, the parrot Loulou becomes as "a son, a lover" (31) to
her. Once she believes him lost, but he returns to her. Stuffed, she sees in
him the Holy Spirit and reveres him. Sacrificing everything, she cares for
the poor and the sick, only to be discarded and forgotten like an old piece
of furniture by the son of her mistress, whom she had raised. The house
where she lives in complete loneliness as she grows old falls into disrepair:
it rains through the roof. For a whole winter she lies on a wet mattress,
and she begins to spit blood after Easter. She lives and dies as Flaubert had
originally wanted Madame Bovary to live and die, "a virgin, living in the
nowhere land of the province, growing old in sorrow and thus attaining
the last stages of mysticism."[10]

As she breathes her last breath, with a Corpus Christi procession to
some chapel pausing at her window, Félicité is united in ecstasy with the
Heavenly Bridegroom. In this ecstatic death of the Bride of Christ the
pattern of the legend is fulfilled and simultaneously destroyed: it reverts
back to antiquity. In its refinement the description must be weighed word
by word. This rapture in death takes back the failed Christian world into
the fold of the destructive power of the classical schema from which it
had originated. Flaubert inverts the typology and with it the Pauline hermeneutic figure founding Christianity, according to which both the Old
Testament and the adumbrating texts of the ancients can be fully grasped
only in the light of Revelation. For this form of reading Paul's figure of
the living spirit and dead letter was decisive.[11] In "A Simple Heart," the
truth of the New Testament is overturned; the new becomes legible in
the light of the old. *Figura* and *implementum* are reversed. This readability is effected exclusively through the letter of the tradition and not by a
kerygmatic event, which is deconstructed by the writings of the ancients.
Antiquity does not become an adumbration; rather, the devastating truth
of Christianity is fully disclosed in the light of antiquity.

A cloud of blue incense smoke rose up to Félicité's room. She opened wide her nostrils as she breathed it in deeply, in an act at once sensual and mystical. She closed
her eyes. Her lips smiled. Her heartbeats grew steadily slower, fainter every time, like
a fountain running dry, like an echo fading; and as she breathed her last, she thought
she saw, as the heavens opened, a gigantic parrot hovering over her head. (40)

Fatal Fortune: The Ruined State of the World

Characterizing the patristic exegesis of the relation between the New and Old Testaments, "A Simple Heart" is structured by the figure and its fulfillment (*figura* and *implementum*). All motifs are taken up twice. Yet, by virtue of the reversal of this structure, it is not a promise come true, but deception finally disclosed. This letter does not lead to life but to death. The world, as described in "A Simple Heart," shows nothing but the signs of the times, traces of ruin and decay. At the level of plot this continuous ruin occurs because of the sensuous attraction of deceptive appearances. This falling victim to the weakness of the flesh is a typical moment in the *vanitas* topos. Madame Aubain is ruined by "a handsome but impecunious young man" (3), who gambles away her property and leaves nothing but debts and two little children after his premature death. Again, her final undoing comes about because she is enthralled by appearances: she falls prey to the respectable demeanor of the notary Bourais, with whom she spends many an hour alone poring over her accounts behind closed doors, in Monsieur's *cabinet*. The notary cheats Madame Aubain both financially and erotically, taking his own life after falling destitute, having squandered her capital, and making another woman pregnant with his child. The disillusionment Madame Aubain first experiences with her "young fellow who was good-looking but badly-off" is thus doubled and repeated more poignantly, acting as the catalyst for her death.

Madame Aubain's house is described from the very beginning as a grave-like shell of souvenirs (3), an ossified sign of reified memory. The shroud is evoked in the dust covers of the drawing-room furniture; the grave, through the humidity of the parlor: "The whole room smelt a little musty, as the floor was on a lower level than the garden" (ibid.). In the end, the house disintegrates into a ruin. Madame Aubain's farms at Toucques and Geffosses, which she was able to save from the financial debacle of her marriage, are likewise both little more than ruins. At the Toucques farm only the ruined remains of a better past are left; the wallpaper is in tatters and trembles in the wind. *Vanitas* discerns in the living world nothing but an absurd and chaotic doom, symbolized by the apple trees, once heavenly but now diseased in trunk and crown and collapsing under their own fertility: "and they all bent under the weight of their apples" (11). Their life brings death; their fertility is their death sentence. In their decay none of the described houses reflect well-established order, but rather ruinous disorder. In their random accumulation of motley odds and ends, they are ciphers of the meaningless, decaying, and overflowing arbitrariness of the universe: the thresholds are all of different heights; the thatched roofs are all of different thicknesses.

Nature does not provide an image of harmonious order either. The beauty of nature is described without the slightest hint of kitsch, only for the effect to be shattered by the platitude of the next sentence: "and the immense vault of the heavens arched over everything [*tout cela*]" (12). "Tout cela" swallows the image of sea and cliff up into the spleen and senselessness of a random, disjointed coexistence. After a poetic flight, one smacks headfirst into bottomless banality: it is as if Flaubert is anxious when faced with the beauty of his language. In an act of self-censorship, he cannot but systematically destroy it. Nature is presented as the image of mourning or death: "here and there a tall dead tree traced against the blue sky the zigzag pattern of its branches" (ibid.). Historical events in the shape of three changes of political regime—the revolutions of 1830 and 1848 and the coup d'état of 1851—make no sense either. They simply make no difference. The July Revolution is announced by the driver of the post coach and arbitrarily leads to an absolutely trivial replacement of one prefect by another. Time is given rhythm only through the decay of the houses, which literally brings death: Félicité's father falls from scaffolding and dies. Later, "in 1827 a part of the roof fell into the courtyard and narrowly missed killing a man" (26). Félicité dies because of the leaking roof of the house, now reduced to a ruin. Her life follows the rhythm of the slow disappearance and death of friends: "Bourais went mysteriously absent; and old acquaintances gradually departed" (ibid.).

Death is the perfect example of the mechanical return of the selfsame, which has nothing edifying, comforting, or noble about it. Stylistically, Flaubert models this crass, irredeemable material decay of the corpse in the language of anatomy, which is intent on gaining knowledge of life by studying the dead. In Victor's case, death becomes pandemic, wiping out all individuality. Humanity is reduced to a mass of cattle destined for slaughter. The protagonists of Bernardin de Saint-Pierre's novel *Paul et Virginie,* famous at the time, are the namesakes of Madame Aubain's children. But whereas the virginal body of Virginie remains intact and unscathed by death—*nomen est omen*—and smells sweetly as appropriate to the body of a saint, the corpse of Flaubert's Virginie immediately starts to decay: "At the end of the first vigil, she noticed that the face had turned yellow, the lips blue, the nose was becoming pinched, the eyes more sunken" (24). Even the description of the river, traditionally the wellspring of life with its living water, becomes an image of death through its evocation of the suicide of Shakespeare's Ophelia: "The meadows were empty, the wind ruffled the river; on the bottom long weeds streamed out like the hair of corpses floating in the water" (22). In the senselessness of this decaying world, in which Fortuna is fatal and beauty only appears in the image of death, the heavens intervene, in destructive Flaubertian irony, only to reveal a higher calling to the vocation of accountancy: "at thirty, by some heaven-sent inspiration, he had suddenly discovered the right path: Registration Office for Deeds" (35).

This ruined world is sentenced to death through avarice and deception, scorn, boredom and unkindness, desperation and pride. Christianity, which speaks of a love stronger than death, has itself become the agent of deadly reification: one goes to church out of blind routine, girls are sent to the convent to get an education so that they can become paragons of conventionality; the names of saints appear everywhere but no longer mean anything to anyone. Easter, Assumption, and All Saints' Day mark time in mechanical deadliness;[12] no one remembers the promise of salvation. What remains are signs, traces of time marking the body on its way to death: "The sun shone brightly on these shabby things, showing up the stains, and creases caused by movements of her body" (27).

The undoing of the promise of redemption reaches its literary climax in the legend of the woman with the simple heart, who carries bliss in her name. Moths are one of the most striking symbols of this undoing. When Félicité finally takes it upon herself to clean up the dead Virginie's room, moths have eaten away her fur coat and flutter out of the wardrobe (26–27). Flaubert does not use the usual French term for clothes moths, *mites*, but *papillons*, which can also be translated as "butterflies." The butterfly is the symbol of the resurrection of the soul as it leaves behind its earthly cocoon: like the butterfly arising from the ugly larva, the soul soars free from its earthly cover to attain beautiful immortality. In an aggressive recasting of this topos, the butterfly becomes nothing but the crass sign of the decay of all things earthly. In disastrous irony the word *papillon* is there to register the disavowed promise of immortality.

As has been frequently noted, this ruinous irony is also apparent in the naming in "A Simple Heart," often with the religious promise of the suggestive names turning out to be a lie, starting with Félicité, whose life is anything but blissful in worldly terms. The man who betrays Félicité's love out of selfish calculation is called Théodore, the gift of God. Félicité's mistress, "who was not however a very likeable person" (3), is called Aubain, evoking *aubaine*, or "godsend." One could hardly call Madame Aubain a godsend to Félicité, at least not by any human standard. Victor, Félicité's nephew, does not die in victorious triumph, but as a deckhand: "He had been taken to hospital with yellow fever, and they had bled him too much. Four doctors had held him at once. He had died immediately, and the head one had said: "Right! One more . . . !" (22). Félicité's sister, Nastasie, who carries the promise of resurrection in her name, treats her child barbarically and displays the exploitative, loveless cruelty of destitution. In contrast to her illustrious namesake in Bernardin de Saint-Pierre's *Paul et Virginie*, Virginie remains only physically *virgo intacta*. She never recovers from once being charged by a black bull. Adulated as a saint, Bernardin de Saint-Pierre's Virginie is completely free of such sexual, hysterical neuroses. The body of Flaubert's Virginie thus rots, whereas that of her namesake remains untouched by decay, with the sweet smell of holiness.

Mothers, Carnal and Spiritual

Félicité's fate can be paraphrased with Philippians, which accentuates the provocation of the Savior for classical antiquity by stating that he "made himself of no reputation, and took upon him the form of a servant, and was made in the likeness of men: And being found in fashion as a man, he humbled himself, and became obedient unto death." Indeed, he degraded himself and suffered the most shameful and contemptuous of deaths, "even the death of the cross" (Phil. 2:7–8).[13]

Unlike those of Madame Arnoux, Madame Bovary, Salammbô, Rosanette, or Salome, the portrait Flaubert paints of Félicité is not sketched after a painting, be it a Raphaelesque Madonna or an Ingres-like odalisque. It is this turning into an image, into an idol, that sparks lust. Sex and idolatry turn out to be two sides of the same coin. Félicité, on the other hand, devoid of charm, is not composed based on an image and thus turned into an image. She is rather based on a text: on the portrait Lamartine draws of his servant Geneviève.[14] In the guise of the servant, Félicité presents the figure of the human in the most humble form. In her "dog-like devotion"

(27) she almost disfigures the figure of the human. Derided, jeered, offended, abandoned, betrayed, and beaten, she represents her servile status in contrafactual blessedness. However, her transcendence is strained to the aporetic opposite of a hopeless immanence: alienated into the form of an *automaton*, Félicité has no beauty that can captivate our eyes, no appearance that could capture our love, to put it in the terms of Isidore of Seville's commentary. "A Simple Heart" is an inverted bildungsroman. Félicité does not form into a self; she lacks all thirst for knowledge. She knows simply nothing about the world she lives in and has no sense of history. The more limited she becomes in her understanding, to the point of actual blindness and deafness, the greater the goodness of her heart. Félicité, the degree zero of the norms of modern subjectivity, is in every respect *"assujetti"*; subjecting herself, she is certainly not a self-controlled, self-confident, and self-determined subject. She is never self-centered or self-assertive—she never says "I"—but surrenders unconditionally. Without a will of her own, she is pure being-for-another. She lovingly gives herself over to others who are indifferent or exploitative toward her, only to leave her behind in disgust. The unconditional love Félicité offers them is misunderstood and disdained. They never return love for love. Nobody comforts Félicité about the death of Virginie; nobody comforts her about the death of Victor. As with her love, her suffering is equally disregarded. Félicité's life is the loving—misjudged and denied—surrender to the other. But those whom she loves are destined to die—Madame Aubain, Virginie, Victor, the parrot—and her *imitatio* concerns the way of dying: like Virginie and Madame Aubain, she dies of pneumonia.

Félicité's life is a displacement and condensation of the Passion of Christ; she follows him by surrendering herself to the vileness of the modern world. The stations of the cross lead her from the false promise of the beautiful mountain "Beaumont"—the place of her amorous encounter with God's gift, Théodore, her first, betraying love—to the true Calvary, the place of the skull, the "Calvaire" (*Trois contes*, 44) of the always recurring deprivation of love. Like Jesus with Judas, she will be betrayed for thirty pieces of silver (Matt. 26:14–16). One after the other, she loses all those she loves. Before the loss of the beloved lie arduous, agonizing, and frightening journeys in the loneliness of the night, during which she will be abandoned by everyone, just like Christ on the Mount of Olives. Lashed by a furious coachman on the road to Honfleur, thrown to the ground and left bleeding in a ditch, Félicité continues her stations of the cross. The "vinaigrette" (*Trois contes*, 66), a beef salad the Polish refugee eats in her kitchen, carries the word *vinaigre* in its name—the sponge soaked in vinegar extended to the crucified Christ to quench his thirst. The desperate bitterness of being forsaken by God on the cross threatens to suffocate Félicité, who is abandoned by God and mankind: "and her wretched childhood, her first unhappy love affair, her nephews' departure, Virginie's death, all came back to her at once like a rising tide, and welling up in her throat made her choke" (32–33). Like Christ, Félicité forgives those who leave her brokenhearted, trampling on her love. The clearest allusion to the iconography of the Passion is perhaps Félicité positioned like Mary under the cross: Stabat Mater. She prays for her nephew Victor at the hill called Calvaire after his departure for the colonies: "As Félicité went past the Calvary she wanted to commend to God all that she held most dear; and she stood praying for a long time, her face wet with tears, her eyes lifted up to the clouds" (19).[15] The tale Flaubert tells here is no run-of-the-mill erotic love story—"She had had, like everyone else, her love-story" (4)—but the incredible story of an incomparable love and *imitatio Christi*. Here, Flaubert inscribes himself into an existing genre of religious broadsheets dating back to the fourteenth century, in which the reader is admonished to remember the crown of thorns when putting on a bonnet, or the Last Supper when serving food.[16] The difference Flaubert introduces into this tradition is that Félicité exclusively stages the *suffering* of Christ. The Eucharist and Pentecost are there to highlight the absence of the divine. When taking the Communion, Félicité feels no communion with Christ, but only with Virginie. At Pentecost, no all-embracing love reaches her heart. Instead, because of her increasing deafness, Félicité loudly proclaims her lack of sin during confession (*Trois contes*, 79).

"A Simple Heart" is not the first instance in which Flaubert created a maidservant called Félicité with a lover called Théodore, who has a mistress, but to whom the maid, fulfilling her destiny, yields completely. *Félicité*, bliss, is something Madame Bovary finds neither in her marriage nor in her adultery. However, she has a maid named Nastasie, like the sister of the Félicité of "A Simple Heart," and as her successor she employs a maid called Félicité, whose lover is named Théodore. Since evening prayer does not furnish Emma Bovary's maid Félicité with spiritual sweetness, she steals something literally sweet: sugar.[17] She is hopelessly entangled, as is her mistress, in the materiality of the world and later even steals what is left of Madame Bovary's precious wardrobe after the latter's death. She thus literally invests herself in the dazzling materiality of the world, which led to Madame Bovary's ruin. Succumbing to her desires, she achieves what was denied to her mistress: she runs away with her lover, thus realizing the promise of bliss in her name, which Emma searches for in vain. Prefiguring the other Félicité, she does this under the sign of the Holy Spirit at Pentecost, "running off with Théodore and carrying away with her everything that remained of Emma's wardrobe."[18]

Nevertheless, both Félicités remain faithful until death to their mistresses in their own way. Emma's Félicité remains loyal to her mistress in fulfilling Emma's desire: she elopes with her lover. Knowing Flaubert, her story will probably end as ruinously as Madame Bovary's. Félicité of "A Simple Heart" remains faithful to her mistress even in the way she dies: "like Madame" (37) she dies of pneumonia. On the one hand, Flaubert contrasts the selfless love of the second Félicité with the earthly, voluptuous love of the first. Madame Bovary's Félicité relates to the Félicité of "A Simple Heart" as the self-blinding worldliness of the Old Testament relates to the New Testament. On the other hand, however, this contrast is subverted by a more profound parallelism, since, despite being exact opposites, both loves lead to the same end: death. "A Simple Heart" is a rejoinder to *Madame Bovary*. Worldliness stands out against the renunciation of the world, sensuous love against spiritual love. In addition, this reply is marked by the recasting of the story of the martyred pair of Perpetua and Felicity, mistress and slave.[19]

Renunciation of the world is pitted against worldliness in "A Simple Heart." In the reworking of the legend of Perpetua and Felicity, carnal motherhood is opposed to spiritual maternity. This legend, widely known in the nineteenth century, belongs to the tradition of Pauline Pneumatism. It is famous for its visions, and thus for the working of the Holy Spirit,[20] venerated by Félicité in "A Simple Heart" in the form of a parrot. Flaubert uses the legend in order to recast its central point. To the coarsely foregrounded, wholly carnal motherliness of the ancient saints he opposes the spiritual motherliness of his Félicité. Whereas Emma and her Félicité pine for mundane pleasures of this world, the love of the martyred pair Perpetua and Felicity in the second century CE (presumably in the year 203) is not of this world. But nonetheless, it remains stuck within this world.

The allusion to the martyrdom of mistress and slave, who are to be thrown to the animals during the birthday party of Caesar Geta under Septimius Severus for the entertainment of the Romans occupying Carthage, appears in Flaubert's novel most violently in the motif of cattle, *bovinae*: a wild cow is set loose on both martyrs in the arena. Cows and their signifiers constantly appear in "A Simple Heart." Félicité watches over a cowherd at the beginning, and at the end Mère Simon looks through a bull's-eye window, or *œil-de-bœuf* (*Trois contes*, 80), at the moment of Félicité's death. Thematically, the clearest manifestation is the raging bull—by no means a mad cow—who appears out of the evening fog in the Normandy meadows—instead of in the sun-drenched Carthaginian arena—and who gallops toward Félicité, Madame Aubain, and her children. At the risk of her own life, Félicité throws clods of earth in the eyes of the furious bull. She saves her mistress and children and escapes with her life as if by a miracle (9–10).

A glance at the *Acta Sanctorum* shows how Flaubert transforms the carnal motherliness of the Late Roman saints into Félicité's spiritual motherliness. He thereby follows Saint Augustine, who comments on the legend in his *Sermons*. Augustine highlights the ideal of the chaste, fertile Bride of Christ who is victorious over the matron. He thus reworks the primal scene of carnal motherliness, which realizes itself in the extreme in the martyrdom of the original legend. In Augustine's commentary, motherliness completely recedes into the background. Augustine rather foregrounds the masculinity or asexuality of both saints; motherhood is nothing but a soft spot the devil can take advantage of.[21] According to the *Acta Sanctorum*, Perpetua, the mistress, has a baby who shortly before the martyrdom and by the will of God has no more desire to be nursed. Miraculously, she is not stricken by inflammation of the breast: "Then because my child had been wont to take suck of me and to abide with me in the prison. . . . And as God willed, neither is he fain to be suckled any more, nor did I take fever; that I might not be tormented by care for the child and by the pain of my breasts."[22] Felicity, the heavily pregnant handmaiden, prays for a premature birth to secure her crown of martyrdom. Pregnant, she would have to be spared and could not be thrown to the animals.

As for Felicity, she too received this grace of the Lord. For because she was now gone eight months (being indeed with child when she was taken) she was very sorrowful as the day of the games drew near, fearing lest for this cause she should be kept back (for it is not lawful for women that are with child to be brought forth for torment) and lest she should shed her holy and innocent blood after the rest, among strangers and malefactors.[23]

Her prayers are answered, and in time for her martyrdom at the birthday of Caesar Geta, she gives birth to a daughter in her prison cell at the eight-month mark.

Incontinently after their prayer her pains came upon her. And when by reason of the natural difficulty of the eighth month she was oppressed with her travail and made complaint, there said to her one of the servants of the keepers of the door: Thou that thus makest complaint now, what wilt thou do when thou art thrown to the beasts, which thou didst contemn when thou wouldst not sacrifice?[24]

Fortunate in having given birth, she can now die the glorious martyr's death: "Felicity likewise, rejoicing that she had borne a child in safety, that she might fight with the beasts, came now from blood to blood, from the midwife to the gladiator, to wash after her travail in a second baptism."[25] The milk dripping from her breasts as she stands there postpartum, naked in the arena, is too much even for the hardened Roman soldiers in the audience. "The people shuddered, seeing one a tender girl, the other her breasts yet dropping from her late childbearing."[26]

The motherliness—the breast-feeding and childbirth—of both of these women is hyperbolically sublated in the martyrdom through which their motherhood fulfills itself. The femininity of both martyrs is emphasized once again through distortion: an animal of their gender, a female animal, a cow, is unleashed on them. The legend already perceives in it a diabolical comment. The rage of this cow ostensibly represents the furor of their sex: "But for the women the devil had made ready a most savage cow, prepared for this purpose against all custom; for even in this beast he would mock their sex."[27] By contrast, Flaubert's Félicité does not become a mother. Her femininity is erased; she becomes sexless as well as ageless. However, there is nothing sublime about this sexlessness. Before spiritual motherhood was elaborated by the Church Fathers of late antiquity to become the absolute Christian ascetic ideal in the late Middle Ages, absence of sexual activity and the resulting infertility were seen as something monstrous. Augustine did everything to banish this eunuch-like monstrosity from the new ideal of chaste virginity. Flaubert surreptitiously reinscribes this monstrosity into the spiritual motherhood of his Félicité. Her spiritual motherhood manifests itself in the most unspectacular ways, in the humblest of tasks: feeding, mending, tying shoes, tucking in sheets, combing hair, wrapping up pears, violets, and jam. Her love widens from a small, known, or related circle into a love that embraces all those who suffer. She looks after the needy and weak, provides drink to soldiers, takes care of cholera victims, and nurses the dying "Père Colmiche, an old man reputed to have committed atrocities in 1793" (27), without flinching from either the ideological enemy or his festering cancerous abscesses. Flaubert invokes all the clichés of the lives of saints and does not omit what impressed modernity most of all: the overcoming of the disgust at the sight of pus in Christian charity. The hagiographic catachresis into which religion has been largely reified in Félicité's world is overcome by the new language of *caritas* and self-renunciation Flaubert invents. The petrified religious commonplaces are broken open and infused with new life.

Félicité's simple heart, deaf and blind to the temptations of this world, inverts the voluptuous worldliness of Emma Bovary's Félicité. In her humble simplicity of heart she also exceeds her martyr ancestors' heroic love of God in that she longs to attain the everlasting bliss embodied in her name. While the two ancient martyrs are intent on gaining the crown of martyrdom—thereby attaining the renown of *gloria passionis*—Félicité risks life and limb in a completely unthinking and unselfish way, attesting to an unconditional love for the other, without thinking of any glory for herself. "This event was talked about for many years at Pont-l'Évêque. Félicité took no pride in it, and had no idea that she had done anything heroic" (10). Unlike in the legend of late antiquity, in Flaubert's story the contrast between spiritual and carnal motherliness separates mistress from maidservant, pitting the bodily motherhood of Madame Aubain against the spiritual motherhood of Félicité. In the legend of late antiquity, mistress and handmaid overcome class division at the moment of their martyrdom and become equal; the mistress goes to the aid of the slave when she is struck down by the cow: "So she stood up; and when she saw Felicity smitten down, she went up and gave her her hand and raised her up."[28] In "A Simple Heart," mistress and maidservant remain separate; in Flaubert the classes function as metaphors for the kindness of the heart, and thereby of course also serve as metaphors for different kinds of motherliness. Félicité, the virgin, seems completely purified through her spiritual motherhood, while the class snobbery of her bourgeois mistress limits her to the most egotistical kind of motherly love. This cold-hearted motherly love that only loves its own flesh and blood is most conspicuous when Félicité tries to comfort Madame Aubain about the fact that a letter from her daughter has failed to arrive:

Trying to console her with her own example, Félicité said to her: "But Madame, I haven't had any for six months!" "From whom . . . ?" The servant quietly replied: "Why, from my nephew!" "Oh! your nephew!" And shrugging her shoulders Madame Aubain resumed her pacing, which meant: "I never thought of him! . . . Besides, what do I care! A worthless cabin boy, of no account! . . . Whereas my daughter . . . Just imagine!" (20)

This contrasts sharply with the absolute love Félicité feels for Madame Aubain's children: "The two children were of equal importance to her; they were united by the bond in her heart, and their destiny should be the same" (ibid.). Their destinies are indeed the same: the children are unified in barren ruin. They are safeguarded in the heart of Félicité, the locus of spiritual motherliness. However, they are born to death, not to life. With this in mind, it becomes evident that Flaubert overturns the model of spiritual motherhood developed in late antiquity from Gregory of Nyssa up to Augustine and which remained so powerful within the Catholic world up to the nineteenth century. The spiritual mother bore to life, the mother in the flesh to death. The birth in the flesh was conceived of as sterile in the last instance, while the birth from the heart was fertile.

Flaubert uses self-commentary and the form of the legend to play out carnal against spiritual love, physical against spiritual motherliness. Félicité's spiritual motherliness is sharply profiled within these pages; she is purely and simply the unsurpassable *summum* of this motherhood. Madame Bovary's Félicité and Madame Aubain seem to relate to Félicité the way pagan antiquity did to the Gospel of Christianity. If the former stands under the sign of deceptive, sensual love and the old love of carnal motherliness, then the latter is characterized by the spiritual love of the Virgin Mary. Flaubert constructs the opposition between carnal and spiritual motherliness according to the mold of Christian doctrine, but only to better subvert it. This so carefully crafted opposition is demolished by a deeper-lying identity. It finds its expression in the only kiss exchanged between Félicité and Madame Aubain, in their shared pain over the death of Virginie. This kiss makes them equal, just like the two martyrs of late antiquity: "Their eyes met, filled with tears; finally the mistress opened her arms, the servant fell into them; and they embraced, appeasing their grief in a kiss which made them equal" (27). Nonetheless, this kiss is the sign of a fatal equality. It does not confirm a motherhood finding its triumphant fulfillment in martyrdom. The motherhood of both is indiscriminate without difference, in that it only births death. Despite all their glaring differences, Madame Aubain and Félicité are in the end equal. Flaubert's Félicité follows the path of a loving heart: the more limited the horizon of her ideas becomes, the greater the goodness of her heart.[29] From mechanical, external piety—going to church every day and falling asleep in front of the fireplace holding a rosary—we move toward loving inwardness: "Her natural kindness began to develop" (ibid.). As a spiritual mother she carries her children in her heart. What she brings into the world, however, is not a birth destined to life, but a birth to death. Félicité's spiritual motherliness does not become fertile, but remains infertile. This brings us to the core of kenotic intensification. It originates with the famous first sentence of the story, in which Félicité appears as the epitome of the virgin and maiden, the subjected and subjugated subject living to serve: "For half a century the good ladies of Pont-l'Évêque envied Madame Aubain her servant Félicité. For hundred francs a year she did the cooking and housework, sewing, washing, and ironing, she could bridle a horse, fatten up poultry, churn butter, and remained faithful to her mistress, who was not however a very likeable person" (3).

Félicité is an example of reification and alienation: Marx could not have dreamt up a better case to study. Flaubert painted another example of a life reduced to servitude, the maidservant in *Madame Bovary*, Catherine Leroux. She is presented by a smug middle-class amongst prize-winning pigs as a cynical example of true servitude at the agriculture fair. As a reward for an entire life of servitude, she receives the magnanimous sum of twenty-five francs. Félicité is disassembled like a machine according to her functions, which she performs on the cheap. She adds her loving heart free of charge. Among all of Madame Aubain's possessions, she is without a doubt the one generating the most surplus value.[30] Through her labor she loses all resemblance not only to a woman but to a human being as such. Alienated, she is transformed into a mechanical and soulless thing: "She had a thin face and a sharp voice. At twenty-five she was taken for forty. Once past fifty she could have been any age; and with her perpetual silence, straight back, and deliberate gestures she looked like a wooden dummy, driven by clockwork" (4). Mechanical reification has become her innermost being.[31] If Flaubert enlivens the stereotyped catachresis of hagiographies in their respect for abjection and suffering on the one hand, he literalizes their spiritual metaphors for saintliness on the other: Félicité does not become—as the topos demands—metaphorically deaf and blind to the world so as to see better with the eyes of the heart. She simply becomes deaf and blind. Her simple heart is not—or rather, not only—the sentimental education of the heart out of the flesh that is opposed to the Pauline notion of a heart of stone; she really is an idiot. Her love for her parrot is not the spiritual love of the Mother of God and the Bride of Christ, but remains marked by Eve's erotic desire.

Mary, Mary, Quite Contrary: Birds and Bees?

With the questions of spiritual and carnal motherliness we have come to the paradigm of spiritual motherhood: Mary. While in late antiquity, the spiritual virginity of the Bride of Christ was central, the high Middle Ages fully elaborated the concept of spiritual motherliness as the highest ideal of perfect love. Although the connection of Félicité to Mary becomes explicit only once, when Félicité considers joining the lay order of the "demoiselles de la Vierge" (*Trois contes*, 83), the matrix of "A Simple Heart" is the Annunciation. In Félicité, *antitypus Mariae*, Flaubert reverses the moment in which the fecund understanding of the Word becomes flesh. "A Simple Heart," which is thus a story of knowing, grasping, understanding on the model of the Gospel, is a classic allegory of reading. In order to gauge the radicalness of Flaubert's revision of the Marian paradigm it is necessary to turn to the most successful and most complete representation of Marian platitudes of spiritual motherhood in the nineteenth century: Lamartine's *Geneviève: Histoire d'une servante* (1850).

The connection between handmaiden and Mary, founded on Mary's reply to the angel that "I am the handmaid of the Lord; let it be to me according to your word" (Luke 1:38), is a—if not *the*—topos of handmaiden literature.[32] As such, the primal scene of this genre is Mary's Conception and links to issues of spiritual motherhood. Flaubert takes apart Lamartine's *Geneviève* like a jigsaw puzzle in order to reassemble the parts in a new way. He treats the text in the way that Christian authors mined the ancient writers, as a source of signifiers whose meanings could be twisted around. Flaubert twists Lamartine's words. What is at stake is first and foremost a reversal of the glad tidings. The Gospel is read in the light of the Old Testament and classical antiquity. And this is Flaubert's anti-Gospel: love is not stronger than death, but remains fatal.

It looks very much like a Freudian slip that Lamartine excludes Mary's Annunciation scene—with the classical iconographical tradition showing the Holy Spirit as a dove hovering over Mary—from his main storyline. Instead he transposes the bird into an ancient erotic scene à la Catullus. In his foreword Lamartine has such a poem in the elegiac tradition written by another female servant, Reine, featuring a bird. Thus, the motif, where the bird is eroticized as the placeholder for the absent lover, persists in the foreword. In "A Simple Heart" Flaubert superimposes these two scenes: the Immaculate Conception with the spiritual bird above is coupled with the ancient tradition of the phallic bird, which combines multiple strands of ancient motif.[33]

In his programmatic introduction, Lamartine argues for the creation of a new, living literature; it is a new Gospel for the masses, who may be able to read, but who do not read in the right way—such a reading will be possible after they have been made literate according to the ideal of the simple heart.[34] The epitome of such *sancta simplicitas* is Lamartine's heroine Geneviève. The vertiginous entanglement of spiritual and carnal maternity that Lamartine deploys is anything but "simple." Geneviève, Lamartine's simple heart, got engaged to a man whom she loves very much. For lack of money, Geneviève would upon marriage have to leave behind her little sister, whom she has been raising as a daughter. The sister, benumbed by the expected pain of separation, soon almost dies in an accident. Geneviève nurses her sister back to life and vows to Mary to renounce her marriage. Out of her spiritual motherhood she renounces earthly family ties, possessions, and reproduction. The sister, a true daughter of Eve, for whom Geneviève has sacrificed all that was dear to her, repeats her first fall in a second one: she falls in love, becomes pregnant, and dies insane after the birth of her child on hearing that her beloved has died. Geneviève takes her sister's transgression upon herself. She pretends to be the mother of the child, so that her sister can be honored in death by the entire community as an immaculate virgin.

Geneviève's life spans the time from the entry of Christ into Jerusalem on Palm Sunday—as a bride she walks triumphantly into her new domain like a queen "entering Jerusalem"[35]—to the way of the cross, which she must undertake as an apparently illegitimate mother in prison, slandered, ruined, cast out, mocked, and despised by all, and to her elevation from the depths of humiliation when she returns as a beggar to the house of her bridegroom. There she encounters the highly pregnant wife of her former groom who already is the mother of two children. In her, she sees once more what she has renounced. Absolute humiliation is overturned in this household into a miraculous exaltation: Geneviève is restored in the eyes of the world. Whereas she could have ruled the house as its mistress, wife, and mother, she now lives to serve, but only to see the whole family wiped out by a deadly epidemic. While carnal bonds lead to death, thus the moral of the story, a spiritual family is created through Geneviève's loving service to the sick and weak. Her Calvary is crowned by a triumph; while still alive she is already revered as a saint. Those for whom she acts as spiritual mother organize a supplicatory procession,[36] making her a mediator between God and man. This triumph is more glorious than her triumph as a bride; not flowers, but hearts line her path: "There was not a greater triumph on the day you stopped here on the mule's back. This is indeed a different triumph; then the bridge was strewn with poppies, but now, it is covered with heart's-ease."[37]

On top of everything, Geneviève does find her sister's child in the end. Whereas the unhappy, fleshly motherhood of her sister was compared to figures like Venus and Niobe, Geneviève becomes her spiritual mother in emulation of Mary. Throughout the most absurd coincidences the life of this handmaiden is directed by loving Providence. In an exemplary way it illustrates the Pauline dynamic of absolute humiliation and miraculous elevation. Geneviève's life culminates in an idyll, in that as a new Mother Mary she releases Eve from her suffering upon the Fall so as to give her everlasting blessedness here on earth under the Tree of Life. For the sacrifice of her love, for her sacrificial love, she is recompensed. Her spiritual motherhood is fecund.

In "A Simple Heart," Flaubert models his Félicité word for word on Lamartine's *Geneviève*. He takes up countless details to recombine them, but only in order to overturn the structure of Lamartine's story and to reverse its message. Just to give two examples: in Lamartine, we find a dog called Loulou like Flaubert's parrot, and a man who must be bought out of military service by a substitute like Théodore. Flaubert's handmaiden's tale is the precise antithesis to Lamartine's *Geneviève*. If Lamartine's story follows the pattern of *figura* and fulfillment, then Flaubert's story embodies the pattern of *figura* and degradation. In Lamartine a loving heavenly Providence rules, while in Flaubert fatal Fortuna rules. Instead of edification in the humanistic-Christian mold, giving us a patriarchal literature propped up by spiritual motherhood, "A Simple Heart" treats us to the absolute ruination of patriarchy through general corruption. Ultimately, Lamartine's story confirms a divinely ordained social structure; in spite of all insistence on equality, the hierarchy of sexes and classes prevails. Against this, Flaubert deconstructs the patriarchal order grounded in theology; patriarchy does not originate in spiritual motherhood but in Eve's blind desire for the male, and it is thus nothing but the outcome of the Fall. Instead of an author who is not willing for one nanosecond to give up his class privilege—Lamartine keeps his handmaiden with the simple heart at the appropriate distance and never allows her to speak directly, but makes her dependent on his voice—Flaubert identifies with Félicité on her path of suffering. Instead that of a handmaiden who can act and judge autonomously, Flaubert tells the story of a subject who is subjugated in every respect, a character in which the human is disfigured into the monstrous and the animal. Instead with a woman who successfully follows the *imitatio Mariae*, we are confronted with a woman burdened with the task of erasing the Marian promise of love and understanding by means of a love that can rival that of Mary any time. In her apparently blessed death, Félicité leaves us all the more hopeless. Félicité not only lives a hard life up to her death; it is her elevation in death that reverts the Annunciation. The woman whose desire is fulfilled in this hysterical erotic vision is an inverted Mary. She forces us to read the indissoluble entanglement of even the purest love with the sexual. A fatal desire, any love is death-bound.

Through her boundless love, Félicité erases the promise of a love stronger than death, the promise of bliss locked in her name. Lamartine's Geneviève already redeems life while here on earth; she converts the curse of Eve into the blessing of Ave, thus delivering humanity from sin and death. This heavenly moment is announced in the dog, whose name is Loulou and who sleeps like the lion in paradise peacefully alongside the lamb. At the end, Geneviève sits like a weaving Mary in Eden under the Tree of Life. By contrast, Flaubert risks everything to infuse the Marian imitation of his handmaid with an erotic charge by superimposing the moments of Eve in Lamartine onto his Marian figure: even in a completely self-renouncing love, there is no escape from the effects of the Fall, sex and death. Félicité's incomparable love is thus, in the truest sense of the phrase, "for nothing." Because of the ingratiating, patriarchal, and condescending representation of the "people," nothing remains of Lamartine's so extremely successful saint. Geneviève, like her author, is almost forgotten. In Félicité, with whom he identifies tooth and nail, Flaubert has through his honing of language created a figure who to this day puts the great, brilliant figures of world literature in the shade, darkened by idiotic humility.

Flaubert has read Lamartine closely. He lets his Félicité twice succumb to the seductive attraction of the world, which is in Lamartine the sign of Eve's children. The only shortcoming of the dazzling beauty Josette, Geneviève's unhappy sister, is her sensuous intoxication, which leads to her fall: "but motion, music, the heat and excitement of the waltz intoxicated her. . . . That was the only fault I ever found in her."[38] It is precisely Eve's shortcoming that Félicité suffers from, blinding her at the feast: "From the start she was dazed and bewildered by the noise of the fiddles, the lamps in the trees; the medley of gaily coloured dresses, the gold crosses and lace, and the throng of people jigging up and down" (19).

The shining, brilliantly colored objects spread out on the Corpus Christi altar, crowned by Félicité's parrot, are fetishized, shown in the perspective of *curiositas*. The counterpart to this arrangement is a scene in Lamartine. Josette's son, just as blindingly beautiful as his mother, under the sign of femininity, a real child of Eve, carefully arranges his colorful and tempting toys on the table: "They were wooden boxes, painted with large red and yellow flowers, needles and pins in little packages, children's toys, rosaries with little black and red beads, to be worn around the neck, pewter rings. . . ."[39] This inscription of Eve onto Mary is most evident in the motif of the bird. In Lamartine's programmatic preface, a poem by a handmaiden is presented, which mourns the death of her goldfinch, her only love, in the elegiac tradition of Catullus. Lamartine erases all erotic moments characteristic of the elegiac tradition so as to rearrange the poem according to the topoi of spiritual motherhood. The motif of the bird, strangely transposed, plays no role in the main story. However, in his housemaid's tale Flaubert foregrounds this motif to overturn Lamartine's thrust. The parrot, reiterating the Ovidian motif, is for Félicité the substitute for the dove that would represent the Holy Ghost in the Annunciation. Thus the primal scene of spiritual motherhood is eroticized. An erotic topos of classical antiquity is superimposed onto the story. The primal scene of the virgin Church's birth as constituting a new covenant of pure love redeeming mankind from original sin is secretly stained.

The hermeneutic dimension is decisive for the scene of the Annunciation: at this moment, Mary, blessed amongst readers, undergoes the miracle of living understanding, fertile legibility.[40] Mary is excluded from the consequences of the Fall; through the Ave, Eve is overturned. In Mary's act of understanding, Babel is also overturned, thereby announcing Pentecost. The letter, which turns to life, leads to a love stronger than death. The central poetological-hermeneutic event of Flaubert's tale is substitution: the parrot is substituted for the dove that floats above or toward the Virgin in the iconography of the Annunciation. Mary conceives with the heart, and the word becomes flesh. Mary's virginity is less sexual than it is a gift of mercy by an understanding heart, as Saint Augustine decreed, insisting on the hermeneutic dimension of this scene and spiritual motherliness:

Therefore Mary is more blessed in receiving the faith of Christ, than in conceiving the flesh of Christ. For to a certain one who said, "Blessed is the womb, which bare Thee," he Himself made answer, "Yea, rather, blessed are they who hear the Word of God, and keep it" (Luke 11:27–28). . . . Thus also her nearness as a Mother would have been of no profit to Mary, had she not borne Christ in her heart after a more blessed manner than in her flesh.[41]

The word for this birth out of the heart would later become the spiritual, virginal, and fruitful motherhood that does not bear unto death but unto life, and that has its origin in Mary. Virginity is a spiritual, ecclesiastical concept, which finds its earthly expression, its allegory, in sexual intactness. Love is an allegory of reading.

The substitution of the parrot for the dove, symbol of the Holy Spirit, is first of all an error in reading, namely, a literalization. This lapse in reading corresponds to an erotic affect; both are the fatal outcomes of the Fall. Fetishism and sexualization are the poetological-hermeneutic reversals of the Annunciation, reversals occurring through the replacement of the dove by the parrot. Flaubert marks the reified kenosis of his Félicité with the great stigmata that an enlightened perspective inscribed into nineteenth-century piety: the stigmata of idolatrous Moors, fetishistic "savages," and of sexually dissatisfied sanctimony. As such, in the figure of the parrot's unparalleled eroticization of the Annunciation, Mary's Annunciation is read back into what should have been sublated and overcome through her.

An ancient motif is inscribed with the parrot as a substitute for the dove of the Holy Spirit onto the iconography of the Annunciation: the sexual union of human women—or boys like Ganymede—and gods who, metamorphosed into birds, descend to have intercourse. Flaubert carries out this sexualization with all the means of his art not in order to mock or insult his saint, as enlightened philosophers and male science did when they dismissed such sexualization as a symptom of sexually frustrated women. Flaubert simply does not believe in the healing, therapeutic power of sexuality. Nor does he believe in the straight man who would set them straight. In contrast to his contemporaries, who put their faith in straight sexuality and straight men, Flaubert resists the straightforward normalization and standardization of femininity. The discourse of the nineteenth century has featured this finally sexually fulfilled femininity with unprecedented aggressiveness. Flaubert is not intent on contrasting the two ideals, namely, the ideal of the Bride of Christ—judged as perverse by his contemporaries and depicted as an unattractive, lonely spinster—and the sexually fulfilled wife and fertile mother. No one dismantled this new feminine ideal of wife and mother as forcefully as Flaubert did with Madame Bovary and Madame Aubain. No less magnificent is his shattering of the healing promise of a "fulfilled" sexuality. Flaubert does not cast the hysterical eroticization of Félicité's spiritual love in a malicious light the way contemporary medical discourse did, which triumphantly also had the remedy at hand, the full-blooded man. Rather, the real tragedy of this story lies precisely in the inescapability of eroticization. All love is fatal. In an often-cited letter to Edma Roger des Genettes, Flaubert takes pains to prevent "A Simple Heart" from being confused with an enlightened religious satire, saying: "This is not ironic at all, as you might suppose, but on the contrary very serious and very sad."[42]

The story Flaubert tells, with the replacement of the dove by the parrot, of the spiritual messenger by a phallic bird, is no enlightened song praising liberated sexuality. The stereotype of all mystic-religious phenomena really being symptoms of repressed sexuality is not confirmed, but contradicted. For Flaubert, sexuality cannot be liberated. It is in the firm grip of illusion and death; as the result of original sin, it has no potential for redemption. Even full-blooded "real men" are of no use. The promise of the Annunciation lights up more intensely when confronted with enlightened discourse. The happiness of this promise reveals its full beauty in the very moment when it turns out that it has always already been lost. Félicité is the most perfect of all of Christ's followers: "By our patience let us show we are their brothers, intent on imitating the Lord, seeing which of us can be the more wronged, robbed, and despised" (Ignatius to the Ephesians 10:3). Félicité is also the most perfect of all spiritual mothers. Nevertheless, she—and one must stress, *even* she—remains wholly entangled in Eve's deadly and deceptive desires. An unbearable burden is placed on her shoulders: to disappoint the hope in the promise embodied in the figure of Mary. This promise was nothing more than, and could never amount to more than, a promise.

The basic differentiation with which monotheistic religions set themselves apart in their own self-understanding from all other religions revolves around the difference between crude idolatry and true belief. If idolatry separates heathens from Christians, then in the nineteenth century, fetishism became roughly synonymous with idolatry, differentiating "civilized" Europe from the "savages" in the colonies. Both fetishism and idolatry were used to stigmatize the cultic obscurantism of the Catholic Church in anticlerical propaganda. Thus Stendhal and Michelet, for example, labeled the cult of the Sacred Heart *cordolatrie*. Idolatry and fetishism are the hallmarks of the Church of his time, as a disgusted Flaubert diagnoses them in the aberrations with Pius IX: "Pius IX—the martyr of the Vatican—will have been a disaster for Catholicism. The devotions he promoted are hideous. Sacred Heart, Saint Joseph, Mary's bowels, [Our Lady of La] Salette, and so on. They resemble the cult of Isis and Belone in the last days of paganism."[43] Catholics behave toward their God as the "savages" would toward their fetish:

And above all the priests, who constantly carry this name in their mouth, get on my nerves. It's a kind of habitual sneezing: the goodness of God, the anger of God, to outrage God—this is how they talk. It is as if God were a man, and worse, a bourgeois. They are also set on decorating him with attributes, like the savages who put feathers on the fetishes.[44]

In the wake of the idolatry that makes the Church look like a decadent pagan cult, the fetishism of the West is apparent; with the triumph of the bourgeoisie, everybody is turned into a heathen worshipper of gold and sex.

What Europe is anxious to distance from itself as the other lives within it. This comes to the fore most eloquently in the Madonna in the church built at Yonville during the Restoration, where throne and altar promote each other without scruples. Idolatry reigns supreme. "Ahead, where the nave narrows, stands the confessional, opposite a statuette of the Virgin; she wears a satin gown and a tulle veil sprinkled with silver stars, and her cheeks are painted scarlet, like an idol from the Sandwich Islands."[45] Nothing could have better symbolized fetishism and idolatry than the exotic-erotic bird *d'outre-mer*, infatuating Félicité's simple heart. He overturns the order of media lying at the heart of the Gospel as the scene of the origin of the Church, namely, the order between word and image. Mary stirs words in the heart; in her the word becomes flesh. To the illiterate Félicité only the image makes sense, and only in its most clichéd and cheapest form: as Épinal kitsch images. Sexuality and fetishism—antithetical to the Annunciation—are united in the parrot. The phallic connotations of the exotic-erotic bird captivated a nineteenth century in the grips of a parrot craze. Rather than the swan or the eagle in whose guises Zeus makes love to Leda and Semele, the parrot became the erotic lovebird par excellence during the eighteenth and nineteenth centuries.[46] Félicité drops to her knees for one such parrot: "[she] fell into the idolatrous habit of saying her prayers on her knees in front of the parrot" (36).

The comic-heroic poem *Ver-Vert ou le Voyage du perroquet de Nevers* by Jean-Baptiste-Louis Gresset (1734) tells of a parrot who plays the role of the lover. As *mignon* amongst the Order of the Visitation of Holy Mary, he takes all hearts by storm. These Brides of Christ yearn for nobody but the parrot. Like all nuns the Sisters of Visitation follow the example of Mary; their special connection with Mary is underscored by the name of the order, remembering the Visitation of the pregnant Mary by pregnant Elizabeth. Like Flaubert, Gresset superimposes the ancient topos of the sexual union between bird and woman upon the Christian topos of the mystic love of the Bride for the Heavenly Bridegroom. As in Flaubert, the parrot is a prophetic bird announcing the truth in all its clarity: with Gresset this is the naked truth of sex; with Flaubert it concerns the dead externality of the letter. As with Flaubert, Gresset develops a poetics that finds its allegory in love.

The punchline of Gresset's *Ver-Vert* is that the erotic language of devotion is translated into overtly sexual terms. As "the idol of delight,"[47] the parrot spends its nights turn by turn in the alcoves of the most attractive novices and watches them "[t]ill milder Venus glitter'd in the sky,"[48] happily indulging in voyeurism while they complete their toilet. Finally, the parrot outstrips the predestined role of the father confessor who is the usual candidate as the nuns' lover and makes the nuns, now sighing and cooing like doves, "happy."[49] Their rapture has little mystical about it and is clearly of a sexual kind.[50] The crude sexual meaning of this equivocal tenderness is furnished later on in the words that the shameless parrot learns on a sea voyage to another cloister of the Order of the Visitation: "With words obscene thus passing through his beak, / The younger sisters deem'd he dealt in Greek."[51] By the end of the piece, the erotic subtext comes to the surface through the citations of classical literature and by the association with Venus. With the parrot it is the *petite mort* that leads to his real death. He dies too many times in the arms of too many nuns, and, finally exhausted, he dies for good. Though he does not end up in heaven, Ver-Vert does reach the pantheon, where he joins Ovid, Corinna's beloved. Ovid is not only *the* author of libertine erotica, but also substitutes for Catullus's rather harmless sparrow as the bird of Venus a grotesquely puffed up parrot, for whom Corinna is made to weep (*Amores* 2.6). Ovid ushers in the genre of the comic grotesque.

Love's victim he, with kind attentions tir'd,
Quite overdone, in Pleasure's arms expir'd.
'Twas thus they duly watch'd their much-lov'd bird,
And his last words with admiration heard.
Now beauteous Venus kindly interpos'd,
And with a gentle hand his eyelids clos'd;
And then this parrot, with convenient haste,
She bore away,—and lastly him she plac'd
Midst groves Elysian, hero-birds among,
Near him Corinna's lover wept and sung.[52]

The nuns immortalize their parrot through his embroidered and painted portraits, inspired by love:

his picture next they drew;
More hands than one, and Love amidst the train,
At once essay'd to give him life again;
And many a striking likeness there, I ween,
In water, oil, and needlework was seen[53]

In Gresset's poem, sexually satisfying love leaves behind all ascetic mysticism and triumphs in the successful revival of the beloved in art. In Flaubert, it all comes to nothing. Félicité's erotic fulfilment is a hysterical hallucination; the *petite mort* is nothing but a sign of her final death. Death will not be overcome by love, as the Gospel promises; rather, love is a figure of death as the ancients knew. The attempt to breathe a second life inspired by love into the parrot fails: Félicité's stuffed parrot is not vividly immortalized as Ver-Vert, but looks paler than death.

Chronologically closer than this mock heroic poem, which is intertextually intertwined into "A Simple Heart," is Gustave Courbet's contemporary scandal image of *Woman with a Parrot* (1866). The painting unmistakably evokes the sexual act between bird and woman. In an alcove before a landscape, a woman lies on her back in ecstatic nakedness, with disheveled hair, offering her fondling hand for the parrot to land on with its stretched wings. The colored plumage of the stretched-out wings corresponds to the loosened locks, in which the light plays. With the naked woman before a landscape, Courbet cites the Venus motif, most exemplary in Titian or Giorgione, only to eroticize it. This Renaissance Venus reflects harmoniously in her perfect body the quiescent beauty of the landscape. The serpentine figure of the woman twists the harmonious, self-sufficient beauty of Venus. She lacks something; she wants the parrot. Courbet's promise of erotic fulfillment in the love play with the parrot is shattered in Manet's sad *Young Lady* (1866): a lemon points to her sour widowhood. All beauty has been taken away from the bird between the pole and the prosaic feeding bowl, only to be withdrawn into the shining silk sateen of the house frock covering the woman from neck to toe. In Manet, the parrot does not promise sexual fulfillment but stands for its absence. The painting is an allegory of the five senses, which here only point to a lack. The absence of fulfillment is evident in the heartbroken expression of the lonely woman. Courbet, who replaces Catullus's sparrow with Ovid's parrot, illustrates a poem of Catullus's in which the lover plays in innocent covetousness with the beaked sparrow, pars pro toto for the male member. With Manet, the parrot becomes a symbol for the absent lover. As the companion of the lonely woman, it symbolizes her present or even systematic frustration.

Félicité substitutes the erotic-phallic bird par excellence, the parrot, for the spiritual bird par excellence, the dove in the Annunciation, when the Holy Spirit descends in the guise of a dove to Mary. The moment is depicted for her by a stained-glass window in the church in Pont-l'Évêque that shows "the Holy Spirit above the Virgin" (14). In the *diptyque* of the Annunciation on the church window, she concentrates upon the half with

Mary and the dove.[54] In one of three sentences that the parrot Loulou is able to say, "Hail Mary!" (28), the performance of redemption—Ave Maria—congeals into mechanical babbling. The dove, Félicité concludes, must in reality have been a parrot, since he can speak: "The Father could never have chosen to express himself [*pour s'énoncer*] through a dove, for those creatures cannot speak, but rather one of Loulou's ancestors" (34). This thought comes to Félicité while looking at a kitschy print in which the Holy Spirit descends upon Christ accompanied by the voice of God the Father from the heavens: "This is my beloved Son" (Matt. 3:17). According to Félicité, in this picture the dove looks more like a parrot:

In church she always gazed at the Holy Spirit, and noticed that he looked something like the parrot. The likeness seemed still more evident in a popular print [*image d'Épinal*] of Our Lord's baptism. With his purple wings and emerald green body he was the very image of Loulou. (34)[55]

Moreover, the word *énoncé* also plays with the signifier *annoncé*, thus once more recalling the motif of Annunciation. In the background of Félicité's idea that the parrot must be able to speak, the strangely material notion flashes up that Mary conceives literally through the ear. In Marian hymn, this is of course a metaphor: she conceives hearing the angel's address.[56] In the greeting "Hail Mary!" (28)—Loulou's babbling repetition as a parody of the speech act of the Annunciation—the word becomes flesh. Through the metamorphosis of the dove into the parrot, Mary's Conception is transformed into a fruitful coitus after the ancient pattern in which a god is present in the form of a bird lying with a mortal. Félicité's taking the dove, not as a symbol but as the Holy Spirit itself, only to substitute the parrot for it,[57] replaces conversion with metamorphosis. According to the doxa, the hermeneutic conversion originates in Mary, when the Word becomes Flesh. From now on, the world is readable in the light of the living spirit. Flaubert reverts this conversion back into the antique pattern of metamorphosis: a mere transformation of bodies.

Félicité fulfills the role of Virgin Mary and dies at the moment when the latter blissfully conceives: the bird hovers over her. Félicité's death scene is a sexualization of the Annunciation. The gigantic proportion of the parrot—"a gigantic parrot hovering over her head" (40)—glaringly points to erotic overpowering. Félicité is overcome by the phallic bird, which dominates her with its sheer size. In Félicité's perception, the dove (usually a small dove approaching Mary's ear) is already dominating the Virgin (*dominait la vierge*) in the church window.

The political dimension of these patriarchal relations of domination together with the doctrine of the divine right of kings—we are between the Restoration and Louis Philippe's constitutional monarchy—is conjured up through the replacement of the portrait of the comte d'Artois, Charles X (the last king of the Bourbon line, ruling from 1824 to 1830), by the Épinal pictures in which the Holy Spirit appears as the "portrait" of Loulou: "She bought the print and hung it up in place of the Comte d'Artois" (34). By means of the signifier "hovering" (*planer*), the parrot is inserted into the patriarchal status of both Madame Aubain's late husband and the successor to the throne: "At first she lived there in a state of fear and trembling brought on by 'the kind of house' it was and the memory of 'Monsieur' hanging over [*planant*] everything" (7). Husband and successor to the throne are again connected by the signifier "Monsieur": the comte d'Artois is called "Monsieur frère du roi." The late husband of Madame Aubain is affiliated with the ancien régime of the comte d'Artois through his clothes. In the portrait, "Monsieur" is portrayed *en costume de muscadin* (*Trois contes*, 10). The *muscadins* were the aristocratic, counterrevolutionary "gilded youth" (*jeunesse dorée*) who fought the sansculottes after the fall of Robespierre. The patriarchal claim to authority, which saw in the figure of the king the representative of God on earth and in the *pater familias* the latter's representative, is ridiculed by this dressed-up, "handsome but impecunious young man" (3), or, as the parrot puts it, *charmant garçon* (*Trois contes*, 68). This charming man is certainly a terrible husband and father. He squanders the fortune of his wife and leaves her behind in ruin—with two children to care for. The parrot is simultaneously the crowning and the inversion of this male ridicule, since he is linked into this chain through substitution and the repetition of words and is crowned with flowers at the end like the portrait of the husband. The stuffed parrot is thus the final, utterly grotesque link in this patriarchal chain of God's representatives on earth, disfiguring them once and for all. He makes apparent the grotesqueness of the patriarchal claim, perpetuated as it is by the blindness of female desire. The parrot brings the idea of the divine right of kings and its bourgeois, patriarchal reincarnations to its most absurd conclusion.

The figure of God's representative on earth in the *pater familias* is ruined and defaced in "A Simple Heart." The first husband of Madame

Aubain—the "charmant garçon"—leaves her with debts. Precipitated by the bull into a nervous, premature sexuality, their daughter dies early; their son stubbornly continues his father's ruinous work. In the manuscript version the husband is a thief and gambler, cheating his wife in every respect. The notary Bourais takes his place and completes his work of ruin. Betraying Madame Aubain, the notary begets an illegitimate child with another woman and embezzles what is left of the fortune Madame Aubain has so painstakingly saved after her first marriage:

The following week came news of M. Bourais's death, in Lower Brittany, in an inn. Rumours of suicide were confirmed; doubts were raised as to his honesty. Madame Aubain examined her accounts, and it was not long before she came aware of the catalogue of his infamies: embezzlement of arrears, disguised sales of timber, forged receipts, etc. In addition he had fathered a natural child, and had had "relations with a person from Dozulé." (35)

In the figure of the parrot, Flaubert subverts the patriarchal alliance between altar and throne. The earthly family is ruled by the husband and thus marked by gender hierarchy. The woman, eternal Eve, is condemned to desire male beauty. She is thus subjected to her husband in more than one sense. Sex and money unite and disunite these families. In matters of sex and money, husband and wife cheat and defraud the other. The man becomes God's representative on earth only by female, carnal desire. More radical still than the Church Fathers, Flaubert reveals that these earthly families are destined to be ruined. The price a woman has to pay for her sensual idolatry of the male is her property, which charming husbands and lovers squander with the utmost regularity in Flaubert. The children born out of this bond die prematurely or remain infertile. Flaubert is no Zola; without exception, sexuality is ruinous and leads to death. His Félicité would gain nothing by abandoning her sterile virginity, marrying the right man, and bearing him children to people a new France like the Mary of Zola's novel *Lourdes*. So much for fleshly motherliness.

Nevertheless, spiritual motherhood does not fare much better in Flaubert. The two types of motherhood are connected by the parrot. On the one hand, the parrot is inserted into the chain with "Monsieur" and thereby aligned with the patriarchal family. On the other hand, the relation between the parrot and Félicité cites the spiritual love bond signified by *fils* and *amoureux*. Félicité loves the parrot the way Mary loved Christ, her son and beloved. In the final version, Flaubert subdued the erotic explicitness between Félicité and Loulou.[58] What remains in the final version, rehearsing Mary's overwhelming love for her doomed son, are only Félicité's conversations with her parrot: "In her isolation Loulou was almost a son, a lover to her. He would climb up her fingers, nibble her lips, cling to her bodice; and as she bent forward, wagging her head as nurses do, the wide wings of her bonnet and those of the bird quivered in unison" (31). Following the Fathers of the Church in late antiquity, spiritual love should become fertile in everlasting bliss, in contrast to deadly erotic love.[59] However, Félicité's love remains, as a reversal of the Christian promise of salvation, a love destined to death. Flaubert makes Félicité the paragon of spiritual motherhood. But her *imitatio Mariae* is only staged to make the opposition collapse: Mary did not invert Eve. No redemption has taken place. The task with which Flaubert burdens his housemaid is to make this catastrophe legible. In the words of the old English nursery rhyme: Mary, Mary, quite contrary. Here, too, Flaubert belongs to a long tradition which does not conclude with him. In the wake of Flaubert's work, literature will almost obsessively articulate its allegories of readability or unreadability with reference to the Annunciation scene. Claude Simon can be considered the most prominent of Flaubert's heirs for this very specific version of Marian literature.[60]

Félicité becomes the paradigm of a state of language in modernity in which the word, shorn of all life-giving power, remains but dead letter. A language petrified into clichés only touches deaf hearts of stone that understand nothing. In *Madame Bovary*, Flaubert, in a very auctorial voice, compares the tragic inadequacy of language with a cracked kettle that makes bears dance, but cannot mollify the stars, that is to say, fate. The "cracked kettle" is a transposition of "sounding brass and a tinkling cymbal" (1 Cor. 13:1): when listened to without love, it all comes to nothing. Rodolphe, incapable of understanding Emma's heartfelt love talk, only hears clichés he thinks he has heard a thousand times already. Against this discordant language condemned to cliché, "A Simple Heart" pits the heart of Félicité, which fills the eternally repeated, pointless babbling, with love, and thereby turns it into the language of the heart (31). Contrary to modernity Félicité fills the empty husks of words, the mechanical parrot speech, with all her heart. But what she in all her simplicity fills with love is not destined for life but bound for death. The theological core of this intensified kenosis is the renunciation of the promise held in Mary's Annunciation that the word can come to life and overcome death. Félicité's heartfelt love is not just lacking in beauty; worse, is it not salvific either. Modern literature is thus an elegy to Mary, or to keep in tune with the birds of antiquity, a swan song to the salvific promise embodied in the Virgin Mother, Queen of Heaven.

The Holy Ghost Upside Down: Parrot Stories

The parrot carries the stigmata of definite deadliness in a dispirited modern world. The attributes of the Holy Spirit, which Flaubert drew from the missal of Lisieux and the breviary of the choirmaster, are fatally inverted and scattered through the text. Instead of a fullness of spirit that transcends the letter, we are left with the crudest literalness. According to liturgy, the Holy Spirit is the breath of God, an omnipotent inspiration kindling everything into life. The pouring out of the Holy Ghost, its arrival in fiery tongues and bursts of wind, ended Babel's confusion of tongues; people speak in tongues and everybody understands everything. "She found it hard to visualize what he looked like, for he was not just a bird, but a fire as well, and at other times a breath" (15). Hermeneutically, the Holy Spirit is precisely the phenomenon that makes the material outwardness of the letter transparent, dissolving all mediality in immediate understanding. In "A Simple Heart," the idolatrous picture takes the place of the Word, mechanical droning takes the place of mindful speech, and senseless aping takes the place of true understanding. The life-endowing effects of tongue and breath are scattered throughout the text in inverted, lethal literalness. The parrot suffers from a swelling under the tongue from which he almost dies (29). His life is also threatened by the smoke of a Havana cigar, blown in his direction to reach his nostrils (29–30)—an inversion of breathing in new life. Félicité imagines Havana filled with cigar smoke—rather than with the Holy Spirit. Madame Aubain's tongue seems covered with smoke (*paraissait couverte de fumée* [*Trois contes*, 84]). The wind howling in the chimney—like the storm the Holy Spirit inflicts on the disciples—makes Félicité think of her nephew suspended in mortal danger. Madame Aubain, her daughter, and Félicité all die of lung disease, of a lack of *pneuma*. Through his screeching, Loulou prevents anyone from understanding their own words. The confusion of Babel dominates Félicité's world, manifested in human and animal roaring muddled into an undifferentiated din.

The parrot stands for the mechanical aping of the human word instead of the Word's spiritual breath of life. Thus voided of all sense, it becomes a purely rote, spiritless imitation. The text stresses this mechanical lack of wit by making the parrot imitate machine sounds: "he would reproduce the regular clicking of the spit turning . . . the sawing of the carpenter who lived opposite" (31). In the same mechanical materiality, Félicité is illuminated by a sunbeam reflected by the parrot's glass eye. Here, too, Flaubert places Félicité in the—now inverted—Marian succession when taking up the iconography of Annunciation scenes in which Mary is illuminated by a ray of light, as for example in the Venetian Annunciation by Titian: "Sometimes the sun coming through the skylight, would catch his glass eye, so that a great beam of light flashed out from it, and this entranced her" (36). Thus it is the outwardness of the letter and the arbitrariness of the signs that motivate the replacement of the Holy Spirit by a parrot in a pun: for Félicité, the most outstanding quality of the parrot is that of the consoler, and this is indeed what the Holy Spirit is called: the Paraclete. While Félicité is abandoned by everyone and left with nothing, the parrot whom she thought lost on two occasions twice returns to her, the first time alive, the second taxidermized. Against the misleading likeness of outward appearances, a true resemblance of sounds speaks forth from the text. It is the homophony *paraclet/perroquet* that motivates the substitution of the Holy Spirit through the dove. This wordplay would be wasted on Félicité. Nevertheless, for the reader it is an echo of the analogy of all things in the Book of Nature, which may comfort us briefly.

In the most pointed and ironic distortion of the essence of the Holy Spirit, which, as the immaterial and ever-changing, blocks out every reification in the form of an image, the stuffed parrot illustrates precisely what absolute rigidity is. The crudest hypermateriality is stressed, which merely appears to be liveliness. But this appearance of liveliness never stands a chance against death; drastically, death is inscribed onto the most artificial allegorical body of appearances possible, a suspended fetish: "Although he was not a corpse, he was all worm-eaten, one of his wings was broken, the stuffing was coming out of his stomach" (38). What the art of mummification had intended to make last forever does not even resemble anything lifelike.

The Holy Spirit empties himself out by taking up the form of the modern world (*kenosis*). He, who in the economy of the Trinity would vouchsafe the life of the resurrected, goes to ruin in the figure of the parrot, in a world abandoned by the enlivening spirit of love, amid complete annihilation—kenosis in the literal sense of the word. He takes the form of the world upon himself and thus makes the world readable: it is a senseless world, not inspired by enlivening spirit, but dominated by the letter that kills. In this respect the parrot fulfills the double, at first contradictory, meaning Flaubert ascribes to him. Parrots parrot mechanically without understanding even one word of what they are saying, as Flaubert remarks in his unpublished piece "Les trois frères" about a painting entitled *Pays de Perroquets*: "Repeating words they've learned, but don't understand, all they utter is clichés."[61] It is precisely because of this that the parrot is a prophetic bird, a bird who speaks the truth in the most literal sense: the truth of a world that has congealed into the blind repetition of clichés no one understands any longer with the heart—a world in which nothing affirms life as much as it affirms death. Félicité faithfully collects the remains on this way to death in her room, the leftover, disdained signs of the times no longer wanted by anyone. You can hardly move in her chamber, both a bazaar and chapel, since it is stuffed with souvenirs. Félicité embraces the *vanitas* of the world, lovingly gathering decay and the reified, the numb memory traces of lost love.

What remains are agony and apotheosis. For one brief moment of illusion one might think that the parrot verges on the performative strength of the Holy Spirit just this one time. On the Corpus Christi altar, while Félicité is dying, he animates the dead remains that are assembled on the altar as an allegory of ruin. The definitive death of the world lying there in fragments of disjointed, disdained ruins of memory is infused with life: shine, color, light, and scents. Flaubert's stylistic ideal—*enargeia,* to present things vividly, "faire clair et vif," as he told Turgenev[62]—seems to be realized. What is described here, however, in all its clarity and vividness, is death. The altar on which the parrot is placed at the time of Félicité's death throes is heaped with knickknacks of all kind, bric-à-brac from China to South America, a motley collection from all four corners of the earth, colorful, sparkling, glittering. In gray Normandy, it is a sensuous explosion of colors, scents, and tones. It is not by chance, though, that what seems to be animated comes in the guise of a dazzling deception, namely, framed within the discourse of curious ocular desire, *concupiscentia oculorum*: "rare objects caught the eye" (39). It is not by chance that the typical symbols

of the overcoming of death through resurrection fossilize into mere ornament—like the violets painted on porcelain, whose sweet scent was traditionally believed to promise resurrection. All life—fragrance, movement,
warmth—is on this altar "metamorphosed into a Parnassian, mineralized
tableau, a reliquary of eternal durability."[63] The price of eternity is a petrifying death that turns everything to stone. This is the effect of all fe-
tishizing aestheticization. That which appears to make the miracle of the
Pentecost come true turns out, once again, to be its Babylonian retraction:
fragments of delusion, scattered across the whole world. In its guise as the
Holy Spirit, the parrot should overturn Babel, but it has become the cen-
terpiece of the Babylonian scenario. Nothing testifies more forcefully to
God's forsaking of the world than the feast of the body of Christ, Corpus
Christi, where rather than the divine real presence, the only thing that
shines through is the idolatrous golden dazzle of the monstrance, turning
the occasion into an idolatrous dance around the Golden Calf. Only this
petrified, gold-plated ornament can be shown so vividly, killing that which
once promised a life after death.

Félicité starts coughing up blood after Easter. When she dies, it is
the Feast of Corpus Christi, and like the dove in pictures of the Annunciation, the parrot hovers above her, "gigantesque" (*Trois contes*, 94; in
manuscript versions it is even called "monstrous"—*monstrueux*).[64] Flaubert blows up the proportions of the iconography of the Annunciation,
where the bird is small compared to Mary. In this reversal of proportions,
antiquity breaks into the scene. The gigantic bird is Zeus as an eagle, who
plucks Ganymede like a lamb and carries him away into the skies. He
descends or pounces on the objects of his desire, who for the most part
are pictured lying down, like Félicité, rather than kneeling, sitting, or
standing, like Mary, expecting the Word. In his painting *The Apotheosis
of Semele* (ca. 1585), Catherine de' Medici's court painter Antoine Caron
portrayed Zeus with French flair as lightning bolt, his true form, zapping
the human woman, who is stretched out naked on an altar. In fulfilling
her desire, he cannot but kill her. The painting belonged to a private collector, and it is unlikely that Flaubert knew it. Nevertheless, a better illustration of the mythical motif of a god making love to a human woman
is hardly imaginable. In this case, Flaubert inscribes the deadly nature of
Eros into the ravishment of the Bride of Christ that Félicité experiences
in her ecstatic death.[65] Showing the conversion to everlasting life to be a

lethal promise of love, always already erased by death, deadly rape is portrayed here as ecstatic rapture.

In the rhythm of the sentences with which Flaubert lets his exemplary saint pass away, we hear the echo of the irregular heartbeat of vanishing life. With the dying echo, in its last lines, the text references an Ovidian metamorphosis.[66] The nymph Echo, whom Hera, the queen of heaven, deprives of meaningful speech, leaving her with only the senseless reverberation of the words—language reduced to pure sonority—represents the outwardness of Félicité's passion, learned mechanically, by heart. In the emphatic inversion of the Marian promise of the Word, which becomes flesh by moving the heart, Félicité becomes the figure through which Flaubert stages the failure of this promise. Living spirit has turned into dead letter; it has coagulated into fetishistic, clichéd idolatry of the image, which can only be fulfilled by Félicité's simple heart, senselessly brimming with love. She dies in a state of complete illusion, a delusion that we peruse in all its idolatrous outwardness. "A Simple Heart" is a monument to her incomparable love, hopelessly deluded but overwhelmingly true, which is all that remains of her after the ruin of everything edifying and constructive. What remains is the love of literature and Loulou, the code name for all the loves Flaubert ever lost. Their monuments are erected in the ruins of his writing.[67]

"SAINT JULIAN THE HOSPITALIER"

Your poetry became a part of me like my nurse's milk.

Flaubert to Victor Hugo, July 15, 1853

Nimrod, Mighty Hunter in Defiance of the Lord

Flaubert's legend of Saint Julian is not only the legend of a saint, but also a legend in the sense of a text that explains an image. It is written as a caption to a stained-glass window in Notre-Dame de Rouen Cathedral with the legend as its subject: "And that is the story of Saint Julian the

Hospitaller, more or less as it can be found in the stained-glass window of a church in my part of the world" (70).[1] Flaubert was well acquainted with the window through his art teacher Eustache-Hyacinthe Langlois, who gave an account of it in his *Essai . . . sur la peinture sur verre*.[2] This "more or less," suggestive of the discrepancy between the legend and the window, between word and image, is emphasized by Flaubert in his correspondence. Anyone having viewed the actual window must have wondered after having read the text: "At the end of Saint Julian I wanted to reproduce the stained-glass window from the Rouen cathedral. . . . Comparing the picture with the text, the reader would have been puzzled, and would have wondered how I derived the one from the other."[3] This chapter addresses the question of what might have motivated this radical departure from the legend, while apparently following it so faithfully.

The source material Flaubert uses goes back to Jacobus de Voragine's thirteenth-century *Golden Legend* (Legenda aurea).[4] The nobly born Julian tracks down a deer during a hunt. The deer foretells his future ruin: "One day, savage heart, you will murder your father and your mother!" (51). Julian leaves the parental castle in order to evade the curse and enters into the service of a foreign ruler; for his loyalty, he is awarded the hand in marriage of his master's daughter and a castle. Meanwhile, Julian's parents are searching high and low for their son. Finally, after a long odyssey, they arrive at his castle, are recognized by Julian's wife and, as a token of hospitality, are invited to sleep in the marital bed to rest after their arduous journey. Julian, returning from the hunt in the early morning, suspects his wife of adultery and stabs both sleepers. After the murder, when leaving the castle, he comes across his wife. He acknowledges that the deer's prophecy has come true. Julian intends to atone for his crime, but cannot leave his wife to her own devices, so they abandon everything and take to the road. They end up at the bank of a big river, a deserted wasteland where they build an asylum, a hospital for the poor and sick while ferrying people across the river. One night Julian hears a voice calling from the other bank and discovers a half-frozen leper. Despite the storm, Julian takes him across the river, gives him food and drink, and lays him in his bed to warm him. In other versions, the married couple lie down together with their guest in their bed. The leper arises in glorious splendor. He is Christ himself, and tells Julian that the Lord has accepted his penance and that he will soon rest in Him.

Flaubert deviates from this and all other versions of the legend in three specific points. First, there is the hunt, which does not play a central role in the legends, but which Flaubert foregrounds in his version. Nowhere is Julian's hunt described as such a voluptuously sadistic massacre. Second, Julian is not joined by his wife in the wilderness; his charity no longer fulfills a social function enabling his integration into the community to serve its needs. Instead, he lives the life of an outcast, a pariah, a stigmatized outsider.[5] Third, literally united in an apotheosis of love with the leper, Julian ascends to heaven, whereas no mention is made of such an ascension in any of the other versions of the story.

Flaubert's legend is first and foremost a transmission: an all-embracing transfer, one is tempted to say, of ancient myth into the form of the legend.[6] In an arguably similar case, it is foretold to Oedipus that he will kill his father and sleep with his mother. After Oedipus has fulfilled his destiny by doing so, he is banished from the sight of man and exiled from the inhabited world to live as an outcast (*Oedipus at Colonus*). But other parallels might also be invoked: Ajax, who in his boundless rage slaughters animals instead of people; Actaeon, who is transformed into a stag and is torn apart by his own pack of hounds;[7] Ulysses, who after his homecoming is recognized by his wet nurse because of a hunting scar; Narcissus, who misrecognizes his own reflection in the river; Acheron, the ferryman who transports the often cursing passengers across the Styx into the underworld.

Flaubert does the same thing with the characters of his legend that Julian does with people as a ferryman: he transfers them, carries them over. When, during the final and crucial transference, Julian is surrounded by darkness and white, foaming stormy waters, followed by the ink-black surface of the water with its white tips, this is more than just a reference to the romantic treatments of the legend by Jacobus de Voragine.[8] As an allusion in "black and white" to writing, it is a representation of Flaubert's poetic method. This antique transference is most evident in what seems to be the legend's Christian event par excellence, namely Julian's ascension to heaven. It will turn out that rather than the ancient sources adumbrating it, Christianity lives in the shadow of antiquity.

The legend of Saint Julian is—as Shoshana Felman has elaborated— a story of writing, language, and interpretation.[9] The legend tells of the marking of the human body; God marks this body either with a mark of love or with a mark of rejection. In what follows I am concerned with uncovering the patristic theological moments in this story of writing that have been overlooked until now. While the plot is modeled on the *Legenda aurea*, the deep structure of the narrative is organized according to a subtext that only now and then rears its head. At the heart of Julian's story is the Augustinian opposition between the City of God and the City of Man. Sartre's intuition of an ultra-Jansenist conception of original sin is right on target.[10] As opposed to the traditional reception of Saint Augustine, it is the illusion of the City of God on earth that Flaubert attempts to extirpate.

"Saint Julian the Hospitalier" is perhaps the text where Flaubert plays most clearly on the Augustinian frame of reference. The Roman Empire, Saint Augustine's City of Man, and the Church, en route to the City of God, are already jointly present in the architecture of the parental castle: the tiles at the court are "clean as the floor of a church" (41), while a "Roman steam bath" (42) is some distance away, unused. The chapel is as luxuriant as the "oratory of a king" (ibid.). Basil and heliotrope adorn the windowsills of the castle; the heliotrope, also the attribute of John the Baptist, stands for divine inspiration (City of God), while basil symbolizes rage and cruelty (City of Man).[11] From this coexistence, no harmony will ensue, which would have pointed to the establishment of the City of God here on earth. Instead, both will soon disintegrate in perfect dissonance.

The story is only putatively set in a concrete historical setting; it illustrates—despite all the romantic-medieval historicism—the state of worldly peace according to the criteria of Augustine's *The City of God*. This state of affairs is always the result of war, and Augustine describes it as deficient by the standards of the City of God. The castle evinces such a state of peace following war: "They had lived in peace for so long that the portcullis was not lowered any more; the moat was overgrown with grass; swallows nested in the slits of the battlements; and the archer who patrolled the castle walls all day long withdrew to the watchtower as soon as the sun's heat became too much for him, and there he dropped off to sleep like a monk in his stall" (41). That there was continuous warfare prior to this peace is evident from the castle's armory, where weapons of war from all over the globe and all times, "weapons of every age and nation" (42), are gathered peacefully, almost like in a museum. Following Augustine, there is no doubt that worldly peace is a blessing, but it is only a worldly good wrested from war: "Thus, it [the earthly city] desires earthly peace, albeit only for the sake of the lowest kind of goods; and it is that peace which it desires to achieve by waging war. . . . It is for the sake of this peace that wearisome wars are fought, and it is by victories which are deemed glorious that this is achieved" (*De civitate Dei* 15.4).[12]

In the signifying material of the legend as well as in the consciousness of the protagonists, the City of God seems to have been realized on earth—this consciousness is perhaps the "medieval" moment of the story. Church and world are in perfect harmony. The man of the Church can speak indiscriminately in the name of God, of honor, and of the forefathers: "Finally, the old monk, in the name of God, honour, and his forebears, bade him resume the activities of a nobleman" (52). This ostensible fulfillment of the City of God on earth appears in the consecrated patterns of the just ruler, the regulated household, the well-run marriage: "Always wrapped in a fox-fur mantle, he would walk round his home, dispensing justice to his vassals and acting as peacemaker in his neighbours' quarrels, . . . [and] chatting to the peasants and giving them advice" (42). Yet all three areas—Church, household, marriage—appear hollow in Flaubert; they are nothing but the stereotypical husks of bourgeois ideology, lacking the glow of love. As a stereotype of the middle-class male, the lord of the castle has found himself a suitable match after many an erotic adventure: "After many adventures he had taken to wife a lady of high degree" (42). Modesty, as symbolized by the fair skin of the lord's wife, is the corresponding norm for the bourgeois wife. In Rousseau, that preacher of bourgeois paternalistic morality, the ideal family mother is walled in like a nun in the convent—but lacking the slightest hint of God's love. Julian's mother runs a monastic household: "Her household routine was as regular as that of a monastery; every morning she assigned tasks to her serving-women" (ibid.). However, monastic life is reduced here to the mechanical regularity of the clock. Inside the castle, this peace manifests itself in the exclusively material aspects of comfort, homeliness, and prosperity. If the lord of the castle used to indulge in carnal lust, war, and hunting, then the core of the monastic chastity of the lady of the castle is nothing but pride, which is conveyed through her long train and her bonnet, whose tip is so high that it touches the door frame.

In keeping with bourgeois family ideology, the child born from their union is stylized as an infant Jesus. Completely heeding the trend of the new middle-class configuration of wife and mother, which merges biological maternity with sacred motherliness, the son is the result of an Immaculate Conception: "At length her prayers were answered and she bore a son" (42). Both prophecies the parents receive follow the stereotypes of gender-specific literature: the prophecy intended for *maman* is formulated in the style of devotional literature, while *papa* receives his in the style of the gothic novel. Thus, the only seemingly contradictory prophecies bespeak the harmony of holiness and rule: as a saint, the child would partake of an otherworldly empire, while as emperor, the kingdom of this world would belong to him. "Mother, rejoice! Your son will be a saint!" (43), and to the father is revealed: "Ah, ah, your son . . . ! much blood! . . . much glory . . . ! Always good fortune! An emperor's family!" (43). Both parents consider their son to be "marked out by God" (44). Like Jesus, Julian teethes without pain. He is laid to sleep in valuable embroidered cushions and clothes, in a bed that, in its tender preciousness, recalls the craftsmanship of the medieval beguines. However, the only thing remaining of the devoted piety of the needlework is the outside cover, the surface. The Holy Spirit appears as a lamp in the form of a dove—the light of truth ossified into a commodity fetish.

The two prophecies realize the narcissistic fantasies of both parents. In their eyes, holiness and worldly empire are compatible. There were indeed holy kings: Saint Louis, for instance. For the mother, saintliness does not entail a self-denying renunciation of the world, but success within Church hierarchy. She interprets holiness according to the worldly social criterion of success: she sees her son as a high dignitary of the Church, as an archbishop. Flaubert unmasks the ostensible actualization of the City of God on earth as merely illusory through a pre-formulated language that is mechanically memorized and riddled with clichés. Against the backdrop of the romantic version of the Middle Ages, the bourgeois world with its reification of the spiritual into commodity fetishes and dead mechanics comes to the fore. Julian has come to destroy the synthesis of both empires. He brings to light the fallenness of all worldly things. He is marked by God to uncover the objective nature of mankind, which, despite the coming of the Messiah, is still in a state of absolute depravity and as unredeemed from original sin as before the coming of Christ. This nature of man will reveal itself in Julian as maculated and maculating. The marks of salvation are overwritten with the marks of damnation.

This brings us to the crux of Flaubert's legend, namely, the meaning of the hunt. To say that the latter is central is somewhat of an understatement. The legend is structured by the two hunts, mutually referring to each

other.[13] The first part is a crescendo-like swelling of Julian's orgiastic intoxication with murder ending in a massacre of cosmic proportion. In the end,
a family of deer is slaughtered and Julian is damned to parenticide by the
stag. Julian leaves the parental castle in horror after almost inadvertently fulfilling the curse. The second part is governed by Julian's raging urge to hunt.
But when he finally gives in to his desire, it turns out that, being incapable
of killing any more, he is unable to satisfy it. It is precisely this frustration
that leads him to slaughter his parents instead of animals. That the father
serves as a stand-in for the animals to be shot is made clear through the
figure of the fox, fueling Julian's desire for the hunt. It refers to his father's
"fox-fur mantle" (42). However, apart from its structuring function within
the legend, the hunt also stands out, since it evinces the most marked diver-
gence from all other sources due to its radical, sadistic, and orgiastic description of bloodlust. In Flaubert's version, Julian's story is that of a bloodthirsty
boy and man, who finds fulfillment of his lust through slaughter: "Bloodlust possessed him again; failing animals, he would have liked to slaughter
men" (61). The hunt is a figure for dissolution, but above all—and this is
wholly Flaubert's invention—a literal cancellation of redemption.

Julian succumbs to the desire to commit senseless murder, the desire to destroy all life. The hunt becomes the passion taking over his entire life. It condemns him to a solitary life and bars him from the pleasure
of community with other people. Flaubert exerts himself in juxtaposing
Julian's uncivilized hunting methods to the notion of the hunt as a perfect
example of a civilizing technique. By hunting, Julian abandons the community of man. Paradoxically, his solitude simultaneously bespeaks the
figura Christi—as indicated by the crown of thorns—as well as the figure
of the wild animal: "he would . . . come back in the middle of the night,
covered in mud and blood, his hair full of thorns, and reeking of wild
animals. He became like them" (48). The solution to the riddle of the hunt
can be found in Augustine's *City of God*. In the simple form of the legend, Flaubert narrates the story of the cosmic struggle between good and
evil, the war of the founders of the City of Man with the precursors of the
City of God. Unaware of the Augustinian background, scholarship has remained blind to the symbolic meaning of the hunt. This is doubly mys-
tifying given that it is precisely this symbolic meaning that is so glaringly
obvious in one of the intertexts of the legend of Saint Julian, which Flaubert even names in his correspondence: Victor Hugo's legend of the hand-

some Pécopin, whose fate he recounts in "La légende du beau Pécopin et de la belle Bauldour" in his collection *Le Rhin* (1842). For Augustine—as for Hugo—the most important figure in the cosmic struggle between the founders of both empires is Nimrod.

Who is Nimrod? In Augustine's *City of God*, he is the successor of the fratricidal Cain and the founder of Babylon as the City of Man. This makes him the predecessor of the founders of Rome, the new Babylon on the banks of the Tiber, which Augustine, referring to Lucan, presents as the embodiment of the City of Man. The constantly recurring motif in the description of the City of Man is that people are worse than wild animals—this motif as well was taken from the *Pharsalia*. The motif of the metamorphosis of men into creatures more bloodthirsty than wild beasts that plays so crucial a role in the legend is already traced out *here*.[14] Nimrod is the antagonist of all those who enter into a covenant with God, those who are marked by God to become patriarchal figures of the City of God: he is the antitype of Abel, Noah, Abraham—"God's beloved"—who, in exile on earth, are the predecessors of Christ, precursors of the City of God. Nimrod is also marked by God: he inherits the mark of Cain. The giant Nimrod is described in the Bible as a "hunter against the Lord,"[15] and Augustine regularly confers this epitaph on him. Nimrod's qualification is foregrounded when Augustine explicates the sense of the word "against" through biblical exegesis.

Not a few translators have failed to understand this, being misled by an ambiguity in the Greek, and so have rendered it as "before the Lord" rather than "against the Lord.". . . It occurs . . . in the Book of Job, where it is written, "Thou hast turned thy spirit against God." But it is in this latter sense that we are to understand it in the description of the giant Nimrod, who was a "mighty hunter against the Lord." For what does this word mean, what is a "hunter," if not a deceiver, an oppressor, a slayer of earth-born creatures? (*De civitate Dei* 16.4, 703)

Before he dies, the stag condemns Julian to murder his parents; he is "solemn as a patriarch, or a judge" (51). The patriarchs and judges are the counteracting forces against the giant Nimrod; they are the governors of the City of God, the progenitors of Christ. With the killing of the stag, which represents the patriarch and judge, Julian becomes a hunter against those, who, as the forefathers of Christ, are the founders of the City of God.

In another text by Hugo, *La fin de Satan*—an overlooked intertext just as important as "La légende du beau Pécopin et de la belle Bauldour"— Nimrod appears in an outspoken Augustinian context as "this man, / this hunter, as the whole world calls him."[16] The figure of the hunt against God becomes a literal hunt for God in Hugo's cosmic drama: Nimrod shoots an arrow at God, and the text suggests that his arrow struck Him, because he falls to earth all bloodied. This Hugoesque literalization of the hunt not only against, but for God is taken up by Flaubert. As a descendant of Cain and heir to his weapons of warfare, the giant Nimrod visits ruin and destruction upon humanity in Hugo's epic.[17] His hunt or war is interpreted as a direct consequence of original sin, which he spreads like a contagious disease over the face of the earth through his war frenzy and carnage: "The Hindu, . . . the Assyrian, have eaten flesh as Eve has eaten from the apple."[18] War is regarded as "the monstrous worm of Creation's fruit."[19] The violence of the process of undoing is read as a continuation of original sin: "What God creates, mankind destroys."[20] In Hugo, Nimrod also becomes the antitype of Noah, harbinger of devastation and death.[21] However, in "La légende du beau Pécopin et de la belle Bauldour," and more explicitly in his cosmic epic, Hugo posits a creative love—*caritas* as well as *eros*—as a counterforce to destruction. To illustrate that, Hugo doubles Nimrod as a eunuch. It is his sterility, his inability to love and bring new life into being, that engenders his hatred of and striving for revenge against all living things. While all life testifies to and partakes in God's work, the eunuch has vowed to annihilate all Creation and to further death: "and the pigeon mates with the dove, but I, the eunuch, have chosen the grave as my wife!"[22] In Hugo as in Augustine, Nimrod is explicitly the opponent of God, and the figure for his destructive activity is the hunt.

Hugo's "Légende du beau Pécopin" recounts how the devil dissuades men from pursuing their happiness, love, and women, and tempts them to hunt instead. The handsome Pécopin is estranged from his happy life with the beautiful Baldour. The passion for hunting overtakes love's passion[23]—this is how the birds sum up the moral of the story. The dove, the cooing bird of love that whispers sweet nothings, ends the story in the name of the beloved: "Baldour, Baldour, Baldour!"[24] Pécopin goes hunting instead of making love and, in the eyes of Hugo, thereby rescinds his happiness. The devil tempts him to one last hunt, which, contrary to what Pécopin believed, does not last one night but a hundred years. When he finally rejoins the beautiful Baldour, she has turned into a hideously decrepit old woman. It is no coincidence that Flaubert closely associates the motif of love's desire and the desire for the hunt with the strangulation of the pigeon. Julian experiences his first orgiastic desire while killing the dove, the bird of Venus, which, with the name of the star-crossed lover in its beak, has the last word in Hugo. This is not the case in Flaubert: "Its persistent hold on life angered the boy. He began to throttle it, and the bird's convulsions made his heart beat faster, filling him with wild, turbulent ecstasy. When it finally grew stiff he felt quite faint" (46). Julian's lust is murderous.

In Hugo, the hunt signals aberration, deviation, temptation. As in Flaubert, the first and second hunts are synchronized so that they reciprocally illuminate one another. In Hugo as well as in Flaubert, the second hunt brings to light the true character of the first hunt. Only when three birds of prey, the kite, buzzard, and eagle, which Pécopin has shot during the first hunt, fly midair with the arrow pierced through their bodies and the wind calling out the names of three castles through which the hunt had passed—"Heimburg," "Vaugtsberg," "Rheinstein"[25]—does Pécopin recall the count palatine's first hunt. "Pecopin now recalled to mind the chase of the Palsgrave, in which he had performed such prodigies."[26] The devil, to whom one of Pécopin's former squires betrayed Pécopin's weakness for hunting, tempts Pécopin to this second, uncanny, cosmic hunt across the world for a monstrous black eight-point stag. Place and time are suspended. The second hunt, *chasse noire*, ends in Nimrod's castle with a black mass: the deer that had been hunted across the world is finally consumed. The company gathered there, consisting of all the world's hunters, is served the roasted deer, dished up by the devil on a huge gold platter, "the sixteen-horned stag, smoking in a sea of gravy."[27] This sinister reversal of the Banquet of Love seals a covenant of destruction.

However, the deer is not just any animal, but a *figura Christi*. In the slaughtering and serving of the deer, Hugo portrays a travesty of the Holy Communion. For the covenant Nimrod forges through this supper is made in dedication to original sin and war—in short, it pays homage to Rome: "The jennet dashed up the flight of steps, carrying the knight into a splendidly illuminated hall, of which the tapestry represented subjects taken from the Roman history. . . . The remaining parts of the pavement represented in mosaic the siege of Troy."[28] Above the door an inscription is emblazoned referring to the connection between food and the Fall: "Adam found the meal; Eve came up with the dessert."[29] In a world redeemed by Christ, reborn through love and freed from the curse of Rome, this community of hunters is doomed to a ghostly existence in the shadows. It vanishes in the resplendent light of day. Both in *La fin de Satan* and the legend of the handsome Pécopin, where the hunter Nimrod features so prominently, Hugo accords victory to the forces of good. Nimrod/Satan stays behind as the vanquished opponent, virtually dead. Lifeless, he crashes down to earth after his death-defying, soaring flight in *Fin de Satan*; in the legend of the handsome Pécopin, the crowing of the cock dispels his ghost. Nimrod fades away and so does his new, perverted covenant. Daybreak brings us back to the true world: a world redeemed. A covenant of love.

In Flaubert, the opposition between good and evil collapses. This becomes clear when keeping in mind that Hugo's Nimrod and the leper—who, as a figure of Christ, is the latter's antagonist—are both inscribed within Flaubert's Julian. Whereas Nimrod-cum-eunuch, who cannot bring forth life, wants to destroy Creation out of revenge, the leper still loves the very Creation that has rejected him. Julian's ostracism from humanity, spurned as he is from Creation and even death, is modeled on Hugo's leper:

Lord, oh Lord, I am in a miserable prison.
Creation sees my face and tells me: out!
The city of the living repels me and the dead
Reject me, the disgust of the catacombs;
The worm of the grave abhors the worm of the leper.
God! I am neither dead nor alive.
I am the shadow that suffers, and men think
That the cancer that ravages and saps the damned who drags along,
Is not enough and they add hate.
The crowd, O Lord, while singing and laughing, in passing by
Throw stones until I bleed, me the innocent, the dying.
They walk over me as they would walk over mud,
I have no wound that wasn't hit by a stone.[30]

For Hugo, war and destruction are symptoms of the incapacity to love and procreate. Destructive hatred is opposed to creative love; Satan stands against Christ. By contrast, Flaubert's Julian is at the same time modeled on Christ and on his satanic antagonist.[31] Hugo's leper blesses those who torment him, those who turn away in horror and curse him:

Little child that clutches your mother's skirt,
You who say, when seeing me dreaming of the infinite,
Mother, who is this monster? be blessed!

And you men who laugh at my tears,
O my brothers who throw stones at me,
Be blessed. Be blessed on earth and in heaven!
Be blessed, fathers in your children and sons in your forefathers!
. . . .
And heaven, since my eye sees your eternal face,
Your benediction must fill my eye!
. . . .
It is my right to consecrate the earth
Since I am the most abject and the most miserable being!
It is my right to bless since I am damned.[32]

Conversely, Julian's curse becomes a blessing in Flaubert; his erasure of all things created, his erasure of the marks of love becomes the very condition of salvation. Unlike Hugo, Flaubert does not put love and war in an antithetical relation; sexuality and slaughter—and herein he follows Augustine—are the same. Both tarnish and stain; both are a fatal continuation of the stain of original sin. In Flaubert's legend, Nimrod/Julian is not condemned as merely one of God's creations, as is the case in Hugo; rather, Flaubert's Julian is unique in that he brings to light the damnation of the whole of Creation. Stamped by God with the mark of Cain, he is destined to re-signify the signs of Christ's redemption, the stigmata of the Passion, into indices of original sin. Flaubert leaves the entirety of Creation unredeemed and condemned. Creation is utterly loveless and thus fixated on sex and slaughter, irremediably maculated by the stains of original sin. Julian has come into the world in order to reveal this. Christian peace turns out to be of a worldly nature; the human condition is that of the City of Man. The apparently triumphant synthesis of City of Man and City of God conceals the truth of fallenness. Julian is marked out—condemned and elected—to ruin this world right back to its fallen origin. He is marked out to kill the whole of Creation and Christ with it, to reinflict the holes, the stigmata, the deadly wounds of His Passion as signs of irredeemability.

Marked by God

In what follows, I concentrate on the stains, stigmata, and inscriptions on the body, reading "Saint Julian the Hospitalier" as a story of inscription—of writing—in an attempt to reveal the patristic underpinning of Shoshana Felman's psychoanalytic interpretation.[33]

Julian's parents consider their child, the offspring of an immaculate conception, marked by God. But their sweet little Jesus soon sets out to produce marks of an altogether unholy kind, stains of blood and murder. His first sacrificial victim is an innocent white church mouse, whose blood is smeared on the church floor: "A drop of blood stained the flagstones" (45). His most fateful re-signifying, his literal re-marking occurs at the climax of the first major hunting scene. Instead of naming and thereby creating things, as Adam did, Julian annihilates everything; instead of preserving life, as Noah did, he hunts it down. In accordance with his configuration as Nimrod, Julian negates Adam's founding act and Noah's act of preservation. From this point on, Julian re-marks the holy wounds of the martyrs, who were executed in Roman arenas because of their beliefs:

Then he advanced through an avenue of great trees, whose lofty tops formed a kind of triumphal arch at the entrance to a forest. . . . An extraordinary sight brought him up short. Some stags filled a valley shaped like an amphitheater; and, huddling close together, they warmed each other with their breath, which rose steaming in the haze. . . . [T]he sky was red as a pool of blood. Julian leaned against a tree. He gazed wide-eyed at the enormity of the massacre, without understanding how he could have done it. (50–51)

The triumphal arch and the circus point to Rome; the description draws on the massacre of Christians in Rome as depicted by Michelet in his *Histoire romaine*.[34] This hunting scene is, like that in Hugo, outside of space and time: "He was out hunting, he knew not where, nor for how long" (50). Julian, the hunter in defiance of God, exterminates the animals Adam named on the first day of Creation. As in Noah's case, the animals present themselves to him in all their abundance of species, but instead of saving them, he kills them all. The arch also alludes to the Church, where all nations live together peacefully. Here, however, bestial cruelty reigns. Flaubert leaves no doubt as to the cosmic dimensions of this bloodbath: "the sky was red as a pool of blood." Julian finally kills the stag, the figure of patriarchs and judges, but above all the figure of Christ as the endpoint and full actualization of the precursors of the City of God. Through this murder, Julian re-inscribes the stigmata of all stigmata, namely, the wounds of the Passion. The finale of the hunting orgy puts both the Old and the New Testaments under erasure, since Julian wipes out Christ's figurations as well as Christ himself.

The deer is no "blank slate" for Flaubert. Already in *A Sentimental Education*, we encounter Saint Hubert's stag with the cross between its antlers in the forest of Fontainebleau. Victor Hugo is the direct source of Flaubert's stag—"which was black and of monstrous size, carried sixteen antlers, and had a white tuft of beard"—in "Saint Julian the Hospitalier" (51); compare Hugo's "colossal black outline of a huge sixteen-horned stag," later called a "monstrous stag."[35] The Hugoesque intertext underscores the Christological nature of the animal. In Hugo's legend, the satanic hunt that keeps Pécopin from making love to the beautiful Baldour ends with a black mass in Nimrod's castle, where all the hunters of the world are united in a sinister perversion of the communion of love to form a covenant of hate and ruin instead. The stag is consumed as a figure of Christ.

Another important source for Flaubert is Alfred Maury's *Essai sur les légendes pieuses du moyen âge*, where the symbolic force of the Christologically overdetermined stag is unfolded. The stag, as Maury tells us, while also referring to Saint Julian in this regard, is mistaken for the unicorn, and hence interpreted as a symbol of Christ. The stag is also seen as the animal bearing the cross, the instrument of the Passion, on its forehead: "The first Christians imagined they saw the mark of *thau*, the sign of the cross, on the forehead of the deer."[36] However, the deer is also an image of the soul thirsting after God in the way a deer thirsts after a waterhole: "As the heart panteth after the water brooks, so panteth my soul after thee, O God" (Ps. 42:1–2).[37] By contrast, Julian only thirsts for blood and murder, as the text literally tells us.

The legend of Saint Hubert is a variation on the conversion of Paul. What the deer says to Hubert is what the Lord said to Paul: "Saul, Saul, why do you persecute me?" Subsequently, in what has been interpreted as an invisible stigmatization, the Lord inscribes the cross on Saul's brow, transforming him into Paul. Since it bears the cross between its antlers, the deer, which is often linked to Paul in iconography, "makes the stigma on his forehead more visible."[38] Julian overwrites and reinscribes this cross: "Julian shot his last arrow at him. It struck him in the forehead, and stayed embedded there" (51). He thus refashions the redeeming sign of love into a mark of hate. Julian's failed conversion, his irrecoverable accursedness is thereby drastically underlined. Paradoxically, however, this crossing out of the cross is the condition for Julian's holiness. The deer curses him: "Cursed! Cursed! Cursed! One day, savage heart, you will murder your father and your mother!" (ibid.).

The second part fulfills the *figura* of the first part. Again, in a reversal of the hermeneutic figure of patristic tradition, what was prefigured and is subsequently fulfilled is not the promise of salvation but a curse that reverses and undoes redemption. From the start, Julian takes part in a war of cosmic proportion. In this socially accepted war with its suggestion of the crusades, he wins a wife and riches and becomes the son-in-law of an emperor. The universal scope of the novella, which unites the Occident and the Orient, becomes clear in that Julian first lives in a Christian castle in Europe, after which he moves to a Moorish castle in the East. Through marriage, Julian experiences the power of lust. The seductive power of the sultan's daughter, which, incidentally, is modeled on Christ's temptation in the desert, is subtly highlighted. At this stage, Julian is like his father only, *à l'orientale*: "Julian no longer waged war. He took his ease, surrounded by a peaceful people; and every day a throng passed before him, genuflecting and handkissing in the oriental manner. Clothed in purple" (56). Unlike his father, however, Julian is not able to satisfy his thirst for blood within socially sanctioned boundaries. He continues to dream of the hunt. The missing signifiers "Adam" and "Noah," which were merely alluded to in the first part of the narrative, now materialize: "Sometimes in a dream he would see himself like our forefather Adam in the midst of Paradise, among all the animals: stretching out his arm, he would put them to death; or else, they would file past, two by two, in order of size, from elephants and lions down to stoats and ducks, as on the day when they went into Noah's ark" (56). Julian is accentuated as the antitype who destroys. As the new Nimrod, Julian brings not life, but death, not salvation, but damnation.

The second great hunt takes place under the sign of temptation. However, rendered incapable of killing through the intervention of higher powers, Julian cannot give in to this temptation. The hunt leads to a place of doom and destruction, a Golgotha of fallen crosses and ruins: "Flat stones were scattered among ruined vaults. He stumbled over the bones of the dead; here and there worm-eaten crosses leaned over piteously" (59–60). This place evokes, *ex negativo*, paradise. The scorn with which the animals greet him and the plans of revenge they seem to harbor—"A mocking irony was evident in their stealthy movements. . . . They seemed to be contemplating some plan of revenge" (61)—evoke, in a distorted manner, the paradisiacal harmony of the animals that gather around peacefully. What is significant, iconographically speaking, is that *after* the Passion of Christ, Julian does not walk in a garden redeemed through the Passion, but rather in a wholly unredeemed, desolate, barren garden where men and animals tear each other apart. The cross is precisely the sign of the triumph over death, which should transform the Calvary, the place of suffering as depicted in countless medieval paintings, into the Garden of Life. Julian, however, wanders through a landscape where death and decay triumph uncontested, while the collapsed and moss-grown cross has itself become a sign of unredeemed *vanitas*. The landscape Julian traverses is a reversal of the Garden of Life restored by the Passion.

Julian's unsatisfied bloodlust will drive him to murder his parents. This murder will, quite literally, stain Christ on the cross anew with blood. The two consequences of original sin are acted out through the convergence of the lust for murder and the lust for sex. Both bring forth death. Julian stabs his parents in his marital bed, believing that he has caught his wife defiling it through adultery with another man. Fuming with rage, he kills his parents rather than making love to his wife. The act of stabbing and the sexual act are associated; the dagger Julian uses to stab his mother is a metaphor for the male sexual organ. Christ and his parents suffer maculation through this act in the same way that Julian is already stained: it was the description of Julian's skin, the description of his birthmark, that convinced his wife that her two guests were indeed his parents, "they proved that it was so by describing distinguishing marks on his skin" (58).[39] And just as Julian's skin is already marked from the outset, his parents will now receive the maculating stain of his murderous act.

Splashes and stains of blood showed starkly against the whiteness of their skin, on the sheets, on the floor, down an ivory crucifix hanging in the alcove. The crimson reflection from the stained-glass window, just then catching the sun, lit up those red patches and scattered others still more plentifully about the room. (62–63)

The stain of original sin is retrospectively inscribed into his mother's immaculate conception in the blood that oozes through the mattress on the floor: "Drops oozing from the mattress fell one by one upon the floor" (63). After the murder, at their funeral, Julian positions himself as he did on the cadaver of the buck, "prostrated in the middle of the doorway" (64), while the outstretched arms of his dream (56) have become "les bras en croix" (*Trois contes*, 150).

The murder scenes of the first part of the story are fulfilled in the second. The murder of the family of deer prefigures the murder of his parents. Julian himself was then the spotted fawn, "the dappled fawn clung to her teat" (51). His father's death rattle blends into that of the deer: "At first hesitant, this long-drawn-out cry of pain came ever nearer, swelled, became cruel; and terror-struck he recognized the belling of the great black stag" (62). There could be no better illustration of the Augustinian idea that murder and sex are the consequences of original sin than this super-imposition and eventual interchangeability of the hunt, murder, and sex. All three are directed against God; all three inflict lethal wounds on God.[40]

In the third part, Julian, now the marked man, becomes the *homo sacer* by virtue of his divestiture. Nothing in him is as it was before; even his voice has changed. He leaves behind his possessions and his wife to atone for his transgression, which was not really his. He committed the crime while being "out of his mind," so to speak. This means that he did not commit the most unimaginable crime of his own will, but of the will of God: "He did not rebel against God who had inflicted such a deed upon him, and yet he was in despair at the fact that he had been able to do it" (65). The stainer has become the stained who is expelled from the commu-nity of fellow human beings. However, Julian does not become a new man: there is no *conversio*. What is missing—as Sartre has pointed out—are the three cardinal Christian virtues of faith, hope, and love, of which there is no trace in Julian. Instead, he succumbs to the utter desperation of *ace-dia*, which is a deadly sin. His despair runs so deep that he considers the sin of all sins, suicide, after all his attempts to die in the service of others have been shattered: "His own body filled him with such revulsion that, in the hope of winning freedom from it, he exposed himself to the greatest dangers. He saved the palsied from fires, children from deep chasms. The abyss cast him back, the flames spared him" (65).[41] This perversion of the hagiographical pattern does not have to be made explicit, since the norms of a saint's life are specific to the genre: although a saint should be willing to sacrifice his own life for the sake of the other, he cannot make the de-struction of his own life the motive of his actions.

Julian sees himself as stigmatized, marked, cast out, and fallen—in short, he acknowledges himself as the embodiment of the fallen human condition. This entails that he is no longer at home in the world. His being in the world has become a being in exile. Neither man nor beast, not even death, is willing to touch him—he is like Oedipus at Colonus and also like Cain, who is marked by God as a murderer. Julian is forever alone with his endlessly repeating murder. If higher powers were fundamental to this act, God has now completely receded from his life. The whole of nature is transformed into a spectacle, displaying, not the greatness of God, but the horror of his parenticide, his deicide—in short, the horror of his hunt, his Nimrodian essence. "But the wind brought to his ears moans like a death rattle; dewdrops pattering to the ground reminded him of other drops falling so much more heavily. Every evening the sun streaked the clouds with blood; and every night, in his dreams the murder of his parents began all over again" (65). The bloodstained cadavers of his parents, the maculated body of the Lord on the cross block out the sight of the "splendour of the tabernacles" (ibid.), the transfigured, redemptive body of Christ: "But his thoughts were relentless, dimming the splendour of the tabernacles" (ibid.). Unlike the saint in the precursory legends who founds and builds in and for the community, Flaubert's Julian is thrust out of the community of the living and the sacred bond of marriage.

In Flaubert, this community appears under the sign of radical irredeemability, which may well be *the* topos, *the* hermeneutical locus of all realist literature. In *Effi Briest*, Theodor Fontane depicted the society of his time as governed by the Old Testament, which is not informed by the spirit of love but by the deadly letter of the law. Flaubert inscribes the Church within this context of irredeemability. Church bells do not call the community to the love of God: religious celebrations merely give those in power an opportunity to flaunt their domination. For the people, the event merely serves as a conduit for indulging their carnal lust. It does not foster *caritas*, but rather promotes the *libido dominandi* and the *superbia* of the rulers, while fueling the *concupiscentia* of the people (38). Flaubert spells out the results arising from all this beer and dancing: the children bouncing on the knees of their grandparents only *appear* idyllic. The text consistently depicts the "air bestial" (*Trois contes*, 152) of the common people: "But the brutish faces, the din of the different trades, the heedless chatter, chilled his heart" (64).[42] The people's radical lack of hospitality, of *caritas*, is particularly poignant in their treatment of Julian. Under blasphemous curses they chase him away and leave him with—in a mockery of charity—their garbage and rags. They threaten and throw stones precisely at the one who embodies the human condition and who bears it as his cross. The murderer of animals has become an animal lover with Franciscan overtones: "he would gaze with pangs of love at foals in the meadows, birds in their nests, insects on the flowers; all, as he drew near, would run away, hide in terror, quickly fly off" (65).

The lust for the hunt is converted to the asceticism of a hermit. He devotes his life in complete isolation to the service of others. Yet he remains ostracized from any form of human communality. Julian, alone from beginning to end, becomes a pariah cast out by all, accepting his suffering in the midst of an inhuman wasteland of mud. He becomes consubstantial with the stinking decay around him, with this place where nothing grows and prospers and which recalls Ovid's desperately absurd description of his exile in Tomis.

Inverted Conversion

At the end of "Saint Julian the Hospitalier," the leper arrives at Julian's. His three calls identify him as Christ: three times the child Christ has to call out to Saint Christopher to get ferried across the river. Burdened with the sins of the world, the child becomes heavy just like the leper does in Flaubert's story. His voice—"and the voice rang out like a church bell" (67)—also points to Christ, since it refers to the deer, the *figura Christi*, who was murdered while a bell was ringing in the distance. His body is marked, just like Julian's; the leper with his skin covered with stains is a stigmatized outcast, a body rotting while alive, a living skeleton. Leprosy was read as an allegorical disease, as a mark of God, of Cain. It was regarded as a stigmatization, as a reinscription of what had been washed away by the blood of Christ. The leper's *maculae* are contagious. They mark everything he gets into contact with: "the table, the bowl, and the knife handle bore the same spots as were to be seen on his body" (68).

Julian is hospitable to the point of absolute self-renunciation: risking his own life in the terrible storm, he transports the leper to the other side of the river. He offers him the last of his food, keeps him warm in his bed, comforts him with his body. Julian incarnates the virtue of hospitality, which is a mark of *caritas*, to the extreme of utter self-sacrifice. He exposes himself completely to the leper.[43] The leper works miracles; like Christ at the wedding at Cana, he turns water into wine. The wedding prefigures the union of love between Julian and the leper. Instead of erotic temptation, hinted at in the serpent of paradise—"colder than a snake" (69)—we have pure, selfless *caritas*. The bed in which the leper and the outcast lie is a reversal of the bed that was stained by desire and thus also by murder and blood. As naked as on the day he was born—he will be reborn, radiantly unblemished—Julian lies down, mouth to mouth, face to face with the one who bears the marks of God's repudiation in his leprosy. He takes the leper, both stainer and stained, in his care; they even become one flesh. And Julian, who ushers in death through the contact with these contagious blemishes, finds eternal life in this loving embrace. The stains turn into rays of light, the stench becomes a sweet scent, the rotting flesh is transfigured into an astral body. Julian, an exile on earth, departs in the arms of the leper for his true fatherland.

Julian, as the one who is maculated and who maculates others, is also the one who renders the marks of original sin—the stains of murder and sex, in short, all the hallmarks of the Fall—drastically visible in the world. He not only inscribes himself within the economy of these marks but he makes them his own, that is to say, he transforms his entire being into these marks. His immaculate conception through his milk-white mother is retroactively maculated by the blood seeping from the mattress. Julian's maculations, his murders, occur in a space where the City of God and City of Man are seemingly united through piety and redemption. The white mouse is killed in a church. The animals are slaughtered in Noah's ark, *figura ecclesiae*. The Church, built from the blood of the martyrs, is evoked in the massacres in the Roman circus. The leaded-glass window transforms the bedroom into a church-like space. The Church, as it appears here, becomes the counterimage of the ecclesiastical self-image. This becomes particularly striking when taking into account the central place that the motif of the stained-glass window occupies in the narrative: in the rays of the colored church windows the divine truth of Creation enlightens everything with its beauty. The contemplation of the church window amounts to an immersive *contemplatio divinae*. However, the windows in "A Simple Heart" are a medium for the misrecognition of God: via the image of the Annunciation on the church window, it dawns on Félicité that God must have sent, not a dove, but a parrot. The stained-glass window initially darkens the bedroom in such a way that Julian cannot recognize anything and murders his parents. The stained-glass window then becomes a medium, not of God's Glory, but of the annihilation of God. Not the beauty of Creation, but the blood of parenticide and deicide is horrifyingly multiplied through its ray.[44] "The crimson reflection from the stained-glass window, just then catching the sun, lit up those red patches and scattered others still more plentifully about the room" (63).

Julian converts the marks of redemption—the stigmata—that wash away the stains of original sin into the stigmata of damnation. He commits the most inconceivable of all sins, the murder of God. However, his becoming *maculator* and maculated is necessary to bring out the fallen condition of the world and therefore to put an end to the deadly deception of immaculacy. According to Flaubert, the world *tout court*, but above all the middle-class world of the nineteenth century, is caught up in this disastrous self-deception. In Flaubert's radicalized Augustinian, Pascalian view, the world is not redeemed. The realization of the City of God in the here and now is but a fateful illusion. Julian is marked out by God to expose the unredeemed horror of all Creation, to revert the stigmata of grace back to the stigmata of original sin. He turns himself into a leper, an outcast bearing the stamp of death, exiled from all forms of community. But in the end, this maculation is transformed into a sign of grace.

This brings us to the crux of all interpretations, namely, Julian's ascension in the arms of Jesus. First it should be noted that Flaubert's Nimrod, that is, Julian—as opposed to Hugo's—does not end up as the vanquished enemy. He is saved as an instrument of God—he alone becomes in perfect *imitatio* similar to Christ. Indeed, he is the only one who undertakes a true *imitatio* in the spirit of *caritas*. Everybody else, the whole of Creation, is irrevocably condemned. It seems that only Satan will be redeemed. Julian seems to be born again, not out of the lust of the flesh, but out of the love of the heart in the spirit of *caritas*. In this transfiguration, he seems to overcome sin and death in a very happy, beatific ending indeed. It is nevertheless at this very moment that the act of writing itself, of scripture, comes to the fore. Writing comes *à l'antique*, in the garments of antiquity. What is at stake is a truly disastrous translation of antiquity into Christianity that we are already familiar with from "A Simple Heart," and that we shall find later in "Hérodias." The literal black and white of writing is already evoked by the black and white of the passage across the river: "All lay in deep darkness, rent here and there by the white caps of the tossing waves" (67). Later, the water turns blacker than ink: "the water, blacker than ink, raged" (68). The ancient moment is inscribed in the Savior, when, with royal dignity, he stands motionless on the boat, as "immobile as a pillar" (ibid.). However, the ancient substratum is the clearest in the image of the file. The skin of the leper is "colder than a snake and rough as a file" (69). The file is the instrument of every *ars poetica*, which works upon and polishes the coarseness of the outer layer in order to reveal the inner beauty of language, the way the rough human integument is sloughed off, like the skin of a snake, to release the astral body.

Flaubert transposes ancient myth and the central plot of the Old Testament, as retold by Augustine, into the simple form of the legend. While the ancient myths are distorted with respect to their content, the message of the Bible is reversed. Julian is an anti-Adam, an anti-Noah, who slaughters instead of creating life through name-giving and kills instead of preserving life. At the heart of the matter is the crossing out of the redemptive wounds of the Cross. Through Julian—the *figura Christi* who paradoxically also bears the mark of Cain—the wounds are turned into marks of original sin. Only thus can the Babylonian, unredeemed state of Creation be revealed. Marked out to kill both Christ's precursors as well as Christ himself in a satanic act, Julian ultimately goes so far in his love as to sacrifice himself to the leper and to become one flesh with him. He thus becomes like all saints, to quote Jacobus de Voragine, the Temple of God. At this very moment, within a Christian horizon, Julian's transfiguration should happen. A saint's ecstasy in death is usually described through erotic metaphors. At the moment of rapture in everlasting life, the earthly-carnal sense of these figures is overturned into their anagogical-spiritual, original sense. They refer to the transfigured body, and with that to their original, their proper sense:

Then the leper embraced him; and his eyes suddenly shone as bright as stars; his hair streamed out like the rays of the sun; the breath from his nostrils as sweet as roses; a cloud of incense rose from the hearth, the waters sang. Meanwhile delights in abundance, a superhuman joy came flooding into the soul of Julian, who lay in a swoon; and the one whose arms still clasped him tight were larger, larger, until his head and his feet touched the walls of the hut. The roof flew off, the firmament unfolded—and Julian rose up into the blue of space, face to face with Our Lord Jesus, who bore him off to heaven. (69–70)

However, are we dealing here with transfiguration? The most obvious intertext for this scene of a conversion of decomposing flesh into heavenly rays is yet again Hugo's leper, whose festering torments are the seeds of infinite splendor, whose leprous wounds shine forth, his sores becoming the stars that reveal the truth to everyone:

I throw my torture into the radiant sky,
My night, my thirst, my fever and my raggy bones,

And the pus of my wounds and the tears of my eyes,
I sow infinite splendors into the furrow,
So that the Good, Virtue, and Harmony may come out of my sufferings!
Leprosy, spread out over life and creation,
Over men and children, and become a ray of light!
Open up, abscesses, and sow stars on my brothers, benighted by veils![45]

Hugo stages the Pauline dynamic of the conversion on the road to Damascus, where, having gone through the depths of despair, the highest epiphany is attained. With characteristic concision, Hugo formulates conversion as "a transfiguring fall [*une chute transfiguration*]," and thereby renders it as the epitome of the sublime. The Christian God is superior to the pagan god: whereas the pagan god only illuminates through lightning bolts, the true God enlightens to an absolute inner clarity in a sudden epiphany. Everything is transfigured.[46]

Julian's ascension, though, is not so much a transfiguration as a metamorphosis: a sudden change in bodily form, limited to the purely sensuous and cut off from the spiritual dimension of any final insight into the truth.[47] It is no coincidence that this ascension takes the form of an allegory of the five senses: sight, hearing, smell, taste, and touch are invoked. Like the ancient gods, the leper becomes a constellation of stars in the firmament (70). In this ancient, pagan apotheosis wholly situated on the sensuous level, there is no need of *noli me tangere*. The purely physical moment of change is grounded in a radical desublimation. Flaubert turns the figurality of the transfiguration upside down: the union in love of Julian and Christ, in which Julian, according to the female role of the soul, acts the female part, is not sublimated but sexualized instead. The almost factual nature of this enlargement, further emphasized through the repetition of getting "larger, larger" (70),[48] conjures up the image of a gigantic erection. In this case, what grows is not the spiritual—"the awakening of a spirit by the interruption of light," to cite Hugo's rendering of Saul's experience on the road to Damascus[49]—but sexuality. The power of love reveals itself as an exclusively sexual force; the ascension can therefore be read as a moment of orgiastic, phallic pleasure.

The typical erotic metaphors in which spiritual ecstasy is described as a swoon (*pamoison*) and flood (*inondation*) are sexualized in terms of orgasm and ejaculation. Flaubert's description of the ascension is posited as a comforting fairy tale, as pure fiction; it is a fictitious self-empowerment, a phallic hallucination. The promise of the resurrection thus becomes legible as a phallic remnant from classical antiquity that is as illusionary as it is idolatrous. The Pauline conversion of the spirit is written back into a metamorphosis of bodies, divested of all sublimity. In this respect, the ascension prefigures the phallic moment of the scriptural riddle, "He must increase, but I must decrease" (John 3:30), while pointing back to the overwhelming (*gigantesque*) phallic parrot in Félicité's ecstasy. The sexual moment of this homosexual love scene is highlighted by a word that simultaneously alludes to the art of polishing a text and to the sexual act: *limer* (to file). The fact that homosexual love, associated with classical antiquity, is seen as a satanic practice by Christianity makes it all the more fitting.[50] The blasphemous moment of the homosexual ascension in the arms of the Savior is further highlighted by a direct citation, "Notre Seigneur Jésus [Our Lord Jesus]," which Flaubert took from the heading of Lemaître de Sacy's Bible translation, *Le Nouveau testament de Notre Seigneur Jésus-Christ*. To this, Flaubert opposes his own New Testament, "in my part of the world" (70).

With the words *face à face*, Paul's "face to face" encounter is invoked, which is a metaphor for knowing to the full: "For now we see through a glass, darkly; but then face to face: now I know in part; but then shall I know even as also I am known. And now abideth faith, hope, love, these three; but the greatest of these is love" (1 Cor. 13:12–13). Nevertheless, this knowledge of God does not have the same sense in Flaubert as it has in Genesis: as a metaphor for the act of love, knowing—as a pivotal event in the *conversio*—is sexualized. The New Testament is read back into the Old Testament and classical antiquity, thus reversing Paul's typological progression. Hugo's sublime figure, whose Pauline moment points humanity onto the right path of the "chute transfiguration," is turned into a "transfiguration chute."

The legend of Saint Julian is the testament of the successful self-creation of a poet, who, by taking up the cross of crossing out the Cross as the sign of redemption, demonstrates that the Christian hope of transfiguration is nothing but a fictitious, ancient remnant from classical antiquity, a metamorphosis. Hospitality thereby becomes a metaphor for intertextuality: like Saint Julian, Flaubert completely opens up to the other and, in a welcoming gesture, makes the texts of the tradition his own. Nevertheless, this Christian virtue par excellence of devotion leads to a complete distortion of Christian figures, starting with the typological order that is inverted—the

Old is not read in light of the New; rather, the New is read in light of the Old Testament—and the notion of *conversio*, which is turned into metamorphosis. With acidic irony, Flaubert thus also crosses out the texts of the Fathers. His first target is Hugo, the consecrated poet-priest.[51]

Poetologically, Flaubert's writing turns into a dead—one is tempted to say deadening—letter at the moment when he recounts the event that should give rise to a jubilantly living spirit: the ascension. While the ascension is shown as a metamorphosis, as an exclusively sensuous change of form, all spirituality is killed through literalization. Language, deader than dead, comes as cliché. If Flaubert's language kills off what is to have everlasting life, then it animates what is condemned to death: Julian's hunt is portrayed with striking vivacity, but equally vivid is his truly loving hospitable devotion, from which every hope for transfiguration is barred.

In his overturning of the history of redemption through his act of rewriting, Flaubert clears a space for literature against the Church, which he sees as a part of the ruinous City of Man. This oeuvre, erected against the Church and in this case more specifically a work composed from the material of Rouen Cathedral and directed against the message of this cathedral "in my part of the world," is not of a material nature. It is neither a church building nor the foundation of a city, which often originated from a hospital or asylum. Being grounded in *caritas*, it is built against the empires of this world. With the metaphor of the hospitable body, Flaubert seems to refer to the Pauline metaphor of the living body of the Church composed of the limbs of the believers.

Just as Flaubert's text stands out against the temple in the sense Peter gave it, it also opposes the Pauline doctrine.[52] Through literalization, this literature destroys every trace of the living spirit and thus reverses the key principle of Pauline hermeneutics stating that it is the letter that kills and the spirit that animates. In Flaubert's so patiently crafted and cryptic texts, which, just like some churches, are built from the spoils of tradition, composed of classical and Christian stones alike, the edifying message of Christianity is razed to the ground. Pauline hermeneutics is inverted.

Antiquity is neither subsumed nor transcended by Christianity; rather, Christianity remains overshadowed. In a vertiginous reversal of the Pauline dynamic of kenosis, the promise of resurrection is the catastrophe. At first, it may appear as if the revocation of the glad tidings of the redemption was necessary for the heralding of an even happier message, namely that Nimrod, a satanic figure and enemy of God, has now come to incarnate love itself, and has thus not been defeated, but redeemed. But since Satan now resembles Christ, the Ascension of Christ can be deciphered as the phallic, idolatrous illusion of homosexual, so-called "ancient love." Only a radical re-marking of the history of redemption, which would ruin the phallic illusion of the resurrection, can open up a new space for literature, as a space of an endless and faithful *imitatio Christi* maintained to the bitter end: Gustave l'Hospitalier.

The story Flaubert tells us follows, "more or less," rather, less than more, the life of Saint Julian as depicted on the window in Rouen Cathedral. The radical difference that is instilled into it is also a difference of medium. His differing from the story on the stained glass is not of a visible order. It is anything but transparent, and must be deciphered: it thus hinges upon the difference that writing engenders.

"HÉRODIAS"

[Flaubert's] style, which immobilizes everything, is our literature's most singular petrifying fountain.

Jean Prévost, "Aspects du roman moderne"

Christianity is the formula for exceeding *and* summing up the subterranean cults of all varieties, that of Osiris, that of the Great Mother, that of Mithras, for instance: in his discernment of this fact the genius of Paul showed itself.

Friedrich Nietzsche, *The Anti-Christ*

Iaokanann, or the Birth of the Roman Church out of the Demon Babel

"Hérodias," the last of Flaubert's *Three Tales*, was generally regarded when it appeared as too dark and incomprehensible. Its reception thus contrasted sharply with that of the other two tales, which were deemed accessible and readable. This impression, still widely shared today, is deceptive. For while "Hérodias" may seem somewhat unreadable, one is blindly trapped in an illusion of readability when it comes to the other two tales. *Three Tales* is a trilogy about readability, telling a story that, as it moves toward modernity, is characterized by a growing infatuation with the delusion of an apparent comprehensibility. The blindness is due to the repression of a crucial primal scene of Christianity, which Flaubert reads against the grain of tradition. From Flaubert's perspective, Christianity requires a repressed past in proclaiming its Gospel. He reverses the historical order by beginning with the deluded darkness of modernity, its failure to understand, in favor of a misleading readability, the constitutive unreadability. And he ends with what he identifies as the primal event at the bottom of this unreadability, uncannily transmitted in the story of "Hérodias." Flaubert routinely rejects the idea that "enlightened" modernity attains the light of understanding. Instead, he turns back, in an "archeological" undertaking—a metaphor coined by Rousseau and Freud, recently refashioned by Foucault—to the story that contains the prehistory of the Christian disaster of history.

Formally, "A Simple Heart" and "Saint Julian the Hospitalier" reverse the simple form of the saintly life. "Hérodias," on the other hand, is a rewriting of the Gospel itself that deals with the message of Christianity in the complex form of a classical tragedy. The unities of place and time are strictly applied: The story of John the Baptist's beheading in the fortress of the Tetrarch Herod lasts exactly twenty-four hours, from sunrise to sunrise.[1] Indeed, "Hérodias" is a story about the sun/son. Its dramatic character is intensified by a massive employment of direct speech. At the obscure moment of the birth of Christianity, history itself is brought to light in this third tale. John, the first, proto-Christian martyr, testifies to Jesus being the Messiah. Why is the birth of Christianity conceived of as tragedy and dressed in a garb commonly considered to have been *overcome* by Christianity? Such is the riddle posed in the story of "Hérodias." Flaubert turns the Good News of the Gospel into the bad news of an anti-Gospel.[2] Earthly history is nothing other than the perversion of the Gospel; it does nothing but recall the promise of salvation by inadvertently inverting it. The Christian events of salvation eternally determine everything we call history for all time. The Word, which was in the beginning and from which all life proceeds in the Gospel of John, is inverted by Flaubert into a word that ossifies everything. In its hermetic, monumental grandeur, "Hérodias" is a finally genuine New Testament that bears witness against the preaching of the Gospel. Its capacity as a *testa-mentum* is emphasized in the head (*tête*, *teste*) of this first martyr, borne by his disciples out of the fortress toward Jerusalem. The fortress's vertical line is crossed by the horizontal; its form is a cross. Thus, John's head does not, in fact, confirm Jesus as Messiah, it just "shows" the way to the cross. In this respect, the Baptist is Christ's predecessor in the true sense of the word. The capital division of history to which the decapitation of the Baptist is supposed to be the prelude has not happened. No break has taken place. Christ does not mark a turning point, with a before and an after. Everything stays the same in getting worse and worse. Flaubert's tale is a testament to the truth of a suffering that worldly politics can be relied upon to produce again and again. The ultimate figure of this suffering, it should be kept in mind, is the Cross. Hérodias, whose name stands at the head of the novella as its title (as the titulus crucis "INRI" on the head of the cross), is in such a surprising, dominant position because it is of her, not of the Virgin Mary, that the supposedly new—but in fact old as ever—era is born.

The deceptiveness of the Gospel is reflected in the polished surface of Hérodias's story. Born at Pentecost, along with the all-encompassing Church, the Gospel promises the overcoming of death and the resurrection of the flesh through a love stronger than death, in an other-worldly realm in which all will be united in a spiritual covenant of love. The promise has not been fulfilled; it remains nothing but an illusion, against the grain of which Flaubert interprets the birth of the Church in its historical pagan and Jewish context. Alternative testimonies are mobilized and seamlessly worked together into one compact narrative, containing the Jew Flavius Josephus as well as the Roman Suetonius, along with their reprocessing by Flaubert's contemporaries, most prominently by Renan. Flaubert's story is state-of-the-art, representing the contemporary avant garde of historical research on the sources of the New Testament. Taking into account the historical value of that Testament and thereby reducing its redemptive scope, "Hérodias" counters the New Testament, showing it up as the flagrant globalization of an unredeemable Babylonian disaster of older origin: world history is nothing other than the ongoing defeat of the Christian promise.

The word most frequently used in connection with "Hérodias" is "obscurity." The long procession of those who have lamented its unreadability begins in Flaubert's time with Hippolyte Taine, Aglaé Sabatier,[3] and Sainte-Beuve and includes, most recently, Gérard Genette.[4] The strong impression of incomprehensibility shared by every reader is even stranger considering that Flaubert tells a well-known story from the Bible. The intrigue of the decapitation of the Baptist deals with power, murder, sex, and has obvious political implications: Hérodias wants to maintain a kingdom won by the power of sex, breaking Jewish marriage laws. She wants to solidify her rule precisely through the power of her sex.[5] The Evangelists Matthew and Mark agree with the historian Flavius Josephus in this interpretation, which Flaubert incorporates in accordance with the research of his time, which he extensively studied. It is no minor side issue that his handling of the available data shows him to be a great historian, which was, one has to realize, part of his ambition—this undercurrent in his earlier work surfaces in "Hérodias."

For Flaubert, what happened runs roughly as follows: Hérodias, whose marriage to Herod was publicly cursed by John the Baptist as incestuous and adulterous,[6] persuades her husband—possibly against his intention—to eliminate this dangerous political opponent for her. Herod therefore "laid hold on John, and bound him, and put him in prison for Herodias's sake, his brother Philip's wife. For John said unto him, It is not lawful for thee to have her" (Matt. 14:3–4). According to Matthew, Herod does not dare to have the Baptist killed because the people consider him a prophet and Herod fears their wrath. According to Mark, Herod fears and protects John because he knows he is "a righteous and holy man" (Mark 6:20). Flaubert follows the general tendency of Mark, which underscores the antagonism between Hérodias and Herod, saying that she attempted to kill the Baptist in his dungeon with snakes. In both Gospels, however, Hérodias gets what she wants: the head of John, who threatened her rule by seeking to get her husband to repudiate her. With a woman's weaponry, she instrumentalizes Herod, aware of his erotic excitability. As a means to this end, she deploys Salome, her daughter from her first marriage to Herod's brother. Excited beyond all measure by Salome's dance during the festival celebrating his birthday, Herod promises her anything she wants. Obedient to her mother—we know the scene, which captured the imagination of the nineteenth century—she asks for John's head on a platter (a detail emphasized by Mark). Bound by his promise, but with grim premonitions of the consequences for Hérodias's hopes, Herod gives Salome the head on the notorious platter, vividly testifying to the depravity of the pagan banquet, a perverse precursor of the Last Supper, the ritual installation of the Eucharist.

The emblematic event represents an error in reading on Salome's part.[7] She takes the desire of her mother all too literally and does not grasp the rhetorical figure—the head as a metonym of execution. In Flaubert's rendition, Salome's dance indicates exactly what is at stake. Flaubert models his version of her dance on the dance of the Egyptian courtesan Azizeh, which he recalls in great detail in his *Voyage en Égypte*. In his words, Azizeh "dances" a decapitation: her dance evokes a "frightening effect of decapitation [*effet de décapitement effrayant*]."[8] The platter, whose astounding art-historical career did not just debut in the art of the fin de siècle, is a literary feature rare within the Gospels; it has always fascinated as an uncanny kind of "reality effect," which shows how much more than reality is at stake in such detail. Mark and Matthew do not recount any popular intrigue from the horror show of Roman imperial politics; the platter preserves a pre-Christian scenery, in which the salvific thrust of the Eucharist originates from its perversely prefiguring ground—a prefiguration equivalent, as Flaubert recognizes, to John's role as precursor to the Messiah and all political martyrs that succeeded Christ. To John, Jesus assigned the task of testifying to his messianic identity; John was the one who preceded him and blindly announced him. Salome's complementary blindness was able to open Herod's eyes for only a brief moment, which came too late to open his eyes for good.

It requires remarkable skills to alienate a story as well known as this one and render it incomprehensible. Flaubert's most obvious strategy is a shift in perspective: "Hérodias" places the birth of Christianity in an unfamiliar, purely Roman imperial context, which was utterly alien to the Evangelists. The obviousness of Rome's dominance emerges in all its implications from every word of the text. "Caesar" is the word with which Hérodias steps onto the stage; it is constantly on her lips. All conflicts are embedded in the Roman world, whose power interests, assumed to be known by the reader, are always implied. This defines Herod's title: those in Roman command of that region were "tetrarchs" until Constantine's reign. The power struggles that developed in conflict with Roman rule remain in the background of the Gospels, like the dependence of local powers and many other effects of Romanization. In Flaubert's text, Palestine, Galilee, Judea, and Samaria are represented as the Roman colonies they were. The disputes of Jewish sects and their shifting alliances with Rome, as well as the wars with the Arabs, take place in that colonial context.

This defamiliarization entails a de-automatized reading of the Christian tradition and its modes of interpreting. At its heart, Flaubert excavates a latent retraction of the proclaimed content of the Gospels. This radical re-historization does not serve the modern purposes of a demystification of the biblical sources, as intended by the research of his contemporaries. Flaubert reveals the historical truth of the Gospel in his own "testament" by elaborating its Roman context. The theme of "Hérodias" is the *translatio* of Roman antiquity and Judaism into Christianity, a translation that had been hidden until Flaubert brought it to the light of his day. The key to the transformation is named in the title; it is the Jewish but completely Romanized *mediatrix* Hérodias who is the link between the Jews and their Roman rulers.[9] The Roman-Jewish origin, the inextricable Roman influx, spoils the Good News from the beginning. For Flaubert, Rome and Jerusalem remain a Babylon, from which the Jewish Exodus did not escape. "Hérodias" tells of the birth of a Church that is born out of Babel and proves Babel to be its all-embracing "catholic" source in the very sense of the word. Aptly, Flaubert illustrates this true state of the Christian tradition in a Babylonian mode. His testament is not exoteric like the Gospel, but esoteric. This true story of Christianity's origin is an anti-Gospel already in its rhetorical frame. While Epiphany and Pentecost exemplify the global reliance on the evidence for those who are of good will, the intertextual complexity of Flaubert's text decomposes the exemplary thrust of the Good News in the light of the discarded ancient sources and their devastating counterevidence.

The Roman state of history is utterly Babylonian. This topos—of Augustinian origin—is illustrated.[10] The linguistic confusion of Babel marks the theme of "Hérodias," and a disturbed comprehension results. This novella appears hermetically sealed against hermeneutics. What is set vividly before our eyes is the lack of kerygma, the deadliness of letters upon which no spirit of love has ever breathed. Flaubert illustrates this stony state of the literal in the Babylonian fashion of multilingual confusion: his figures speak Latin, Hebrew, Syrian, Greek, Arabic, Gallic, Germanic—a Pentecostal scene without a Holy Ghost in sight. No one understands anyone or anything at all. Instead, everyone is led by blind prejudice and deaf self-interest. In arbitrary parataxis, everything becomes indifferent. Flaubert does not level out or soften the encounter of strange languages; with each step one stumbles over foreign words and names.[11] Even readers well versed in the intricate uses of Tacitus or Flavius Josephus find navigating through the tangle of changing names used for the same person hard to impossible: Caius and Caligula; Aulus and Vitellius; and at least three names for Herod himself, which are furthermore easily confused with those of his father and at the same time grandfather-in-law, Herod the Great. It is not as though there were no reason for the variation, but its *ratio* remains in the remote darkness of a plot as confused as its linguistic references. Confused and misled, we the readers take part in confused relationships, and the scent we follow leads again and again to scarce results. Thus, we do not learn before the last chapter that Jacob, the murdered captain of Tiberius's garrison, and a witness to the miracle-man Jesus of the same name are in fact the same person. Among these ornaments of unreadability, the name John sticks out, which is recorded in exotic Hebrew as Iaokanann, as if it were, like the name of Yahweh itself, unutterable. With the familiar Latin version of the Vulgate (which is, of course, historically much younger), Flaubert ignores transmission. The names, whose outlandish appearance extends to their typographic format, are hardly adequate to ascertain— they are in fact meant to disturb—the identities necessary for understanding the plotline. The disturbance thus represented presents us with the Babylonian state of a history rhetorically remastered to the false, deluded exemplarity of Christ's Church.

The primordial theme of "Hérodias" is thus interpretation itself and its breakdown. The figure of the translator stands prominently between Babel and the Pentecost. The translators' task is not easy; often enough, they simply give up. The interpreter of the emperor Aulus Vitellius hesitates to translate Aulus's blasphemous jokes about the Jewish religion, for example, and it evidently takes him some time to decide how to translate "messiah," a concept central to the Jewish conception of history, into Latin. What he finally does translate is no longer Jewish, but emphatically Roman: Flaubert condenses one of the crucial moments of the history to come in this translation scene: that of the Messiah becoming a political figure in the circuit of power and wealth, within which he is to liberate Israel from the political rule of Rome. But the translation does not simply go wrong, it betrays a deep division in Jewish thought, an unbridgeable difference of political concepts. For quite some time—since the Maccabees at least—the Messiah had become a political code word among the Jews, which is exploited both ways by Christ's precursor John the Baptist.[12]

The growing inability to understand is illustrated in this crucial question of the Messiah's kingdom to come. The Tetrarch Herod Antipas understands the proclamation of the Messiah to arrive through the genealogical lines of dynasties. A kingdom not of this world is unimaginable to him: "your kingdom will be eternal, Son of David!" says Flaubert's John (89).[13] Herod knows himself endangered by the House of David like his father, Herod the Great, who unleashed the murder of Bethlehem's children. Hérodias has an easy job depicting John as a political insurgent who threatens Roman rule. Understanding John's true mission would have required a Herod capable of surpassing the horizon of a politically complicated dynastic state of affairs and going against his political instincts.

In addition, considerable blanks in the narrative increase the darkness emerging in the story of "Hérodias" and obfuscate the familiar perspective of the Bible. It remains fragmented right up to the pensive mood of Herod. More often called by his surname Antipas in "Hérodias," he has the look of a king who suffers from Baudelairean spleen. Melancholy is the figure of shattered sense, of a senseless incoherence. The ruler's notorious melancholy points to the allegory of a history falling to pieces, which carries in its dispersed fragments only the memories of meaning. Antipas is the only character in the story who does not furiously pursue his goal-oriented power play but contemplates history for a quickly vanishing moment. Aside from this, everything in this story stays in a fractured limbo: figures are not explained, background information is not given, the complicated structure of intrigue between people whose social and religious identities are barely indicated remains puzzling. This is caused by Roman affairs that are never explained, but thoroughly implied, on the one hand, and these interfere, on the other hand, with equally unexplained conflicts—religious differences papered over in the biblical telling of the story—between Sadducees, Pharisees, and Essenes, on the Jewish side, not to speak of the Samaritans, who acquire a completely different, unfamiliar profile. Obviously, the relationship of Jesus and John must be also determined by these conflicts. The Gospel's harmonious resolution of the issue was to make John forerunner of Jesus. The answer John awaits to the question of whether Jesus is indeed the Messiah comes too late. John is not enlightened; not knowing what he does nor who he is, he remains trapped in the darkness of world history's Babylonian confusion—he may, however,

have a certain sense of that historical condition, beyond which his documented intention seems directed.[14]

The Roman-Jewish world of "Hérodias" is a world in which everyone talks past one another. The failure of the translator illustrates a general
impossibility of understanding as the universal condition that has emerged
with Babel. Between the sexes, between religions and races, hate and contempt hold sway. This speechlessness does not only extend to customs and
morals, but also to the understanding of representation, of what language
can do and what images are. The Tetrarch's hangman, who casts a curse on
Jerusalem, believes in the destructive power of words. The Tetrarch does
not share this perception. The Jews accuse the Romans of idolatry. The
only language that is universally practiced is the language of sex and violence. Language threatens, curses, wounds, incriminates, leads to killing.
Sexual understanding does not become fruitful in unification, but leads in
lovely regularity to murder and manslaughter.

Hermeneutics in the original sense of the word is the theme of "Hérodias." It is concerned with a pair of parallel-constructed riddles. The first
one turns around the relationship of John to Christ: Who is John? This
question contemplates the all-decisive identity of the Messiah: Is Christ the
awaited Messiah? The second riddle's concern is the identity of the beautiful Salome. Who is she? While the first puzzle is of a linguistic nature, the
second one is pictorial.

Who is Flaubert's Iaokanann? In the only dialogue deserving of the
name, the concern is with two biblical verses, including a kind of riddle
that forms the focal point of "Hérodias": "He must increase, but I must
decrease" (John 3:30).[15] If that verse's meaning must remain completely incomprehensible to Herod and his executioner, then even more so the second verse, a piece of "big news [*grande nouvelle*]" that is meant to clarify
the relationship of John to Jesus, but is left unstated in the text. As a matter
of fact, "Hérodias" is written around the omission of the "big news" that
will become the Gospel. The all-important missing sentence, the proof of
the identity of Jesus and thus of John, is the void center of the text. A lacuna is its basis. The "long hoped-for reply" (105) comes too late for John.
His head, saved from the remains of the meal, is too heavy to be carried
by one person alone. Those who carry it are the returning messengers John
had sent out to discover whether or not Jesus is the Messiah. Jesus lets the
glad tidings be known to John and unveils the Good News of his true iden-

tity. One of the two, the Essene Phanuel, is enraptured by this revelation.

Now when John had heard in prison the works of Christ, he sent two of his disciples, And said unto him, Art thou he that should come, or do we look for another? Jesus answered and said unto them, Go back and shew John again those things which ye hear and see: The blind receive their sight, and the lame walk, the lepers are cleansed, and the deaf hear, the dead are raised up, and the poor have the gospel preached to them. And blessed is *he* whosoever shall not be offended in me. (Matt. 11:2–6)

Renan's paraphrase went as follows:

"Art thou he that cometh? Or look we for another?" Jesus, who, from that time forth, had no longer any doubt with respect to his own position as the Messiah, enumerated to them the works which ought to characterize the coming of the kingdom of God—such as the healing of the sick, and the good tidings of speedy salvation preached to the poor.[16]

In *Madame Bovary*, Flaubert had refuted the Gospel of Matthew point by point. This world is a world where the poor remain poor and despised, the lame lame, the blind blind, and the dead dead. No kingdom of God is in sight. There, in the novel, the good news announced to the poor servant girl Catherine Leroux is a mocking curse; the operation on the lame Hippolyte leads to his becoming even more lame; and the blind beggar stays blind in spite of the pharmaceutical miracle hoped for. In "Hérodias," the missing sentence from Matthew triggers the single instance of understanding in the whole story. What is understood by Phanuel the Essene is the all-important confirmation of Christ as the Messiah. "Now the Essene understood these words: 'For him to increase, I must decrease'" (105). The reader of "Hérodias" will understand Phanuel's understanding only if he is able to supplement the missing piece of the text. He is only able to solve the riddle when he can fill the lacuna left by Flaubert, since the enlightening words from the Gospel are literally missing from the text.

That is a point of method. The structurally most significant intertexts of the story are Augustine's two homilies on John the Baptist. The Church, Augustine expounds, celebrates only two birthdays: those of John and Christ. Reading the sentence "He must increase; I must decrease," Augustine relates the birthdays of the two figures to the winter and summer solstices. But then he also relates the waning and waxing of the sun to their individual deaths: with his decapitation John shrinks like the sun that decreases on his birthday, whereas Christ is raised on the cross like the sun that grows on his birthday. Moreover, Augustine defines their relationship as that between voice and word: "John was asked who he was, whether he was the Christ, whether Elijah, whether the prophet: *I am not, he said, the Christ, nor Elijah, nor the prophet. And they said, So who are you? I am a voice crying in the desert* [John 1:22–23]. He called himself a voice. You have John as a voice; what have you got Christ as, if not as a word?"[17] Augustine defines the relationship of voice and word as the relationship between a sound in itself not yet meaningful, which does not yet convey anything, and the spoken word that carries meaning. "It is a kind of formless sound, bearing or carrying a noise to the ears, without any meaning to the intelligence." The word gives meaning to the voice. For Augustine, John becomes the voice of all voices, the voice in general: "So gather together all the voices which preceded the Word as into one man, and lump them all together in the person of John. He was cast in the symbolic role of all of them, he alone was the sacred and mystical representative or person of them all. That's why he is properly called the voice, as the sign and sacrament of all voices" (Augustine, Sermon 288, 115). Augustine refigures the relationship of *figura* and *implementum* with the example of voice and word: the voice as the non-signifying vehicle acquires meaning through the word. The voice of John becomes filled with sense by the word of Jesus and so it finally signifies—"In the beginning was the Word, and the Word was [with] God" and "the word became flesh," as Augustine cites the Gospel of the other John, the apostle.

The Baptist is the epitome of the voice also for Flaubert. One never sets eyes on him; the only presence he has on stage is his voice and his cut-off head. John is voice, the voice as such: "Suddenly a distant voice, as though issuing from the bowels of the earth . . . ," is how he enters (72). "The voice answered . . ." (89). And so on. In the word of Christ the voice is fulfilled. In Flaubert's narrative the voice speaks in an intertextual overlapping of all of the prophets' voices and thus exemplifies the *figura* that the Old Testament is to the New. This representation of the *figura* through the body of John the Baptist remains the unfulfilled echo of an uncertain future. His story is built on and constructed around the missing words of Jesus. The news of who Jesus is comes too late. The two miss one another, and John's voice remains empty, his prophecies senseless. Flaubert inverts the meaning of John's and Jesus's typological foundation of Christianity. He also inverts the mode of interpreting the solstice metaphors for the deaths of the two figures. As we shall see, while the Church Father Augustine sublimates the metaphor of the sun, Flaubert sexualizes it. And in the sexual reinvestment of that metaphor—by the way, the true meaning of sublimation, discovered a little later by Freud—comes to the fore what Flaubert would call its continued perversion.

Augustine took the decrease literally: John is made shorter like the day, shorter by a head. He read the death on the cross—the very point that marks the change from a carnal to a spiritual understanding—spiritually. Christ is raised on the cross. Undoing the metaphorological thrust from carnal literalness toward spiritual elevation—the Church Fathers' economy of Christian interpretation—Flaubert relocates the elevation on the cross to the sexual context of castration and erection. The reversal of figuration corresponds to their difference in interpretation concerning the typological relation between Old and New Testaments. The New, Augustine maintains, fulfills, with and in Christ, the Old in Spirit. Flaubert, by contrast, has the New Testament carry forward both ancient and Jewish literalness in the carnality of the letter. In "Hérodias" it is contained, sublated without solution, in a veritable "pseudomorphosis" of the tradition.[18]

The story of the birth of Christianity reconstituted in "Hérodias" against the grain of the Gospels and their authoritative patristic interpretations erases their very point: the promise of this birth. In short, the story in "Hérodias" interprets earthly history against the transmitted backdrop of the glad tidings. Only as a perversion of the universal covenant of love's promise does history become decipherable, does it make sense. The chaotic cacophony of Flaubert's many voices implicates the counterimage of the linguistic miracle of the Pentecost. The birth of Christianity reconstrued by Flaubert presents the Church that came into its own on Pentecost as propagating what it thought it had overcome, Babylon. Already at the beginning of "Hérodias," the doves at Herod's court invoke the event of Pentecost, the Holy Ghost's appearance: "doves flying out from the friezes, wheeled above the courtyard" (87). John the Baptist baptizes with water to announce Him who would baptize with the Ghost. The *Three Tales* echo one another in the shared motif of that Ghost. The miracle of Pentecost that brings the linguistic confusion of Babel to an end is the precondition for worldwide evangelization. It should inaugurate an unprecedented way of life—unheard of in a Babylonian world—that consists of the selfless self-surrender prophetically articulated in the Bible quote "For him to increase, I must decrease." John himself does not yet fully grasp this maxim; it is understood only *post factum* and envisioned by Phanuel in a rapture. But was this fact, which Phanuel the astrologer did, in fact, understand, not already written in the stars, in the eclipse of John by Jesus? Phanuel carries the ambivalence of understanding in his name; his name indicates the place where Jacob sees God face to face without recognizing him (Gen. 32:30).[19]

Christianity in "Hérodias," as we have seen, is the result of a disavowed and denied Roman *translatio*. It is, as we shall see, yet another "pseudomorphosis" of the cult of Cybele, just another idolatrous form of phallus worship. The birth of the Roman Church out of the more ancient Cybele cult is the irony of the Roman *translatio,* which Flaubert—informed by Georg Friedrich Creuzer's seminal rewriting of ancient symbolism and mythology—proposes as an answer to the theological pretensions of the political *translatio* theories advocated in his time. Christianity, Flaubert demonstrates, rests on a deeply buried mythical stratum, misjudged even by Renan. Flaubert's conclusion is that the Catholic Church is really nothing other than the most influential, globalized continuation of the Cybele cult. According to the sources and literature he consulted—again, we must not underestimate his competence as a historian in these matters—the cult of Cybele had already become the dominant Roman state cult at the time of Christ's birth.[20] The birth of Christianity therefore is not the moment in which Pentecost led to a universal bond of love, but rather the reverse. Babel comes into its all-encompassing, earth-spanning, truly catholic existence in the Roman Church. Everything became, no, remained Babylonian, Augustine's City of Man, without even a glimpse of a City of God.

As a variant of the oriental cults that would have already undermined Rome's republican *virtus*, Christianity was the fruit of an arcane but established *translatio*. In the rise of the oriental milieu, the Roman and the Jewish heritage merge and add to the number of orgiastic oriental cults of the phallus reaching for worldwide domination in the Rome of the empire. In short, Flaubert discovered that the Christian Occident had been oriental in origin from the start. In a pseudomorphosis advanced by the syncretism of the time—a false metamorphosis without the substance of translation—the Roman Catholic Church participated in and profited from the oriental cults that rose to prominence in the later Roman republic. This was a *translatio Romae* of an altogether different kind, which had nothing to do with the *translatio Romae* imagined by Flaubert's contemporaries: this *translatio imperii* was not about classical ideals, male virtue, clemency, and glory. By the same token, all world history is nothing but the perversion of the Christian promise of an unheard-of love, a love not based on the concupiscence cultivated in the oriental cults. History after Christ, Flaubert recognizes, only preserves this promise in the negative.

Flaubert deciphers the world of "Hérodias" against the backdrop of the New Covenant related in the Gospels. The human condition of Babylonian confusion, in which sex and violence, both equally fatal, are the universal media, is a perversion *avant la lettre* of Pentecost, in which the Holy Ghost unites and illuminates in divine love. To an equal extent, Herod's banquet perverts the love sacrifice of the Eucharist. The political body, as it is staged on the Tetrarch's birthday, is not only a perversion of the political body in the style of Suetonius's *Lives of the Caesars*, but even more so an inversion of the representation of the body of Christ by the Church. The death of all flesh—the head of John on the platter is carrion among carrion—is the counterimage of the transfiguration and resurrection of the flesh. The Christian matrix remains unthematized, but "Hérodias" discloses its historical meaning to those who recognize it to be a reverse image, a photographic negative. In "Hérodias," the events of the year 30 CE cryptically include the birth of the Church, whose self-understanding is indirectly invoked. It is to be deciphered in the light of a political, hermeneutical, theological scheme that did not exist during the time at which the narrative takes place. It would not appear until later, when it would be formed by Paul and further developed by Augustine. In spite of all its historical detail, despite its meticulously precise research, "Hérodias" is not a historical novella. It timelessly puts the general, eternal condition of all things human—say, our Being-toward-death—vividly before our eyes. "To place vividly before the eyes" means to signify its mortality and make it recognizable. Flaubert follows the understanding of world history presented in Augustine's diagnostic work *The City of God*: fratricide and incest indisputably reign as the clearest manifestations of a political body torn apart and ruled by self-love. History in the Hegelian sense of progress, of a coming into itself, does not exist for Flaubert. The parallel drawn by Flaubert between Herod and a prefect of the French Second Empire underlines this idea of history as the return of the unchanging catastrophe. This Augustinian view sets Flaubert sharply apart from the historicism of his time, including the secular philosophies of history influenced by Hegel.

In his entire work Flaubert only ever "illustrates" one history: the story of Babel. The type of "Babel," a topos reshaped and deepened in the distinction of *civitates* in *The City of God*, is delivered in Flaubert's work with its full patristic charge. The basic difference for Flaubert, as well as for Augustine and his tradition, remains the distinction between self-love and a selfless, Christian love, of *caritas* opposed to carnal *concupiscentia*. The consequences of self-love in the *civitas terrena* connected with the name of Babel are twofold: the *libido dominandi* leads to fratricide and civil war, while the *concupiscentia carnis* leads to individual corruption of body and mind. Lust of the flesh and civil war are evident consequences of the Fall. They determine the course of the world. As the overarching paradigm of the City of Man, Rome serves as the politically updated Babel in Augustine's view. The fratricide committed by Romulus at Rome's beginning repeats the biblical murder by Cain of Abel. Fratricide returns, not only in the Roman civil wars, but in all history from beginning to end. In the respect that it remains Babylonian, all history turns out to be inescapably Roman. With the end of the republic, with the accession of Tiberius at the latest, palace secrets (*arcana domus*) emerge as the dominant feature of Roman politics. In his discussion of the secrets of the imperial state (*arcanum imperii*), Flaubert's literary precursor Tacitus stresses incest as the hidden motive for fratricide.[21]

The universality of fratricide is an unspoken assumption in Flaubert, as in Tacitus. Whether Flaubert writes about contemporary history, namely of the Revolution of 1848 (in *A Sentimental Education*), or about antiquity (in *Salammbô*), fratricide is always the hidden figure lurking in the background. Fratricide prevails as the foundational scheme for the disjointedness of any political body ruled by the self-interests of its members. Motivated by concupiscence, it finds its fulfillment in civil war. Together, fratricide and civil war remain determining in the wake of the world empires through Flaubert's nineteenth century. True to Tacitus's diagnosis, he incorporates the motif of incest in this tableau. Shakespeare, whom Flaubert admired, also exposes the motif of incest as a family secret (*arcanum domus* is Tacitus's term) linked to fratricide, patricide, and matricide. The war of brothers and incest both found and destroy the social body. In contrast to their treatment by the classical Roman authors, fratricide, incest, and their acting out in civil war are not perversions of the political or social body; fratricide and incest are their arcane foundations and secretly guarantee their functions in Flaubert as in Augustine.

For Lucan, Augustine's foremost model, the Roman civil war, which lay only a few generations in the past, was a perverse effect of the striving for absolute power. It had destroyed the Republic, in hindsight, the best sociopolitical order conceivable. For Tacitus and also Suetonius, incest in the imperial house was the symptom through which the perversion of the Republic (which survived only in name) was becoming obvious; a symptom in which the monstrous magnitude of inversion expressed itself. Thus the lynched body of Vitellius, who became emperor because he was the catamite of Tiberius, reveals the brutal violence ruling the empire after Tiberius. The disfigurement practiced upon his body symbolized the disfigurement of the political body; the lapidary representation of his lynched body in Suetonius is not a mere matter of factual description, but a scathing criticism of tyranny: in other words, a description still aware of a political alternative.

Saint Augustine's consequence is another. For Augustine—and Flaubert accordingly—there is no worldly alternative to this politics based on fratricide and incest. Augustine gives up on earthly politics and features the City of God instead. Against the pretension of an earthly "empire without end" preordained by God—the "*imperium sine fine*" cited by Augustine from the prophecy of Vergil's Jupiter—he positions the Kingdom of Christ, which is only figured in this world and not realized in the Church. In Flaubert's reading the prediction of Rome's unlimited reign related by Vergil has ironically come true. In a pointedly ironic inversion of Origen, whose earlier Christian optimism Augustine refuted, this promised empire without limits in time or space indeed came true, and this is the catastrophe of history. By carrying on the *translatio Romae*, the Roman Catholic Church universalizes the reign of Babel. Babel rules without limits in time and space—an empire without end—in the Roman Church. Instead of overcoming the Babylonian logic, this Church promotes it. However, in promoting it, the promise of an altogether other love is kept alive, albeit in the negative.

The topos of Babel has, firstly, a historical-theoretical aspect in Flaubert's revision of Augustine (the return of unchanging terror), secondly, a hermeneutic aspect (heart of stone and heart of flesh), but thirdly also a poetological aspect, which I would like to specify as anti-Paulinian (the words becoming flesh, the living spirit versus deadly letters). Only the illustration of earthly history—of that which is fatally bound to happen—preserves the Christian matrix as the perverted backdrop of worldly history. World history itself testifies through inversion to the Testaments. Here, Flaubert differs radically from Augustine. Unlike Augustine, who separated world history from salvation history, for Flaubert history and salvation are related. In an utterly negative dialectic, the one is pressed to testify to the other. In Flaubert, history is—or remains—readable against the background of the evangelical promise, so conversely this promise shines forth through its perversion in history. It no longer has a positive location. In "Hérodias," the history of the City of Man becomes readable as a testament, the one and only possible new testament. In the testament given in Flaubert's work, world history is constituted from the beginning to eternity as a perversion—and in this a testament to the promise of salvation. History is thus not secular. Down to the smallest detail, it is determined by the promise of salvation. The perversion of the Christian scheme binds the *Three Tales* together and links them to the rest of Flaubert's oeuvre.

The similarity between the Pharisees of the year 30 and the socialists of 1848 depicted in the "Club de l'Intelligence" of *A Sentimental Education* is of a structural nature. Although they discuss absolutely unrelated subjects, the Babylonian topos informs the structure of their discussions. There is no living spirit, no understanding, only the dead letter that leads to murder. Flaubert inverts the "ruses of reason" with which Hegel replaced the Providence diagrammed in the work of Church Fathers like Origen. It is bitterly ironic that history providentially produced the Roman Empire and its everlasting peace for the spread of Christianity. What seems like a good-humored irony until Hegel, appears in "Hérodias" as the self-assertion of Babel. Flaubert's text reveals the unredeemable condition of all political constitutions after Rome. The Catholic Church and its secularized, political others, like the French Republic, all embody this constitution.

Flaubert turns Augustine ironically against Hegel. For it is under cover of promoting the kingdom not of this world that the empire of this world gains power. The triumph of the City of Man is total and global. As the most effective of Cybele cults, the Catholic Church leads to the ultimate world-historical triumph of Rome and Babel. Christianity never overcame its pagan rivals; it became the most successful among them.

Reckoning with the cult of Cybele, against which Augustine had to assert Christianity, Flaubert draws on the two most sensitive issues for the rivalry of the two cults: on the sacrifice practiced by the priests of Cybele in their self-mutilation and on the reaction of Roman authorities against human sacrifice. For Augustine, the self-mutilation of the priests of Cybele is a stumbling block, which the modern reader has to detour around. They were said to practice castration on themselves. According to Augustine, this not only perverts natural sexuality but, more important, counterfeits the chastity of the new families in Christ. The fear behind Augustine's disgust is the closeness with which this act of self-mutilation approaches the ideal of chastity propagated by the Fathers of the Church. The new sublimely erotic norm of love that he advocates is conceived of as spiritual maternity or virginity, which both women and men can achieve. To establish this new norm against the Old Testament, which regards chastity as virtually monstrous, was difficult enough. The families in Christ are the foil against which Cybele's cult must have appeared as the latest symptom of depravity. With self-castration, the cult of the Great Mother exceeded the most hateful of crimes. As an unsurpassable perversion of natural sexuality, it was even more perverse than all acts of incest committed by the pagan gods, more perverse even than Jupiter's homosexuality.

More decisive than the perversion of nature was the perversion of the Christian cult that came with it: the parallelism of the sacrifice of sexuality, which seemed a feature shared by the families in Christ and the Cybele cult. In condemning the Cybele cult as the most depraved of all, Augustine's intention is to render these sacrifices, close to one another as they seem, as antithetical in every respect possible. For him the Cybele cult is the most repulsive of all ancient cults, because its priests do not sublimate their sexuality in their castration, but rather regress to the most carnal of all levels: feminized men turn into catamites. In them sexuality is not sublimated, but carnally powered. Augustine is particularly disgusted by the feminine transvestitism of the Cybele priests:

Concerning the effeminates consecrated to the same Great Mother, in defiance of all modesty which belongs to men and women, Varro has not wished to say anything, nor do I remember reading anything concerning them anywhere. These effeminates, no later than yesterday, were going through the streets and palaces of Carthage with anointed hair, whitened faces, relaxed bodies, and feminine gaits, exacting from the people the means of maintaining their ignominious lives.[22]

In the "bloody sacrifices" offered in "monstrous obscenity" to Cybele, the male member is mutilated, not in effigy, but in fact; through the blood sacrifice Cybele turns her priests into eunuchs and catamites. While natural families and a fortiori these perverse cult communities are held together by *concupiscentia*, the families in Christ are joined by *caritas*. They transform spirit and soul, while the Cybele priests change bodies and clothes. For Augustine, castration is not an overcoming of sexuality, but the epitome of the sexual. This is an important point for Flaubert's interest in the archeology of the Christian Babylon and, as we shall see, a point of stylistic consequence.

The two forms of love, *caritas* and *concupiscentia*, are brought together in "Hérodias." The spiritualization of the bonds of the flesh, which converts men and women into spiritual sisters and brothers, into spiritual fathers and mothers who are united not by blood but love, is the aim of the families in Christ. *Caritas* takes the place of *concupiscentia*. A passion for one's self is transformed into a love that gives itself up for the other. The name for that love was chastity, a term no longer comprehensible since, to use Foucault's term, we have to do here with the *dispositif* of the sexual. The Virgin Mary incorporated the idea of this spiritual love.

The juxtaposition of the two types of love and the two kinds of families shows itself in the doubled riddle that concludes every chapter of "Hérodias." Phanuel the Essene is a member of a sect whose commitment to chaste poverty anticipates the structures of monastic life.[23] Flaubert fashions the Essenes as a pre-Christian sect, foreshadowing the communists of *A Sentimental Education*. They practice celibacy, live in poverty, defend the equality of all, and keep no slaves. Phanuel tries to understand what John the Baptist means by the mysterious statement "For him to increase, I must decrease." It is a first formula of Christian love, the surrender of self for the sake of another.[24] Phanuel's appropriate question is: Who is this Christ? Is he the awaited Messiah? In the end, Phanuel solves the puzzle and finds the love he seeks. Even Herod's quest is to be read in parallel with Phanuel's quest for love. At the end of every chapter Herod catches sight of a girl whose fleeting appearance excites him and awakens vague memories. Who is this girl? Women in Flaubert, it is important to note, can only be arousing when they appear as artworks, as idols, for which Jews and Christians alike reproached the Romans: "a bare arm stretched out, a youthful, charming arm, that could have been fashioned in ivory by Polycleitus" (93). At the peak of carnal desire triggered in idolatry, the secret is unveiled. Herod recognizes the girl who has attracted him time and again from the distance: "Up on the dais she took off her veil. It was Herodias, as she used to look in her youth" (101). Herod desires the daughter of his wife and brother. Families united by idolatry are bound in incestuous concupiscence. They are the opposite of families bound to one another in spiritual love by the medium of the word.

The ground on which the story of salvation is supposed to play out proves to be the Earth herself, Mother Cybele. The new will be born out of her mountains, out of her stones, basalt, namely, out of her city, in which her emblem, the tower crown, became stone.[25] It will not be born out of the intact womb of a virgin in which God's Word becomes flesh.[26] Fatal premonitions more than messianic hopes announce this coming. The bloody birth of the Church, a cosmic event like the birth of the Messiah prefigured by the stars, ruptures the womb of the Earth Mother Cybele, whose representative is Hérodias. If the birth out of the virgin is sublime, that of the political pairing of Aulus Vitellius and Hérodias is perverse, bordering on the grotesque. The new here is conceived by a ruler made sterile by incest and who has come to power through an act of incestuous adultery, according to John's continuously repeated accusation. The catamite Aulus owes his empire to his having been Tiberius's favorite "sphincter"— thus his nickname. Herod fearfully awaits this birth, which he expects to be bloody. Its token is the severed head of John.

At the end of "Hérodias," the heaviness of the cross is foreshadowed by John's heavy head dragged by the hair. The blind exchange of looks between the dead John and the blind drunk Aulus bears exact witness, not to a love stronger than death, but to the same deadly violence. Salome's dance, performed with a face as motionless as a pantomime's, figures a cross that the governor Vitellius perceives without recognizing. Her performance points the way to those carrying John's head to Galilee: "Her neck and her spine were at right angles" (102). Christ's cross is inscribed onto the beheading of John by Salome's pantomime. Evidently, she neither understands the one—the beheading of John—nor has a clue about the other—the cross of Christ.

The punch that Flaubert pulls in "Hérodias" is a double one: he hits at both the Catholic Church and nineteenth-century humanism— including those who, like Sainte-Beuve, imagined a genteel antiquity and Europe and Paris as inheritors of the Roman tradition's humane qualities. The Rome whose heir France had considered itself since the Renaissance falls victim to the Babylonian curse. Thus also its self-declared heir Napoleon III and the Second Empire. The apologists for Christianity who opted in favor of an enlightened Humanism—Renan's study, where Jesus is a hero, whose true genius remains to be discovered—do not fare any better. Flaubert takes aim at both of France's dominant constructions of history: Paris as the new, truer, better Rome and France as the oldest, most loyal daughter of the Church.[27] The rebirth out of the spirit of antiquity is blocked. Rome's severity, its pride, its *virtus*, and masculinity are done for. Every *translatio* of antiquity, whether it presents itself as Catholic or republican, humanist or imperial, is nothing but a travesty of Babylonian cults, to which Christianity had fallen even before it began. If one follows Flaubert, orientalism is always already far more foundational for Europe than Edward Said ever dreamed. The Orient must serve as the Other, because it is at the roots of the self-centered foundation of a politics that is perpetually in disguise and hypocritically Babylonian.

Again, Flaubert's vision of the Roman Catholic Church stands in stark contrast to that of Augustine, who took care to separate the Church from Rome and salvation history from a mundane world history that was thoroughly Roman. For Flaubert, all history remains Roman. At stake is not the progress of salvation, but the translation of an ever-recurring Babylonian curse. The Catholic Church and its secular after-formations epitomize the City of Man, beyond which there is no City of God. Thus the doom of political theologies is also sealed. In the guise of the promise of a kingdom not of this world, the empires of this world go global and triumph fatally. The Church is nothing but a travesty of all things Babylonian. Fratricide rages all the more staggeringly under the cover of brotherly love, travestied as Christian. Binding together kingdom and salvation, victory and the cross, the Church carries on the Roman curse well into its political aftermath, into the French Empire and Republic alike, onward into the nineteenth-century present. Flaubert subverts the possibilities of a theologically grounded politics as practiced in secularization (*laïcité*). It was not the Jews who triumphed under this sign, as Nietzsche holds in his notorious antisemitism, but Babel. That is the bad news, the anti-Gospel, that Flaubert proclaims in "Hérodias" to be history's greatest joke. It underlies the allegorical reflection of the dead look that links Aulus and John the Baptist: "Through their open lashes the dead eyes and the vacant eyes seemed to be telling each other something" (104). The future Roman emperor wakes out of his bender and looks the prophet in his dead eyes. The deadness of the eyes announces his own death, while Herod, by the grace of Rome, anticipates the late melancholy of the nineteenth century. The century that pictured itself as a new and better Rome and saw itself even on the road to the Heavenly Jerusalem blindly promoted nothing, in Flaubert's equally merciless analysis, but Babel's continued rule.

Flaubert's last story completes the destruction of the Catholic Church as an institution that was damned before its beginnings and through its beginnings. Only literature can deliver a testament to this devastation, and only literature can testify to the promise of redemption that finds itself so awfully travestied by this Church. Literature is thus itself the missing testament to the martyrdom of Christ and of all who suffered in the sign of the Cross in his wake. Holding fast to the maxim "For him to increase, I must decrease," Flaubert's Hérodias not only challenges the Roman constitution of the Church and the modern secular institutions that have arisen in its wake, but counters lay priests à la Hugo, self-proclaimed imperialist evangelists à la Zola, and, last but not least, the "transvaluation of all values" by a virtuous superman à la Nietzsche.

Incest and Fratricide According to Flavius Josephus

Flaubert succinctly illustrates the fatality of the City of Man, marked by incest and fratricide. The opening tableau of "Hérodias" depicts a petrified *nature morte* in the form of the black basalt landscape of the Dead Sea—"mer Morte" (71). The story opens at a fortress marked by its vertical dynamic. A towering worldly rulership is negotiated in this beginning. The fortress of the Tetrarch Herod Antipas, Machaerous, evokes Cybele's stone crown, with "here and there, towers set like florets . . . , suspended over the abyss" (71).

As Herod surveys the land over which, by the grace of Rome, he has jurisdiction, the dynamics of his gaze rebounds on him, however, and he falls prey to fear. The Tetrarch is impotent, the classical nineteenth-century motif of melancholy. The inversion of power into impotence, of standing into falling (with a phallic connotation), dominates the political dynamic. In spite of all of the realism of the fortress Machaerous, which is emphasized time and again and well documented, the allegorical register is obvious. Like the Bible, Flaubert's story has a *sensus allegoricus* alongside the *sensus historicus*.

The phrase "mer Morte"—the Dead Sea and dead mother—is re-iterated: "A mist was floating; it parted, and the contours of the Dead Sea [*la mer Morte*] appeared" (62). Nearby, the red morning sky assumes bloody overtones; one thinks of a birth out of the Earth Mother. With a tower soaring into the sky, a new Babel emerges out of Jerusalem: "the enormous cube of Antonia tower dominated Jerusalem" (71). A bit later, vainglory completes the Babylonian association: "It was like a luminous mountain, something superhuman, crushing everything with its opulence and pride" (74).[28] The vertical dynamic remains determining. Fertile fields are reduced in this petrified landscape to mere geometric, dead, inorganic forms. Even the water is no source of life, but becomes crystallized and petrified in the metaphor of snow: "Meanwhile the Jordan flowed over the arid plain, which in its total whiteness dazzled like a sheet of snow. The lake now seemed to be made of lapis-lazuli" (72). In lapis lazuli, of which the blue on the head of Félicité's parrot is resonant, but also in the general petrification, this scene is tied to the altar of the Corpus Christi celebration in "A Simple Heart." Flaubert en passant, but thoroughly, reverses the art of Parnassus that petrifies everything in order to preserve it lifelike forever. Here by contrast he petrifies in order to place death in life permanently. This is not about the living spirit written onto a heart of flesh, but about dead letters written in stone.

Herod Antipas symbolizes incest. He has married his brother's wife: "They were the troops of the Arabian king, whose daughter he had put away so that he could take Herodias, the wife of one of his brothers, who lived in Italy with no pretensions to power" (72). It is not simply a matter of war, but of a war between brothers: "Philip, his third brother, ruler of Batanea, was arming in secret" (72). The outcome of this politics is right before the Tetrarch's eyes: the landscape shows the eternal ruin of all power; nature supplies the image of an ancient site of ruins, as in the forests of "Saint Julian the Hospitalier" and Fontainebleau in *A Sentimental Education*: "he was filled with despondency at the sight of the wilderness, with its chaotic landscape calling to mind ruined amphitheatres and palaces" (72). As traces of human violence, ruins merge with the cities of Sodom and Gomorrah, destroyed by acts of enraged divine violence.[29] "The hot wind smelling of sulphur seemed to bring with it exhalations from the cursed cities, now buried below shore level beneath the weight of the waters. These signs of an undying wrath filled his mind" (74).

The landscape of "Hérodias" renders Flaubert's historical theory in a nutshell. It is a Babylonian story, determined by the vertical—the proud, soaring tower—and its collapse. History, a series of catastrophes, leaves nothing behind it but the traces of human and divine destruction. Noah's Flood is alluded to in the petrified waves that make up the landscape. An end to this kind of history, in which the empires of this world follow one another in their ruins, is nowhere in sight. At precisely this historical moment in the Holy Land, the eternal story of incest and fratricide, powered by *libido dominandi* and *concupiscentia carnis*, takes place once again. Again the result will be devastated ruin: it is only a question of time until the hollowed-out stone crown towering over the abyss falls. The human bond is Babylonian and will fall like its tower. Men are joined in hate and lust; and full of envy, contempt, and jealousy they blindly and deafly pursue nothing but their own interests.

Both Herod Antipas and Hérodias come on stage under the sign of incest and fratricide. Mentioned nowhere in the historical sources, the fratricide is in Hérodias's case Flaubert's pointed invention. But let us first look into the classical motif of incest. Herod Antipas, the son of Herod the Great, is Hérodias's uncle and her brother-in-law. She leaves her first husband for his (also already married) brother because of the latter's governorship, and their union violates Jewish marriage law. The Bible presupposes this; Renan follows suit in his retelling of the account given by Josephus.[30] Hérodias's dominant libidinal impulse is the will to power: "Since she was a child she had nourished dreams of a great empire" (77). In this desire she feels frustrated by her husband: "It was in furtherance of that ambition that she had left her first husband and joined this one, who had made a fool of her" (ibid.). Now she tries to prevent disaster by getting rid of John the Baptist, whose incitement of the people could lead her husband to cast her off: "She was wondering too whether the Tetrarch, yielding to public opinion, might not decide to put her away. Then all would be lost!" (ibid.).

Up to this point, Flaubert follows his sources. His one and only innovation is to make Hérodias the murderer of her brother. Upon her first entrance, Hérodias appears as a seductive Eve with snake, a lock of her black hair slithering between her breasts. The first word of this woman, who already as a child dreamed of nothing other than the empire, is "Caesar." She immediately reveals herself as a schemer who will do anything for power.

What she says seems at first completely incomprehensible: "'Caesar is our friend! Agrippa is in prison!' 'Who told you so?' 'I know!' She added, 'It is because he wished that the empire might pass to Caius [or Gaius, nicknamed Caligula]'" (74–75). Only a few lines later is the perceptive reader able to discover what she is talking about. The reason why she is so ecstatic that she dashes out of her room unadorned to announce the good news is to be inferred from the next sentence, which betrays the struggle between Agrippa and Herod: "While living off their charity he had intrigued for the title of king, to which they aspired as much as he" (75). Hérodias not only has her rival Agrippa jailed, but indicates that she plans to get rid of him entirely. No one can be sure of surviving one of Tiberius's prisons, and he could be poisoned there—she will see to it that this happens. The reader realizes the extent of Hérodias's wickedness only on learning that she is the sister of the man whose incarceration she has thus successfully schemed for and whose death she thereby hopes to accomplish: "Then she revealed what measures she had taken: clients bribed, letters disclosed, spies at every door, and how she had managed to seduce Eutychus the informer" (ibid.).

Neither the Bible nor Flavius Josephus nor Renan, who follows Josephus's version, tie Hérodias to attempted fratricide in her struggle for power. In Flaubert's account she is presented as the mastermind of a scheme that she historically had nothing to do with; it did not take place until the year 36, six years after the Baptist's death. The story of the attempted murder of her brother and rival is to be credited to Flaubert alone. In spite of his obsession with historical detail, Flaubert falsified the facts. He followed his higher insight in order to embody incest and fratricide in the figure of Hérodias thereby all the more forcefully, illustrating the deeper historical truth of his story.

To this end, he condensed and relocated what were in Flavius Josephus's text two separate moments: first, the story of Hérodias's brother Agrippa's denunciation by his coachman Eutychus and his incarceration under Tiberius, and secondly, an episode in which Hérodias urged her spouse to do whatever was needed to acquire the royal title for himself. Hérodias's contempt for her husband's lack of the will to power comes from Josephus. In contrast, in Flaubert this motivates Hérodias to commit fratricide. Whereas according to Josephus she knows only how to fight with the weapons of a woman, instrumentalizing Herod Antipas, in

Flaubert's version of the story, she acts autonomously, intervenes effectively in politics, and is in every respect more "masculine" than her husband.

Agrippa and Caligula are close friends, and Agrippa's freedman and chariot driver Eutychus overhears them praying for the emperor Tiberius's death so that Caligula can succeed him. When Eutychus is later brought to court on a charge of theft, he informs the judge that he has something to tell the emperor. He is accordingly sent to Tiberius on Capri, where he succeeds in ingratiating himself with the emperor, whom he tells that he has heard Agrippa express the wish that Tiberius might die and that Caligula might become emperor in his place. The paranoid Tiberius believes him and has Agrippa imprisoned. But unlike in "Hérodias," Agrippa was in fact treated well in prison and was freed after Tiberius's death. Caligula then made him ruler of his homeland. Hérodias reenters the game only at this point in Josephus's text.[31]

According to Josephus, then, the power struggle for the royal title, which Hérodias urges on her husband out of envy of her brother, does not occur until years after the intrigue with the coachman, and no longer under Tiberius but under Caligula. Hérodias does her utmost to get her husband to "leave no stone unturned in order to be king."[32] She proposes that the two of them go to Rome to achieve this.[33]

It is not Hérodias who denounces her brother, but Agrippa who denounces Herod, who correctly conjectures in Flaubert's text that Agrippa had maligned him to the emperor. In Josephus, Caligula receives letters from Agrippa that accuse Herod of having plotted with the Parthians against Rome under Tiberius and of now being "confederate with Artabanus, the king of Parthia, in opposition to the government of Caius."[34] The liaisons with the Parthians against Rome also play a role in Flaubert: Agrippa "was hesitating between two plans: soothing the Arabs or concluding an alliance with the Parthians" (72). In Josephus's version, he tells Caligula that Herod possesses arms for 70,000 men:

Caius was moved at this information, and asked Herod whether what was said about the armor was true; and when he confessed there was such armor there, for he could not deny the same, the truth of it being too notorious, Caius took that to be a sufficient proof of the accusation, that he intended to revolt. So he took away from him his tetrarchy, and gave it by way of addition to Agrippa's kingdom; he also gave Herod's money to Agrippa, and, by way of punishment, awarded him a perpetual banishment, and appointed Lyons, a city of Gaul, to be his place of habitation.[35]

Although exempt from this banishment as the sister of Agrippa, Hérodias goes into exile with her husband. According to Josephus, Herod and Hérodias are driven into exile in Lyon by the libelous letters of Hérodias's brother Agrippa. The wearying struggle for the royal title shows a couple to whom there remains only exhaustion from the former passion on his part, and on her end the insatiate urge for power, deep contempt for her husband, and envy of her brother following his promotion by sheer Fortuna.

The portrait drawn by Josephus depicts the connection between power and sex. Flaubert stresses this link. He emphasizes the transformation of Herod's previous erotic fascination with Hérodias to languid indifference. Hérodias tries hard to stir her husband with crocodile tears in a scene resembling a Strauss operetta. She recalls how she unhesitatingly gave up everything for him: she even left her only child behind in Rome. No longer blinded by lust, however, Herod wonders "what had caused this sudden rush of affection" (75). Hérodias can no longer arouse Herod: "She looked at him as she used to, rubbing up against his chest, fondling him. He pushed her away. The love she was trying to revive was so far away, now!" (ibid.). In the past, only war ensued from his love. Herod forgets that lesson, however, whereas Hérodias recognizes sex as a means to power. She is deeply satisfied when she recognizes the flames of desire in her husband's eyes—a desire that no longer applies to her, but does not concern her any less. Her strategy has succeeded. We have the same interchangeability of sex and murder as in "Saint Julian the Hospitalier." Without much ado, Hérodias switches from failed seduction to manslaughter: "Kill him!" (76).

Josephus draws the following moral from his story of Herod and Hérodias: "And thus did God punish Hérodias for her envy at her brother, and Herod also for giving ear to the vain discourses of a woman."[36] God's punishment may for once be just; the story that Josephus otherwise tells is not about divine justice, but rather determined by Fortuna, who controls the fate of men. Fortuna's most defining figure is irony: what usually happens in Josephus is the exact opposite of what was intended. Flaubert's interest is in the catastrophic, ruinous schemes of all history. In defiance of facts he knew perfectly well, for the sake of the deeper truth of history, he places his Hérodias under the sign of fratricide. She is simply faithfully carrying on a family tradition: "Antipas understood her, and although she was Agrippa's sister, her appalling intention seemed to him to be justified.

Such murders were in the nature of things, inevitable in royal houses. In Herod's family they were now too numerous to count" (75).

Like murder, sex stays in the family. Both are means to the same end, in Rome and Jerusalem alike. Incest is the sign under which Hérodias rules. Incest, not the transgression of Jewish divorce law, is the core reproach in John the Baptist's prophecy in Flaubert. Herod's fascination with Salome, the daughter of his wife and brother, repeats the incestuous desire once more: "It was Herodias, as she used to look in her youth" (101). In Jewish and Roman ruling families alike, members were murdered for the sake of power. Incest is a common topic in the Old Testament long before there was a Roman Empire. From Jerusalem to Rome, Flaubert shows in "Hérodias," incest and fratricide are the foundation of world history. It consists of perverted family stories, in which the bonds of nature are disfigured. At the same time the political body is disfigured when man cannot govern himself but is governed by lust. The sexual hierarchy is turned upside down, as well as the generational order. The son is ruling the father, as Aulus Vitellius does.

Despite their all too obvious differences, Jews and Romans are fatally the same: fratricide and incest are the backbone of their political praxis. In Roman literature they are seen as phenomena of decadence, not a homegrown product, but a foreign import. Renan follows the Roman ideology and judges the decadence of *virtus* to be an oriental perversion of the Roman political body: incest, fratricide, orgiastic homosexuality, and effeminate, ostentatious displays of splendor are pointedly enacted in Suetonius's *Lives of the Caesars*. Flaubert pulls the rug out from under this ultimately calming xenophobia. Tacitus and Suetonius, the sources for Flaubert's "Hérodias," tell of Caesars having gone "oriental." Nero, on whose life Suetonius modeled his account of Vitellius, is their prime example, and hence Flaubert's template. In this respect, Nero was not so much a monstrous exception as proof of the rule. His predecessor Claudius, who married his cousin Agrippina, Nero's mother, had been incestuous before him.

Perverted Eucharist: Aulus Vitellius's Great Pig-Out

The third act of "Hérodias" tells of the feast served by the Tetrarch Herod Antipas at his birthday celebration. The story is dominated by the signifying chain of sacrifice, meal, transformation, flesh, wine. Themati cally, the question of the resurrection of the flesh stands in the background, "on the third day risen from the dead." This question is coupled with the political question of "My kingdom is not of this world" or "Thy kingdom come."[37] Meat and its consumption is the stuff of this text. The interchangeability of human flesh and butcher's meat—the Lamb of Christ, the scapegoat—plays the central role. What constitutes the text is the almost unbearable narrative distortion of love sacrifices and love meals, of Crucifixion and Eucharist.[38]

In addition to the implicit matrix of the Eucharist and Christ's sacrifice on the cross, we find the Pentecost complex. The living spirit—its glaring absence—is the backdrop for the banquet scene. Pentecost, the Church's official birth hour, constitutes a new covenant of love as the living body of the Church. This miracle is an overcoming of Babel: everybody understands everybody beyond linguistic borders. Implicitly framed as the opposite of Pentecost, Herod's birthday party is genuinely Babylonian. A worldly empire under the stark rule of the flesh figures as an insatiable appetite for butcher's meat and thus stands against the promise of a Catholic, all-encompassing covenant of love. The flesh alludes, of course, to Saint Paul's exposition of the hermeneutic dimension: the blind eyes of the flesh stand against the spiritual eyes of the heart, eyes that can see, since they are blind to the world. Vitellius is shown fighting even during this banquet for his *imperium*, since, in crass defiance of all table manners, he bears not only the insignia of imperial power, but also his weapons. He correctly interprets Herod's meal as a demonstration of power and as potential warfare, in which he must be able to act at any time. The meal in honor of the Tetrarch unites everybody present—Romans, Samaritans, Jews, Pharisees, Sadducees, Germans, Gauls—in a crescendo-like swelling of hate and shared lust. It is not for nothing that the celebration is walled in by Babylonian fabrics: "Babylonian wall-hangings enclosed it in a kind of tent" (94). And not for nothing is the feast orchestrated by Hérodias, apostrophized by John the Baptist as "daughter of Babylon" (90). Hérodias enters for the second time with "Caesar" on her lips: "Long live Caesar" (100).

The promise of the kingdom not of this world remains a dead letter. Jacob claims that Jesus is the Messiah, but the Romans do not have the faintest idea of what a Messiah might possibly be. The interpreter translates the Messiah into political, Roman terms: a Messiah is a political insurgent against the Roman occupation and promises the Jews what the Romans have already achieved. He is "what they called a liberator who would bring them enjoyment of all earthly goods and dominion over all peoples" (96). The expectation of the Messiah is parodied as absurd: "for centuries they had been expecting him at any minute" (ibid.).

Miracles, seen as a revelation of the divine on earth, are unthinkable in such a world: Jesus is nothing but a trickster. The deceitful, magic aspect of miracles is emphasized by the mention of Simon the Magician, who attempted to buy the secret of Jesus's most beautiful miracle from Peter to use it peddling door to door. This smacks of the reproach of simony that the Church had to work through during the Middle Ages: "The talk was of Iaokanann and suchlike people. Simon of Gitta washed away sins with fire. A certain Jesus . . ." (95). Everything in the world is decipherable through the senses only, perceptible with the bare eye, countable, measurable. The most exalted things are treated like prescriptions and reduced to naked, shallow facts. The supernatural only exists in the form of the commonly shared superstitious beliefs in demons with hellish powers.

The anti-Pentecostal, Babylonian momentum contaminates the syntactical devices: the conjunction "and" does not link together, but places the unconnected absurdly side by side. The reference of personal pronouns is unclear. Conversations are interrupted by violence, howlings, mockeries, threats, condemnations, misunderstandings, slander, insult. People's hatred of and contempt for each other surfaces in corrupt sentences. As a continuous interruption, a tireless tearing apart of the syntactical fabric of language, this text is onerous, even painful to read. The feast of Herod is a feast of linguistic contamination, which cuts to the bone of communication.

It is a party at which everyone perceives everyone with eyes of the flesh, unmediated by a language crippled by what it is meant to conceive. This seeing with the eyes of the flesh is illustrated against the topos of the eye that sees with the heart without a need for language. The double coding, as both sacred and worldly, of the party's location, allegorizes this perspective, in which the sacred remains implicit. The historically correct description of the three-naved basilica evokes the space of the Roman churches, which developed out of this structure and into which the former is later transformed in the text. The "vessel [*vaisseau*]," an architecturally neutral term, turns into a "nave [*nef*]," the *terminus technicus* for the axial middle space of a cathedral.

As already noted, the banquet that turns into a sacrificial meal with John's beheading offers a perversion of the Eucharist. The Father's love goes so famously far that he sacrifices his beloved Son. By shouldering the sin of the world, Jesus, the Lamb of God, the scapegoat, conquers death; as a consequence, bodies can rise to eternal life. In the memory of this sacrifice of love, a new covenant is constituted during the Eucharist by sharing the sacrificed body—flesh and blood in the form of bread and wine. This new covenant is made of people who, in an *imitatio Christi*, reenact this sacrifice in self-sacrifice: they become dead to the world in order to rise to life with Christ.

The link between flesh and resurrection is the main topic of the conversation—a howling, rather—during the banquet. Thus, the resurrection of the flesh comes up in immediate proximity to carefully described mountains of meat: "Bulls' kidneys were served, dormice, nightingales, vine-leaves stuffed with mincemeat; the priests went on discussing resurrection" (98). Mention of the prophet Elijah comes up repeatedly in the discussion.[39] In the biblical tradition, he is twice linked to resurrection; he raises the son of the widow of Zarephath from the dead, and he himself ascends to heaven. The return of Elijah, his resurrection from the dead, is central because it adds to the question of who is Christ. The coming of the Messiah is to be announced, according to the Scriptures, by the return of Elijah.[40] The followers of Christ see Elijah returned in John the Baptist. The Romans, on the other hand, keep to the materialist Lucretius, who held that all bodies die and remain dead: "Nec crescit, nec post mortem durare videtur": life "neither grows nor seems to last after death" (Lucretius, *De rerum naturae* 338, ed. Kenney, 47), a sentence of great prominence in Flaubert's intellectual milieu. The sexualization of the resurrection is stressed by comparing the Latin quotation with the central maxim of the text, "For him to increase, I must decrease." Its phallic point is evident in the (etymologically grounded) alliteration of the Latin *crescit* and the French *croisse*—to become large, to grow.

Aulus is a most breathtaking example of the link between death, flesh, and butcher's meat. Consumed by greed, he quite literally almost gorges himself to death. Embodying the appetite of the flesh, he is the repulsive perversion of the body politic in Flaubert's text, just as he was in Suetonius earlier. Aulus doesn't try to master his consuming gluttony, which would later astonish the Roman world. He is tyrannically ruled by his passions.[41] His effeminacy is underlined by ostentatious luxury: "and a sapphire necklace sparkled on his bosom, plump and white as a woman's" (94). He allows himself to be governed by sexual lust just as dissolutely as he submits to gluttony. The beautiful youth Aulus has fallen for is called "the Asiatic" (94), confirming Roman decadence's oriental reputation.[42]

. . .

Up to this point, Flaubert follows Suetonius. But for Flaubert, the figure of Aulus has yet another purpose. He is not only the embodiment of the perversion of the body politic. Flaubert relies on the topos of Roman decadence when he shows Aulus vomiting during the banquet. But he also emphasizes a change in form: the transformation of food into vomit. On the other hand, he underlines the danger of death that proceeds from gluttony—both aspects are missing from Suetonius's account. The threat of death through gorging becomes manifest in the image presented by Aulus's body at the end: "He lay [*il gisait*] with a heap of food in front of him" (100). The *gisait* recalls a corpse, so that Aulus ends as a mountain of meat next to a mountain of meat. The dead eyes with which he meets the dead eyes of John the Baptist underscore his eating himself to death.[43] Aulus's great pig-out is the evident counterfigure to the Holy Communion. Only the tails of lamb—rolls of fat, the text says—with which he stuffs himself are able to satiate him; a dark allusion to Christ, the Lamb of God.

Given the Eucharist as formative matrix of Herod's feast, Aulus's complaint about food that is not sufficiently transformed takes on a peculiar ring. For the Eucharist is all about the change of form and substance, called transubstantiation. For Aulus's decadent taste, the dishes served are by far too close to nature; they are not sufficiently dressed. They do not meet a taste refined far beyond the primitive nature of food. He thus obliquely refers to a transubstantiation that is not taking place: "he was not enjoying the meal, the dishes were too ordinary and crudely prepared" (100). Christ's image was fused with that of Bacchus in the iconography of later times under the sign of wine and sacrifice. The sober inebriation of the Gospel is anticipated by the drunk Aulus in the opposite sense, the blind sense of the letter: The god of the Jews is Bacchus, Aulus says, and they worship the god of intoxication; hence the grapevine in their temple.[44] The Galilean translator hesitates to translate the insult— no *translatio* (86). The drunkenness that reigns at the banquet is obviously no sober inebriation that sees the Loving God in the lesson of the Gospel, but simple drunkenness, which leads to anger, scorn, destruction, and, finally, murder. In Aulus all the elements that make up the Eucharist are concentrated and perverted. In the economy of the story, he thereby gains special weight—if one may say so in view of his extraordinary girth.

The "sacrificial meal" is conjured up on the Jewish side in the conflict over the sacrificial privilege awarded by the Romans to the Jewish High Priests.[45] Communion and sacrifice are the complexes used by Flaubert to sketch out a patchwork of religious practices. The Jews are introduced as consumers of the remains of sacrificial cults: "A dozen of them, scribes and priestly servants, who fed on the leavings from the sacrifices" (99). That points to a Jewish custom of leaving the meat of the sacrificial animal that was not burned by the fire, but only well roasted, to the priests and their servants.[46] Which meat one may consume, and which gods one insults in doing so, is the most important topic at the banquet. The Pharisees lament: "They had been served Maecenas' favourite dish, wild ass in a stew, an unclean food" (99). The Shechem do not eat squab, because they deify a dove: "and men from Sichem would not eat any turtle-doves in deference to the dove Azima" (98).[47] Vitellius suspects that the Jews sacrifice children and perhaps also eat them: "Their god might well be Moloch, whose altars he had encountered on the roadside; and he recalled the child sacrifices, and the story of the man whom they fattened up mysteriously" (100).

In this setup, John the Baptist becomes the scapegoat.[48] Two moments unify the guests at this party, who otherwise are divided by everything: their lust for Salome and their scapegoating of John: "'What a trouble-maker!' said Jonathan. 'No one will have any money left if he goes on!' added the Pharisees. And from all sides came recriminations: 'Protect us!' 'Let's make an end of him!'" (99). The love to which John falls victim is not the *caritas* of the Father, but the incestuous love of Herod for his niece. What is consumed at this party is not flesh and blood in the form of bread and wine, but gallons of wine and mountains of meat. The eternally dead quality of this meat is highlighted in the description of the anatomical parts of dismembered corpses—tongues, tails, kidneys. The carrion quality, as dead as dead can be, of the consumed meat is alluded to in the vultures who feed on carrion (95). The head of John also appears as carrion in the end; it remains behind on a platter in the *genre* of a Flemish still life:

"Then he showed them the mournful object on the dish, amidst the remnants of the feast" (105).

The deadness of the flesh is also present in the anatomic register that Flaubert uses to describe the severed head of John: "The sharp blade of the weapon, slicing downwards, had caught the jaw. The corners of the mouth were drawn back in convulsion. Blood, already clotted, lay sprinkled on the beard" (104). The execution of John parallels the slaughter of the scapegoat. Notions of butchering and slaughter are associated not only with the head of John, but also with Aulus, whose lynched body was carried through Rome and exposed to the mob. This future scene related in Suetonius is already latently present in the banquet and alluded to by the Pharisees. They threaten Antipas with knives as though they want to slaughter him (99). Images of the interchangeability of man and animal converge in the idea of the Lamb of God that takes away the sins of the world as its scapegoat. The foundational reversability between humans and animals—animals with human traits, humans with animal qualities—leads to a terrible consequence in the slaughtered scapegoat. The beastly beheading of John is nothing but the sacrifice of another scapegoat that prefigures the failure of Christ's sacrifice on the cross: this sacrifice will not end the practice of sacrifices for times to come. The caesura that severs the head of John is capital insofar as it precisely does not represent a capital caesura. Like John, Christ will be only one more scapegoat and will change nothing in the practice of sacrificial cults ancient and modern. Only in this respect is John the predecessor of Christ, the proto-martyr of a continuing martyrdom.

Resurrection and the Pentecost Turned Upside Down: The Dance of Salome

Just as the figure of Aulus assembles and weirdly contains the components of the Eucharist in perverted form, the dance of Salome turns Pentecost upside down. It leads to a reaction that is the perversion of the outpouring of the Holy Ghost. When the Ghost descends to the assembled community at Pentecost in the form of tongues of fire, everyone is enflamed by divine love.[49] Similarly, the men at the Tetrarch's banquet are ignited in lust by the invisible sparks that are released from Salome: "from her arms, her feet, her clothes invisible sparks shot out, firing the men with excitement" (102). Beyond all dividing differences they are united by *concupiscentia*: "and the nomads accustomed to abstinence, the Roman soldiers skilled in debauchery, the avaricious publicans, the old priests soured with controversy, all with flaring nostrils shivered with lust" (102). When Salome lisps as she says John's name, which she cannot remember, this is a sign of her childishness. This recapitulates a motif we have already encountered in *A Sentimental Education*, that of a little girl prostituted by her mother.[50] Allegorically the prostitution of the daughter by the mother refers back to the matriarchal succession of the whorish cities. Yet Salome's lisp is in its resistant fleshliness—you lisp when your tongue wrongly touches your teeth—and in her repetition of a word that remains a dead letter to her, also the counterimage of the Pentecostal tongues of fire.[51]

The dance of Salome is performed under the sign of both erection and castration, death and resurrection. Flaubert confronts the Church's Covenant of Love founded on the Pentecost with a covenant of an altogether different kind of love. He has us read the story of Salome's dance and the beheading of John as a version of the phallic cult of Cybele. He does so according to Georg Friedrich Creuzer's *Symbolik und Mythologie der alten Völker* (*Symbolism and Mythology of the Ancients*, 1810–12), translated by J.-D. Guigniaut (1825–51), which he carefully worked through. In Creuzer we find, to begin with, Herod's beautiful horses, which have remained an unsolved riddle to interpreters. They are animals dedicated to the Sun god, hence connected to the cults of the Sun and the Phallus.[52] In "Hérodias," their herdsman is suitably a Babylonian: "As soon as Iakim entered they came to him, like sheep when their shepherd appears" (86). Creuzer traces all religions back to the one scheme of the dying away and reappearance of the sun as a principle of fertility and thereby of life. According to him, pre-Christian religions do nothing other than symbolize and stage this death and rebirth of nature in human sexuality and above all in the phallus cults, whose original pattern we find in the story of Isis and Osiris. These cults are idolatrous inasmuch as the phallus of Osiris is a crafted simulacrum, "the tool of generation that was lost and reproduced in image."[53]

Incest and fratricide are essential for Isis and Osiris *ab ovo*, one is tempted to say. "Already in the mother's womb, the myth begins, the two siblings Isis and Osiris were inflamed with love for one another and copulated" (2: 40). After the consummation of the mystical wedding in the body of their mother, they came into the world coupled not only as twins but as a wedded pair. Sister and wife, brother and husband reigned as the divine pair of Egypt.

"However, Osiris had an evil brother filled with envy and suspicion against him, Typhon, who would gladly have used the absence of his brother to take his place on the throne" (ibid.). And Typhon kills Osiris. So fratricide was not only in the beginning of mankind according to Genesis but also according to Egyptian myth: "So the savior Osiris must die at the hands of his brother" (2: 20).

Typhon hides the corpse, but Isis finds it:

She hides the corpse and coffin in a lonely place deep in the woods. A hunt called forth by the wild hunter Typhon leads to the discovery of the casket. It is opened, at which point Typhon attacks the corpse, cuts it up and divides it into fourteen pieces. Isis discovers the loss, she searches on a papyrus boat for the hacked up corpse of Osiris and travels through all seven mouths of the Nile until she finally gathers together thirteen pieces; only the fourteenth member, the masculine, she cannot find, because certain fish, cursed ever since, have eaten it. She pieces the corpse together and the missing member is replaced with a replication out of sycamore wood. Isis dedicates the phallus and its cult to his memory. (ibid.)

Central for Creuzer's cosmological interpretation of the Isis and Osiris myth is the loss and re-erection of the male member. The cutting off and the devouring by fish correspond to the decrease of the sun in fall and winter. Castration symbolizes the dying of nature. The re-erection of the male member as phallus symbolizes the winter solstice, in which the sun begins to climb and revive everything. The celebration of the summer solstice is the moment when Osiris's inseminating power is rediscovered: "the phallus is instituted, which means that now the sun comes up again, has made it through the dark" (2: 36). Creuzer reads the myth as a popular tale—as "the legend—of the natural and chronological history of the Egyptian land" (ibid.); it tells of the condition of all natural life. For Creuzer the cult of Cybele is a variation of the Isis and Osiris cults.

The service of Cybele overtook, Creuzer writes, "the entire old world, and set up its seat in the metropole of the world, great Rome" (2: 364). All of the Middle East were followers of her, "and the imperial Romans distinguished this cult, among only a few others in their city, with the most important privileges" (2: 365). The Cybele cult was at that time then, according to Creuzer, a state religion and, as the state religion of the Roman

Empire that preceded the Christian Church of Rome, a world religion. Rome shows itself to be already fully oriental, Asian, and not for the first time with Flaubert's text, but already in Creuzer's work. According to Creuzer, the cult that became a world religion with Rome was originally a Syrian, Phrygian, Babylonian, and in any case an oriental cult.

Cybele was at the time of Christ's birth a pantheon of gods, a kind of syncretistic super-goddess. Her most consistent attributes were the crown of towers and the two lions beneath her throne (2: 377). Hérodias appears at the Tetrarch's banquet in exactly this way to take over. What are the determining practices of this cult? According to Creuzer, the Cybele cult was a lavish one, and by that he meant it was wild, lecherous, orgiastic. He finds this lavishness especially among "the sensuous people of Babylon," where Cybele was honored under the name of Mylitta:

More opulent than in Persia was the service of this goddess in the sensuous people of Babylon. The lecherous tribute that the female sex rendered in the temple of the great Mylitta, where every Babylonian woman once in her life had to give herself to every chooser (Herodotus 1.199), broke through the strict protections that were otherwise inflexibly drawn around women by Asian custom." (Creuzer, 2: 377)

Salome's lascivious dance would count as a form of temple prostitution, and Renan rightly wondered how even high-ranking women—here the daughter of the queen—could exhibit themselves publicly in such a shameless way. The Babylonian carpets refer implicitly to the temple prostitution and lend the appropriate framework. Unlike Flaubert, Renan was either unfamiliar with Creuzer or did not believe the cult of Cybele was practiced in the region under Herod.

As it had been for the Isis cult, fall and erection of the phallus is basic for the Cybele cult, though in a clearly sharpened form. Unlike the Isis cult, the Cybele cult is not determined by animal sacrifices but by representative sacrifices. In fact, the male member is sacrificed: under intoxication Cybele's priests unman themselves in cultic celebration. Cybele has a lover, Attis, and the entire cult turns around the departure and rediscovery of Attis, around his unmanning and re-erection. Attis unmans himself because he was unfaithful to Cybele. According to the wish of the gods, however, no member of Attis should perish. Like Osiris, Attis serves, according to Creuzer, as incarnation of the sun, whose path symbolizes unmanning and re-erecting male energy. With recaptured energy Attis celebrates his wedding with Cybele anew every year. The wedding ceremony takes orgiastic, enthusiastic forms; it is accompanied by music and dance, in which castration and lovemaking appear to be the same (2: 367). To quote Lucretius: "The Galli come: / and hollow cymbals, tight-skinned tambourines resound around to bangings of their hands; / the fierce horns threaten with a raucous bray; / the tubed pipe excites their maddened minds / in Phrygian measures; they bear before them knives, / wild emblems of their frenzy."[54] Creuzer himself writes:

The disappearance and recovery of Attis determines in this religion, as in similar forms of nature worship, the two essential celebratory periods. With the beginning of spring the festival began. A day of mourning, the 21st of March, inaugurated the whole thing. On this day one raises up the pine tree [until today the word for the male member in Romance languages] and plants the tree in the goddess's temple. One designated this day and its symbolic treatment with a saying: *Arbor intrat.* The second day was the day of horns. Horns would be blown incessantly. On the third day Attis was found and the jubilation over this discovery carried the long held-back masculine power beyond every boundary and drove it up to the peak of joy into fanatical anger and bloody acts. The intoxicating tone of the cymbals and hand drums, pipes and horns, accompanied the enthusiastic dances of armed priests. . . . Among other festive preparations and in another regard the castration took place, through which the priests became eunuchs. . . . The masculine would thereupon be carried forward in reality, instead of just a symbolic phallus being carried forward in the procession. This castration had a metaphorical relationship to the extinguished production of nature in winter. (2: 366–67)

The dance of Salome and the subsequent decapitation of John combine displaced elements from Cybele's cult. Hérodias appears as Earth Mother, like Cybele with two lions, and emblematically preludes the themes of passion, sacrifice, and death developed in the dance of her daughter: "With two stone monsters, like those in Atrides' treasure, standing against the door, she looked like Cybele flanked by her lions" (100). The name of the "Atrides" points to the family that has become proverbial for incest and matricide. Flaubert unites these ancient families with the Jewish families under the sign of Saint Augustine's Babylon. The motif of death is announced by the two lions, which resemble the lions that guard the sepulchral entrance of Mycenae.[55] Pertinent to Flaubert is the warlike element, in which men, in exuberant joy over the immortality of Attis's member—over the rise of the life-giving sun—not only mutilate themselves, but fiercely grasp for their weapons. Significantly, the men praying to the goddess wear feminine clothing, as Creuzer reports. The same warlike sentiment and transvestite tastes are unmistakable among the men gathered for the Tetrarch's celebration. Salome dances to her mother's tune: "drums thunder from strikes of the hand, therein / to murmur the hollow cymbals, and the tone of raw-voiced horns blares" (2: 366). Flaubert illustrates Lucretius's description found in Creuzer, who cites precisely this passage. To proceed with the metaphor, Salome is a well-practiced instrument in the hands of her mother, as willing as she is indifferent. She is prostituted and abused for the sake of her mother's power. Her stockings are embroidered with mandrake, a flower reputed to grow under the gallows and regarded as the strongest aphrodisiac. According to legend, it sprouts from the seed ejaculated by the hanged at the moment of death. The longevity of the motif has been only recently demonstrated by Bruce Nauman's neon light sculpture *Hanged Man*.[56] Mourning music is played for the dance, just as it accompanies the cult of Cybele: "the mournful sound of the gingras" (101). Salome anticipates the outcome of the dance—the severed head—in the image of a decapitation that her dance figures: "her neck and spine were at right angles" (102). In his *Voyage en Égypte*, Flaubert is more explicit as to what this image is about, and he registers at the same time the fear triggered by the danced form: "Her neck slides on the back spine forth and more often to the side, as if the head would fall off any moment—one gets the terrible impression of a decapitation."[57] As if unmanned, the Tetrarch collapses after the excitement: "The Tetrarch collapsed, shattered" (103). The beheading of John is obviously a displaced castration and corresponds to the unmanning.[58] The phallus in these scenarios is not in good shape, it collapses. The rule that has been rigidly towering over the abyss will collapse according to the logic of history, because the mountain on which it was built is already hollowed out, just as the aroused Herod Antipas collapses in excitement after Salome's dance. The severed head of the Baptist references this metaphor of castration.

But Flaubert goes even further in the condensation of myth and appropriates the sun motif that symbolizes the decrease and increase of the sun in unmanning and re-erection. John the Baptist murmurs his leitmotif, "For him to increase, I must decrease," in a cave, his prison cell, which is itself a symbol of the mother goddess, so that he speaks and repeats this sentence endlessly from her womb. "So that he gets longer, so that he grows, I must become smaller, shorter, shrink." The final meaning of these words emerges from the resonances of the Cybele cult: Christ is born at the winter solstice, when the sun's elevation in the sky starts to increase and the days become longer; John, at the summer solstice, when sunlight is decreasing and the days start to become shorter. Flaubert restores the relationship between John and Christ within the sun cult. The proclamation of Christ as the awaited Messiah takes place at sunrise: "as the sun was rising, two men, sent out earlier by Iaokanannn, arrived with the long hoped-for reply. . . . Now the Essene understood these words: 'For him to increase, I must decrease'" (105). Translated back into the sexual symbolism from which it originated, this means that Flaubert's analysis concludes with the reinscription of Christianity into the pagan phallic castration cults.

Flaubert's archeology identifies Christianity as phallus worship, a pseudomorphosis of pagan rites. In Hérodias/Salome, the Cybele cult and the story of Isis and Osiris—the motifs of incest and fratricide—are merged together. Cybele/Hérodias is completely of this world and rules the political world through phallus worship, fratricide, and incest. "Hérodias" tells of the globalization of this religion under the cover of the emergence of the Catholic Church. This new institution, in whose guise Babel goes global under inverted signs, is born of the worldly rule of the emperor Aulus Vitellius and Hérodias. Both are sterile: Hérodias an incestuous wife, Aulus a former catamite whose turn it is to love toy boys.[59] Out of sterility, the new is born, which turns out to be worse than the old foresaw. Both Hérodias and Aulus have special places in Flaubert's novella, because the Good News is inverted, but is still, and in a memorable way, remembered through them. They reduce the Eucharist and Pentecost to pure, mortal flesh and butcher's meat—sex, gorging, violence. In this blind literalness there is no trace of spirituality left that would allow for a loving understanding. Decisive in this syncretism is a political-historical point that turns on the state of the empire.[60] Flaubert merges historical texts (Tacitus, Suetonius, Flavius Josephus) and mythologies (Creuzer). He deliberately makes up historical facts and rewrites their mythical underpinnings. The result is a doubled genealogy of the Christian world.

On the one hand, this Christian world continues with a political theology under more devastating conditions. With the Roman Catholic Church, born of Aulus and Hérodias, the claim of a salvific kingdom of this world became global, driven forward by the pretense of a kingdom not of this world. The distinctions that run between Orient and Occident, other and self, sensual and rational, the effeminized tyrannical and the masculine upright, idolatry and belief, between Babylon and Rome, but also between Jerusalem and Babylon, collapse. Basic for the Roman Empire, for medieval and modern Europe, its heir, basic above all for the Roman Catholic Church, this historical construct breaks down. Jews and Romans are in this breakdown of history as oriental as they are catholic, occupied with the continuing empires of this world, entangled in the worldly politics of fratricide and incest. Political theology is the mask of sexual politics.

Let me resume the evidence and add one last significant point: Hérodias, the romanized Jewish queen, makes Caesar's politics her own; the alliance that comes about at Herod's banquet between Hérodias and the Sadducees advances the murder of John. Incest and fratricide as principles of politics in Rome and Israel alike proliferate: "'No matter! I am most unfairly treated!' said Antipas. 'After all Absalom slept with his father's wives, Judah with his daughter-in-law, Amnon with his sister, Lot with his daughters'" (91). With ease, the Tetrarch sums up the incests upon which the Old Testament thrives. Herod the Great's family history reads as follows: "He it was who drowned Aristobulus, strangled Alexander, burned Matathias alive, beheaded Zozimus, Pappus, Joseph, and Antipater" (103). Flaubert's commentary notes: "*Aristobule*, drowned in year 33, was his brother-in-law, *Joseph*, decapitated in the same year, was his uncle, *Alexander*, strangled in year 6, and *Antipater*, beheaded two years later, were none other than his sons."[61] Thus, the state of the affairs, whose foremost paradigm, Tiberius's succession that followed the Divine Augustus's reign, was documented by Tacitus and appropriately named *arcana domus*. The role of the Old Testament is reduced from its prophetic status to that of an arbitrary historical source for the same *arcana imperii*: incest and fratricide.

Hérodias/John is a *figura* of a confrontation fulfilled in Julian/Christ: the hunter in defiance of God, founder of the earthly city, and Christ, founder of the heavenly city, are opposed to one another in "Saint Julian the Hospitalier." Hérodias and Julian fit together under the sign of the hunt. The key to the symbolic meaning of Hérodias, like the meaning of the deer in Julian's legend, can be found in Alfred Maury's *Croyances et légendes du moyen âge*. Readers have always been surprised that Hérodias's reaction to the happy outcome of her efforts, her triumph in the face of her dead enemy on the tray, is absent from the story. Hérodias, who gives the story her name, disappears without further ado, because she went hunting.

We find in Maury that the Middle Ages believed that after John's execution, Hérodias was cursed to wander the woods every night until cockcrow. But that is not all. For Hérodias is also, we read in Maury, another name for Diana, the goddess of the hunt, or Venus: "The goddess Holda, whom the Romans identified as Diana or Venus . . . was also called . . . Hérodiade."[62] In Hérodias, the huntress—allegorically the huntress against the Lord—and the goddess coincide in carnal love. This huntress has nothing about her of the chaste Diana. On the contrary, Hérodias is an infernal Diana ("Diane infernale"), the supremely arousing femme fatale par excellence. Flaubert took Henri II's mistress Diane de Poitiers, whose portrait Frédéric encounters in the palace of Fontainebleau, to have been an infernal Diana of this type. In a famous sentence from *A Sentimental Education*, Flaubert depicts the infernal queen of the hunt as the quintessential object of desire: "The loveliest of all such famous women had had herself portrayed, on the right, in the shape of Diane the Huntress or even of the Queen of the Night, no doubt to assert her infernal powers beyond the grave. . . . Frédéric felt a sudden, indescribable retrospective concupiscence."[63] All erotically enticing women in Flaubert are daughters of Babylon; all of them have something oriental about them as daughters of the Great Whore.

Thus, while the Catholic Church achieves the globalization of Babel under Vitellius and Hérodias, these two exponents of power also testify with satanic irony to the Christian promise of the Resurrection and Pentecost. This function of a negative profiling, which is occupied by Nero as Anti-Christ in Renan, is assigned to Hérodias and Aulus Vitellius in Flaubert. For "Hérodias" is not a critique, but a deconstruction of Christianity. In the perversion offered in the story, the perverted is affirmed, a promise of love unto death, if only just until death. The disciples carry the head of John out of the fortress; it does not remain with Hérodias, as is most likely in the Bible version. They carry the heavy head of John, his *testa-mentum*, with difficulty. In unknowing anticipation of the stations of the cross, they head for the cross that lies before them and will complete the work of the Baptist. One could almost say that the Petrine weight of this head renders the spirituality of Pauline Christianity speechless. The capital caesura, which the birth of Christ was meant to be, turns out to be literally nothing but the beheading of John, through which pagan antiquity is carried onward under updated devastating conditions. On the other hand, John's beheading is a capital caesura in the metaphorical sense, a historical turning point: in the cross the transcendental immanence of a thus unsurpassed love becomes manifest. From the beginning and for all eternity, history turns out to be a testament to a promise that it has latently, in the negative, inverted form, transmitted nonetheless.

There remains the blue. Flaubert wrote *Three Tales* on blue paper. Blue shines in the manes of the horses, in the hair of the Tetrarch, in the lapis lazuli of the sea, on the forehead of the parrot, in the open skies. Blue is the color of Mary, the color of the stained glass in the cathedral of Notre-Dame de Chartres, which bathes the interior in an unearthly, heavenly light. Chartres is the city of Madame Arnoux, the Mary of *A Sentimental Education*, who bears the Annunciation in her name. Flaubert shades his testament with the color blue, which, despite everything, illuminates his cathedral.

REFERENCE MATTER

Notes

Crossed Out

This chapter was translated by Aarnoud Rommens.

Epigraph: Friedrich Nietzsche, *The Anti-Christ, Ecce Homo, Twilight of the Idols and Other Writings*, ed. Aaron Ridley and Judith Norman, trans. Judith Norman (Cambridge: Cambridge University Press, 2005), 14.

1. "Pro captu lectoris habent sua fata libelli [Texts have their fate based on the capacity of the reader]": Terentianus Maurus (ca. first and second centuries CE), *De litteris, de syllabis, de metris*, ed. Chiara Cignolo (Hildesheim: Olms, 2002) = Collectanea grammatica latina 6.325–413.

2. Barbara Vinken, "Maculature ou De la difficulté de lire. *Leçon de choses* de Claude Simon," in *Lectures allemandes de Claude Simon*, ed. Irene Albers and Wolfram Nitsch (Villeneuve d'Ascq: Presses universitaires du Septentrion, 2013), 149–70.

3. In most contexts, especially sociology, "secularization" refers to the defeat of the sacred and God's receding from human affairs altogether, or at least the reduced prominence of practices of signification centered on religion. This disenchantment with the world is the fantasy that with the "death of God," we have finally become free of this entire tradition, since now "everything is permitted." However, it could be argued that we are still dealing with the *Nachträglichkeit* of Christianity today and the structure of messianism in particular, as Derrida shows in *Specters of Marx*. Lacan observes that it is only with the death of God that "nothing is permitted."

4. See Jean-Paul Sartre, *The Family Idiot: Gustave Flaubert, 1821–1857* (Chicago: University of Chicago Press, 1981), vol. 1.

5. Cf. Barbara Vinken, "Aufhebung ins Weibliche: Mariologie und bloßes Leben bei Joseph Ratzinger, Benedikt XVI," in *Ratzinger-Funktion* (Frankfurt/Main: Suhrkamp, 2006), 24–55.

6. "Quoiqu'elle n'eût plus de jeunesse ni de beauté, elle le gouvernait avec un empire si absolu que l'on peut dire qu'elle était maîtressse de sa personne et de l'Etat." See also Jean-Michel Delacomptée, *La Princesse de Clèves: La mère et le courtisan* (Paris: Presses universitaires de France, 1990), 115.

7. Octave Mannoni quoted in André Green, *Le complexe de castration* (Paris: Presses universitaires de France, 1995), 64.

8. Flaubert, excerpts and comments from and to Samuel Cahen's translation of the Song of Songs (trans. BV), MS Morgan Library & Museum, New York: "Les femmes riches avaient des esclaves qui portaient leurs chaussures dans les étuis. Plaute les appele *sandaligerulae*. Benoit Baudoin qui etait cordonnier et qui s'étant mis à l'étude s'est appliqué à ce qui regarde la chaussure à compter jusqu'à vingt sept sortes de souliers divers."

9. Flaubert MS, "Voltaire—Mélanges, critique littéraire et historique" (unpublished excerpts, trans. BV), Morgan Library & Museum, New York: "Un prince héritier d'une grande monarchie n'aimait que les pieds. On dit qu'en Espagne ce goût avait été assez commun. Les femmes par le soin de les cacher avaient tourné vers eux l'imagination de plusieurs hommes."

10. Cf. Marthe Robert, *Roman des origines et origine du roman* (Paris: Gallimard, 1972).

11. Michel Foucault, "Foreword," in Gustave Flaubert, *The Temptation of Saint Anthony* (New York: Modern Library, 2001), xiii–xliv.

12. Janet Beizer, "The Physiology of Style: Sex, Text, and the Gender of Writing," in *Ventriloquized Bodies: Narratives of Hysteria in 19th Century France* (Ithaca, NY: Cornell University Press, 1994), 77–98.

13. This is treated in exemplary fashion in Harold Bloom's *The Anxiety of Influence: A Theory of Poetry* (Oxford: Oxford University Press, 1997).

14. In "Three Questions to Hans-Georg Gadamer," Jacques Derrida argues against Gadamer's authority principle of tradition. See *Dialogue and Deconstruction: The Gadamer-Derrida Encounter*, ed. Diane P. Michelfelder and Richard E. Palmer (Albany: State University of New York Press, 1989), 52–55.

15. Friedrich Nietzsche, *The Anti-Christ*, trans. H. L. Mencken (New York: Cosimo, 2005), 16.

16. Ibid., 4.

17. For the significance of kenosis in the formation of the modern subject, see Marcus Coelen, *Die Tyrannei des Partikularen: Lektüren Prousts* (Munich: Wilhelm Fink, 2007), 152–61.

18. Nietzsche, *Anti-Christ*, trans. Mencken, 31.

19. Ibid., 26.

20. Ibid., 32.

21. Ibid., 28.

22. Ibid., 30.

23. Ibid., 35.

24. Ibid., 32.

25. Ibid., 28.

26. Ibid., 32.

27. Flaubert, *Madame Bovary: Contexts, Criticism*, trans. Paul de Man and Eleanor Marx Aveling, ed. Margaret Cohen (New York: Norton, 2005), 275.

28. Cf. Claude Lefort, "La permanence du théologico-politique," *Le temps de la réflexion* 11 (1981): 13–61.

29. Flaubert to Louise Colet, September 4, 1852, in *The Letters of Gustave Flaubert*, ed. and trans. Francis Steegmuller (Cambridge, MA: Belknap Press of Harvard University Press, 1980–82), 1: 169.

30. Acts 10:39, KJV. All subsequent biblical citations are from the King James Version.

31. My use of the rhetorical term catachresis as "dead metaphor" owes its specific historical point to Fontanier's reevaluation of tropes and his redefinition of the "abuse" named in the Latin translation of catachresis as *abusio*: Pierre Fontanier, *Les figures du discours* (1827), with preface by Gérard Genette (Paris: Flammarion, 1968), part III, pp. 209ff. The last great attempt at a new linguistic refashioning of rhetoric, Group M's *Rhétorique générale* (Paris: Larousse, 1970), p. 95, dedicates a footnote to the French genealogy of the term in Fontanier's precursor Dumarsais's *Des Tropes* (1730), preface by Françoise Douay-Soublin (Paris: Flammarion, 1988), chap. II, p. 182, where catachresis is valued as a radicalized overextension of metaphor and thus, in the eyes of the *Rhétorique générale* is overused in the old sense of *abusio* in Quintilian; reduced to a purely instrumental use, catachresis is no longer a figure at all: *A General Rhetoric*, trans. Paul Burell and Edgar Slotkin (Baltimore: Johns Hopkins University Press, 1981), p. 239, note 8 to chap. IV. Paul Ricoeur has drawn his conclusion from Fontanier under the telling title *La métaphore vive* (Paris: Seuil, 1975), a point unfortunately missed in the English title *The Rule of Metaphor*, trans. Robert Szerny (London: Routledge & Kegan Paul, 1977). From "dead metaphor" a new Pauline understanding of writing originates.

32. Jacques Derrida, *On the Name* (Stanford: Stanford University Press, 1995), 54.

33. "L'illustration est antilittéraire. . . . Voulez vous que le premier imbécile venu dessine ce que je me suis tué à ne pas montrer?" This is Flaubert's indignant response, as reported by Pascal Quignard, to his publisher Gervais Charpentier's suggestion of illustrated editions of his work. In Pascal Quignard, *Petits traités* (Paris: Gallimard, 1997), 1: 131.

34. Theodor W. Adorno and Max Horkheimer, *Dialectic of Enlightenment*, ed. Gunzelin Schmid Noerr, trans. Edmund Jephcott (Stanford: Stanford University Press, 2002), 18.

35. John 3:30: "He must increase, but I must decrease" (KJV). Gustave Flaubert, *Three Tales*, trans. A. J. Krailsheimer (Oxford: Oxford University Press, 2009), 74.

"Quidquid volueris": The Monstrosity of Civilization

This chapter was translated by Susan L. Solomon.

1. For a contextualization of this motif, see Gerhard Neumann and Barbara Vinken, "Kulturelle Mimikry: Zur Affenfigur bei Flaubert und Kafka," *Zeitschrift für deutsche Philologie* 126 (2007): 126–42.

2. Sigmund Freud, *General Introduction to Psychoanalysis*, trans. G. Stanley Hall (New York: Boni & Liveright, 1920), pt. 3, ch. 23, para. 25.

3. Flaubert, "Whatever You Want," in id., *Early Writings*, trans. Robert Griffin (Lincoln: University of Nebraska Press, 1991), 78 (this is the source of all the quotations here, subsequent page numbers for which are given parenthetically in the text). "Quidquid volueris—Études psychologiques," in Flaubert, *Œuvres de jeunesse*, vol. 1 of *Œuvres complètes*, ed. Claudine Gothot-Mersch and Guy Sagnes (Paris: Gallimard, 2001), 245.

4. See Barbara Vinken, "'Tränen zum Leben, Tränen zum Tode': Katharina von Siena, Petrarca, Boccaccio, Theresa von Avila, Zola," in *Tränen*, ed. Beate Söntgen and Geraldine Spiekermann (Munich: Wilhelm Fink, 2008), 17–26.

5. Jean-Paul Sartre's biographical reading of "Quidquid volueris" in *L'idiot de la famille—Gustave Flaubert de 1821–1857* (Paris: Gallimard, 1971), 1: 29–35, concentrates on this. English translation: *The Family Idiot: Gustave Flaubert, 1821–1857* (Chicago: University of Chicago Press, 1981).

6. Translation modified—BV.

Madame Bovary: Mœurs de province—Provincial Manners

This chapter was translated by Aarnoud Rommens.

1. See Stephen Heath, *Madame Bovary* (Cambridge: Cambridge University Press, 1992), and on consumer fetishism, see Joachim Küpper, "Das Ende von Emma Bovary," in *Geschichte und Text in der Literatur Frankreichs, der Romania und der Literaturwissenschaft. Rita Schober zum 80. Geburtstag*, ed. Hans-Otto Dill (Berlin: trafo, 1999), 71–93. For a very different reading of this phenomenon, seen as a commentary on utilitarianism, see Frances Ferguson, "Emma, or Happiness (or Sex Work)," in *Pornography, the Theory* (Chicago: University of Chicago Press, 2004), 96–124.

2. For an example of the *amazone*, see Édouard Manet's painting *The Amazon or Horsewoman*, ca. 1882, Villa Flora Winterthur (Collection Hahnloser).

3. Proudhon in the Dictionnaire Larousse, s.v. "adultère," cited by Michael Riffaterre, "Flaubert's Presuppositions," *Diacritics* 11 (1981): 5. My translation—BV.

4. Ibid., 6, quoting *Les Français peints par eux-mêmes* (Paris: L. Curmer, 1841), 3: 265 (http://gallica.bnf.fr/ark:/12148/bpt6k2079830/f348.image).

5. Riffaterre, "Flaubert's Presuppositions," 9.

6. "I committed fornication against you [*Et fornicabar abs te*]," Augustine, *Confessions. Books I–IV*, ed. Gillian Clark (Cambridge: Cambridge University Press, 1995), 1.13.21 (p. 39).

7. Saint Augustine, *Confessions*, trans. Henry Chadwick (Oxford: Oxford University Press, 1991), 115–16: "quae fiebat non amando te, deus, lumen cordis mei et panis oris intus animae meae et vitus maritans mentem meam et sinum cogitationis meae? Non te amabum et 'fornicabar abs te' (Ps. 72: 27). . . . 'Amicitia' enim 'mundi huius fornicatio est abs te . . .'"

8. All citations are from the Norton Critical Edition, *Madame Bovary*, ed. Margaret Cohen, trans. Eleanor Marx Aveling and Paul de Man (London: Norton, 2005). Page numbers are given in the text. Citations in the French original are from *Madame Bovary: Mœurs de province*, ed. Claudine Gothot-Mersch (Paris: Classiques Garnier, 1971). For valuable comments, see also *Madame Bovary: Mœurs de province*, ed. Jacques Neefs (Paris: Librairie générale française, 1999), and Pierre-Marc de Biasi, *Madame Bovary: Mœurs de province* (Paris: Imprimerie nationale, 1994).

9. Augustine, *Confessions* 1.12.

10. For the ramifications of this discussion, see Barbara Vinken, "Der Ursprung der Ästhetik aus theologischem Vorbehalt. Ästhetische Kontroversen von Port-Royal bis Rousseau und Sade" (PhD diss., Yale University, 1991).

11. On the motif of the healing Christ, see Gerhard Fichtner, "Christus als Arzt. Ursprünge und Wirkungen eines Motivs," *Frühmittelalterliche Studien* 16 (1982): 1–18.

12. This observation would tend to support the thesis put forward by Jonathan Culler in "The Uses of Madame Bovary," *Diacritics* 11 (1981): 74–81, on the anachronism of Flaubert's procedures, which run counter to his radical modernity.

13. As formulated by Louise Kaplan, *Female Perversions: The Temptation of Madame Bovary* (New York: Doubleday, 1991).

14. Gustave Flaubert, *Madame Bovary*, ed. Maurice Bardèche (Paris: Librairie générale française, 1972), appendix, "Le procès. Le ministère public contre Gustave Flaubert. Réquisitoire de M. l'avocat impérial M. Ernest Pinard," 413–37; 426, 423.

15. Micheline Hermine, *Destins de femmes. Désir d'absolu. Essai sur Madame Bovary et Thérèse de Lisieux* (Paris: Beauchesne, 1997).

16. Flaubert to Marie-Sophie Leroyer de Chantepie, May 30, 1857, conceives of Emma Bovary as "vierge, vivant au milieu de la province, vieillissant dans le chagrin et arrivant ainsi aux derniers états du mysticisme et de la passion rêvée." Quoted in Martine Reid, *Flaubert correspondant* (Paris: Sedes, 1995), 61.

17. See Erich Auerbach, *Mimesis* (Bern: Francke, 1964), trans. Willard R. Trask as *Mimesis: The Representation of Reality in Western Literature* (Princeton, NJ: Princeton University Press, 1953, 2013); Jean-Pierre Richard, *Littérature et sensation* (Paris: Seuil, 1954); Victor Brombert, *The Novels of Flaubert* (Princeton, NJ: Princeton University Press, 1966).

18. Culler, "Uses of Madame Bovary," 11.

19. Avital Ronell, *Crack Wars: On Mania, Addiction and Literature* (Lincoln: University of Nebraska Press, 1992). For a rather idiosyncratic psychoanalytic reading, see Ion K. Collas, *Madame Bovary: A Psychoanalytic Reading* (Ghent: Librairie Droz, 1995).

20. Flaubert, *Madame Bovary*, ed. Bardèche, appendix, "Le procès," 423.

21. "Voilà deux jours que j'essaie d'entrer dans les rêves de jeune fille et que

je navigue pour cela dans les océans laiteux de la littérature à castels et de troubadours à toques de velours à plumes blanches." Flaubert to Louise Colet, March
3, 1852, in *Correspondance*, ed. Claude Pichois (Paris: Bibliothèque de la Pléiade,
1973), 2: 56.

22. Cf. Klaus Lange, "Geistliche Speise. Untersuchungen zur Metaphorik der
Bibelhermeneutik," *Zeitschrift für deutsches Altertum und deutsche Literatur* 95, no.
2 (1966): 6–122. On the renaissance of the Patristic tradition in the nineteenth
century, see *Migne et le renouveau des études patristiques,* ed. André Mandouze
and Joël Fouilheron (Paris: Beauchesne, 1985), and A. G. Hamann, *Jacques-Paul
Migne: Le retour aux Pères de l'Eglise* (Paris: Beauchesne, 1975).

23. Flaubert to Louise Colet, April 13, 1853, in *Correspondance*, ed. Pichois, 2: 304.

24. Janet Beizer, "Les lettres de Flaubert à Louise Colet: Une physiologie de
style," in *L'œuvre de l'œuvre: Études sur la correspondance de Flaubert,* ed. Raymonde
Debray-Genette and Jacques Neefs (Saint Denis, Paris: Presses universitaires de
Vincennes, 1993), 63.

25. Flaubert, *Correspondance*, ed. Jean Bruneau (Paris: Bibliothèque de la Pléiade,
1973–2007), 1: 48 and 2: 387.

26. Charles Baudelaire, "Madame Bovary, by Gustave Flaubert," in *Madame
Bovary*, ed. Margaret Cohen (New York: Norton, 2005), 410.

27. On the psychoanalytic implications of this convergence of hysteria, feminine lust, and the Medusa, and the male anxiety articulated therein, there is much
to say. But this will have to be taken up on another occasion.

28. At the mention of the wet nurse's name by her unfortunate daughter, Emma
turns her head away. The nurse is a connection in multiple scriptural senses. The
milk of the breast of Christ is "sweeter than wine"; and above all in exegeses of the
Song of Songs, milk is a metaphor for the spiritually nourishing, sweet meaning of
the Scriptures. The breasts of Berthe's nurse are not, however, "sweeter than wine."
The nourishment the baby gets is tainted with brandy, for which, the text insinu-
ates, the nurse trades her milk. It makes Berthe ill, and it is at the wet nurse's home
that Emma's dress is stained with vomit for the first time, prefiguring the black
fluid that will leak posthumously from her corpse.

29. J.-B. Pitra's *Spicilegium solesmense* (Paris: Firmin Didot, 1855) had appeared
two years earlier.

30. Cf. Karin Westerwelle, *Ästhetisches Interesse und nervöse Krankheit. Balzac,
Baudelaire, Flaubert* (Stuttgart: Metzler, 1993).

31. On the motif of the spider and the inscription of Flaubert into the Ovidian
tradition, see Edi Zollinger, *Arachnes Rache. Flaubert inszeniert einen Wettkampf im
narrativen Weben: Madame Bovary, Notre-Dame de Paris und der Arachne-Mythos*
(Paderborn: Fink, 2007).

32. Quoted in Pierre-Marc de Biasi, *Madame Bovary: Mœurs de province* (Paris:
Imprimerie nationale, 1994), 524.

33. Ibid., 604n483.

34. Jonathan Culler, *Flaubert: The Uses of Uncertainty* (Ithaca, NY: Cornell University Press, 1974), 79.

35. Gustave Flaubert, *Salammbo*, trans. A. J. Krailsheimer (New York: Penguin Books, 1977), 241.

36. "Victime d'un sacrifice expiatoire, Mme Bovary rassemble le mal répandu à Yonville comme le bouc émissaire des Hébreux. Elle est en même temps sacrificatrice." See Michel Butor, *Improvisations sur Flaubert* (Paris: Éditions de la Différence, 1984), 106.

37. Madame Bovary is a woman who fully accepts her desires, Alain Buisine remarks. See *Emma Bovary*, ed. Alain Buisine (Paris: Autrement, 1997), 7.

38. Jean Racine, *Phaedra* 1.3.306 in id., *Iphigenia, Phaedra, Athaliah*, trans. John Cairncross (London: Penguin Books, 1970), 161.

39. Quoted in Butor, *Improvisations sur Flaubert*, 81. "En outre, son futur roman l'occupait; il me disait: 'J'en suis obsédé.' Devant les paysages africains il rêvait à des paysages normands. Aux confins de la Nubie inférieure . . . pendant que nous regardions le Nil se battre contre des épis de rochers en granit noir, il jeta un cri: 'J'ai trouvé! Euréka! euréka! je l'appellerai Emma Bovary'; et plusieurs fois il répéta, il dégusta le nom de Bovary en prononçant l'*o* très bref." My translation—BV.

40. See Agnès Bouvier, "Jéhovah égale Moloch: Une lecture antireligieuse de *Salammbô*," *Romantisme* 136 (2007): 113.

41. For a discussion of the reversal of contemporary orientalism under the sign of Babel, see Chapter 5 in this book on *A Sentimental Education*.

42. Quotations refer to the translation by Margaret Mauldon (Oxford: Oxford University Press, 2004), here 233.

43. Cf. Friedrich Nietzsche, *The Will to Power*, ed. Walter Kaufmann, trans. Walter Kaufmann and R. J. Hollingdale (New York: Vintage Books, 1968).

44. Saint Augustine, "Ad Pollentium de adulterinis coniugiis," 2.5–7, in *Corpus Scriptorum Ecclesiasticorum Latinorum*, vol. 41, ed. Joseph Zycha (Vienna: F. Tempsky, 1900), 387: "quamvis enim sit mors adulterium non corporis, sed quod peius est animae."

45. Elfriede Jelinek elaborates magnificently on the metaphoric constellation of sex and slaughter in *Lust* (1989), trans. Michael Hulse (London: Serpent's Tail, 1992).

46. I quote here from the Oxford edition. The Norton translation is somewhat palid: "But the more Emma grew conscious of her love, the more she repressed it, hoping thus to hide and to stifle her true feeling" (90).—Trans.

47. The objectification is less pronounced (except in the final remark) in the English translation, where the original French passages are rendered as "How bored she gets!" "How she'd want to" and "she'd adore me" (106).—Trans.

48. The Oxford translation has "it." Translation changed.

49. For more on the apricot as a metaphor for the female genitalia, see Neefs's commentary in *Madame Bovary*, ed. Neefs, 317.

50. *Madame Bovary*, ed. Cohen (cited n. 8 above), 165. A direct reference to the ram disappears in Margaret Mauldron's translation of *Madame Bovary* (cited n. 42 above), where when Emma reads Rodolphe's letter "her heart began to thump, pounding her chest with great hammer-blows" (182).

51. See Antonia Fonyi, "Sa 'vie nombreuse', sa 'haine nombreuse,'" in *Emma Bovary*, ed. Alain Buisine (Paris: Éd. Autrement, 1997), 122–44.

52. See Charles Baudelaire, "*Madame Bovary*, by Gustave Flaubert" (cited n. 26 above), 403–10. Ever since Baudelaire's spectacular analysis, Emma's androgyny has become a commonplace in scholarship, which for the most part places all emphasis on psychological or psychoanalytic elements.

53. For more on Rouen as amphitheater, see Flaubert, *Madame Bovary*, ed. Gérard Gengembre (Paris: Magnard, 1992), 603, 625. On the obviousness of this Babylonian topos, see also Flaubert to Louis Bouilhet, May 24, 1855: "(je suis en plein Rouen) . . . Le mot est lâché: *Babylone* y est, tant pis! Tout cela, je crois, frise bougrement le ridicule. C'est *trop fort*" (*Correspondance*, 2: 575).

54. On the importance Flaubert accorded to his *turbans alimentaires*, see his letter to Louis Bouillhet cited in the preceding note.

55. The homophony of *sang* and *sens* is, of course, lost in translation, but the joke about Homais's lack of (common) sense remains the same.—Trans.

56. "Dans *Mme Bovary* comme dans *L'éducation sentimentale*, la banqeroute, prologue funèbre, se traduit par le démembrement d'une garderobe. La carrière d'Emma se boucle avec la saisie de son linge," Roger Kempf observes in *Madame Bovary: Mœurs de Province*, ed. Gérard Gengembre (Paris: Magnard, 1992), 118.

57. Manfred Fuhrmann, "Proscriptio," in *Realencyclopädie der classischen Altertumswissenschaft*, 23, chap. 2 (Stuttgart: Druckenmüller, 1959), 2443.

58. See, e.g., Sallust, *De coniuratione Catilinae* 60.29–34, and Plutarch's *Lives* (a source Flaubert knew well), especially the lives of Marius (44.10) and Sulla, e.g.:

Those who fell victims to political resentment and private hatred were as nothing compared with those who were butchered for the sake of their property, nay, even the executioners were prompted to say that his great house killed this man, his garden that man, his warm baths another. Quintus Aurelius, a quiet and inoffensive man, who thought his only share in the general calamity was to condole with others in their misfortunes, came into the forum and read the list of the proscribed, and finding his own name there, said, "Ah! woe is me! my Alban estate is prosecuting me." And he had not gone far before he was dispatched by someone who had hunted him down.

Plutarch, *Lives*, vol. 4, trans. Bernadotte Perrin (London: Loeb, 1916), 429. I thank Michèle Lowrie for the wealth of information on this comparison with Flaubert, which had been completely ignored.

59. Fuhrmann, "Proscriptio," in *Realencyclopädie*, 2443. For the literary elaboration of the motif, see John Henderson, *Fighting for Rome: Poets and Caesars, History and Civil War* (Cambridge: Cambridge University Press, 1998).

60. Ovid, *Metamorphoses*, trans. Charles Martin (New York: Norton, 2004), 193.

61. Such desires are unknown to the Homais household and that is why I think Neefs is incorrect in saying that the "border" of Athalie—the fatal apothecary's daughter—is a misprint, and should be *broder* (embroider). Neefs's suggestion in his edition of *Madame Bovary* (above note 8) is simply unintelligible.

62. Cf. Edi Zollinger, *Arachnes Rache. Flaubert inszeniert einen Wettkampf im narrativen Weben: Madame Bovary, Notre-Dame de Paris und der Arachne-Mythos* (Paderborn: Fink, 2007).

63. "Sa chemise entr'ouverte découvrait son cou gras. Son pantalon à pieds, de flanelle rousse, lui dessinait la musculature des cuisses, et toute la rancune d'Emma s'évanouissait à l'enchantement de la force et de la virilité" (*Madame Bovary*, ed. Neefs, 539).

64. Jean Bellemin-Noël, "Le sexe d'Emma," in *Emma Bovary*, ed. Alain Buisine (Paris, 1997), 52–78, 53.

65. Until the second half of the twentieth century, women underwent a purification ritual about five weeks after giving birth (like Mary between December 25 and the Feast of the Purification of the Virgin on February 2), which obviously parallels Jewish custom.

66. By contrast, Jacques Neefs's comments in his 1999 edition of *Madame Bovary* (cited n. 8 above) are exclusively concerned with the wolves of Normandy (p. 73).

67. See Florence Emptaz, *Aux pieds de Flaubert* (Paris: Grasset, 2002), 51.

68. Jean Racine, *Iphigenia, Phaedra and Athaliah* (London: Penguin Books, 2004), 184. The French has: "Je sais mes perfidies / Oenone, et ne suis point de ces femmes hardies / Qui goûtant dans le crime une tranquille paix, / Ont su se faire un front qui ne rougit jamais." Racine, *Phèdre*, in id., *Oeuvres complètes*, vol. 1, ed. Raymond Picard (Paris: Bibliothèque de la Pleiade, 1950), 777. All French quotations from the play refer to this version; all English translations to the Penguin edition.

69. Ibid., 184.

70. Ovid, *Metamorphoses* 6.46–49.

71. Racine, *Iphigenia, Phaedra and Athaliah*, 213.

72. Ibid., 211. For the link between sacrifice and tragedy, see Walter Burkert, "Greek Tragedy and Sacrificial Ritual," in *Savage Energies: Lessons of Myth and Ritual in Ancient Greece*, trans. Peter Bing (Chicago: University of Chicago Press, 2013), 1–36. See also Walter Burkert, *Homo Necans: Interpretationen altgriechischer Opferriten und Mythen* (Berlin: De Gruyter, 1972).

73. Ibid.

74. Sigmund Freud, "The Taboo of Virginity," in *Sexuality and the Psychology of Love* (New York: Touchstone, 1997), 60–76.

75. The Latin text can be found in the Augustine volume of the Vienna *Corpus Scriptorum Ecclesiasticorum Latinorum* 41 (Vienna: Tempsky, 1900). How impor-

tant Augustine deemed the treatise *De adulterinis coniugiis* can be gleaned from the overview of the *Retractiones*, which Flaubert made use of.

The English translation of the text, under the title "Adulterous Marriage," can be found in *Saint Augustine: Treatises on Marriage and Other Subjects* in *Fathers of the Church: A New Translation*, vol. 27, ed. Roy J. Deferrari, trans. Charles T. Wilcox et al. (Washington, DC: Catholic University of America Press, 1955), 55–134. All quotations in English are from this edition.

76. Cf. Jean-Marie Privat, *Bovary charivari: Essai d'ethno-critique* (Paris: CNRS, 1994).

77. Augustine, "Adulterous Marriage," 107–8. See also the authoritative account by Philip Lyndon Reynolds, *Marriage in the Western Church: The Christianization of Marriage during the Patristic and Early Medieval Periods* (New York: Brill, 1994), 207ff. Through contextual relativization rather than reconstructing a narrow dogmatics, Reynolds shatters the usual interpretation of Augustine's dialogue with Pollentius as a dogmatic reading of Matthew (211). A chapter further, when Reynolds cites the Carolingian court jurist Theodulf of Orleans, he could have already found in him an unequivocal example attesting to Augustine's influence (215), which, incidentally, agrees with Flaubert's reading of the Augustinian text (with Flaubert having knowledge of the Carolingian capitulars dating back to 802 CE).

78. Augustine, "Adulterous Marriage," 110. On adultery as an exemplary theme of realism, see also Barbara Vinken, "'Schlusen.' *Effi Briest* und die 'rechte Liebe,'" in *Allegorie. DFG-Symposion 2014*, ed. Ulla Haselstein (Berlin: De Gruyter, forthcoming 2015).

79. "I committed fornication against you [*Et fornicabar abs te*]," Augustine, *Confessions*, ed. Clark, 1.13.21 (p. 39); "I had no love for you and 'committed fornication against you' (Ps. 72:27)," in Augustine, *Confessions*, trans. Henry Chadwick (Oxford: Oxford University Press, 1991), 16. Augustine, "Adulterous Marriage," 108 ("in adulteras adulteri saeviunt") and 120.

80. Ibid., 106.

81. Ibid., 108–9, 125ff.

82. Jacques Seebacher refers to this historical moment in "Chiffres, dates, écritures, inscriptions dans Mme Bovary," in Centre culturel international de Cerisy-la-Salle, *La production du sens chez Flaubert* (Paris: Union générale d'éditions, 1975), 291.

83. "Il [M. Rouault] s'était cassé la jambe, la veille au soir, en revenant de faire les Rois, chez un voisin" (Flaubert, *Madame Bovary*, ed. Gothot-Mersch, 70). Although Emma's father was only attending a Feast of the Epiphany party, the signifier knows that he plays king. The reference to royal authority is lost in Mauldon's English translation: "'He had broken his leg the evening before on his way home from a Twelfth-night feast at a neighbor's'" (15).

Salammbô

This chapter was translated by Aarnoud Rommens.

Epigraphs: "Ah ! que je voudrais être savant ! ce que je ferais un beau livre sous ce titre : De l'interprétation de l'Antiquité ! Car je suis sûr d'être dans la tradition, ce que j'y mets de plus, c'est le sentiment moderne." Flaubert to Louise Colet, March 27, 1853; quoted in Eugenio Donato, "Flaubert and the Question of History: Notes for a Critical Anthology," *MLN* 91, no. 5 (1976): 867.

"Je n'ai pas eu la prétention de faire l'Iliade ni la Pharsale": Flaubert's response to C.-A. Sainte-Beuve, published in the *Constitutionnel* on December 8, 15, and 22, 1862, in Flaubert, *Œuvres*, ed. Albert Thibaudet and René Dumesnil (Paris: Bibliothèque de la Pléiade, 1951), 1: 1001.

1. Charles Baudelaire to Poulet-Malassis, December 13, 1862, in Baudelaire, *Correspondance*, ed. Claude Pichois (Paris: Bibliothèque de la Pléiade, 1973), 2: 271.

2. Michel Butor, *Improvisations sur Flaubert* (Paris: Éd. de la Différence, 1984), 113–14.

3. For the repeated ironic effect of this soft porn, see Francesco Vezzoli's *Trailer for a Remake of Gore Vidal's Caligula* (2005).

4. "Le bruit devint surtout énorme, après qu'une grande dame se fut risquée en costume de Salammbô dans un bal des Tuileries": Émile Zola, *Les romanciers naturalistes: Balzac, Stendhal, Gustave Flaubert, Edmond et Jules de Goncourt, Alphonse Daudet, les romanciers contemporains* (Paris: G. Charpentier, 1881), 199.

5. This is expressed most poetically in *Henri Scepi présente "Salammbô" de Gustave Flaubert* (Paris: Gallimard, 2003), where Scepi compares the novel to an "astre lointain et peut-être mort" (11).

6. Cf. Gisèle Séginger, *Flaubert: Une poétique de l'histoire* (Strasbourg: Presses universitaires de Strasbourg, 2000), 167: "Flaubert fait bouger cette opposition traditionnelle [of barbarism and civilization, BV] en montrant que la civilisation carthaginoise institutionnalise la barbarie."

7. Flaubert, *Correspondance*, ed. Jean Bruneau (Paris: Bibliothèque de la Pléiade, 1973–2007), 2: 338. Quotations from Flaubert's correspondence all cite this edition.

8. "le corps de l'ennemi (hostie) est une chose religieuse." As de Maistre explains, every enemy was guilty; and it was only one step from enemy to stranger. *Hostis*, "guest," also signifies "enemy, stranger," and, of course "victim, sacrifice." See Joseph de Maistre, *Éclaircissement sur les sacrifices*, in id., *Œuvres complètes* (Lyon: Vitte & Perrussel, 1884), 5: 309.

9. English page numbers in the text cite *Salammbo*, trans. A. J. Krailsheimer (New York: Penguin Books, 1977); French citations are from *Salammbô*, ed. Gisèle Séginger (Paris: Flammarion, 2001).

10. See, e.g., the manuscript in an envelope labeled "*Iliade*," Heineman Collection MS 85, Morgan Library & Museum, New York.

11. Sainte-Beuve, *Le Constitutionnel*, December, 8, 15, and 22, 1862, cited in Flaubert, *Œuvres*, ed. Thibaudet and Dumesnil, 1: 1000.

12. Further strengthening the quid pro quo between Mâtho's and Christ's way of the cross, Gisèle Séginger points out that Christ's way of the cross is modeled on that of Mâtho in the second *Tenation* (*Flaubert: Une poétique de l'histoire* [Strasbourg: Presses universitaires de Strasbourg, 2000]).

13. "In all, Flaubert's works are repeated formal experimentations of one single concept," Joachim Küpper asserts in "Erwägungen zu *Salammbô*," in *Konkurrierende Diskurse: Studien zur französischen Literatur des 19. Jahrhunderts*, ed. Brunhilde Wehinger (Stuttgart: Steiner, 1997), 272.

14. Butor, *Improvisations sur Flaubert*, 117. "Carthage c'est non seulement l'envers de Rome, c'est l'envers de Paris, l'envers d'Yonville. Nous retrouvons les mêmes personnes d'une cité à l'autre sous des déguisements extraordinaires." My translation—BV.

15. Ibid. "Tout dans la ville est double: ici et ailleurs, antiquité et nous, aujourd'hui et autrefois." My translation—BV.

16. For more on the totalitarian structure of the political order in Carthage inspired by Claude Lefort, see Jacques Neefs, "Le parcours du zaïmph," in Centre culturel international de Cerisy-la-Salle, *La production du sens chez Flaubert*, ed. Claudine Gothot-Mersch (Paris: Union générale d'éditions, 1975), 233.

17. This is what grounds Georg Lukács's analysis in *The Historical Novel* (Lincoln: University of Nebraska Press, 1983). Like Sainte-Beuve, Lukács sees Carthage as a part of antiquity detached from its historical-philosophical teleology, which would therefore be of no consequence to the present, at least on his rather superficial reading. And concerning the historical pessimism of the bourgeoisie, which surrendered its role as bearer of the world spirit for good with the 1848 Revolution, one must agree with Althusser's dictum that Lukács's view is "tainted by a guilty Hegelianism." See Louis Althusser, *For Marx*, trans. Ben Brewster (London: Verso, 2005), 114n29.

18. For a historical perspective, see Richard Miles, *Carthage must be destroyed—The Rise and Fall of an Ancient Civilization* (New York: Penguin Books, 2010).

19. The Bible was more than just Flaubert's bedside book. As preparation for *Salammbô*, he reread the eighteen volumes of the Old Testament translated by Cahen (French and Hebrew) on the train over a period of two weeks, while providing detailed explanations and excerpts. On July 26, 1857, he writes to Jules Duplan: "et je viens en quinze jours d'avaler les 18 tomes de la Bible de Cahen, avec les notes et en prenant des notes" (*Correspondance*, 2: 747).

The Cahen translation, dedicated to the "Citizen King" Louis Philippe, is an homage to humanistic France, which, thanks to decrees emancipating the Jews passed under the latter, Cahen writes, has become the actual promised land of

Israel. Furthermore, it is an apologia of Judaism against a Christianity that has championed the cause of charity only to be able to live free of guilt for its cold-heartedness. Although the echoes of this translation in *Salammbô* cannot be reduced to citing "sources," its pages are haunted by the biblical complex of sacrifice, idolatry, outspoken thirst for revenge, howls of triumph, and actions at the expense of the lives of others. After reading Flaubert's novel, the Old Testament has to be read differently. Algernon Coleman's chapter "Salammbô and the Bible," in *Sources and Structure of Flaubert's Salammbô*, ed. Percival Bradshaw Fay and Coleman (Baltimore: Johns Hopkins University Press, 1914), 37–55, is to be seen as a defensive strategy.

20. This has been condemned most sharply by Paul Valéry, himself no stranger to erudition: "Mais les produits forcés de l'érudition sont nécessairement impurs," in "La tentation de (saint) Flaubert," in *Œuvres*, ed. Jean Hytier (Paris: Bibliothèque de la Pléiade, 1987), 1: 615.

21. Erich Auerbach, "Figura," trans. Ralph Manheim, in *Scenes from the Drama of European Literature* (Minneapolis: University of Minnesota Press, 1984), 11–76; esp. 16.

22. Cf. Jacques Neefs, "*Salammbô* et la cité antique," in *Flaubert, la femme, la ville*, ed. Marie-Claire Bancquart (Paris: Presses universitaires de France, 1983), 109–21.

23. Wilhelm (known as Christian-Guillaume) Froehner, quoted in Flaubert, *Œuvres*, 1: 695.

24. For the most extravagant theses on Mâtho's supposed hysteria, see Benjamin F. Bart, "Male Hysteria in *Salammbô*," *Nineteenth-Century French Studies* 12, no. 3 (1984): 313–21, and Janet Beizer, *Ventriloquized Bodies: Narrative of Hysteria in Nineteenth-Century France* (Ithaca, NY: Cornell University Press, 1994). See also Nancy Rubino, "Impotence and Excess: Male Hysteria and Androgyny in Flaubert's *Salammbô*," *Nineteenth Century French Studies* 29, nos. 1–2 (2000–2001): 78–99. Mark S. Micale, "Charcot and the Idea of Hysteria in the Male," *Medical History* 34 (1990): 363–411, detects in Flaubert a Charcot *avant la lettre* whose work already illustrates the connection between religious mysticism and hysteria posited some time later by the latter.

25. "Lèpre d'Egypte, elephantasis" (MS, Morgan Library & Museum, New York). This is only one example where Flaubert possibly excerpts in his "Notes sur la traduction de la Bible" from Cahen's Deuteronomy, but there are numerous others.

26. René de Chateaubriand, *Les martyrs*, in id., *Œuvres romanesques et voyages* (Paris: Bibliothèque de la Pléiade, 1969), 2: 483ff. Cf. the reprint of the passage in the "Documents" in Flaubert, *Salammbô*, ed. Séginger, 456. Bernard Masson points to additional myths: Prometheus, Orpheus and Eurydice, the search for the Holy Grail, and Iphigenia, among many others. See Masson, "*Salammbô* ou la barbarie à visage humain," *Revue d'histoire littéraire de la France* 81 (1981): 585–96.

27. The roman à clef thesis is presented by Monika Bosse and André Stoll in "Die Agonie des archaischen Orients: Eine verschlüsselte Vision des Revolutions-zeitalters," the afterword to the German translation, *Salammbô*, ed. ids., trans. Georg Brustgi (Frankfurt/Main: Insel, 1979), which frames *Salammbô* as a story about the France of the late ancien régime and sees in Hamilcar a possible portrait of Napoleon I. In *Flaubert and the Historical Novel: Salammbô Reassessed* (Cambridge: Cambridge University Press, 1982), Anne Green too believes that Flaubert writes in a roundabout way about the 1848 Revolution, with the revolutionary days of 1848 in particular appearing quite explicitly. Behind the uprising of the mercenaries, the great revolutionary movements of the nineteenth century stand out. It is exactly this transparent, even if not perfectly perceived, relation that accounts for the choice of theme. See also François Laforge, "*Salammbô*: Les mythes et la révolution," *Revue d'histore littéraire de la France* 85 (1985): 26–40.

28. Cf. Mircea Eliade, *Images et symboles. Essais sur le symbolisme magico-religieux* (Paris: Gallimard, 1952): "Le roman du 19e siècle ... en dépit de toutes les 'formules' scientifiques, réalistes, sociales, a été le grand réservoir des mythes dégradés" (12).

29. Donato, "Flaubert and the Question of History," provides a clear debunking of the theory of evasion and sees in distant Carthage the France of the nineteenth century.

30. "Les juifs demandent des miracles et les Gentils cherchent la sagesse, quant à nous, nous prêchons JC crucifié, qui est un scandale aux Juifs et une folie aux Gentils." MS excerpting from Corinthians in the Morgan Library & Museum, New York, in an envelope endorsed in Flaubert's handwriting with the words "les Actes des Apôtres; Épîtres de Saint Paul aux Romains, Corinthiens, Galates, etc. Épître de Saint Jacques, Épîtres de St. Pierre, Épître de St. Jean, Épître de St. Jude," p. 4.

31. See *Henri Scepi présente "Salammbô,"* 130.

32. For more on the gift of tears, a fortiori for the nineteenth century, see Barbara Vinken, "'Tränen zum Leben, Tränen zum Tode': Katharina von Siena, Petrarca, Boccaccio, Theresa von Avila, Zola," in *Tränen*, ed. Beate Söntgen and Geraldine Spiekermann (Munich: Wilhelm Fink, 2008), 17–26.

33. Philippe Dufour, "Salammbô, un tigre de marbre," in *Gustave Flaubert*, vol. 5, ed. Gisèle Séginger (Paris: Minard, 2005), 195, 197, 198, 204.

34. Ibid., 203: "stylistique de l'indifférence."

35. Ibid., 198: "calme connaissance anatomique."

36. Ibid., 199: "tranquille méditation sur le vif de la mort."

37. On *faire vif*, see Flaubert to Ivan Turgenev, October 28, 1876, in *Correspondance*, 4: 127.

38. Dufour, "Salammbô, un tigre de marbre," 212.

39. The correspondence between George Sand and Flaubert is especially revealing with reference to this question of providing the reader with signposts for interpretation. Flaubert's *impassibilité* does not entail that the author is untouched

by what he narrates or is completely impartial. It merely registers that the author is not going to prescribe to the reader what he or she should feel. Rather, the reader must be able to draw his or her own conclusions from the description alone, which offers no explicit judgment.

40. Butor, *Improvisations sur Flaubert*, 138. "De même que nous agonisons avec Mme Bovary, nous agoniserons avec lui [Mâtho], et il est en partie son propre sacrificateur."

41. For the praxis of writing as living testimony, as a form of martyrdom, as *donner à voir à vif*, see Jacques Derrida, *Le monolinguisme de l'autre, ou la prothèse d'origine* (Paris: Galilée, 1996).

42. Flaubert to Louis Bouilhet, October 8, 1857, in *Correspondance*, 2: 769.

43. "La littérature, d'ailleurs, n'est plus pour moi qu'un supplice." Flaubert to Charles d'Osmoy, July 22, 1857, in *Correspondance*, 2: 746.

44. See the elegant essay by Françoise Gaillard, "La révolte contre la révolution. *Salammbô*: un autre point de vue sur l'histoire," in *Gustave Flaubert, procédés narratifs et fondements epistémologiques*, ed. Alfonso de Toro (Tübingen: Narr, 1987), 43–54.

45. Ibid., 46. "Ce n'est pas l'histoire qui manque à sa mission, mais [c'est . . .] la mission qui lui manque."

46. Gustave Flaubert, *Sentimental Education*, trans. Robert Baldick (1964), rev. with an introduction and notes by Geoffrey Wall (London: Penguin Books, 2004), 364.

47. "The Roman people threatened the Republic with immediate hostility unless it paid 1,200 talents and the whole island of Sardinia. They had accepted alliance with the Barbarians, and sent them flat boats laden with flour and dried meats" (204). And when Rome later takes the side of Carthage, it does so purely out of self-interest. "A deeper reason brought help to Carthage; people knew very well that, if the Mercenaries won, from the soldier to the scullion there would be general insurrection, which no government, no household would be able to resist" (245).

48. Cf. Séginger, *Flaubert, Une poétique de l'histoire*, following Gaillard.

49. Gaillard, "La révolte contre la révolution," 44. "Car l'écriture, ou l'art, pour parler comme Flaubert, ont cette supériorité sur l'opinion, qu'ils inversent le néant idéologique des valeurs en valeur esthétique du néant."

50. Ibid.: "fureur fratricide qui vient de plus loin qu'eux," "le sentiment de leur fraternité révélée par l'identité de leur courage et de leur virilité, les jette encore plus sauvagement l'un contre l'autre."

51. "Carthago's brutal struggle with the mercenary army is as pointless as is the contemporary moment in European civilization," Charles Bernheimer maintains in "The Decadent Subject," *L'esprit créateur* 32, no. 4 (1992): 55. However, is it not more accurate to say that the novel offers an analysis of mechanisms of power that take hold always and everywhere—including France during the Second Empire—and is therefore indeed anything but reassuring? Where would the pathos of the Flauber-

tian text so purposely overlooked by such attributions to decadence otherwise stem from? Doesn't it get too much under our skin, as for example with the murder of the insurgent boy in *A Sentimental Education* or the sacrifice of the slave child? And isn't the brushing aside of this in the name of "decadence" or "nihilism" not just a defense mechanism in the reader? Are Flaubert's texts not a cry for the sake of this anguished creature, awakening in the reader compassion bordering on agony? The thesis of decadence or nihilism was already presented by Paul Bourget, "Gustave Flaubert" (1883), in *Essais de psychologie contemporaine: Études littéraires*, ed. André Guyaux (Paris: Gallimard, 1993), 113–73. On this reading, Flaubert sees nothingness in everything and sentences every human endeavor to failure. However, to my mind it is not that Flaubert sees "nothing" but that he registers great suffering.

52. Gaillard, "La révolte contre la révolution," 49. "Le futur Hannibal doit moins hériter d'une histoire à faire que d'une haine inexpiable à reconduire. Et la forme que prend son destin dans les rêves de son père, est celle de la perpétuation non celle de l'accomplissement."

53. Butor, *Improvisations sur Flaubert*, 114. "Rome a pour nous deux aspects fondamentaux, qui sont les deux piliers de notre histoire culturelle, les deux testaments sur lesquels toute notre civilisation est fondée: d'une part, la Rome impériale et par conséquent l'antiquité classique, celle des humanistes, des études grècques et latines, et d'autre part la Rome chrétienne, le siège de Pierre."

54. Ibid., 117: "la face cachée de ses deux aspects fondamentaux: antiquité et christianisme."

55. Charles Augustin Sainte-Beuve, *Nouveaux lundis* (Paris: Calmann Lévy, 1885), 4: 34.

56. "On pourrait croire que les raffinements de cruauté qu'ils y exercent l'ont tenté, et qu'il y a vu une suite de scènes appétissantes pour un pinceau que la réalité, quelle qu'elle soit, attire, mais qui, tout en cherchant, en poursuivant partout le vrai, paraît l'aimer surtout et le choyer s'il le rencontre affreux et dur" (ibid., 40ff.).

57. "Que me fait à moi le duel de Tunis et de Carthage? Parlez-moi du duel de Carthage et de Rome, à la bonne heure! J'y suis attentif, j'y suis engagé. Entre Rome et Carthage, dans leur querelle acharnée, toute civilisation future est déjà en jeu, la vôtre elle-même en dépend." Ibid., 84.

58. "Et vous vous étonnez que des barbares qui sont vaincus, désespérés, enragés, ne leur rendent pas la pareille, n'en fassent pas autant une fois, et cette fois-là, seulement? Faut-il vous rappeler Mme de Lamballe, les Mobiles en 48, et ce qui se passe actuellement aux États-Unis? J'ai été sobre et très doux, au contraire." Flaubert to Sainte-Beuve, December 23–24, 1862, in *Correspondance*, 3: 281.

59. "Vous me demandez où j'ai pris une 'pareille idée du Conseil de Carthage'? Mais dans tous les milieux analogues par les temps de Révolution, depuis la Convention jusqu'au Parlement d'Amérique." Ibid., 279.

60. "Je crois même avoir été moins dur pour l'humanité dans Salammbô que dans Madame Bovary." Ibid., 283.

61. Cf. Guy Rose, "Civilisation et humanité: le virage du texte," in *"Salammbô" de Flaubert. Histoire, fiction,* ed. Daniel Fauvel and Yvan Leclerc (Paris: Champion, 1999), 79–93. Susanne Dürr points to the fundamental difference between the violence of the mercenaries and that of the Carthaginians. See Dürr, "Functions of Violence in Flaubert's *Salammbô,*" in *The Aesthetics and Pragmatics of Violence,* ed. Michael Hensen and Annette Pankratz (Passau: Stutz, 2001), 211–24.

62. Flaubert models these victims after the *homo sacer,* which for him also counts as the foundation of Christian sacrifice. Through the sacrifice of Christ, in Flaubert's vision, *homo sacer* is affirmed and redeemed; this perspective then no longer refers to that of those who sacrifice, but to the sacrificed, to those who sacrifice themselves. De Maistre elaborates on the peculiar ambivalence of the word *sacer,* signifying both "holy" and "rejected." *Homo sacer* is offered to God and his reckoning fulfilled. Desacralization is a release from sin in which one is cleared of stains: "dé-sacré (expié) on les a lavés d'une souillure qu'ils avaient contractée." They are consecrated by God, "voués," and through his sacrifice they are "dé-voués" (de Maistre, *Eclaircissement sur les sacrifices,* 307ff.).

63. Speaking of sadism, Flaubert even invoked Bonald, a character in de Sade, for inspiration and thus positioned himself directly as successor to de Sade.

64. Cf. Karl Heinz Bohrer, *Ästhetische Negativität. Zum Problem des literarischen und philosophischen Nihilismus* (Munich: Hanser, 2002), and Sabine Friedrich, *Die Imagination des Bösen: Zur narrativen Modellierung der Transgression bei Laclos, Sade und Flaubert* (Tübingen: Narr, 1998).

65. Flaubert uses the *Histoire de Polybe, nouvellement traduite du grec par Dom Vincent Thuillier . . . Avec un commentaire ou un corps de science militaire enrichi de notes critiques et historiques,* ed. Jean-Charles de Folard, 6 vols. (Paris: P. Gandouin, 1727–30).

66. Cf. Séginger, *Flaubert: Une poétique de l'histoire,* 170.

67. Jules Michelet, *History of the Roman Republic,* trans. William Hazlitt (New York: Miller, Orton & Mulligan, 1856), 138.

68. Ibid., 143.

69. Ibid., 137.

70. Ibid., 134.

71. Ibid., 133.

72. Ibid., 128.

73. Ibid., 132.

74. For a comparison between Michelet and Flaubert, see Joseph Jurt, "Literatur und Archäologie: Die *Salammbô*-Debatte," in *Literatur und Wissenschaft,* ed. Brigitte Winklehner (Tübingen: Stauffenburg, 1987), 101–17.

75. Butor, *Improvisations sur Flaubert,* 117.

76. A small detail points to Flaubert's intimate knowledge of de Maistre's text. Froehner deplores that Flaubert allows the priest to tear Mâtho's heart from his body at the end to display it to the sun. In his documentation, Flaubert refers to

this "Trait emprunté aux religions du Mexique" (quoted in Séginger, *Flaubert: Une poétique de l'histoire*, 168).

77. Joseph de Maistre, "Elucidation on Sacrifices," in *St. Petersburg Dialogues, or, Conversations on the Temporal Government of Providence*, trans. and ed. Richard A. Lebrun (Montreal: McGill-Queen's University Press, 1993), 367.

78. Ibid., 365–67.

79. Flaubert to Sainte-Beuve, December 23–24, 1862, in *Correspondance*, 3: 275–76.

80. Chateaubriand, *The Martyrs*, ed. O. W. Wright (New York: Derby & Jackson, 1859), 440.

81. Chateaubriand, "*Les martyrs*," 489. To this day, the word *hostie* in French, designating the transubstantiated body of Christ, is still associated with older sacrificial methods in the meaning "victime offerte en sacrifice." *Le nouveau Petit Robert: Dictionnaire alphabétique et analogique de la langue francaise* (Paris: Le Robert, 2008), s.v. "hostie."

82. Chateaubriand, *Martyrs*, 450.

83. Ibid.

84. Ibid., 450–51.

85. De Maistre, "Elucidation on Sacrifices," 384–85.

86. Ibid., 385.

87. Sainte-Beuve, *Nouveaux lundis*, 4: 77.

88. Augustine, *De civitate Dei* 16.32,745–46, ed. and trans. R. W. Dyson as *The City of God Against the Pagans* (Cambridge: Cambridge University Press, 1998). All quotations from *De civitate Dei* refer to this edition.

89. Vergil, *Aeneid* 4.39–42, trans. Frederick Ahl (Oxford: Oxford University Press, 2007). All quotations from the *Aeneid* refer to this edition. Further source notes are given parenthetically in the text.

90. Cf. Angela Cozea, "*Salammbô* dans une perspective romane: La traduction d'Hannibal comme 'survie,'" *Canadian Review of Comparative Literature* 17, nos. 3–4 (1990): 307–17.

91. Sainte-Beuve, *Nouveaux Lundis*, 4: 77. "Si l'auteur a voulu montrer en action une de ces religions infâmes, infernales, écrasantes, qui ne tenaient nul compte de la vie des hommes, et dont le Christ a débarrassé le monde, il a réussi."

92. Cf. Bohrer, *Ästhetische Negativität*.

93. The lion as *figura* for the *implementum* of Christ is also found in other places: "Judah is a lion's whelp" (Gen. 49:9).

94. *Pontife*, derived from Latin *pontifex*, "Ministre du culte, dans l'Antiquité romaine," "hauts dignitaires catholiques, évêques ou prélats," "*Le souverain pontife*: le pape." *Petit Robert*, s.v. "pontife."

95. This parallel between the Passion and the torment of love is already evident in Petrarca's *Canzoniere*, whose *passio* begins on Good Friday in the church, in remembrance of the Passion of the Lord.

96. For more on the cult of the Sacred Heart of Jesus, see Barbara Vinken, "Herz Jesu und Eisprung: Jules Michelets 'devotio moderna,'" in *Stigmata. Poetiken der Körperinschrift*, ed. Bettine Menke and Barbara Vinken (Munich: Fink, 2004), 295–318.

97. The epigraph to this section is quoted from Friedrich Nietzsche, *The Gay Science*, trans. Josefine Nauckhoff, ed. Bernard Williams (New York: Cambridge University Press, 2001), 193.

98. "Son supplice—par les rues—le jour où l'on va célébrer les noces de Pyrrha, regard de la jeune fille sur le corps déchiré de Mâtho—elle l'aime—c'est lui, l'époux—ils ont été marié par la mort—elle pâlit, et tombe dans le sang de Mâtho." Flaubert's summary quoted in Bernard Gagnebin, *Flaubert et Salammbô: Genèse d'un texte* (Paris: Presses universitaires de France, 1992), 60.

99. Chateaubriand, *Martyrs*, 446.

100. Ibid., 204.

101. "She sat behind some shrubs that were half-stripped of their foliage: thus the poet represents the shade of Dido" (ibid., 201). In this case, the poet is of course Dante and not Vergil. See French ed., 55. Here Astarté, who also bears the name Salammbô, is addressed by this name.

102. Flaubert excerpts from Cahen's Bible translation, in MS, Morgan Library & Museum, New York: "J'ai trouvé plus amère que la mort la femme, qui est du même un piège et dont le cœur est un filet et les mains des liens."

103. Euripides, *Iphigenia in Aulis*, in *The Plays of Euripides*, trans. Edward P. Coleridge (London: George Bell & Sons, 1891), vol. 2.

104. In his letter to Sainte-Beuve, December 23–24, 1862 (*Correspondance*, 3: 277), Flaubert calls *Salammbô* "une espèce de sainte Thérèse."

105. "Salammbô était devenue bourgeoise. Plus d'exaltation, elle envisageait les choses telles qu'elles étaient." See Flaubert, *Salammbô*, ed. Séginger, 306.

106. In "Impotence and Excess: Male Hysteria and Androgyny in Flaubert's *Salammbô*," Nancy Rubino impressively documents the clinical sources for Flaubert's hysterical figuration of Mâtho and also demonstrates the relation between modern pathology and Christian pathos. Nonetheless, by making Flaubert a Charcot *avant la lettre* and by observing a transference in *Salammbô* from the religious to the scientific, she more or less completely misjudges Flaubert's intention.

107. Cf. Jean Rousset, "Positions, distances, perspectives dans *Salammbô*," in *Travail de Flaubert*, ed. Raymonde Debray-Genette (Paris: Seuil, 1983), 79–92, and Lucette Czyba, *Mythes et idéologie de la femme dans les romans de Flaubert* (Lyon: Presses universitaires de Lyon, 1983), 157.

108. In his excerpts from the Song of Songs (MS, Morgan Library & Museum, New York, Misc. Heineman), Flaubert summarizes the function of these small foot chains under the heading "Chainettes de jambes": "Les chainettes de jambes, prévenaient les accidents qui arrivent aux filles en faisant de trop . . . enjambées. Cette sorte d'entrave avait pour but de conserver les signes de la virginité."

109. "Je suis la plaie et le couteau," Baudelaire writes in his poem "L'Héautontimorouménos." English translation from Lewis Piaget Shanks, *Flowers of Evil* (New York: Ives Washburn, 1931).

110. Cf. Mary Jacobus, "Judith, Holofernes and the Phallic Woman," in *Reading Woman. Essays in Feminist Criticism* (New York: Columbia University Press, 1986), 110–36: "the sleeping and clearly postcoital Holofernes" (122).

111. Section epigraph from Flaubert to Sainte-Beuve, December 23–24, 1862, in *Correspondance*, 3: 281: "C'était une opinion primitive que Noga et Cochab (Vénus et Mars) étaient au-dessus du Soleil, contrairement à ce que les modernes ont decidé." In "La bible, traduction de Cahen, Ezechiel" (MS), Flaubert excerpts this comment by a Professor d'Aborbanel, cited by Cahen.

112. Flaubert to Sainte-Beuve, December 23–24, 1862.

113. For more on this, see the "Dossier" in *Salammbô*, ed. Séginger, 436. In the chapter he left out, Flaubert explains: "Baalet-Tanit, à la fois Junon, Diane et Vénus, c'est à dire la Lune qui se lève dans les espaces de l'autre côté du soleil, l'élément humide, la nuit profonde, l'immense ovaire où germaient les choses" (394).

114. Quotations from the Latin here are all from Vergil, *Aeneis: lateinisch-deutsch*, trans. Maria and Johannes Götte (Zurich: Tusculum, 1983).

115. "je prépare actuellement un coup, le *coup* du livre. Il faut que ce soit à la fois cochon, chaste, mystique et réaliste! Une bave comme on n'en a jamais vu, et cependant qu'on la voie." Flaubert to Ernest Feydeau, October 21, 1860, in *Correspondance*, 3: 122.

116. Bart, "Male Hysteria in *Salammbô*," 316.

117. "Quel pauvre amant je fais ! n'est-ce pas !—Sais-tu que ce qui m'est arrivé avec toi ne m'est jamais arrivé ? (J'étais si brisé depuis trois jours et tendu comme la corde d'un violoncelle.) Si j'avais été homme à estimer beaucoup ma personne j'aurais été amèrement vexé. Je l'étais pour toi. Je craignais de ta part des suppositions odieuses pour toi, d'autres peut-être auraient cru que je les outrageais, elles m'auraient jugé froid, dégoûté ou usé. Je t'ai su gré de cette intelligence spontanée qui ne s'étonnait de rien quand moi je m'étonnais de cela comme d'une monstruosité inouïe. Il fallait donc que je t'aimasse, et fort, puisque j'ai éprouvé le contraire de ce que j'avais été à l'abord de toutes les autres, n'importe lesquelles." Flaubert to Louise Colet, August 13, 1846, in *Correspondance*, 1: 299ff.

118. "Alors il la couvre avec le manteau—comme avec un linceuil, il l'étreint sur sa poitrine, et finalement la baise." Quoted in Gagnebin, *Flaubert et Salammbô*, 60.

119. For more on the female body as a metaphor for poetics in the work of Émile Zola, see Barbara Vinken, "Zola: Alles sehen, alles wissen, alles heilen; Der Fetischismus im Naturalismus," in *Historische Anthropologie und Literatur: Romanistische Beiträge zu einem neuen Paradigma der Literaturwissenschaft*, ed. Rudolph Behrens and Roland Galle (Würzburg: Königshausen & Neumann, 1995), 215–26.

120. Naomi Schor, "Salammbô enchaînée, ou femme et ville dans *Salammbô*," in *Flaubert, la femme, la ville,* ed. Marie-Claire Bancquart (Paris: Presses universitaires de Paris, 1983), 98. Schor cites Guy Rosolato: "pour trouver dans le *gland* même, dans l'organe, l'initial brillant tégumentaire, mais justement atteint au sommet de l'érection, hors de toute enveloppe, apparaissant. Arrêtons-nous à ce point pour marquer combien il se doit pour le fétichiste de trouver ce miroitement, témoin de celui de son désir." See Guy Rosolato, "Le fétichisme dont se 'dérobe' l'objet," *Nouvelle revue de psychanalyse* 2 (1970): 38.

121. "la seule étreinte qu'il leur accorde, il la raconte privativement." Rousset, "Positions, distances, perspectives," 86.

122. This body brings to mind a torn hymen. See "Salammbô ou les dangers du dévoilement," in Alain Buisine, *L'orient voilé* (Paris: Cadeilhan, Éd. Zulma, 1993), 127–48. "Dans cet homme qui n'est plus qu'une grande blessure, dans l'organique obscénité de cette chair violentée et meurtrie, il m'est impossible de ne pas voir aussi une sorte de figuration pitoyable et lamentable d'un sexe défloré puisqu'aussi bien tout le tissu textuel ne cesse d'entrecroiser le manteau de la déesse et la virginité de la fille d'Hamilcar" (130).

123. Homer, *The Iliad*, trans. Robert Fagles (London: Penguin Books, 1991). All quotations from the *Iliad* refer to this edition, with page numbers in it following book and line numbers.

124. Not only is Hector's corpse violated by the Greeks; it even inspires an enraged Achilles to express what he would like to do most: "to hack your flesh away and eat you raw" (*Iliad* 22.409; 553).

125. More fitting than the example of the baroque Rome, Lacan could have adduced Ovid as exemplifying the irruption of the Real, i.e., the rejected, repressed body—the unrepresentable that stages representation. See Jacques Lacan, "On the Baroque," in *Seminars of Jacques Lacan*, vol. 20, *On Feminine Sexuality: The Limits of Love and Knowledge*, trans. Bruce Fink, ed. Jacques-Alain Miller (New York: Norton, 1998), 95–117.

126. Ovid, *Metamorphoses*, trans. Charles Martin (New York: Norton, 2005). All quotations from the *Metamorphoses* refer to this edition.

127. Cf. Myriam Saguy in Centre culturel international de Cerisy-la-Salle, *La production du sens chez Flaubert*, ed. Claudine Gothot-Mersch, 250: "Je signale que zaïmph, en hébreu, c'est l'organe mâle" (the minutes indicate that everyone laughed).

128. This downward movement of the side wound to the hip seems at most secondarily motivated by a pictorial description of Grünewald's Crucifixion scene at the Isenheim altar, as Séginger suggests.

129. Cf. Jacobus, "Judith, Holofernes and the Phallic Woman."

130. For more on this, see Chapter 2, "Quidquid volueris," in this volume.

131. With the Prophets, Flaubert noted, "il n'est pas question . . . ni de l'arbre divin, ni de la tentation du Serpent, ni du déluge, ni de la tour de Babel." MS in a

folder marked "*Juifs, Doctrines*" in Flaubert's handwriting, excerpting from Michel Nicolas, *Études critiques sur la Bible: Ancien Testament* (Paris: Michel Levy frères, 1862), Morgan Library & Museum, New York.

132. As Christopher Wild noted during a discussion at the conference "Kunst, Zeugung, Geburt" (Munich, April 2000), the real meaning of the body before the Fall and the fallen body revolves around the introduction of inauthenticity through sexuality.

133. Claude Lefort, "La permanence du théologico-politique," *Le temps de la réflexion* 11 (1981): 13–61.

134. "demeure que dans le firmament, qui enveloppe tout l'univers, nous voyons diverses figures formées par les étoiles et les planètes pour nous annoncer les choses cachées et de profonds mystères. Aussi sur la peau qui entoure notre corps il y a les formes et les traits qui sont comme les planètes ou les étoiles de notre corps. Toutes ces formes ont un sens caché et sont un objet d'attention pour les sages qui savent lire dans le visage de l'homme." Excerpted by Flaubert from Adolphe Franck, *La Kabbale, ou la Philosophie religieuse des Hébreux* (Paris: Hachette, 1843). MS, Morgan Library & Museum, New York.

135. Frédéric Baudry to Flaubert, October 27, 1859, Morgan Library & Museum, New York, commenting on Ernest Renan, "Nouvelles considérations sur le caractère général du peuple sémitique, et en particulier sur leur tendance au monothéisme," *Comptes rendus des séances de l'Académie des Inscriptions et Belles-Lettres* 3, no. 3 (1859): 67–100: "Je livre à vos méditations cette nouvelle transformation du peplos, qui cette fois ne serait plus un pallium, un manteau, mais une étoffe couverte d'écriture."

136. "Depuis que la littérature existe, on n'a pas entrepris chose plus insensé. Donner aux gens un langage dans lequel ils n'ont pas pensé." Flaubert to E. Feydeau, December 19, 1858, in *Correspondance*, 3: 845.

137. "À chaque ligne, à chaque mot, la langue me manque." Ibid.

138. See the letter to E. Feydeau, end of November 1857, in *Correspondance*, 3: 783.

139. "Le verbe chrétien est comme le verbe juif le créateur du monde." Excerpt by Flaubert from Michel Nicolas, *Les doctrines religieuses des Juifs pendant les deux siècles antérieurs à l'ère chrétienne* (Paris: Michel-Lévy frères, 1860). MS, Morgan Library & Museum, New York.

A Sentimental Education: The Story of a Young Man

This chapter was translated by Aarnoud Rommens.

Epigraph: Victor Hugo to Rioffrey, secretary-general of the Comité de protection artistique de la forêt de Fontainebleau, December 1872, in *Correspondance de Victor Hugo*, 3: "Un arbre est une édifice, une forêt est une cité, et entre toutes, la forêt de Fontainebleau est un monument."

1. Flaubert to Ivan Turgenev, November 13, 1872, in *Correspondance,* vol. 2 (Paris: Gallimard, 1973), 200.

2. Horace, *Epodes* 16.2: "Suis et ipsa Roma viribus ruit."

3. See John Henderson, *Fighting for Rome: Poets and Caesars, History and Civil War* (Cambridge: Cambridge University Press, 1998), "Introduction," for the pivotal role Lucan played.

4. Augustine, *De excidio urbis Romae sermo, A Critical Text and Translation with Introduction and Commentary,* ed. Sister Marie Vianney O'Reilly (Washington, DC: Catholic University of America Press, 1955), 8.1–4.

5. Jerome, *Epistolae* 125, in J.-P. Migne, *Patrologia latina* (Paris: J.-P. Migne successores, 1865), 12.

6. Vergil, *Aeneid* 1.278–79: "His ego nec metas rerum nec tempora pono / imperium sine fine dedi."

7. Augustine, *De civitate Dei* 30.

8. Pointedly illustrated in Edgar Salin, *Civitas Dei* (Tübingen: Mohr, 1926).

9. See Valérie Huet, "Napoleon I: A New Augustus?" in *Roman Presences: Receptions of Rome in European Culture, 1789–1945,* ed. Catharine Edwards (Cambridge: Cambridge University Press, 1999), 53–69.

10. "Hegel remarks somewhere that all great, world-historical facts and personages occur, as it were, twice. He has forgotten to add: the first time as tragedy, the second as farce." In Karl Marx, "The Eighteenth Brumaire of Louis Bonaparte," in *The Marx-Engels Reader,* ed. Robert C. Tucker (New York: Norton, 1978), 594.

11. "Préface," in Jean Racine, *Andromaque,* in *Œuvres,* ed. Edmond Pilon and René Gross (Paris: Gallimard, 1940), 124.

12. Victor Hugo, "À l'Arc de Triomphe," in *Œuvres complètes. Poésie I,* ed. Claude Gély (Paris: Robert Laffont, 1985), 819–31. See also Barbara Vinken, "Forget Virgil? Baudelaire and the Truth of Modernity," *Literary Imagination* 8, no. 3 (2006): 417–40.

13. Barbara Vinken, "Nana: Venus *à rebours,*" in *Venus as Muse: From Lucretius to Michel Serres,* ed. Hanjo Berressem, Günter Blamberger, and Sebastian Goth (Leiden and Boston: Brill Rodopi, 2015), 173–97.

14. See Barbara Vinken, "'Rom, Tochter Babylons': Augustinus' Verkehrung der Roma aeterna" and "Emile Zolas Neues Rom," in *Rom rückwärts. Europäische Übertragungsschicksale von Lucan bis Lacan,* ed. Judith Kasper and Cornelia Wild (Paderborn: Fink, forthcoming, 2015).

15. "Quid est enim aliud omnis historia, quam romana laus?" (What else, then, is all history, if not the praise of Rome?). Francesco Petrarch, "Invectiva contra eum qui maledixit Italie," in id., *Prose,* ed. Guido Martellotti (Milan: Ricciardi, 1955), 790.

16. Frederik Ahl's account in his *Lucan: An Introduction* (Ithaca, NY: Cornell University Press, 1976) exemplifies this.

17. All references to *Pharsalia* are to Lucan, *Pharsalia*, trans. and ed. Jane Wilson Joyce (Ithaca, NY: Cornell University Press, 1993).

18. See Amos Funkenstein, *Heilsplan und natürliche Entwicklung: Formen der Gegenwartsbestimmung im Geschichtsdenken des hohen Mittelalters* (Munich: Nymphenburger Verlagshandlung, 1965). See also Henri-Xavier Arquillière, *L'Augustinisme politique* (Paris: Vrin, 1934), which summarizes the state of the historical reappraisal of medieval research in the later nineteenth century after Flaubert.

19. Augustine's *Civitas Dei* does not appear in the catalogue of Flaubert's books, which is, however, incomplete. See *La bibliothèque de Flaubert*, ed. Ivan Leclerc (Rouen: Presses universitaires de Rouen, 2001). Luis Bertrand's edition of *Tentation de St Antoine* (Paris: Charpentier, 1908) contains another fragmentary list ("Lectures de Flaubert pour la version de 1874"). Flaubert excerpted from an authoritative Paris edition, "La foi, l'espérance, la charité," in Augustine, *Opera omnia*, vol. 6, 1.333–410, and, on demons, from *La Cité de Dieu*, ed. and trans. Émile Saisset, 4 vols. (Paris: Charpentier, 1855), which he apparently consulted in detail.

20. Joseph Ratzinger [Pope Benedict XVI], "Herkunft und Sinn der Civitas-Lehre Augustins," in *Geschichtsdenken und Geschichtsbild im Mittelalter*, ed. Walther Lammers (Darmstadt: Wissenschaftliche Buchgesellschaft, 1961), 62. Cf. Ratzinger's useful standard comparative analysis of Augustine research in *Volk und Haus Gottes in Augustins Lehre von der Kirche* (Munich: Karl Zink, 1954). On sources of *Civitas Dei*, see also Henri-Irénée Marrou, *Saint Augustin et la fin de la culture antique* (Paris: Boccard, 1958).

21. Franz Hofmann, *Der Kirchenbegriff des heiligen Augustinus in seinen Grundlagen und in seiner Entwicklung* (Munich: Hueber, 1933), 506.

22. Wilhelm Kölmel, *Regimen Christianum: Weg und Ergebnisse des Gewaltenverhältnisses und Gewaltenverständnisses. 8. bis 14. Jahrhundert* (Berlin: De Gruyter, 1970), 20.

23. "La conversion signifiait littéralement la découverte d'une nouvelle histoire depuis Adam et Ève jusqu'aux événements contemporains." Arnaldo Momigliano, "L'historiographie paienne et chretienne au IVe siècle après J.-C.," in *Problèmes d'historiographie ancienne et moderne* (Paris: Gallimard, 1983), 149 (without reference to any later reception like that of the nineteenth century and Flaubert).

24. Augustine, *The City of God Against the Pagans*, trans. and ed. Robert W. Dyson (Cambridge: Cambridge University Press, 1998), 640 (unless otherwise noted, all English quotations from *City of God* cite this edition). Lucan, *The Civil War (Pharsalia)* (1928; Cambridge, MA: Harvard University Press, 1988), 1.95.

25. Augustine, *De civitate Dei* 15.5. *City of God*, 639.

26. Augustine, *De civitate Dei* 15.1. *City of God*, 635.

27. All citations of the French original are from Flaubert, *Éducation sentimentale*, ed. Pierre-Marc de Biasi (Paris: Hachette, 2002), here p. 479, translation supplied. Robert Baldick's translation, from which the English quotations are drawn

unless otherwise indicated, renders this passage as "the inevitable impermanence of all things" (*Sentimental Education*, trans. Baldick [1964; rev. ed., London: Penguin Books, 2004], 349).

28. See Barbara Vinken, *Du Bellay und Petrarca: Das Rom der Renaissance* (Tübingen: Niemeyer, 2001), chap. 4.

29. "Bruderkrieg ist mein Lied." Friedrich Hölderlin, "Lucans Pharsalia," in id., *Sämtliche Werke*, vol. 5, ed. Friedrich Beißner (Stuttgart: Kohlhammer, 1954), 319.

30. In *Une forêt pour les dimanches. Les romantiques à Fontainebleau* (Paris: Grasset, 2003), Jean Borie pinpoints the function of the forest in *A Sentimental Education* when he observes that it represents "le moment peut-être le plus historique de *L'Éducation sentimentale* . . . précisément parce que l'histoire y est congédiée" (331). See also Jeanne Bem, "La forêt de Flaubert. Retour sur un épisode de *L'Éducation sentimentale*," in *Orients littéraires. Mélanges offerts à Jacques Huré*, ed. Sophie Basch et al. (Paris: Champion, 2004), 58.

31. Lucan, *Civil War (Pharsalia)* 1.71–73.

32. Ibid., 9.985 and 264.

33. Ibid., 1.72–80.

34. Cf. Rainer Warning, *Die Phantasie der Realisten* (Munich: Fink, 1999).

35. Lucan, *Civil War (Pharsalia)* 4.211.

36. This is not without a Flaubertian pun, since a *régisseur* is "une personne physique qui dirige une régie intéressée" (*Petit Robert*, s.v.).

37. Flaubert notably used only right-wing newspapers to document the February Revolution, while drawing exclusively on left-wing publications as sources for the June Days and coup.

38. "Le samedi, au haut d'une barricade, dans la rue Lafayette, un gamin enveloppé d'un drapeau tricolore criait aux gardes nationaux: 'Allez-vous tirer contre vos frères!' Comme ils s'avançaient, Dussardier avait jeté bas son fusil, écarté les autres, bondi sur la barricade, et, d'un coup de savate, abattu l'insurgé en lui arrachant le drapeau. On l'avait retrouvé sous les décombres, la cuisse percée d'un lingot de cuivre" (499).

39. "Mais, sur les marches de Tortoni, un homme,—Dussardier,—remarquable de loin à sa haute taille, restait sans plus bouger qu'une cariatide. Un des agents qui marchait en tête, le tricorne sur les yeux, le menaça de son épée. L'autre, alors, s'avançant d'un pas, se mit à crier:—Vive la République! Il tomba sur le dos, les bras en croix. Un hurlement d'horreur s'éleva de la foule. L'agent fit un cercle autour de lui avec son regard; et Frédéric, béant, reconnut Sénécal" (614). The English translation does not retain the reference to the cross.

40. See Marcel Proust, "À propos du 'style' de Flaubert," *Nouvelle Revue Française* 76 (1920, collected in the Pléiade edition, *Contre Sainte-Beuve. Précédé de Pastiches et mélanges et suivi de Essais et articles*, ed. Pierre Clarac and Yves Sandre [Paris: Gallimard, 1971]).

41. For more on the historical sources for this scene, see Pierre-Marc de Biasi,

"Qu'est-ce que cela veut dire, la réalité? Le cryptage du réel dans *L'Éducation senti-mentale*," in *Le Flaubert réel*, ed. Barbara Vinken and Peter Fröhlicher (Tübingen: Niemeyer, 2009), 61–78.

42. Christopher Prendergast cites this excerpt to point to an instance of mani-fest and ostentatious absence of irony in Flaubert. See *The Order of Mimesis: Bal-zac, Stendhal, Nerval, Flaubert* (Cambridge: Cambridge University Press, 1986), 339.

43. For more on this, see Frank Paul Bowman's monumental history *Le Christ des barricades, 1789–1848* (Paris: Cerf, 1987).

44. Flaubert to George Sand, July 5, 1868, in *The Letters of Gustave Flaubert: 1857–1880*, ed. and trans. Francis Steegmuller (Cambridge, MA: Harvard Univer-sity Press, 1982), 116.

45. "Il avait une mission, il devenait Christ" (278).

46. This according to Wetherill's edition of the *Éducation*, which draws at-tention to the Balzacian intertext (601), but also to "le groupe des premiers ro-mantiques qui, vers 1825, se réunissait autour de Victor Hugo et de Sainte-Beuve" (444), where the term *cénacle* also appears as the name they chose for themselves.

47. "Flaubert's *Education* culminates in his critique of the myth of history. The novel questions at the same time the historical reason and the meaning of the per-sonal experience of his romantic 'hero,'" Hans Robert Jauß says in "Die beiden Fassungen von Flauberts 'Éducation sentimentale,'" *Heidelberger Jahrbücher* 2 (1958): 115.

48. Cf. Augustine, *City of God*, 704–5.

49. Ibid., 609; *De civitate Dei* 14.13.

50. Goncourt Journal, March 29, 1862, cited by Pierre-Marc de Biasi in *Flau-bert: L'éducation sentimentale*, 18 ("un immense roman, un grand tableau de la vie, relié par une action qui serait l'anéantissement des uns par les autres").

51. Cf. C. S. Lewis, *The Allegory of Love* (Oxford: Clarendon Press, 1936), one of Paul de Man's theoretical intertexts.

52. Cf. Jonathan Culler, *The Uses of Uncertainty* (Ithaca, NY: Cornell Univer-sity Press, 1985).

53. For the republican-democratic variation, see Agnès Antoine, *L'impensé de la démocratie* (Paris: Fayard, 2003).

54. For the renewed boom in readings of Paul—following Giorgio Agamben and Alain Badiou—see the study oriented on Flaubert's century (alas, without naming it as such) by Jean-Michel Rey, *Paul ou les ambiguïtés* (Paris: Éditions d'Olivier, 2008), especially 45.

55. Barbara Vinken, "Tränen zum Leben, Tränen zum Tode," in *Tränen*, ed. Beate Söntgen and Geraldine Spiekermann (Munich: Fink, 2008), 17–25.

56. For the strictly conceived parallel between love and politics, see Jean-Pierre Duquette, *Flaubert ou l'architecture du vide, une lecture de L'Éducation sentimentale* (Montréal: Presses de l'Université de Montréal, 1972), 85.

57. "il [M. Dambreuse] avait fait prononcer par le Tribunal de commerce, non

seulement la condamnation d'Arnoux, mais celle de sa femme, qui l'ignorait, son mari n'ayant pas jugé convenable de l'en avertir" (602).

58. Such happy imbroglios are exemplified in Dominique-Vivant Denon's erotic novel *Point de lendemain* (1777–1812; Paris: Gallimard, 1995).

59. See Mary Orr, *Flaubert: Writing of the Masculine* (Oxford: Oxford University Press, 2000), and Richard Halperin, *How to Do the History of Male Homosexuality* (Chicago: University of Chicago Press, 2002).

60. The English translation, "reconciled . . . by that irresistible element in their nature which always reunited them in friendship" (456), is more circumspect than the original "par la fatalité de leur nature qui les faisait toujours se rejoindre et s'aimer" (621).

61. "À partir de ce jour, l'intimité fut complète" (58). Again, the English translation prefers the less ambiguous trope of "friendship."

62. The French original contains the sexual connotations: "Monsieur le censeur prétendait qu'ils s'exaltaient mutuellement" (60).

63. "On surveilla leurs relations. Ils ne s'en aimèrent que davantage" (60–61).

64. "Il ne découchera pas" (64), Deslauriers tells Frédéric's mother. The ambiguity of *découcher*—to stay out all night (with the connotation of sleeping around)— is lost in the English.

65. Robert Baldick's translation says simply that it was his "friend" (57).

66. As already indicated by Flaubert's notes for "A Simple Heart," which follows the teleological pattern of salvation history then customary, Babel is associated with Sodom and Gomorrah: "elle croyait voir le paradis, le déluge, la tour de Babel, des villes en flammes"; cited in Gustave Flaubert, *Drei Erzählungen—Trois Contes*, trans. and ed. Cora van Kleffens and André Stoll (Frankfurt/Main: Insel, 1983), 61.

67. "On vit de loin Babel, leur fatal complice, / Regarder par-dessus les monts de l'horizon." Victor Hugo, "Le feu du ciel," in *Odes et ballades: Les Orientales* (Paris: Nelson, 1960), 419. See www.gutenberg.org/files/8775/8775–8.txt.

68. Cf. Timothy Hampton, "'Turkish Dogs': Rabelais, Erasmus, and the Rhetoric of Alterity," *Representations* 41 (1993): 58–82.

69. A better illustration of Réné Girard's "désir médiatisé" is hardly imaginable.

70. As shown by Joseph Jurt's "Die Wertung der Geschichte in Flauberts *Éducation sentimentale*," *Romanistische Zeitschrift für Literaturgeschichte* 7 (1983): 141–68, its multiplicity of factually corroborated historical details, verification of information by different sources, and extraordinary documentation all make *A Sentimental Education* a source for historical research. However, its historical veracity does not preclude its subsumption of historical details under a unifying topos, under the guiding light of which the narrative is organized. As such, it resembles the Bible: although its narrated events contain a kernel of historical truth, everything is organized to bring out an allegorical significance.

71. On the flagrant discrepancies in chronology, see *L'Éducation sentimentale*, ed. Peter Michael Wetherill (Paris: Garnier, 1984).

72. See Jeanne Bem, "La production du sens chez Flaubert: La contribution de Sartre," in *La production du sens chez Flaubert*, ed. Claudine Gothot-Mersch (Paris: Union générale d'éditions, 1975), 155–74.

73. For *histoire* and *discours*, see Gérard Genette, *Discours du récit* (Paris: Points, 2007). In this respect, the *Éducation* is in its Babylonian poetics also rhetorically speaking an anti-Gospel: it is a hermeneutic countertext to the New Testament.

74. For an allegorical reading of the parallel structures, see Dolf Oehler, "Zum gesellschaftlichen Standort der Neurose-Kunst. Sartres *Idiot de la Famille* und Flauberts *Éducation sentimentale*. Versuch einer vergleichenden Lektüre," in *Sartres Flaubert lesen*, ed. Traugott König (Reinbek: Rowohlt, 1980), 149–90. Flaubert's works have been described as proto-cinematic, as in Pierre Danger's *Sensations et objets dans le roman de Flaubert* (Paris: Colin, 1973). For me, it revolves around a parallel with the film cut, as practiced by Eisenstein's metaphoric montage. In contrast to Flaubert, Eisenstein mobilizes clearly "unrealistic" moments, with the metaphor helping to explicate what happens, while Flaubert almost always sticks to a realistic register.

75. As for the rest, this praxis overturns the classical relations of overlapping that Roman Jakobson postulated for literature and centered around Goethe for the theory of metaphor. See *Theorie der Metapher*, ed. Anselm Haverkamp (Darmstadt: Wissenschaftliche Buchgesellschaft, 1983).

76. Maxime Du Camp, *Souvenirs littéraires*, ed. D. Oster (Paris: Aubier, 1994), 583, quoted in Adrianne J. Tooke, "Preface," in *Éducation sentimentale* (Ware, Herts., UK: Wordsworth Editions, 2001), xiv.

77. "D'ailleurs, le père Roque n'hésitait jamais devant une saisie; puis il rachetait à bas prix les bien hypothéqués, et M. Dambreuse, voyant ainsi rentrer ses fonds, trouvait ses affaires très bien faites. Mais cette manipulation extra-légale le compromettait vis-à-vis de son régisseur. Il n'avait rien à lui réfuser. C'était sur ses instances qu'il avait si bien accueilli Frédéric" (368).

78. "Canailleries de famille provinciale faisant pendant à celles du monde parisien"; quoted in *Éducation sentimentale*, ed.Wetherill, 475.

79. For a reversal in the literal sense of the Balzacian provinces—Paris topos, see Peter Brooks, *Reading for the Plot: Design and Intention in Narrative* (New York: Knopf, 1984), 171–93.

80. "Le don de l'observation ne peut appartenir qu'à un honnête homme, car pour voir les choses en elles-mêmes, il faut n'y apporter aucun intérêt personnel." Gustave Flaubert, "Notes de voyage," in *Œuvres complètes*, vol. 2, ed. Louis Conard (Paris: Conard, 1910), 360.

81. "L'artiste doit s'arranger de façon à faire croire à la postérité qu'il n'a pas vécu." Quoted in *Éducation sentimentale*, ed. Wetherill, xxx.

82. Flaubert to Louise Colet, September 26, 1853, *in Lettres,* 2: 440: "Les héros

pervers de Balzac ont, je crois, tourné la tête à bien des gens. . . . Ce n'est plus Werther ou Saint-Preux que l'on veut être, mais Rastignac ou Lucien de Rubempré (épiciers fourvoyés)."

83. Wetherill has summed up this common observation in his edition of *Éducation sentimentale* in terms of an increased darkening of the text.

84. Cf. Ulrich Schulz-Buschhaus, "Zeugma und zeugmatische Erfahrung in Flauberts *L'Éducation sentimentale*," *Zeitschrift für Französische Sprache und Literatur* 95 (1985): 33.

85. For the French original, see note 38 above.

86. *Éducation sentimentale*, ed.Wetherill, cix.

87. See ibid., 434. Flaubert read the *Mémoires* (Paris, 1841) of Marie Lafarge, convicted of murdering her husband with arsenic in 1840. Charles de Choiseul-Praslin commited suicide with poison while on trial for the murder of his wife in 1847.

88. Flaubert does not write a bildungsroman in the classical sense, because he does not accept its prerequisites: the freedom of the individual and the idea that humanity determines the course of its history. The following quotation can suffice to illustrate Flaubert's anti-humanistic stance: "Je nie la liberté individuelle parce que je ne me sens pas libre; et quant à l'humanité, on n'a qu'à lire l'histoire pour voir assez clairement qu'elle ne marche pas toujours comme elle le désirerait." Flaubert to Louise Colet, September 18, 1846," in *Correspondance*, 2: 349.

89. The German-speaking world overlaps with the French in many respects. See Andrea Polaschegg, *Der andere Orientalismus. Regeln deutschmorgenländischer Imagination im 19. Jahrhundert* (Berlin: De Gruyter, 2005).

90. One is reminded here of Louise's first husband in Balzac's *Mémoires de deux jeunes mariées*.

91. "Il avait le charme des putains par le seul développement de sa vie analogue à la leur." *Éducation sentimentale*, ed. Wetherill, 502.

92. Section epigraph above: "Medusa e l'error mio m'an fatto un sasso / D'humor vano stillante" (Petrarch, "Vergin bella, che di sol vestita"), trans. A. S. Kline, www .poetryintranslation.com/PITBR/Italian/PetrarchCanzoniere306-366.htm.

93. For Flaubert this is no compliment: "Je crois que le succès auprès des femmes est généralement une marque de médiocrité" (*Éducation sentimentale*, ed. Wetherill, 502).

94. Flaubert to Marie-Sophie Leroyer de Chantepie, October 6, 1864, in *Letters: 1857–1880*, ed. and trans. Francis Steegmuller (Cambridge, MA: Harvard University Press, 1982), 80. Emphasis in original.

95. "Montrer que le sentimentalisme (son developpement depuis 1830) suit la politique et en réproduit les phases," Flaubert says in an oft-quoted formula in *Carnets de Travail*, ed. Pierre-Marc de Biasi (Paris: Balland, 1988), 296. The fact that the word "sentimental" in the novel's title is meant pejoratively has become somewhat of a commonplace. A study of the associations with the German ro-

mantic tradition is still lacking, but Frédéric was originally to have been named Fritz; he plays German waltzes and reads *Werther*. For tentative steps in the direction of such an inquiry, see Michel Brix, "*L'Éducation sentimentale* de Flaubert: De la peinture de la passion 'inactive' à la critique du romantisme français," *Études littéraires* 30, no. 3 (1998): 107–19. And on the sentimental as a form of narcissism in Fénelon, see Robert Spaemann, *Reflexion und Spontanität. Studien über Fénelon* (Stuttgart: Klett-Cotta, 1990).

96. Cf. Michel Crouzet, "Passion et politique dans *L'Éducation sentimentale*," in *Flaubert, La femme, la ville* (Paris: Presses universitaires de France, 1983), 39–71. Crouzet points to an "identité de nature entre passion et politique" (42). The thesis of a historical novel onto which the love story is merely grafted has been argued at length by J.-P. Duquette, whose *Flaubert ou l'architecture du vide: Une lecture de L'Éducation sentimentale* (Montréal: Presses de l'Université de Montréal, 1972) systematically expounds the entanglement of love and politics. The issue, however, is how this convergence is to be interpreted.

97. "All the Christianity I find in Socialism appalls me!" Flaubert to George Sand, July 5, 1868, in *Letters of Gustave Flaubert: 1857–1880*, ed. and trans. Steegmuller, 116. Flaubert cites Louis Blanc, transcribing one of the "little notes now lying on my [Flaubert's] table" as an example: "This system [Louis Blanc's own] is not a system of disorder. For it has its source in the Gospels. And from this divine source *there cannot flow* hatred, warfare, total conflict of interest. For the doctrine formulated from the Gospels is a doctrine of peace, union and love" (ibid., emphasis in original). In a subsequent letter, again to George Sand, dated September 29, 1868, he says: "Neo-Catholicism on the one hand and Socialism on the other have made France less intelligent. Everything is either the Immaculate Conception or workers' lunches" (ibid., 120).

98. Cf. Barbara Vinken, *Unentrinnbare Neugierde: Die Weltverfallenheit des Romans; Richardsons "Clarissa" und Laclos' "Liaisons dangereuses"* (Freiburg im Breisgau: Rombach, 1991).

99. Flaubert, *Madame Bovary: Mœurs de Province*, ed. Jacques Neefs (Paris: Librairie générale française, 1999), 226.

100. "Il ne regretta rien. Ses souffrances d'autrefois étaient payées" (618). The English does not put it in such explicitly economic terms.

101. "Je comprends les Werther que ne dégoûtent pas les tartines de Charlotte" (618).

102. "Le milieu hypocrite où il se trouve l'a pris. L'énèrvement causé par le demi-monde l'a préparé aux bassesses du vrai monde. Ses idées changent, il devient froid et bassement sceptique—et dans l'état de fausseté qui le révoltait autrefois. Alors l'ambition politique sous sa forme la plus vulgaire le prend" (*Éducation sentimentale*, ed. Wetherill, 498).

103. Ibid., 452: "les honneurs déshonorent, le titre dégrade, la fonction abrutit."

104. "Cet immense désir sans but (sans égoïsme), où l'idée d'un profit personnel n'entrait pas" (ibid., 433).

105. "Son apparition chez Mme Arnoux, une fille chez une sainte" (ibid.).

106. "Elle s'en coupa, brutalement, à la racine, une longue mèche" (621).

107. Flaubert sees this contrast as stemming from a male childhood illness. "La jeunesse a l'esprit tragique et n'admet pas les nuances—en fait de femmes deux classes seulement—ou putains comme Messaline ou immaculées comme la Ste Vierge" (*Éducation sentimentale*, ed. Wetherill, 435). For more on the subversion of this confrontation/comparison, see D. A. Williams, "Sacred and Profane in *L'Éducation sentimentale*," *Modern Language Review* 73 (1978): 786–98.

108. *Éducation sentimentale*, ed. Wetherill, xxv.

109. "Sophie Arnoux . . . tout le monde connaît ça." For further on Sophie Arnauld, see Simone de Beauvoir, *Le deuxième sexe* (Paris: Gallimard, 1949), 115.

110. *Éducation sentimentale*, ed. Wetherill, xxvii.

111. This opposition between a fulfilled, self-identical, true eternity and a divided time, which is merely a countdown to death that attempts to reconcile the fragments of time into a true and wholesome unity by means of delusional idols, informs Petrarch's *Canzoniere*, which contrasts Mary, the Queen of the Heavens, "chiara, bella, di sol vestita, pura, intera, santa, unica, intacta, stabile et eternal," with Laura, who becomes a deceitful image of sensual fascination, like Medusa, and crumbles to dust in the end. Here the *conversio*, which is a hermeneutic *conversio*, already runs aground and is deconstructed.

112. In the French original, the reader is left in suspense on account of the ambiguity of the possessive pronoun in "dans l'éblouissement qui lui envoyèrent ses yeux" (47), which the English translation of necessity resolves.

113. The title of Rousset's study, *Leurs yeux se rencontrèrent. La scène de la première vue dans le roman* (Paris: José Corti, 1981), 24–27, is the locus classicus of Flaubert scholarship.

114. Frédéric's eyes blind his heart, thus perverting the traditional theological model of love. See Harald Nehr, "Sehen im Klischee—Schreiben im Klischee. Zum Verhältnis von Wahrnehmung, bildender Kunst und Künstlern in Gustave Flauberts *Éducation sentimentale*," *Romanistische Zeitschrift für Literaturgeschichte* 27 (2003): 117–130. Nehr very convincingly also shows the effects of the transformation of the relation of possessive pronouns through a comparison with the manuscripts. Indeed, as both Nehr and Warning suspect, what is at stake is not the theology of love but the Annunciation.

115. Wetherill, ed., *Éducation sentimentale*, 260: "on dirait une vierge de Raphael."

116. "[E]t son nez droit, son menton, toute sa personne se découpait sur le fond de l'air bleu" (47).

117. See also Flaubert, *Voyage en Égypte*, trans. Pierre-Marc de Biasi (Paris: Grasset, 1991), 280.

118. Sara Danius's *The Prose of the World: Flaubert and the Art of Making Things Visible* (Uppsala: Uppsala University, 2006) is basic to this discussion of the visual.

119. Another example of precocious female sexuality is Louise Marthe, the daughter of the Arnoux family. This is not only apparent from the incestuous overtones of her love for her father, but also appears in the scene with the eels—obvious phallic symbols—with which the little girl plays, thus spoiling them for everybody.

120. Sigmund Freud, "On the Universal Tendency to Debasement in the Sphere of Love," in *The Standard Edition of the Complete Psychological Works*, trans. and ed. James Strachey, Anna Freud, Alix Strachey, and Alan Tyson (London: Hogarth Press, 1964), 11: 177–90.

121. "sa poitrine se gonflait, ses bras s'écartaient, son cou d'où s'échappaient ses roulades se renversa mollement comme sous des baisers aériens" (106).

122. "l'univers venait tout à coup de s'élargir" (41).

123. For more on this form of curiosity described by Augustine, see Hans Blumenberg, *Der Prozeß der theoretischen Neugierde* (Frankfurt/Main: Suhrkamp, 1973), and Barbara Vinken, "Curiositas/curiosity," in *Historisches Wörterbuch ästhetischer Grundbegriffe*, ed. Karlheinz Barck et al. (Stuttgart: Metzler, 2000), 794–813.

124. "des amulettes sur la peau et des pudeurs dans la dépravation" (539).

125. "Avec un peu de blanc d'Espagne, ça brillera!" (609). The English loses the reference to the opening scene and what Frédéric fancies to be Madame Arnoux's "Andalusian origin" (9).

126. "Mais ce n'est pas curieux" (609). The link with *curiositas* is unclear in the English translation.

127. For an elucidation on the relation with the Roman specter of proscription, see Chapter 3 in the present volume.

128. Thomas Hobbes's posthumously published book *Behemoth* discusses the struggle of the Church, Behemoth, against the state, Leviathan; through the Church's claims to power, the state is constantly undermined, thus resulting in an eternal civil war. This perhaps explains why Madame Dambreuse's second husband is an Englishman.

129. "Animals of the Bible," in *The Jewish Encyclopedia*, http://jewishencyclo pedia.com/articles/1539-animals-of-the-bible, ed. G. Hirsch et al.

130. Cf. Giorgio Agamben, *The Open: Man and Animal* (Stanford: Stanford University Press, 2003).

131. "le partage de ces reliques, où il retrouvait confusément les formes de ses membres, lui semblaient une atrocité, comme s'il avait vu des corbeaux déchiquetant son cadavre" (608).

132. Cf. Stanley Cavell, *Disowning Knowledge in Seven Plays of Shakespeare* (Cambridge: Cambridge University Press, 2004), 165.

133. "et de toutes ses forces, lançant son âme dans les hauteurs, elle offrit

à Dieu, comme un holocauste, le sacrifice de sa première passion, de sa seule faiblesse" (419).

134. For more on the image of birth, which in the case of men brings forth constitutions, see Lynn Hunt, *The Family Romance of the French Revolution* (Berkeley: University of California Press, 1993).

135. The constitution was passed on November 4, 1848, and abrogated on January 14, 1852, with the proclamation of the Second Empire.

136. For variations of the manuscript, see Peter Michael Wetherill, "C'est là ce que nous avons eu de meilleur," in *Flaubert à l' œuvre*, ed. Raymonde Debray-Genette et al. (Paris: Flammarion, 1980), 35–68.

137. A passage from "A Simple Heart" also brings out the idolatrous nature of the Corpus Christi procession: "The priest slowly mounted the steps and set on the lace the great golden sun, which shone radiantly. All knelt." Gustave Flaubert, *Three Tales*, trans. A. J. Krailsheimer (Oxford: Oxford University Press 1991), 39. In "Hérodias," the sun is what unites Christianity with the idolatrous sun cults.

Three Tales

This chapter was translated by Aarnoud Rommens.

Epigraph: "T'es-tu nourrie de la Bible? Pendant plus de trois ans je n'ai lu que ça le soir avant de m'endormir." Flaubert to Louise Colet, October 4, 1846, in id., *Correspondance*, ed. Jean Bruneau (Paris: Bibliothèque de la Pléiade, 1973–2007), 1: 375. Citations of Flaubert's letters all refer to this edition.

1. Erich Auerbach, "Sermo humilis," in *Literatursprache und Publikum in der lateinischen Spätantike und im Mittelalter* (Bern: Francke, 1958), 25–64.

2. See the reintroduction of Auerbach in Jacques Rancière, *Politique de la littérature* (Paris: Galilée, 2007), but Rancière ignores the Christological point, which Auerbach took over from Hegel.

3. Cf. Alexandre Leupin, *Fiction et incarnation: Littérature et théologie au Moyen Âge* (Paris: Flammarion, 1993), who, following Kojève, speaks of a "coupure épistémologique chrétienne" (10). Jean-Claude Milner reiterates the Kojevian theorem: "Il n'y a jamais aucune synonymie entre une notion appartenant au système de pensée païen et une notion chrétienne, c'est à dire moderne" (ibid.). Leupin adds: "L'effort d'un Tertullian, par exemple, n'est autre qu'une vaste tentative d'homonymiser les noms de l'ancienne rhétorique pour leur faire dire autre chose—la réalité/vérité de l'Incarnation" (ibid.).

4. On this logical paradox, see, e.g., Boethius in *Contra Eutychen et Nestorium* (ca. 512), writing against two heresies: "Quelle grande et nouvelle chose—unique et non-répétable en aucune époque—que la nature de celui qui est seul Dieu se joigne à la nature humaine (entièrement différente, elle, de Dieu), et forme ainsi une seule personne par la conjonction (*copulatio*) de natures différentes!" (quoted in Leupin, *Fiction et incarnation*, 11).

5. Erich Auerbach, "Sermo Humilis," cites Augustine, *Enarrationes in Psalmos* 96.4 (CCSL, 39, 1356ff. = PL, xxxvii, 1239), 36. "Ille qui stetit ante iudicium, ille qui alapas accepit, ille qui flagellatus est, ille qui in ligno suspensus est, ille cui pendenti in ligno insultatum est, ille qui in cruce mortuus est, ille qui lancea percussus est, ille qui sepultus est: ipse resurrexit."

6. See Georg Wilhelm Friedrich Hegel, "Die romantische Kunstform: Der religiöse Kreis," in id., *Vorlesungen über die Philosophie der Kunst*, ed. Annemarie Gethmann-Siefert (Hamburg: Meiner, 1998), 187.

7. Gerald Wildgruber, "Kunst—Religion—Wissenschaft: Zur Konstellation dreier Terme im Spätwerk Flauberts," *Hofmannsthal-Jahrbuch* 7 (1999): 322.

8. Friedrich Nietzsche, "Nietzsche contra Wagner: From the Files of a Psychologist," in *The Anti-Christ, Ecce Homo, Twilight of the Idols, and Other Writings*, ed. Aaron Ridley and Judith Norman, trans. Judith Norman (Cambridge: Cambridge University Press, 2005), 272.

9. Wildgruber, "Kunst—Religion—Wissenschaft," 322.

10. In a certain—paradoxical—*cura sui* between Catholics and Protestants, kenotic thought continued in Germany in certain theological debates on Christ's human nature, which reflected internal differences within Protestantism according to J. Webster, "Kenotische Christologie," in *Religion in Geschichte und Gegenwart*, vol. 4 (Tübingen: Mohr Siebeck, 2001), 929–31. In Flaubert and the many kenotically inclined writers, the theological differences are not thematized.

11. Cf. Barbara Vinken, "Aufhebung ins Weibliche: Mariologie und bloßes Leben bei Joseph Ratzinger, Benedikt XVI," in *Ratzinger-Funktion* (Frankfurt/Main: Suhrkamp, 2006), 24–55.

12. Jacques Le Brun, *Le pur amour: De Platon à Lacan* (Paris: Seuil, 2002), 200: "cette impensable éclipse de la divinité."

13. Ibid., 202: "un Père, dont la Volonté a laissé le désespoir envahir le fils abandonné."

14. Most strikingly presented by Hans Urs von Balthasar, *Herrlichkeit: Eine theologische Ästhetik*, vol. 3.2 (Einsiedeln: Johannes, 1969).

15. "J'honore donc ce dénuement, que l'Humanité de Jésus a de sa propre subsistance . . . je renonce à toute la puissance, autorité et liberté, que j'ai de disposer de moi, de mon être. . . . Je passe outre ; et je veux qu'il n'y ait plus de MOI en moi; . . . et que je ne sois plus qu'une nue capacité et un vide en moi-même." Pierre de Bérulle, "Discours de l'état et des grandeurs de Jésus, par l'Union ineffable de la Divinité avec l'Humanité," in *Œuvres complètes du Cardinal de Bérulle* (Monsoult: Maison d'institution de l'Oratoire, 1960), 1: 183 (quoted in Wildgruber, "Kunst—Religion—Wissenschaft," 331). A wonderful modern literary example of this specific *imitatio Christi* is the opening prayer in Paul Claudel's *Le soulier de satin*.

16. "Car nous devons nous anéantir en cette action et y être purs membres de Jésus-Christ, offrant et faisant ce qu'il offre et ce qu'il fait, comme si nous n'étions

pas nous-mêmes." Carles de Condren, "Letter 74," in id., *Œuvres completes*, ed. Abbé Pin, vol. 1 (Paris: Guyot & Roidot, 1857), 276.

17. "Voilà ce que tous les socialistes du monde n'ont pas voulu voir, avec leur éternelle prédication matérialiste. Ils ont nié la *Douleur*, ils ont blasphémé les trois quarts de la poésie moderne, le sang du christ qui se remue en nous.—Rien ne l'extirpera, rien ne la tarira. Il ne s'agit pas de la dessécher, mais de lui faire des ruisseaux. Si le sentiment de l'insuffisance humaine, du néant de la vie venait à périr (ce qui serait la conséquence de leur hypothèse), nous serions plus bêtes que les oiseaux, qui au moins perchent sur les arbres." Flaubert to Louise Colet, September 4, 1852, in *Correspondance*, 2: 151, trans. Francis Steegmuller, ed., in *The Letters of Gustave Flaubert: 1830–1857* (Cambridge, MA: Belknap Press of Harvard University Press, 1980), 169.

18. Wildgruber, "Kunst—Religion—Wissenschaft," 332.

19. Ibid., 341. For discourse-analytical reformulations, see André Jolles, *Einfache Formen: Legende, Sage, Mythe, Rätsel, Spruch, Kasus, Memorabile, Märchen, Witz* (Halle: Niemeyer, 1930), and Anselm Haverkamp, *Typik und Politik im Annolied: Zum Konflikt der Interpretationen im Mittelalter* (Stuttgart: Metzler, 1979), pt. 1, 10.

20. Wildgruber, "Kunst—Religion—Wissenschaft," 334.

21. For the link between kenosis and atheism, see Xavier Tilliette, "L'exinanition du Christ: Théologies de la kénose," *Les quatre fleuves* 4 (1975): 48–59.

22. "La première qualité de l'Art et son but est l'*illusion*." Flaubert to Louise Colet, September 16, 1853, in *Correspondance*, 2: 433.

23. "Je pourrais donc en 1857 fournir du Moderne, du Moyen Âge et de l'Antiquité." Flaubert to Louis Bouilhet, June 1, 1856, in *Correspondance*, 2: 614, quoted in Claude Mouchard and Jacques Neefs, *Flaubert: Une vie, une œuvre, une époque* (Paris: Balland, 1986), 305.

24. Cf. Per Nykrog, "Les *Trois Contes* dans l'évolution de la structure thématique chez Flaubert," *Romantisme* 6 (1973): 55–66.

25. Alan W. Raitt, in *Flaubert: Trois Contes* (London: Grant & Cutler, 1991), counts as many as sixty ternary structured sentences in "A Simple Heart" alone.

26. It is fascinating to see how this topic can provoke 360 pages of paraphrase without any thesis to speak of, such as in Adrianne Tooke, *Flaubert and the Pictorial and Arts: From Image to Text* (Oxford: Oxford University Press, 2000).

27. "dans mon pays" (166). Quotations in English are from *Three Tales*, trans. A. J. Krailsheimer (New York: Oxford University Press, 1991), occasionally modified.

28. See Friedrich Ohly's famous essay, "Die Kathedrale als Zeitenraum," in *Schriften zur mittelalterlichen Bedeutungsforschung* (Darmstadt: WBG, 1977), 171–273; as well as, not far from Flaubert and closest to Proust: John Ruskin, *The Seven Lamps of Architecture* (London: Smith, Elder, 1855), esp. chap. 2, "The Lamp of Truth."

29. "Phanuel . . . eut un ravissement" (248). In a close comparison of the MSS, Ulrich Schulz-Buschhaus, "Die Sprachlosigkeit der Félicité: Zur Interpretation

von Flauberts Conte *Un cœur simple*," *Zeitschrift für französische Sprache und Literatur* 93 (1983): 113–30, explains Flaubert's *procedere* as "progressive spiritual purification" that follows closely the "typological scheme of hagiography" (116) and is captured in all its finesse in the finally published text: "The *explicitness* of the hagiography is hidden by means of Flaubert's disarticulating *écriture*" (117).

30. Thus the exemplarity of the little Thérèse de Lisieux according to Hans Urs von Balthasar, *Thérèse von Lisieux: Geschichte einer Sendung* (Cologne: Hegner, 1950).

31. See Michel Tournier's preface to *Trois Contes*, ed. Samuel S. de Sacy (Paris: Gallimard, 1973), 14.

32. "Que ferons-nous? Toi à coup sûr, tu vas faire de la *désolation* et moi de la *consolation*." George Sand to Gustave Flaubert, December 18–19, 1875, in *Correspondance*, 4: 998.

33. For a striking example, see Émile Gérard-Gailly, *Flaubert et "les fantômes de Trouville"* (Paris: Renaissance du Livre, 1930).

34. "Si je continue, j'aurai ma place parmi les Lumières de l'Église. Je serai une des colonnes du temple. Après saint Antoine, saint Julien, et ensuite saint Jean-Baptiste, je ne sors pas des saints. Pour celui-là, je m'arrangerai de façon à ne pas, 'édifier.'" Flaubert to Edma Roger des Genettes, June 19, 1876, in *Correspondance*, 5: 56.

35. On the contemporary business with texts of the Church Fathers, see R. Howard Bloch, *God's Plagiarist: Being an Account of the Fabulous Industry and Irregular Commerce of the Abbé Migne* (Chicago: University of Chicago Press, 1994).

36. Harold Bloom, *The Anxiety of Influence: A Theory of Poetry* (Oxford: Oxford University Press, 1997).

37. "Votre poésie est entrée dans ma constitution comme le lait de ma nourrice." Flaubert to Victor Hugo, July 15, 1853, in *Correspondance*, 2: 383.

38. On the Christological metaphorics of assimilation surrounding Flaubert, see Jules Michelet, *Le peuple: Nos fils* (Paris: E. Flammarion, 1869); and see also Barbara Vinken, "Wo Joseph war, soll Prometheus werden! Michelets männliche Mütter," in *Kunst—Zeugung—Geburt. Theorien und Metaphern ästhetischer Produktion in der Neuzeit*, ed. Christian Begemann and David E. Wellbery (Freiburg im Breisgau: Rombach, 2002), 251–70.

39. "Voilà deux jours que je tâche d'entrer dans des *rêves de jeunes filles* et que je navigue pour cela dans les océans laiteux de la littérature à castels, troubadours à toques de velours à plumes blanches." Flaubert to Louise Colet, March 3, 1852, in *Correspondance*, 2: 56.

40. Gustave Flaubert, *Sentimental Education*, trans. Robert Baldick (1964), rev. with an introduction and notes by Geoffrey Wall (London: Penguin Books, 2004), 432.

41. Gustave Flaubert, *Madame Bovary*, trans. Geoffrey Wall (London: Penguin Books, 2004), 284.

42. "Leur poésie [de l'école de Lamartine] est une bavachure d'eau sucré. Mais

ceux qui ont sucé le lait de la louve (j'entends le suc des vieux) ont un autre sang dans la veine." Flaubert to Louise Colet, April 21, 1853, in *Correspondance*, 2: 300.

43. Paul Bénichou, *Le sacre de l'écrivain, 1750–1830: Essai sur l'avènement d'un pouvoir spirituel laïque dans la France moderne* (Paris: Corti, 1973), and *Le Temps des prophètes: Doctrines de l'âge romantique* (Paris: Gallimard, 1977).

44. "Il faut que Dieu suscite un génie populaire, un Homère ouvrier, un Milton laboureur, un Tasse soldat, un Dante industriel, un Fénelon de la Chaumière . . . un commencement de littérature, une poésie; une sensibilité du peuple!" Alphonse de Lamartine, *Geneviève: Histoire d'une servante* (Paris: Lib. nouvelle Jaccottet, Bourdilliat, 1857), 25–26.

45. "L'évangile du sentiment est comme l'évangile de la sainteté: il doit être prêché d'abord aux simples et dans un langage aussi simple que le coeur d'un enfant!" Ibid., 44.

46. "une édition vivante . . . et aimante." Ibid., 35.

47. Ibid., 40.

48. Irène Rosier-Catach, *La parole efficace: Signe, rituel, sacré* (Paris: Seuil, 2004), chap. 2, 99–184.

49. The "second cénacle" and "petit cénacle" so devastatingly depicted in Flaubert's *A Sentimental Education* are already to be found in Balzac's *Illusions perdues;* see Bénichou, *Sacre de l'écrivain.*

50. See Geoffrey Mehlman, *Revolution and Repetition: Marx/Hugo/Balzac* (Berkeley: University of California Press, 1977).

51. Victor Hugo, *Actions de grâces,* cited in Bénichou, *Sacre de l'écrivain,* 391.

52. Victor Hugo, *La lyre et la harpe,* cited in Bénichou, *Sacre de l'écrivain,* 389.

53. Victor Hugo, *Le poète,* cited in Bénichou, *Sacre de l'écrivain,* 391.

54. "Le grandissement d'un esprit par l'irruption de la clarté, la beauté de la violence faite par la vérité à une âme, éclate dans ce personnage. C'est-là, insistons-y, la vertu du chemin de Damas. Désormais quiconque voudra de cette croissance-là suivra le doigt indicateur de saint Paul. . . . La lumière . . . croîtra en intensité; après avoir été la révélation, elle sera le rationalisme; mais elle sera toujours la lumière. Paul, après sa chute auguste, s'est redressé armé, contre les vieilles erreurs, de ce glaive fulgurant, le christianisme; et deux mille ans après, la France, terrassée de lumière, se relèvera, elle aussi, tenant à la main cette blazes épée, la Révolution." Victor Hugo, cited in Jean-Michel Rey, *Paul ou les ambiguïtés* (Paris: Éditions de l'Olivier, 2008), 30.

55. Theodor W. Adorno and Max Horkheimer, *Dialectic of Enlightenment*, trans. John Cumming (New York: Verso, 1997), 57.

56. See Karin Westerwelle, "Saint Julien et le mythe de Narcise: Les images du christianisme chez Gustave Flaubert," in *Le Flaubert réel,* ed. Barbara Vinken and Peter Fröhlicher (Tübingen: Niemeyer, 2008), 109.

"A Simple Heart"

This chapter was translated by Aarnoud Rommens.

Epigraph: Jacques Derrida, *On the Name*, ed. Thomas Dutoit, trans. David Wood, John P. Leavey, and Ian McLeod (Stanford: Stanford University Press, 1995), 54.

1. See Jean-Paul Sartre, *L'idiot de la famille: Gustave Flaubert de 1821–1857* (Paris: Gallimard, 1971), 1: 13ff.

2. Flaubert to Louise Colet, September 2, 1853, in id., *Correspondance*, ed. Jean Bruneau (Paris: Bibliothèque de la Pléiade, 1973–2007), 2: 423. All quotations from Flaubert's letters are from this edition.

3. Flaubert to Edma Roger des Genettes, June 19, 1876, in *Correspondance*, 5: 56.

4. The reading of "A Simple Heart" as a satire on religion has been most forcefully advocated by Michael Issacharoff in *L'espace et la nouvelle: Flaubert, Huysmans, Ionesco, Sartre, Camus* (Paris: Corti, 1976), 35ff. Ben Stoltzfus follows the same direction in "Point of View in *Un cœur simple*," *French Review* 35, no. 1 (1961): 19–25. See also the epilogue by Andre Stoll and Cora van Kleffens in Gustave Flaubert, *Drei Erzählungen: Trois Contes*, trans. and ed. ids. (Frankfurt/Main: Insel, 1983). Karin Westerwelle also proposes an ironic reading in *Ästhetisches Interesse und nervöse Krankheit: Balzac, Baudelaire, Flaubert* (Stuttgart: Metzler, 1993). For an interpretation that hinges on "crut voir," with which the author supposedly signals that the story is nothing but the erotic hallucination of a frustrated spinster, see the textual exegesis of Marshall C. Olds in *Au pays des perroquets: Féerie théâtrale et narration chez Flaubert* (Amsterdam: Rodopi, 2001): "Le sens de *croire voir* dans cette citation n'est aucunement *ne rien voir de réel*, mais bien, *maintenir avoir vu ce que les autres sont incapables de voir et par conséquent de disputer*. Selon cet emploi de l'auxiliaire (emploi tout à fait légitime), l'expérience visionnaire n'est point niée" (166). Stirling Haig argues in a similar vein with comparative passages from the entire oeuvre in "The Substance of Illusion in Flaubert's *Un Cœur simple*," *Stanford French Review* 7, no. 3 (1983): 309ff. Victor Brombert, "La chambre de Félicité: bazar ou chapelle?" in *George Sand et son temps: Hommage à Annarosa Poli*, ed. Elio Mosele (Geneva: Slatkine, 1994), 1: 73–86, opts resolutely for undecidability: "le motif hagiographique est à la fois sérieux, parodique et démystificateur" (83).

5. Following Henri Guillemin's image of Flaubert, William J. Beck sees "A Simple Heart" as a triumph of hope, and Félicité as the embodiment of the eight beatitudes preached by Jesus in the Sermon on the Mount. See "'Un Cœur simple' de Flaubert: Le chemin de la sainteté," *University of Dayton Review* 20, no. 1 (1989): 109–15. Lewis J. Overaker is of the same opinion, stating that "in re-evaluating the role of the parrot in the tale, we find ourselves witnesses to a serious and triumphant spiritual journey in which the workings of the Holy Ghost are disclosed" (119). See "Manifestations of the Holy Ghost in Flaubert's *Un Cœur simple*," *Re-*

nascence 53, no. 2 (2001): 119–48. However, following Brombert, "Chambre de Félicité," he does in the end—with "the parrot . . . being simultaneously a mystical fetish for the character and an instrument of irony for the author"—make room for a double focus: "Flaubert, as a sceptic, may have regarded Félicité's final vision of the parrot as a laughable, if not indeed meaningless, hallucination, while, as imaginative participant in the maidservant's inner world, he simultaneously treated it as an authentic apotheosis" (141).

6. See Haig, "Substance of Illusion," who resolutely hides the theological question in order to read "A Simple Heart" as the expression of a religion of aesthetics. The confrontation between the sterile, gray upon gray world of Madame Aubin and the bright, colorful, and fertile world of Félicité is mobilized in a phenomenological vein: "So we must state too that *Un Cœur simple* is a closed text, seeking its only transcendence (its justification, even its Derridean 'presence') in its own intransitive play of signifiers" (315). The most interesting reading of "A Simple Heart" as the mise en scène of its own aesthetics, as a poetological writing, comes from Ross Chambers, "Simplicité de cœur et duplicité textuelle: Étude d'*Un Cœur simple*," *MLN* 96 (1981): 771–91, who reads Félicité's fetishism, which she shares with the bourgeoisie of Pont-l'Évêque, as a condemnation of realistic aesthetics. Her ability to reach mystical ecstasy, which sets her radically apart from the world of Pont-l'Évêque, functions as the expression of an idealist "religion du beau" favored by Flaubert, but which he yet again charges with irony.

7. Friedrich Nietzsche, *The Anti-Christ, Ecce Homo, Twilight of the Idols, and Other Writings*, ed. Aaron Ridley and Judith Norman, trans. Judith Norman (Cambridge: Cambridge University Press, 2005), 26.

8. Derrida, "la pire des violences," quoted in Hent de Vries, *Philosophy and the Turn to Religion* (Baltimore: Johns Hopkins University Press, 1999), 316.

9. All quotations for the English version of the text refer to Gustave Flaubert, "A Simple Heart," in *Three Tales*, trans. A. J. Krailsheimer (Oxford: Oxford University Press, 1991), 3–40.

10. "vierge, vivant au milieu de la province, vieillissant dans le chagrin et arrivant ainsi aux derniers états du mysticisme." Flaubert to Marie-Sophie Leroyer de Chantepie, March 30, 1857, in *Correspondance*, 2: 697.

11. Cf. Leonhard Goppelt, *Typos: Die typologische Deutung des Alten Testaments im Neuen* (Darmstadt: Wissenschaftliche Buchgesellschaft, 1966).

12. "Then years went by, all alike and without incident, apart from the great festivals as they came round: Easter, Assumption, All Saints" (25–26).

13. Cf. Lucien Cerfaux, "L'hymne au Christ-Serviteur de Dieu," in *Miscellanea Historica in honorem Alberti de Meyer* (Louvain-La-Neuve: Bibliothèque de l'Université, 1946), 1: 117–30, and more generally in Paul Henry, "Kénose," in *Supplément au Dictionnaire de la Bible* (Paris: Letouzey & Ané, 1957), 5: 7–161.

14. Movement "of the eye without sight, an eternal but objectless march, action without repose, mechanical life, living death. Such was Genevieve"; she "appeared

to be thirty-five or forty years of age, though years were less legible on her features than fatigue" (45, 48). Alphonse de Lamartine, *Genevieve; or, Peasant Love and Sorrow*, trans. Fayette Robinson (New York: Stringer & Townsend, 1850).

15. For a mid-seventeenth-century example of such a Madonna, see Philippe de Champaigne, *La vierge de douleur au pied de la croix*, Musée du Louvre, Paris. As the manuscript version has it, "comme on représente les saintes femmes au pied de la croix"; quoted in Giovanni Bonaccorso, *Corpus Flaubertianum* (Paris: Les Belles Lettres, 1983), 1: 198.

16. See, e.g., Eva Eßlinger, *Das Dienstmädchen, die Familie und der Sex: Zur Geschichte einer irregulären Beziehung in der europäischen Literatur* (Munich: Fink, 2013), 194–95.

17. "Félicité every evening took a small supply of sugar that she ate alone in her bed after she had said her prayers." Gustave Flaubert, *Madame Bovary: Contexts, Criticism*, ed. Margaret Cohen, trans. Paul De Man and Eleanor Marx Aveling (New York: Norton, 2005), 51.

18. Flaubert, *Madame Bovary: Mœurs de Province*, ed. Jacques Neefs (Paris: Librairie générale française, 1999), 304.

19. Hippolyte Delehaye, *Les passions des martyrs et les genres littéraires* (Brussels: Société des Bollandistes, 1966), 49: "Les Actes de Perpétue et Félicité sont, pour l'ampleur et le pathétique, le chef-d'œuvre de la littérature hagiographique. Tout le monde les a lus, et nous pouvons nous dispenser de les résumer." See *Passion de Perpétue et de Félicité: Suivi des Actes*, trans. and ed. Jacqueline Amat (Paris: Cerf, 1996), 38–41, where the question of inspiration is elaborated.

20. This question is surrounded by an entire scholarly debate around Tertullian and Montanism. See Delehaye, *Les passions des martyrs et les genres littéraires*, 51ff.; *Passion de Perpétue et de Félicité*, trans. and ed. Amat, 38–40.

21. Augustine, *Sermons* 280, 281, and 282.

22. *The Passion of SS. Perpetua and Felicity MM*, trans. W. H. Shewring (London: Sheed & Ward, 1931), 28.

23. Ibid., 35.

24. Ibid., 36.

25. Ibid., 38.

26. Ibid., 39–40.

27. Ibid., 39.

28. Ibid., 40.

29. Cf. Ulrich Schulz-Buschhaus, "Die Sprachlosigkeit der Félicité. Zur Interpretation von Flauberts Conte *Un cœur simple*," *Zeitschrift für französische Sprache und Literatur* 93 (1983): 113–30.

30. Cf. Shoshana Felman, "Illusion et répétition romanesque," in *La lecture sociocritique du texte romanesque*, ed. Graham Falconer and Henri Mitterand (Toronto: Stevens, 1975), 240.

31. Schulz-Buschhaus, "Sprachlosigkeit," sums up the problem nicely: "From

the outset she thus appears in a position that contradicts all the ideas of bourgeois emancipation and personal autonomy" (125).

32. See Eßlinger, *Dienstmädchen*, 182–90.

33. Pairs of male doves and parrots can already be found in Ovid, *Amores* 2.6.11–16. All quotations from the *Amores* refer to Ovid, *The Love Poems*, trans. A. D. Melville (Oxford: Oxford University Press, 1990).

34. Lamartine, *Genevieve*, 30.

35. Ibid., 78.

36. Ibid., 145.

37. Ibid., 146.

38. Ibid., 93.

39. Ibid., 151.

40. Cf. Anselm Haverkamp, *Begreifen im Bild: Methodische Annäherungen an die Aktualität der Kunst: Antonello da Messina, August Sander* (Berlin: August, 2009).

41. Augustine, "Of Holy Virginity," in *Seventeen Short Treatises of Saint Augustine* (Oxford: J. H. Parker, 1847), 309–10.

42. "Cela n'est nullement ironique, comme vous le supposez, mais au contraire très sérieux et très triste." Flaubert to Edma Roger des Genettes, June 19, 1876, in *Correspondance*, 5: 57.

43. "Pie IX—le martyr du Vatican—aura été funeste au catholicisme. Les dévotions qu'il a patronnées sont hideuses! Sacré Cœur, Saint Joseph, entrailles de Marie, Salette, etc. cela ressemble au culte d'Isis et de Belone, dans les derniers jours du paganisme." Flaubert to Mme X***, December 1879, in *Œuvres complètes*, ed. Louis Conard, vol. 11, *Correspondance*, vol. 8, *Correspondance (1877–1880)* (Paris: L. Conard, 1930), 343.

44. "Les prêtres surtout, qui ont toujours ce nom-là à la bouche, m'agacent. C'est une espèce d'éternuement qui leur est habituel : *la bonté de Dieu, la colère de Dieu, offenser Dieu,* voilà leurs mots. C'est le considérer comme un homme et, qui pis est, comme un bourgeois. On s'acharne encore à le décorer d'attributs, comme les sauvages mettent des plumes sur leur fétiche." Flaubert to Edma Roger des Genettes, December 18, 1859, in *Correspondance*, 3: 67.

45. Flaubert, *Madame Bovary*, ed. Neefs, 65.

46. The parrot as attribute signifying Mary's immaculate purity—sin runs off her like water off a parrot's plumage—belongs to a different tradition. See Wilhelm Molsdorf, *Christliche Symbolik der mittelalterlichen Kunst* (Leipzig: Hiersemann, 1926), 148; 217. In another tradition pertinent to "A Simple Heart" the parrot is the bird of the mediation of divine truth, which presumably explains why popes kept them as pets in their *camera dei papagalli*, the dictation room. Cf. the iconography of Saint Jerome sitting at his desk translating the Bible, where his lion is often attended by a parrot, as in Lucas Cranach the Elder's *Cardinal Albrecht of Brandenburg as St. Jerome in His Study* (1526), John and Mable Ringling Museum of Art,

Sarasota. See Brigitte Le Juez, *Le papegai et le papelard dans "Un cœur simple" de Gustave Flaubert* (Amsterdam: Rodopi, 1999), 45–47.

47. Jean-Baptiste Louis Gresset, *The Parrot, and Other Poems*, trans. T. S. Allen (London: Longman, Orme, Brown, Green & Longman, 1848), 8.

48. Ibid., 7.

49. Ibid., 10.

50. Ibid., 15.

51. Ibid., 27.

52. Ibid., 31–32.

53. Ibid., 32.

54. Cf. the glass window in Jean Lafond, "Une victime de la guerre: La vitrerie de l'église Saint-Michel de Pont-l'Évêque," *Bulletin de la Société des antiquaires de Normandie* 56 (1961–62): 569–86.

55. This is less of a zoologically correct description of an Amazonian parrot than it is a quotation from Ovid's *Amores* 2.6.21–22: "Your wings could dim the blaze of brittle emeralds, / Your crimson beak was tinged with saffron hue."

56. "Gaude, Virgo, mater Christi, Quae per aurem concepisti"; "Deus per angelum loquebatur et Virgo per aurem impregnabatur." Quoted in Le Juez, *Le papegai et le papelard*, 46. For an "enlightened" interpretation, in which sexual repression gets the final say, see Ernest Jones, *Essays in Applied Psycho-Analysis* (London: Hogarth Press, 1951), 2: 322–41.

57. Flaubert found instances of such misreadings in Alfred de Maury's *Essai sur les légendes pieuses du moyen âge* (Paris: Ladrange, 1843). Maury attributes inability to understand allegory, confusing the representation with what it represents, to the naive populace, the uneducated. See Pierre-Louis Rey's commentary in his edition of *Trois contes* (Paris: Presses Pocket, 1989), 153ff.

58. "Reste en extase devant l'oiseau. Et la nuit le met dans sa chambre. Félicité en jouissant, comme d'un amant caché. Elle le voyait de dedans son lit à son reveil," is how the text ran in the first version. Cf. *Trois contes*, ed. Pierre-Louis Rey, 82, 91, 71, 93.

59. Cf. Susanna Elm, *Virgins of God: The Making of Asceticism in Late Antiquity* (Oxford: Clarendon Press, 1994).

60. See Barbara Vinken, "Makulatur oder Von der Schwierigkeit zu lesen: Claude Simons *Leçon de choses*," *Poetica: Zeitschrift für Sprach und Literaturwissenschaft* 21 (1989): 403–28.

61. "Tous donnant dans les idées reçues, répétant des mots appris et qu'ils ne comprennent pas." Flaubert, "*Les trois frères*," in *Œuvres complètes*, vol. 12, *Œuvres diverses, Fragments et ébauches. Correspondance* (Paris: Club de l'honnête homme, 1974), 222–27; 226.

62. Flaubert to Ivan Turgenev, October 28, 1876, in *Correspondance*, 4: 127.

63. Haig, "Substance of Illusion," 309; 313.

64. "monstrueux" (Bonaccorso, *Corpus Flaubertianum*, 1: 473).

65. See Barbara Vinken on the death of Clarissa Harlowe, *Unentrinnbare Neugierde: Die Weltverfallenheit des Romans; Richardsons "Clarissa" und Laclos' "Liaisons dangereuses"* (Freiburg im Breisgau: Rombach, 1991).

66. Cf. Jörg Dünne, *Asketisches Schreiben: Rousseau und Flaubert als Paradigmen literarischer Selbstpraxis in der Moderne* (Tübingen: Narr, 2003), 346.

67. Cf. Jacques Derrida, "Une idée de Flaubert: La lettre de Platon," in *Psyché: Inventions de l'autre* (Paris: Galilée, 1987), 305–25.

"Saint Julian the Hospitalier"

This chapter was translated by Aarnoud Rommens.

I would like to express my gratitude to those who discussed this text with me. Some of the key ideas of this essay are owed to discussions at the Poetics Institute in New York and at Johns Hopkins University—BV.

Epigraph: "Votre poésie est entrée dans ma constitution comme le lait de ma nourrice." Flaubert to Victor Hugo, July 15, 1853, in *Correspondance*, 2: 383. All French quotations from Flaubert's letters are from Jean Bruneau's edition (Paris: Bibliothèque de la Pléiade, 1973–2007); English quotations from them are from *The Letters of Gustave Flaubert: 1830–1880*, ed. and trans. Francis Steegmuller (Cambridge, MA: Belknap Press of Harvard University Press, 1980–82).

1. All quotations from the English version of the text are from "The Legend of Saint Julian the Hospitaller," in *Three Tales*, trans. A. J. Krailsheimer (Oxford: Oxford University Press, 1991), 41–70.

2. Eustache-Hyacinthe Langlois, *Essai historique et descriptif sur la peinture sur verre ancienne et moderne* (Rouen: E. Frère, 1832), 32–39.

3. *Letters of Gustave Flaubert: 1857–1880*, ed. and trans. Steegmuller, 251. Cf. Flaubert to Georges Charpentier, February 16, 1879, in *Correspondance*, 5: 543.

4. Langlois, *Essai historique et descriptif sur la peinture sur verre ancien et modern*, 32–39, quoted in Benjamin F. Bart and Robert Francis Cook, *The Legendary Sources of Flaubert's Saint Julien* (Toronto/Buffalo: University of Toronto Press, 1977), 170–73. Cf. Lecointre-Dupont's rendering of the legend and Joseph de La Vallee, *La chasse à tir en France* (1853; 5th ed., Paris: Hachette, 1873), 254–57, quoted in Bart and Cook, *Legendary Sources*, 174–75. That Flaubert had read the Latin original is evident from the Latinism "occis," in "et quand il les eut tous occis" (116). "Julienus qui utrumque parentem nesciens occidit [Julian who unwittingly killed both of his parents]," in Jakobus de Voragine, *Jacobi a Voragine Legenda aurea vulgo Historia lombardica dicta*, ed. Johann Georg Graesse (Bratislava: Koebner, 1890), 142.

5. Julian's total isolation, and its autobiographical dimension in the shunning of all human ties, has been emphasized by Victor Brombert in "Flaubert's *Saint Julien*: The Sin of Existing," *PMLA* 81, no. 3 (1966): 297–302.

6. On the underlying topos of Latin literature and the European Middle Ages, see Cornelia Wild, "*Saint Julien l'hospitalier* de Flaubert: Un face à face entre la

littérature européenne et le Moyen Âge latin," in *Le Flaubert réel*, ed. Barbara Vinken and Peter Fröhlicher (Tübingen: Niemeyer, 2008), 125–38.

7. "[A]nd when the stag began to moan from the pain of their bites, he would swiftly despatch it, and then delight in the frenzy of the hounds as they devoured their prey, cut into pieces, on the steaming hide" (48).

8. Bart and Cook, *Legendary Sources*, view the romantic reworking as more pertinent than the *Legenda aurea*.

9. Shoshana Felman, "La Signature de Flaubert: *La Légende de St. Julien l'hospitalier*," *Revue des sciences humaines* 181 (1981): 39–57.

10. Cf. Jean-Paul Sartre, *L'idiot de la famille: Gustave Flaubert de 1821–1857* (Paris: Gallimard, 1971), 2: 2109–10: "C'est sous cette forme ultra-janséniste qu'il conçoit la malédiction d'Adam: tous damnés, tous vicieux jusqu'aux moelles, tous hantés dans leur sexe par l'impérieux désir de tuer. Bref, au départ, l'espèce est foutue: . . . La nature humaine est telle qu'elle ne peut se vivre authentiquement que dans le dégoût."

11. For the symbolic meaning of both plants, see J.-K. Huysmans, *La cathédrale* (1897), which is quoted in Édouard Maynial's edition of the *Trois Contes*, (Paris: Garnier frères, 1960), 281; 293.

12. Augustine, *The City of God Against the Pagans*, ed. and trans. R. W. Dyson (Cambridge: Cambridge University Press, 1998), 639. All quotations from *The City of God* here refer to this edition.

13. See René Descharmes, "Saint-Julien l'Hospitalier et Pécopin," *Revue biblio-iconographique* 3, no. 12 (1905): 1–7 and 67–75. Pierre-Marc de Biasi regards the second hunt as the exact opposite of the first: see Flaubert, *Trois Contes*, ed. de Biasi (Paris: Flammarion, 1999), 21.

14. This is a motif also apparent in Victor Hugo, *La fin de Satan*, in *La legende des siècles. La fin de satan. Dieu*, ed. Jacques Truchet (Paris: Bibliothèque de la Pléiade, 1955), 785, where Nimrod strangles a tiger, which is afraid of him: "Les bêtes ne savaient s'il était homme ou bête."

15. Cf. *De civitate Dei* 16.4, 703.

16. "cet homme, / Ce chasseur, c'est ainsi que la terre le nomme."

17.

Lorsque Caïn, l'aïeul des noires créatures,
Eut terrassé son frère, Abel au front serein,
Il le frappa d'abord avec un clou d'arain,
Puis avec un bâton, puis avec une pierre;
Puis il cacha ses trois complices sous la terre
Où ma main qui s'ouvrait dans l'ombre les a pris.

Hugo, *La fin de Satan*, 781.

[When Cain, the forefather of all the creatures of the Dark,
Had beaten serene Abel to the ground,
He first hit him with a bronze nail,

Then with a stick, then with a stone;
He then hid his three accomplices in the Earth
Where my hand, opening in the shadow, has taken them.]

18. "L'hindou, . . . l'assyrien, / Ont mordu dans la chaire comme Ève dans la pomme." Ibid., 787.

19. "le ver monstrueux du fruit de la création." Ibid., 788.

20. "Ce que Dieu fit, les hommes le défont." Ibid.

21. Ham, his ancestor, is "le fils au rire infâme, / Dont Noé dans la nuit avait rejeté l'âme [the son with the infamous laughter, whose soul Noah has pushed back into darkness]." Ibid., 783.

22. "et que le ramier s'accouple à la colombe, / Moi l'eunuque, j'ai pris pour épouse la tombe!" Ibid., 789.

23. "Tu fis la chasse à l'aigle, au milan, au vautour. Mieux eût valu la faire au doux oiseau d'amour!" Victor Hugo, "Légende du beau Pécopin et de la belle Baldour," in *Œuvres complètes de Victor Hugo*, 9 vols., *Le Rhin*, vol. 1 (Paris: Nelson, n.d.), 379. All quotations from the English translation are from Victor Hugo, *The Rhine* (New York: Wiley & Putnam, 1845).

24. Ibid., 379.

25. Hugo, "Légende du beau Pécopin et de la belle Baldour," 351.

26. "Alors Pécopin se souvint de la chasse du pfalzgraf, où il s'était laissé entraîner, et il frisonna." Ibid., 352. Trans., 213.

27. "un immense plat d'or vert dans lequel gisait, au milieu d'une vaste sauce, le cerf aux seize andouillers, rôti, noirâtre et fumant." Ibid., 362. Trans., 221.

28 "Les murailles de cette salle étaient couvertes de tapisseries figurant des sujets tirés de l'histoire romaine. . . . Le reste du pavé était une mosaïque représentant la guerre de Troie." Ibid., 356; trans., 215. For Hugo's negative assessment of Rome—and here he obviously follows Augustine—see his epic *La fin de Satan*, and also "À l'Arc de Triomphe," where the depravity of Rome's foundation through bloodshed stands out as the antitype of an immaculate Paris.

29. "Adam inventa le repas, Ève a inventé le dessert." Ibid., 359; trans., 217, modified.

30.
Seigneur! Seigneur! je suis dans le cachot misère.
La création voit ma face et dit : dehors!
La ville des vivants me repousse, et les mort
Ne veulent pas de moi, dégoûts des catacombes;
Le ver des lèpres fait horreur au ver des tombes.
Dieu ! Je ne suis pas mort et ne suis pas vivant.
Je suis l'ombre qui souffre, et les hommes, trouvant
Que pour mordre et ronger le damné qui se traîne,
C'était trop peu du chancre, ont ajouté la haine.
Leur foule, ô Dieu, qui rit et qui chante, en passant

Me lapide saignant, expirant, innocent;
Ils vont marchant sur moi comme sur de la terre;
Je n'ai pas une plaie où ne tombe une pierre.

> Hugo, *La fin de Satan*, 791ff. English translation in the text by the author.

31. This strange confusion between imitators and opponents of Christ is already evident in the main source for Flaubert's story, i.e., the *Legenda aurea*, where among the various Julians the figure of the apostate appears, who has renounced his faith and washes away the stain of Christian baptism with the blood of a bull in the *taurobolium* of the Mithras cult, and who has declared war on the sect of the Galilean. The *Legenda aurea* portrays him as someone who indulges in the practice of animal sacrifice, and by that token he is given the nickname "victimaire."

32.
Petit enfant qui tiens la robe de ta mère,
Et qui, si tu me vois songeant sous l'infini,
Dis :—Mère, quel est donc ce monstre?—sois béni!
Vous, hommes, qui riez des pleurs de mes paupières,
O mes frères lointains qui me jetez des pierres,
Soyez bénis, bénis sur terre et sous les cieux!
Pères, dans vos enfants, et, fils, dans vos aïeux!

. . . .

Et, ciel, puisque mon œil voit ta face éternelle,
La bénédiction doit emplir ma prunelle!

. . . .

J'ai le droit de sacrer la terre vénérable,
Étant le plus abject et le plus miserable !
J'ai le droit de bénir puisque je suis maudit.

> Hugo, *La fin de Satan*, 791ff. English translation in the text by the author.

33. Felman, "Signature de Flaubert."

34. Flaubert read Michelet from an early age; his history teacher, Adolphe Chéruel, was a former student of Michelet's.

35. Hugo, "Légende du beau Pécopin et de la belle Baldour": "colossale silhouette noire d'un énorme cerf à seize andouillers" (349; trans., 211); "le monstrueux cerf de la nuit bramait dans les halliers" (352; trans., 213).

36. Alfred Maury, as quoted in *Trois Contes*, ed. Pierre-Louis Rey (Paris: Presses Pocket, 1989), 155. "[C]'est que les premiers chrétiens s'imaginaient voir sur le front du premier animal, la marque du Thau, le signe de la croix." In Ezekiel 9:4, tau, the last letter of the Hebrew alphabet, is a sign of God, to be marked on the foreheads of the saved. Transcribed as the Greek tau by the early Christian authors, it was seen as marking the reversal of the old Adam into the new Adam through the Cross.

The tau is especially relevant to our discussion since Francis of Assisi and the followers of Saint Antony used the Tau cross as protection against leprosy. Francis of Assisi adopted this sign of the leper.

37. "As the hart panteth after the water brooks, so panteth my soul after thee, O God. [Quemadmodum desiderat cervus ad fontes aquarum, ita desiderat anima mea ad te, Deus]" (Ps. 42:1).

38. Maury quoted in *Trois Contes*, ed. Pierre-Louis Rey, 156: "rendait plus visible le stigmate qu'il portait sur le front."

39. This too is an allusion, but also a peculiar twist on the Ulysses myth. In the *Odyssey* it is the nurse who recognizes Ulysses by his birthmarks or scars, while in Flaubert, it is the parents who are identified through their child's birthmarks. Allusions to such reversals of ancient myth occur regularly in the text.

40. Unlike Oedipus, Julian does not both kill his father and sleep with his mother. The incest, the "piercing" of his mother, is his murder of her. Flaubert merges incest and murder as early as "Quidquid volueris." Following Freud, one might speak of an Oedipus complex that has not been resolved by the castration complex: the mother is not given up as an object of desire. At the same time, Flaubert remains at the level of the childlike interpretation of the primal scene: the father with whom he identifies does make love to the mother, but kills her. To make love to someone whom one is in love with signifies, from this perspective, to wound the other and oneself. The castration threat persists—it is accepted and internalized—in order not to give up the object of desire. For an elegant, Lacanian interpretation, see Jean Bellemin-Noël, *Le quatrième conte de Gustave Flaubert* (Paris: Presses universitaires de France, 1990), 55–79.

41. Flaubert's investigation of Julian's self-alienation is aptly illustrated here in what amounts to a clinical presentation of schizophrenia: Julian endangers his persona rather than himself. Such conflation of clinical language and hagiography is already apparent in "A Simple Heart."

42. "Mais l'air bestial des figures, le tapage des métiers, l'indifférence des propos glaçaient son cœur" (French ed., 152).

43. Cf. René Scherer, *Zeus hospitalier. Éloge de l'hospitalité. Essai philosophique* (Paris: Armand Colin, 1993), 28: "Derrière la charité, l'humilité de l'hospitalier . . . , il faut déceler autre chose: une folie de Dieu, la recherche de l'abandon absolue de 'Soi', une affirmation de l'exil terrestre. Là se situe le point extrême de la vertu hospitalière. L'exilé est accueilli, mais parce que celui qui accueille se reconnaît, en lui et grâce à lui, comme un être d'exil."

44. For the function of the church window and Abbot Suger of St. Denis, see Georges Duby's *Le temps des cathédrales: L'art et la société 980–1420* (Paris: Gallimard, 1976). For an especially felicitous contemporary example, one could take Gerhard Richter's "symphony of light" stained-glass windows in Cologne Cathedral, where the cross is made to shine forth in an electrifying randomly colored pattern.

45.

Dans le ciel radieux je jette ma torture,
Ma nuit, ma soif, ma fièvre et mes os chassieux,
Et le pus de ma plaie et les pleurs de mes yeux,
Je les sème au sillon des splendeurs infinies,
Et sortez de mes maux, biens, vertus, harmonies!
Répands-toi sur la vie et la création,
Sur l'homme et sur l'enfant, lèpre, et deviens rayon!
Sur mes frères que l'ombre aveugle de ses voiles,
Pustules, ouvrez-vous et semez des étoiles!

> Hugo, *La fin de Satan*, 792–93. English translation in the text by the author.

46. Victor Hugo, *William Shakespeare*, quoted in Jean-Michel Rey, *Paul ou les ambiguïtés* (Paris: Éditions de l'Olivier, 2008), 27.

47. Cf. Karin Westerwelle, "Saint Julien et le mythe de Narcisse: Les images du christianisme chez Gustave Flaubert," in *Le Flaubert réel*, ed. Barbara Vinken and Peter Fröhlicher (Tübingen: Niemeyer, 2008), 108–23. Westerwelle analyzes a superimposition of the Ovidian mythos of Narcissus, the model for all metamorphosis, distorting the topoi of Christian Ascension. The entanglement of transfiguration and metamorphosis, of biblical sources and Ovid, determines the entire scene of the visitation of the leper. See also *Trois Contes*, ed. de Biasi, 126, who sees the conversion of water into wine as an allusion to the wedding in Canaan. Reference to the Philemon and Baucis metamorphosis in Ovid is detected in this passage by Alain Montandon, "Mythes et représentation de l'hospitalité," in *Mythes et représentation de l'hospitalité*, ed. id. (Clermont-Ferrand: Presses universitaires Blaise Pascal, 1999), 20. The systematic nature and aim of closely linking classical antiquity and Christianity does however get somewhat overlooked in these close readings.

48. "Et celui dont les bras le serraient toujours grandissait, grandissait, touchant de sa tête et de ses pieds les deux murs de la cabane. Le toit s'envola" (French ed., 166).

49. "le grandissement d'un esprit par interruption de la clarté." Victor Hugo, *William Shakespeare*, quoted in Rey, *Paul ou les ambiguïtés*, 30.

50. Pierre-Marc de Biasi underlines the general quid pro quo of Christ and Satan and their inversion, which is already evident from the window in the cathedral. "Jésus-Lépreux-tentateur-sodomite, c'est à dire Jésus-Diable" (98). See Pierre-Marc de Biasi, "Le palimpseste hagiographique: L'appropriation ludique des sources édifiantes dans la rédaction de 'La Légende de saint Julien l'Hospitalier,'" in *Gustave Flaubert*, 2 vols., *Mythes et réligions*, vol. 1, ed. Bernard Masson (Paris: Minard, 1996), 69–124.

51. For more on the laicist priesthood of poets and Hugo's mission, and how he incarnates this priesthood, see Paul Bénichou, *Le sacre de l'écrivain, 1750–1830: Essai sur l'avènement d'un pouvoir spirituel laïque dans la France moderne* (Paris: Corti, 1973), 380–407.

52. For a more comprehensive account of the theological-political topicality of the question regarding the foundations of nation and community in Flaubert's France, see Cécile Matthey, *L'écriture hospitalière: L'espace de la croyance dans les "Trois contes" de Flaubert* (New York: Rodopi, 2008), 179–93.

"Hérodias"

This chapter was translated by Susan L. Solomon.

Epigraphs: "Son style, qui rend tout immobile, est la plus singulière fontaine pétrifiante de notre littérature": Jean Prévost, "Aspects du roman moderne," *Confluences* (Lyon) 3 (1943), 21–24, *Problèmes du roman*, special issue, ed. id., 3.

Friedrich Wilhelm Nietzsche, *The Antichrist* (New York: Knopf, 1920), 171; "Der Antichrist," in id., *Werke. Kritische Gesamtausgabe*, ed. Giorgio Colli and Mazzino Montinari (Berlin: De Gruyter, 1969), vol. 6, no. 3, 245.

1. On its theatrical character, see Jean Bellemin-Noël, *Le quatrième conte de Gustave Flaubert* (Paris: Presses universitaires de France, 1990), 81.

2. Hans Peter Lund, *Flaubert—Trois Contes* (Paris: Presses universitaires de France, 1994), 88.

3. On Aglaé Sabatier, see Gustave Flaubert, *Trois Contes* (Paris: Louis Conard, 1910), 225–26.

4. Gérard Genette, "Demotivation in *Hérodias*," in *Flaubert and Postmodernism*, ed. Naomi Schor and Henry F. Majewski (Lincoln: University of Nebraska Press, 1984), 201.

5. Flavius Josephus, *The Antiquities of the Jews,* in *The Works of Flavius Josephus*, trans. William Whiston (Whitefish, MT: Kessinger, 2006), 18.5.1; German edition consulted, Flavius Josephus, *Jüdische Altertümer*, trans. Heinrich Clementz (1899; Wiesbaden: Fourier, 2004), 1: 885.

6. Cf. Michel Butor, *Improvisations sur Flaubert* (Paris: Éditions de la Différance, 1984), 180: "Hérode Antipas épouse une femme qui est à la fois sa nièce et sa belle-sœur."

7. René Girard, "Scandal and the Dance: Salome and the Gospel of Mark," *New Literary History* 15 (1984): 318.

8. Pierre-Marc de Biasi, editorial commentary in *Trois Contes*, ed. id. (Paris: Librairie générale française, 1999), 173n3.

9. Philippe Borgeaud, *La Mère des Dieux: De Cybèle à la Vierge Marie* (Paris: Seuil, 1996), trans. as *The Mother of the Gods: From Cybele to the Virgin Mary* (Baltimore: Johns Hopkins University Press, 2004).

10. On the topos of Babylon, see Arno Borst, *Der Turmbau zu Babel* (Stuttgart: Hiersemann, 1957–63).

11. Cf. Alan W. Raitt, *Flaubert—Trois Contes* (London: Grant & Cutler, 1991), 67.

12. Cf. Josephus's version in Ernest Renan, *Life of Jesus*, trans. William G.

Hutchison (London: Walter Scott, 1898). Renan speaks of John the Baptist simply as "censor of the established authorities" (69). Herod Antipas was supposedly unsettled about the "political leaven which was so little concealed by John in his preaching" (ibid.). Renan also follows Flavius Josephus's interpretation in this appraisal. He calls John's speech a "harsh continuous invective" (66) and claims that the idea of an empire not of this world would have been completely foreign to him. Flaubert's John follows these appraisals; his John is a political agitator entirely of this world.

13. All quotations from Flaubert's *Three Tales* refer to A. J. Krailsheimer's translation (New York: Oxford University Press, 1999).

14. Cf. Per Nykrog, "'Les Trois Contes' dans l'évolution de la structure thématique chez Flaubert," *Romantisme* 6 (1973): 60.

15. This and all subsequent quotations from the Bible are from the King James translation.

16. Ernest Renan, *Renan's Life of Jesus*, trans. William G. Hutchison (London: Walter Scott, 1898), 125. French original: *Histoire des origines du christianisme* (1863), vol. 1, *Vie de Jésus* (Paris: R. Laffont, 1995).

17. Sermon 288, in *The Works of Saint Augustine*, Sermons III/8 (273–305A), trans. Edmund Hill (New York: New City Press, 1994), 112. The King James Bible renders John 1:22–23 thus: "Then said they unto him, Who art thou? that we may give an answer to them that sent us. What sayest thou of thyself? He said, I am the voice of one crying in the wilderness, Make straight the way of the Lord, as said the prophet Esaias."

18. Hans Jonas adapts the concept of pseudomorphosis from Spengler to describe religious (mostly gnostic) intermingling in *Gnosis und spätantiker Geist* (Göttingen: Vanderhoeck & Ruprecht, 1934).

19. On this point, see Cécile Matthey, *L'écriture hospitalière. L'espace de la croyance dans les Trois Contes de Flaubert* (New York: Rodopi, 2008), 77.

20. Whether this is still to be considered historically accurate is not of concern here. Flaubert mostly follows G. F. Creuzer's *Symbolik und Mythologie der alten Völker* (1810–12; Hildesheim: Olms, 1973), ed. and trans. J.-D. Guigniaut as *Religions de l'antiquité considérées principalement dans leurs formes symboliques et mythologiques*, 10 vols. (Paris: Treuttel & Würtz, followed by J.-J. Kossbühl and Firmin-Didot frères, 1825–51), and Michelet's *Histoire romaine*.

21. Anselm Haverkamp, "Arcanum translationis. Das Fundament der lateinischen Tradition," in *Tumult. Schriften zur Verkehrswissenschaft*, vol. 30 (Berlin: Diaphanes, 2006), 19–31.

22. Saint Augustine, *City of God*, trans. Marcus Dods, ed. Philip Schaff, vol. 2 (Grand Rapids, MI: Eerdmans, 1997), 7.26, p. 324.

23. See Josephus, *Jüdische Altertümer*, trans. Clementz (2004), 874, and Renan, who follows Josephus in regard to this point.

24. This comes close to Renan, who writes: "By his self-abnegation he has at-

tained a glorious and a unique position in the religious pantheon of humanity" (130, 147).

25. The attributes of Cybele in the description of the landscape in "Hérodias" can be found in Raymonde Debray-Genette, *Métamorphoses du récit. Autour de Flaubert* (Paris: Seuil, 1988), 200.

26. On the blasphemous conflation of Maria and Cybele in *The Temptation of Saint Anthony*, see Matthey, *Écriture hospitalière*, 96.

27. Flaubert broaches this in an early essay, "Lutte du sacerdoce et de l'empire," in id., *Œuvres de jeunesse* (*Œuvres complétes*, vol. 1), ed. Claudine Gothot-Mersch and Guy Sagnes (Paris: Bibliothèque de la Pléiade, 2001), 1137.

28. Flaubert partially follows Renan as far as the signifiers are concerned: "Jérusalem avait comblé la mesure. Cette ville qui tue les prophètes, lapide ceux qu'on lui envoie, flagelle les uns, crucifie les autres, est désormais ville de *l'anathème*" (Renan, *Vie de Jésus*, 1: 58; emphasis added). Similarly, Mannaei casts an anathema against the hated city: "jeta un *anathème*" (174).

29. See most recently Martin Harries, *Forgetting Lot's Wife: On Destructive Spectatorship* (New York: Fordham University Press, 2007).

30. Here is the synopsis of Joseph in Renan:

Herodias, granddaughter of Herod the Great, a violent ambitious, and passionate woman, who detested Judaism and despised its laws. She had been married, probably against her own inclinations, to her uncle Herod, son of Mariamne, who had been disinherited by Herod the Great. The subordinate position of her husband, as compared with that of other members of the family, gave her no peace; she determined to be sovereign at whatever cost. Antipas was the instrument of whom she made use. This man of weak will having fallen violently in love with her, promised to marry her, and to repudiate his first wife. The almost incestuous union of Antipas and Herodias then took place. The Jewish laws of marriage were a constant stone of offence between the irreligious family of the Herods and the strict Jews. (69–70)

31. Josephus 18.6, 5.

32. Ibid., 7, 2.

33. Ibid., 7, 1.

34. Ibid., 7, 2.

35. Ibid.

36. Ibid.

37. Renan regarded the Christian promise of a kingdom not of this world as the crucial element in Christianity,

of which the "kingdom of God" will be eternally the root and the stem. On this phrase all the social revolutions of humanity will be grafted. But, tainted by a gross materialism, and aspiring to the impossible—that is to say, to the foundation of universal happiness upon political and economic measures, the socialistic endeavors of our time will remain unfruitful, until they take as their guiding principle the true spirit of Jesus, by which I mean absolute idealism—the principle that to possess the world we must renounce it. (182)

38. I would on the other hand not speak of "carnivalization," because this is not a matter of passionate affirmation, but rather of denouncing what is unbearable and blood-curdling.

39. Flaubert again references Renan, who asserts that everyone was waiting for the reappearance of the prophet Elijah, who as the predecessor of the Messiah was supposed to smooth the way: "That, with these ideas, Jesus and his disciples could have no doubt as to the mission of John the Baptist is easily understood. . . . the Scribes raised the objection that it was still a question whether the Messiah could really have come, since Elias [Elijah] had not yet appeared from the dead" (127–28). The soldier Jacob, Jesus's disciple, who later tries to protect John and is killed as a result, gives this explanation too.

40. Cf. Matt. 11:14: "And if ye will receive *it*, this is Elias [Elijah], which was for to come."

41. Cf. Suetonius, *The Lives of the Caesars*, vol. 2, trans. J. C. Rolfe (Cambridge, MA: Harvard University Press, 1979), 314: "Being besides a man of an appetite that was not only boundless, but also regardless of time or decency, [Vitellius] could never refrain, even when he was sacrificing or making a journey, from snatching bits of meat and cakes amid the altars, almost from the very fire, and devouring them on the spot ; and in the cookshops along the road, viands smoking hot or even those left over from the day before and partly consumed." French edition consulted: Suetonius, *Vies des douze Césars*, ed. Henri Ailloud, vol. 3 (Paris: Les Belles Lettres, 1993).

42. This Babylonian-Asiatic has a special point. As Flaubert excerpts from the *Stories of the Apostles*, the Holy Ghost excludes Asia *expressis verbis* from the proclamation of the Good News: "L'asie ne doit pas être chrétienne," notes Flaubert and cites as a reference: "le Saint Esprit leur defendit d'annoncer la parole de Dieu en Asie" (MS, Morgan Library & Museum, New York, excerpts from the *Stories of the Apostles*).

43. "through their open lashes the dead eyes [of John the Baptist] and the vacant eyes [of Vitellius] seemed to be telling each other something" (104).

44. The link between Bacchus, Adonis, and Christ would be followed up here; Aulus alludes to it, because not Bacchus but Adonis was killed by a boar ("pourceau," "grosse bête," 236).

45. The debate over "sacrament" played no role at all during this time: "Flaubert invente [the dispute over Moses' sacrificial fire] pour le besoin du récit: en fait, Caïphe, le Grand Prêtre alors en charge de la sacrificature, connut au contraire une carrière exceptionnellement longue en gardant sa fonction une dizaine d'années" (de Biasi in *Trois Contes*, ed. id., 165n3). The "besoin du récit" is specifiable: the debate on the sacrificial privilege is introduced by Flaubert to profile the Jewish side of the theme too.

46. Ibid., 168n3.

47. Excerpting from Leon de Modena's *Cérémonies et coutumes parmi les Juifs*,

trans. Richard Simon [Recared Scimeon] (Paris: L. Billaine, 1674–81), Flaubert notes that the Jews allege that the Samaritans deify the image of a dove in their temple (MS, Morgan Library & Museum, New York).

48. Girard, "Scandal and the Dance," encapsulates the dynamic of the City of Man without naming Augustine. This precarious social covenant unites mimetic, that is rivaling, fraternal, and incestuous interests through human sacrifice: "The dreadful paradox of these desires is that they can make peace with each other only at the expense of some victim" (320).

49. Acts 2:1–8.

50. In making Salome so childish, Flaubert stands in the biblical tradition and against the view of her as decadent. See Helmut Pfeiffer, "Salome im Fin de Siècle. Ästhetisierung des Sakralen, Sakralisierung des Ästhetischen," in *Das Buch der Bücher—gelesen*, ed. Steffen Markus and Andrea Polaschegg (Berlin: Lang, 2006), 303–36.

51. I owe this observation to Gabriele Brandstetter. See also Brandstetter and Söntgen's analysis of Salome's dance in "Hérodias" in Gabriele Brandstetter and Beate Söntgen, *Renaissancen der Passion* (Berlin: August, 2012).

52. In his synopsis of the Book of Kings in the Cahen translation of the Bible, Flaubert notes of the king who wants to put an end to idolatry and has the horses dedicated to the sun removed from the temple: "Il fit disparaître de l'entrée de la maison de l'Éternel les chevaux que les rois de Behouda avaient consacré au soleil, auprès de la cellule de . . . l'eunuque qui demeurait dans Parvarime et il brûla au feu les chariots du soleil" (MS, Morgan Library & Museum, New York).

53. Creuzer, *Symbolik und Mythologie* (1973), 2: 40, trans. Susan Solomon. Further quotations from this with page numbers given parenthetically in the text are from the same source.

54. Lucretius, *On the Nature of Things*, trans. William Ellery Leonard (New York: Dutton, 1921), bk. 2. Latin original quoted by Creuzer.

55. On the uncovering of this commentary, see Flaubert, *Trois contes*, ed. de Biasi, 170.

56. Bruce Nauman, *Hanged Man* (Dia Art Foundation, Beacon, NY).

57. Cited in Flaubert, *Trois Contes*, ed. de Biasi, 173.

58. Cf. Mary Jacobus, "Judith, Holofernes and the Phallic Woman," in *Reading Woman* (New York: Columbia University Press, 1986), 110–36.

59. "He spent his boyhood and early youth at Capri among the pathics of Tiberius, being branded for all time with the nickname Spintria and suspected of having been the means of his father's first advancement at the expense of his own chastity." Suetonius, *The Lives of the Caesars*, 308.

60. The promise of another kingdom is explained by the situation of Palestine, which was under Roman rule. The Messiah is therefore understood as a Jewish religious as well as political figure, who rebelled against Roman rule. John the Baptist's prophecies are of a thoroughly political nature. Jesus's strength, however,

according to Renan, was supposedly in his separation of the political from the religious: My kingdom is not of this world. Christianity radically depoliticized the messianic expectation of the Jews and precisely in that way established its specific attraction for Rome. For Renan, it opened up a space beyond the political for the Romans, in which, for better or worse, one was not obliged to be a political animal. Renan also shows how the Roman Empire was related to the promise of a kingdom not of this world: Nero for instance becomes the Antichrist as the embodiment of satanic irony. See Renan, *Histoire des origines du christianisme*, 2: 382.

61. "mais *Aristobule*, noyé en 33, était son beau-frère, *Joseph*, décapité la même année était son oncle, *Alexandre*, étranglé en 6 et *Antipater*, décapité deux ans plus tard, n'étaient autres que ses fils" (*Trois Contes*, ed. de Biasi, 174).

62. "La déesse Holda, identifié par les Romans à Diane et à Vénus: on l'appelait aussi . . . Hérodiade." Alfred Maury, *Croyances et légendes du Moyen Age* (Paris: H. Champion, 1896), cited in a note in *Trois contes*, ed. Pierre-Louis Rey (Paris: Presses Pocket, 1989), 157.

63. Flaubert, *A Sentimental Education: The Story of a Young Man*, trans. Douglas Parmée (New York: Oxford University Press, 1989), 350. *L'Éducation sentimentale*, ed. Pierre-Marc de Biasi (Paris: Librairie générale française, 2002), 477.

Select Bibliography

Flaubert Translations Used

Madame Bovary: Contexts, Criticism. Translated by Eleanor Marx Aveling, revised by Paul De Man. 2nd ed. Edited by Margaret Cohen. New York: Norton, 2005.

Salammbo. Translated by A. J. Krailsheimer. New York: Penguin Books, 1977.

Sentimental Education. Translated by Robert Baldick. 1964. Revised with an introduction and notes by Geoffrey Wall. London: Penguin Books, 2004.

Three Tales. Translated by A. J. Krailsheimer. New York: Oxford University Press, 1991.

"Whatever You Want." In *Early Writings*, trans. Robert Griffin. Lincoln: University of Nebraska Press, 1991.

All Other Titles

Adorno, Theodor W., and Max Horkheimer. *Dialectic of Enlightenment.* Translated by John Cumming. New York: Verso, 1997.

———. *Dialectic of Enlightenment.* Edited by Gunzelin Schmid Noerr. Translated by Edmund Jephcott. Stanford: Stanford University Press, 2002.

Agamben, Giorgio. *The Open: Man and Animal.* Stanford: Stanford University Press, 2003.

Ahl, Frederick. *Lucan: An Introduction.* Ithaca, NY: Cornell University Press, 1976.

Althusser, Louis. *For Marx.* Translated by Ben Brewster. London: Verso, 2005.

Antoine, Agnès. *L'impensé de la démocratie.* Paris: Fayard, 2003.

Arquillière, Henri-Xavier. *L'Augustinisme politique.* Paris: Vrin, 1934.

Auerbach, Erich. "Sermo humilis." In *Literatursprache und Publikum in der lateinischen Spätantike und im Mittelalter*, 25–64. Bern: Francke, 1958.

———. *Mimesis.* Bern: Francke, 1964. Translated by Willard R. Trask as *Mimesis: The Representation of Reality in Western Literature* (Princeton, NJ: Princeton University Press, 1953, 2013).

———. "Figura." Translated by Ralph Manheim. In *Scenes from the Drama of European Literature*, 11–76. Minneapolis: University of Minnesota Press, 1984.

Augustine (Saint Augustine). *Les Confessions de S. Augustin.* Translated by Arnaud d'Andilly. Paris: Le Petit, 1736.

―――. "Of Holy Virginity." In *Seventeen Short Treatises of Saint Augustine,* 309–10. Oxford: J. H. Parker, 1847.

―――. "Ad Pollentium de adulterinis coniugiis." In *Corpus Scriptorum Ecclesiasticorum Latinorum,* vol. 41, ed. Joseph Zycha, 2.5–7, 347–410. Vienna: F. Tempsky, 1900.

―――. "Adulterous Marriage." In *Fathers of the Church: A New Translation,* vol. 27: *Saint Augustine: Treatises on Marriage and Other Subjects,* ed. Roy J. Deferrari, trans. Charles T. Wilcox et al., 55–134. Washington, DC: Catholic University of America Press, 1955.

―――. *De excidio urbis Romae sermo: A Critical Text and Translation with Introduction and Commentary.* Edited by Sister Marie Vianney O'Reilly. Washington, DC: Catholic University of America Press, 1955.

―――. *Confessions.* Translated by Henry Chadwick. Oxford: Oxford University Press, 1991.

―――. *The Works of Saint Augustine. Sermons III/8 (273–305A).* Translated by Edmund Hill. New York: New City Press, 1994.

―――. *Confessions. Books I–IV.* Edited by Gillian Clark. Cambridge: Cambridge University Press, 1995.

―――. *The City of God.* Translated by Marcus Dods. Edited by Philip Schaff. Grand Rapids, MI: Eerdmans, 1997.

―――. *The City of God Against the Pagans.* Translated and edited by Robert W. Dyson. Cambridge: Cambridge University Press, 1998.

Balthasar, Hans Urs von. *Therese von Lisieux: Geschichte einer Sendung.* Cologne: Hegner, 1950.

―――. *Herrlichkeit: Eine theologische Ästhetik.* Vol. 3.2. Einsiedeln: Johannes, 1969.

Bart, Benjamin F. "Male Hysteria in *Salammbô.*" *Nineteenth-Century French Studies* 12, no. 3 (1984): 313–21.

Bart, Benjamin F., and Robert Francis Cook. *The Legendary Sources of Flaubert's Saint Julien.* Toronto: University of Toronto Press, 1977.

Baudelaire, Charles. *Flowers of Evil.* Translated by Lewis Piaget Shanks. New York: Ives Washburn, 1931.

―――. "Madame Bovary par Gustave Flaubert." In *Curiosités esthétiques. L'art romantique et autres œuvres critiques,* ed. Henri Lemaitre, 641–51. Paris: Classiques Garnier, 1962.

―――. *Correspondance.* Vol. 2. Edited by Claude Pichois. Paris: Bibliothèque de la Pléiade, 1973.

———. "*Madame Bovary*, by Gustave Flaubert." In *Madame Bovary*, ed. Margaret Cohen, 403–10. New York: Norton, 2005.

Beauvoir, Simone de. *Le deuxième sexe*. Paris: Gallimard, 1949.

Beck, William J. "'Un Cœur simple' de Flaubert: Le chemin de la sainteté." *University of Dayton Review* 20, no. 1 (1989): 109–15.

Beizer, Janet. "Les lettres de Flaubert à Louise Colet: Une physiologie de style." In *L'œuvre de l'œuvre. Études sur la correspondance de Flaubert*, ed. Raymonde Debray-Genette and Jacques Neefs, 59–83. Saint Denis: Presses universitaires de Vincennes, 1993.

———. *Ventriloquized Bodies: Narratives of Hysteria in Nineteenth-Century France*. Ithaca, NY: Cornell University Press, 1994.

Bellemin-Noël, Jean. *Le quatrième conte de Gustave Flaubert*. Paris: Presses universitaires de France, 1990.

———. "Le sexe d'Emma." In *Emma Bovary*, ed. Alain Buisine, 52–78. Paris: Éd. Autrement, 1997.

Bem, Jeanne. "La production du sens chez Flaubert: La contribution de Sartre." In Centre culturel international de Cerisy-la-Salle, *La production du sens chez Flaubert*, ed. Claudine Gothot-Mersch, 155–74. Paris: Union générale d'éditions, 1975.

———. "La forêt de Flaubert. Retour sur un épisode de *L'Éducation sentimentale*." In *Orients littéraires. Mélanges offerts à Jacques Huré*, ed. Sophie Basch et al. Paris: Champion, 2004.

Bénichou, Paul. *Le Sacre de l'écrivain, 1750–1830: Essai sur l'avènement d'un pouvoir spirituel laïque dans la France moderne*. Paris: Corti, 1973.

———. *Le Temps des prophètes: Doctrines de l'âge romantique*. Paris: Gallimard, 1977.

Bernheimer, Charles. "The Decadent Subject." *L'esprit créateur* 32, no. 4 (1992): 53–62.

Biasi, Pierre-Marc de. "Le palimpseste hagiographique: l'appropriation ludique des sources édifiantes dans la rédaction de 'La Légende de saint Julien l'Hospitalier.'" In *Gustave Flaubert*, vol. 1 of *Mythes et réligions*, ed. Bernard Masson, 69–124. Paris: Minard, 1996.

———. Editorial commentary to Gustave Flaubert, *Trois Contes*, ed. P.-M. de Biasi. Paris: Librairie générale française, 1999.

———. "Qu'est-ce que cela veut dire, la réalité? Le cryptage du réel dans *L'Éducation sentimentale*." In *Le Flaubert réel*, ed. Barbara Vinken and Peter Fröhlicher, 61–78. Tübingen: Niemeyer, 2009.

Bloch, R. Howard. *God's Plagiarist: Being an Account of the Fabulous Industry and Irregular Commerce of the Abbé Migne*. Chicago: University of Chicago Press, 1994.

Bloom, Harold. *The Anxiety of Influence: A Theory of Poetry.* Oxford: Oxford University Press, 1997.

Blumenberg, Hans. *Der Prozeß der theoretischen Neugierde.* Frankfurt/Main: Suhrkamp, 1973.

Bohrer, Karl Heinz. *Ästhetische Negativität. Zum Problem des literarischen und philosophischen Nihilismus.* Munich: Hanser, 2002.

Bonaccorso, Giovanni. *Corpus Flaubertianum.* Vol. 1. Paris: Les Belles Lettres, 1983.

Borgeaud, Philippe. *La Mère des dieux: De Cybèle à la Vierge Marie.* Paris: Seuil, 1996.

———. *The Mother of the Gods: From Cybele to the Virgin Mary.* Baltimore: Johns Hopkins University Press, 2004.

Borie, Jean. *Une forêt pour les dimanches. Les romantiques à Fontainebleau.* Paris: Grasset, 2003

Borst, Arno. *Der Turmbau zu Babel.* 6 vols. Stuttgart: Hiersemann, 1957–63.

Bosse, Monika, and André Stoll. "Die Agonie des archaischen Orients: Eine verschlüsselte Vision des Revolutionszeitalters." Afterword to Gustave Flaubert, *Salammbô,* ed. Monika Bosse and André Stoll, trans. Georg Brustgi. Frankfurt/Main: Insel, 1979.

Bourget, Paul. "Gustave Flaubert." 1883. In *Essais de psychologie contemporaine: Études littéraires,* ed. André Guyaux, 113–73. Paris: Gallimard, 1993.

Bouvier, Agnès. "Jéhovah égale Moloch: Une lecture antireligieuse de *Salammbô.*" *Romantisme* 136 (2007): 109–20.

Bowman, Frank Paul. *Le Christ des barricades, 1789–1848.* Paris: Cerf, 1987.

Brandstetter, Gabriele, and Beate Söntgen. *Renaissancen der Passion.* Berlin: August, 2012.

Brix, Michel. "*L'Éducation sentimentale* de Flaubert: De la peinture de la passion 'inactive' à la critiqe du romantisme français." *Études littéraires* 30 (1998): 107–19.

Brombert, Victor. "Flaubert's *Saint Julien:* The Sin of Existing." *PMLA* 81, no. 3 (1966): 297–302.

———. *The Novels of Flaubert.* Princeton: Princeton University Press, 1966.

———. "La chambre de Félicité: bazar ou chapelle?" In *George Sand et son temps: Hommage à Annarosa Poli,* ed. Elio Mosele, 1: 73–86. Geneva: Slatkine, 1994.

Brooks, Peter. *Reading for the Plot: Design and Intention in Narrative.* New York: Knopf, 1984.

Buisine, Alain. "Salammbô ou les dangers du dévoilement." In id., *L'orient voilé,* 127–48. Cadeilhan: Éd. Zulma, 1993.

———, ed. *Emma Bovary.* Collection Figures mythiques. Paris: Éd. Autrement, 1997.

Butor, Michel. *Improvisations sur Flaubert.* Paris: Éd. de la Différence, 1984.

Camp, Maxime du. *Souvenirs littéraires.* Edited by D. Oster. Paris: Aubier, 1994.

Cavell, Stanley. *Disowning Knowledge in Seven Plays of Shakespeare*. Cambridge: Cambridge University Press, 2003.

Cerfaux, Lucien. "L'hymne au Christ-Serviteur de Dieu." In *Miscellanea Historica in honorem Alberti de Meyer*, 1: 117–30. Louvain: Bibliothèque de l'Université, 1946.

Chambers, Ross. "Simplicité de cœur et duplicité textuelle: Étude d'*Un Cœur simple*." *MLN* 96 (1981): 771–91.

Chateaubriand, François-René de. *The Martyrs*. Edited by O. W. Wright. New York: Derby & Jackson, 1859.

———. "Les martyrs." In *Œuvres romanesques et voyages*. Vol. 2. Paris: Bibliothèque de la Pléiade, 1969.

Coelen, Marcus. *Die Tyrannei des Partikularen: Lektüren Prousts*. Munich: Fink, 2007.

Coleman, Algernon. "*Salammbô* and the Bible." In *Sources and Structure of Flaubert's Salammbô*, ed. Percival Bradshaw Fay and Algernon Coleman, 37–55. Baltimore: Johns Hopkins University Press, 1914.

Collas, Ion K. *Madame Bovary: A Psychoanalytic Reading*. Geneva: Librairie Droz, 1995.

Condren, Charles de. "Letter 74." In id., *Œuvres complètes*, ed. Abbé Louis-Marie Pin, 1: 276. Paris: Guyot & Roidot, 1857.

Cozea, Angela. "*Salammbô* dans une perspective romane: La traduction d'Hannibal comme 'survie.'" *Canadian Review of Comparative Literature* 17, nos. 3–4 (1990): 307–17.

Creuzer, Georg Friedrich. *Symbolik und Mythologie der alten Völker*. 1810–12. 4 vols. Hildesheim: Olms, 1973.

———. *Religions de l'antiquité considérées principalement dans leurs formes symboliques et mythologiques*. Translated and edited by J.-D. Guigniaut et al. 10 vols. Paris: Treuttel & Würtz, followed by J.-J. Kossbühl and Firmin-Didot frères, 1825–51.

Crouzet, Michel. "Passion et politique dans *L'Éducation sentimentale*." In *Flaubert, la femme, la ville*, ed. Marie-Claire Bancquart, 39–71. Paris: Presses universitaires de France, 1983.

Culler, Jonathan. *Flaubert: The Uses of Uncertainty*. Ithaca, NY: Cornell University Press, 1974.

———. "The Uses of Madame Bovary." *Diacritics* 11 (1981): 74–81.

Czyba, Lucette. *Mythes et idéologie de la femme dans les romans de Flaubert*. Lyon: Presses universitaires de Lyon, 1983.

Danger, Pierre. *Sensations et objets dans le roman de Flaubert*. Paris: Colin, 1973.

Danius, Sara. *The Prose of the World: Flaubert and the Art of Making Things Visible*. Uppsala: Uppsala University, 2006.

Debray-Genette, Raymonde. *Métamorphoses du récit: Autour de Flaubert*. Paris: Seuil, 1988.

Delacomptée, Jean-Michel. *"La Princesse de Clèves": La mère et le courtisan*. Paris: Presses universitaires de France, 1990.

Delehaye, Hippolyte. *Les passions des martyrs et les genres littéraires*. Brussels: Société des Bollandistes, 1966.

Derrida, Jacques. *Spurs: Nietzsche's Styles*. Translated by Barbara Harlow. Chicago: University of Chicago Press, 1979.

———. "Une idée de Flaubert: La lettre de Platon." In id., *Psyché: Inventions de l'autre*, 305–25. Paris: Galilée, 1987.

———. "Three Questions to Hans-Georg Gadamer." In *Dialogue and Deconstruction: The Gadamer-Derrida Encounter*, ed. Diane P. Michelfelder and Richard E. Palmer, 52–55. Albany: State University of New York Press, 1989.

———. *On the Name*. Edited by Thomas Dutoit. Translated by David Wood, John P. Leavey, and Ian McLeod. Stanford: Stanford University Press, 1995.

———. *Le monolinguisme de l'autre, ou La prothèse d'origine*. Paris: Galilée, 1996.

Descharmes, René. "Saint-Julien l'Hospitalier et Pécopin." *Revue biblio-iconographique* 3, no. 12 (1905), 1–7, 67–75.

Donato, Eugenio. "Flaubert and the Question of History: Notes for a Critical Anthology." *MLN* 91, no. 5 (1976): 850–70.

Duby, Georges. *Le temps des cathédrales: L'art et la societé 980–1420*. Paris: Gallimard, 1976.

Dufour, Philippe. "Salammbô, un tigre de marbre." In *Gustave Flaubert*, ed. Gisèle Séginger, 5: 193–214. Paris: Minard, 2005.

Dünne, Jörg. *Asketisches Schreiben: Rousseau und Flaubert als Paradigmen literarischer Selbstpraxis in der Moderne*. Tübingen: Narr, 2003.

Duquette, Jean-Pierre. *Flaubert, ou L'architecture du vide: Une lecture de l'Éducation sentimentale*. Montréal: Presses de l'Université de Montréal, 1972.

Dürr, Susanne. "Functions of Violence in Flaubert's *Salammbô*." In *The Aesthetics and Pragmatics of Violence*, ed. Michael Hensen and Annette Pankratz, 211–24. Passau: Stutz, 2001.

Eliade, Mircea. *Images et symboles: Essais sur le symbolisme magico-religieux*. Paris: Gallimard, 1952.

Elm, Susanna. *Virgins of God: The Making of Asceticism in Late Antiquity*. Oxford: Clarendon Press, 1994.

Emptaz, Florence. *Aux pieds de Flaubert*. Paris: Grasset, 2002.

Eßlinger, Eva. *Das Dienstmädchen, die Familie und der Sex: Zur Geschichte einer irregulären Beziehung in der europäischen Literatur*. Munich: Fink, 2013.

Euripides. *Iphigenia in Aulis*. In *The Plays of Euripides*, trans. Edward P. Coleridge, vol. 2. London: George Bell & Sons, 1891.

Felman, Shoshana. "Illusion et répétition Romanesque." In *La lecture sociocritique du texte romanesque*, ed. Graham Falconer and Henri Mitterand. Toronto: Stevens, 1975.

———. "La Signature de Flaubert: *La Légende de St. Julien l'hospitalier.*" *Revue des sciences humaines* 181 (1981): 39–57.

Ferguson, Frances. "Emma, or Happiness (or Sex Work)." In id., *Pornography, the Theory: What Utilitarianism Did to Action*, 96–124. Chicago: University of Chicago Press, 2004.

Fichtner, Gerhard. "Christus als Arzt. Ursprünge und Wirkungen eines Motivs." *Frühmittelalterliche Studien* 16 (1982): 1–18.

Flaubert, Gustave: *Tentation de St Antoine*. Edited by Luis Bertrand. Paris: Charpentier, 1908.

———. *Trois contes*. Paris: Louis Conard, 1910.

———. "Notes de voyage." In *Œuvres complètes*, vol. 2, ed. Louis Conard. Paris: Louis Conard, 1910.

———. *Correspondance (1877–1880)*. Edited by Louis Conard. Vol. 8 of *Correspondance*. Vol. 11 of *Œuvres complètes*. Paris: L. Conard, 1930.

———. *Œuvres*. Vol. 1. Edited by Albert Thibaudet and René Dumesnil. Paris: Bibliothèque de la Pléiade, 1951.

———. *Trois contes*. Edited by Édouard Maynial. Paris: Garnier frères, 1960.

———. *Madame Bovary: Mœurs de province*. 1856. Edited by Claudine Gothot-Mersch. Paris: Classiques Garnier, 1971.

———. *Les trois frères*. In *Œuvres diverses, Fragments et Ébauches. Correspondance*, vol. 12 of *Œuvres completes*, 222–27. Paris: Club de l'Honnête Homme, 1974.

———. *Drei Erzählungen: Trois contes*. Edited and translated by Cora van Kleffens and Andre Stoll. Frankfurt/Main: Insel, 1982.

———. *The Letters of Gustave Flaubert: 1830–1880*. Edited and translated by Francis Steegmuller. 2 vols. Cambridge, MA: Belknap Press of Harvard University Press, 1980–82.

———. *Éducation sentimentale*. Edited by Peter Michael Wetherill. Paris: Garnier, 1984.

———. *Carnets de travail*. Edited by Pierre-Marc de Biasi. Paris: Balland, 1988.

———. *Trois contes*. Edited by Pierre-Louis Rey. Paris: Presses Pocket, 1989.

———. *A Sentimental Education: The Story of a Young Man*. Translated by Douglas Parmée. New York: Oxford University Press, 1989.

———. *Voyage en Égypte*. Edited by Pierre-Marc de Biasi. Paris: Grasset, 1991.

———. *Madame Bovary*. 1856. Edited by Gérard Gengembre. Paris: Magnard, 1992.

———. *Madame Bovary: Mœurs de province*. 1856. Edited by Pierre-Marc de Biasi. Paris: Imprimerie nationale, 1994.

————. *Madame Bovary: Mœurs de province*. 1856. Edited by Jacques Neefs. Paris: Librairie générale française, 1999.

————. *Trois contes*. Edited by Pierre-Marc de Biasi. Paris: Flammarion, 1991; Librairie générale française, 1999.

————. "Lutte du sacerdoce et de l'empire." In *Œuvres complètes*, vol. 1: *Œuvres de jeunesse*, ed. Claudine Gothot-Mersch and Guy Sagnes. Paris: Bibliothèque de la Pléiade, 2001.

————. "Quidquid volueris—Études psychologiques." In *Œuvres complètes*, vol. 1: *Œuvres de jeunesse*, ed. Claudine Gothot-Mersch and Guy Sagnes, 243–72. Paris: Gallimard, 2001.

————. *Salammbô*. Edited by Gisèle Séginger. Paris: Flammarion, 2001.

————. *The Temptation of Saint Anthony*. Translated by Lafcadio Hearn. Edited by Marshal C. Olds. New York: Modern Library, 2001.

————. *Éducation sentimentale*. Edited by Pierre-Marc de Biasi. Paris: Hachette, 2002.

————. *L'Éducation sentimentale*. Edited by Pierre-Marc de Biasi. Paris: Librairie générale française, 2002.

————. *Correspondance*. 5 vols. Edited by Jean Bruneau. Paris: Bibliothèque de la Pléiade, 1973–2007.

————. *Madame Bovary*. Translated by Geoffrey Wall. London: Penguin Books, 2004.

————. *Madame Bovary: Provincial Manners*. Translated by Margaret Mauldon. Oxford: Oxford University Press, 2004.

Fonyi, Antonia. "Sa 'vie nombreuse', sa 'haine nombreuse.'" In *Emma Bovary*, ed. Alain Buisine, 122–44. Paris: Éd. Autrement, 1997.

Foucault, Michel. Foreword to Flaubert, *The Temptation of Saint Anthony*, trans. Lafcadio Hearn, ed. Marshal C. Olds, xiii–xliv. New York: Modern Library, 2001.

Freud, Sigmund. *General Introduction to Psychoanalysis*. Translated by G. Stanley Hall. New York: Boni & Liveright, 1920.

————. "On the Universal Tendency to Debasement in the Sphere of Love." In *The Standard Edition of the Complete Psychological Works*, 11: 177–90. Translated and edited by James Strachey, Anna Freud, Alix Strachey, and Alan Tyson. London: Hogarth Press, 1964.

————. "The Taboo of Virginity." In *Sexuality and the Psychology of Love*, 60–76. New York: Touchstone, 1997.

Friedrich, Sabine. *Die Imagination des Bösen: Zur narrativen Modellierung der Transgression bei Laclos, Sade und Flaubert*. Tübingen: Narr, 1998.

Fuhrmann, Manfred. "Proscriptio." In *Realencyclopädie der classischen Altertumswissenschaft*, vol. 23, chap. 2: 2439–44. Stuttgart: Druckenmüller, 1959.

Funkenstein, Amos. *Heilsplan und natürliche Entwicklung: Formen der Gegenwarts-bestimmung im Geschichtsdenken des hohen Mittelalters.* Munich: Nymphen-burger Verlagshandlung, 1965.

Gagnebin, Bernard. *Flaubert et Salammbô: Genèse d'un texte.* Paris: Presses univer-sitaires de France, 1992.

Gaillard, Françoise. "La révolte contre la révolution. *Salammbô*: un autre point de vue sur l'histoire." In *Gustave Flaubert: Procédés narratifs et fondements episté-mologiques*, ed. Alfonso de Toro, 43–54. Tübingen: Narr, 1987.

Genette, Gérard. "Demotivation in *Hérodias*." In *Flaubert and Postmodernism*, ed. Naomi Schor and Henry F. Majewski. Lincoln: University of Nebraska Press, 1984.

———. *Discours du récit.* Paris: Points, 2007.

Gérard-Gailly, Émile. *Flaubert et "les fantômes de Trouville."* Paris: La Renaissance du Livre, 1930.

Girard, René. "Scandal and the Dance: Salome and the Gospel of Mark." *New Literary History* 15 (1984): 311–24.

Goppelt, Leonhard. *Typos: Die typologische Deutung des Alten Testaments im Neuen.* Darmstadt: Wissenschaftliche Buchgesellschaft, 1966.

Green, André. *Le complexe de castration.* Paris: Presses universitaires de France, 1995.

Green, Anne. *Flaubert and the Historical Novel: Salammbô Reassessed.* Cambridge: Cambridge University Press, 1982.

Greenblatt, Stephen. *Renaissance Self-Fashioning.* Chicago: University of Chicago Press, 1980.

Gresset, Jean-Baptiste Louis. *The Parrot, and Other Poems.* Translated by T. S. Allen. London: Longman, Orme, Brown, Green & Longman, 1848.

Haig, Stirling. "The Substance of Illusion in Flaubert's *Un Cœur simple*." *Stanford French Review* 7, no. 3 (1983): 301–15.

Halperin, Richard. *How to Do the History of Male Homosexuality.* Chicago: Uni-versity of Chicago Press, 2002.

Hamann, A. G. *Jacques Paul Migne: Le retour aux pères de l'Eglise.* Paris: Beauchesne, 1975.

Hampton, Timothy. "'Turkish Dogs': Rabelais, Erasmus, and the Rhetoric of Alterity." *Representations* 41 (1993): 58–82.

Harries, Martin. *Forgetting Lot's Wife: On Destructive Spectatorship.* New York: Fordham University Press, 2007.

Haselstein, Ulla. "Un réalisme d'un genre nouveau: *Trois contes* de Flaubert et *Trois vies* de Gertrude Stein." In *Le Flaubert réel*, ed. Barbara Vinken and Peter Fröhlicher, 165–82. Tübingen: Max Niemeier, 2009.

Hausmann, Frank-Rutger. "Im Wald von Fontainebleau: Sehnsuchtsort oder Metapher des Erzählens?" In *Sehnsuchtsorte, Festschrift zum 60. Geburtstag von Titus Heydenreich.* Tübingen: Stauffenburg, 1999.

Haverkamp, Anselm. *Typik und Politik im Annolied: Zum Konflikt der Interpretationen im Mittelalter.* Stuttgart: Metzler, 1979.

———. "Christ's Case, and John Donne, Seeing Through His Wounds: The Stigma of Martyrdom Transfigured." In *How the West Was Won: On the Problems of Canon and Literary Imagination, with a Special Emphasis on the Middle Ages,* ed. Willemien Otten and Hent de Vries, 55–65. Leiden: Brill, 2006.

———. "Arcanum translationis. Das Fundament der lateinischen Tradition." In *Tumult. Schriften zur Verkehrswissenschaft,* vol. 30, ed. Walter Seitter and Cornelia Vismann, 19–31. Berlin: Diaphanes, 2006.

———. *Begreifen im Bild: Methodische Annäherungen an die Aktualität der Kunst: Antonello da Messina, August Sander.* Berlin: August, 2009.

———. *Shakespearean Genealogies of Power.* London: Routledge, 2010.

———, ed. *Theorie der Metapher.* Darmstadt: Wissenschaftliche Buchgesellschaft, 1983.

Heath, Stephen. *Madame Bovary.* Cambridge: Cambridge University Press, 1992.

Hegel, Georg Wilhelm Friedrich. "Die romantische Kunstform: Der religiöse Kreis." In *Vorlesungen über die Philosophie der Kunst,* ed. Annemarie Gethmann-Siefert. Hamburg: Meiner, 1998.

Henderson, John. *Fighting for Rome: Poets and Caesars, History and Civil War.* Cambridge: Cambridge University Press, 1998.

Henry, Paul. "Kénose." In *Supplément au Dictionnaire de la Bible,* 5: 7–161. Paris: Letouzey & Ané, 1957.

Hermine, Micheline. *Destins de femmes. Désir d'absolu. Essai sur Madame Bovary et Thérèse de Lisieux.* Paris: Beauchesne, 1997.

Hofmann, Franz. *Der Kirchenbegriff des heiligen Augustinus in seinen Grundlagen und in seiner Entwicklung.* Munich: Hueber, 1933.

Hölderlin, Friedrich. "Lucans Pharsalia." In *Sämtliche Werke,* ed. Friedrich Beißner, vol. 5. Stuttgart: Kohlhammer, 1954.

Homer. *The Iliad.* Translated by Robert Fagles. London: Penguin Books, 1991.

Huet, Valérie. "Napoleon I: A New Augustus?" In *Roman Presences: Receptions of Rome in European Culture, 1789–1945,* ed. Catharine Edwards, 53–69. Cambridge: Cambridge University Press, 1999.

Hugo, Victor. "Légende du beau Pécopin et de la belle Baldour." In *Œuvres complètes de Victor Hugo,* vol. 1: *Le Rhin.* Paris: Nelson, n.d.

———. *The Rhine.* New York: Wiley & Putnam, 1845.

———. *La fin de Satan.* In *La legende des siècles. La fin de satan. Dieu,* ed. Jacques Truchet, 765–942. Paris: Bibliothèque de la Pléiade, 1955.

———. "Le feu du ciel." In *Odes et Ballades: Les Orientales,* 419. Paris: Nelson, 1960.

———. "À l'Arc de Triomphe." In *Œuvres complètes,* ed. Claude Gély, vol. 1: *Poésie,* 819–31. Paris: Robert Laffont, 1985.

————. *Poems by Victor Hugo.* Available at www.gutenberg.org/files/8775/8775–8
.txt.

Hunt, Lynn. *The Family Romance of the French Revolution.* Berkeley: University of
California Press, 1993.

Issacharoff, Michael. *L'Espace et la nouvelle: Flaubert, Huysmans, Ionesco, Sartre,
Camus.* Paris: Corti, 1976.

Jacobus, Mary. "Judith, Holofernes and the Phallic Woman." In id., *Reading Woman:
Essays in Feminist Criticism,* 110–36. New York: Columbia University Press, 1986.

Jauß, Hans Robert. "Die beiden Fassungen von Flauberts 'Éducation sentimentale.'" *Heidelberger Jahrbücher* 2 (1958): 96–116.

Jelinek, Elfriede. *Lust.* Reinbek bei Hamburg: Rowohlt, 1989. Translated by Michael Hulse (London: Serpent's Tail, 1992).

Jolles, André. *Einfache Formen: Legende, Sage, Mythe, Rätsel, Spruch, Kasus, Memorabile, Märchen, Witz.* Halle: Niemeyer, 1930.

Jonas, Hans. *Gnosis und spätantiker Geist.* Göttingen: Vanderhoeck & Ruprecht,
1934.

Jones, Ernest. *Essays in Applied Psycho-Analysis.* Vol. 2. London: Hogarth Press, 1951.

Josephus, Flavius. *Jüdische Altertümer.* Translated by Heinrich Clementz. 1899.
Wiesbaden: Fourier, 2004.

————. *The Antiquities of the Jews.* In *The Works of Flavius Josephus,* trans. William Whiston. Whitefish, MT: Kessinger, 2006.

Jurt, Joseph. "Die Wertung der Geschichte in Flauberts *Education sentimentale.*"
Romanistische Zeitschrift für Literaturgeschichte 7 (1983): 141–68.

————. "Literatur und Archäologie: Die *Salammbô*-Debatte." In *Literatur und
Wissenschaft,* ed. Brigitte Winklehner, 101–17. Tübingen: Stauffenburg, 1987.

Kaplan, Louise. *Female Perversions. The Temptation of Madame Bovary.* New York:
Doubleday, 1991.

Kasper, Judith, and Cornelia Wild, eds. *Rom rückwärts. Europäische Übertragungsschicksale von Lucan bis Lacan.* Munich: Fink, 2015.

Kölmel, Wilhelm. *Regimen Christianum: Weg und Ergebnisse des Gewaltenverhältnisses und Gewaltenverständnisses. 8. bis 14. Jahrhundert.* Berlin: De Gruyter, 1970.

Küpper, Joachim. "Erwägungen zu *Salammbô.*" In *Konkurrierende Diskurse: Studien zur französischen Literatur des 19. Jahrhunderts,* ed. Brunhilde Wehinger,
269–310. Stuttgart: Steiner, 1997.

————. "Das Ende von Emma Bovary." In *Geschichte und Text in der Literatur
Frankreichs, der Romania und der Literaturwissenschaft. Rita Schober zum 80.
Geburtstag,* ed. Hans-Otto Dill, 71–93. Berlin: trafo, 1999.

Lacan, Jacques. "On the Baroque." In *Seminars of Jacques Lacan,* vol. 20: *On Feminine Sexuality: The Limits of Love and Knowledge,* ed. Jacques-Alain Miller,
trans. Bruce Fink, 95–117. New York: Norton, 1998.

Lafond, Jean. "Une victime de la guerre: La vitrerie de l'église Saint-Michel de Pont-l'Évêque." *Bulletin de la Société des antiquaires de Normandie* 56 (1961–62): 569–86.

Laforge, François. "*Salammbô*: Les mythes et la revolution." *Revue d'histore littéraire de la France* 85 (1985): 26–40.

Lamartine, Alphonse de. *Geneviève, histoire d'une servante*. 1850. Paris: Lib. nouvelle Jaccottet, Bourdilliat, 1857.

———. *Genevieve; or, Peasant Love and Sorrow*. Translated by Fayette Robinson. New York: Stringer & Townsend, 1850.

Lange, Klaus. "Geistliche Speise. Untersuchungen zur Metaphorik der Bibelhermeneutik." *Zeitschrift für deutsches Altertum und deutsche Literatur* 95, no. 2 (1966): 6–122.

Le Brun, Jacques. *Le pur amour: De Platon à Lacan*. Paris: Seuil, 2002.

Le Juez, Brigitte. *Le papegai et le papelard dans 'Un cœur simple' de Gustave Flaubert*. Amsterdam: Rodopi, 1999.

Leclerc, Ivan. *La Bibliothèque de Flaubert*. Rouen: Presses universitaires de Rouen, 2001.

Lefort, Claude. "La permanence du théologico-politique." *Le temps de la réflexion* 11 (1981): 13–61.

Leupin, Alexandre. *Fiction et incarnation: Littérature et théologie au Moyen Âge*. Paris: Flammarion, 1993. Translated by David Laatsch as *Fiction and Incarnation: Rhetoric, Theology, and Literature in the Middle Ages* (Minneapolis: University of Minnesota Press, 2003).

Lewis, C. S. *The Allegory of Love: A Study in Medieval Tradition*. Oxford: Clarendon Press, 1936.

Loiseau, Jean. *Le Massif de Fontainebleau*. 1935. 4th ed. Paris: Vigot frères, 1970.

Lucan [Marcus Annaeus Lucanus]. *The Civil War (Pharsalia)*. With an English translation by J. D. Duff. Loeb Classical Library. 1928. Cambridge, MA: Harvard University Press, 1988.

———. *Pharsalia*. Translated and edited by Jane Wilson Joyce. Ithaca, NY: Cornell University Press, 1993.

Lucretius [Titus Lucretius Carus]. *Of the Nature of Things*. Translated by William Ellery Leonard. New York: Dutton, 1921.

———. *De rerum natura*. Edited by E. J. Kenney. Cambridge: Cambridge University Press, 1971.

Lukács, Georg. *The Historical Novel*. 1937. Translated by Hannah and Stanley Mitchell. Lincoln: University of Nebraska Press, 1983.

Lund, Hans Peter. *Flaubert: Trois contes*. Paris: Presses universitaires de France, 1994.

Maistre, Joseph de. *Éclaircissement sur les sacrifices*. 1810. In *Œuvres completes*, vol. 5. Lyon: Vitte & Perrussel, 1884.

———. "Elucidation on Sacrifices." In *St. Petersburg Dialogues, or, Conversations on the Temporal Government of Providence*, trans. and ed. Richard A. Lebrun. Montreal: McGill-Queen's University Press, 1993.

Mandouze, André, and Joël Fouilheron, eds. *Migne et le renouveau des études patristiques*. Paris: Beauchesne, 1985.

Marrou, Henri-Irénée. *Saint Augustin et la fin de la culture antique*. Paris: Boccard, 1958.

Marx, Karl. "The Eighteenth Brumaire of Louis Bonaparte." In *The Marx-Engels Reader*, ed. Robert C. Tucker. New York: Norton, 1978.

Masson, Bernard. "*Salammbô* ou la barbarie à visage humain." *Revue d'histoire littéraire de la France* 81 (1981): 585–96.

Matthey, Cécile. *L'écriture hospitalière. L'espace de la croyance dans les Trois Contes de Flaubert*. New York: Rodopi, 2008.

Maury, Alfred. *Essai sur les légendes pieuses du Moyen âge*. Paris: Ladrange, 1843.

———. *Croyances et légendes du Moyen âge*. Paris: H. Champion, 1896.

Mehlman, Geoffrey. *Revolution and Repetition: Marx/Hugo/Balzac*. Berkeley: University of California Press, 1977.

Micale, Mark S. "Charcot and the Idea of Hysteria in the Male." *Medical History* 34 (1990): 363–411.

Michelet, Jules. *History of the Roman Republic*. Translated by William Hazlitt. New York: Miller, Orton & Mulligan, 1856.

———. *Le peuple: Nos fils*. Paris: E. Flammarion, 1869.

Migne, Jacques-Paul. *Patrologiae cursus completus. Series Latina*. Paris: J.-P. Migne successores, 1844–91.

Miles, Richard. *Carthage Must Be Destroyed: The Rise and Fall of an Ancient Civilization*. New York: Penguin Books, 2010.

Molsdorf, Wilhelm. *Christliche Symbolik der mittelalterlichen Kunst*. Leipzig: Hiersemann, 1926.

Momigliano, Arnaldo. "L'historiographie paienne et chretienne au IVe siècle après J.-C." In id., *Problèmes d'historiographie ancienne et moderne*. Paris: Gallimard, 1983.

Montandon, Alain. "Mythes et représentation de l'hospitalité." In *Mythes et représentation de l'hospitalité*, ed. Alain Montandon, 11–21. Clermont-Ferrand: Presses universitaires Blaise Pascal, 1999.

Mouchard, Claude, and Jacques Neefs. *Flaubert: Une vie, une œuvre, une époque*. Paris: Balland, 1986.

Neefs, Jacques. "Le parcours du zaïmph." In Centre culturel international de Cerisy-la-Salle, *La production du sens chez Flaubert*, ed. Claudine Gothot-Mersch, 227–41. Paris: Union générale d'éditions, 1975.

————. "*Salammbô* et la cité antique." In *Flaubert: La femme, la ville*, ed. Marie-Claire Bancquart, 109–21. Paris: Presses universitaires de France, 1983.

Nehr, Harald. "Sehen im Klischee—Schreiben im Klischee. Zum Verhältnis von Wahrnehmung, bildender Kunst und Künstlern in Gustave Flauberts *Éducation sentimentale*." *Romanistische Zeitschrift für Literaturgeschichte* 27 (2003): 117–30.

Neumann, Gerhard. "Der Blick des Anderen. Zum Motiv des Hundes und des Affen in der Literatur." *Jahrbuch der deutschen Schillergesellschaft* 40 (1996): 87–122.

Neumann, Gerhard, and Barbara Vinken. "Kulturelle Mimikry: Zur Affenfigur bei Flaubert und Kafka." *Zeitschrift für deutsche Philologie* 126 (2007): 126–42.

Nietzsche, Friedrich Wilhelm. *The Anti-Christ*. Translated by H. L. Mencken. 1918. New York: Cosimo, 2005.

————. *The Will to Power*. Edited by Walter Kaufmann. Translated by Walter Kaufmann and R. J. Hollingdale. New York: Vintage Books, 1968.

————. "Der Antichrist." In *Werke. Kritische Gesamtausgabe*, vol. 6, ed. Giorgio Colli and Mazzino Montinari. Berlin: De Gruyter, 1969.

————. *The Anti-Christ, Ecce Homo, Twilight of the Idols and Other Writings*. Edited by Aaron Ridley and Judith Norman. Translated by Judith Norman. Cambridge: Cambridge University Press, 2005.

Nykrog, Per. "Les *Trois Contes* dans l'évolution de la structure thématique chez Flaubert." *Romantisme* 6 (1973): 55–66.

Oehler, Dolf. "Zum gesellschaftlichen Standort der Neurose-Kunst. Sartres *Idiot de la Famille* und Flauberts *Éducation sentimentale*. Versuch einer vergleichenden Lektüre." In *Sartres Flaubert lesen*, ed. Traugott König, 149–90. Reinbek bei Hamburg: Rowohlt, 1980.

Ohly, Friedrich. "Die Kathedrale als Zeitenraum." In id., *Schriften zur mittelalterlichen Bedeutungsforschung*, 171–273. Darmstadt: Wissenschaftliche Buchgesellschaft, 1977.

Olds, Marshall C. *Au pays des perroquets: Féerie théâtrale et narration chez Flaubert*. Amsterdam: Rodopi, 2001.

Orr, Mary. *Flaubert. Writing of the Masculine*. Oxford: Oxford University Press, 2000.

Overaker, Lewis J. "Manifestations of the Holy Ghost in Flaubert's *Un Cœur simple*," *Renascence* 53, no. 2 (2001): 119–48.

Ovid. *The Love Poems*. Translated by A. D. Melville. Oxford: Oxford University Press, 1990.

————. *Metamorphoses*. Translated by Charles Martin. New York: Norton, 2004.

Passion de Perpétue et de Félicité: Suivi des Actes. Translated and edited by Jacqueline Amat. Paris: Cerf, 1996.

The Passion of SS. Perpetua and Felicity MM. Translated by W. H. Shewring. London: Sheed & Ward, 1931.

Petrarch, Francesco. "Invectiva contra eum qui maledixit Italie." In id., *Prose*, ed. Guido Martellotti. Milan: Ricciardi, 1955.

Pfeiffer, Helmut. "Salome im Fin de Siècle. Ästhetisierung des Sakralen, Sakralisierung des Ästhetischen." In *Das Buch der Bücher—gelesen*, ed. Steffen Markus and Andrea Polaschegg, 303–36. Berlin: Lang, 2006.

Pitra, Jean-Baptiste. *Spicilegium solesmense complectens sanctorum patrum scriptorumque ecclesiasticorum anecdota hactenus opera.* 4 vols. Paris: Firmin Didot, 1852–58.

Plutarch. *Lives.* Vol. 4. Translated by Bernadotte Perrin. London: Loeb, 1916.

Polaschegg, Andrea. *Der andere Orientalismus. Regeln deutschmorgenländischer Imagination im 19. Jahrhundert.* Berlin: De Gruyter, 2005.

Prendergast, Christopher. *The Order of Mimesis: Balzac, Stendhal, Nerval, Flaubert.* Cambridge: Cambridge University Press, 1986.

Prévost, Jean. "Aspects du roman moderne." In *Problèmes du roman*, special issue, ed. id., of the review *Confluences* (Lyon) 3 (1943), 21–24.

Privat, Jean-Marie. *Bovary Charivari: Essai d'ethno-critique.* Paris: CNRS, 1994.

Le procès. Le ministère public contre Gustave Flaubert. Réquisitoire de M. l'avocat impérial M. Ernest Pinard. Appendix to *Madame Bovary*, by Gustave Flaubert, ed. Maurice Bardèche, 413–37. Paris: Librairie générale française, 1972.

Proust, Marcel. "À propos du style de Flaubert." *Nouvelle Revue française* 76 (1920).

Quignard, Pascal. *Petits traités.* Vol. 1. Paris: Gallimard, 1997.

Racine, Jean. *Andromaque.* In id., *Œuvres*, ed. Edmond Pilon and René Gross. Paris: Gallimard, 1940.

———. *Phèdre.* In id., *Œuvres complètes*, ed. Raymond Picard, 1: 745–803. Paris: Bibliothèque de la Pleiade, 1950.

———. "Phaedra." In id., *Iphigenia, Phaedra, Athaliah.* Translated by John Cairncross. London: Penguin Books, 1970. Rev. ed. 2004.

Raitt, Alan W. *Flaubert: Trois Contes.* London: Grant & Cutler, 1991.

Rancière, Jacques. *Politique de la littérature.* Paris: Galilée, 2007.

Ratzinger, Joseph. *Volk und Haus Gottes in Augustins Lehre von der Kirche.* Munich: Karl Zink, 1954.

———. "Herkunft und Sinn der Civitas-Lehre Augustins." In *Geschichtsdenken und Geschichtsbild im Mittelalter*, ed. Walther Lammers, 55–74. Darmstadt: Wissenschaftliche Buchgesellschaft, 1961.

Reid, Martine. *Flaubert correspondent.* Paris: Sedes, 1995.

Renan, Ernest. *Renan's Life of Jesus.* Translated by William G. Hutchison. London: Walter Scott, 1898.

————. *Vie de Jésus*. 1863. Vol. 1 of id., *Histoire des origines du christianisme*. Paris: Robert Laffont, 1995.

Rey, Jean-Michel. *Paul ou Les ambiguïtés*. Paris: Éditions de l'Olivier, 2008.

Reynolds, Philip Lyndon. *Marriage in the Western Church: The Christianization of Marriage During the Patristic and Early Medieval Periods*. New York: Brill, 1994.

Richard, Jean-Pierre. *Littérature et sensation*. Paris: Seuil, 1954.

Riffaterre, Michael. "Flaubert's Presuppositions." *Diacritics* 11 (1981): 2–11.

Robert, Marthe. *Roman des origines et origine du roman*. Paris: Gallimard, 1972.

Ronell, Avital. *Crack Wars: On Mania, Addiction and Literature*. Lincoln: University of Nebraska Press, 1992.

Rose, Guy. "Civilisation et humanité: Le virage du texte." In *"Salammbô" de Flaubert. Histoire, fiction*, ed. Daniel Fauvel and Yvan Leclerc, 79–93. Paris: Champion, 1999.

Rosier-Catach, Irène. *La parole efficace: Signe, rituel, sacré*. Paris: Seuil, 2004.

Rosolato, Guy. "Le fétichisme dont se 'dérobe' l'objet." *Nouvelle Révue de psychanalyse* 2 (1970): 31–39.

Rousset, Jean. *Leurs yeux se rencontrèrent. La scène de la première vue dans le roman*. Paris: José Corti, 1981.

————. "Positions, distances, perspectives dans *Salammbô*." In *Travail de Flaubert*, ed. Raymonde Debray-Genette, 79–92. Paris: Seuil, 1983.

Rubino, Nancy. "Impotence and Excess: Male Hysteria and Androgyny in Flaubert's *Salammbô*." *Nineteenth Century French Studies* 29, nos. 1–2 (2000–2001): 78–99.

Ruskin, John. *The Seven Lamps of Architecture*. London: Smith, Elder, 1855.

Sainte-Beuve, Charles Augustin. *Nouveaux Lundis*. Vol. 4. Paris: Calmann Lévy, 1885.

Salin, Edgar. *Civitas Dei*. Tübingen: Mohr, 1926.

Sartre, Jean-Paul. *L'idiot de la famille—Gustave Flaubert de 1821–1857*. 2 vols. Paris: Gallimard, 1971.

————. *The Family Idiot: Gustave Flaubert, 1821–1857*. Vol. 1. Chicago: University of Chicago Press, 1981.

Scepi, Henry. *Henri Scepi présente "Salammbô" de Gustave Flaubert*. Paris: Gallimard, 2003.

Scherer, René. *Zeus hospitalier. Éloge de l'hospitalité. Essai philosophique*. Paris: Armand Colin, 1993.

Schor, Naomi. "*Salammbô* enchaînée, ou femme et ville dans *Salammbô*." In *Flaubert, la femme, la ville*, ed. Marie-Claire Bancquart, 89–108. Paris: Presses universitaires de Paris, 1983.

Schulz-Buschhaus, Ulrich. "Die Sprachlosigkeit der Félicité: Zur Interpretation von Flauberts Conte *Un cœur simple*." In *Zeitschrift für französische Sprache und Literatur* 93 (1983): 113–130.

————. "Zeugma und zeugmatische Erfahrung in Flauberts *L'Éducation senti-mentale*." *Zeitschrift für Französische Sprache und Literatur* 95 (1985): 28–40.

Seebacher, Jacques. "Chiffres, dates, écritures, inscriptions dans Mme Bovary." In Centre culturel international de Cerisy-la-Salle, *La production du sens chez Flaubert*, ed. Claudine Gothot-Mersch, 286–96. Paris: Union générale d'éditions, 1975.

Séginger, Gisèle. *Flaubert: Une poétique de l'histoire*. Strasbourg: Presses universitaires de Strasbourg, 2000.

Spaemann, Robert. *Reflexion und Spontanität. Studien über Fénelon*. Stuttgart: Klett-Cotta, 1990.

Spitz, Hans-Jörg. *Die Metaphorik des geistigen Schriftsinns. Ein Beitrag zur allegorischen Bibelauslegung des ersten christlichen Jahrtausends*. Münstersche Mittelalter-Schriften 12. Munich: Fink, 1972.

Stoltzfus, Ben. "Point of View in *Un cœur simple*." *French Review* 35, no. 1 (1961): 19–25.

Suetonius [Gaius Suetonius Tranquillus]. *Vies des douze Césars*. Vol. 3, ed. Henri Ailloud. Paris: Les Belles Lettres, 1993.

————. *The Lives of the Caesars,*. Vol. 2. Translated by J. C. Rolfe. Cambridge, MA: Harvard University Press, 1979.

Tilliette, Xavier. "L'exinanition du Christ: théologies de la kénose." *Les quatre fleuves* 4 (1975): 48–59.

Tooke, Adrianne. *Flaubert and the Pictorial and Arts: From Image to Text*. Oxford: Oxford University Press, 2000.

————. "Preface." In Gustave Flaubert, *Sentimental Education*. Ware, Herts., UK: Wordsworth Editions, 2001.

Tournier, Michel. Preface to Gustave Flaubert, *Trois contes*, ed. Samuel S. de Sacy. Paris: Gallimard, 1973.

Valéry, Paul. "La tentation de (saint) Flaubert." In id., *Œuvres*, vol. 1, ed. Jean Hytier. Paris: Bibliothèque de la Pléiade, 1987.

Vergil. *Aeneis: lateinisch-deutsch*. Translated by Maria and Johannes Götte. Zurich: Tusculum, 1983.

————. *Aeneid*. Translated by Frederick Ahl. Oxford: Oxford University Press, 2007.

Vinken, Barbara. "Makulatur oder Von der Schwierigkeit zu lesen: Claude Simons *Leçon de choses*." *Poetica: Zeitschrift für Sprach und Literaturwissenschaft* 21 (1989): 403–28.

————. "Der Ursprung der Ästhetik aus theologischem Vorbehalt. Ästhetische Kontroversen von Port-Royal bis Rousseau und Sade." PhD diss., Yale University, 1991.

————. *Unentrinnbare Neugierde: Die Weltverfallenheit des Romans; Richardsons "Clarissa" und Laclos' "Liaisons dangereuses."* Freiburg im Breisgau: Rombach, 1991.

———. "Zola: Alles sehen, alles wissen, alles heilen. Der Fetischismus im Naturalismus." In *Historische Anthropologie und Literatur: Romanistische Beiträge zu einem neuen Paradigma der Literaturwissenschaft*, ed. Rudolph Behrens and Roland Galle, 215–26. Würzburg: Königshausen & Neumann, 1995.

———. "Curiositas/curiosity." In *Historisches Wörterbuch ästhetischer Grundbegriffe*, ed. Karlheinz Barck et al., 794–813. Stuttgart: Metzler, 2000.

———. *Du Bellay und Petrarca: Das Rom der Renaissance*. Tübingen: Niemeyer, 2001.

———. "Wo Joseph war, soll Prometheus werden! Michelets männliche Mütter." In *Kunst—Zeugung—Geburt. Theorien und Metaphern ästhetischer Produktion in der Neuzeit*, ed. Christian Begemann and David E. Wellbery, 251–70. Freiburg im Breisgau: Rombach, 2002.

———. "Herz Jesu und Eisprung: Jules Michelets 'devotio moderna.'" In *Stigmata. Poetiken der Körperinschrift*, ed. Bettine Menke and Barbara Vinken, 295–318. Munich: Fink, 2004.

———. "Aufhebung ins Weibliche: Mariologie und bloßes Leben bei Joseph Ratzinger, Benedikt XVI." In *Ratzinger-Funktion*, 24–55. Frankfurt/Main: Suhrkamp, 2006.

———. "Forget Virgil? Baudelaire and the Truth of Modernity." *Literary Imagination* 8, no. 3 (2006): 417–40.

———. "'Tränen zum Leben, Tränen zum Tode': Katharina von Siena, Petrarca, Boccaccio, Theresa von Avila, Zola." In *Tränen*, ed. Beate Söntgen and Geraldine Spiekermann, 17–26. Munich: Fink, 2008.

———. "Nana: Venus à rebours." In *Venus as Muse: From Lucretius to Michel Serres*, ed. Hanjo Berressem, Günter Blamberger, and Sebastian Goth. Leiden and Boston: Brill Rodopi, 2015.

———. "'Schlusen.' *Effi Briest* und die 'rechte Liebe.'" In *Allegorie. DFG-Symposion 2014*, ed. Ulla Haselstein. Berlin: De Gruyter, forthcoming 2015.

Voragine, Jakobus de [Giacomo da Varazze]. *Jacobi a Voragine Legenda aurea vulgo Historia lombardica dicta*, ed. Johann Georg Graesse. Bratislava: Koebner, 1890.

———. *The Golden Legend of Jacobus de Voragine*. Edited and translated by Granger Ryan and Helmut Ripperger. 1941. New York: Arno Press, 1969.

Vries, Hent de. *Philosophy and the Turn to Religion*. Baltimore: Johns Hopkins University Press, 1999.

Warning, Rainer. *Die Phantasie der Realisten*. Munich: Fink, 1999.

Webster, John. "Kenotische Christologie." In *Religion in Geschichte und Gegenwart*, vol. 6, ed. Hans Dieter Betz et al., 929–31. Tübingen: Mohr Siebeck, 2001.

Westerwelle, Karin. *Ästhetisches Interesse und nervöse Krankheit. Balzac, Baudelaire, Flaubert*. Stuttgart: Metzler, 1993.

————. "Saint Julien et le mythe de Narcisse: Les images du christianisme chez Gustave Flaubert." In *Le Flaubert réel*, ed. Barbara Vinken and Peter Fröhlicher, 108–23. Tübingen: Niemeyer, 2009.

Wetherill, Peter Michael. "C'est là ce que nous avons eu de meilleur." In *Flaubert à l'œuvre*, ed. Raymonde Debray-Genette et al., 35–68. Paris: Flammarion, 1980.

Wild, Cornelia. "*Saint Julien l'hospitalier* de Flaubert: Un face à face entre la littérature européenne et le Moyen Âge latin." In *Le Flaubert réel*, ed. Barbara Vinken and Peter Fröhlicher, 125–38. Tübingen: Niemeyer, 2008.

Wildgruber, Gerald. "Kunst—Religion—Wissenschaft: Zur Konstellation dreier Terme im Spätwerk Flauberts." *Hofmannsthal-Jahrbuch* 7 (1999): 307–44.

Williams, D. A. "Sacred and Profane in *L'Éducation sentimentale*." *Modern Language Review* 73 (1978): 786–98.

Zola, Émile. *Les Romanciers naturalistes. Balzac, Stendhal, Gustave Flaubert, Edmond et Jules de Goncourt, Alphonse Daudet, les Romanciers contemporains.* Paris: G. Charpentier, 1881.

Zollinger, Edi. *Arachnes Rache. Flaubert inszeniert einen Wettkampf im narrativen Weben: Madame Bovary, Notre-Dame de Paris und der Arachne-Mythos.* Paderborn: Fink, 2007.

Cultural Memory in the Present

Lambert Wiesing, *Artificial Presence: Philosophical Studies in Image Theory*

Jacob Taubes, *Occidental Eschatology*

Freddie Rokem, *Philosophers and Thespians: Thinking Performance*

Roberto Esposito, *Communitas: The Origin and Destiny of Community*

Vilashini Cooppan, *Worlds Within: National Narratives and Global Connections in Postcolonial Writing*

Josef Früchtl, *The Impertinent Self: A Heroic History of Modernity*

Frank Ankersmit, Ewa Domanska, and Hans Kellner, eds., *Re-Figuring Hayden White*

Michael Rothberg, *Multidirectional Memory: Remembering the Holocaust in the Age of Decolonization*

Jean-François Lyotard, *Enthusiasm: The Kantian Critique of History*

Ernst van Alphen, Mieke Bal, and Carel Smith, eds., *The Rhetoric of Sincerity*

Stéphane Mosès, *The Angel of History: Rosenzweig, Benjamin, Scholem*

Pierre Hadot, *The Present Alone Is Our Happiness: Conversations with Jeannie Carlier and Arnold I. Davidson*

Alexandre Lefebvre, *The Image of the Law: Deleuze, Bergson, Spinoza*

Samira Haj, *Reconfiguring Islamic Tradition: Reform, Rationality, and Modernity*

Diane Perpich, *The Ethics of Emmanuel Levinas*

Marcel Detienne, *Comparing the Incomparable*

François Delaporte, *Anatomy of the Passions*

René Girard, *Mimesis and Theory: Essays on Literature and Criticism, 1959-2005*

Richard Baxstrom, *Houses in Motion: The Experience of Place and the Problem of Belief in Urban Malaysia*

Jennifer L. Culbert, *Dead Certainty: The Death Penalty and the Problem of Judgment*

Samantha Frost, *Lessons from a Materialist Thinker: Hobbesian Reflections on Ethics and Politics*

Regina Mara Schwartz, *Sacramental Poetics at the Dawn of Secularism: When God Left the World*

Gil Anidjar, *Semites: Race, Religion, Literature*

Ranjana Khanna, *Algeria Cuts: Women and Representation, 1830 to the Present*

Esther Peeren, *Intersubjectivities and Popular Culture: Bakhtin and Beyond*

Eyal Peretz, *Becoming Visionary: Brian De Palma's Cinematic Education of the Senses*

Diana Sorensen, *A Turbulent Decade Remembered: Scenes from the Latin American Sixties*

Hubert Damisch, *A Childhood Memory by Piero della Francesca*

José van Dijck, *Mediated Memories in the Digital Age*

Dana Hollander, *Exemplarity and Chosenness: Rosenzweig and Derrida on the Nation of Philosophy*

Asja Szafraniec, *Beckett, Derrida, and the Event of Literature*

Sara Guyer, *Romanticism After Auschwitz*

Alison Ross, *The Aesthetic Paths of Philosophy: Presentation in Kant, Heidegger, Lacoue-Labarthe, and Nancy*

Gerhard Richter, *Thought-Images: Frankfurt School Writers' Reflections from Damaged Life*

Bella Brodzki, *Can These Bones Live? Translation, Survival, and Cultural Memory*

Rodolphe Gasché, *The Honor of Thinking: Critique, Theory, Philosophy*

Brigitte Peucker, *The Material Image: Art and the Real in Film*

Natalie Melas, *All the Difference in the World: Postcoloniality and the Ends of Comparison*

Jonathan Culler, *The Literary in Theory*

Michael G. Levine, *The Belated Witness: Literature, Testimony, and the Question of Holocaust Survival*

Jennifer A. Jordan, *Structures of Memory: Understanding German Change in Berlin and Beyond*

Christoph Menke, *Reflections of Equality*

Marlène Zarader, *The Unthought Debt: Heidegger and the Hebraic Heritage*

Jan Assmann, *Religion and Cultural Memory: Ten Studies*

David Scott and Charles Hirschkind, *Powers of the Secular Modern: Talal Asad and His Interlocutors*

Gyanendra Pandey, *Routine Violence: Nations, Fragments, Histories*

James Siegel, *Naming the Witch*

J. M. Bernstein, *Against Voluptuous Bodies: Late Modernism and the Meaning of Painting*

Theodore W. Jennings, Jr., *Reading Derrida / Thinking Paul: On Justice*

Richard Rorty and Eduardo Mendieta, *Take Care of Freedom and Truth Will Take Care of Itself: Interviews with Richard Rorty*

Jacques Derrida, *Paper Machine*